Exploring Gogol

STUDIES OF THE HARRIMAN INSTITUTE,
COLUMBIA UNIVERSITY

Robert A. Maguire

EXPLORING GOGOL

STANFORD UNIVERSITY PRESS

STANFORD, CALIFORNIA

Stanford University Press
Stanford, California
© 1994 by the Board of Trustees of the
Leland Stanford Junior University
Printed in the United States of America

CIP data appear at the end of the book.

Stanford University Press publications
are distributed exclusively by Stanford
University Press within the United States,
Canada, Mexico, and Central America;
they are distributed exclusively by
Cambridge University Press throughout
the rest of the world.

Original printing 1994
Last figure below indicates year of this printing:
04   03   02   01   00   99   98   97   96   95

For Hugh McLean

Contents

Preface

WHEN I first encountered Gogol, longer ago than now seems plausible, he did not conform to my expectations of what a "great" nineteenth-century fiction writer should be. For one thing, the corpus was modest: a mere fourteen volumes (albeit substantial ones) in the only existing complete works, of which seven covered the stories, plays, and *Dead Souls*, and the rest, nonfiction. I found few ontological excursions of the kind that make Tolstoy, Dostoevsky, and Stendhal so discussable, by casual readers as well as scholars. There were virtually no exciting or even very interesting plots of the kind that take us back again and again to Pushkin, Poe, and Dickens. There were none of those rounded characters, to borrow E. M. Forster's once fashionable term, whom we can treat almost like real human beings, such as Raskolnikov, Emma Bovary, and Becky Sharp. At most I could identify two or three well-made stories of the kind that readers of Chekhov and Maupassant enjoy as a matter of course. It was all but impossible to paraphrase a story by Gogol, and I was usually hard put, on finishing one, to say with much confidence what it was "about." Yet the simplicity was only apparent. Except in format, these works were not really prose fictions at all, but tightly knotted poems, which produced a profound, disturbing, unforgettable impression. Reading Gogol was like visiting a house where the door was open and welcoming but we were admitted only part way. We had to be satisfied with what we could see by craning our necks from the well-lighted hallway, but we yearned to explore the whole house, particularly the attic and the basement. Over the years I

have returned to that house again and again, with exploration as my purpose. The book offered here has been written in the first instance as an
account of these explorations, and in the second instance as a testimony to
my belief that Gogol is accessible not only to specialists but to readers with
no knowledge of Russian. In fact, it is to them that I primarily address
myself.

Gogol has intrigued and baffled critics ever since the 1830's, when his
first works began to appear. I am well aware of the enormous weight of
commentary that has accumulated since then. Indeed, the whole history of
Russian literary criticism could be written around the various strategies
that have been devised for dealing with what early came to be known as
"the Gogol problem." Having fallen off steeply under Stalinism, criticism
in what was then the Soviet Union began to revive about twenty years ago;
and it is Gogol who has been attracting some of the most subtle and powerful readers, like Sergei Bocharov, Yury Lotman, and Yury Mann. Understandably, foreign critics discovered Gogol much later than did the Russians, really only in the past half century. First came the Germans, then the
French, and then, beginning in the 1960's, the British and Americans. Ever
since, the level of awareness about Gogol has been steadily rising in the
English-speaking world. When I was a graduate student, more than thirty
years ago, almost no one wrote Ph.D. dissertations on Gogol. Neither did
I. Now, however, they are common, and many are of such high quality that
they can pass into print with little revision. This growing critical achievement confirms that Gogol's magic continues to travel and to work its spell.
An outstanding recent instance of Gogol scholarship is the volume entitled
Essays on Gogol, edited by Fusso and Meyer, which includes contributions
by several of our best specialists.

Critical writing on Gogol, in Russia and abroad, has moved in essentially four directions. One considers an aspect, such as the grotesque, or
Ukrainian elements, or rhetorical devices, and follows it throughout. Another discovers a key to everything in a single theme, like demonism, or in
a dominant psychological trait, like homosexuality. A third sees Gogol as
a reflection of certain social and political issues of his time. The fourth
studies specific texts to determine how they work as self-contained verbal
entities. This last approach is the least common, and has been the preserve
mainly of recent Anglo-American critics. "Diary of a Madman," "The
Overcoat," and "The Nose" have been the chief beneficiaries. Virtually all
the other works have yet to be treated in this way. Even *The Inspector General* and *Dead Souls* await microsurgery, although Yury Mann, among others, has been pointing the way in brilliant and stimulating studies. The sizable body of nonfiction has so far remained largely closed to this kind of
reading, but promising beginnings have been made by imaginative critics

like William Mills Todd, in his essay on the letters. For other scholarly writings on Gogol, in several languages, readers may consult the exhaustive bibliography compiled by Philip Frantz, which covers works published through 1988.

Few studies in any language have considered Gogol's achievement as a whole. The ones that do all date from the twentieth century. Among the Russians who have made the attempt, I most admire Vasily Gippius, Grigory Gukovsky, and Andrei Sinyavsky. Otherwise, the best work has emanated from the English-speaking world. The first study of this kind—which, however, ignores the nonfiction—was Vladimir Nabokov's *Gogol*. It does not look markedly original in the context of *Russian* criticism, being heavily indebted to Symbolist and Formalist approaches; but in 1944, it was entirely new to Anglo-American readers, offering quirkily persuasive evidence that Gogol was something far more important than merely the "realist" or "local colorist" of long repute. Since then, the most important attempts at giving us the whole writer have been the books by Victor Erlich (1969), Donald Fanger (1979), and Richard Peace (1981). I should also add the book by Gippius, inasmuch as it first appeared in English translation in 1981.

The book I offer here belongs to this genre as well. I need hardly say that I owe much to my predecessors, consciously and unconsciously. But my own readings yield quite a different picture, criticism being an interpretive art, and the subject in this case being so complex, elusive, and still inadequately explored in so many important respects.

Fanger insists that Gogol "will not yield to frontal assault, but must be taken like Jericho" (p. x). On the contrary, I think that frontal assault is very likely the only way; otherwise, we are left at the mercy of Gogol's own games of indirection, feint, and evasion, which we cannot hope to play nearly so well. The critic's equivalent of the soldier's maneuver is confrontation with the realia of the texts, in courageous acknowledgment that they can and must be explicated, even if the result can never be a definitive victory. Thus I began with close readings of all the texts. It soon became clear that a book consisting only of these would run to many volumes. So I decided to focus on works that have been inadequately studied, notably "A Terrible Vengeance," "Old-World Landowners," "The Tale of How Ivan Ivanovich Quarreled with Ivan Nikiforovich," "The Portrait," "Taras Bulba," Part 2 of *Dead Souls*, and some of the nonfiction as well, like "An Author's Confession" and *Meditations on the Divine Liturgy*. Certainly "Diary of a Madman" does not lack for critical attention, but I treat it in some detail nonetheless, because I think I have something to add. On the other hand, I do not devote the space to "The Overcoat" and "The Nose" that works of such quality would seem to warrant, simply because I think they have been well accounted for by others. Among my omissions are *Marriage* and *The Gamblers*, mainly because they do not speak to me. Although the longest chapter in the book is devoted to *Dead Souls*, I do not aim at anything like a "full" treatment of so difficult a work, which warrants a hefty book all its own (none yet exists in English); instead, I use it to explore Gogol's ways with language.

For that matter, I am not attempting a "full" treatment of any work. Even if such a venture were theoretically possible, it would be endless. I am convinced that there is nothing superfluous in a work of art; everything is a necessary part of the whole. When the artist is Nikolai Gogol, who revels in minutiae and in what the rhetoricians like to call auxesis, the critic either risks madness or selects. What has guided my selections from Gogol's corpus is the pattern that emerges from a scrutiny of all the texts. This pattern, I believe, organizes itself around three major themes, closely intertwined, yet distinguishable. I call them "place," "the apprehending eye," and "word." All are simultaneously present in Gogol from beginning to end. But one or the other dominates at a particular time, and defines a "period." "Place" marks the years 1831–36; "the apprehending eye," 1836–42; and "word," 1842–52. This chronology was recognized by Gogol himself, and has been accepted by virtually all his critics. I accept it too, and use it to identify the three large sections of my book. However, I interpret it very differently. In a larger sense, "place" refers to the ways Russians have tried, from the earliest times to the present, to contend with a deep-rooted fear of social and personal chaos by creating bounded systems. Gogol's version, which is especially apparent in the works written between 1831 and 1836, represents a unique response to a powerful cultural imperative. By the mid-1830's, however, he was beginning to show considerable interest in the way the verbal artist relates to the world at large. The artist, he thought, is, or should be, one who sees, and then creates verbal pictures to record his perceptions. Gradually and reluctantly, however, Gogol grasped that "seeing" could not account for the way his own art worked. Almost all his stories are narrated in highly marked, idiosyncratic language that is not pictorial or iconographic but dynamic and polyvalent. With *Dead Souls* (1842), he set out to explore the theme of language, or "the word," in a variety of senses; and from that point on, "word" became his dominant concern. Through it he focused on a number of problems central to his art and his life, such as the mission of an artist in an increasingly secular and fragmented society. His failure to find satisfactory answers to, even formulations of, these problems eventually robbed him of the ability to write, and he lapsed into silence and death.

Rather early on, I discovered that fiction was only part of the Gogol story, albeit the best known. "Text" had to include the nonfiction too, the letters, the essays, in fact everything Gogol had committed to writing. And it had to extend to his "life." More than for most writers, the distinction that convention makes between "life" and "work" is meaningless for Gogol. This is so not just because the quotidian details of his existence outside of writing are sparse and uninteresting—so much so that biographical studies usually resort to looting the fiction—but also because Gogol in a very real sense created a life that is one of his texts. Since lives are lived in time, and since most of us appreciate some guideposts when traveling someone else's road, I attach a brief chronology of the major events of his life, as well as a list of all his works that I mention in this study.

"Text" also embraces a larger world. Insofar as this world includes the society in which Gogol lived and worked, I give it relatively scant attention, since that society has been splendidly accounted for by Fanger and by Todd (especially in *Fiction and Society in the Age of Pushkin*). Instead I concentrate on art, religion, and ideas, with particular attention to those aspects that have been neglected. They include eighteenth-century literature; the visual arts, especially painting; Eastern Orthodox Christianity; German Romantic aesthetics; the Greek and Roman classics; historiography; and certain theories of language, especially philosophical grammar. Gogol's strange but crucial relationship with Pushkin comes in for fresh evaluation, as does the so-called "spiritual crisis" of his later years, which was really a literary crisis. "Gogol," then, defines a rather large and complex phenomenon, in which everything is interrelated, as in any healthy organism. But I have been always mindful of what might be called the fallacy of irrelevance, the danger that a critic may end up talking around, not about, his main subject. Any excursions I make into the wider world are intended to help us better read the texts, by which I mean everything Gogol wrote down.

What remains is the most pleasant part of my job: extending thanks to the people who have helped me see it through. In the first instance, I owe an enormous debt to my students, particularly at Columbia, but also at Yale and Princeton, who over the years have served not only as sounding boards but also, in more cases than I can name or remember, as creative collaborators in the great adventure of exploring Gogol. Of the individuals who have known about the book in progress, Harry Fogarty, William Johnston, Judith Kornblatt, Cathy Popkin, Marc Raeff, Irina Reyfman, Mark von Hagen, and Richard Wortman steered me to some valuable materials that I would otherwise have overlooked. Marina Ledkovsky gave me knowledgeable advice on details of Russian realia, particularly religious practices. Frank Miller helped me cope with some of Gogol's odder Russian usages. James Coulter, Matthew Santirocco, and Alexander Ulanov provided expert guidance in Greek and Latin literature. Michael Flier put at my service his expertise in linguistic theory. Paul Valliere served as a *peritus* on matters of Eastern Orthodox theology. Ellen Chances was always ready with an understanding mind and a sympathetic ear to let me try out ideas. Helen Tartar, the humanities editor of Stanford University Press, took an interest in this project before any of it existed on paper, inquired about my progress at regular intervals, and had faith that a completed manuscript would eventually emerge. John Feneron, associate editor at Stanford Press, showed much patience and friendly forbearance, for which I was especially grateful during the final stages of preparing the book. As a manuscript editor, Nancy Atkinson was well-nigh perfect; her meticulous and wise ministrations have made my text incalculably better than it was.

Hugh McLean and William Mills Todd, both outstanding students of Gogol, interrupted their own busy lives to read my long manuscript in its entirety, and offered detailed and incisive commentary. Without their sharp eyes, sound taste, sophisticated sensibilities, and generosity of mind and spirit, my book would be much the poorer.

My debt to Richard Gustafson is of a very special kind. For thirty years, first as a fellow graduate student, then as a colleague, he has responded to my ideas, enthusiasms, and doubts with wisdom, patience, and encouragement. It is a privilege to count him as a friend.

Among my nonspecialist friends, I owe grateful thanks to Harry Fogarty (again), Alexander Kirschenbaum, and Raymond Matta. Their skillful and creative services have kept *soma* and *psyche* connected and intact.

Of particular importance to me during the writing process has been my friendship with Carl Plansky. He not only shared with me his profound knowledge of European painting, but commented imaginatively and constructively on sticky parts of the manuscript, helped me arrive at better formulations, and offered warm support throughout.

I have to say another word about Hugh McLean. For nearly all my scholarly career, he has read my writings, in manuscript and in print, has given me the benefit of thoughtful and candid criticism, and has been generosity itself in sharing his own insights with me. Although I have never studied formally with him, he has been all that one could wish in a mentor. It is with pleasure that I dedicate this book to him.

New York
Robert A. Maguire
1993

Three Notes to the Reader

TEXTS

Because I want my nonspecialist readers to orient themselves readily in the full texts from which I quote, I use translations of the fiction and plays that are currently in print. Most frequently I refer to *The Complete Tales of Nikolai Gogol*, in two volumes, which is the original Constance Garnett translation, as edited by Leonard J. Kent. In my citations, the Roman numeral designates the volume, the Arabic the page, and "Garnett/Kent" this particular work. For *Dead Souls*, the best translation is by Bernard Guilbert Guerney, in the Modern Library. It has, unfortunately, long been out of print, although there is talk of reissuing it. I therefore have chosen the less satisfactory but readily available translation by David Magarshack, in the Penguin series. In every case, however, I have consulted the Russian original, and made corrections, both silent and explicit, when I deem them essential. For works out of print, never translated, or, in my judgment, not translated satisfactorily, I offer my own renditions. The canonical Russian text of Gogol's works is *Polnoe sobranie sochinenii*, in fourteen volumes, edited by various hands and published in Moscow and Leningrad by the Soviet Academy of Sciences between 1937 and 1952. I refer to it as *PSS* when some indication of the title is needed; usually, however, I cite it only by volume and page numbers, using Roman and Arabic numerals respectively. For fuller bibliographical information on these and other editions and translations, see the entries under "Gogol" below in Works Cited.

TRANSLITERATION

I use a transliteration system that seems easiest on English-oriented eyes, with no concern for scholarly accuracy or even consistency. For the benefit of those who know Russian, I add the palatalization marker to names in the Notes and Works Cited, and to Russian phrases and titles throughout.

OTHER PRACTICES

Unless otherwise indicated, all italics in quotations from Gogol are mine.

The Julian calendar, or Old Style (o.s.), remained officially in force in Russia until 1918, when the Gregorian, or New Style (n.s.), was adopted, as it had generally been in Western Europe in the eighteenth century. Unless otherwise indicated, dates are in o.s. when referring to Russia, in n.s. when referring to Europe. (Days are dated roughly eleven dates later in n.s. than in o.s.)

Major Events in Gogol's Life

1809	Mar. 20: Born in Bolshie Sorochintsy, Poltava Province, Mirgorod District, Ukraine.
1821	Enters Gimnaziya at Nezhin.
1825	Death of father.
1828	Finishes Gimnaziya. Dec.: Leaves for St. Petersburg.
1829	Publishes *Hanz Kuechelgarten*, an "idyll in verse," under the pseudonym "V. Alov." Aug.–Sept.: First trip to Europe (Germany). On returning, he unsuccessfully attempts to become a professional actor. Nov.: Enters civil service as a minor official.
1830	Begins publishing prose fiction ("Bisavryuk, or St. John's Eve," and one chapter of *The Hetman*, an unfinished historical novel).
1831	Becomes a history teacher in the Patriotic Institute. May 20: Meets Pushkin for the first time. Sept.: Publishes *Evenings on a Farm Near Dikanka*, Part 1.
1832	Publishes *Evenings on a Farm Near Dikanka*, Part 2.
1833	Works on various articles and stories.

1834	Appointed adjunct professor of world history, St. Petersburg University.
1835	Jan.: Publishes *Arabesques*.
	Mar.: Publishes *Mirgorod*.
	Dec.: Dismissed from teaching position.
1836	Apr. 19: Premiere of *The Inspector General*, St. Petersburg.
	June 6: Goes abroad, travels through Western Europe the rest of the year.
1837	Jan. 29: Death of Pushkin.
	Mar. 26: Arrives in Rome.
1838–41	Lives in Rome, travels in Europe, makes two trips to Russia.
1842	In Russia. Prepares edition of collected works; publishes first two volumes.
	May: Publishes *Dead Souls*, Part 1.
	June: Returns to Europe.
	Dec. 9: Premiere of *Marriage*, St. Petersburg.
1843	In Europe.
	Jan.: Publishes third and fourth volumes of collected works.
	Feb.: Premiere of *Marriage* and *The Gamblers* in Moscow.
1844–46	In Europe. Works on *Dead Souls*, Part 2.
	June–July 1845: Burns manuscript.
1847	In Europe.
	Jan.: Publishes *Selected Passages from Correspondence with Friends*.
	June–July: Works on apologia (posthumously published as "An Author's Confession").
1848	In Europe.
	Mid-Feb.: Travels to Holy Land.
	Apr. 11: Returns to Russia, there to remain.
1849–51	In Russia; works on *Dead Souls*, Part 2.
1852	In Russia.
	Feb. 11–12: Burns manuscript of *Dead Souls*, Part 2.
	Feb. 21: Dies.
	Feb. 25: Buried.

Works by Gogol Cited in the Text and Notes

THE following list includes all works cited in text and notes except for outlines and sketches. Brackets ⟨ ⟩ indicate titles supplied by later editors. In nearly all cases the dates are dates of publication; exceptions will be obvious.

POETRY

| 1829 | *Hanz Kuechelgarten* | *Gants Kyukhel'garten* |
| 1829 | Italy (attributed) | Italiya |

FICTION

1830–32	*The Hetman* (one chapter from the projected novel, never completed)	*Get'man*
1831–32	*Evenings on a Farm Near Dikanka* (2 vols.)	*Vechera na khutore bliz Dikan'ki*
	Christmas Eve	Noch' pered Rozhdestvom
	The Fair at Sorochintsy	Sorochinskaya yarmarka
	Foreword (Part 1, Part 2)	Predislovie
	Ivan Fyodorovich Shponka and His Aunt	Ivan Fedorovich Shpon'ka i ego tetushka
	A May Night	Maiskaya noch'
	A Terrible Vengeance	Strashnaya mest'
1835	*Arabesques*	*Arabeski*

	Diary of a Madman	Zapiski sumasshedshego
	Nevsky Prospekt	Nevskii Prospekt
	The Portrait (1st version)	Portret
1835	*Mirgorod*	*Mirgorod*
	Old-World Landowners	Starosvetskie pomeshchiki
	Taras Bulba (1st version)	Taras Bul'ba
	The Tale of How Ivan Ivanovich Quarreled with Ivan Nikiforovich	Povest' o tom, kak possorilsya Ivan Ivanovich s Ivanom Nikiforovichem
	Viy	Vii
1836	The Carriage	Kolyaska
1836	The Nose	Nos
1842	*Dead Souls*, Part 1	*Mertvye dushi*
1842	The Overcoat	Shinel'
1842	The Portrait (revised)	Portret
1842	Taras Bulba (revised)	Taras Bul'ba
1842	Rome	Rim

PLAYS

1832–34	*The Order of St. Vladimir, Third Class* (remaining fragments published under different titles)	*Vladimir tret'ei stepeni*
1836	*The Inspector General*	*Revizor*
1842	*Marriage*	*Zhenit'ba*
1842	*The Gamblers*	*Igroki*
1842	*Leaving the Theater After the Performance of a New Comedy*	*Teatral'nyi raz' 'ezd posle predstavleniya novoi komedii*

ARTICLES AND OTHER PIECES

1831	Woman	Zhenshchina
1831	*Boris Godunov. A Long Poem by Pushkin* (publ. 1881)	*Boris Godunov. Poema Pushkina.*
1835	From *Arabesques*:	
	A Few Words About Pushkin	Neskol'ko slov o Pushkine
	Al-Mamun	Al-Mamun
	⟨Foreword⟩	⟨Predislovie⟩
	The Last Day of Pompeii	Poslednii den' Pompei
	Life	Zhizn'
	A Look at the Making of Little Russia	Vzglyad na sostavlenie Malorossii
	On the Architecture of the Present Day	Ob arkhitekture nyneshnego vremeni
	On Little-Russian Songs	O malorossiiskikh pesnykah

PART ONE

PLACE

1

Bounded Space

PROSE presupposes place. Writer and reader require a sense of topography, however rudimentary, within a prose text, even in the most artless forms like the office memorandum, the letter, the diary entry. There a mere specification of date, time, and locale may suffice. Fiction must work harder to create the necessary semblance of ordinariness, which is then explored, as in realism, or departed from, as in fantasy and the grotesque, sometimes in more detail, as in the novel, sometimes in less, as in the short story. Much depends on genre, convention, and authorial predilection.

And much depends on cultural imperatives as well. For Russians, one of the most powerful and enduring imperatives has been a fear of disorder or placelessness, and a corresponding need for structure and discipline. The account of the founding of the Russian state, under the years 860–62 in the *Primary Chronicle* (Povest' vremennykh let, twelfth century), tells of a society in such disarray that the inhabitants turn to foreigners, the Varangians, with the following request: "Our whole land is great and rich, but there is no order in it. Come to rule and reign over us." By the twelfth century, an ordered society had been created, but it was under constant threat from disruptive forces, internal as well as external. The greatest work of old Russian literature, *The Song of Igor's Campaign* (Slovo o polku Igoreve, 1187), records one instance that was to become paradigmatic. Four princes, among them Igor, leave their towns and set out for the open steppes beyond the Donets River to do battle with the Kumans, or Polovetsians. These nomads had been defeated a year earlier by Igor's cousin; now Igor himself, in the words of Vladimir Nabokov, "was moved by the spirit of rash emulation in undertaking his own expedition without consulting the senior prince."[1] The battle was lost, and the princes were captured. The *Song* is about the wages of arrogance, disobedience, and rashness, for individuals and for Russia as a whole. It is also about the contrast between the enclosed, ordered places represented by walled towns, and the boundless, featureless, and therefore dangerous world of the open steppes. Eventually Igor returns from captivity to his town, which is welcoming, nurturing, and safe.

Subsequently, the ideal enclosure took many forms—the monastery, the church, the garden, the country manor, the city, the modern state. Many found parallels in Western Europe, while manifesting peculiarly Russian characteristics. Ultimately the most Russian of these characteristics may be less a particular mode of embodiment than the persistence and intensity of the need for enclosure. This need has taken on the quality of myth. It resembles what Mary Douglas, in a very different context, calls a "bounded system," with "external boundaries, margins, internal structure"; it can form "a complex set of Chinese boxes, each sub-system having little sub-systems of its own."[2] Beyond enclosure lies the realm of nonplace, which is variously represented as amorphous, unclean, chaotic, indifferent, and hostile, and is to be kept at bay by physical boundaries and by elaborate routines, rituals, and taboos. Although it has often assumed harsh and oppressive form, the ideal of an ordered enclosure in a disordered world remains intact to this day. A cartoon in a recent issue of *Literary Gazette* (Literaturnaya gazeta, No. 43, Oct. 30, 1991, p. 16), published when the Soviet system was already disintegrating, shows Gorbachev seated at a table facing a group of top-hatted, cigar-smoking capitalists, obviously representing the Group of Seven, which he was unsuccessfully trying to join. Issuing from his mouth is a balloon that contains only the lines from the *Primary Chronicle* we quoted earlier. There are no quotation marks and no attribution. None are necessary, for every Russian knows these words by heart.

The myth of enclosure has proved endlessly nourishing to writers, whose explorations in turn have rooted it still deeper. None was more sensitive to it than Gogol. A "bounded system" underlies his conception of the world in all his writings, fictional and nonfictional. In fact, he mediated it in ways that have proved decisive for many of the great writers who followed him, whether Goncharov in *Oblomov* (1859), Dostoevsky in *Crime and Punishment* (1866), Bely in *Petersburg* (1916), or Solzhenitsyn in *Cancer Ward* (1968), all of which are built on elaborate interplays of enclosures—social, individual, spiritual, intellectual, and moral.

It is especially in the works of the first period, 1831 through 1836, that Gogol was intent on working out a poetics of bounded space. We can see it at its starkest in "A Terrible Vengeance."

"A TERRIBLE VENGEANCE"

This story forms part of the second volume of *Evenings on a Farm Near Dikanka* (1832). A brief summary will help orient us. A Cossack wedding feast is under way in a section of Kiev. Among the guests are three of the characters on whom the story eventually centers, Danilo Burulbash; his wife, Katerina; and their infant son. As the host, a Captain of Cossacks, raises the icons to bless the newlyweds, one of the guests turns into a sorcerer, causing fear and confusion, after which the feast winds down to a drunken and silent end. Danilo and his family make their way home by boat on the Dnieper, talking about Katerina's father, a gloomy and unfriendly man who has returned to live with them after 21 years abroad. He disapproves of Danilo; the two come to blows; only Katerina's pleas induce her husband to back off and apologize, which he does with heavy heart. At night he goes to a sinister castle nearby, and watches as his father-in-law turns into the sorcerer and calls up Katerina's soul. Later he locks the sorcerer/father in a cellar, but the compassionate Katerina releases him, whereupon the old man flees to the Poles, who are planning to attack the Cossacks. Tragedies ensue: Danilo is killed by his father-in-law, as is the child; Katerina loses her mind and is eventually murdered by her father, who comes disguised as a friend of Danilo's. The sorcerer/father, tormented by his crimes, kills a holy hermit who refuses to pray for the salvation of his soul, then flees to the highest mountain of the Carpathians. Here he meets an awesome figure on horseback, who strangles him and drops him into an abyss, where he is gnawed for all eternity by other corpses. In the final chapter, a blind bandore-player explains all these events as the fulfillment of a curse that avenges a much earlier crime of fratricide, whereby the last descendant of the murderer—the sorcerer/father—shall be "the worst criminal that has ever been seen," and must suffer accordingly.

This account may suggest why "A Terrible Vengeance" is one of the least studied works in the Gogol canon.[3] It does not engage everyday reality, but verges on exemplum; it sustains a hieratic tone until the final chapter; it is devoid of humor; the tonality is dark throughout; the characters are scarcely more than cartoons. But a mere summary conveys nothing of the unexpected power, even poignancy, of this apparently simple story, of the ingenious ways in which Gogol turns the myth to his own purposes. And it was probably this work, more than any other by Gogol, that made the myth usable for his successors, as a careful study of Dostoevsky, Turgenev, Bunin, and others would show.

As is often the case in Gogol, the opening scene (comprising the first chapter or section) establishes the main theme and direction of the story as a whole. The wedding party is represented as a social collective, whose unity is conveyed stylistically in the first line: *Shumit, gremit konets Kieva* ("There was a bustle and an uproar in a quarter of Kiev"). This contains two assonances (*-mit, -mit*) and two alliterations (*k-, k-*), and scans as three iambs and a dactyl: *Shu-mít/gre-mít/ko-néts/Kí-e-va*. In fact, rhythmic prose predominates throughout the story. Drawing heavily as it does on the oral traditions of folk literature and formal rhetoric, it further suggests that the telling is ritualized. Ritual is explicit here too: in the wedding itself, the feast that follows, and especially the blessing of the couple with icons. Religious ritual in particular has a way of setting a collective apart and endowing it with a sense of what Mary Douglas calls "wholeness and completeness."[4] Apartness is further marked by another stylistic device common in folklore and rhetoric: a series of negations that define non-place and thereby confirm the identity of true place. They apply first to Katerina's father: "[the guests] marveled still more that her old father had *not* come with her. . . . No doubt he would have many strange stories to tell. How could he *not* have them, after being so long in *foreign* parts! Everything there is *not* the same: the people are *not* the same, and there are *no* Christian churches. ... But he had *not* come." The next clustering of negatives occurs in the second paragraph: "[The icons] had *no* rich setting, there was *no* gleam of either [lit., *neither*] gold or [lit., *nor*] silver on them." The icons are "good" because they are *not* adorned with the traditionally suspect metals, and they are capable of reinforcing the boundary between place and non-place: "*no un*clean power dares [lit., does *not* dare] approach [*ni-kakaya nechistaya sila ne posmeet*]" (I, 136).[5]

Another negative attaches to a Cossack "standing in their midst" whom "*nobody* knew" (lit., *nobody* did *not* know: *ni*kto *ne* znal). What is alien is now present; a boundary has been crossed. Moreover, the icons have the power to define the distinction for all to see. The moment the host raises them in blessing, this Cossack's face undergoes a complete transformation: "his nose grew longer and twisted to one side, his rolling eyes turned from brown to green, his lips turned blue, his chin quivered and grew pointed like a spear, a tusk peeped out of his mouth, a hump appeared behind his head, and the Cossack turned into an old man" (136–37). Transformation works in two ways here, either pulling things out of their proper place or substituting one thing for another. In either case it violates boundaries and threatens the collective. The point is reinforced by the sudden lapse into ordinary Russian, which contrasts with the prevailing high style. Particularly disturbing is the sorcerer's ability to move in and out of the guise of a Cossack. A "real" Cossack is nothing but Cossack; he is bounded by the set of gestures, thoughts, and actions that have been assigned him from birth by the collective. The only kind of acceptable "change" might be a spiritual one, which would involve no physical dislocations or transmutations, although this does not figure in "A Terrible Vengeance" or for that matter in Gogol's work through most of the 1830's. Here, on the contrary, change is accompanied by fragmentation as body parts are enumerated and compared to nonhuman orders (lance, tusk). Fragmentation is an attribute of death, so it is not surprising that an "old man" is the result.

The collective fears and tries to protect itself against the kind of change represented by the sorcerer. As its spokesman, the captain "stepped forward and, turning the icons toward him, said in a loud voice: 'Away, image of Satan! This is *no place* for you!' " (137). One of the epithets traditionally attached to Satan is "unclean power" (it is actually mentioned earlier in the scene). We are mindful of what Douglas calls "the old definition of dirt as matter out of place" (35). What is dirty or unclean, that is, out of place, must be swept away, sent back, as it were, to its own place, which in effect is "not here." The young people ask the question: "What sort of sorcerer is this? [*Chto eto za koldun?*]" This suggests that there is something mysterious not so much about sorcerers in general as about this particular one. Victor Turner has called attention to "a widely prevalent social tendency *either* to make what falls outside the norm a matter of concern for the widest recognized group," often by sacralizing it, "*or* to destroy the exceptional phenomenon."[6] Russian folk belief recognizes the so-called "wedding sorcerer," who is invited to the feast and given the place of honor lest he spoil the ceremonies and bring harm to the young couple and the guests. But Gogol's sorcerer is not of this kind. The power of ritual at first seems capable of mustering the collective's defenses against the intrusion. Another stylistic shift, however, intimates that something is amiss. Dialogue appears for the first time, and in a colloquial Russian: " 'It's him! It's him!,' shouted the crowd [*krichali*]. . . . 'The sorcerer has appeared again!' cried [*krichali*] the mothers."[7] A cry or shout also marks a violent intrusion into the harmony of ceremony and music. These sounds are further associated with suddenness and with change, which offend the bounded order: "all at once [*vdrug*] the children playing on the ground cried out [*zakrichali*] in terror" as they saw how "at once [*vdrug*] the Cossack's face completely changed." All three images—change, unpleasant sound, and suddenness— are caught up in the final aspect of the sorcerer: "hissing and clacking his teeth like a wolf, the strange old man vanished." He is no longer present, but he is not entirely absent either. One sign is that diversity now prevails, first as "talk and conjecture," *tolki i rechi*, both plural nouns in Russian, then as discrete groups of people, each of which has its own version of the sorcerer's identity: "almost everyone told [the story] differently." A final flourish of negations hints that the boundary between place and non-place is no longer so firm: "*no one* could tell anything [lit., 'could *not* tell'] certain about him" (137).

The festive atmosphere of the story's beginning seems restored as activities resume: "A barrel of mead was rolled out and many gallons of Greek wine were brought into the yard. The guests regained their light-heartedness. The orchestra struck up—the girls, the young women, the gallant Cossacks in their gay-colored coats flew around in the dance." But this is immediately followed by a hint that returns of any kind are no longer possible: "After a glass, old folks [*star'e*] of ninety, of a hundred, began dancing too," in a kind of *Totentanz*. With these ancient folk comes a dimension of time, hitherto absent, as they remember "the years that had passed." Boundaries are crossed laterally by the dispersal of most of the guests, and the remaining space is fragmented as the Cossacks "[drop] to sleep uninvited *under* the benches, *on* the floor, *by* their horses, *by* the stables" (137). But there is no corresponding individualization of characters. On the contrary, the personages in this final scene are designated by collective adverbs and by nouns that are singular in number and mostly neuter in gender: "The guests began to disperse, but only a *paucity* [*malo*] made its way home; *a multitude* [*mnogo*] stayed to spend the night . . . ; and even more Cossackry [*kazachestvo*] dropped to sleep . . . wherever *the Cossack head* [*kozatskaya golova*] stumbled, there *it* [subject unexpressed in Russian] lay," and so on. My literal translation is awkward, but it is meant to show how Gogol makes the point that until now, people have been marked by name, rank, age, social position, and, where appropriate, by plurals. The effect has been to suggest that it is only in and through the collective that people attain individuality. Conversely and ironically, the destruction of the collective means the destruction of individuality and the imminence of death, as the first of the series of collective nouns, *star'e*, "old folkery," neatly hints. The point is restated in the concluding phrase: *lezhít i khrapít na ves' Kíev* ("lay and snored for all of Kiev to hear"). This parallels the opening *Shumít* [*i*] *gremít konéts Kíeva*; but instead of dancing, immobility and sleep prevail, to the accompaniment of the "music" of snoring.

"All of Kiev" marks a considerable expansion of the "quarter of Kiev" in which the story begins. Foreshadowed is the steady enlargement of boundaries throughout, from Kiev to the Cossack Ukraine, then to the Carpathian Mountains, and finally to the universe. With every swing of the narration back to Kiev, the original place becomes distended. By chapter 14, the Carpathians are visible from it, as they literally are not; and when we reach the final chapter, this place is gone, has disappeared altogether, like a huge bubble that has swelled and burst. Instead, we find ourselves in the otherwise insignificant town of Glukhov, where a blind bard explains the meaning of the story to a group of awed listeners.[8] Read this way, the story describes a movement from a small, well-enclosed place to any place, or no place at all. This is the general direction followed by most of Gogol's fictions.

Expansion is caused by the intrusion of an alien element into a social body that is already full and integral. Again this holds in a general way throughout Gogol's work. In "A Terrible Vengeance," the element takes three different forms. One comes from the outside, most graphically as the sorcerer. Another consists of people who leave the collective and return, as Danilo does when he visits the castle and then goes home. Returns are always charged with danger in Gogol, because they bring with them whatever lies outside. A third, more subtle and probably even more typical of Gogol, is an incongruous or discordant internal element that at first is all but undetectable. One example will suffice: "Among others the Dnieper Cossack Mikitka came on his sorrel horse straight from a riotous orgy at the Pereshlay Plain, where for seven days and seven nights he had been entertaining the Polish king's soldiers with red wine" (136). This is cast in a stylized folk diction—*Priékhal na gnedóm koné svoém i zaporózhets Mikítka prýamo s razgúl'noi popóiki s Pereshlyáya pólya*, and so on, which is euphonious in itself and enables the sentence to fit smoothly into the larger context of happy revelry. It even looks semantically neutral, since the battle/feast comparison is a topos of folk literature. Here, however, the terms are reversed, with the feast likened to a battle. This hints at the potential for violence in the collective, particularly as the "battle" refers to the very real Polish-Cossack conflict then rampant. The stakes of this battle are higher than those of the kind of personal bravery addressed in Mikitka's situation, as soon becomes plain. For "Poles" occupy the same semantic field as "sorcerer," "devil," and "Antichrist," and therefore menace the Cossack community at large. It does not matter that the Poles are still "out there"; the sorcerer is very much "in here."

Boundaries may be violated from without or within. We find an almost exact parallel here with three of the four kinds of "social pollution" identified by Douglas: "The first is danger pressing on external boundaries; the second, danger from transgressing the internal lines of the system. . . . The fourth is danger from internal contradiction" (122).[9] The third, "danger in the margins of the lines," is also present in Gogol's story, primarily in the natural world, which is meant to stand as a counterpart to the bounded system of Cossack society. This world is first evoked in the description of the Dnieper River at the beginning of chapter 2. That this large but benevolent stream represents a harmonious center is conveyed by the use of rhythmic prose, again with folkloric stylizations, and by the simple device of making it reflect the surrounding landscape: "Those mountains are not mountains: they end in peaks below, as above, and both under and above them lie the high heavens. Those forests on the hill are not forests: they are the hair that covers the shaggy head of the wood demon. Down below he washes his beard in the water, and under his beard and over his head lie the high heavens. Those meadows are not meadows: they are a green girdle encircling the round sky; and above and below the moon hovers over them" (138). Conventionally, mountains, fields and forests are boundary markers, but they do not fulfill that function here: instead, the emphasis is on a wholeness and oneness so vital and energetic that it does not require clear definition.

In chapter 10, the Dnieper returns in a famous set piece that has been memorized by generations of Russian schoolchildren. The first sentence establishes a rhythmic prose of considerable complexity, which is sustained throughout the entire scene: "Lovely is the Dnieper in tranquil weather when, freely and smoothly, it speeds its waters through forests and mountains": *Chúden Dnepr pri tíkhoi pogóde, kogdá vól'no i plávno mchit skvoz' lesá i góry pólnye vódy svoí*. Here we find internal rhymes or half-rhymes: *pri/ti* (-khoi) *pog* (-ode)/*kog* (-da); *go* (-ry)/*po* (-lnye)/*vo* (-dy); at least one mirror rhyme—(chu-) *den/Dne* (-pr)—and an insistent pulse. The scene is surveyed horizontally and vertically to create the impression of a coherent whole, unbounded by space, where heaven and earth join to form a "center [*seredina*]" that stands for the ongoing life of the people, as is clear from its personification as a Cossack mother weeping over her son when he sets out for battle. All this looks like an amplified version of the opening of chapter 2. But there is one important difference. The river's reflective properties now do not extend to the surrounding landscape; only the "forests on the banks . . . are never tired of gazing and admiring their bright visages, and smile and greet it with nodding branches." Even so, there is an important qualification: "Into mid-Dnieper they dare not look; none but the sun and the blue sky gaze into it" (160). The river has now so expanded that "it is a rare bird that flies to the middle." No mention is made of hills, mountains, or meadows; they are no longer incorporated into the "center"; in the intervening chapters, these boundaries have become transitional places and are therefore potentially dangerous.

Retrospectively, we see that something is amiss in the earlier Dnieper scene as well. The negatives in the passage we have quoted do not define the distinction between place and non-place, as in chapter 1, but dislocate boundaries and thereby eradicate an essential distinction in the image system of the story. The consequences are suggested by the way in which the hills are treated. As Danilo and his family float down the Dnieper in a boat, they see a graveyard, on the bank, presumably at the top.[10] From it rise in succession three shrieking corpses, with long beards and fingernails. Danilo says: "It is the sorcerer who frightens people so that they will not break into his foul lair," which is a castle—itself a foreign object in any Eastern Slavic land—that is situated behind an earthen wall (*val*, another boundary) atop another hill overlooking the river. Thereafter hills are consistently associated with actions inimical to the Cossacks. Many scenes later, for example, the invading Poles "covered the mountainside"; "the festival [the battle] was kept on the mountains"; and at length Danilo died when the sorcerer "stood on the hillside aiming his musket at him. . . . Then came the crack of a shot—and the sorcerer vanished behind the hill" (158–59).

"Behind (or beyond) the hill" may remind readers of the refrain in the *The Song of Igor's Campaign*: "O Russian land, you are already beyond the hill! [*O Ruskaya zemle! Uzhe za shelomyanem esi!*]." Here the bard tells us that Rus, as it was originally called, has, in the person of the disobedient Prince Igor, crossed the boundary (of the town in the first instance, of the Donets River in the second) that delimits its proper place, and must suffer the consequences. We may also be hearing an echo of Pushkin's one-act play *The Covetous Knight* (Skupoi rytsar', 1830), where the miser accumulates a "hill" of coins, from whose "height" and "crest" he surveys and rules, "demonlike," his "vast domains," which have no "bounds."[11] In the topography of Gogol's story, beyond the hill lie open fields, which, like the miser's domains, lack boundaries and are therefore hostile. There live the Poles, the archenemy. It is an interesting though perhaps coincidental fact that the word "Pole" (*polak* in Polish, *polyak* in Russian) is derived from the common Slavic word for "field" (*pole* in both Russian and Polish). The significance of this topography is tellingly summed up by the narrator: "A thatched roof came into sight *behind the mountain*: it was Danilo's ancestral home. *Beyond* it was another *mountain*, and then the *open plain*, and there you might travel a hundred miles and *not see a single Cossack*" (141). The situation of Danilo's house on the margin of Cossack territory, behind a mountain, suggests, as we shall see, that his position in the collective is precarious.

Eventually these hills expand to become huge mountains, which also mark a boundary between place and non-place: "just beyond the mountains there are still here and there echoes of our native tongue," after which non-Cossack territory unambiguously begins: "but further beyond, faith is *no longer* the same [*uzhe ne ta*], and speech is *no longer* the same [*uzhe ne ta*]."[12] The Dnieper has now disappeared, seemingly absorbed by the mountains, which resemble a huge river viewed from above: "There are no such mountains in our country [cf.: 'There is no river like it in the world,' 160]. The eye shrinks from viewing them and no human foot has climbed to their tops [cf.: 'Into mid-Dnieper they dare not look; none but the sun and the blue sky gaze into it'].'' They are "wondrous" to behold, the same adjective in the same form being used here as for the Dnieper in chapter 10: "*Chuden* i vid ikh" (cf. "*Chuden* Dnepr"). And the wondrousness motivates a rhetorical flourish that all but confirms the parallelism: "Were they perhaps caused by some angry sea that broke away from its wide shores in a storm and threw its monstrous waves aloft only to have them turn to stone, and remain motionless in the air? Or did heavy storm clouds fall from heaven and cumber up the earth? For they have the same gray color, and their white crests flash and sparkle in the sun" (163). This is an early instance of what Yury Mann has called the "poetics of petrifaction" in Gogol, which recurs throughout his works in many different forms. It always signifies "the immobilization of the living," appears suddenly and unexpectedly, and is "linked with some very powerful experience or shock." Here it sets the scene for the final judgment of the sorcerer, which is pronounced by the apocalyptic horseman who drops him into an abyss. This abyss (*proval* or *propast'*) stands in the same spatial relationship to the mountain as did the Dnieper to the surrounding hills. Danilo has stated that if Katerina was the one who released the sorcerer from the cellar, he would sew her up in a sack and drown her in the middle of the Dnieper (156). The river is the place in which troublesome, chaotic elements can be deposited and reconciled. As the final habitation of the sorcerer, the abyss serves the same mythic function: the curse has been fulfilled, and he has found his "place." Gogol may here be hinting at the well-developed "theology of the abyss" in Orthodox iconography, although, as John Breck points out, the abyss is also "a universal symbol for death and for the power of hell."[13] This in fact seems more appropriate to a story that aspires to myth and gives short shrift in other respects to specifically Christian elements.

Water has either become petrified or been confined to small landlocked lakes located "among the mountains," in faint parodies of the Dnieper: "They are still as glass and reflect bare mountaintops and the green slopes below like mirrors" (163). Ultimately they too disappear. We find only three or four further mentions of water in the entire story, all trivial or general. The last chapter, in which the blind bard explains the meaning of the events, contains not a single reference to water; he describes a *nature morte*, dominated by mountains. There is no longer a life-giving center.

Let us now turn to the human characters of the story. When we first encounter Danilo and Katerina, they inhabit a well-ordered, harmonious place. In part, these qualities reflect a scrupulous adherence to the tradition-bound roles of husband and wife. Katerina devotes herself to rearing the child, keeping the house, and lending unquestioning support to the man she calls "my lord Danilo." He is a warrior who lives exclusively by the male Cossack code and will not tolerate the slightest wifely infringement on his preserve. When Katerina expresses doubts about the wisdom of attacking the sorcerer in his lair, he retorts: "Hold your tongue, woman! . . . If one has dealings with you, one will turn into a woman, oneself" (139). Each of these roles carries with it a set of gestures, habits, thoughts, and speech-patterns fixed according to constantly invoked Cossack norms: "That's our way here" (142).

The presence of Katerina's father in the household creates complications. When he insists that Katerina tell him why she returned so late the night before, Danilo immediately breaks in: "It is not her but me you should question about that, father-in-law [reminding him of his rank or place]! Not the wife but the husband is responsible [clearly defining the roles]" (142). But the old man reaffirms his own primary role: "Who, if not a father, should watch over his daughter!" Danilo then takes on the role of Cossack warrior as he casts his father-in-law into the role of adversary (without yet knowing that he is also the sorcerer) and asperses his courage and loyalty. The exchange of words escalates into physical violence. Katerina tries to intervene by recovering the now discarded roles of "son-in-law" and "old man incapable of fighting": "Danilo! . . . think what you are doing, madman, see against whom you are lifting your hand! Father, your hair is white as snow, but you have flown into a rage like a senseless boy [behavior entirely inappropriate to his age]!" (143). She is set back into her proper role by Danilo—"Wife! . . . You mind your woman's business!"—who then proceeds to do battle with the old man. The fight ends when Katerina successfully appeals to other roles: Danilo as father of his son, and the son as future Cossack: "But look at your son, Danilo, look at your son! Who will cherish the poor child? Who will be kind to him? Who will teach him to race on the black stallion, to fight for faith and freedom, to drink and carouse like a Cossack?" (143). Immediately Danilo relents: "Give me your hand, Father! Let us forget what has been between us! For the wrong I have done you I ask pardon" (144). There is no question of psychological verisimilitude: Danilo's apology is motivated entirely by the larger need to honor the strictures of his proper place.

Nevertheless, he is deeply troubled by the apology. He broods that he may have acted "badly and in a non-Cossack way in asking pardon when he had done no wrong" (144). Actually, he is caught in a dilemma: he must *not* do his Cossack duty—to defend the ethos by getting rid of his father-in-law—in order to ensure the survival of that ethos. He gives up an immediate Cossack good for a distant one, thereby introducing the future,

which intrudes on the timeless present he has always inhabited. Here begin
the psychological dislocations that eventually pull him out of his place.
Soon he leaves the Cossack collective, for the first time as far as we know,
and goes to the sorcerer's castle, which stands on alien territory. There,
through the window from his vantage point on a tree limb, he watches as
his father-in-law turns into the sorcerer and summons up Katerina's soul.
Such displacements inspire reactions inappropriate to a young Cossack
warrior: he feels a "thrill of fear in his Cossack heart," and, profoundly
shaken, he leaves the castle muttering "terrible, terrible [*strashno*]" (151).

Killing the sorcerer/father-in-law would be a drastic but legitimate
method of exorcising an alien presence from the Cossack body. But Danilo
plans it in a fatally wrong way. By locking the sorcerer in the cellar of his
own house, he effectively sanctions his continued residence within the collective. His exemption of Katerina from punishment—"nothing would
make me abandon you. The sin all lies at your father's door" (152)—shows
his failure to understand the responsibility she bears for introducing her
father into this society, and ultimately the responsibility he himself has in-
curred by marrying her. Personal displacement is the price he must pay.

At the beginning of chapter 9 he complains: "I am sad, my wife! . . . My
head aches and my heart aches. I feel weighed down." Physical and psychic
malaise promptly finds spatiotemporal equivalents: "It seems my death is
hovering *not far away*" (157), which indicates that the "other," or "not,"
is nearly present. Danilo has never been given to negations, but suddenly
they appear and cluster, and with them comes an uncharacteristic shift into
the future tense, in yet another displacement: "do *not* desert our son when
I am [lit., 'will be'] *no* more. God *will* give you *no* happiness either [lit.,
neither] in this world or [lit., *nor*] the next if you [will] forsake him. Sad
it will be for my bones to rot in the damp earth; sadder still *it will be* for
my soul!"(157). Katerina accuses him of talking like a "weak woman,"
thereby creating a counterpart to the role-reversal that he has earlier
warned her against, and providing further confirmation that his own place
has become shaky. Again he invokes death, only this time it is "near [*bliz-
kuyu*]," not merely "not far away." There remains only the salvific possibility of the past, the one time-dimension that has not yet been invoked:
"Ah, I remember, I remember the good years. . . . Those were golden days,
Katerina!" (157). But he is well aware that "they will not return": "I shall
never fight like that! One would think I am *not* old . . . yet . . . I live doing
nothing [lit., 'without work'] and know *not* what I live for. There is *no*
order in the Ukraine . . . there is *no* chief over them all." The negations to
which he resorts may represent a last desperate attempt to define a place
for himself, as they do for his society at large in the opening chapter of the
story. By now, however, they have the very different function of confirming
that non-place is present as place, or, conversely, that place has become

non-place. With the future lethal, the present invalid, and the past beyond recall, he no longer has a place, and there is no further need for him, as he himself acknowledges: "I know *not* what I live for" (158). As in the first scene, the negations introduce the motif of change—"Our gentry have *changed* [*peremenilo*] everything" (157–58, omitted in Garnett/Kent)— which is reified when Danilo tells the boy to "go to the *cellar* [*podval*]" (158) and bring him a jug of mead. "Cellar" is an image of death, being not only a foreshadowing of the grave that awaits Danilo but a reminder of the place where the sorcerer had been confined, which in turn looks ahead to the "abyss" into which he will be dropped at the story's end. All this is immediately followed by the arrival of the Poles "from the direction of the meadow" (non-place), and the onset of the battle on the hills. Danilo then goes forth to meet them, and perishes at the hands of the sorcerer.

Katerina is considerably more complex. She first becomes vividly aware that she occupies more than one place when she dreams that her soul has been summoned from her body by the sorcerer. Actually, it is no dream: Danilo has witnessed it through the window of the castle. At first the sorcerer keeps the two entities, body and soul, separate: "soul" is his daughter, "body" is "Katerina," that is, the Cossack wife. So when he says "Katerina shall love me," he is not proposing incest with his daughter but adultery with his son-in-law's wife, with an eye to the eventual corruption and destruction of the Cossack family as a whole. Danilo overhears the sorcerer make this statement, but, unfailingly obtuse, he does not grasp what is meant. He thinks that he has witnessed nothing more than what we would today call an out-of-body experience, where the soul is in danger of falling into the clutches of the devil; and he says to his wife, drawing heavily on popular superstition: "You do not know a tenth part of what your soul knows. . . . [T]he Antichrist has the power to call up every man's soul; for the soul wanders freely when the body is asleep" (151–52). Katerina is terrified by the experience, but it seems to be a terror inspired not so much by the danger to her soul as by the danger to the integrity of her person: "daughter" and "wife," she seems to see, call on very different and utterly incompatible allegiances. From now on, her main concern is to reconcile the conflicting roles. But she starts off in a fatally wrong way, as she renounces her father and says to Danilo: "You are my father!" (152). In this way she eradicates the boundaries that have marked her roles as wife and daughter, and creates a relationship that is unthinkable not only within the Cossack ethos but in human society generally. This relationship works in two ways, of course: if husband is father, then father is also husband. It is therefore not surprising that the incest theme eventually becomes explicit. When the sorcerer/father returns in the guise of one Kopriyan, who claims to have been Danilo's closest friend, and tells Katerina that it was her husband's dying wish for him to marry her, she recognizes him as her father, who has killed her child; she tries to kill him, but is herself killed. Incest, infanticide, and parricide spell the end of the Cossack family and of the Cossack ethos as well.

Katerina in fact comes to embody at least three different roles (or places) in the story: wife, mother, and daughter. Each is defined in different ways and occupies a different place, with its own boundaries. None of them, in Cossack society, counts as a position of authority. Rather, they are what we may call, borrowing again from Douglas (99), "dangerously ambiguous roles," which require her to operate in several subsystems simultaneously. In the tightly bounded role-system of Cossack society as described here, this ambiguity places her in a hopeless position. She learns that these subsystems neither separate nor combine readily. For instance, she releases the sorcerer from the cellar because he appeals to her role as daughter; but she immediately understands that her action is inconsistent with her role as a Cossack wife: "I let him out! . . . What answer shall I give my husband now? I am undone. There is nothing left but to bury myself alive!" (155). Instead, she decides to lie to Danilo, thereby creating still another role, which, as an enactment of a private self, has no place in the very public repertory of roles played out in a rigidly organized society. Deception becomes essential. The result is an unbearable tension, which eventually fragments her personality and finds expression as insanity.

The mad scene begins in chapter 13 when Katerina says to the nurse: "You are hideous: there are iron pincers coming out of your eyes ... ugh, how long they are, and they blaze like fire!" (164). This displaces one of the striking physical features of the sorcerer onto the servant. "Pincers [kleshchi]" are a visual counterpart of the "tusk" seen in chapter 1 and of the "crooked tooth" that protrudes from the sorcerer's mouth in the castle scene, but are further displaced from mouth to eyes. Temporal displacements also occur, as Katerina supposes her husband and son to be still alive, and her nurse capable of becoming young again. Like the sorcerer, she is seen in constant motion, itself a sign of placelessness. She does a mad dance "regardless of time or tune," and sings a song that confuses "lines from different songs." Gradually each of her roles or places has disappeared: wife (with Danilo's death), mother (with her son's death), daughter (with her renunciation of her father, her attempt to kill him, and her awareness of imminent incest), and finally, soul (with madness and attempted murder). Once the last of these roles is played out, nothing remains but death, the final expression of non-place: "a terrible deed was done: the father killed his crazed daughter" (166).

Danilo disappears from the story in chapter 9, Katerina in chapter 13. We are surprised to discover that we have come to care about them in ways that seemed inconceivable at the beginning of the story. By binding them up with the broader, inescapable issues of place, Gogol enlarges them and gives them greater claim to our pity than to our contempt.

Sorcerer, father, father-in-law, Cossack, traitor: these are the roles played by the remaining major character. They prove far more unstable than the roles of Danilo and Katerina. For this figure really has no place at all. He moves easily and rapidly across boundaries, usurping places that belong to others, often changing his own form and that of the places he temporarily inhabits. Now he is with the Cossacks, now with the Poles, now in the castle, now in his daughter's home; now he is Katerina's father, now her would-be lover, finally her murderer. In the castle he presides over a scene filled with transformations, rapid movement, and striking dislocations of time and space. In the father-guise with which this scene begins, he is suddenly invested in an oriental costume, and his face turns into that of the sorcerer. As he walks around the table, "the symbols on the wall began changing more rapidly, the bats flitted more swiftly up and down and to and fro" (149). Boundaries are erased in a kind of synesthesia: "accompanied by a faint ringing sound the rosy light flooded the room again. . . . The sounds grew louder and deeper, the delicate rosy light shone more brilliant." This culminates in oxymorons, which are rhetorical eradications of logical boundaries: "her lips were pale crimson . . . her brows were faintly dark" (149–50). And the room suddenly opens up to reveal the night sky, then Danilo's own room, and finally the misty floating figure of a woman, who turns out to be Katerina's soul.

Mutability is characteristic of demonic figures generally. In their Russian versions, they torment others but are gnawed by the awareness that they lack a proper place. Mikhail Lermontov's long poem *The Demon* (Demon, 1829–39) illustrates the type: a figure who is in love with a mortal woman but is doomed to perpetual solitude. Although Gogol's sorcerer does not know love, he experiences a feeling of acute isolation, whose spatial correlative is his inability to find his way:

Leaping on his horse he rode straight to Kanev, thinking from there to go through Cherkassy direct to the Crimean Tartars, though he knew not why. He rode one day and a second and still Kanev was not in sight. The road was the same; he should have reached it long before, but there was no sign of Kanev. Far away there gleamed the cupolas of churches; but that was not Kanev but Shumsk. The sorcerer was amazed to find that he had traveled the wrong way. He turned back toward Kiev, and a day later a town appeared—not Kiev but Galich, a town further from Kiev than Shumsk and not far from Hungary. At a loss what to do he turned back, but felt again that he was going backward as he went on. (168–69)

One essential difference between the sorcerer and other demons is that he does not create his fate through an act of defiance, but is the vehicle of a curse pronounced centuries before. We come to pity him too. Ironically, he is the only character eventually assigned a permanent place, in the abyss. To see this as a reward for his suffering is to appreciate Gogol's penchant for black humor.

The sorcerer and the Cossack collective represent extremes. The first has no proper place at all. The second is utterly lacking in the kinds of flexibility that make for a healthy society. For one, no allowance is made in the story for what Victor Turner, in a very different but I think relevant context, calls "liminality," a state "betwixt and between the positions assigned and arrayed by law, custom, convention, and ceremonial," yet recognized and acknowledged as a necessary aspect of society as a whole (95). Despite her comparative complexity, Katerina does not exemplify liminality: her roles as wife, mother, daughter are rigidly prescribed by convention; her secret life, if made public, would result in her banishment, probably by death, beyond any *limen*, or threshold. Gogol's story shows that societies can and must deal with threats to their stability, as in the case of the sorcerer. If the danger cannot be seen, as with Katerina, the consequences are fatal, particularly when the society is as rigidly structured as the one in "A Terrible Vengeance," or, for that matter, in most of Gogol's fictions.

'THE INSPECTOR GENERAL'

The mechanisms of displacement and isolation are employed in a similar but far more sophisticated fashion in *The Inspector General* (1836).[14] The play is set in a small, remote, unnamed provincial town, which is visited by Khlestakov, a minor civil servant from St. Petersburg. Even though he is stupid, self-indulgent, and vacuous, the officials take him for the inspector general they have been fearfully awaiting, treat him with great deference, and offer him bribes. Unaware of the misunderstanding, he lets himself be carried along, and ends by proposing marriage to the mayor's daughter. Her ecstatic parents envision moving to the capital and becoming important people. Meanwhile, Khlestakov's wise servant Osip persuades him that matters have gone far enough. Khlestakov leaves on the pretext of visiting a rich uncle, promising to return the next day. When the leading citizens assemble to offer insincere congratulations to the mayor and his family, the postmaster reads aloud an intercepted letter written by Khlestakov to a friend, which shows that he has finally figured things out and is capable of characterizing the principals in sharp and amused terms. Amidst general consternation, a gendarme enters to announce that an official from St. Petersburg has arrived and commands their presence.

Before Khlestakov turns up, the town appears to be a smoothly functioning body politic. Everyone knows his place and takes care not to overstep. Even the pervasive corruption of the officials is part of the system. At first Khlestakov creates anxiety but no dislocations: the system has a place for inspectors general and for swindlers, as seen in the accepted practice of offering bribes. Nevertheless, profound displacement of an unexpected kind occurs.

Khlestakov is himself already displaced. For one thing, he is virtually a cipher, intellectually, culturally, morally, and socially. For another, he comes from St. Petersburg, which, as we shall see in a subsequent chapter, is consistently denied the attributes of real place in Gogol's universe. Finally, he leads a migratory life, and is capable of assuming the identities and thereby the places of others with little difficulty. This is no doubt why many Russian critics, most notably Dmitry Merezhkovsky, have tended to see him as a demonic character.[15] In the exchanges with Anna Andreevna in Act III, he borrows the language and ethos of Sentimentalism the more effectively to woo her, and in the process arrogates to himself an astonishing repertory of places occupied by others: commander-in-chief; intimate of Pushkin; composer of the works of Mozart, Meyerbeer, and Bellini; author of books by Senkovsky, Bestuzhev-Marlinsky, Polevoy and Zagoskin; head of a government department; and imminently, field marshal. Placeless, he functions mainly to displace the other characters.

Khlestakov enables many of the townsfolk to become aware of their real feelings and psychic needs, which are at variance with the places they occupy and have therefore been repressed. Strongest of all is their desire to be recognized as unique individuals. Hence Zemlyanika's vicious though possibly accurate characterizations of the other officials, all the more amusing since they come from the director of charities ("Welfare Commissioner" in Garnett/Kent); Dobchinsky's confession that his son was born out of wedlock but has extraordinary qualities; and Bobchinsky's plea that Khlestakov, on returning to the capital, should say to all the "great gentlemen"—senators, admirals, even the tsar—that "in such and such a town there lives a man called Pyotr Ivanovich Bobchinsky." The mayor's wife and daughter, nourished on Sentimentalist literature, entertain fantasies of a grander life lived far from this provincial town. Until now, these fantasies have not moved beyond harmless and ineffectual day dreams. Khlestakov's arrival turns them into possibilities, then expectations, then virtual realities as he and the daughter become engaged and the mayor and his wife look forward to becoming persons of consequence.

When the final scene comes, everyone has been mentally displaced by the imagined consequences of the impending marriage. As such displacements work in Gogol, there is no going back. But then the postmaster reads Khlestakov's letter, which effects a further displacement of the officials it names, only in just the opposite direction from the one they anticipate, socially downward and ultimately into the realm of animals and inanimate objects. According to the letter, the postmaster is "the very image of our porter, Matveyev." The judge is "awfully *mauvais ton*." The superintendent of schools reeks of onions; one more step and he would *be* an onion. Such a step is nearly taken in the case of the mayor, who is called "as stupid as an old gray gelding" (*merin*: the Garnett/Kent translation has "horse," but that is too tame). This is still simile, but the outraged repetitions that follow (a favorite device of Gogol's) make it almost metaphor:

> *Postmaster (reads):* "First and foremost the mayor—as stupid as an old gray gelding."
> *Mayor:* It can't be, it isn't there!
> *Postmaster (shows him the letter):* Read it yourself!
> *Mayor (reads):* "As an old gray gelding." It can't be, you wrote it yourself.
> *Postmaster:* How could I have written it?
> *Artemy Filippovich:* Read!
> *Luka Lukich:* Read!
> *Postmaster (goes on reading):* "The mayor—as stupid as an old gray gelding."
> *Mayor:* Oh, damn it all! You need not repeat it! We all know the words are there!
> *Postmaster (goes on reading):* Hm ... hm ... hm ... "old gray gelding . . ."
> (670–71)

The word "gelding" would be offensive to most males. It fits the mayor's situation particularly well, as a man whose ambition has been, so to speak, abruptly cut off. He may also of course be reacting to the word "stupid"; but undoubtedly he is thinking, as any Russian speaker would, of the saying *vret kak sivyi merin*, "lies like a gray gelding," or "is an out-and-out liar," which accurately characterizes the way he performs his official duties, as well as his fantasies of rising to social prominence.[16] Full transformation is achieved in the case of Zemlyanika, who is called "a regular pig in a skullcap." His rejoinder, which also employs the device of repetition, draws attention to the displacement: "It is not even witty! A pig in a skullcap! *Who has ever seen* a pig in a skullcap?" He appears to react not so much to the "pig" label as to the absurdity of the skullcap, as if trying to displace the label from himself, for it does seems apt: he is described in the stage directions as "very fat, slow, clumsy."

The labels are as offensive in their way as the "gander" in "The Two Ivans" (see below, Chapter 3). And they have something of the same effect, even though they come at the end of the play. They transform, lower, and individualize the characters to whom they are affixed, as "mayor" and "Welfare Commissioner" do not: those particular designations attach to countless other officials in countless other towns. Khlestakov, though now physically absent, performs the same service for these officials as he has face to face for the other characters: he brings out a private self that would otherwise have remained hidden under titles and rituals. In this sense, he is indeed an "inspector general," and not such a "false" one at that.

The mayor's mortified response is structured as a displacement fantasy, which lowers, fragments, and depersonalizes. "I see nothing; nothing but pigs' snouts of faces. . . . Silly old sheep, I am in my dotage! . . . To take a suckling, a rag like that, for a man of consequence! ... I'd tie you all in a knot, pound you all to a jelly and into the lining of the devil's cap! . . . you bobtailed magpies!" To which Zemlyanika adds: "You potbellied shrimps!" (670–74). Ironically, the mayor is mimicking the phraseology of Khlestakov's letter, and thereby confirming that he too lacks a proper place. Is it mere coincidence that he mentions the devil, who also has no place?

In another irony, Khlestakov's and the mayor's labels "place" the officials, but in so doing, displace them irrevocably from the larger collective. The old system has been shattered; the town is no longer a society but a collection of isolated individuals. It never was a true place. The stage has been cleared for whatever drama is to follow upon the arrival of yet another inspector general, of whose authenticity we have no more reason to be sure than of Khlestakov's, despite Gogol's retrospective interpretation. The mute scene that closes the play suggests that at the moment of truth, each character is isolated in an awareness of his own position vis-à-vis all the others. As Gogol explained this scene a decade later: "Each personage should be assigned a pose appropriate to his personality, the degree of fear he feels, and the shock that ought to be created by the words announcing the arrival of the real inspector general. It is necessary that these poses should not complement each other, but should instead be diverse and distinctive."[17]

The very isolation of the town is what enables the play to work as it does. The inhabitants are so removed in time and space from society at large that they have no standards for judging unfamiliar phenomena, and are therefore capable of the kind of drastic misjudgments that ultimately destroy their stability and equilibrium. Of course the equilibrium is illusory, inasmuch as it does not take account of the powerful emotions that lurk beneath, waiting only to be set loose by an alien intrusion in the person of Khlestakov. In a real sense, the play gradually gives substance to incongruous elements already present in an apparently harmonious social body.

2

Displacement: "Old-World Landowners"

In "A Terrible Vengeance," memory proves profoundly disruptive, for it does not form an integral part of Danilo's personality but instead emerges from the realm of non-place, which is represented as both past and future. The same theme is treated in a similar but more sophisticated way in "Old-World Landowners," a story published in 1835 in the collection *Mirgorod*.

The story line is one of Gogol's simplest. The narrator, presumably a city dweller, sometimes ventures to the rural Ukraine to visit an old couple, Afanasy Ivanovich and Pulkheria Ivanovna, on their isolated estate. Their life seems blessed with happiness, good order, and prosperity. One day, however, Pulkheria's little gray cat disappears into the forest beyond, returns, then disappears again, whereupon she decides that her death is imminent. To Afanasy's despair, she stops eating, wastes away, and dies. Inconsolable, he goes into a decline. One day he hears her voice calling to him, and joyfully prepares to join her in the next world. After his death, the now nearly ruined estate passes to a distant relative, then to a board of trustees; but all efforts to revive it are fruitless, and it soon ceases to exist.

So tight are the boundaries of this estate that they create an "extraordinarily secluded life in which not one desire flits beyond the palisade surrounding the little courtyard, beyond the hurdle of the orchard filled with plum and apple trees, beyond the village huts surrounding it," a life so "humble and bucolic," so remote from "fashionable dress coats in the noise and crowd," "so quiet, so quiet," that one "imagines that those passions, desires, and restless promptings of the evil spirit that trouble the world have no real existence" (II, 1–3). This is the timeless world of the idyll, a favored genre of Sentimentalism, whose most illustrious Russian representative, Nikolai Karamzin, was still much read and admired in Gogol's time. Its layout, however, calls more to mind the enclosed garden, or *hortus conclusus*, that was cultivated in the Middle Ages, particularly in monasteries, as a replication of the original Eden. In Dmitry Likhachev's words, it was "free from sin, holy, abounding in everything essential to man, in all kinds of trees and plants, and inhabited by animals [horses and a little gray cat in Gogol] living together peacefully." The monastery (here the courtyard) was itself enclosed; beyond it lay a small orchard of fruit trees, symbolic of Paradise, also enclosed; still further began unenclosed, wild nature.[1]

That earlier nature, though unorganized, tended to be benevolent. In Gogol's hands, as later in Goncharov's, it was anything but that. (Chapter 5, below, explores this topic in greater detail.) He subtitled *Mirgorod* "tales serving as a continuation of *Evenings on a Farm Near Dikanka*" (omitted in Garnett/Kent); and the treatment of unenclosed nature is one of the continuities, even if, for present purposes, we restrict the comparison to "A Terrible Vengeance" and "Old-World Landowners." But there is one important difference. Pulkheria Ivanovna and her husband are far slower than Danilo and Katerina to acknowledge that the world beyond their enclosures is hostile. The reasons will become clearer after we look at the text in some detail.

Early in the story, Pulkheria Ivanovna drives out of the palisade to "inspect her forests." That this is no ordinary journey is signaled by the elaborate description of the carriage and its progress, which arrests the attention and prepares us for something momentous, very much as in, say, Homer, who invented this technique for European literature: "a chaise was brought out with immense leather aprons which, as soon as the coachman shook the reins, and the horses, who had served in the militia, set off, filled the air with strange sounds, so that a flute and a tambourine and a drum all seemed suddenly audible; every nail and iron bolt clanked so loudly that even at the mill it could be heard that the mistress was driving out of the yard, though the distance was fully a mile and a half." On arriving, she notices "the terrible devastation in the forest and the loss of the oaks, which even in childhood she had known to be a hundred years old." She asks the steward why, and is told: "They have fallen down! They have simply fallen: struck by lightning, gnawed by maggots—they have fallen, lady, they have fallen," although in truth he has been cutting and selling them. The Russian for the phrase after the dash is *propali, pani, propali*. This may be intended to echo the saying *libo pan, libo propal*, which the *Oxford Russian-English Dictionary* translates as "all or nothing." A more literal rendition, however, has greater resonance for this text: "either you're the master or you're done for." This could be a commentary on the "lady's" helplessness before her servant, and before her gradual loss of control in managing the enclosed part of the estate. In this context, *propali* could carry the meaning of "done for," "lost," and, by the rules of Russian grammar, could refer not only to the trees but also to Pulkheria. In any event, we are told that Pulkheria is "completely satisfied" with the steward's answer, and that "on arriving home [she] merely gave orders that the watch should be doubled in the garden near the Spanish cherry trees and the big winter pears" (7).

The scene is prevented from being merely comic by a strange use of verb tenses. We are told, "*On only one occasion* did Pulkheria Ivanovna [conceive the] desire to inspect her forests"; and the question she puts to the steward seems to have been asked on only this one occasion as well, since the perfective form of the verb "she said" is used, *skazala*. But the steward's answer—"they have fallen down"—is what "he *would usually say [govarival obyknovenno]*," that is, on more than one occasion, the adverb's meaning being strengthened by the iterative form of the verb. Repeated and one-time actions are logically incompatible. Indeed, Garnett/Kent obviously finds the situation so odd that it simply omits the word "usually." The inconsistency suggests that there may have been earlier visits, which the steward (like the narrator) remembers but which Pulkheria, faced with the spectacle of devastation, death, and lost childhood, represses, although not fully: her "satisfaction" with the steward's explanation does not square with her desire to double the watch inside the palisade. In fact, the very existence of a "watch [*strazha*]" hints at her awareness of the possibility that non-place and all it represents may have already taken up residence within the palisade. What is being guarded against might seem to amount to no more than the stealing of fruit, which would even be beneficial in this self-contained world that produces far more than can be consumed; but the doubling of the watch shows that Pulkheria knows far more is involved. For the moment, it is an unconscious knowledge: the house servants are perpetrating "*terrible robberies [strashnye khishcheniya]*," a phrase more commonly associated with major crimes than with petty thievery, yet they "went *completely unnoticed*." What she does not understand is that she herself may be the vehicle by which violence has entered the household, for she enacts the familiar Gogolian pattern of leaving a place, then returning and carrying with her at least part of the outside world, which may be "forgotten" or "repressed" but which works in deadly ways. As we shall soon see, this is not the only occasion on which she fulfills this function.

Actually, non-place has already established an almost undetectable presence, as is usually the case in Gogol. One clue comes in the pictures that adorn the walls of the house. Pictures are miniature places, whose boundaries are well marked by frames. Gogol makes frequent use of them in his stories. Sometimes they simply mirror the larger place of which they are part. But sometimes they are incompatible with it, and function as alien intrusions. In "Old-World Landowners," they at first look like mere decor, "a few pictures in old-fashioned narrow frames," which mean nothing to the old couple, who in fact "had themselves long ago forgotten what they represented, and if some of them had been taken away, they would probably not have noticed it" (4–5). But the passage is organized in such a way as to ensure that we readers do notice. We see a progressive narrowing of focus, from "a few pictures" to "two big portraits painted in oil." One of them depicts an anonymous bishop. But the other is said to represent Tsar Peter III, and is complemented by a second named picture, showing "a fly-blown Duchess de La Vallière" looking out "from a narrow frame." Hereafter the description again falls off to "numbers of little pictures [unnamed] which one grew used to looking upon as spots on the wall and therefore never examined."

The two named portraits look anomalous in the simple surroundings of the old couple's house. But anomaly is the point of the passage, as well as the reason why the old couple "forgets." These portraits represent historical subjects, and as such occupy the same dimension of non-place as the forest of Pulkheria's childhood, which she also "forgets." Furthermore, as any Russian reader knows, Peter III was the husband of the future Empress Catherine the Great; the marriage was probably unconsummated, she turned to other men, and Peter was soon murdered, presumably with the foreknowledge if not the complicity of his wife, who then ascended the throne. The Duchess of La Vallière was not the wife but the mistress of Louis XIV. Although there was no lack of consummation and no murder, the portrait nonetheless is said to be "flyblown," in an obvious suggestion of death, which is subtly strengthened by the mention of "[fly-]spots on the wall" in the next sentence and, a page or so later, by the frame around the mirror, "which the flies had covered with black spots" (6). The subjects of these two paintings, then, are violence, illicit sex, sterility, and death. All are characteristic of non-place in Gogol's world generally. In this particular story, they take other forms as well: sterility in the childlessness of the old couple; illicitness in their shared patronymic, Ivanovich/Ivanovna, which symbolically gives them the same father and explains why they seem more like brother and sister than husband and wife; rampant sexuality in the mysterious pregnancies of the servant girls and in the "ardent young men, chilled with the pursuit of some dark charmer," who run in to warm their hands in rooms that are grotesquely overstuffed and overheated, thus introducing those "passions, desires, and restless promptings" that in the very first paragraph are identified as issuing from the "evil spirit"; death in the relentless outpouring of produce from the estate's garden, a fertility gone cancerously wild. It is probably significant too that Peter III was the tsar who issued the edict of February 18, 1762, which absolved the gentry from obligatory service, making it possible for people like Afanasy Ivanovich to shut themselves up in their estates, forget about the world beyond, and live entirely off the labor of others.

However, it is mainly Afanasy Ivanovich himself who embodies an alien presence long resident within the enclosure. In this respect, he is a counterpart of Katerina in "A Terrible Vengeance."

At one time in his youth Afanasy Ivanovich was in the service and had been a lieutenant major; but that was very long ago, that was all over, Afanasy Ivanovich himself *scarcely ever recalled it* [*vspominal*]. Afanasy Ivanovich was married at thirty, when he was a fine fellow and wore an embroidered coat; he even rather neatly *carried off* [*uvez*] Pulkheria Ivanovna, whose relations opposed their marriage, but he *remembered* [*pomnil*] *very little* about that now—at any rate, he never spoke of it. (3–4)

His former profession and his virtual abduction of Pulkheria Ivanovna[2] hint at a past that was a good deal more violent than his now hebetudinous existence might lead us to suspect. In failing to remember it, he is acting as does his wife when faced with violence in the realm of non-place. Presumably he "carried off" his bride from her parental home. But where they went we are not told, nor do we know how they acquired the estate on which they now live. It is very likely that same parental estate, inasmuch as the forest to which Pulkheria journeys is said to be familiar to her from her childhood. If so, she is responsible for having brought Afanasy and all he represents into the ancestral enclosure, as Danilo did with Katerina, and she therefore embodies the motif of the polluting return that occurs so frequently in Gogol's work, reflects a deep-seated belief among Russians generally, and finds counterparts in many other societies as well.[3]

As in "A Terrible Vengeance," here these anomalies, inconsistencies, and discrepancies prepare the way for actual displacements, whose imminence is signaled by the following statement: "Sometimes, if it was fine weather and rather warm indoors, Afanasy Ivanovich, being in good spirits, liked to make fun of Pulkheria Ivanovna and talk of *something extraneous* [*postoronnem*]" (10). It is not immediately clear why good spirits should be a precondition for teasing, a form of cruelty. Apparent non sequiturs are stylistic displacements, which often prepare the way for spatial displacements. Here the word "extraneous" (omitted by Garnett/Kent) translates literally as "on the other side," or "beyond," which at the least would mean outside the confines of the routine life the couple has led, and at the most, outside the confines of the estate. Retrospectively it confirms that the preceding dialogue has been "in place." That dialogue has been devoted exclusively and at length to food, which has been synonymous with a smoothly functioning, well-ordered estate. We are alerted that something important is about to happen.

Afanasy proceeds to make three "little jokes" (the magic number suggests that we are entering the realm of the fairy tale) by way of postulating situations in which place, as they both know it, is violated. First, he asks seven times (also a magic number) what would happen if the house burned down. Pulkheria's alarmed reaction shows that she regards these questions as more than a joke: she knows that words have power and are not to be trifled with (a subject we will discuss in the next chapter). Yet her proposed solutions play into the speculation: "[W]e would move into the kitchen. You would have for the time the little room that the housekeeper has now. . . . [W]e would move into the storeroom while a new house was being built" (10). They would no longer occupy their proper places. Imaginative displacement would become actuality.

The second "little joke" occurs after guests have arrived. They are pressed to stay the night, as required by the rules of hospitality; but Afanasy Ivanovich also raises the specter of robbers on the road. Again Pulkheria Ivanovna objects: "God preserve us from robbers! . . . And why talk of such things at night? It's not a question of robbers, but it's dark, it's not fit for driving at all" (11). There is more truth than meets the eye here: guests participate in the life of the estate as long as they remain; when they leave its bounds, they take with them some of that life, which is then subject to whim, fate, or depredation. We are reminded of the fairy-tale motif of guests who are never allowed to leave.

The third "joke" combines the first and the second in that it envisages a situation whereby Afanasy Ivanovich, ostensibly a permanent member of the estate, actually leaves. Again guests are present; the talk turns to the possibility of war with France; Afanasy, "pretending not to look at Pulkheria Ivanovna," says: "I think I shall go to the war myself; why shouldn't I go to the war?" She rises to the bait: "There he goes again! . . . How could an old man like him go to the war! The first soldier would shoot him." This merely encourages Afanasy, who then runs through a list of the weapons he would use. Now Pulkheria is indignant: "I know he is only joking, but yet I don't like [lit., 'it is unpleasant'] to hear it." The Russian of this last statement restates the displacement theme in highly compressed form: *Ya i znayu, chto on SHUTIT* [is joking], *a vse-taki NEPRIYATNO* [unpleasant] *slushat'*, where "joking" creates "unpleasantness," the displaced state of the "pleasantness" that reigns in an idyllic world as mediated through

Sentimentalism. Far from being chastened, Afanasy is "pleased at having scared Pulkheria Ivanovna a little," and he laughs (12).

In all three exchanges, time is displaced to the future, not the past. But there is no real difference. What matters, as in "A Terrible Vengeance," is the distinction between present and non-present, here and there, the former comprising the estate and its contents, the latter being everything outside. This is confirmed by the fact that the future contains all the ingredients of the past that have supposedly been forgotten: violence, misfortune, and death. In effect, the future is a memory of the past. For the moment it intrudes only rhetorically as a "what if" statement, but it soon becomes actuality, in the form of "a very melancholy incident which transformed forever the life of that peaceful nook," an incident that "is the more impressive because it arose from such an insignificant cause": the "little gray cat [*seren'kaya koshechka*]," which Pulkheria pets and spoils, more out of habit than affection (13).

This cat is also the subject of one of Afanasy's little jokes, and thus becomes a candidate for displacement: he "often teased her [*podshuchival*: the same word is used for the earlier joking incidents] about her affection for it. 'I don't know, Pulkheria Ivanovna, what you find in the cat: what use is she?' . . . [H]e only said it to tease [*podshutit'*] Pulkheria Ivanovna a little" (14). One day the cat is lured out of the garden into the "big forest" beyond by the wild cats who live there. This is presumably not the same forest earlier visited by Pulkheria, for it "had been completely spared by the enterprising steward, perhaps because the sound of the ax would have reached [her] ears." In fact it is far more dangerous because it abuts the enclosure, and it is far more elemental, being "wild and neglected; the old tree stumps were covered with overgrown nut bushes and looked like the feathered legs of trumpeter pigeons." There the wild cats "mew in a coarse, uncultured voice. . . . In fact, they are unacquainted with any noble sentiments; they live by plunder, and *murder little sparrows in their nests*." Finally they entice Pulkheria's "gentle little cat" away. At first she handles this situation like other manifestations of non-place: "at last she forgot." When the cat comes back, she reverts to habit and plies it with food; but when she extends her hand to stroke it, the cat leaps out the window never to be seen again. Pulkheria immediately concludes: "It was my death coming for me!" (14–15).

The association of the cat with misfortune is of course a staple of folklore. But it also grows out of the structure of the story. Pulkheria has "forgotten" the cat after the first disappearance, but when it returns, she "remembers" it. Specifically, she remembers those elements of otherness that she has repressed on her visit to the more distant forest, and that the cat now makes present to her: chronological time ("three days passed" before she forgets the cat; it "was evident that [the cat] had not tasted food for several days"); change (the cat "had grown very wild during her absence"); sex and violence (the cat "had evidently grown too accustomed to the ways of wild cats") (14–15). The animal's second escape shows Pulkheria that she is powerless to control these elements by "forgetting." Perhaps too the cat helps her "remember" things about her relationship with Afanasy of which she has been largely unconscious. After all, she treats him in much the same way she does the cat, pampering and overfeeding him, more like a mother than a wife. To be sure, the cat is female; but the fact that the spouses are really more like siblings prepares us for the possibility of gender interchangeability, as does the constant invocation of the fairy tale, with its possibilities for transformation. In the seduction of Pulkheria's female cat (*koshka*) by the male cats (*koty*) of the forest—"at last they enticed her away, as a company of soldiers entices a silly peasant girl"—we detect an echo of the soldier Afanasy's "abduction" of Pulkheria. Finally, Afanasy himself has accomplished at least one "escape" from the estate by means of his "little jokes." Pulkheria's reaction—indignation, anger, irritation—shows that she feels insecure about her role as a nurturer. The feeding of dependents, whether Afanasy or the cat, has been her vocation. If that does not suffice to keep a cat at home, then what about a husband? This question is never asked, but her calm acceptance of death shows that she no longer has a reason for being.

From this point on, the story is dominated by drastic displacement, or loss, as foreshadowed in the account of the ravaged forest and in the disappearance of the cat. Pulkheria disappears, like the cat, and is assigned a new place, a grave by the church fence. Five years later Afanasy himself is laid to rest beside her. The original "place" ceases to exist: "The little house was now completely emptied. The enterprising steward and the elder hauled away to their huts all that were left of the old-fashioned goods and furniture, which the housekeeper had not been able to carry off" (21).

The childlessness of the old couple, which may at first have seemed quaint and charming, now proves lethal, because the estate cannot survive their death. Gogol explored this idea again some six years later, in chapter 6 of *Dead Souls*. There Chichikov visits Plyushkin, a miser who lives alone in utter squalor. Yet, we are told, he was once married with children, and was known for the "wise thriftiness" with which he ran a flourishing estate. But his wife died, his children left, and the estate has slowly declined, along with its master. Nothing can be done to restore it. Although Plyushkin has children, as most of Gogol's characters do not, they have forever abandoned the place in which they were brought up, and are as dead to it as their mother is. Even the two most memorable children in Gogol's work, those of Manilov in *Dead Souls*, have the ludicrous Greek-sounding names of Alcides (Alkid) and Themistoclus (Femistoklyus, with a Latin ending!), which serve the double purpose of mocking the recent vogue for things classical and establishing a decidedly non-Russian presence in this estate. And these children are destined to leave too, since their father wishes them to enter the diplomatic service.[4]

We have to interpret this in the larger context of an underlying metaphor that informs all Gogol's ideas about place: that of a living organism. It is a very old idea. Even the briefest account might begin with the fable of Aesop in which the belly and the feet "were vying with each other about their strength. The feet kept on saying that they must be much stronger than the belly, because they actually carried it about. 'That's all very well, my friends,' replied the belly; 'but if I stop supplying you with nourishment you won't be able to carry me.'" The same story is repeated and extended to political and social bodies by many other writers, including Livy, Shakespeare, and, among eighteenth-century Russians, Vasily Maikov and Aleksandr Sumarokov. Readers of Plato and Aristotle will remember striking instances of somatic imagery used for similar purposes. For Christians, the locus classicus is found in 1 Corinthians 12:4–30, where Paul, after enumerating the various gifts of the Holy Spirit, insists that they are all "the work of one and the same Spirit," and by way of illustration brings in the parts of the body, each of which has its own function, and all of which together are essential to the proper workings of the body as a whole, just as, in a further extension, each individual Christian is a member of the Body of Christ. Among Gogol's more immediate predecessors, the German Romantics developed organic views of society in contrast to the prevailing mechanistic models. Especially important was the idea that bodies politic were like living beings, not the result of conscious design. As Friedrich Schleiermacher put it: "Never has a state, even the most imperfect one, been made."[5]

We do not have to read far below the surface to see that for Gogol, too, a bounded space must ideally be organic. This is as true for the world of Pulkheria Ivanovna and Afanasy Ivanovich as for any of his other fictional worlds. Insofar as this old couple is part of a living organism, it is a very sick organism indeed, suffering from a kind of edema that eventually kills it. But there is a strong suggestion, as we have seen, that the disease has been introduced. And there are hints as well that the old couple, Pulkheria Ivanovna in particular, looks on the estate less as an organism than as a mechanism.

The first indication comes in the narrator's reaction to the way Pulkheria handles the cat: "I cannot say that Pulkheria Ivanovna was excessively fond of [the cat]; she was simply attached to her from being used to seeing her about" (14). This looks ahead to the question rhetorically posed by the

narrator as he contemplates the spectacle of a widowed and ruined Afanasy: "What is stronger in us—passion or habit?" (20). The answer, in all
likelihood, would be "habit." And habit, routine, custom, any thought,
emotion, or gesture repeated to the point where it is automatic or unre-
membered is for Gogol always a symptom of mechanical thinking, a denial
of the vitality that any healthy organism must enjoy.

Pulkheria's preparations for dying also reflect this mechanical thinking.
A change in roles and functions, which cannot occur among the members
of any healthy body, now takes place. It is Afanasy's turn to be frightened
by predictions of dire events, as his wife informs him that she will soon die:
" 'God knows what you are saying, Pulkheria Ivanovna!' said Afanasy Ivanovich. 'Death may be a long way off, but you are really frightening me by
talking this way' " (16). Now it is he who urges her to eat, in virtually her
own previous words: "Perhaps you would eat a little of something, Pulkheria Ivanovna" (17; cf. 10: "Hadn't you better eat something, Afanasy
Ivanovich?"). The production and consumption of food have been the symbol if not the agent of their shared life and the integrity of the estate. Now
we cannot help but conclude that Pulkheria starves herself to death, in an
ironic reversal of her earlier obsession with food (although students of eating disorders recognize that self-deprivation is the obverse of gluttony). Instead, she introduces the new motif of clothing, and makes it ironically
clear that unlike food, clothes can be shared even when one person is gone:
"Put my gray dress on me, the one with the little flowers on a brown background. Don't put on me my satin dress with the crimson stripes; a dead
woman has no need of such a dress—what use is it to her?—while it will
be of use to you [again the androgynous motif]: have a fine dressing gown
made of it, so that when visitors are here you can show yourself and welcome them, looking decent" (16). Clothing and food are often interchangeable for Gogol. Either may have sexual connotations as well. This is certainly the case, as we shall see, in "Ivan Fyodorovich Shponka" and "The
Tale of How Ivan Ivanovich Quarreled with Ivan Nikiforovich." In "Old-
World Landowners," it is tempting, and valid up to a point, to see food as
a substitute for sex in the old couple's marriage. Once it can no longer be
shared—a situation for which Pulkheria prepares her husband by refusing
to eat—the dress could serve as a symbolic substitute. But as I read this
story, Gogol is far more interested in using the dress to advance the theme
of place. What Pulkheria proposes, in effect, is what we would today call
cross-dressing, and with it, Afanasy's assumption of her old role as mistress
of the house. The consequence is a further displacement of Afanasy while
he is still living. Pulkheria also proposes a substitute for herself, in the person of the housekeeper Yavdokha, whom she enjoins to perform for Afanasy precisely the services she herself has performed: "[W]atch over him

like the apple of your eye, like your own child. Make certain that what he likes is always cooked for him in the kitchen; that you always give him clean linen and clothes; that when visitors come you dress him in his best" (16). The fact that she moves Yavdokha out of her appointed place is further evidence that she regards the estate as a machine that can be fixed by replacing a damaged or missing part. In any event, Yavdokha does not heed her mistress, as Afanasy's condition five years later demonstrates, but avails herself of his progressive enfeeblement to help loot the estate, as if in revenge for Pulkheria's presumptuousness in upsetting an ordained order of things.

Pulkheria Ivanovna's question about the dress, "what use is it [to a dead woman]? [*na chto ono ei*]," ironically echoes Afanasy Ivanovich's teasing question about the cat: "what use is it? [*na chto ona?*]" The syntactic parallel prompts another question in the reader's mind: what do "cat" and "dress" have in common? We know that the cat has been "useful" as a harbinger of death. "Dress" is of course explicitly associated with death in this passage, but more generally it points to still another question about usefulness that has remained unasked throughout the story: have Pulkheria's housewifely pursuits served any end beyond mere accumulation? Rather early in the story we are told:

Pulkheria Ivanovna's room was all surrounded with chests and boxes, big and little. Numbers [*mnozhestvo*] of little bags and sacks of flower seeds, vegetable seeds, and melon seeds hung on the walls. Numbers [*mnozhestvo*] of balls of different-colored wools and rags of old-fashioned gowns made half a century ago were stored in the little chests and between the little chests in the corners. Pulkheria Ivanovna was a notable housewife and saved everything, though sometimes she could not herself have said to what use it could be put afterwards. (5)

This paragraph does not really follow from what precedes, and does not organically connect with the next: its isolation on the page makes it the more conspicuous. The key term is *mnozhestvo*, which means a multitude of anything. It has appeared in the "picture" scene in the preceding paragraph—"numbers [*mnozhestvo*] of little pictures"—and recurs frequently in the three or four pages that follow: as "a terrible number [*strashnoe mnozhestvo*] of flies" (6); "preserving countless masses [*beschislennogo mnozhestva*] of fruits" (7); "a dreadful number [*strashnoe mnozhestvo*] of plums and apples" (8); and "the blessed earth produced everything in such abundance [*v takom mnozhestve*]" (8). It indicates an enormous, unnecessary, and useless profusion of things, which are elsewhere referred to as *dryan'* and *dryazg*, meaning, respectively, "rubbish" and "refuse."[6] Rubbish and refuse consist of things or pieces of things no longer useful or alive, which, if collected, as in "a heap of all kinds of refuse [*kuchu vsyakogo dryazgu*]" (18), do not form an organic or necessary unit: they can be added to or subtracted from at will. We are prepared to discover that the estate is a "heap" of just this kind. Once its components begin to disappear, it slowly dwindles to nothing. Gogol would explore this same theme on a grander scale in chapter 6 of *Dead Souls*, where Plyushkin's house has turned into an undifferentiated heap of rubbish, its owner along with it.

One attempt is made to revive the old couple's estate. It passes into the hands of a relative, a "terrible reformer," who "saw at once the great slackness and disorganization in the management of the land" and "made up his mind to change all that radically, to improve things and bring everything into *order*." To that end he "bought *six* splendid *English* sickles, pinned a special *number* onto each hut, and managed so well that within *six months* his estate was put under the supervision of a board of trustees" (21). Such efforts, Gogol thought, are bound to be chimerical. For one thing, they involve the importation of still more alien elements into what is left of the enclosure. The relative himself is "distant" by blood, and comes from "I don't know where." He brings the implements of a far more distant place, England, and with them, a desire to imitate traits popularly ascribed to the English in the nineteenth century: efficiency and a knack for administration, all regulated by calendar and calculation. Everywhere in Gogol these count as foreign and therefore negative qualities, characteristic of an urban, mercantile ethos he thought was being imposed on Russia, much to its detriment. But he took for granted that Russia was still an organism, while the estate in this story has ceased to be that, if in fact it ever was. Actually, the well-meaning relative is doing no more than repeating consciously what Pulkheria Ivanovna had done mostly unconsciously: introduced alien elements and assumed that they would somehow find their place. That never works in Gogol's world. Such efforts are themselves "rubbish." The final paragraph makes the point graphically. The new owner "drives about to all the fairs in Little Russia" but "only buys small trifles such as flints, a nail to clean out his pipe, in fact nothing which exceeds at the utmost a ruble in price" (22). That single ruble stands in stark contrast to the prosperity and abundance, unreckonable in currency, that characterize the estate as the story opens. But is the contrast of the two value-systems ultimately meaningful? An estate that is not an organism but instead has been assembled out of discrete units resembles a heap of money, whose total value could be reckoned in multiples of one. Its diminution would eventually reduce it to its basic unit, one ruble.

At the beginning of the story, Gogol likens the hospitable old couple to Philemon and Baucis. An editorial note reminds us that these were the "devoted couple, in Greek legend, who graciously supplied food and shelter to Zeus and Hermes after they had been turned away by others, and, as a result of their kindness, survived the flood Zeus unleashed to destroy their neighbors" (3). But neither the note nor the narrator goes on to tell the rest of the story, which is really the most significant part here. The two gods throw off their disguises as ordinary travelers and reveal themselves to the old couple. Not only does the humble house survive the flood, but it turns into a magnificent temple. In Ovid's more familiar version: "Marble columns took the place of the forked wooden supports; the straw grew yellow and became a golden roof; there were gates richly carved, a marble pavement covered the ground." As if that were not reward enough, Zeus asks the old couple to name "any boon you will." Philemon consults with his wife, then requests that "we may be your priests, and guard your temple." Then he makes another request, which is more important for Gogol's purposes: "since we have spent our lives in constant company, we pray that the same hour may bring death to both of us—that I may never see my wife's tomb, nor be buried by her." These requests are granted; and as they die, they turn into "two trees standing close together, and growing from one double trunk."[7] Read in these terms, what happens to Pulkheria and Afanasy looks like a punishment. They begin with an opulent estate, which crumbles away into nothing, and the wife predeceases her husband by five years. We do not expect them to turn into trees, of course; but there is nothing to mark their graves, not even a conventional weeping willow or a tuft of flowers. They simply disappear.

What are they "punished" for? Not for a lack of hospitality as the ancient Greeks saw it. Rather, perhaps, for forgetting that hospitality, broadly conceived, requires a receptivity to the variety of the world's body, in all its parts. It is not merely, or even mainly, that they are inhospitable to nature around them, walling themselves off from it instead of respecting and working with it, as the mythical model prescribes. They are also inhospitable to nature inside the enclosure, with the "chemical laboratory" that reduces fruits to comestibles far in excess of what can be consumed even by these gluttons, and with their failure to comprehend how their servant girls could possibly be getting pregnant. By contrast, the hospitality of Baucis and Philemon bespeaks moderation and respect toward the world at large. Appropriately enough, their first gift from the gods is a self-filling mixing bowl that never overflows.

Gogol seems to be saying that the estate of Pulkheria and Afanasy could have been a vigorous, healthy bounded space were it not for human fears, frailties, and mistakes. As in "A Terrible Vengeance," the protagonists do not set out deliberately to ruin what they have. Things are never that simple for Gogol. The old couple are vaguely aware of forces quite beyond their control. Their main fault, if fault it is, springs from an inability to recognize, name, and acknowledge those forces. Had they done so, they might have gained in nobility, and we might then have found them tragic rather than pathetic; but the outcome would probably have been the same.

3

Equilibrium as Place:
"The Two Ivans"

A SMOOTHLY functioning collective rests on a delicate balance of all the components. Once disturbed, they can never be restored to their original positions. This is the mechanism, or plot, of many of Gogol's works. Nowhere is it more conspicuous than in the last of the four stories in *Mirgorod* (1835): "The Tale of How Ivan Ivanovich Quarreled with Ivan Nikiforovich," hereafter referred to as "The Two Ivans." Here we are told how two apparently inseparable friends quarrel, become bitter enemies, and bring libel suits against each other that drag on, never to be resolved.

The story is set in Mirgorod. But it is not so much the town that is treated as enclosure now; rather, attention falls on the personal place that defines each of the Ivans. Much is made of the differences between the two men: "In spite of their great affection, these rare friends were not at all alike. Their characters can best be understood by comparison" (II, 172). The comparisons that follow are really contrasts: Ivan Ivanovich is tall, thin, and eloquent, Ivan Nikiforovich short, fat, and taciturn, and so on, for the better part of two pages. What otherwise would be two very different places interact, or so it would seem, to form a larger and more dynamic kind of place than we have seen in the earlier stories. So well balanced syntactically is this long list of comparisons—"on the one hand / on the other"—that, as Alexander Slonimsky formulates it, we are lulled in "a cradle of logic" and may very well fail to detect the narrator's sudden introduction of an orange into a basket of apples: "Ivan Ivanovich is rather

of a meek character. Ivan Nikiforovich, *on the other hand*, wears trousers
with such ample folds that if they were blown out you could put the whole
courtyard with the barns and the outhouses into them" (173).[1] Incompatibility masked by a verbal device, whether mellifluous prose, as in "A Terrible Vengeance," or syntactical symmetry, as in the story we are now discussing, is a trick beloved by Gogol, and often alerts us to the presence of
far deeper incompatibilities in the work as a whole. It serves that function
here too, as the two friends become aware that they are really enemies. The
twist, however, is that their enmity depends on similarities that are at least
as important as their differences. But that is also true of verbal constructs
built on logical illogicalities; and it is therefore not surprising that Gogol
reinforces the point by ending the first chapter with a grammatically sound
but semantically nonsensical statement: "In spite of some dissimilarities,
however, both Ivan Ivanovich and Ivan Nikiforovich are excellent people"
(173).

Trouble begins, as it usually does in Gogol, with a violation of place. One
day, as Ivan Ivanovich lies on his porch surveying his domain with rich self-
satisfaction, his eyes move "over the fence into Ivan Nikiforovich's yard,"
that is, into another's place, and are "involuntarily caught" by the "curious
spectacle" of a servant woman hanging a peculiar assortment of articles
on a clothesline: an old uniform, trousers, vests, various coats, a dead
grandmother's petticoat, a saddle and a saddlecloth, a sword, and finally,
a gun. Ivan Ivanovich understands that the clothes symbolize Ivan Nikiforovich—large, musty, useless—and do not in this sense violate the place
he has assigned his friend in his own mind. Even the sword does not look
unusual (although it inspires a Homeric simile on the part of the narrator).
But it is the gun that instantly strikes him as anomalous: "What is the
meaning of it? . . . I have never seen a gun at Ivan Nikiforovich's. What
does he want with that? He never shoots, but keeps a gun! What use is it
to him?" (175). The conversation he then has with the woman is humor-
ously silly, but serves further to mark the object:

> "What's that you have got there, my good woman?"
> "You see yourself—a gun [*ruzh'e*]."
> "What sort of gun [*Kakoe ruzh'e*]?"
> "Who can say what sort [*kakoe*]! If it were mine, I might know, maybe, what it
> is made of; but it is the master's. . . . It's made of iron [*zheleznoe*], one would
> think. . . ."
> "Hm! made of iron [*zheleznoe*]. Why is it made of iron [*zheleznoe*]?" (175–76)

So strong is Ivan Ivanovich's desire to obtain the gun for himself that he
violates his routine, leaves his yard in the heat of day, and goes to his neighbor's house. Even though "one could climb over the fence" that separates
the two yards, he proceeds by way of the street, then into a very narrow

alley, through the gate, across the courtyard, and into the house, with a leisurely tour of the sights en route. His trip is structured as a quest, rich in obstacles that enhance the value of the final goal.

In itself the gun is no more out of place on a clothesline than a sword. By the logic of the scene, it too stands for Ivan Nikiforovich. And this is what Ivan Ivanovich finds profoundly disturbing, for the gun deranges the balance of dissimilarity between the two men and creates an equality that he is not prepared to grant. The threatening equality may in part be sexual. Although he does not use the expression, Ivan Ivanovich considers himself a "real man." He was married, though he has been a widower for ten years. The union produced no offspring; but his servant girl Gapka "has children and they often run about the yard. . . . Gapka is a sturdy wench, she goes about in a skirt, has fine healthy calves and fresh cheeks" (170–71). No mention is made of a husband. We are left to draw our own conclusions, and it seems obvious what they should be. By contrast, Ivan Nikiforovich is endowed with characteristics that are stereotypically "feminine"—indolence, corpulence, self-indulgence. He is even rumored to have been "born with a tail." Although the narrator pooh-poohs this on the ground that only witches have tails, it does enable him to make the point that witches are females (as, therefore, is Ivan Nikiforovich). We remember too that the ornate man's vest that is hauled out for airing on the clothesline is "soon covered by the old petticoat of a deceased grandmother," who must have been built along the same lines as her grandson, for the garment "had pockets in which one could have stowed a watermelon" (175). This odd juxtaposition has occasioned no comment from Ivan Ivanovich, and we may therefore presume that he considers the petticoat to be as meaningful an emblem of his friend as are the unmistakably "masculine" clothes that accompany it on the line. The only living woman in Ivan Nikiforovich's life is the mysterious Agafya Fedoseevna, a shrewish figure who once "bit off the tax assessor's ear" and is no doubt capable of biting off more essential organs.

Nonetheless, Ivan Nikiforovich is in possession of a gun, an obvious symbol of masculinity, albeit in this case a flawed one: we are told that he had "bought it from a Turk" when he was beginning his military service; that it is a hunting weapon (*ruzh'e*), not a rifle (which would be *vintovka*); that it is rusty; that the lock is broken; that Ivan Nikiforovich himself "never shoots" and has "not been created by the Lord for shooting" (178). The gun and its owner cannot fulfill their proper function militarily, any more than the owner can fulfill his proper function sexually (or so Gogol implies). Yet the gun is profoundly disturbing to Ivan Ivanovich. To be sure, he makes no reference to its sexual symbolism. His argument for acquiring it moves in quite another direction: "You have a dignified figure and deportment," he tells his friend, in a delicate allusion to his corpulence. "How could you go trailing about the bogs when your apparel, *which it is not quite proper* [*prilichno*] to call by name on every occasion, is still getting a good airing [on the clothesline] as it is? What would the situation be like then [out hunting]? . . . Yes, you must behave *properly* [*vam nuzhny prilichnye postupki*]. Listen, give [the gun] to me!" (178–79, much modified: Garnett/Kent is misleadingly inaccurate). What he really says here is that the gun is an attribute of the gentleman. Among other things, it is associated with the "gentlemanly" sport of hunting. Ivan Nikiforovich evidently cannot qualify, being slothful, inelegant, and, perhaps most important, lacking in what Ivan Ivanovich calls *prilichie*, meaning "decency," "propriety," "decorum," the sure mark of the gentleman, as far as he is concerned. Possession of the gun sets Ivan Nikiforovich on the same level in the one way that truly matters to his friend. The point is also made linguistically. One of the qualities of *prilichie*, for Ivan Ivanovich, is elegant speech, in which he is adept: "If Ivan Ivanovich offers you snuff, he always first licks the lid of the snuffbox, then taps on it with his finger, and offering it to you, says, if you are someone he knows: 'May I make so bold as to ask you to help yourself, sir?' Or if you are someone he does not know: 'May I make so bold as to ask you to help yourself, sir, though I have not the honor of knowing your name and your father's and your rank in the service?'" By contrast, Ivan Nikiforovich "puts his horn of snuff straight into your hands and merely adds, 'Help yourself'" (173).

Prilichie is also a code word of Sentimentalism, which cherished circumlocution. Ivan Ivanovich knows how to draw on the code for other terms as well. On first seeing the gun, for instance, he says: "[I]t is a *nice* thing [*veshchitsa slavnaya*]! I have been *wanting* [*khotel*] to get one like that for a long time past. I should *very much like* [*ochen' khochetsya*] to have that gun; I *like to amuse* myself [*lyublyu pozabavit'sya*] with a little gun. . . . It's a *fine* thing [*khoroshaya veshchitsa*]" (175–76). He takes for granted that fluency in this special language also marks the gentleman. As such, he puts it off limits to the decidedly ungentlemanly Ivan Nikiforovich. However, he soon discovers that his friend is capable of mimicking it effectively, for Ivan Nikiforovich later calls the gun "a *very interesting* [or curious] *entertainment* [*lyubopytnaya zabava*], besides being a very *agreeable ornament* to a room [*ukrashenie . . . priyatnoe*]" (181). *Zabava*, "entertainment," is built from the same root as Ivan Ivanovich's *poZABAVit'sya*, "amuse oneself"; and the adjective that modifies it, *LYUBopytnaya*, "interesting," contains the same root as Ivan Ivanovich's *LYUBlyu* (*lyublyu pozabavit'sya*). Both instances in turn echo *LYUBopytnoe zrelishche*, the "curious spectacle" of the clothesline that opens this long scene. "Agreeable" (or "pleasant") does not find a literal counterpart in Ivan Ivanovich's speech, but as the most common code word of Sentimentalism, it is implicitly present there. Ivan Nikiforovich introduces these statements by re-marking that the gun is a "gentlemanly thing [*veshch' blagorodnaya*]," which clearly shows that he also lays claim to the "gentlemanliness" that his friend has arrogated to himself. The tables are turned: Ivan Ivanovich has set out to encroach on Ivan Nikiforovich's place, only to find that his friend encroaches on his. An equality has been established, much to Ivan Ivanovich's chagrin.

The oft-cited exchange that precipitates the break is not long in coming:

"You go on about your gun, Ivan Nikiforovich, *like a crazy child with a new toy* [*kak duren' s pisanoyu torboyu*]. . . ."

"And you, Ivan Ivanovich, are a regular [or 'real': *nastoyashchii*] gander [*gu-sak*]." (181)

Here each man remains true to form linguistically, Ivan Ivanovich being florid, Ivan Nikiforovich being terse. Gogol heightens the contrast with italics (omitted by Garnett/Kent). *Duren' s pisanoyu torboyu* is a common enough expression. The literal meaning is something like "a simpleton with a painted bag." It can also be rendered as "making a big fuss" or a "song-and-dance" about something. The words *duren'* and *torba* are not them-selves of particularly high frequency. *Gusak* is as ordinary a word as one could wish, yet it has anything but an ordinary effect on Ivan Ivanovich: "How dare you, sir, forget propriety [*prilichie*] and respect for a man's rank and family and insult him with such an infamous name?" The two friends become implacable foes.

We may wonder why Ivan Ivanovich is so upset at being called a gander. Certainly, being equated with a barnyard fowl would not in general be re-garded indifferently. Here the victim is especially susceptible. The bird mocks his appearance: both are long-necked, strutting, and pompous. To someone so particular about his lineage, the gander also parodies a heral-dic bird, displacing the usual eagle or owl. No doubt there are sexual con-notations too. Gogol appends a footnote explaining that a "gander," a *gu-sak*, is a "male goose," something of which no native speaker of Russian would have to be apprised. In the official complaint that Ivan Ivanovich later lodges against Ivan Nikiforovich, he himself all but links "gander" with shameful, hidden sexual activity: his adversary, he says, built a goose-pen "with no other design but to emphasize the insult paid me . . . solely to compel me to witness *unseemly* [*nepristoinye*, virtually a synonym of *neprilichnye*, 'indecent'] *incidents*; forasmuch as it is well known that no man goes into a pen, above all a goose pen, for any *proper* [*prilichnogo*] purpose" (192). What is "unseemly" in Ivan Ivanovich's own life may well be explained by the presence of Gapka and her children: his gentlemanly dignity would never allow him to acknowledge a liaison with a servant girl.

More to the point is the threat of displacement through transformation. If Ivan Ivanovich is a "real gander," then by implication he is an "unreal" human being. To move him into the animal world is to make him equal to Ivan Nikiforovich, or at least equal to Ivan Ivanovich's perception of his friend. This represents another turning of the tables (a common device in Gogol). In the long dialogue that leads up to the fateful words (177–81), Ivan Ivanovich proposes exchanging the gun for a sow and two sacks of oats. Ivan Nikiforovich will not hear of it, and is offended. He does not say why, but perhaps he sees the oats as a mockery of his preoccupation with food, and the pig as a commentary on his physical appearance. Perhaps too oats and pig are a silent joke about his ambiguous sexuality: although *svin'ya* may refer to animals of both sexes, the one in this story is probably female; at least, there is a later reference to Ivan Ivanovich's "sow in farrow [*suporosnaya svin'ya*]," presumably the same one that has figured throughout. As a porcine female, it does not really "belong" in Ivan Ivanovich's world, at least as he conceives it, any more than a gun "belongs" in his friend's. And if, as at least one reader has suggested, the sow and two sacks of oats represent a penis and testicles, the sexual ambiguity and the joke are further served.[2] But perhaps the most important consideration is that Ivan Ivanovich's offer would take away the one token of nobility and masculinity left to Ivan Nikiforovich—the gun—and confirm him in his visceral, effeminate self. Ivan Nikiforovich is insulted, but not mortally so. Perhaps he is just a pig and a sack of oats, but he still has the gun. And he knows how to reply to the insult: turning Ivan Ivanovich into an animal would be sweet revenge. As a gunless gander, Ivan Ivanovich would lose everything he values. His fine speech would become an anserine honking (as Ivan Nikiforovich seems to understand when he asks him, after delivering the deadly word, why he is "cackling"); he would be deprived of the clothing that is essential to his keeping up appearances, and would be set on a level with his friend, who has received him "in a state of nature . . . without anything on, not even his shirt . . . in full beauty completely unadorned" (177, 182); his animal passions, which have presumably been indulged with Gapka, would be exposed for all to see; his aristocratic dignity would be just a memory. In fact, he would sink even lower than Ivan Nikiforovich, and the inequality that he has striven so hard to maintain would, ironically, be preserved. Could Gogol have been thinking here of the Russian proverb "The goose is no friend of the pig" (*gus' svin'e ne tovarishch*)? Real friends they may not be, but they still have to live in the same barnyard.

The word "sow" very nearly acquires the same transforming power as "gander." In chapter 5, the police captain decides to try his hand at bringing the two neighbors together, and pays a visit to Ivan Ivanovich. He warms to his main topic with a lengthy discussion about his host's sow, which has stolen Ivan Nikiforovich's petition (199–201). The captain informs Ivan that since the sow is his property, he himself is to blame, to which Ivan replies sarcastically: "I am very much obliged to you for putting me on a level with a sow" (199). Actually, the captain has made the pig human. He reminds Ivan, "anyone who steals a legal document in a court of law is liable like any other criminal to be tried in a criminal court." This law he interprets as follows: "Nothing is here defined as to species, sex, or calling; therefore, an animal, too, may be guilty." Now, Ivan Nikiforovich is also a "pig," suggestively in appearance and indubitably in his erstwhile friend's eyes. If Ivan Ivanovich acknowledges his own pig to be equal to himself, then in effect he sanctions an erosion of the boundary between his human and animal selves, as well as equality with his adversary. But he refuses to entertain this possibility, upon which the police captain drops the matter and proposes that the pig be cut up and eaten. Symbolically, this would rid Ivan Ivanovich of his enemy; the catch is that Ivan Nikiforovich would be transformed into what he likes best, food, whereas Ivan Ivanovich would remain transformed into what he hates most, a gander. Reconciliation is clearly doomed.

That is why Ivan Ivanovich's task throughout the story is to maintain a distance, lest each man resemble his adversary too closely. Conversely, Ivan Nikiforovich's task is to bring them together, in acknowledgment of their essential oneness. "Gander" establishes a semblance of equilibrium between the two, which Ivan Ivanovich promptly undoes by breaking off the friendship. Ivan Nikiforovich tries to reestablish the equilibrium by building the goose-pen. Ivan Ivanovich restores disequilibrium by sawing down the offending structure and lodging a written complaint with the district court. By now an alternating rhythm of equilibrium and disequilibrium has set in, making the next development predictable: Ivan Nikiforovich submits a complaint of his own, thus restoring equilibrium. Ivan Ivanovich's sow steals this document, creating a new disequilibrium. Ivan Nikiforovich then hands in a fresh complaint, and thereby seems to "win," for he finally achieves equilibrium: both complaints stand, now and forever.

There may well be another dimension to *gusak*. As it is used here, the word seems to function much like a curse.[3] Gogol relies on the reader to remember two earlier instances of birds. It is Ivan Ivanovich who introduces them. First he says: "It's strange that the quails [*perepela*] still don't come at the birdcall. . . . I don't know why it is they don't come" (178). This follows immediately on Ivan Nikiforovich's observation that he cannot understand why his mention of the devil has so offended his friend. The abrupt change of subject—a favorite attention-calling device of Gogol's—highlights the juxtaposition of "devil" and "quails," making us wonder

whether they may be related, and if so, how. Shortly thereafter Ivan Ivanovich brings up another bird and links it with the gun. In arguing that
Ivan Nikiforovich has no need of such a weapon, he asserts: "You have
never yet killed a single *kachka* as far as I know" (178). Here Gogol appends one of his rare footnotes (omitted in Garnett/Kent), explaining that
kachka means "duck." (His own name signifies a certain kind of duck as
well, a "golden-eye," according to the *Oxford Russian-English Dictionary*.) *Kachka* is listed in standard Russian-Russian dictionaries as a re-
gionalism, and probably does require explanation for most native speak-
ers; but in this context, the note also serves further to mark the bird theme.

The third and last bird mentioned is the "gander" in Ivan Nikiforovich's
retort. It too is marked with a footnote (though again, not in Garnett/
Kent), and unnecessarily so, as we have seen, if the author's only intention
is to save us a trip to the dictionary. Since we take for granted that a footnote conveys information that is not available in or evident from the text,
and since we are not dealing here with a parody of scholarly writing, we
conclude that "male goose," as the note has it, aims at raising the motif of
sexuality and prompting us to reflect on other possible meanings of "gander." When we do, we notice that the decisive exchange repeats the cue/
response pattern that has been established virtually from the moment Ivan
Ivanovich enters his friend's house. This time, to be sure, Ivan Nikiforovich
does not literally repeat Ivan Ivanovich's "you are a simpleton with a
painted bag," to take the more literal translation. Yet in a sense, "gander"
really is a terse recapitulation: a goose is famously foolish; it is also osten-
tatiously preening and vain, as suggested by the image of the "painted bag."
More important, "gander" picks up the bird theme introduced many pages
earlier by Ivan Ivanovich. The difference is that in this instance, there has
been a long delay between cue and response: an extensive dialogue has intervened, during which no mention has been made of any bird. Yet this
dialogue is essential for bringing about what amounts to a demonization
of "gander." In much abridged form:

[*Ivan Ivanovich*]: "It's a very fine day."

[*Ivan Nikiforovich*]: "Don't praise the weather, Ivan Ivanovich. *The devil* take
it! There's no doing anything for the heat!"

[*I. I.*]: "So you must bring *the devil* in. Aie, Ivan Nikiforovich! you will remember my words, but then it will be too late; you will suffer in the next world for your
ungodly language [lit., 'words']. . . . I'll give you the gray *sow*. . . . A splended
sow! . . ."

[*I. N.*]: "What use is your *sow* to me? Am I going to give a banquet at *the devil's*
wake?"

[*I. I.*]: "Again! You must keep bringing *the devil* in! It's *a sin*, it really is *a sin*,
Ivan Nikiforovich!"

[*I. N.*]: "How could you really, Ivan Ivanovich, give me *for the gun the devil knows what—a sow*?"

[*I. I.*]: "Why is she *the devil* knows what, Ivan Nikiforovich?"

[*I. N.*]: "Why is she? . . . This is a gun, a thing everyone knows; while that—*the devil only knows what to call it—is a sow!*" . . .

[*I. I.*]: "I'll give you *two sacks of oats* besides *the sow*. . . . Two sacks, not empty, but *full of oats*; and have you forgotten *the sow*?"

[*I. N.*]: "You can go and kiss *your sow or the devil*, if you prefer him!"

[*I. I.*] "Oh! you'll see, your tongue will be pierced with red-hot needles for such *ungodly sayings* [lit., 'words']." (177–81)

Two of the words in this dialogue, "devil" and "gun," have already been paired with the bird words interjected by Ivan Ivanovich. They are now not only repeated by both men but also, in keeping with the direction taken by most Gogolian stories, like "A Terrible Vengeance," expanded to pull in other words, here "sow" and "sack of oats." Furthermore, repetition attunes our ear to receive these words as significant units. (I will have more to say in Chapter 11 about this use of repetition.) Here again the cue/response pattern prevails. Only now far more is at stake than Ivan Nikiforovich's skill at mimicry, far more even than his desire to establish an equality with his friend. Every time Ivan Nikiforovich repeats one of the key words, he also pronounces the word "devil [*chert*]." Russian culture is hardly unique in regarding this as a taboo word. Many people to this day avoid saying it lest it summon up the reality. Ivan Ivanovich's protests prompt us to conclude that he is among them. But Ivan Nikiforovich has no such fears. He is the one who first utters it and then harps on it throughout the dialogue. His primary purpose may well be to upset his adversary, but the effect reaches beyond that. For he is also the one who ties the words "sow," "gun," and "sack of oats" to "devil," just as the devil, according to Anton Prokofievich Pupopuz, has "tied" the two Ivans together in eternal friendship. Through association, these terms become virtually synonymous with "devil." "Gander" as such is not present. But we note that embedded in the dialogue, repetitively and obsessively, are the two words that were originally paired with birds: "devil" and "gun." We expect to find birds matched with these words now; instead, we find other items in the same semantic fields (rural life, food, and sex): "sow" and "sack of oats." It is almost as if birds have already become taboo. When a bird is mentioned again, as "gander"—and in such an unexpected and highly marked way—all the earlier associations and pairings, actual and surrogate, are likely to arise in the reader's mind, as they may well do in Ivan Ivanovich's, given his violent reaction to this word. "Gander," we may say, is virtually demonized by association.

When we ask ourselves why no mention is made of birds in this dialogue, we have to give credit in the first instance to Gogol's delight in working by indirection and in catching his readers unawares. Just when we have forgotten all about quails and ducks—assuming we have noticed them at all—he comes out and says in effect: "You think *I've* forgotten about the birds just because I didn't mention them in the dialogue? On the contrary, they are the most important thing!" Thereupon we go back, if we are good readers, and take a closer look at those earlier birds. In the process we are reminded, once again, that to read Gogol is often to re-read him. It may be that the omission of bird words in the dialogue serves the characterization of Ivan Ivanovich as well. He too is addicted to indirection, though not for the same reasons as Gogol. And since it is he who has initially created the associations of bird/gun/devil, perhaps he dimly intuits during the long exchange that bird words are potentially dangerous, especially if picked up by his sharp-tongued friend, and are best avoided in the present circumstances. Finally, Gogol may be making a point that would eventually become crucial to his whole idea of verbal creativity: that any ordinary word, once uttered, may take on a life of its own, often quite at variance with the original intention of the speaker or writer, and can pull other words, often quite unrelated semantically, into its field of energy.

Ivan Nikiforovich could have come back in the final exchange with "you are a real devil," instead of "you are a real gander." This would have made a better semantic match for "simpleton" since we tend to think of the devil as being invested in human form. But one of the themes of the story is also the underlying desire of the two men to reestablish their friendship. Even though "gander" proves far more damaging than Ivan Nikiforovich had imagined—judging, as we shall presently see, by his attempts to soften it— "devil" would have put reconciliation out of the question. Ivan Nikiforovich could certainly have effected a symbolic transformation of his adversary into a lower order of being with "sow" or "sack of oats." But for the reasons we have already stated, "gander" has far greater resonance than any of those others.

Ivan Ivanovich has endured rude remarks from his friend before, but this is one he does not let pass: "'What was that you said, Ivan Nikiforovich?' he asked, raising his voice." The other man, as if taken aback, replies: "I said that you were *like* a gander, Ivan Ivanovich." But that is *not* what he said: there is no "like" in the fateful utterance; it is a naming and a symbolic if not actual fact. Accordingly, Ivan Ivanovich becomes even more outraged: "How dare you, sir, forget propriety [*prilichie*] and respect for a man's rank and family and insult him with such an infamous name?" Ivan Nikiforovich retorts that he sees nothing "infamous" about it, but then, as if confirming his erstwhile friend in his new identity, likens him to some kind of hysterical winged creature: "And why are you waving your hands about like that [*chego zhe . . . tak razmakhalis' rukami*]? . . . Why have you set up such an incredible cackling [*chto vy tak raskudakhtalis'*]?" Even so, the verb "cackle" does not properly apply to geese in English any more than does its equivalent, *raskudakhtat'sya*, in Russian. Hens cackle, geese honk (*gogochut*). As a man close to rural life, Ivan Nikiforovich surely knows the proper word; his failure to use it may represent another attempt to soften the force of the original insult. But Ivan Ivanovich will not be mollified; the friendship ends; and later Ivan Nikiforovich, just as stubbornly, seems further to confirm Ivan Ivanovich in his new identity by building a goose pen that encroaches on his neighbor's land.

It does not take the townspeople long to find out what has happened. They decide that steps must be taken to restore the friendship. What they try to do, in effect, is to re-create and then alter the circumstances in which the fateful word originally became empowered. Ivan Ivanovich is present at a party; the others decide to "send on the sly for Ivan Nikiforovich and bring them together." As the emissary they at first choose Ivan Ivanovich— "not *the* Ivan Ivanovich," we are told, "but the other one who squinted" (204; the italics are Garnett/Kent's). Of course *this* Ivan Ivanovich is not affected by the curse, since it has not been laid directly on him. By substituting a "clean" person bearing the same name as the cursed one, they may hope to confuse, as it were, the power of the curse and undo it. This is not stated in the story; but so much is made at this point of the otherwise unimportant second Ivan Ivanovich that we are invited to read more deeply. Ultimately, Gogol sends someone else on the errand, as if to tell us in advance that there is no fooling the power of the curse. The task devolves upon Anton Prokofievich Golopuz, who brings it off successfully. The enemies find themselves in the same room, with all the leading citizens of the town in attendance.

Reconciliation seems imminent. But then Ivan Nikiforovich says: "You took offense over *the devil knows* what, over *my calling you a 'gander.'"* And all is as before: "Ivan Nikiforovich was instantly aware that he had committed an indiscretion in uttering that word; but *it was too late: the word had been uttered*" (212). Why then does he repeat the "indiscretion," knowing that it was the cause of the break in the first place? He seems himself to be under the spell of the word, which once again comes into play as soon as he recreates the original verbal pattern: "the devil . . . my calling you . . . gander." The power inherent in precisely this last word is further underscored by the narrator's assertion: "[H]ad he said 'bird' and not 'gander,' the position might still have been saved. But—all was over!" (212).

Throughout most of the story, each Ivan has occupied a distinct place. When the narrator returns to the town after twelve years, he finds both of them inside the church, a public place that belongs to nobody in particular but to all collectively. Each man is now beginning to resemble the other physically. Ivan Nikiforovich is "an old man with grizzled hair," who has "changed" enormously; we are not told how, but since corpulence has been his most striking trait, he has perhaps lost much weight. Ivan Ivanovich has become a "thin, wasted figure," whose face is "covered with wrinkles," and whose hair is "completely white." Each devotes himself to the identical goal of winning the lawsuit. Yet each still thinks of himself as an individual. Ivan Nikiforovich tells the narrator that he has "positive information that the case will be settled next week and *in my favor*." Ivan Ivanovich, using virtually the same words, says: "Tomorrow *my case* will positively be settled; the court has told me so for certain" (213–14). "My" is the operative word for both. But it is the "my" of an alter ego, distinct, yet partaking of the qualities of the other. This might account for the strangely powerful attraction Ivan has always felt for Ivan. It could also explain other apparent anomalies, such as the sow's belonging to Ivan Ivanovich, whereas "logically" it should belong to his friend, who in turn owns a gun that would better suit the other man: the sow represents the "lower" self of the "higher" Ivan Ivanovich, and the gun the "higher" self of his "lower" friend. Each man needs the other, for by himself he is incomplete.

The relationship between the two Ivans also raises the kinds of questions that are often asked about identical twins. Are they one? Or are they two? Can two people occupy the same place? Victor Turner offers a helpful parallel from Ndembu society. Even though twins there are considered "mystically identical," the rules of the kinship system prescribe that "there is only one position in the structure of the family or corporate kin-group for them to occupy." The solution is either to "deny the social existence of the biological fact" or to accept the fact and "try to cope with it" in various ways.[4] The society in which the two Ivans live not only accepts the "fact" of the relationship but tries to mend it when it fails. Perhaps that is because an absent twin creates a peculiar kind of empty space, one that is not fully occupied by the remaining twin and that therefore threatens the integrity of the collective as well as of the individual. A tempting solution lies at hand in the person of the "other" Ivan Ivanovich. As we have said, the narrator makes much of the fact that he is "not *the* Ivan Ivanovich," and that he is to be distinguished from his namesake by his squint. But the one essential difference is a similarity too, because we have already been told that the "real" Ivan Ivanovich sees life in a very imperfect fashion: the gun on the clothesline represents the "truth" of his friend's situation, but he cannot "see" it; and when he enters Ivan Nikiforovich's house, at the begining of the scene that culminates in the quarrel, he at first fails to see his friend at all because the room is so dark. So this "other" Ivan Ivanovich is essentially a twin of the "real" one, and therefore, by extension, of Ivan Nikiforovich too. Presumably his job is to act as a surrogate, who would restore the essential twinning relationship temporarily, until the "real" principals can be brought together. However, as a virtual copy of the other Ivan, he would also be duplicating the conditions that led to the quarrel in the first place. Possibly this is another reason why he is not sent. Possibly his own position is too anomalous. As a character whose identity finds expression only in terms of someone else, he lacks a real place of his own, and therefore points up the potentially fatal flaw in any twin relationship, and with it, the danger posed by any "placeless" character in a tightly bound collective.

The person who does go is Anton Prokofievich Golopuz. He is as full-blooded a secondary character as we find in this story, enjoys good relations with both men, and would in all these respects seem to be an ideal go-between. Actually, he is a far riskier bet than the "other" Ivan Ivanovich. Presumably this is the same character who was reported, in the first chapter, as saying, "the devil himself had tied Ivan Nikiforovich and Ivan Ivanovich together with a string; where the one went the other would turn up also" (172). In both places he wears a brown frock coat with blue sleeves, and bears the same first name and patronymic. There is, however, an odd discrepancy in the surname. On first occurrence he is called "Pupopuz"; on second, "Golopuz." (Garnett/Kent uses "Golopuz" for both.) To be sure, the names are close. They are built on the same root, *puz-*, from *puzo*, "belly."[5] Only the first element differs, and it remains within the same semantic field: Pupo- is from *pup*, "navel," and Golo- from *golyi*, "naked," the state in which the navel can be seen. The textual variants, as recorded in the *Complete Works* (PSS, II, 588ff.), make no mention of the name in either form, so we must assume that the discrepancy existed from the beginning. Carelessness on Gogol's part is unlikely, since he had a chance to make corrections for the 1842 edition of his works. Assuming that the discrepancy is deliberate, I attribute it not only to playfulness and a love of mystification (never to be discounted in any text by Gogol) but also to a desire to draw attention to the larger problem of naming, and with it, placing.[6]

If the figures having almost but not quite the same name in separate parts of the story are the same character, he can be seen as a twin of himself. If so, he can also be seen as the "twin" of each of the Ivans in some respects. The components of his name, in both versions, describe Ivan Nikiforovich's most salient physical characteristics and Ivan Ivanovich's moral and psychological situation after he has been "made naked" by his enemy. So what we may have is not one set of twins but at least four: Ivan Ivanovich–Ivan Nikiforovich; Pupopuz-Golopuz; Pupopuz–Ivan Ivanovich; Pupopuz–Ivan Nikiforovich. Does this represent eight personae occupying one place, or one place fragmented into eight personae? Either possibility destroys the idea of "place" in the Gogolian sense, and signals that in the Mirgorod of this story, displacement and placelessness are already rampant as symptoms of a profound and irreparable disorder. As we know, they are demonic characteristics in Gogol's world. It is significant that the narrator, close to the end, launches into a fairly extensive characterization of Golopuz and makes disorder his salient trait. We are told that he wears a winter coat in summer and a summer coat in winter. More important, he has no home (or "place") of his own, and is therefore forced "to spend his nights at different houses." And as we have seen, he cannot even be "placed" by name: is it Golopuz, Pupopuz, or both? Finally, his main task is also demonic: reconnecting the tie with which the devil himself has bound the two Ivans.

It is quite true, as Richard Peace points out, that "the argument which begins over a gun is really about social status, noble origins and ultimately the claim to be a true Cossack."[7] In a deeper sense, however, it is an argument about one's fundamental place in the world.

4

Place Within: "Diary of a Madman"

"DIARY of a Madman" was written in 1834 and published the follow-ing year in Part 2 of *Arabesques*. Gogol had originally planned to call it "Diary of a Mad Musician" (Zapiski sumasshedshego muzykanta). The hero would have joined the small company of Gogol's fictional artists in stories like "Nevsky Prospekt" (1835) and "The Portrait" (1835, 1842). But in the final version he made his hero a middle-level civil servant with a taste for the popular theater. The change from musician to clerk enabled him to explore the motif of rank (which would otherwise have probably been irrelevant) through a character who works in words, that is, in the same medium as a writer, and is driven by many of the same impulses. Akaky Akakievich would be a later instance ("The Overcoat," 1842). This is as close as Gogol came to dealing with his own craft in fiction; "serious" writers figure as characters only in his articles and essays.

The madness motif remained. It ties the story to "The Portrait" and to the unfinished play *The Order of St. Vladimir, Third Class* (1832–34), as well as to the extensive literature of madness then popular in Russia, West-ern Europe, and the United States.[1] As Gogol sees madness, it means a fail-ure to find one's proper place, or the compulsion to occupy a place to which one is not entitled. The Russian word for madness, *sumasshestvie*, trans-lates literally as "going out of one's mind." In view of the importance of spatial imagery throughout the story we are now considering, a better ren-dition of the title might be "Diary of a Man Who Has Gone Out of His

Mind." In any event, by 1836 the locus of the theme of place had progressively narrowed, from a whole people ("A Terrible Vengeance"), to a small town ("The Two Ivans"), then to a single estate ("Old-World Landowners"), and finally to one individual ("Diary"). Correspondingly, the external world had become less vivid, until in "Diary" it became almost abstract, perhaps because Gogol wished it to stand entirely as a mental construct of his hero, just as Petersburg, where the story is set, had by then become mythologized as a mental construct of its founder, Peter the Great. (We will have more to say about this in the next chapter.) "Diary" is the only work in which Gogol explores the theme of place as a wholly internalized phenomenon, and the only work, logically enough, to be narrated consistently in the first person. I mean the only fictional work: the imagery of place and non-place also undergirds all the first-person nonfiction, as we shall see at a later point in this book. And it represents an early instance of a theme that Gogol was to amplify in his most important writings of the 1840's: the health or sickness of society at large depends on the mental and spiritual condition of each constituent member.

Aksenty Ivanovich Poprishchin is a clerk in a government office in the capital. His job consists in copying documents and sharpening the director's quills. He is looked down on by his fellow clerks, considers himself superior to them in every way, and resents his position. Secretly he is smitten with the director's daughter, Sophie, and gradually becomes convinced that he can attain a rank high enough to win her. He gains imaginative access to her through letters written, so he claims in his diary, by her dog, Madgie, which he steals and reads. In them he learns that she is engaged to be married, whereupon he realizes that he can never possess her. He then drops her and devotes all his psychic energies to bettering his official position. With the doors in Russia closed to him, he concludes that he is king of Spain, quits his job, and is locked up in an asylum, where he is treated so badly that he can think only of escaping from this world in "a troika and horses swift as a whirlwind."

Despite the simplicity of the plot, this story operates on many levels simultaneously, and is one of Gogol's most subtle and powerful works. In particular, its treatment of the relationship between power and sex has engaged some of the best critics.[2] I suggest, however, that the main issue of the story may well be the place a person is or is not entitled to occupy.

The first entry betrays great confusion in Poprishchin's mind about his *mesto*, his place, in the specific sense of "job" and the more general sense of situation in the world. (Like the English, the Russian carries both meanings.)

Today an extraordinary event occurred. I got up rather late in the morning, and when Mavra brought me my cleaned boots I asked her the time. Hearing that it was long past ten I dressed quickly. I admit I wouldn't have gone to the department at all, knowing the sour face the chief of our section would make at me. For a long time past he has been saying to me: "How is it, my man, your head always seems in a muddle? Sometimes you rush about as though you were crazy and do your work so that the devil himself could not make head or tail of it, you write the heading with a small letter, and you don't put in the date or the number." The damned heron! He must be jealous because I sit in the director's room and sharpen quills for his Excellency. (I, 239)

It is not clear what "event" he has in mind, and in what sense it is "extraordinary." There would seem to be several possibilities in the lengthy account of his day that follows: the encounter with Sophie and the talking dogs is the most spectacular; but perhaps he means the meeting with his section chief, or his lateness to work. We simply do not know: one thing seems as important to him as another. Undoubtedly, though, "long past ten" violates a fixed routine; "I wouldn't have gone to the department" looks ahead to the time when he will not go there at all. Confusion and haste, everywhere in Gogol, are demonic characteristics, as we are reminded here by the mention of the devil. The substitution of small letters for capitals and the omission of dates and numbers are minor but telling violations of the kind of place that must be honored by the routine-bound copy clerk, as well as signs of incipient madness, which later burgeons in the chaotic headings of the diary entries.

In professional terms, Poprishchin's *mesto* is determined by the Table of Ranks, where he occupies Grade 9, or titular councillor.[3] This is the same rank that would later be held by another Gogolian copy clerk, Akaky Akakievich, in "The Overcoat." Akaky pays it no mind: his obsessions run in a different direction. But for Poprishchin, it is of enormous significance. He already holds so-called "personal" or lifetime nobility (*lichnoe dvoryanstvo*), which was conferred by Grade 12; but a promotion now to just one grade higher (or lower, in the reverse numeration of the system) will automatically elevate him to hereditary nobility. He never does attain it, and in this sense his rank becomes another indication of his marginality. The place he occupies in the office confers only an official identity, which requires personal anonymity. "The flunkey set," as he calls them, "are always lolling about in the hall and don't even take the trouble to nod to me"; the section chief "put on a look as though he did not see me come in"; and the director "always sits silent" (242–45). Poprishchin yearns for a personal place that is somehow different from the official. But any attempt he makes, however tentatively, to assert his right to such a place is immediately noticed and followed by a reminder that his proper place is no place at all: "Why, you are a nonentity [lit., 'zero,' *nol'*] and nothing else!" (243). In these senses he is the prototype of what would become a familiar character in later Russian fiction, particularly in Dostoevsky, Tolstoy, and Chekhov, the person whose public and private selves occupy very different and irreconcilable places.

For Poprishchin, these two places are identified by different kinds of writing. In the office he is a mere copyist, doing what everyone else of his rank does. Were he to resign or die, he would be instantly replaced. His replaceability shows that his official place is not true place in the Gogolian sense; for, as we shall see in Chapter 6, true place is unique place. The diary, however, is his own creation, in his own language, a record of a private self in a form of writing he cannot practice at work. Or so it might seem. Actually, he is too limited intellectually and culturally (a master stroke of Gogol's) to generate any kind of inner life that in itself would be worth recording. Mainly he records his reactions to stimuli from the world outside, using the diary form to manipulate and control that world as he pleases. We may assume that Sophie, the section chief, his servant, Mavra, in fact all the characters do have some kind of independent existence. Not only is Poprishchin incapable of inventing them, but he is heavily dependent, as we soon begin to see, on externals of another kind, words as created by others, especially in the form of letters, newspaper articles, and fiction. Simon Karlinsky has noted the "delicious mini-parodies, scattered throughout the story," such as "the parody of police investigation novels ('I need to have a talk with your little dog'); of the literary critics who demand a human-interest angle at all costs ('Give me a human being! I want to see a human being, I require spiritual nourishment that would sustain and delight my soul,' Poprishchin exclaims, disgusted at having to read about Madgie's canine love affairs); and of the editorial style of commenting on current political affairs ('England will not tolerate such and such, France has such and such interests to consider, etc.')."[4] All this belongs to the kind of "low" or "popular" literature that a man of Poprishchin's level would find accessible and even profound. In his attempt to make plausible stories or at least extended anecdotes out of this material, he bears some earmarks of the professional writer.[5] He is also vaguely reminiscent of the popular conception of the Romantic artist, a sensitive, misunderstood creature who is forced to spend his life among philistines. More specifically, he operates as Gogol elsewhere stated a writer should: by drawing on materials from the ordinary world to create something new and organically whole, as does his diary, itself a recognized literary genre.[6] In fact, Poprishchin and Gogol turn out to have much in common, in the ways they express their anxieties about the place they occupy in the world. Yet Poprishchin could not possibly be a genuine writer, as Gogol conceives him. He looks at the outside world not to discover what lies beneath the surface but to manufacture a personal identity out of ready-made materials.

The diary gives Poprishchin some sense of being in control of the world "out there," insofar as he can erase the boundary and bring it in "here." If that were all there was to it, we would be reading an account of the fantasies and delusions of a happy man. On the contrary, he is chronically dissatisfied, indeed acutely wretched most of the time. This is evidence of his awareness that a world does exist independently of what he is capable of registering in his diary. He fears it, tries to flee it, but knows that it is essential to finding his proper place. He acknowledges its presence in various ways, most notably through the device of letters written by the dog Madgie to her friend Fido.

Obviously, Poprishchin himself must have written the letters, thereby creating a dialogic monologue, as perhaps all diaries do. Certainly Madgie's attitudes are compatible with what we know about him. She is fastidious, with pretensions to gentility and the kind of snobbery often found among underlings. Her remarks on Sophie's "papa," the man for whom Poprishchin works, reflect the master-slave relationship that prevails in the office. Her proximity to Sophie, particularly her access to the boudoir, amounts to wish fulfillment on Poprishchin's part: "My young lady . . . loves me passionately" (247). Her more circumstantial account of Sophie's meetings with Teplov, the court chamberlain, speak to Poprishchin's own sense of utter insignificance: "I don't know, *ma chère*, what she sees in her Teplov. Why she is so enthusiastic about him" (250). Finally, like Poprishchin, Madgie has mastered the clichés of the philistine: "It seems to me that to share one's ideas, one's feelings, and one's impressions with others is one of the greatest blessings on earth. . . . Ah, my dear, how one feels the approach of spring! My heart beats as though I were expecting someone" (247, 249). Yet Poprishchin takes these letters as being written by another, to the point of commenting on them like a literary critic. This he can plausibly do because Madgie herself treats him as if he were not the author of the diary but "that clerk that sits in papa's study," and because the letters are generically different from the kind of diary text in which they are embedded. And since they are written by a female dog with a foreign name, he presumably could not be their author.

What do the letters tell him about himself that he does not already know? For one, they suggest that he is sexually inadequate: both dogs involved in the correspondence are female, and their values contrast sharply with those of male canines, whom Madgie considers crude, self-important, or unwelcomely attentive. For another, they tell him that Sophie is too remote to be attainable, as suggested by the French form in which her name consistently appears. Through Madgie he can walk into her boudoir; but Madgie, as a female and a dog, presumably cannot enjoy the sexual fantasies that would visit a "real man" in such a situation. He learns too that he is unworthy of possessing a beautiful, well-placed woman like Sophie, perhaps any woman. Madgie writes: "Sophie can never help laughing when she sees him" (250). To this he takes vehement exception, but it is an objectification of his own unacknowledged attitude toward himself. Finally, the letters confirm his own contradictory ideas about rank: either it is utterly unimportant, "gentlemanliness" being the main thing, or it is important to the exclusion of everything else. Certainly it seems more important than sex appeal: Sophie's engagement, he insists, is the result not of any outstanding physical qualities on the part of his rival but of his loftier rank. As a court chamberlain, Teplov occupies either Ranks 3–4 or 5–8, as against Poprishchin's Rank 9; he even outranks the daunting section-chief's court councillorship, which is Rank 7. If a "mere" court chamberlain can win a girl like Sophie, then how much greater could be the conquest of, say, a general.

Characteristically, Poprishchin handles these unpleasant truths through displacement. A first displacement attributes Sophie's laughing at him to jealousy on the part of the section chief, who has already been displaced in the very first entry when Poprishchin makes him a "damned heron." A second displacement removes matters even further, to the fateful workings of the Table of Ranks: "Everything that's best in the world falls to the court chamberlains or the generals" (251). A third displacement makes Sophie unworthy of him in any event. She loves to attend balls: that proves she is too frivolous for a serious man like him. And she is willing to settle for a "mere" court chamberlain, when Poprishchin has already decided that he can be much more. However, the discoveries have all been embedded in the diary text even before Poprishchin gets hold of the letters. As he has self-righteously noted, he is no crude clerk running after pretty legs in the street. The only women in his life have been Sophie and his stupid servant, Mavra, the one too high, the other too low to be a plausible mate. His very first entry has sounded a note of disapproval about Sophie: "And why does she drive out in such rain [to go shopping]! Don't tell me that women have not a passion for these rags" (240). Every day of his life he has had to contend with the world's perception of him as a nonentity. He has insisted on the superiority of "gentlemanliness" to any rank, yet is obsessed with making a steady, sometimes dramatic rise through the Table of Ranks. The letters restate and focus these motifs in a safely distanced and authoritative way: he is sexually inadequate, women are unworthy, rank is all that counts, and his place in the scheme of things is very insecure. More important, the letters assure Poprishchin, however unpleasantly, that he exists in the world outside his own head, and thereby enable him to undertake a serious quest for his real place, which he always tries to define in the publicly recognized terms of rank and social position. But he already knows from his experiences in the office that public selves run the danger of being appropriated to larger identities that take no account of the individual. He must therefore retain a private self that will enable him to ogle, monitor, and comment. Any time these two selves come too close to each other, his very existence is threatened.

His quest for an authentic public self begins with a series of rhetorical questions posed in the entry for December 3: "Why am I a titular councilor and on what grounds am I a titular councilor? Perhaps I am not a titular councilor at all? Perhaps I am a count or a general, and only somehow appear to be a titular councilor. Perhaps I don't know myself who I am. . . . I should like to know why I am a titular councilor. Why precisely a titular councilor?" He promptly comes up with an answer that contains a solution: "How many instances there have been in history: some simple, humble tradesman or peasant, not even a nobleman, is suddenly discovered to be a great gentleman and sometimes even a great lord [or tsar: the Russian *gosudar'* can mean both] ... If a peasant can sometimes turn into something like that, what may not a nobleman turn into?" (251–52).[7] The syllogism is constructed as follows: A peasant can become a great lord, even tsar; therefore a nobleman can become a . . . ? If we take *gosudar'* to mean "tsar" here, which seems legitimate in the light of Poprishchin's radically rising expectations, the syllogism demonstrates that the nobleman has no place to go in Russia: after all, there is nothing higher than the tsar either in the Table of Ranks or in that vague realm of "gentlemanliness" that Poprishchin so often evokes. He could of course promote himself to tsar, but that position can be filled by only one man, and is already occupied. The only solution is to find a different system, one that resembles but is not the Russian. He solves this problem through displacement too; only this time, it is himself that he displaces, not others.

With his limitations, Poprishchin is incapable of accomplishing this task alone. Again an outside authority comes to hand. Poprishchin is a regular reader of the newspapers. In some ways they resemble the letters, being self-contained places inhabited by others over whom he has no control, their very shape marking a distinct boundary between their place and his. In other works of Gogol, they may also function as mirrors. For example, in "The Portrait," Chartkov himself supplies and pays for a laudatory review of his paintings. Poprishchin's first reference to newspapers leads us to suppose that they function in the same way: he tells of reading about "two cows who went into a shop and asked for a pound of tea," which looks like a product of his fantasy but may well represent Gogol's snide commentary on a well-known brand of philistine journalism, virtually synonymous with *The Northern Bee* (Severnaya pchela), of which Poprishchin is an avid reader, as we discover in the October 4 entry.[8] (Newspapers that print this kind of thing are not of course unknown even in our late twentieth century.) For Poprishchin, however, newspapers are even more authoritative than letters because they have the impersonality of print and depend on "others," often anonymous, for their content. Most important, they deal with events more remote than Sophie's boudoir or the director's office; significantly, he is mainly interested in news of the French and English, and the doings of a gentleman from Kursk, which lies several hundred miles from St. Petersburg. And they allow him to nourish the thought that he is in control of his life, for they do not so much mirror him as offer an array of items from which he selects those that fit his situation.

The diary entry for December 5 reads as follows:

I spent the whole morning reading the newspaper. Strange things are going on in Spain. In fact, I can't really understand it. They write that the throne is vacant, and that they are in a difficult position about choosing an heir, and that, as a consequence, there are insurrections. It seems to me that it is extremely peculiar. How can the throne be vacant? They say that some Donna ought to ascend the throne! A Donna cannot ascend the throne, she cannot possibly. There ought to be a king on the throne! "But," they say, "there is not a king." It cannot be that there is no king. A kingdom can't exist without a king. There is a king, only probably he is in hiding somewhere. He may be there, but either family reasons or danger from some neighboring state, such as France or some other country, may compel him to remain in hiding, or there may be some other reasons. (252)

Here is an empty space that meets all Poprishchin's requirements. It is "noble," designed for a male, and high. In fact, it is so high that there can be none above it (all Gogol's obsessives are oblivious to God). It therefore marks a boundary that is secure from incursion except from ambitious people below; that partly explains the ruthlessness toward subordinates that figures in Poprishchin's picture of what it would be like to be a general. The empty-space device is identical to the one introduced in "The Two Ivans" when Ivan Ivanovich, while surveying his domain, suddenly wonders what it is that he does not *yet* possess, and finds the answer in the gun he descries on his neighbor's clothesline. In "Diary," Poprishchin finds the missing fourth element of his syllogism of rank in the newspaper story: "There is a king of Spain! He has been discovered. I am that king" (252). At this point, he has apparently not been going to the office for several days; physical displacement has literally begun. Mental displacement, expressed in spatial or geographical terms, is not far behind.

The first concrete sign appears in the dating of the entry in which he proclaims himself king: 2000 A.D., April 43. From now on, the dates become progressively more disordered or vague.⁹ To clear the way for his own displacement, he begins, in another characteristically Gogolian reversal, by displacing the office. This works in two ways. First he transforms the director into a smaller, inanimate object: "He is a cork, he is not a director. An ordinary cork, a plain cork and nothing else—such as you cork a bottle with" (254). He has already used this displacement technique against his section chief in the milder form of simile—"his face is somewhat like a druggist's bottle" (243)—and has had it used against him by Madgie: "[H]e looks like a turtle in a bag. . . . The hair on his head is very much like hay" (250). This last remark is the one that upsets him. Even though it is a simile, and thus only a threatened transformation, it does envisage changing a person into a thing, which is probably the most extreme form of boundary violation.[10] He then simply eliminates the director by usurping his place, and in writing, thus giving it greater authenticity in his eyes: "[T]hey put a paper before me to sign. They thought I should write at the bottom of the paper, So-and-so, head clerk of the table—how else should it be! But in the most important place, where the director of the department signs his name, I wrote 'Ferdinand VIII' " (254). Then, in a decisive self-displacement, he walks out, never to return. From there he goes to the director's house and invades Sophie's boudoir, in fulfillment of the fantasy entertained in the entry of November 11: "I long to have a look . . . into her boudoir. . . . I long to glance into her bedroom" (245). There he makes a speech (which we will consider in a moment), and then leaves. This is followed by a tirade against the treacherous nature of "woman," who is "in love with the devil." It culminates as follows: "You will see her from a box in the first tier fixing her lorgnette. You imagine she is looking at the fat man with decorations. No, she is looking at the devil who is standing behind his back. There he is, hidden in his coat. There he is, beckoning to her! And she will marry him, she will marry him" (254).

This passage contains three interconnected images: concealing, revealing, and clothing, which, as Gogol uses them, are versions of place. They have been established by remarks in the first entry from which we have already quoted, when Poprishchin sees Sophie darting from a carriage that has pulled up to what is presumably a dressmaker's shop, and comments: "Don't tell me that women have not a *passion* for these *rags*." He is ashamed of his own "rags," and tries to conceal himself from her: "She didn't know me, and indeed, I tried to muffle myself up all I could, because I had on a very muddy, old-fashioned overcoat" (240). An association is established between passion and clothes, between clothes and concealment, and thus between passion and concealment. Passion can be indulged from a safe distance. The moment Poprishchin has an opportunity to act on it, in the boudoir scene, he merely makes a speech, couched in the clichés he has picked up from vaudevilles: "I only told her that there was a happiness awaiting her such as she could not imagine, and that in spite of the wiles of our enemies we should be together" (254). He then walks out, never to see her again. From his experiences at the office, he has learned that self-revelation brings punishment. His declaration to Sophie puts him in no real danger because he does not disclose to her his "real" identity as king of Spain but further conceals it under ordinary clothes. Concealing with clothes is what the devil does in the theater passage, and what he conceals is also his real identity, one of placelessness that pretends to be place. Poprishchin, in other words, already intuits that his real place is no place at all.

For a time he continues to conceal his royal persona, viewing the world voyeuristically: "I walked incognito along Nevsky Prospekt. His Majesty the Tsar drove by. All the people took off their caps and I did the same, but I made no sign that I was the king of Spain. I thought it improper to reveal myself so suddenly before everyone, because I ought first to be presented at court" (255). Finally he decides to reveal himself in an appropriate costume, a royal mantle made from an old uniform. That this is a futile attempt to assert his proper place is suggested by the heading of this entry, with its lack of date and place and its reference to the devil: "I don't remember the date / There was no month either / The devil knows what to make of it" (255). Indeed, there is no place in Russia for a king of Spain. Hence the need for still another displacement, this time to what he supposes is Spain itself (of course it is the madhouse), unquestionably his proper place if he is king.

Under the entry "Madrid, February thirtieth," he reports: "And so here I am in Spain, and it happened so quickly that I can hardly believe it. This morning the Spanish delegates arrived and I got into a carriage with them. The extraordinary rapidity of our journey struck me as strange. We went at such a rate that within half an hour we had reached the frontiers of Spain" (256). The moment he tries to assert his prerogatives as ruler, he is beaten; the pattern of revelation and punishment repeats itself. At length it dawns on him that something is wrong, whereupon "Spain" ceases to be a real place and becomes only one way of naming a place that is not "here." That is why he can say: "I discovered that Spain and China are one and the same country, and it is only through ignorance that they are considered to be different kingdoms. I recommend everyone to try to write Spain on a piece of paper and it will always turn out China" (256). Even rank and title no longer matter: if the king of Spain cannot function in Spain, there is no place for him at all, at least not on this earth.

This discovery is followed by the oft-quoted passage about the moon. It seems to be motivated within the text by a newspaper report (always authoritative for Poprishchin) of an impending eclipse, as forecast by a foreign (and therefore even more authoritative) source. (There are also parallels in Russian literature before Gogol.)[11] "Tomorrow at seven o'clock a

strange phenomenon will occur: the earth will sit on the moon. The celebrated English chemist Wellington has written about it" (256). It continues
as follows:

I must confess that I experience a tremor at my heart when I reflect on the extreme
tenderness and fragility [*nezhnost' i neprochnost'*] of the moon. You see the moon
is usually made in Hamburg, and very badly made too. I am surprised that England
hasn't taken notice of it. It was made by a lame barrel maker, and it is evident that
the fool had no idea what a moon should be. He put in tarred cord and one part
of lamp oil; and that is why there is such a fearful stench all over the world that
one has to stop up one's nose. And that's how it is that the moon is such a tender
sphere [*nezhnyi shar*] that man cannot live on it and nothing lives there but noses.
And it is for that very reason that we can't see our noses, because they are all in
[*sic*: not 'on'] the moon. And when I reflected that the earth is a heavy body and
when it falls [or "sits": *nasevshi*] may grind our noses to powder, I was overcome
by such uneasiness that, putting on [*nadevshi*] my shoes and stockings, I hastened
to the hall of the Imperial Council to give orders to the police not to allow the earth
to sit on the moon. (256–57)

This passage brings together elements from oral and literary traditions,
as well as from popular science and mythology, all shaped to Poprishchin's
special needs, and thereby grotesquely displaced. The earthly origins of the
moon have a basis in geological fact, of which Poprishchin seems generally
aware. Appropriately, then, his syntax draws on the rhetoric of scientific
discourse—"that is why [*ottogo*]," "that's how it is [*ottogo*]," "it is for that
very reason [*po tomu-to samomu*]," "because [*ibo*]"—and is yet another
instance of Gogol's penchant for wrapping apparent nonsense in verbal
structures that look logical. (This is also characteristic of the discourse of
schizophrenics.) Certainly a moon made in Hamburg looks like sheer nonsense. But is it? Here Gogol may be inviting us to proceed by creative inference. It is possible that popular anecdotes about worlds made of cheese
were circulating at the time.[12] An English speaker, on reading this passage,
might think of the expression "the moon is made of green cheese," which
goes back at least five hundred years and usually refers to attempts to deceive. Although there seems to be nothing comparable in Russian, a handy
albeit coincidental fit can be made: "green" means new or ill-smelling, and
self-deception is the larger theme of this entire entry. This passage in fact
contains three references to England, two explicit and one, "Wellington,"
implicit. These facilitate another association with cheese, specifically with
certain English cheeses, like Stiltons, which are "malodorous" or "rotten"
(*gnoenye*). So they are described in the dictionary by Vladimir Dal, a contemporary of Gogol. There is no possibility that Gogol could have known
this work, since it was published long after his death. Yet Dal recorded
usages current during Gogol's lifetime. Both authors, then, may have

drawn on a common source, popular speech. Dal goes on to define "German cheese [*nemetskii syr*]" as "disc-shaped [*krugami*]," which reminds us of the Hamburg-made moon in Gogol's story; and, among the "French cheeses [*iz frantsuzskikh*]," he identifies Brie as "soft [*myagkii*]" and "fragile [*neprochnyi*]," almost the same terms Gogol uses for the moon in the first sentence of the passage quoted above.[13]

Poprishchin makes no mention of France in this particular section; but it is present indirectly in the reference to Wellington. There may have been an English chemist by that name, but any Russian reader would inevitably think of the famous duke. Not only did he defeat Napoleon at Waterloo in 1815, but he had earlier earned his dukedom by routing the French in Spain during the so-called Peninsular War (1808–14). The king of Spain at that time was Ferdinand VII, who was forced by Napoleon to abdicate and was then imprisoned in France. These events are presumably familiar to Poprishchin when he dubs himself Ferdinand VIII. There was no such king in actuality, but Poprishchin's claiming of the succession again enables Gogol to raise the question of his legitimacy, considering how tangled the world of Spanish monarchical politics was at the time, with claimants and counter-claimants coming and going. The way is prepared for the explicit mention of France in the next entry ("January of the same year"), where it is tied to a "nose": "when England takes a pinch of snuff, France sneezes" (257). Effect is displaced from cause.

Further digging would no doubt bare new strata. But the passage we have quoted is straightforward enough on the face of it for the attentive reader. Quite apart from the obvious association of the moon with lunacy, this passage reenacts the sexual fantasy that has attached to Sophie. Readers even in Gogol's time were well aware that writers often used noses as surrogate phalluses. The practice had been initiated by a celebrated passage in Sterne's *Tristram Shandy* (Vol. III, chap. 21), a book widely known throughout Europe and in Russia.[14] By the early nineteenth century, any mention of this organ by a writer in more than the most casual terms was invariably taken as a reference to the other, unmentionable one. Gogol himself made a substantial contribution to the theme with his story "The Nose," which was published a year after "Diary of a Madman." Here the nose detaches itself from the body of Kovalyov, a compulsive skirt-chaser. Deeply ashamed, he goes to great lengths to recover it, only to find it mysteriously restored to its proper place. He is much relieved, but promptly resumes his old ways, quite unaware that the experience is supposed to have been (or so we are led to assume) a punishment for his misuse of this essential appendage.

In the "moon" passage from "Diary," the nose is not explicitly phallic, but literary tradition, if nothing else, makes it so. Nor is it specifically Poprishchin's, but "one's" or "ours"; yet he certainly is talking about himself, if only because a diary is always "about" its author. We also find other clues. The first comes in the entry for December 3. Brooding about the success that the court chamberlain Teplov has had with Sophie, Poprishchin says: "Why, his nose is not made of gold but is just like mine and everyone else's; he sniffs with it and doesn't eat with it, he sneezes with it and doesn't cough with it" (251). It may be "just like mine," but Poprishchin cannot use it as Teplov does unless he makes of his rival, as he does, a surrogate who can enjoy actual physical access to Sophie. Understandably, then, he is more relieved than envious because Teplov enables him to gratify his passion voyeuristically, which is the only way that does not threaten him. We remember that when he has the opportunity for direct action, in Sophie's boudoir, he withdraws. This marks the end of his fantasies about her, or so it seems; and he makes no further mention of Teplov.

With Sophie ostensibly disposed of, it might seem "logical" for him to recover his nose. He does so long enough to notice that the moon is malodorous, and "very badly made" at that. By stopping up his nose, he denies it its proper function, or, more accurately, allows that function to be discharged only in a displaced state, just as, in the next entry, the stopping up of the nose with snuff in England means that it can sneeze only in France. What is its function? To serve as the only remaining "other," all the previous ones having proven inadequate. By setting the nose and the moon at the truly great remove of outer space, Poprishchin can eliminate an unpleasant, malodorous, and disturbing sexual threat while reclaiming the safe vantage point of voyeur. This new arrangement is all the more satisfying: everyone can see the moon, but only he knows that the nose is there. Undoubtedly the moon is a sexual object in this story, as Richard Gustafson has pointed out; but in its proper place, thousands of miles from earth, it represents a generalized, idealized, and unthreatening image of woman. One thinks of the Roman goddess Diana, who is synonymous with the moon, and who displays some of the traits that characterize Sophie: she is "attended with dogs" (like Madgie and Fido), is often seen riding in a chariot (like Sophie in her carriage when Poprishchin first sees her), and sometimes "appears with wings" (like Sophie when she is compared to various birds). Diana's moonlike traits may carry over to Sophie's "gleaming" eyes and eyebrows and to her "white" dress; even her abjuration of marriage would gratify Poprishchin's ideal image of Sophie as a remote, unattainable, virginal being.[15] This image can now be contemplated at leisure, and Poprishchin need not be bothered by any of the stenches that may emanate from women, particularly those who are menstruating, that is, who are "month-" or "moon"-regulated. But Diana also carries a quiver of lethal arrows, and visits a dire punishment on another voyeur, Actaeon, who watches her bathing. This suggests that Poprishchin may not be as safe as he thinks. And so it is, although he conceives of the danger in a different way. The fear that the "heavy" earth (male) may "sit" on the "tender" moon (female) is clearly a fear of sexual intercourse, with its attendant threat, as Freud teaches us, to the integrity of the male organ. That is why Poprishchin is so afraid of the impending eclipse: his nose (penis) may be ground into dust. Of course, his nose is already detached, and already embedded "in" the moon, but at a safe distance of 250,000 miles. The eclipse would merge "here" and "there," "self" and "other" in a way fatal to his identity.

So apprehensive is he that he hurries to the police—after putting on his shoes and stockings. Why does he mention such a detail? In Russian, the word for "putting on" (nadevshi) is identical in structure and sound, except for a single consonant, to the verb used by Gogol for the fearfully anticipated "falling" or "sitting" of the earth onto the moon (nasevshi). But there is more of a connection than this between footwear and the moon. Shoes and stockings are often fetishistically charged objects, and they play just such roles in several of Gogol's stories.[16] "Diary" too hints at such a fetish: several entries earlier Poprishchin has imaginatively placed himself in Sophie's bedroom and has seen "marvels ... a paradise, such as is not to be found in the heavens. To look at the little stool on which she puts her *little foot* [nozhku] when she gets out of *bed* and the way she *puts* [on] [nadevaetsya, the same verb as nadevshi in a different form] a little snow-white *stocking* [chulochek] on that *little foot* [nozhku] ... Aie, aie, aie!" (245). If these marvels are "not to be found in the heavens," then Sophie is still very much on earth, and therefore threatening to Poprishchin. Until she is transferred to the moon, fetishism displaces and refocuses his sexual anxiety in a safer way. Even safer is his decision to put on his own stockings. He becomes his own sexual object; nose and moon are joined; "here" and "there" are interchangeable; he himself has brought about the unthinkable.

In this context, his decision to go to the police reflects a need to be punished for the typically Gogolian sin of self-gratification. He does not have long to wait. In the entry headed "The twenty-fifth," the Grand Inquisitor comes into the room and runs through all Poprishchin's previous identities. Poprishchin describes the scene as follows: "I hid under a chair. Seeing I wasn't there, he began calling me. At first he shouted 'Poprishchin!' I didn't say a word. Then: 'Aksenty Ivanov! Titular councilor! Nobleman!' I still remained silent. 'Ferdinand VIII, King of Spain!'" (258) To none of these, even the last, does he respond. However, the inquisitor, says Poprishchin, "caught sight of me and drove me from under the chair with a stick." Punishment is now meted out for concealing, not revealing; but with the boundaries between place and non-place eradicated, such a distinction is no longer meaningful. All Poprishchin can do is accept the identity imposed on him by the authorities, which, if articulated, might turn out to be "zero [*nol'*]," a status in which rank and identity are irrelevant, as is the case in madhouses and perhaps in some Russian government offices too, which recognize only the rulers and the ruled. In effect, he finds himself back in the same place he occupied at the beginning of the story, in one of the apparent returns that characterize this story and so much of Gogol's work generally: "They won't listen to me, they won't see me, they won't hear me" (258). Any attempt at protest is punished, for protest is nonacceptance of a place decreed by others. There seems in fact to be no place for him in this world or any other, earthly or celestial. Other has become self.

His awareness of this situation is what inspires the strange statement immediately following, that "every cock has a Spain, that it is under his wings [not far from his tail]" (258). Here "Spain" stands for any "other," which is now situated within him. "Wings" might enable him to escape this self/other; but since any possible destination is already present—"under the wings"—there is no point in undertaking such a trip. The bracketed part of the quotation above is supplied in Garnett/Kent, and occurs in variant texts (also as "near the tail"), but Gogol omitted it in the final version, probably because it reintroduces an overtly sexual motif, which Poprishchin (mistakenly) thinks he has long since disposed of. The emphasis now falls on identity and place. But where is Poprishchin now to find his place? The way is clear for the outburst in the final entry:

It's too much for me, I can't endure these agonies, my head is burning and everything is going around. Save me, take me away! Give me a troika and horses swift as a whirlwind! Take your seat, my driver, ring out, my bells, fly upward, my steeds, and bear me away from this world! Far away, far away, so that nothing can be seen, nothing. . . . [O]n one side the sea, on the other Italy; yonder the huts of Russia can be seen. Is that my home in the distance? Is it my mother sitting before the window? Mother, save your poor son! . . . There is no place for him in the world! He is persecuted! Mother, have pity on your sick child! ... (258–59)

Here he entertains a new and ultimate order of displacement, through unending movement. No specific geography is invoked, only a soaring beyond all space and time. But it is expressed as a wish, not as an actuality. Displacement is also signaled grammatically and stylistically. All the verbs are now in the present tense, indicating the absence of otherness that diaries, written after the fact, customarily record in the past tense. And it reveals a sudden flight of language, which may seem inconsistent with the dreary, plodding Poprishchin we have come to know so well, but which does not jolt us, because it corresponds to his rising level of expectation. In any event, it does not really transcend the philistine, and could have been derived from any number of popular novels of the time. Poprishchin has now broken out of everything that provisionally bounded him: his nationality, his job, his rank, his geography, and his language. There is no further place for him, and nothing more for him to say. The entries will soon cease. The last line in the quotation above is the next-to-last line of the story. Gogol could have ended it here, with the three dots betokening a continuation without end. Poprishchin might then have remained fixed in our minds as a forlorn, pitiable creature, reminiscent of Lermontov's demon.

But there is the last line: "And do you know that the Dey of Algiers has a boil just under his nose?" Originally it read: "The French king has a boil just under his nose." Leonard J. Kent, in a note to the English version of the story from which we have been quoting, comments as follows: "Since the word for 'boil' in Russian, *shishka*, is a colloquialism for 'trouble,' the sentence could easily have been interpreted as an irreverent poke at Charles X, who had abdicated in August of 1830, and it is highly probable that Gogol was less than eager to become involved in a postrevolution imbroglio. In its present form, the line refers to the deposal of the last Dey of Algiers, Hussein Pasha, by the French, in 1830" (259). Kent makes a good point. But Gogol could have avoided the possibility of trouble by omitting the line altogether. Why, then, did he retain it? Structurally, the two versions are identical; only the title and nationality of the ruler are different. We are dealing with a complex of images here, which recapitulate Poprishchin's root obsessions. The phrase "Algiers" (or France) catches up the idea of remoteness that has drawn him to "Spain" and "China," but it has no more specific meaning beyond that. The "Dey" is a head of state who, like Poprishchin himself, has been "deposed." A boil, being under the nose (a phallus), suggests venereal disease. But the phrase forms a meaningful whole only when set in parallel to "every cock has a Spain . . . under the wings." Diagrammatically:

cock—Spain—under wings
Dey—boil—under nose

The more "logical" sequence would be cock—boil—nose, which keeps all the sexual imagery together, and Dey—Spain—wings, which concentrates the imagery of remoteness and escape. However, Gogol obviously wants once more to link the themes of politics, distance, and sexuality, and leave them with us as a final statement. The key is in the equivalence of "Spain" and "boil." "Spain" stands for illicit political power, and it is not remote, but right "under the wings." "Boil" stands for illicit sexual activity, which is right "under the nose." Both are the consequence of fake pretensions to rank (Dey) and masculinity (cock). What Poprishchin has been seeking turns out to be very much "here," very much a part of himself. It is not a healthy or attractive self at all, but a sterile, inward-turned, severely bounded self, whose existence he will no doubt acknowledge for all time by ceaselessly intoning the sentence that ends this most disturbing of all Gogol's stories.

There is another way of reading the last line. *Shishka* is also a colloquialism for "big wheel," the kind of personage that Poprishchin has yearned to be, and that the Dey of Algiers in fact is. And because *shishka* is the last word of the sentence in the Russian, it in effect reduplicates the subject, which is "Dey," and it looks back to the "cock" in the previous entry, who is the "big wheel" of the barnyard. Because it is also the last word of the story, it mirrors the "madman" in the title, the more so when we remember that for Gogol, a madman is a displaced person. Poprishchin's madness consists in his wishing to be a *shishka*, a "big wheel," thinking for most of the story that he is, and, with the very last word, restating his conviction, in the distanced way that is so characteristic of him. Obviously he has "learned" nothing. He seems to be the victim of so-called "circular madness," a term psychiatrists sometimes apply to manic-depressive psychosis. Whether or not we wish to read Gogol's story as a case study of such a psychosis (and we could very well do so), we see, once aware of the recapitulative function of this last line, that Poprishchin is doomed to repeat, endlessly, the obsessions that have moved him throughout: sex, power, rank.[17]

We also see that the theme of utter isolation is cleverly encapsulated in the Russian heading of the final entry: "Chi 34 slo Mts gdao. 'larveF [written upside down and backwards] 349." The words before the period are gibberish, assembled from the fragments of the Russian words for "date" (*chislo*), "month" (*mesyats*), and "year" (*goda*). The word after the period is "Fevral'," the Russian for "February." One way of interpreting the entry is to see it as a restatement of the ways in which a fragmented Poprishchin tries to find a whole, authentic self by creating an "other," a mirror image. What he sees, "February," is not fragmented, to be sure, but it is reversed, turned back on itself. The two parts of the entry are therefore an apt representation of the inescapable self-referentiality that awaits him at the story's end. (The Garnett/Kent translation takes only some of the entry—the Arabic numerals, and, written backwards, "February" and "year.") The fragmented words also sound like an imitation of Chinese that might be made by a person with no knowledge of the language. As such, they remind us of Poprishchin's earlier insistence that Spain and China are "one and the same," and that if you try to write the word "Spain," the word "China" appears instead. China, that is to say, is a mirror image of Spain, especially when we consider that to the popular mind, it is on the "other" or "opposite" end of the earth from Europe. (In some editions of the story, though not in the Academy's, the "Chinese" words are actually printed above the reversed "February.") By now Poprishchin understands that he is not Ferdinand VIII; he rejects Spain as his true "place"; China may beckon as an alternative, almost as remote and exotic as the moon; but as he himself already knows, it is only a mirror of Spain, and therefore nonexistent too. Truly, as he himself acknowledges in this final entry, there is no place for him in the world (*emu net mesta na svete*).

The diary form has served Poprishchin well, enabling him to conceal his thoughts and actions (since diaries are intensely private documents), yet to reveal them with impunity, since he does not write for an audience. (Gogol never tells us how this document fell into his hands, or how it acquired a title that was obviously not supplied by Poprishchin himself.) It has also given him a way of creating other versions of himself, with which he can talk and interact. Once the possibility of "others" ceases to exist, however, the scene must shift inward. There is no further need for a diary, and the story must come to an end.

5

Place as Nature

GOGOL'S characters never feel comfortable about the world outside their enclosures. Yet it is very much a presence in many of the works, particularly those of the early period, often colorfully and attractively so: the summer day in "The Fair at Sorochintsy" (I, 8–9), the Ukrainian night in "A May Night" (I, 55), the reapers in "Ivan Fyodorovich Shponka and His Aunt" (I, 184). These are scenes of a "place" that is harmonious, tranquil, and benevolent but bears little on the human characters: they neither communicate with nor contribute to it, but at best stand aside and watch, as merely passive registrants of the view.

In the superbly crafted mowing scene of "Ivan Fyodorovich Shponka," we see through Shponka's eyes the steppe in all its colors, and hear the songs of the workers and the sounds of the insects and birds. We watch as the day moves toward its close and preparations get under way for the evening meal. The narrator calls this spectacle "a source of unutterable pleasure to [Shponka's] gentle heart. . . . [W]hat an evening! How free and fresh the air! . . . Oh, how fresh and delightful it was!" We assume that we are privy to Shponka's emotions. But then the narrator says: "It is hard to say what passed in Ivan Fyodorovich at such times. When he joined the mowers, he forgot to try their dumplings, though he liked them very much, and stood motionless, watching a gull disappear in the sky or counting the sheaves of wheat dotted over the field" (184). Although "with" the mowers, Shponka does not himself do any of their work or even partake of their food. He stands at a distance, watching them and the panorama of nature, and in turn is watched by the narrator. Elsewhere, nature itself may experience human feelings—hence the heavy use of personification—but it does not share them with people. It is very much like the River Psyol, as described in "The Fair at Sorochintsy": "Willful as a beauty in those enchanting hours when her faithful mirror so jealously frames her brow full of pride and dazzling splendor, her lily shoulders, and her marble neck, shrouded by the dark waves of her hair, when with disdain she flings aside one ornament to replace it by another and there is no end to her whims" (10). The beauty accepts admiration but gives nothing in return. This is why the nature scenes throughout Gogol's work tend to be set pieces that have little to do with the story as a whole, and can easily be excerpted.

The landscape of "A Terrible Vengeance" is the most spectacular of all, being drawn on the largest scale if not in the finest detail. At first glance, it might seem to contain a number of what Kant called "sublime objects":

Bold, overhanging, and, as it were, threatening rocks, thunderclouds piled up [in] the vault of heaven, borne along with flashes and peals, volcanoes in all their violence of destruction, hurricanes leaving desolation in their track, the boundless ocean rising with rebellious force, the high waterfall of some mighty river, and the like, make our power of resistance of trifling moment in comparison with their might.[1]

Essential to the sublime effect—an attractive fearsomeness in the objects under contemplation—is a sense that we are standing in a place from which we can safely look on. Certainly the last chapters of "A Terrible Vengeance" offer as "mighty" a landscape as anything in nineteenth-century Russian literature. From Kiev the Carpathians are suddenly visible, and atop the highest peak appears "a horseman, in full knightly armor, with his eyes closed, and he could be distinctly seen as though he were standing close to them" (I, 167). He is not so close, however, that the onlookers in Kiev feel uneasy. Just to be sure, the narrator resorts to a series of distancing tactics. The seeing is first taken over by the sorcerer, who is described as awestruck by the same sight. The eye then pulls back from him to focus on "another," who is "taller and more terrible than all the rest," and presently moves out of the scene to make room for narratorial generalization: "[I]f he had risen he would have overturned the Carpathians and the whole of the Sedmigrad and the Turkish lands. He only stirred slightly, but that set the whole earth quaking, and overturned many huts and crushed many people." Seeing is then explicitly denied, as the narrator refers to "the endless abyss which *no living man has seen*, for none dares to approach it"; and it is finally abandoned altogether as the narration passes to a blind bard who relates the circumstances of the curse, and whose listeners have only a mental picture of the events: "they still stood with bowed heads, thinking of the terrible story of long ago" (169–73). Our eyes follow theirs, and eventually our own vantage point becomes so "safe" that potentially sublime objects cannot possibly, in Kant's words, "raise the forces of the soul above the height of vulgar commonplace, and discover within us a power of resistance of quite another kind, which gives us courage to be able to measure ourselves against the seeming omnipotence of nature." Nowhere in Gogol's work, save in the final pages of *Dead Souls*, are characters or readers enabled to undertake such measuring.

In *Mirgorod* and *Arabesques*, and in some other stories of the 1830's that were published separately, landscape is far less in evidence, with the exception of "Taras Bulba." Detail is now more selective, with a corresponding loss of wholeness and an inclination toward symbolism. The distant forest in "Old-World Landowners," for instance, consists entirely of tall trees; nothing is said about sky, earth, or the fall of light and shadow. Flies, in this same story, stand for the realm of nature, or rather, betoken the presence of a decay and death that are essential to the proper workings of a nature that is never shown as a whole. In "Viy," Khoma Brut flies through the air straddled by the witch, and observes, as through "a transparent veil," that the "forests, the meadows, the sky, the dales, all seemed as though slumbering with open eyes. . . . [T]he shadows of the trees and bushes fell on the sloping plain in pointed wedge shapes like comets." As we shall see in Chapter 7, Gogol regarded a distanced height as the only vantage point from which the truth of life can be seen. And to Khoma's eyes, nature appears to be on the point of yielding itself, as he "bent his head and saw that the grass which had been almost under his feet seemed growing far below him, and that above it there lay water, transparent as a mountain stream, and the grass seemed to be at the bottom of a clear sea, limpid to its very depths." But what he sees "clearly" is, first, "his own reflection with the old woman sitting on his back," and then, in one of the few erotic passages in all of Gogol, a water sprite whose "cloudlike breasts, dead white like unglazed china, gleamed in the sun at the edges of their white, soft, and supple roundness" (II, 140–41). This figure is a corporealization of the "voluptuous sensation assailing his heart" at the beginning of his midnight ride, and thus a counterpart to the old woman who has made sexual advances to him, now sits atop him, and later turns into a beautiful and desirable young girl. Nature becomes a mirror, which gives back to the observer only what he wishes to see. Khoma is too caught up in his own obsession to be capable of "seeing" anything beyond surfaces or even to realize that more exists. The "truth" that passes before his eyes is that of his own self, not of external nature, which remains inviolate and closed.

Of the stories set in the countryside, "Old-World Landowners" is the most heavily indebted to cultural models that celebrate the cooperation of man and nature. One such model is the Renaissance ideal of an enclosed nature, as garden or park, which is rationally and beneficially improved so as to bring out its ideal qualities. Another might well be the Baroque ideal of contrasts that finds expression in the Dutch garden, as in the Catherine Park in St. Petersburg, where one section was devoted to the cultivation of fruit and another to wild nature;[2] this finds a rather neat parallel in the layout of the old-world landowners' estate. Still another is the idyll, which had enjoyed enormous popularity in the eighteenth century. Mikhail Bakhtin observes: "the elements of the ancient matrices most often appear in the idyll in sublimated form; one or another element is partially or entirely omitted." His example is "Old-World Landowners," where he finds certain "elements of the matrix" well represented—"old age, love, food, death"—but labor "altogether absent."[3] This is not accurate. Labor is present, not prominently so, but noticeably enough that we are aware of still another "matrix," that of the georgic. Readers of Virgil will remember that he attributes human feelings to nature, both animate and inanimate, and insists that man must "con [nature's] varying moods of wind and sky / With care—the place's native style and habit," and only then undertake the business of farming. He dramatizes his point by introducing bees, who build a well-regulated enclosure with materials drawn from the natural world and put to good use: "The workshop hums, and the honey reeks of thyme . . . / Such is their love of flowers and such their pride / In generating honey."[4] What we find in "Old-World Landowners" amounts to a parody of this ideal and of the Renaissance passion for "improving" nature. The steward and the village elder are said to be cutting down ancient trees for personal gain. We do not witness that particular "labor" in actual progress, as we would in Virgil or in an eighteenth-century idyll. But we do see Pulkheria and her servants at work. She does not imagine that human beings can act upon nature when it is out "there": it is too large, powerful, awesome, and dangerous for that, and is best ignored. But within her enclosure, she is mistress, or so she thinks, and she subjects nature to the drastic transformations of a sinister and relentless domestic chemistry, in what reads like a burlesque of a georgic catalogue of instructions:

Her house was very much like a chemical laboratory. There was always a fire built under an apple tree; and a cauldron or a copper pan of jam, jelly, or fruit cheese made with honey, sugar, and I don't remember what else, was scarcely ever taken off the iron tripod on which it stood. Under another tree the coachman was forever distilling in a copper retort vodka with peach leaves, or bird-cherry flowers or centaury or cherry stones, and at the end of the process was utterly unable to control his tongue. (II, 6–7)

She engages nature by mutilating it, devouring it, and converting it into food, whence it in turn ultimately becomes excrement: "Such a quantity of all this stuff was boiled, salted, and dried that the whole courtyard would probably have been drowned in it at last . . . if the larger half had not been eaten up by the serf girls, who, stealing into the storeroom, would overeat themselves so frightfully that they were moaning and complaining of stomach-ache all day" (6–7). Yet nature strikes back with an abundance that cannot be organized, contained, or even explained. The serf girls experience another kind of "stomach-ache" with pregnancies that utterly baffle Pulkheria Ivanovna. The flies that swarm over the interior of the house are like Virgilian bees that have been transformed into pointlessly prolific nuisances. And the old couple look like a latter-day version of Virgil's rower, "who scarce propels his boat / Against the stream: if once his arms relax, / The current sweeps it headlong down the rapids" (*Georgics*, I, 202–4). Whether large or small, Gogol seems to say, nature is a powerful and ultimately deadly force. This is what elevates the story above mere parody.

Another kind of bulwark against nature, the town, makes its appearance in these middle-period stories. The Russian word for "town" or "city," *gorod*, is derived from the Indo-European word for "enclosure," and finds its counterpart in the Latin *hortus* ("garden" or "enclosed place"), the German *Garten*, the English "garden," the Church Slavonic *grad* (whose primary meaning is "wall"), the Czech *hrad* ("castle" or "fortress"), and so on. In all Gogol's work, however, there are only two towns-as-enclosures, and they are not Russian at all. I am thinking of Dubno and Warsaw, in "Taras Bulba."

Dubno is described as walled and heavily fortified, an almost impenetrable enclosure within which are located other enclosures, such as cellars, buildings, and rooms that are difficult of access. This is an achievement of the 1842 version, written after Gogol had spent several years in Rome—a point of importance for the story, as we shall soon see. Taras's younger son, Andrii,[5] while a student in Kiev, falls in love with the daughter of the Polish military governor of Kovno, who is visiting the city. Since the Poles are enemies of the Cossacks, this is a forbidden passion, even though it is not at this point consummated. Eventually the governor leaves, taking his daughter with him. Two years later, the Cossacks lay siege to the town of Dubno, which turns out to be under the command of this same man. The girl's servant, a Tartar woman with markedly demonic features, slips into the Cossack encampment and offers to guide Andrii into the town and to her mistress. He accepts, thereby becoming a traitor.

Much is made of the physical obstacles they encounter (II, 66–72). They come to a stream and cross it on a small log; attain a steep bank, thickly overgrown and marshy; make their way "through the reeds"; stop before "a heap of brushwood and fagots"; and discover "an opening in the earth" that is "hardly bigger than the doorway of a bread oven." To enter, Andrii has to bend "as low as he [can]." They find themselves "in complete darkness," then in the catacomb of a church, and finally in front of a "little iron door," which upon being opened reveals "a monk standing on a narrow flight of stairs with keys and a candle in his hands." From there they enter the church, which is described in considerable detail, and at last emerge into the town marketplace. It is said to be "completely empty" and "dead-looking." On closer inspection, Andrii sees motionless bodies, some still alive. These are "the dreadful victims of famine," which has been brought on by the siege. But an equally lethal element is at work within, although it is harder to detect because it masquerades as beauty amidst all the devastation.

In an early article, Gogol declared his enthusiasm for any "ancient German town with narrow little streets, with a variety of small houses and tall belfries," as presenting an appearance that "speaks to our imagination." He is thinking specifically of Gothic architecture, which he regards as a physical expression of that "ardent faith" and devotion to "a single idea" that characterized the Middle Ages for him, as for so many of its earlier devotees among the Romantics. As such, it was a form in which "everything was joined together"—"grandeur and beauty," "luxuriance and simplicity," "weightiness and lightness"—and which "lifted the viewer's eyes up to infinity."[6] At first sight, Dubno, though Polish, might be just such a place: at least, it looks uniform architecturally, with a touch of the Gothic style in the "one-story stone and clay houses with wooden posts and pillars visible in their walls all the way up, with slanting crosspieces of wood . . . all topped with disproportionately high roofs," and with "numbers of dormer windows and apertures in the walls" (69). The word "disproportionate," however, signals a slight incongruity, which presently recurs on a large scale in the main administration building, where the Polish girl also lives. It is "unlike the others," and warrants a highly particularized description such as Gogol rarely lavishes on structures in his fiction: "[I]t was built of fine red bricks and was of two stories. The windows of the lower story were set in high, jutting granite cornices; the upper story consisted of small arches forming a gallery; between them were trellises with heraldic crests on them; there were crests too on the corners of the house. A wide outer staircase of painted bricks led into the market place itself" (71).[7] What we see here is a building in the Italianate style that has been imported—actually, from one of Gogol's letters about Rome—into an essentially Germano-Polish architectural complex. Gogol approved of variety in architecture as long as it answered to a single, all-informing "idea." Otherwise, the result was eclecticism, or an assemblage of mere fragments, which, for Gogol, was symptomatic of decay and death. Dubno is eclectic; it cannot possibly be a vital enclosure; what Andrii sees in the marketplace—itself a lethal enclosure—is the inevitable result.

Ironically, the eclecticism creates an equality of the parts. But it is the equality conferred by death. This is perhaps why, on close examination, the large building looks like a microcosm of the town. It too is guarded by sentries, "one on each side, who *picturesquely* [a word, as we shall see, that had come to betoken stasis at this period of Gogol's career] and *symmetrically* [also suspect] leaned with one hand on the halberd standing beside them, and with the other supported their *bowed heads*, and so *looked more like carved images than living creatures*. They were not asleep nor dozing, but seemed *insensible to everything*" (71), living dead men, one might say. Like the town, the building presents a series of obstacles to be overcome. Andrii and the Tartar woman climb the stairs, encounter a "sumptuously dressed and equipped soldier" at the top, enter "the first room" filled with people, then exit through "a little door in the side wall" into a corridor and then into another room, this one shuttered and dimly lit. Finally the Tartar woman opens "the door into another room," and there stands the Polish girl. She is the object of a conventionally structured quest on the part of the ardent hero, but unconventionally represents death, not life. Spatially, the location of her boudoir is the equivalent of the marketplace. And it is there that Andrii chooses death by renouncing the Cossacks, the only life force in the story, and allying himself with the Poles.

Andrii's spiritual death is emblematic of what may happen to such a force once it is enclosed. The point is made on a larger scale with a group of Cossacks who are captured by the Poles and taken to Warsaw for execution. The gruesome procedure is witnessed by Taras himself. On learning that his son Ostap is among the captives, Taras arranges with the Jew Yankel, a counterpart of the Polish girl's Tartar servant, to enter the city. This he can do only if he subjects himself to various enclosures that are alien to the Cossack spirit. First he is confined in the "narrow cage" of a cart transporting bricks, which then moves through a "dark narrow thoroughfare" of the Jewish section. He is locked in the room of a house with a "little window," obviously a kind of prison cell. Finally he is vested in the disguise of "a foreign count who had arrived from Germany," which makes him so unrecognizable that even "the Cossacks who knew him best" would overlook his true identity. He and Yankel enter a building that looks like "a nesting heron," as incongruous an intrusion as the Italianate structure in Dubno, and move through a "covered court" into a "dark, narrow corridor," then into "a similar hall with a little window high up," then into the dungeon, and finally into the public square, where the executions take

place (113–26). The whole episode resembles Andrii's progress first into
Dubno and then into the large main building. The difference is that Warsaw itself is not enclosed and, for Gogol, cannot be, for it lacks an identity
of its own. It is part of the Russian Empire, but is not Russian. Poles live
there, but it is full of Jews, who are always "placeless" in Gogol and who
here inhabit filthy surroundings (dirt being, as we remember, matter out of
place). The city also draws "foreign counts and barons" who "were often
attracted solely by curiosity to see this half-Asiatic corner of Europe." All
in all, Warsaw represents a faceless cosmopolitanism that Gogol, as we
shall presently see, deemed characteristic of St. Petersburg too.

The only other large non-Russian town that figures prominently in
"Taras Bulba" is Kiev. But it is treated only as the place to which the Cossacks repair for education, good times, and trouble; it does not represent
enclosure. The provincial towns that provide the settings for *The Inspector
General, Dead Souls*, and a few of the stories function more as gathering
places for a cast of characters, not as bounded spaces in their own right.
By contrast, we might expect Gogol to treat St. Petersburg as an instance
of urban enclosure. The theme had been established in the eighteenth century.[8] Vasily Tredyakovsky's poem "Praise to the Izhorsk Land and to the
Reigning City of St. Petersburg" (Pokhvala Izherskoi zemle i tsarstvuyu-
shchemu gradu Sanktpeterburgu, 1752) recognizes two realms, the natural
·and the human: "Oh! Once a wilderness, now so populated!/ In you we
now see a capital city," which is impressively splendid. But in good Baroque
fashion, there is no real conflict. He celebrates the beauties of nature—"No
few good qualities do I see around me: / The streams of your river are light
and pure: / The air is cold, but of a healthy kind"—and sees human endeavor as equally benevolent and salubrious: "The mossy swamps have
been almost all dried up." By the early nineteenth century, the mood had
changed. City and nature now faced each other more as enemies. Eloquent
attestation can be seen in Pushkin's *Bronze Horseman* (Mednyi vsadnik,
1833). In good eighteenth-century fashion, the Introduction extols the
magnificence of the marble-clad city as a product of the "great thoughts"
of Peter I, with nature not so much an opposing force as a formless waste
to be conquered. Part I, however, reduces the city to workaday proportions
and subjects it to a hostile nature, which attacks, "bristling like a beast,"
as wind and rain, creating a huge flood that inundates everything and
causes a later ruler, Alexander I, to muse: "Against God's element / There
is no prevailing for tsars."[9]

All these traits enter into Gogol's view of St. Petersburg too, where they
combine to create a version of the urban landscape that generations of Russian writers, from Dostoevsky through Bely, would draw upon. Gogol's
earliest impressions of the city are recorded in a letter he wrote to his

mother on April 30 (o.s.), 1829, shortly after his arrival there. Far from feeling dazzled by the metropolis, as we might expect of a twenty-year-old from the backwoods of the Ukraine, he tells of a vast, ugly, impersonal urban center, where "an unusual silence reigns," where there is "no flash of spirit in the people," where everyone talks only of business or is utterly self-absorbed, where "everything is crushed, everything is mired in idle, trivial pursuits." The only touch of color comes in his detailed accounting of shop signs (X, 139–40). This is the city that appears here and there in his fiction: in the pouring rain and the unpleasant smells of "Diary of a Madman"; in the dreary, shabby Kolomna District of "The Portrait," where "the future never comes" and "all is still and desolate"; in the "gray Petersburg sky" of "The Overcoat"; and in the nonworking promenaders of "Nevsky Prospekt," who stroll between twelve and two in the afternoon, a detail transferred without alteration from his letter into the story. There is no sense here, or anywhere else in Gogol, of the capital city as enclosure, none of the marbled symmetries celebrated by Pushkin and Tredyakovsky.

Consequently, there is no contrast with surrounding nature. By now, in fact, nature has taken up permanent residence in the city, so that the two are virtually indistinguishable. In what was probably more a coincidence than a borrowing, Gogol here fleshes out a view of the city that had been set forth many years earlier by Karamzin, in his *Memoir on Ancient and Modern Russia* (Zapiska o drevnei i novoi Rossii, 1810–11). He had found nothing "pleasant" or "amiable" about the north or about the city built to tame it. Here was a land of "sands, marshes, sandy pine forests, where poverty, gloom, and disease hold sway." Building a city there was "yet another glaring mistake of Peter the Great," and even "*pernicious*": "Truly, Petersburg is founded *on tears and corpses*." Natural forces and human arrogance inflict the same punishment: the tsars "must strive to the utmost to keep the courtiers and guards from starving to death, as well as to make good the annual loss of inhabitants with newcomers, future victims of premature death! Man shall not overcome nature!"[10] Gogol's urban nature is more nuanced. Like the landscapes of his middle-period stories, it is partly a projection of the onlooker's mind, partly an independent entity. "The Overcoat" (1842) makes it most memorable. At first the city seems to reflect Akaky Akakievich himself: "Whatever [he] looked at, he saw nothing but his clear, evenly written lines" (II, 308). His happy mood after he acquires the coat leads him to discover lively streets, bright lights, and crowds of people. But we are alerted from the outset that another element is present: "There is in Petersburg a mighty foe of all who receive a salary of about four hundred roubles. That foe is none other than our northern frost" (309–10). The only enclosure against it that Akaky finds is the overcoat; and when he loses that, he is at the mercy of the elements, which is to say, the city itself. The vast, deserted square in which he is robbed was built by human beings, but now has become "a fearful desert," where nature has a life of its own.

It may be that such a view of Petersburg is inescapable for writers who, like Gogol, emphasize its foreignness. In the early letter to his mother, he observed that the city was "not at all like other European capitals or like Moscow," and went on to explain how: "In general, every capital is characterized by its people, who impress on it the stamp of nationality, but Petersburg has absolutely no character: the foreigners who have settled here have made themselves at home and are not at all like foreigners, whereas the Russians for their part have turned foreign and have become neither one nor the other" (X, 139). He returns to this idea in an article written in 1837, amplifying it in a somewhat lighter vein. Petersburg is "masculine," German in its passion for order, routine, and cleanliness, obsessed with money and business, intellectually insignificant, socially fragmented, and essentially non-Russian: "There is something about it that resembles a European colony in America: the same dearth of deep-rooted national characteristics, and the same admixture of foreign elements that has not yet amalgamated into a solid mass. It contains just as many different layers of society as there are nations. These societies are completely separate: aristocrats, civil servants, artisans, Englishmen, Germans, merchants—all comprise completely separate circles which rarely mingle, and which live and enjoy themselves largely in ways that are invisible to the others. And if you look more closely, you see that each of these classes is composed of many other small circles that do not mix either."[11] In terms of our model, such a society could not create healthy enclosures, certainly not healthy Russian enclosures.

Elsewhere in his works Gogol offers a different Petersburg, one with an eighteenth-century resonance, or so it might seem at a quick glance. It first appears in "Christmas Eve," one of the *Dikanka* stories (1832):

Petersburg flashed before him, glittering with lights. . . . My goodness! the clatter, the uproar, the brilliant light; the walls rose up, four stories on each side; the thud of the horses' hoofs and the rumble of the wheels echoed and resounded from every quarter; houses seemed to pop up out of the ground at every step; the bridges trembled; carriages raced along; sled drivers and postilions shouted; the snow crunched under the thousand sleds flying from all parts; people passing along on foot huddled together, crowded under the houses which were studded with little lamps, and their immense shadows flitted over the walls with their heads reaching the roofs and the chimneys. (I, 123–24)

This is a good-natured, even positive (or at least not negative) impression of the city as observed by the blacksmith Vakula, who has come from far-off Dikanka to try to acquire the tsarina's slippers. Like any visitor, he is struck by the sparkle and glamour of an exotic realm. The tsarina is Catherine the Great. She was of course German by birth and upbringing, and spoke Russian with a marked accent; but in the fairy-tale atmosphere of this story, foreignness is a virtue when conjoined with wisdom, solicitude, and benevolence, as is the case here. Even so, the city itself lacks coherence and substance; it is all glitter, patches, and impressions. These are usually demonic features in Gogol, and the fact that Vakula is transported to Petersburg by the devil himself, in yet another aerial journey, all but tells us who really rules. And despite Vakula's fascination with the tsarina, he takes advantage of her momentary distraction to order the devil, now concealed in his pocket, "Get me away from here, quickly!," whereupon he "[finds] himself outside the city gates" (130).

Let us set beside this scene a famous episode from "Nevsky Prospekt," written some five years later. Here Gogol describes the young artist Piskaryov as he sets off in pursuit of the girl he has encountered on the Nevsky:

All his feelings were ablaze and everything before him was lost in a sort of mist; the pavement seemed to be moving under his feet, carriages drawn by trotting horses seemed to stand still, the bridge stretched out and seemed broken in the center, the houses were upside down, a sentry box seemed to be reeling toward him, and the sentry's halberd, and the gilt letters of the signboard and the scissors painted on it, all seemed to be flashing across his very eyelash. (I, 215)

This is virtually the same landscape as in "Christmas Eve." But the tonality is very different, largely because Gogol is writing not a fairytale but a kind of physiological sketch, which strives to create an impression of almost documentary reality. A new kind of reality suddenly intrudes as a derangement of the senses. The proximate cause is external—"And all this was produced by one glance, by one turn of a pretty head"—but the pathology is internal, and the city becomes an extrusion of Piskaryov's obsessive fantasy. Because he revels in it, he finds the city as alluring at this point as Khoma Brut does the landscape that floats below him in "Viy." But the broken, reflecting surface prevents him from seeing, until it is too late, the "real" city, which wallows in poverty, drugs, and prostitution. This city emerges imagistically in the final scene of the story. "Dark" as a time of illusion is conventional: "It deceives at all hours, the Nevsky Prospekt does, but *most of all when night falls* in masses of shadow on it, throwing into relief the white and dun-colored walls of the houses." The peculiarly Gogolian touch comes when he makes light part of that illusion too: "when all the town is transformed into noise and brilliance, when myriads of carriages roll off bridges, postilions shout and jump up on their horses. . . ." And the illusion is exposed as grim reality when "*the devil himself lights*

the street lamps to show everything in false colors" (I, 238). This street is
no longer the projection of one fevered human brain, but an independent
realm that embraces both nature and artifice and is ruled by demonic
forces. The best mere mortals can do is try "not to look at the objects,"
and keep their "distance from the street lamp."

Piskaryov embodies the values of a borrowed, superficial, and now thoroughly decadent Romanticism, values much like those that animate Chartkov in "The Portrait," whose urban landscape is very similar. But there is
a deeper source here too, which is indicated by the profusion of light images. St. Petersburg was founded by Peter the Great in 1703 for very practical strategic, commercial, and cultural reasons. Before long, it came to
represent the one towering achievement of the Enlightenment in Russia, in
contrast to the "darkness" of the old, pre-Petrine ways. In *The Bronze
Horseman* Pushkin catches up the literal and figurative senses of the opposition in such lines as these: "From forest gloom [*t'my*, 'darkness,' with
much the same range of meanings as the English word: absence of light,
ignorance, benightedness, etc.], out of the bog of marshlands, / [The city]
has risen splendidly, pridefully. . . . And before the younger capital / Old
Moscow has faded [*pomerkla*, lit., 'grown dark']. . . . And barring the
gloom [*t'mu*] of night / From the golden skies."[12] To be sure, the remainder
of the poem registers skepticism about the perdurability of "light." But Gogol goes beyond skepticism to outright mistrust of the Enlightenment and
all its manifestations, particularly order, symmetry, and reason, with the
corresponding loss of intuition, vitality, emotion, and religion. He seems
to feel not so much that Peter's great idea has disappeared as that there was
never any real idea to begin with, in the sense of a vital, inspiriting principle
like the one he thought had informed the Middle Ages. If so, then Piskaryov
is a parody not only of the Romantic artist but of Peter the Great himself.

The Enlightenment was a foreign concept, which Russians associated
especially with France. I think this explains why Gogol's later landscapes
of Paris are virtually identical to his landscapes of Petersburg, built as they
are on images of light, disorder, fragmentation, and rapid movement. In
"Rome," a story dating from 1842, the young Italian prince goes to Paris
to study, and immediately finds himself *"disconnectedly* caught up in its
enormous exterior, staggered by the *movement*, the *glitter* of the streets,
the *disorder* of the roofs, the *thicket* of chimneys, the architecture*less*, un-
broken *masses* of the houses, onto which *scraps* of shops were *thickly plas-
tered*, the *ugliness* of *bare* free-standing side walls, by the *numberless, jum-
bled crowd* of gold letters. . . . Here it was, Paris, this eternally *seething
crater.*" His reaction is similar to Piskaryov's: "Like one *stupefied, power-
less to collect himself,* he set out through the streets, which were strewn
with *all kinds of people . . . deafened* by the dull sound of the *several thou-*

sand shuffling feet of the densely moving crowd . . . *blinded* by the quivering *glitter* of the shops . . . now stopping in front of posters which *crowded the eyes* in their *multi-colored millions . . . a countless multitude of all kinds* of musical concerts; now *completely losing his head* when in the evening all this *magical heap* flared up in the *magical illumination* of gas" (*PSS*, III, 222–23). The prince comes to see that all the activity masks "a strange inactivity," a frenzied pursuit of novelty for its own sake, and in fact reaches beyond Paris to the nation as a whole, which is "something pale, incomplete, a light comic sketch engendered by itself," devoid of any "majestic and solid idea," displaying only "hints at thought, but no thoughts as such," "semblances of passions, but no real passions." He concludes, "everything was unfinished, everything was thrown together, sketched with a quick hand; the entire nation was a brilliant vignette, and not a picture by a great master." Paris becomes for the prince a "painful desert" (we may remember the "fearful desert" of the deserted square in "The Overcoat"), in which he feels boredom and anguish; and he decides to return to Rome (*PSS*, III, 228–29).

Gogol was by no means the first Russian writer to take a dim view of Paris. Nearly 65 years earlier, the playwright Denis Fonvizin had visited France and found it wanting: "there is not much here that is good or worthy of being imitated." The natives, he admitted, were witty, but were interested only in externals, beneath which they remained dirty and malodorous. Paris was the same thing writ large: "Its exterior is ineffably more magnificent, and its exterior more filthy."[13] Like Fonvizin, Gogol makes his Paris synonymous with all of France, an embodiment of the evils of *esprit*, with no contrasting realm of nature. His Petersburg offers a subtler picture. For one thing, it does not stand for Russia but is an aberration, or at least he seems to hope so. We might therefore expect him to honor convention and look to Moscow as a repository of the national spirit. In fact, he addresses it briefly in the 1829 letter to his mother, when he cites Moscow as a "real" capital. And in the 1837 article, he launches into a two-page, point-by-point comparison of Petersburg and Moscow (much like the comparison between the two Ivans), where the older city comes off distinctly the better, being "feminine," thoroughly Russian in its slovenly, generous, and relaxed ways, and intellectually vital, mainly because it was home to the native version of German Romanticism. He summed up the differences aphoristically as follows: "Moscow is necessary for Russia; for Petersburg it is Russia that is necessary."[14] Oddly enough, Moscow does not figure in his fiction, even though it might have offered a splendid opportunity to explore the problem of a vital bounded space, being laid out in circles and centered on the Kremlin, a walled fortress. One reason, I suspect, is that Gogol shunned solutions until late in his career, when he had pretty much put fiction aside. In its conventional role, Moscow would probably have represented too positive a force for him. For another, he seemed to harbor reservations about Moscow. In the article we have just cited, he hints at philistinism, particularly when he characterizes its "femininity" in ways that would be unworthy of a great spiritual and national center: it boasts a profusion of marriageable girls and a passion for fashions.[15] And its intellectual life, though vigorous, is dominated by Germans of another type, but foreigners all the same, namely Kant, Schelling, "and so on and on." If Petersburg was too cosmopolitan, Moscow was too provincial.

The rectilinearity of Petersburg that intrigued Pushkin in 1833 would be developed more than 80 years later by Andrei Bely into a vast metaphor in his novel *Petersburg*. For Gogol, however, straight lines would probably have defined the city more than he wished, even though, as Bely knew, those lines could be extended to infinity. He preferred to gratify his penchant for ambiguity and treat Petersburg as placelessness incarnate. It was not Russian, to be sure; but having no real form, it could spread all the more easily to any corner of the country. That, it seems to me, is one point Gogol wishes to make with Khlestakov, an amorphous figure and a Petersburger. When Gogol did eventually reach for solutions, his reference point was all of Russia, not Petersburg, or Moscow, or any particular region.

In his attitude toward nature, Gogol departed from the traditions of folklore, where nature constantly warns, celebrates, and mourns its human counterparts. Nor was he in step with Orthodox Christianity, which, in its Russian version, as G. P. Fedotov points out, gave to the Byzantine cosmology a "warmth, spontaneity, and even poignancy which went far beyond the western medieval sense of nature."[16] We would not mistake him for a latter-day representative of either of the two great international literary movements that had just preceded him, Sentimentalism and Romanticism. The Sentimentalists presupposed that man and nature were mutually responsive. As Nikolai Karamzin put it in "Poor Liza" (Bednaya Liza, 1792), virtually a programmatic short story, "I go to the same place in the gloomy days of autumn to grieve along with nature." We find almost nothing of the kind in Gogol: no assumption, as some German Romantics made, that "nature is the necessary product of an external act of the spirit"; nothing of the "analogical correspondence between man and nature" that Paul de Man finds in the early Wordsworth in "so perfect" a form that "one passes from one to the other without difficulty or conflict, in a dialogue full of echo and joyful exchange." Still, as de Man goes on to observe, Hölderlin always assumed that the idea of a correspondence between nature and consciousness must be "surpassed," and Wordsworth himself gradually arrived at this same idea.[17] Among Gogol's Russian predecessors, Pushkin recognized a hostile nature in *The Bronze Horseman*, and even an indifferent one in the ending of a famous poem:

> And at the entrance to the grave
> May young life play,
> And indifferent nature [*ravnodushnaya priroda*]
> Shine with everlasting beauty.[18]

Gogol, however, was the first important Russian writer for whom nature under these troubling aspects became a major theme. The possibility of borrowing apart, I suspect his attitude has much to do with his tendency to treat the world in visual terms. This creates a space between object and viewer, and a corresponding sense of alienation. Whether he employed seeing to create distance, or was first aware of distance and then recorded it in visual terms, is a subject we shall take up in the next section. In either event, these discontinuities offended his more deeply Russian sense of the need for what Tony Tanner, in one of his numerous studies of American Romantic writers, has called "the fruitful *intermingling* of Nature's and Man's creative potencies."[19] In this respect, Gogol stands far closer to them than to their European counterparts. With Americans, though again not with Europeans, he also shares a profound distrust of cities. Geography could have had its say, each country being vast and underpopulated. So could the prophets of the Old Testament, who are famously jaundiced about all human works, among them, cities. They stand as a commanding presence in American culture of the nineteenth century, and may also have left a quiet but decisive imprint on Gogol's view of the human condition.

6

Some Sources of Place

IN most of Gogol's stories boundaries crumble, pollutants preponderate, ritual is merely formalistic. The results are by turn calamitous, frightful, tragic, repugnant. Much of the effect depends on our ability, surely greater if we are Russians, to recognize that Gogol regards bounded space as an ideal, even if it remains obscured, hidden, and unexpressed.

We have traced the origin of this ideal to the *Primary Chronicle*. But the formulation there has been nourished and enlarged through the centuries by countless other sources, so that it is now a complex of related ideas. One of the sources, itself a complex, is to be found in Eastern Orthodox Christianity, which informed not only Gogol's life but his fiction as well.

Gogol's career as a writer of fiction and plays came to an end in 1842, with the publication of his collected works and Part 1 of *Dead Souls*. He spent the decade that remained to him in a relentless and fruitless struggle with a sequel to this book, most of which he consigned to the flames shortly before his death. Critics have always been intrigued by such spectacular failure on the part of a writer who had become a classic in his own time, and have ransacked his life and work for explanations. One event that has quickened the critical pulse is the religious "conversion" he experienced in 1840. Before then, he had been a nominal Christian at best. To be sure, from an early age he had a lively sense that a higher power—not necessarily the Christian God—had marked him out for some great mission. As he wrote to Mikhail Pogodin in 1836: "A will that is not of this earth is guiding my path." He always regarded the great crises of his life as unfolding under divine guidance. Particularly important was a near-fatal illness in 1840: "Only the wonderful will of God resurrected me." Thenceforth, he increasingly identified God with Christ, and vowed to serve Him. He became convinced that he and all others must imitate Christ, "take Him as a model for oneself, and try to act as He acted while still here on earth."[1] This new enthusiasm (obsession would be a better word) was fed by an avid study of theology and philosophy. The letters and notebooks of the 1840's and 1850's reveal an impressive familiarity with a range of ecclesiastical and spiritual writers, especially Russian, Ukrainian, and patristic, but also Western European. Thomas à Kempis was very much in evidence.[2] Although his *Imitation of Christ* had been translated into Russian by M. M. Speransky and published in 1829 (as *O podrazhanii Khristu, chetyre knigi Fomy Kempiiskogo*), Gogol apparently read it in a French translation. He warmly recommended it to his correspondents, "not because there is nothing higher and better, but because I know of no other book that is better for the purpose I will indicate," that is, self-directed spiritual reading.[3] Gogol himself wrote three works that are largely spiritual and specifically Christian in orientation. One is *Meditations on the Divine Liturgy*, which dates from the mid-1840's and was published posthumously. Another is *Selected Passages from Correspondence with Friends*, which appeared in 1847. Here Christ stands solidly in the center as the model for the individual and for a "unified Christian culture." Many of Gogol's readers found the book spiritually arrogant. Their reaction induced him to write the so-called "Author's Confession," an apologia (but not an apology) for his life, with Christ again the exemplar. It was published after his death, at which time the title was supplied by S. P. Shevyryov.

Except for what remains of Part 2 of *Dead Souls*, there are no works of fiction from this period. As a result, many critics, from that day to this, have talked of "the other Gogol," a self-styled thinker and preacher who supposedly betrayed his true talent; have laid the blame, at least implicitly, on the "conversion"; and have treated the whole question of his religious beliefs with hostility, embarrassment, or indifference. Other critics, often religiously inclined themselves, see this "other" Gogol as a worthy, even great figure in his own right. They scrutinize his earlier work for evidence of the origins of his religious opinions, in hopes, as the unsympathetic V. V. Gippius puts it, of finding "threads" that connect with "the religious quests and experiences of [his] later life."[4] Typically, they fasten attention on Gogol's upbringing by a naively pious mother, on his family's regular churchgoing and observance of religious rituals, and on their readings in spiritual literature. The possible influence of Western European religious thought on the young Gogol has been taken into account as well. Certainly it was a strong presence in the Ukraine of the eighteenth century. The Kievan Academy, for instance, was modeled on Polish Jesuit institutions of higher learning, even to the textbooks used. Other Orthodox seminaries generally followed the Kievan model. Gogol's father studied at the Poltava Seminary. The school in Nezhin, where Gogol was a pupil, was more secular, yet heavily mortgaged to foreign theologians and preachers, including Jacques Bossuet, François Fénelon, and Jesuit preachers like Louis Bourdaloue and Jean-Baptiste Massillon. Closer to home, he may have learned much from the style and thought of the religious writings of the Ukrainian Baroque, which had much in common with its European counterparts.[5]

Critics of this persuasion must, however, contend with Gogol's own testimony that he was skeptical about, if not actively hostile to, organized religion as a young man. In 1833, for example, he told his mother that his sister Olga should be brought up in the "principles of religion," for they were "the foundation of everything," but that she should not be subjected to the catechism, which was "double Dutch to a child," or to regular attendance at church, where everything "is also incomprehensible to a child—the language and the rituals. She will develop the habit of looking on it as a comedy." By way of proof, he recalled his own experience: "I looked on everything with indifferent eyes. I went to church only because I was told to go or was taken, but while there, I saw nothing but the chasubles and the priest, and heard only the repulsive bellowing of the deacons. I crossed myself only because I saw everyone else crossing himself."[6]

Gogol's letters and essays from the early through mid-1830's treat Christianity, if at all, mainly as a historical phenomenon. The fiction and plays written during this time show even scantier evidence of Christian themes. For instance, they present hardly any members of the clergy, while otherwise offering a rather full sociology of early nineteenth-century Russia. The few that do appear, as Lorenzo Amberg has shown, are episodic and, especially in the case of seminarians, often treated sarcastically. The Devil in various forms puts in frequent appearances; but as Konstantin Mochulsky has observed, Gogol's demonism owes more to folklore than to Christianity.[7] There are virtually no references to God and Christ in terms that are anything more than manners of speaking. In fact, Gogol's early fictional works strike us as being rooted in a relentlessly material world and largely indifferent to spiritual values. Mochulsky has insisted that insofar as Gogol's outlook in these works is Christian at all, it reflects "a religion of sin and retribution" that rests on "a pagan foundation," on "the experience of cosmic horror and an elemental fear of death" (10). Other readers have reached much the same conclusion on the evidence of a statement Gogol made in the 1833 letter to his mother from which we have quoted: "I asked you to tell me about the last judgment, and you did tell me, a child, in such a clear, understandable, affecting way, about the blessings that await people who have led a virtuous life, and you described in so striking and horrible a manner the eternal torments of the sinners, that it shook me and awakened all my deeper feelings" (X, 282).

Phenomenologically, these critics are undoubtedly right. Like most readers of Gogol, however, they overlook certain underlying structures of thought and traits of style that reflect a worldview of great complexity: the Neoplatonic tradition within Eastern Orthodoxy. "Place" and "placelessness" are prominent among them. Gogol makes frequent reference to "place" in his later works. In his *Selected Passages* (1847), for example, he writes: "It was not for nothing that God ordered each of us to be in that place in which he now stands." In "An Author's Confession," written the same year, he insists: "we are appointed to serve, and our entire life is service." But such service is possible only in a "place [*mesto*]" or "post [*dolzhnost'*]," which everyone, high and low, should occupy. This place is "a means for attaining not an earthly goal but a heavenly goal, in salvation of your soul." Therefore: "It is hardest of all for the person who has not attached himself to a place, has not determined in what his duty consists."[8] We could almost make a small book out of similar passages from his writings of the 1840's and 1850's. They are obviously the fruits of his readings in spiritual literature. But I would suggest that the idea of "place," as a desirable state of being, is present in his work from the outset, even at a time when he was ignorant of theology. No doubt it was one of those ideas he absorbed unconsciously and took for granted. It was embedded in his religious tradition, so much so that it can be located in virtually any of the theologians and spiritual writers of the Eastern Church, major and minor. One could find it in the *Philokalia*, say, or, among Gogol's recent predecessors, in the writings of Hryhory Skovoroda, or Dmitry of Rostov, whose works Gogol may have seen in the library of his uncle, D. P. Troshchinsky, though this is not known for certain. I propose to go far back into the tradition and concentrate on the one thinker whose formulations of the idea of "place" created an especially compelling paradigm: Pseudo-Dionysius the Areopagite.

This is the name conventionally given to the author of mystical writings in Greek that came to light in the early sixth century A.D. Besides ten letters, the most important are *The Celestial Hierarchy*, *The Ecclesiastical Hierarchy*, *The Divine Names*, and *The Mystical Theology*. These works exerted a profound influence on medieval theology both Eastern and Western. Translations were made into Slavic in 1371 by Isai the Serb and in 1675 by Evfimy, a monk of the Chudov Monastery, and into Russian in 1786–87 by Moisei Gumilevsky and by later scholars in 1855 and 1957.[9] With the Renaissance and the Reformation, Dionysius's influence waned in the

Western church, but he has always remained a major figure in the East, which has seen him as "a theological summa for the interpretation of its best [theological] writers."[10] By the nineteenth century, he had become deeply embedded in the mind of the Orthodox Church. As for Gogol, in 1846 he put on his list of required reading the 1786–87 Russian translation of *The Celestial Hierarchy* and *The Ecclesiastical Hierarchy*.[11] Whether he read them or not we do not know. In any event, they would have come far too late to influence his major fiction. What interest us, rather, are striking parallels of language and thought.

Pseudo-Dionysius sees the world structured as a divine hierarchy, each level of which partakes of the whole divinity, but in its own way, according to the particular nature of its being: "It is wholly present to some, present in a diminished fashion to others, and in the extreme it is present to others as each is able to partake of it."[12] In this divine structure, God provides "what is due to all . . . what is proper to each being according to the conceived need of each being." This exemplifies "divine justice" inasmuch as "it distributes those things which are proper to each being according to what is due to each being, and since it preserves the nature of each in its proper order and power" (*DN*, VIII, 7, p. 184). There are those who do not accept the divine hierarchy or their own place within it, and try to usurp a place that is not theirs, typically one that is higher.

It is significant that the Russian word for "crime," *prestuplenie*, literally means "overstepping" or "transgression"; and a crime is of course a violation of someone else's place. Overattentiveness to one's own place to the point of self-isolation also works against wholeness. Like overstepping, it celebrates a false individuality at the expense of a true personhood. This distinction is fundamental to Orthodoxy. As Vladimir Lossky explains it, the "person [*lichnost'*]" is "the whole man in his entirety," who is in the image and likeness of God. Original sin, however, made man also an "individual [*individ*]": "human nature became divided, split up, broken into many individuals." In consequence, man "now has a double character: as an individual nature, he is part of a whole, one of the elements which make up the universe; but as a person, he is in no sense a part: he contains all in himself. . . . A person who asserts himself as an individual, and shuts himself up in the limits of his particular nature, far from realizing himself fully becomes impoverished."[13] Personhood, to rephrase Lossky, is synonymous with true place. The distinction between individual and person extends to social and spiritual corporations, even those as large as the nation. Vadim Borisov, for one, insists that the "individual embodies the opposite of the common measure in mankind, a fragment of the one human nature." Therefore, "[i]ndividual men and individual nations are *impenetrable* to one another." Borisov uses two terms for "individual," *individ* and *indi-*

viduum, both, significantly, of foreign origin, hence well suited to name what he regards as a profoundly non-Russian phenomenon. By contrast, *lichnost'*, "personality" or "person," is a thoroughly Russian word and marks a thoroughly Orthodox idea, inasmuch as it "comprehends the whole within itself" and therefore "*presupposes* the existence of a common measure in mankind." The nation, then, is "a corporate personality endowed with its being by God." Inevitably, each person is sensible of his "metaphysical relationship with the corporate self of the people, and *through* it with the corporate self of mankind." In turn, mankind is defined (in what looks like a paraphrase of Pseudo-Dionysius, but echoes the Orthodox tradition as a whole) as "not a simple combination of its parts, but a definite hierarchy, each level of which, in possessing the quality of personhood, possesses the same fullness as does the whole."[14]

   This is the ideal that informs Gogol's ideas of place from the beginning. He did not use theological terminology: of that he was profoundly ignorant until the 1840's. But he follows the mind of his Church in regarding "individuality" as pernicious, even depicting it in his fiction as fragmentation, disorder, chaos, isolation, and death. These are also the images many Orthodox theologians use to describe the wages of sin. Leonid Ouspensky, for example, writes: "[Man] turned away from God. . . . This led to the *disintegration* of man, the microcosm, which consequently led to a cosmic *disintegration*, a catastrophe in all creation. The whole visible world fell into *disorder*, *strife*, suffering, *death*, and *corruption*."[15] The person so afflicted harms the larger polity since he no longer occupies his proper place; the polity so afflicted becomes merely a collection of individuals, and loses its coherence and its reason for being. But where is the idea of personhood, or for that matter of any "positive" ideal, in these early works? Lorenzo Amberg, without making the distinction we have been discussing, argues that *The Inspector General* contains a "positive" message in various sayings of the mayor that are quotations from or paraphrases of the Bible, and that "these words, in and by themselves, are a fundamental Christian statement, which despite the comic situation preserve their value as truth for the characters as well as for the spectator" (108). To me this argument seems flawed. For one thing, Amberg draws support from the interpretation of the play that Gogol himself made some ten years later, when he had become a devout Christian who saw the world in the light of his new enthusiasm. For another, the "Christian" statements, though undoubtedly present, read like parodies in the context of the play, and therefore serve to point up the enormous gap that exists between this special language and the textual world at large. If *The Inspector General*, like much of Gogol's fictional work, has a "positive" side, that is because of its negative treatment of its world: "placelessness" indicates what true place must be.

Since we are working in a theological context, it is tempting to describe this technique of definition through negation with the term "apophaticism," and to suppose that Gogol must have absorbed it from the Christian tradition to which he was exposed from an early age. Certainly it is a powerful idea. Vladimir Lossky says that apophaticism "constitutes the fundamental characteristic of the whole theological tradition of the Eastern Church." He characterizes it as follows: "All knowledge has as its object that which is. Now God is beyond all that exists. In order to approach Him it is necessary to deny all that is inferior to Him, that is to say, all that is. . . . Proceeding by negations one ascends from the inferior degrees of being to the highest, by progressively setting aside all that can be known, in order to draw near to the Unknown in the darkness of absolute ignorance."[16] Here Lossky is referring specifically to Pseudo-Dionysius, who is responsible for perhaps the most eloquent and influential formulations of the idea of apophaticism in the Eastern Church. For instance, in *The Mystical Theology* he writes:

> It is
>> not soul, not intellect,
>> not imagination, opinion, reason and not understanding,
>> not logos, not intellection,
>> not spoken, not thought,
>> not number, not order,
>> not greatness, not smallness
>> not equality, not inequality,
>> not likeness, not unlikeness,
>> not having stood, not moved, not at rest,
>> not powerful, not power,
>> not light,
>> not living, not life

and so on, for several more lines.[17] The term "apophaticism" really should be reserved for theological discourse. That certainly is not Gogol's purpose. However, negation—the better way of putting it—is so common a trait of Gogol's style in all periods that it may be called characteristic. Rhetorically, there are many different kinds of negation in his works. Some signal absence, whether physical or moral; some denote preterition; some establish a neutral middle by denying extremes (as in the opening of *Dead Souls*); some betoken non-place, as in "A Terrible Vengeance." Many function formally like apophaticism. Gogol was well aware that he was showing Russia "from one side," as he put it in a letter to Pushkin, written on October 7 (o.s.), 1835 (X, 375). By stating what was not, he seemed to have been relying on his readers' awareness that the world presented in these early works was anything but ideal or desirable. Certainly he saw it that way a decade later. At one point in "The Denouement of *The Inspector General*," Nikolai Nikolaich says: "If you present all the rubbish that is in people, and present it in such a way that every member of the audience is utterly disgusted with it, then I ask you: is that not really praise of everything good? I ask you: is that not praise of the good?"[18]

Lest I emulate Amberg and interpret by anachronism, I cannot insist on this passage (and others like it in the same article) as proof of the point I am trying to make about Gogol in the 1830's. But on the evidence of his letters from those years, and for that matter, of his fictional practices, it is plain that he expected his readers and viewers to react in the way prescribed by Nikolai Nikolaich. For the most part, however, readers could not see past the ruined and desolate world of these early works. This is in some measure a tribute to Gogol's power to make the negative so compelling and convincing that no alternative seemed possible. We must always be mindful of the obvious, that Gogol is writing fiction, not chronicles or documentaries. Nor is he a cultural anthropologist, although his stories could provide valuable data to researchers in that field, the more so since generations of readers have taken for granted that the stories reflect and even record the actual state of Russian society at that time.

Were we, for example, to use Gogol's works alone to evaluate the state of Christianity in early-nineteenth-century Russia, we would have to conclude that it had had its day: the spirit had departed, leaving behind only atrophied structures, isolated "individuals," and overhanging apprehension. The ideal as expressed by Pseudo-Dionysius seems remote indeed. What accounts for this gloomy, hope-bereft, profoundly un-Christian view of the world by a man who was at least nominally Christian? Could he have been reflecting the drastic changes that had occurred in the position of the church in Russia since the eighteenth century? As Geoffrey Hosking has reminded us, the government had "expropriated ecclesiastical land and turned the Church into a department of state." It was particularly weak at the parish level, where it had lost touch with the vital life of the community: "The parish was an outgrowth of the bureaucracy rather than of the village community."[19] Amberg makes much the same point when he observes of Gogol's "Viy": "If the church has long since lost its social function—the gathering-place of the villagers is the kitchen—then it has now been robbed of its religious vocation as well. This house of God, which has been assailed by evil, exists neither for God nor for men" (43). More generally, Gogol may have been expressing a pervasive malaise of the time. Throughout Europe, and in Russia as well, there had been a profound sense, since the late eighteenth century, that an old order of things was giving way to something far less stable, reliable, and predictable. The mood had been well documented by the Romantics. In *Fantasies on Art for Friends of Art* (1799),

Wilhelm Heinrich Wackenroder had extolled the sixteenth century as a golden age in which boundaries were clearly marked and the individual had an unshakable sense of "his appropriate place on one of the side branches of the old, venerable family tree," saw himself as "a member and brother of the vast human race," and "did not make himself alone the principal trunk of the world." This position depended on a strong family structure and on a clear sense of God as a higher power, both of which Wackenroder found considerably weakened as the eighteenth century came to a close.[20]

On the evidence of Gogol's works, particularly the early ones, family structure and higher power have all but disappeared. Displacement is now the norm. It can manifest itself in a restless quest for a nurturing stability and security, as in the case of Chichikov, who is trying to acquire an estate to which his placeless condition does not entitle him. But Gogol also registers the desperate ways people devise for resisting or denying displacement, through habit, routine, acquisition of things, and isolation. The results are equally futile. Poprishchin represents the intersection and the culmination of these tendencies, being both totally displaced and totally isolated, with no hope of even the possibility of redemption, as hinted at, for example, in the arrival of the "real" inspector general at the end of Gogol's great play, which was staged the same year "Diary of a Madman" appeared.

Wackenroder's words also invite a consideration of Gogol's personal situation. "Humble" hardly fits Gogol's personality, but neither does the picture of the godless, self-centered man drawn by Wackenroder, one who "wants to make himself God and Ruler of the universe." Even though Gogol had found churchgoing repellent as a child and occasionally demonstrated some anticlericalism as an adult (though far milder than was common among others of his class), there is no evidence that he went through a stage of "free-thinking," let alone invested himself with divinity. He would therefore seem to stand remote from Wackenroder's characterization of such a man as being "in distressing derangement" and enjoying "only the sad, false happiness of a foolish, mad beggar, who thinks he is a crowned emperor" (168). But there is a forlorn, sad, even "deranged" quality to Gogol's life nonetheless. While convinced that people must find their proper place, he seemed unable to do so himself, and became in effect a wanderer, even a beggar.

In 1821, he entered school in Nezhin, nearly 200 crow's-flight kilometers northwest of his family's home, Vasilievka, in the small settlement of Bolshie Sorochintsy, Poltava Province. Except for visits during school holidays, Gogol never again spent much time there. His brother Ivan died in 1819; his father, Vasily Afanasievich, in 1825. At the age of sixteen, Gogol found himself the only male in a family consisting of his mother and three sisters. His relationship with them, which is amply documented by letters, seems to have provided little emotional sustenance on either side. Gogol most often assumed the role of stern, admonishing teacher, husband, and father. It was a role he played with many of his correspondents too. He tried to ensure an education for his sisters and establish them socially, as was expected of any family head. Toward his mother he was variously patronizing, indifferent, irritated, mendacious. Many scholars have tried to fathom this relationship. Whatever the details, he kept her at more than arm's length. Although he enjoyed occasional infatuations with women, they were brief, platonic, and usually unrequited. He never married. No doubt he did experience a profound attachment to Iosif Vielgorsky, the son of a count who performed many useful services for him. The young man died, at the age of 21, in Gogol's arms; and his sentiments on that occasion, when read in the context of his lifelong bachelorhood and his fictional depictions of women as either goddesses or wantons, have led some scholars to suspect that he was homosexual.[21] The evidence is circumstantial, and must in any event be measured against the Russian standards of male friendship, which in turn were strengthened by the still-fresh memories of the Sentimentalist cult of friendship. (A more recent instance in the supposedly chillier Anglo-Saxon world is Tennyson's friendship for Arthur Hallam.) At best, Gogol found himself in the position of the bachelor who is taken up by solidly married couples and their children, such as the Aksakovs and the Balabins. Certainly he never experienced "family" in the sense in which Wackenroder, unconsciously echoing the Orthodox idea of place (though filtered through Neoplatonism), describes it: "The delightfully intertwined chain of kinship was a holy bond: several friends related by blood constituted, as it were, a single, subdivided life, and each felt himself to be the richer in vital power the more the same ancestral blood was beating in other hearts:—the totality of relatives, finally, was the holy, small forecourt to the grand concept of humanity."[22]

Gogol completed his schooling in July 1828, and remained at home until December 13 of that year, when he set out for St. Petersburg. In the summer of 1829, he took his first trip abroad, to Germany, returning to St. Petersburg in September. There he stayed until late June of 1832, when he visited Moscow. From there he went to Vasilievka in mid-July to see his mother. At the beginning of October he was back in Petersburg, where he lived, one trip to Moscow aside, until June 1836. At this point he was 27 years old, had published three collections of stories and essays, and was already known as a writer of impressive achievement and exceptional promise. He rather precipitately embarked on a series of travels to Europe on June 6, 1836, and lived an almost peripatetic life thereafter. Interested readers may consult the detailed chronologies at the beginning of Volumes X through XIV of the *Complete Works* in Russian. He journeyed widely through Europe, returning to Russia only three times during the next twelve years: from September 1839 to May 1840; from July 1841 to June 1842; and from April 1848 to his death, on February 21, 1852. In other words, he lived in his native land for less than five of the seventeen years between 1836 and the end of his life. After he went back for good, he published nothing, and shortly before his death, he abandoned the great work on which he had long labored, Part 2 of *Dead Souls*.

When laid out this way, the chronology suggests great restlessness, even instability, or at the very least the lack of anything that could conventionally be called a home, or a "place."

The trip abroad in 1836 was probably the most important one of all. In a real sense, Gogol's work had reached an end point with "Diary of a Madman." Certainly it is difficult to imagine what more the theme of bounded space so intensely depicted could have yielded. If he was to develop, he had either to construct a whole new view of the world or invigorate the old one. He never abandoned the conviction that people should live fruitfully and creatively within a bounded space, but he offered no vision in his earlier fiction as to how this was possible. He had reached a point of artistic crisis. It was a personal crisis as well: Gogol never could separate the two, nor did he wish to. And, as he would do in the years to come when faced with other crises, he made a drastic change in his own physical place.

The immediate impulse for his departure from Russia in June 1836 was the first performance of *The Inspector General*, on April 19. In an oft-quoted letter to his friend Mikhail Pogodin, he announced:

I am going abroad, and there I will rid myself of the anguish that is daily visited on me by my fellow-countrymen. A writer of contemporary life, a writer of comedy, a writer of manners must stay as far away as possible from his native land. A prophet has no honor in his own country. I am not troubled by the fact that absolutely all classes of people have risen up against me, but it is somehow painful and sad when you see unjustly arrayed against you your own compatriots, whom you love with all your heart, when you see how they take everything in a false and incorrect way, the particular for the general, the exception for the rule.

Actually, the play was anything but a disaster. He admitted in an earlier letter to the actor Mikhail Shchepkin, "They abuse me and they go to the play; you can't get tickets for the fourth performance." There was a mix of reactions, ranging from enthusiasm to dislike. But Gogol could hear only the negatives. Mochulsky is right in observing that he sincerely expected the play to work an immediate spiritual transformation on its audience.[23] When that did not happen, when he detected no unanimity of opinion about it, he concluded that it had failed. And its "failure" in this regard seems to have alerted him to a genuine problem, or so, I think, we can legitimately suppose: that his work in general had reached a dead end, and that he had to find ways of breaking out of the enclosures he had so brilliantly and persuasively created. In these circumstances, his decision to flee Russia was an enactment of what he had to do as an artist: leave his own place for good, see new things, and look back on old things with entirely new eyes. The fact that he was just beginning work on *Dead Souls*, his most important book, must have made his journey all the more imperative. In effect, he was choosing to make himself placeless, clearing the way for the next stage of his work. Eventually he would understand that he need not abandon or even radically transform his art. For it already contained the solutions to the problems of place, and they would become apparent once he took up new vantage points.

PART TWO

The Apprehending Eye

7

The Art of Seeing

GOGOL literally left "place" behind him in 1836 as he moved into Western Europe, which for Russians had always lain well outside the bounded space. Now began the second period of his work, which ran through 1842. He had always been a writer who thought in visual terms, but had made no special point of it. Now he was to concentrate on working out a consistent and artistically viable poetics of seeing, and embodying it in his fiction.

From an early age, he showed a keen interest in the plastic arts. Painting he found especially attractive. He tried his hand at it while still in school at Nezhin. After moving to St. Petersburg in 1829, he continued to dabble, and the following summer he was serious enough to work at the Academy of Arts three times a week for two hours each.[1] Once he settled in Rome, he began, like many other well-born people of his time, to record the sights in watercolors. He wrote Vasily Zhukovsky at the end of February 1839: "My portfolio and paints are ready, and beginning today I am setting off to paint for the entire day, to the Colosseum, I think. . . . If you had stayed here another week, you would no longer have used [just] a pencil." He expressed his reluctance to "leave Rome for even a minute—it is so beautiful and there is such an enormous number of subjects for painting" (XI, 201–3). These early interests extended to his perceptions and practices of literature as well.

POET AS PAINTER

In Gogol's early statements about the arts, literature goes all but unremarked. We have only to look at "Sculpture, Painting and Music," a brief article written in 1834 and published the following year as part of *Arabesques*. The arts enumerated in the title are "three wonderful sisters [*tri chudnye sestry*]," each of which characterizes a main stage from ancient times to the present. What is significant is not the tripartite division, which was conventional, but rather the virtual absence of any mention of the verbal arts. Sculpture is described as "the clear specter of that bright Greek world which has receded from us into the deep removal of the ages, has already become enshrouded in mist, and can be reached only through the thought of the poet." There ensues a specification of traits that can be found only in certain kinds of poetry (undoubtedly Homeric), such as concrete imagery, strong colors, "beauty and sensuality," all of them producing "enjoyment" (a purely sensual quality, as Gogol sees it) in the beholder. Gogol suggests that poetry—at least ancient poetry—does the same kinds of things sculpture does; it has no qualities or functions unique to it; it is a *faute de mieux*. Painting, he goes on to say, is the achievement of the Christian Middle Ages. Being both sensual and spiritual, it looks back to sculpture and ahead to music; it is "music for the eyes"; and in us it evokes mainly "compassion," a spiritual quality. Because it expresses ineffabilities, things "for which there are no words," we presume that it finds no equivalent in poetry; at least, Gogol makes no mention of any. Music is the art of the present and the future. It is all movement, all "impulse [*poryv*]," is larger in scope and resonance than its two sisters, and eliminates all distance between itself and its beholder, for the listener becomes music. No mention at all is made of poetry here either.[2]

Even when he does deal with the verbal arts in this early period of his work, Gogol thinks in visual terms. An early instance is the article entitled "A Few Words About Pushkin," which he started at the end of 1831, completed in 1834, and included the following year in *Arabesques*.[3] It is a paean to Pushkin, not only as the greatest living poet but as the very embodiment of Russian nationality, two propositions that were far from generally accepted at the time. "In him," Gogol writes, "Russian nature, the Russian soul, the Russian language, the Russian character have been reflected . . ." The word "reflect" leads us to expect the image of a mirror. Instead, Gogol goes on to say "reflected with the same purity, the same purified beauty as a landscape on the convex surface of an optical glass" (50). This suggests that Pushkin has been created not by nature but by human hands, those of his fellow Russians, who see themselves focused and sharpened in him. Spatial and visual imagery predominate throughout the article. We are told that Pushkin "moved apart the boundaries" of the Russian language to show "all its expanse" (50), and that every word of his contains "an enormous expanse [*bezdna prostranstva*, lit., 'an abyss of expanse']" and is "unbounded [*neob' 'yatno*]" (55). He is likened to a painter with a bold and rapid brush, who "draws" (or "paints") the Caucasus in vivid "colors," creating "pictures" that are "magic." His short works are "more spacious, more striking [*vidnee*, lit., 'more visible']" and create "a series of the most dazzling [*oslepitel'nykh*, lit., 'blinding'] pictures," in which "there is a quick and vivid glimpse of dazzling shoulders or white arms or an alabaster neck covered with a night of dark curls, or transparent clusters of grapes or myrtle and the shade of trees" (54–55). These images would readily translate into Gogol's own fiction, particularly in the story "Rome" (1842): though remote from Pushkin's world, it also deals with the way people see. The vocabulary of painting extends even to Pushkin's audience: the fickle public resembles "a woman who commissions an artist to paint an utterly faithful portrait of her, but woe to him if he does not succeed in concealing all her blemishes" (52). And the narrator, obviously a version of Gogol, introduces the following anecdote supposedly from his own childhood to illustrate the perils of dealing with the public, although in this case the public is right: "I have always felt a slight passion for painting. I was very much interested in a landscape I had painted, in whose foreground stood a spreading, dried-up tree. I was then living in the country. My experts and judges were the nearby neighbors. One of them looked at the picture, shook his head and said: 'A good painter chooses a tall, healthy tree with fresh leaves, a vigorous tree that's growing, not one that's dried up'" (53–54).

Such an emphasis on seeing, with a corresponding disregard of the word, is surprising for someone who, after all, was a writer. We should remember, however, that the habit of talking about one art in terms of others had been common for centuries. As Paul Oskar Kristeller has pointed out by way of example, music, for the Greeks, "originally comprised much more than we understand by music. . . . Plato and Aristotle . . . do not treat music or the dance as separate arts but rather as elements of certain types of poetry, especially of lyric and dramatic poetry."[4] There is no reason to suppose that Gogol means "music" to stand for poetry, as sometimes seemed to be the case in his later years. But there is no doubt that throughout his life, painting consistently stood for literature. (Sculpture did not much interest him except as a phase in his grand scheme of the arts.) No doubt Eastern Christianity played its part here too. I am thinking in particular of icons. Timothy Ware reminds us: "Orthodoxy regards the Bible as a verbal icon of Christ. . . . [T]he Holy Icons and the Book of the Gospels should be venerated in the same way."[5] Icon and word are identical, and are therefore readily interchanged. We may also look to the ancient classics, which had come into Russia during the eighteenth century, far later than into Western Europe. They flowed through several channels. One was provided by Polish and Ukrainian manuals of rhetoric written in Latin, which became an essential part of the curriculum in the new schools that were being established in Moscow from the mid-seventeenth century on. By the latter part of the eighteenth century, the seminaries had moved toward adopting a classical curriculum, where the language of instruction was commonly Latin.[6] Other channels were opened by translations from the neoclassicists, like Nicolas Boileau, Jean François de LaHarpe, Voltaire, and Pope, and from the ancient writers themselves. Here particular importance attaches to Vasily Tredyakovsky (1703–69), whose prodigious literary endeavors included a Russian version of Boileau's *L'Art poétique* and Horace's *Epistle to the Pisos* (better known as *The Art of Poetry*). His brief article entitled "An Opinion on the Beginning of Poetry and Verses Generally" (Mnenie o nachale poezii i stikhov voobshche, 1752) is remarkable for the number of references to and quotations from classical and neoclassical authors and their works, but it is Horace who predominates. Tredyakovsky begins with a paraphrase of his most famous formulation, *ut pictura poesis*: "Like a picturesque painting, such is Poetry: it is a verbal depiction."[7] To be sure, the comparison of painting and poetry is far older than Horace, and had become a commonplace by his time. But it was his formulation— or rather, the misreading of it in terms far more specific than he ever intended—that was to prove decisive for the centuries that followed, in Europe as well as in Russia. As Lisa Vergara puts it: "Ut pictura poesis carried with it [for Renaissance art theorists] the demand that painters, like poets, imitate illustrious models, choose their themes from established sources (especially from the sister art, poetry), treat subject matter with decorum, and seek both to edify and to delight the viewer."[8] Eventually the poets were expected to act like painters. By the eighteenth century, the association of the two arts, sometimes so close as to suggest interchangeability, was a commonplace everywhere in Europe. When Johnson observed that Pope "had a strong inclination to unite the art of Painting with that of Poetry," readers required no elaboration.[9]

Tredyakovsky's use of the word "picturesque," especially in connection with painting, reminds us that another idea, really an ideology, had made its way from Europe into Russia. Christopher Hussey, the author of the standard work on the picturesque, has neatly described the underlying assumption as the "habit of viewing and criticizing nature as if it were an infinite series of more or less well composed subjects for painting." A whole semantics of painting focused perceptions of nature upon such qualities as "roughness, lusciousness of texture, glinting, sparkling surfaces, the crumbling and decayed," especially as these inhered in objects like "rural scenes and ruins." Painting remained the touchstone; but picturesque expectations soon extended to other arts, among them gardening, architecture, and above all, poetry. Hussey's two prime examples of what he calls "picturesque poets" are James Thomson and John Dyer, who "look at and describe landscape in terms of pictures. Each scene is correctly composed, and filled in with sufficient vividness to enable the reader to visualize a picture after the manner of Salvator [Rosa] and Claude [Lorrain]. Picturesque describes not only their mode of vision, but their method."[10] The first book on picturesque gardens, translated from the English, appeared in Russia in 1778. Translations of picturesque poetry soon followed, with James Thomson's *Seasons* and Edward Young's *Night Thoughts* enjoying an especially high reputation; and it was not long before the Russians were ready to produce their own versions of the picturesque. But Europe persisted as a powerful presence, and with it, the connection to painting. Among the major writers, Nikolai Karamzin looked particularly to England as "the home of descriptive [picturesque] poetry," citing Thomson as one of the "best" English writers since Shakespeare and the one responsible for teaching Karamzin "to enjoy nature."[11] To be sure, Karamzin does not mention painting. For one thing, the Russians had produced no significant landscape painting in the eighteenth century. When it did arise, in the nineteenth, it owed more to Romantic perceptions. Nonetheless, painting is silently present in the assumption that nature poetry is like painting and can instruct the reader to look at nature as if it were a painting.

After Karamzin, the term "picturesque" was gradually so stretched that it no longer embraced a specific repertoire of themes and moods, and came to mean, as it does today in popular speech, "pleasing to the eye." This is the sense in which Gogol himself seems to use it when he praises two poems by Zhukovsky for their "picturesque depictions of nature" and "picturesque detail," although they only faintly represent the style.[12] Nonetheless, a link between poetry and painting remained an ideal among Russians well into the nineteenth century. Vissarion Belinsky, for one, insisted as late as 1847: "if poetry undertakes to portray persons, characters, and events, in a word, *pictures of life* [*kartiny zhizni*], it goes without saying that in doing so it takes upon itself *the same duty as pictorial art* [lit., 'painting,' *zhivopis'*], which is to be faithful to the reality it purports to reproduce." He goes on to qualify this: "poetry must not be *only* pictorial art" but "should contain thought," "should appeal to the reader's mind, should give a certain direction to his view on certain aspects of life." In this crucial sense, poetry would seem superior to painting. But he then restores the pictorial analogy by arguing that "the novel and the story" are the most appropriate forms of "poetry," inasmuch as they are mainly concerned with "*representing social pictures [izobrazhenie kartin obshchestvennosti]*." Gogol himself clung to the poetry/painting analogy throughout his life. As late as 1850, he wrote: "The artistic work is the same in words as in painting, that is, the same as a picture."[13] Painters and paintings are often mentioned in his works, and, where mentioned approvingly, are meant to stand as models for all artists, regardless of medium. However, he did not expect painters or writers to deal directly with life. Distance was essential. In the first instance it might be provided by subject matter. Gogol's taste ran to religious and historical motifs. Favorites among his contemporaries were Karl Bryullov, whose gigantic canvas entitled *The Last Day of Pompeii* (Poslednii den' Pompei) was first exhibited in the Hermitage in 1834, and Aleksandr Ivanov, who spent twenty years completing *The Appearance of Christ to the People* (Yavlenie Khrista narodu).[14] The two ideal paintings in his story "The Portrait" (1842 version) are both on conventional religious themes. The same preferences are evident in his esteem for Titian, Raphael, Michelangelo, Claude Lorrain, and Van Dyck. Contemporary subjects were not forbidden, but distance still had to be maintained, and in a far more literal way.

DISTANCED HEIGHT

As far as I know, Hugh McLean was the first to identify "distance" as a psychological and aesthetic need that persisted throughout Gogol's life; and his solutions to the seemingly impossible task of reading from the evidence of the texts back into Gogol's mind are at once modest, ingenious, and convincing.[15] His article is rich and suggestive enough to warrant development into a full-length book. My own approach here, while much indebted to McLean, is more specifically focused on the problem of seeing.

Distance as a prerequisite for creation had become a commonplace idea among the Sentimentalists and Romantics, European and Russian, in the two or three generations before Gogol. Novalis, for example, insisted: "Nature *per se* cannot be grasped. A *distant* philosophy sounds like poetry. . . . In distance [*Entfernung*], everything becomes *poetry—poem. Actio in distans.* Distant mountains, distant people, distant circumstances, etc. Everything becomes romantic. *quod idem est* [which is the same thing]." Physical removal from one's subject was most commonly prescribed. As Nikolai Karamzin put it: "At first [the writer] is stunned at the sight of the biggest and noisiest city in the world [Paris]. He feels the need to bring his scattered impressions together and, the better to depict Paris, he abandons it. In the delightful Bois de Boulogne, sitting in the shade of trees, alone among the deer that are running and gamboling about him, he describes this capital city, or, rather, his impressions of it." This is a kind of recollection in tranquility of a definite locale.[16] Some twenty years later Konstantin Batyushkov made much the same point when he averred that the poet must depict only what he has actually experienced, while eschewing society. But a new strain sounds: "[A]t the moment of inspiration . . . I would never take up my pen if I should find a heart capable of fully feeling what I feel. . . . Where to find a heart ready to share with us all our feelings and sensations? We do not have it here with us—and we resort to art to try to express our thoughts, in the sweet hope that there are on this earth hearts that are good, minds that are educated."[17] This poet does not require an audience; all that really matters is the "expression [*vyrazhenie*]" of his own thoughts and feelings. Karamzin himself ventures a similar idea in a late article, when he says that the writer naturally creates in the hope of "fame [*slava*]," which will make his works immortal; but if that eludes him, "then there is another most true and vital reward for the writer, independent of fate and people: *the inner delight [enjoyed by] an active talent.* . . . A powerful thought, truth, the beauty of an image, an expressive word suddenly present themselves to the mind and enliven the soul and nourish it with such a pure, full *kindred* pleasure that in these happy moments it forgets all other earthly happiness." Although he goes on to say, "The inner pleasure of the lover of the Muses always acts on the soul of readers as well," self-delight seems primary, as for Batyushkov.[18]

This position could easily lead to isolation and madness, as many writers of the time attested in their fictions. Typically, such a condition was deemed inimical to true art. Paradigmatic was E. T. A. Hoffmann's "The Golden Pot," which was translated into Russian not long after its publication in 1814. The main character, Anselmus, is a student who is employed to copy manuscripts. Like Gogol's Akaky Akakievich (for whom hc may be a source), he finds this work to be "his true passion," which he indulges "with a pure delight which often rose to highest rapture." Although this is not art, Anselmus and his beloved Serpentina are ultimatcly granted a life "in highest blessedness forevermore" in Atlantis, a realm so removed that the ordinary world can be seen only by special dispensation. By contrast, the true artist, who records these events in a series of "vigils," must "again be transplanted" to his garret, where he will live "ensnared among the pettinesses of necessitous existence." This may seem unjust; but in compensation, it is his privilege to be able to communicate what he has seen to his fellow human beings, something Anselmus is pronounced insane for trying to do.[19] This approximates the view expressed by Gogol's great friend, the poet Vasily Zhukovsky. He grants that writing requires privacy, but insists that it should not be all-consuming, for it is a job like any other that one takes seriously and does well. Indeed, life in society—provided it involves "useful activity and high qualities"—is necessary for helping the writer develop a quick wit and a facility with words.[20] Here we see an early version of a view that came to prevail in Russia, where writers were increasingly measured according to their perceived commitments to social and political issues; those who spent much time abroad, like Turgenev, risked disapproval.

For Gogol it is only ordinary people who require an active involvement in society, lest they suffer the fate of Anselmus without the compensating vision (the comparison is mine). So, at any rate, his fictional gallery of warped and deranged solitaries would indicate. By contrast, the artist who deals with the contemporary world must withdraw. He must always keep his subject in view from a distance. Gogol's particular twist is that his subject, though remote, is not recollected, but seen as if it were physically present before him. (Memory is an important theme of Gogol's work; we have noted one aspect of it in "Old-World Landowners" and will consider others in the next section of this book. But for the creating artist it never replaces the actuality of seeing.) And the artist is to depict only what he sees outside him, not what he sees within: "expression" is merely Gogol's shorthand for the method of exposition, not, as in Karamzin, an outpouring of the self. In the article on Pushkin, Gogol watches the poet viewing his native land as if he were standing atop the Caucasus, hereby discerning features closed to its inhabitants: "the more ordinary the subject, the *higher* must be the poet"—a spatial literalism in this article—"in order to extract from it what is extraordinary, and, incidentally, in order that the extraordinary something be the complete truth."[21] This is also a convenient summary of the poetics to which Gogol clung throughout most of his life.

Distanced height is a stance and often a theme that pervades Gogol's work. In "Rome" (1842), the young prince, through whose eyes the story unfolds, at one point "finally stopped, perceiving that he had long . . . been making his way up a hill. . . . So as not to stand in the street, he went up into a little square, from which all of Rome opened before him." There follows an elaborate description of the panorama of the entire city in the setting sun, with all the physical evidence of its long history combining in a single glistening vision (III, 258). Man-made structures can also provide the proper perspective. In his early article on architecture, Gogol wrote: "Huge, colossal towers are essential in a city, quite apart from their importance for Christian churches. . . . [F]or a capital city it is essential to see at least 150 versts [1 verst = 3,500 feet] in all directions; and for that, perhaps only one or two extra stories are needed, and everything changes. As you ascend, the prospect progressively undergoes a broadening. The capital gains an essential advantage by surveying the provinces and foreseeing everything in advance."[22] Nearly twenty years later, the tower on Kostanzhoglo's estate in Part 2 of *Dead Souls* would provide a fictional analogue: "a long avenue stretched from the barns and workshops to the

very house of the landowner, so that the landowner could see everything
that was going on around him; and to crown all, over the roof of the house
there was a glass watch-tower from which the whole countryside for ten
miles around could be seen" (313).

Gogol's idea of distanced height bypasses Sentimentalism and Romanticism and finds a remarkable parallel, if not its very source, in the aesthetics of the Baroque, with its dramatic contrasts of elevation and depth.
Mountains apart, the towers that so intrigued him would have appealed
to the Baroque mind. D. S. Likhachev has observed, in terms that would
fit unobtrusively into any work by Gogol, that "many [Russian] churches
of the end of the seventeenth century answered to the need to survey the
terrain from a height," and to that end were furnished with elevated promenades, reachable by an open stairway. The purpose, according to Likhachev, was to "detach the individual from a 'natural' level and compel him
to feel the unreality of reality, to conquer in himself the sense of being
bound to the earth."[23] Literary analogues come to mind as well. The earliest is in the *Iliad*, where the gods keep track of human activities from
elevations, usually mountaintops, as in the opening lines of Book XIII.
Much later, when poets themselves had taken on godlike qualities, they
frequently availed themselves of far-reaching vision too. The eighteenth-
century triumphal ode, for example, typically begins with a survey of the
scene from above. M. V. Lomonosov's ode on the taking of Khotin, a virtual anthology-piece, begins as follows:

> A sudden rapture has seized my mind,
> It leads me to the top of a high mountain,
> Where the wind has forgotten to sough in the forests;
> There is silence in the deep valley below.

The eye then ranges further as distance expands, a device Gogol employed,
we remember, in "A Terrible Vengeance," and would use again in the final
chapter of *Dead Souls*, where his narrator surveys Russia from his "beautiful afar." In Lomonosov's version:

> Far distant, smoke curls in the fields,
> Is it not Pindus [a mountain range in Greece] that I espy beneath
>   my feet?
>   . . .
> Extend your gaze across steppe and mountains
> And direct your spirit toward those lands
> Where day arises after the dark of night.[24]

Gogol never commented on this ode, but toward the end of his life, in a
substantial article on Russian poetry, he did praise Lomonosov for "surveying *the whole of the Russian land from end to end*, from a radiant

height, feasting his eyes, without sating them, on its *boundlessness* and its virginal nature," thus clustering all the crucial imagery within a single sentence. Although in this same article he finds "no trace of creativity" in Lomonosov's "rhetorically composed odes," which would presumably include the one from which we have just quoted, he much admires the "grandeur" of his manner and particularly the "ecstasy" that "can be heard wherever he touches on something close to his knowledge-loving soul."[25] Gogol could be talking about the numerous places in his own work where he adopts the lofty diction and serious tone of impassioned orator, preacher, or prophet, which invariably signal the imminent revelation of important truths, and which of course are stylistic correlatives of the elevated vantage point he deems essential on such occasions. His articles on history are almost all cast in such a style, and we are to imagine their author perched atop a temporal height, as provided by his own times, from which he looks down upon a past spread panoramically before him. Even in more secular contexts, characters often find that elevations disclose a true picture of what is happening below. From the belfry in his dream, Ivan Fyodorovich Shponka sees unmistakable evidence of the dreadful realities of his future marriage; and the aerial journeys in "Diary of a Madman" and "Viy" reveal the frightening landscape of the traveler's soul.

More subtly, distanced height can also function as a structural principle. Some stories are built on a line marked by progressively "higher" stages. In "The Overcoat," Akaky Akakievich "ascends" to the level of the Person of Consequence, sees the truth of his situation, and then, from the ultimate remove of life beyond the grave, makes the Person see the truth of *his* situation. (I am assuming that the ghost who returns is in fact Akaky.) Stylistically, "low" rhetoric, which is so common in the openings of the stories, is a distancing technique, since we readers remain "above" and look down with amusement and condescension. But "high" rhetoric, which appears sporadically in the fiction and frequently in the nonfiction, compels us to look up. In fact, Gogol's narrators, in ways we will study in detail in Chapter 11, are usually distanced from us and from the stories they tell.

Distanced height is also a major theme of Gogol's own career as a writer. He consistently removed himself from what he purported to depict. All his stories with Ukrainian settings were written while he was living in St. Petersburg. Several of his works about Russia, most notably *Dead Souls*, date from his years in Rome. His historical articles never brought their subject matter past the seventeenth century, and never dealt with Russia directly. To be sure, the so-called "Petersburg stories" (the designation is not Gogol's) were produced, for the most part, while he was in residence there; but as we have seen, he did not regard that city as a real place. In fact, much of the peculiar quality of those stories depends on an absence of distance, with the inevitable absence of truth. Once he returned to Russia for good in 1848, thereby eliminating all distance, he never completed another work of fiction.

Several motives obviously prompted the trip abroad in 1836. Disappointment at the reception of *The Inspector General* was only one. The need for rest and relaxation was another. Further, a wider world beckoned: many of Gogol's letters, written before and immediately after his departure, read like cries for help from a man in danger of suffocation by a Russia that was indistinguishable from the hermetic spaces of his fiction. He was ready to begin serious work on *Dead Souls*, whose subject was not a Ukrainian village, or the capital city, or a provincial town, but all of Russia, which could be properly seen only from a vast remove. As he himself expressed it many years later in "An Author's Confession": "[W]hile among other people . . . you cannot survey the whole. I began to think of a way in which I could extricate myself from others and find some place from which I could see the mass as a whole" (VIII, 449). Although this was written in 1847, after all his great creative work was behind him, it restates a view of the creative process to which he had clung since the beginning of his career.

MEDIATED DISTANCE

From the vantage point of St. Petersburg and Rome, Gogol was obviously too removed from his subjects to "see" them in any literal way. Yet the imperative of elevated distance was literal. How then could he "see" something removed by hundreds or thousands of miles? Mediation was obviously essential.

The readiest form lay at hand in personal letters. As early as April 30 (o.s.), 1829, Gogol wrote from St. Petersburg to ask his mother to send him detailed descriptions of certain Ukrainian customs and costumes (X, 140–42), which, as it turned out, would serve as material for *Evenings on a Farm Near Dikanka*. It is difficult to believe that he was so Russianized as to know nothing of the folkways of his native territory. More likely, he simply could not (or would not) create by recollecting his own observations, and required an "other" to provide the necessary information. This established a lifelong habit. Many years later, for instance, he told A. O. Smirnova, a constant correspondent, that a common friend should write him letters (without expecting any reply), which would contain "almost a diary of his thoughts, feelings and sensations, a lively notion of all the people he happens to meet, his own opinions of them and the opinions of others, and finally any incidents and squabbles with them." The friend should do this, continued Gogol, "so that I can *have a sense of life itself* [Gogol's italics].

Otherwise, I am simply stupid and good for nothing." Elsewhere he supposes that Smirnova takes for granted that he knows Russia like his "five fingers," but that is not the case: "I know absolutely nothing about it." He then asks her to provide the latest gossip, along with circumstantial descriptions of events and individuals, even to their full names: "That is necessary to me."[26]

There was never a question of plunging into "life itself." What he wanted from Smirnova and others was what he variously called "data," "statistics," or "anecdotal facts," raw verbal material that he could then work on. And it had to be as detailed as possible. In the Foreword to the second edition of Part 1 of *Dead Souls* (1846), he asserts, "In this book much has been described inaccurately, not as it is or the way it actually occurs in our Russian land," and he asks that his reader "correct" him, carefully perusing the book "in its entirety, not omitting a single sheet," pen in hand: "after reading several pages [the reader] should call to mind his entire life and that of all the people he has met, and all the events that have taken place before his eyes, and everything he himself has seen or has heard from others that is similar to what is depicted in my book, or dissimilar; all this he should describe in precisely the way he remembers it, and he should send me every sheet as soon as it is finished, until he has read the entire book in this fashion." No correspondent, particularly of lower estate, should feel intimidated, for "before him stands a man who is incomparably inferior to him in education, who has studied practically nothing." It would help if "instead of me [the reader] would picture some country bumpkin whose entire life has been spent in the back woods," and would accordingly provide "a very detailed explanation of every circumstance, in very simple language, as with a child, taking care at every step not to use expressions beyond [my] comprehension." Under no circumstances, however, should the reader try to embroider the data: "There is no need to concern yourself here with style or beauty of expression; the point is the *facts* [dele] and the *truth* of the facts, not the style." In a similar spirit, Smirnova is enjoined not to "hasten to draw conclusions," but simply to "communicate everything to me as soon as you learn about it."[27]

A deeper insight into these extraordinary requests is provided by "An Author's Confession," which dates from 1847. Like any retrospective account, it invites skepticism, especially when, as is here the case, it is written in response to unfavorable criticisms. Gogol is certainly too quick to dismiss all his work before *The Inspector General* as designed to provoke "laughter" in the reader. What is interesting, however, is the explanation he devises: "I was subject to attacks of melancholy, for which I myself had no explanation. . . . In order to distract myself, I would think up as many funny things as I possibly could. I would simply invent funny people and characters, and mentally place them in the funniest situations, with no concern at all as to why I was doing it, for what purpose, and what benefit it would be to anyone." The result was "stupidities." He came to realize that his art was a process of constructing a picture out of a mass of small detail scrupulously drawn from the outside world. "Compared to any other writer, I needed to know much more, because I had only to omit a few details, not take them into consideration, and the lie would be more glaringly obvious than in anyone else's work." The term he uses for this process, *soobrazhenie*, can be variously translated as "reasoning," "consideration," or "understanding," but is best understood literally, as a derivation from *obraz*, "image," prefixed by *so-*, "with" or "together": putting images together to form a picture. It stands in contrast with *voobrazhenie*, "imaging into," that is, "imagining," which he declares alien to his art. "I never created anything in my imagination. . . . Only what I took from real life, from data familiar to me came out well . . . so far my imagination has not bestowed on me a single outstanding character and has not created a single thing that I have not actually noticed somewhere in nature." However, the "noticing" was typically mediated (although this is not Gogol's term) through others. These "others," as Gogol identifies them here, were, in the first instance, "the books written by lawgivers, connoisseurs of the soul, and observers of human nature," which provided a knowledge of "people and the human soul," and, in the second, far preferable instance, the contemporary Russians "of all classes" who, he hoped, would write him letters.[28]

PUSHKIN AS MEDIATOR

By and large, Gogol disregarded the writers of his own time as sources of information, perhaps because few could be expected to refrain from interpretation. But there was one outstanding exception: Alexander Pushkin.

Pushkin's historical play *Boris Godunov* was published in December 1830. Almost immediately Gogol wrote a review destined for *Literary Gazette* (Literaturnaya gazeta), but he never finished it, and it did not appear in print during his lifetime. It has nothing to say about the play itself, but instead documents the effusively enthusiastic reactions of one Pollior. A sensitive young man, he finds in Pushkin a soul mate, and is obviously a fictionalized version of Gogol himself. At this point Gogol had not yet met Pushkin. That occurred on May 20 (o.s.), 1831. Later that same year he began work on "A Few Words About Pushkin," which was not completed until 1834, and appeared in 1835 as part of *Arabesques*.[29] Here Pushkin serves as a focus for ideas about the mission and the role of the artist that Gogol later embellished, deepened, and applied to himself.

Three main ideas can be identified. One, which we have already mentioned, is that of the distanced observer. A second is that of the misunderstood poet, with the "public," conventionally enough, as antagonist. Pushkin had won enormous popularity, Gogol says, with his pictures of the Caucasus. But he was unable, as a truthful observer, to depict Russian life in the same lively and colorful manner, because it was "far more placid and far less filled with passions." He paid dearly for his honesty: "The mass of the public, which represents the nation, is very strange in its desires. It cries: depict us as we are, utterly truthfully, show the deeds of our ancestors just as they were. But let the poet heed its behest and depict everything utterly truthfully and just as it was, and the public will promptly begin saying: that's ineffective, that's weak, that's not good, that bears no resemblance to the way it was" (52). The third theme is that of beneficial exile. Gogol says merely, "Fate cast him [Pushkin] there," that is, to the Caucasus, although any Russian reader would have known that fate's agent was a wrathful Alexander I, who banished Pushkin in 1820. In any event, "There is not a single poet in Russia who has had such an enviable fate as Pushkin" (51) because the experience provided him with new, exotic subject matter, and, in effect, with the distanced elevation essential to the proper depiction of Russia.

No more than a year later, these same themes surfaced, although in a somewhat different sequence, in a letter that Gogol wrote on May 15 (o.s.), 1836, to Mikhail Pogodin, following what he interpreted as the failure of The Inspector General. First comes misunderstanding: "It is sad when you see the pitiable condition in which a writer still lives in our country. Everyone is against him, and there is no counter-force on his side. 'He's an instigator. He's a rebel.'" In particular, Gogol is offended by the theatergoers who saw themselves depicted in the characters of the play. "I deplore their ignorant irritability, which is a sign of a deep, stubborn ignorance that has spread to all classes of our society." Then follows the removal to a distance, as he decides to go abroad in self-imposed exile. But he already knows, perhaps from his version of Pushkin's experience, that his own vicissitudes have been to the good—"Everything that has happened to me has been salutary. All the insults, all the unpleasantness have been visited upon me by Providence for my edification"—and he looks forward to returning "refreshed and renewed" (XI, 45–46).

There is no mention of Pushkin at this point. The two men seem to have fallen out. Gogol told Zhukovsky in a letter of June 28, 1836: in leaving Russia "I did not manage to say goodbye even to Pushkin, nor could I; however, he is to blame for that" (XI, 50). We do not know what really happened. Pushkin respected Gogol's talent and valued him as a contributor to The Contemporary, but kept him at arm's length: he apparently did not much care for him personally, and in any event was a busy celebrity, with little time for the ambitious and touchy younger man. Six months later, in January 1837, Pushkin was killed in the duel with Georges D'Anthès. Gogol heard about it almost immediately, but addressed it only in late March, when he wrote to Mikhail Pogodin and to Pyotr Pletnyov. On the evidence of these letters alone, we could not guess that the two men had been anything but the most intimate friends. The familiar thematology is restated, only now in overwrought and hyperbolized form: "misunderstanding" has become martyrdom; "exile," "distance," and "height" have become death, with the spatial displacements entertained in traditional Christian belief. More important, Gogol's identification with Pushkin is now explicit, and so close that the two become virtually indistinguishable. As he says to Pogodin:

You invite me to come and visit you. What for? Only to repeat the eternal fate of poets in their own land? . . . Why should I come? Do you think I haven't seen that wonderful aggregation of our enlightened ignoramuses? . . . You write that everyone has been affected by this loss, even cold people. And what were these people prepared to do to him while he was alive? Do you think I did not witness the bitter, bitter moments it was Pushkin's lot to experience? . . . Oh, when I remember our judges, our Maecenases, our learned smart alecks, our noble aristocracy ... My heart shudders at the mere thought. There must have been powerful reasons why they compelled me to take the step I otherwise would not have taken [presumably, leaving Russia]. Or do you think I don't care that my friends, that you are separated from me by mountains? Or that I don't love our boundless, native Russian soil?

Entirely new is Gogol's representation of himself as the beneficiary of Pushkin's personal counsel and encouragement:

My loss is the greatest of all. . . . My life, my greatest joy died with him. The bright moments of my life were the moments when I was creating. When I was creating, I saw only Pushkin before me. All the gossip meant nothing to me, I spat on the contemptible crowd which is known by the name of the public; what I cherished was his eternal and immutable word. *I undertook nothing, I wrote nothing without his advice.* Everything that is good about me—I am obligated to him for it all. What I am working on now [*Dead Souls*] is his creation as well. He made me swear that I would write it, and not a single line of it was written without his being present *before my eyes* [again a literal seeing, not a recollection]. I consoled myself with the thought that he would be satisfied, I tried to guess what would please him, and that was my greatest and highest reward. Now no such reward awaits me! What is my work? What is my life now?[30]

Many critics have questioned the sincerity of these statements. Certainly the letter to Pletnyov raises some justified suspicions. It sets out many of these same themes in much the same language, but in far shorter form. Here too Gogol speaks of his "inexpressible anguish," but then, in a jarring shift of gears and without so much as a new paragraph, requests more money and provides elaborate instructions on how it is to be sent. Gogol, no mean literary politician, undoubtedly had much to gain through public identification with the most famous writer of the time. This would not have struck most contemporaries as preposterous. Although he did not become a national icon until the publication of *Dead Souls* some five years later, he was already widely regarded as the most important Russian writer to emerge after Pushkin. The effusions in the letters to Pletnyov and Pogodin could be taken as hyperboles (a characteristic Gogolian mode) of public expectations to which Gogol was finely tuned. Then too, the biographies of the two writers offered suggestive parallels. Pushkin had "African" blood in him, which was reflected in his appearance; in Gogol flowed Ukrainian and Polish blood; both in a certain sense were therefore "southerners." Their use of language was often regarded as not quite "Russian." If the heavy influence of French was detected in Pushkin, then Ukrainian and substandard usages were found in Gogol. As his contemporary Vladimir Dal noted: "You are carried away by his narrative, you avidly gulp down everything, you re-read it again and you don't notice the peculiar language in which he writes. You begin to analyze it minutely, and you see that a person absolutely ought not to write and speak this way. You try to correct it and you spoil it—you can't touch a word. What would happen if he wrote in Russian?"[31] Both suffered from "misunderstanding" and experienced "exile," Gogol's voluntary, Pushkin's not. Gogol's early stories, as collected in the *Dikanka* and *Mirgorod* cycles, dealt with subjects almost as exotic to the Russian reader of the time as the Caucasus of Pushkin. Both subsequently adverted to the contemporary Russian scene. Late in life, both men again took up a new manner of writing, to the bafflement and annoyance of many readers, who expected them to follow the vein that had made them famous. Pushkin turned to prose fiction and versified fairy tales that were often discounted as trivial. Belinsky went so far as to state, in 1834, that Pushkin had written himself out: "Now we do not recognize Pushkin; he is dead or, perhaps, only mute for a time. . . . [T]he year '30 terminated, or rather put a sudden end to, the *Pushkin* period, for Pushkin himself had ended and, with him, the influence he had wielded." As we shall see, Gogol's *Selected Passages from Correspondence with Friends* was greeted with general indignation and derision, Belinsky again weighing in with a savagely disapproving letter to the author, which concluded as follows: "you should now disown with sincere humility your last book, and atone for the dire sin of its publication by new creations that would be reminiscent of your old ones."[32] To complete the parallel, Gogol would have to die young, as Pushkin did at 37. He characterized his departure from Russia, at the age of 27 and several months before Pushkin's murder,

as a "radical turning point [*perelom*],"[33] a term often associated with death
and rebirth, both of which he seemed psychologically to experience as he
abandoned his old life and took up a new one abroad. He did not know at
this point, of course, that a *perelom* was in store for his great mediator,
who was destined to perish at the hand of D'Anthès and to undergo a kind
of rebirth in the person of Gogol himself. In any event, Gogol died at a
relatively young 42. Although we still cannot identify the illness,[34] there is
some evidence that, like his mentor, he not only welcomed death but actively courted it: Gogol refused to eat; Pushkin himself issued the challenge
to his opponent.

Gogol might well have chosen a painter as his model had there been a
Russian visual artist of an eminence comparable to Pushkin's. Yet his
choice of Pushkin was far from incongruous, for his image of Pushkin was
consistent with his image of the identity and mission of the true artist. We
do not of course know whether Pushkin's life created the image, or whether
it had been present in Gogol's mind from the outset, shaped perhaps by the
mythology of Romanticism, and convincingly embodied in the older
writer. Whatever the etiology, Pushkin took up permanent residence in
Gogol's inner world from 1837 on, to emerge whenever the question of a
writer's true nature and direction arose. Hence even if, like many other
readers, we detect a certain note of insincerity in the letters cited above, we
would err, I think, in setting it down merely to self-promotion.

Sometimes, however, Gogol saw no need to name Pushkin. At the beginning of chapter 7 of *Dead Souls*, for example, the narrator describes
two kinds of writers, in the contrastive pairing that is so characteristic of
Gogol and of much writing of the time.[35] The first possesses certain attributes of authenticity, having ascended to a "pinnacle" from which he surveys the world. But he "clouds men's eyes with enchanting incense; he flat-
ters them marvellously, concealing the sad facts of life," showing them only
"the noble man" and ignoring "his poor, insignificant fellow-creatures."
He is showered with praise and admiration, but is not a true writer, because he has deceived his public and made it serve his ambitions. The other
kind of writer "has dared to bring into the open everything that is every
moment before men's eyes and that remains unseen by their unobservant
eyes—all the terrible, shocking morass of trivial things in which our life is
entangled, the whole depth of frigid, split up, everyday characters with
whom our often dreary and bitter earthly path swarms." For his pains, he
earns public contempt as a producer of "low and insignificant" works and
is assigned "an ignoble place in the ranks of writers who have affronted
humanity." Nonetheless, he is the truly authentic one (142–43). Here Gogol is restating points he had made in his article on Pushkin. The visual
element remains strong as well. The writer seems to be a painter, although

at one point he is likened to a sculptor "who dares with the strong power of his relentless chisel." And something like the earlier "optical glass" appears again: "For contemporary public opinion does not acknowledge that the glasses [*stekla*] which survey suns and which convey the movements of unnoticed insects are equally marvellous."[36]

We are intrigued by the spectacle of a younger writer choosing as mentor and mediator an older writer who regarded him with reservations, constructing a fable about him, and keeping him in the center of his consciousness throughout much of his life. A lack of access to Gogol's inner self, in this as in most matters, sets distinct limitations to psychological speculation. Gogol's need for Pushkin is all the more arresting because there could hardly have been two artists more dissimilar. Pushkin may possibly have provided the plots for Gogol's two best works, but not the manner of working them out. No one would have found such a claim convincing anyway: Gogol was immediately perceived as an entirely different kind of artist, so much so that people soon began and to this day continue to distinguish, however impressionistically, a "Pushkin school" and a "Gogol school" in Russian literature. But that might have been precisely what Gogol intended. Pushkin's prestige would legitimize the necessary process of mediation, while indirectly making the equally necessary point that mediation could not possibly be imitation. Or so, we may suppose, Gogol hoped. In point of fact, however, for the period we are now considering, 1836–41, we must look elsewhere for a better understanding of the ways in which Gogol's ideas of seeing, particularly mediated seeing, affected his work as a writer of fiction in particular. We must look primarily to Rome.

8

Rome

THE EYES OF THE TOURIST

Gogol's accounts of his passage through Western Europe in 1836 are not mediated.[1] And for the most part they are so perfunctory, so bland, that he seems not to see what lies before his eyes. In writing to his mother from Frankfurt-am-Main, for instance, he reports that since he left Aachen, "many towns, large and small, have flashed past me, and I can hardly remember even their names." Only a trip on the Rhine "has remained somewhat in my memory"; but what he then proceeds to describe, although drawing on an analogy with picture viewing, is the kind of thing that any not very intelligent or observant tourist might come up with:

The River Rhine is a very remarkable thing in Germany. It is lined on both sides with hills, and dotted with towns. Our journey by ship lasted two days, and *I finally grew tired of the incessant views*. Your eyes get completely worn out, as in a panorama or a picture. Before the windows of your cabin pass, one after another, towns, crags, hills, and old ruined knights' castles. Very many of them are picturesque and still beautiful to this day. All the hills, which consist entirely of nearly bare rock, are covered with vineyards in rows. This is the home of Rhine wine, which is virtually the only one drunk here, and of which there are many different kinds, many of which have never gotten as far as Russia. In Mainz, a large and ancient town, I went ashore. *I did not stop for even a moment, although the town was very much worth a look*, and I took a carriage to Frankfurt.[2]

Nor is this vagueness about matters observed confined to letters to relatives whom he considered naive or to landscapes that were not inherently or traditionally spectacular. From Geneva he wrote as follows to Nikolai Prokopovich, a classmate from Nezhin days and as close a friend as he ever had:

What can I tell you about Switzerland? It's all one view after another, so that I finally begin to get sick to my stomach. . . . I am not writing you anything about all the towns and lands I passed through, first because Danilevsky, whose pen and eye are perhaps livelier than mine, has written you about half of them, and second, *because there is really nothing to write about them.* Of all my memories there remain only the memories of the endless dinners with which gluttonous Europe torments me, and that only because they are preserved in my stomach, not my head.

Later in the same letter he admits that Europe at first creates a striking impression; but no reader could find anything striking in the details he adduces to make his point: "The picturesque little houses, which are now beneath your feet, now over your head, the blue mountains, the spreading lime-trees, the ivy, which along with grapevines covers the walls and fences—that is all pretty and pleasing and new, because it is nowhere to be found in the vast expanse of our Russia; but later, when you keep on seeing the same thing again and again, you get used to it and you forget that it is pretty."[3]

Italy, however, was a very special place for Gogol, as it had been for generations of Russians before him, even though they discovered it two hundred years later than their European counterparts. Many writers, including Pushkin, Dmitry Venevitinov, and Evgeny Baratynsky, had paid it homage in their works. Wealthy Russians had been acquiring Italian and Italianate paintings. Two of the most spectacular specimens of the latter were Claude Lorrain's *Landscape with Battle on a Bridge* and *Landscape with the Rape of Europa*, both dating from 1655, and purchased by Prince N. B. Yusupov in 1798.[4] Even though the general state of Russian art was dismal, and artists were no longer numbered among the creative elite despite assiduous patronage on the part of Nicholas I, a sojourn in Italy was deemed essential to the formation of anyone who aspired to a serious career. Several artists, in fact, had already produced works on Italian themes, such as Bryullov's *The Last Day of Pompeii*, which Gogol considered a masterpiece, and which was one of only two Russian paintings—the other being Aleksandr Ivanov's *Appearance of Christ to the People*, also a favorite of Gogol's—that won recognition throughout Europe between 1812 and 1860.[5]

Gogol had been aware of Italy since his school days. At Nezhin he studied Latin. In the 1830's, he read extensively in the history of Italy through the Middle Ages, and made detailed notes, mostly lists of names, dates, and events. More important, he was familiar with some of the literary conventions for treating Italy. Apparently his first published work was a poem entitled "Italy" (Italiya), which appeared in 1829. It is almost entirely a pastiche of currently fashionable views, images, and phrases, many of which reappeared in his later works. We find, for example, the snowy north set against the warm south; the power of the ever-present past; the brightness and blueness of the "vault" or "arch" of the sky; the contrasting greenness of the foliage; and so on.⁶ An entirely conventional Italy figured in Gogol's subsequent works whenever the subject of painting arose. "A strange phenomenon, is it not? A Petersburg artist," asks the narrator of "Nevsky Prospekt" (1835). "An artist in the land of snows. An artist in the land of the Finns, where everything is wet, flat, pale, gray, foggy. These artists are utterly unlike the Italian artists, proud and ardent as Italy and her skies." The solution is obvious: "They are often endowed with real talent, and if only they were breathing the fresh air of Italy, they would no doubt develop as freely, broadly, and brilliantly as a plant at last brought from indoors into the open air" (I, 213–14). In "The Portrait," one such artist is responsible for creating the ideal picture displayed at the Academy of Arts. In the 1835 version, written before Gogol's trip, the artist "abandoned friends, relatives, and cherished habits, and without any financial assistance hastened to an unknown land [presumably but not explicitly Italy]," where he lived in poverty and "was insensitive to everything except his beloved art." The 1842 version, prepared after Gogol had spent six years in Rome, amplifies this account and specifies the locale: the artist "rushed off to the majestic breeding-ground of the arts—to wonderful Rome, at whose name the fiery heart of the artist beats so fully and powerfully."⁷

When Gogol finally reached Italy, it struck him as being familiar, but not in the ways he had expected. "It feels," he wrote to Alcksandr Danilevsky on April 15, 1837, "as if I have paid a visit to some old-time Ukrainian landowners. The same decrepit house doors, doors that smudge your clothes with whitewash and have a good many useless holes in them; the ancient candlesticks and lamps like those in churches. The dishes are all special, and all in the old-time manner. Up to now [Europe] has presented a picture of change everywhere. Here everything has come to a dead stop and moves no further." At first, Rome itself "looked small" and was generally disappointing. But impressions soon underwent revision. "It seems bigger and bigger the longer I am here. The buildings are larger, the views are more beautiful, the sky is better, and there are enough pictures, ruins and antiquities to look at for a lifetime." He concludes: "You fall in love with Rome very slowly and gradually, and then for a lifetime" (XI, 95).

Before long the city overwhelmed him in a way no other part of Western Europe had or ever would. He was particularly struck by the sky, the air, the colors, the vegetation, and the mixture of the natural and the man-made: "Again the same sky, now all silver, shining in silken garb, now deep blue, as it likes to show itself through the arches of the Colosseum. Again the same cypresses—these green obelisks, the tops of the cupola-like pine trees, which sometimes seem to be floating in the air. The same pure air, the same clear distance. The same eternal cupola [presumably St. Peter's], so majestically rounded in the air."[8] Frequently he frames his reactions to Rome in a stock antithesis of south and north, usually involving weather and topography: "in Petersburg the sky is gray and foggy, and here it is clear and blue, and the sun bathes everything in such a pleasant radiance!" Germany and Switzerland fall into the same "northern" category as Russia: "now that I have visited them after Italy, they strike me as being shabby, vulgar, nasty, gray, cold, with all their mountains and views, and I feel as if I were in Olonetsk Province listening to the God-forsaken sighing of the northern ocean."[9] What is true of the landscape is true of its inhabitants: the Romans "are the first people in the world who are endowed to such a degree with aesthetic feeling, with the instinctive ability to understand what is understood only by an ardent nature onto which the cold, calculating, mercantile European mind has not thrown its bridle. How vile the Germans seemed to me after the Italians, the Germans with all their petty integrity and egotism!" Earlier in the same letter he declared that Rome returns one to the original condition of the soul—young, whole, vital, and untainted by modern civilization: "I saw [in Rome] not my own native land, but the native land of my soul, where my soul lived even before me, before I was born into the world."[10]

Gogol could have made all these observations without having spent a day in Rome. (Venevitinov actually produced "Italy" and other "Italian" poems without ever visiting the country.) Even the idea of the homeland of the soul circulated as common literary currency. Goethe, for one, had written: "the entire history of the world is linked up with this city, and I reckon my second life, a very rebirth, from the day when I entered Rome."[11] Gogol achieved some measure of originality only when he departed from the visual. For M. P. Balabina he trotted out culinary metaphors: "The air is so tender, more tender than the Milanese-style rice you so often ate in Rome . . . all of Italy is a tasty morsel, and I drink its healing air until my throat hurts." Especially arresting are the olfactory images: "What air! When you draw it into your nose, it seems that at least 700 angels are flying into your nostrils. . . . Would you believe that I am often assailed by the mad desire to turn into nothing but a nose, so that nothing else would exist—neither eyes nor hands not feet, just one enormous nose with nostrils the size of huge buckets, so that I could breathe in as much fragrance and spring as possible."[12] Noses had already found their way into his fiction, but they are rare in his impressions of Italy. Instead, he emphasizes the eyes; but paradoxically, the more he comes to know Rome, the more readily he slips into conventions long established by paintings, works of literature, guidebooks, and *vedute*, those mass-produced topographical views of famous places. He knows what he *should* be experiencing, and how. In a letter written to Danilevsky on April 15, 1837, shortly after arriving in Rome for the first time, he had stated: "all of Europe is for looking, whereas Italy is for living" (XI, 95). But the contrast is false: Gogol "saw" even less of Europe than he did of Rome. As it turned out, he served as an attentive and knowledgeable guide for many visiting Russians to the churches, villas, landscapes, and works of art.[13] On the evidence of his letters, however, we would have to fault him as an observer.

How different this is from the impressions recorded by generations of other European travelers to Italy. The most accomplished was no doubt Goethe, whose *Italian Journey*, many years in the making, had been published in full in 1816–17. Although Goethe had been steeped in the classical world since childhood, and in that sense knew what to expect, this was inadequate: "[I want to] see with [my] own eyes the whole which one had hitherto only known in fragments and chaotically. . . . I am convinced that the many treasures I shall bring home with me will serve both myself and others as a guide and an education for a lifetime" (116, 115). His eyes first sought out detail: "The more closely and precisely one observes particulars, the sooner one arrives at a perception of the whole" (161). There is scarcely a more conscientious collector, classifier, and observer in all of world literature: *Italian Journey* teems with descriptions of landscapes, works of art, and people, so precise as to be palpable. And his attitude is that of the explorer, the learner, the adept, whose larger purpose is to find himself in what he sees: "I am very well and more and more finding out who I am, learning to distinguish between what is really me and what is not. I am working hard and absorbing all I can which comes to me on all sides from without, so that I may develop all the better from within" (341).

Gogol's mind was entirely different. Even though he acquired a good knowledge of Italian language and literature, and declared his determination to get to know the Roman people "in depth, its entire character,"[14] he seems to have been largely unaware of engaging a superior culture, still less of using it to enrich his own life and that of his country. It has been said of Goethe that he was "essentially an autobiographical writer, whose life is the most documented of anyone who ever lived; compared with Goethe, even Dr. Johnson is a shadowy figure."[15] This is more or less true of the Romantics, and it is one of the ways in which Gogol does not belong in their company. Much of his work is undeniably "autobiographical," but until the mid-1840's he was not, even in the letters, given to much introspection of the detailed, analytical sort that contemporary readers had learned to expect of writers in this genre. Most important, Gogol "sees" in a very different way. He is mainly interested in light, shadow, color, and movement, not detail. His goal is to re-create not the realia of Rome but his impressions of the city. The richly embroidered diction he adopts in the Roman passages in his letters and in the story "Rome" is that same "high" style to which he resorts throughout his career in order to signal readers that the narrator is speaking for the author and uttering truths that are to be taken seriously. As we shall see, it is also the language of the articles on history, of *Selected Passages from Correspondence with Friends*, and of the so-called "lyrical digressions" in *Dead Souls*.

On the evidence of the letters alone, we might conclude that Gogol did not know how to look. If so, he would be strikingly prefigurative of our "postmodern" times, when we seem to have lost the ability to see things as they are, and instead are mesmerized by things as they should be or by ideas *about* things. We regret the loss, as our enduring interest in certain kinds of poets would suggest, among them Amy Clampitt and Seamus Heaney, who have a gift for registering the ordinary, material world and validating it in its own right, not only as a "symbol" of something else. Likewise, today's better Russian writers, like Andrei Bitov, are showing impatience with abstractions and ideas.

In Gogol's case, however, we must bear several things in mind. One is that many of the letters were addressed to readers who themselves had visited Rome—notably Zhukovsky and Balabina—and who therefore were as familiar as Gogol with the sights he does not describe, or at least with the conventions known to cultivated Europeans. He can become somewhat more specific and descriptive in response to prompting, as, for example, in the account he gives Balabina of the newly discovered mosaics in the catacombs (Nov. 7, 1838, XI, 182–83). Furthermore, unlike Goethe's, these are not literary letters, and were perhaps not even intended for publication (although in the case of celebrities one can never be sure). It was only with *Selected Passages from Correspondence with Friends* that he made a serious venture into that genre; but there the letters deal with large moral, social, political, and literary questions apart from any particular topography. Most important, his letters from Rome, like those from elsewhere in Europe, record experiences from which he had achieved no distance and which therefore could not be "literary" or "artistic" by his definition.

Distance was eventually achieved, and Rome became art. Once again painting played a vital role in the process. The most extensive evidence is offered by the story "Rome," the one piece of fiction that grew directly out of Gogol's Roman experiences.

"ROME" AS A PAINTING

"Rome" is a reworked version of the beginning of what Gogol called a "novel," provisionally titled *Annunciata*, which he conceived and began in 1839. Two years later, an editorial note in *The Muscovite* (Moskvityanin, No. 2, 1841, p. 616) announced a forthcoming story under the title "Madonna dei Fiori." Gogol put it into final form, with its definitive title, "Rome," during a visit to Moscow in early February 1842, and published it in the third issue of the journal for that year. It has never enjoyed much popularity. Rarely is it included in Gogol's selected works in Russian; it is missing from the Garnett/Kent *Complete Tales*; it is not readily available in translation; by and large, the critics have given it a wide berth.[16] Could it be that Belinsky, the great canon-maker, helped determine its fate? He praised its "surprisingly sharp and true pictures of reality," but otherwise found many quirks that disturbed him in a writer whom he had admired almost without reservation, quirks such as "the distorted views of Paris and the myopic views of Rome," as well as certain turns of phrase "reminiscent of Marlinsky's language in their mannered refinement."[17] While I cannot claim that the story represents Gogol at his best—and I will try to indicate why as I talk about it—we would do well to keep two things in mind. For one, though designated by Gogol himself as a "fragment [*otryvok*]," it has the unity and cohesion of a finished work (at least, a finished work by Gogol). For another, he lavished a great deal of effort on it, as my sketchy account of its origins suggests. Most important for our purposes, it is the best fictional evidence we have of the visual cast of his mind at this point in his career.

Most of the story is devoted to the excursions of the hero, a young Italian prince, through Rome and its environs. By this time, the "stroll through the city" had become a subgenre with a substantial history, much of which passed to Russia in the *feuilletons* of Victor Jouy (1764–1846), whose scenes of city life enjoyed great popularity there, especially in the early 1820's. Among Russian writers, Faddei Bulgarin, always on the lookout for what would sell, had tried his hand, with titles like "A Stroll Along the Sidewalk of the Nevsky Prospekt" (Progulka po trotuaru Nevskogo Prospekta, 1824). Gogol's own "Nevsky Prospekt" belongs to the genre as well.[18] In "Rome," it becomes an eloquent travelogue that emphasizes the "marvelous blending into one" of all the contrasting ages and aspects of Rome: "these signs of a populous capital and a desert together: a palace, columns, grass, wild bushes running along walls, a throbbing marketplace

amidst dark, silent bulks screened from below, the living shouts of a fish-
monger by a portico, a soft-drink vendor with an airy, green-painted stand
in front of the Pantheon."[19] This is a very different approach from the one
taken by earlier Russian celebrants of Rome like Nikolai Nadezhdin and
Dmitry Venevitinov, who saw the ancient city being obliterated by centuries of incrustations. It is also very different from the kind of mere an-
tiquarianism with which readers of travel accounts to Rome had long been
familiar, whereby the ancient world is consigned to an eternally dead remove and aestheticized. This practice had been gently mocked, in a Greek
setting, by Stepan Shevyryov a decade earlier in a poem entitled "To a De-
fender of Classicism" (Partizanke klassitsizma), about a lady who prefers
to escape from the modern world into the ancient, where there are no dark
clouds, passions, or bloodshed:

> In the gardens of Homer you wander
> secure and carefree,
> Your hand gently plucking
> Fragrant flowers.[20]

For the young prince, who is also Gogol's mouthpiece, the deepest understanding of his native city comes when he contemplates the masterpieces of art. These include buildings and sculptures. But he takes greatest
interest in paintings, or, more accurately, in scenes of Rome that are presented and contemplated as if they were paintings. I do not agree with Lucy
Vogel that these visual spectacles create "the impression of a somewhat
artless single-dimensional medieval painting."[21] Rather, they call to mind
views of the Roman landscape that were being produced in vast numbers
in Gogol's own time. In attitude and perspective, they also have much in
common with the landscape and genre scenes of Gogol's earlier works, particularly in *Evenings on a Farm Near Dikanka*. This is further evidence
that Gogol's way of looking at the world was formed very early and persisted well into the second period of his life, regardless of changes of
geography.

The story opens (217–19) as follows: "Try to look at lightning, when,
cleaving the storm clouds, black as coal, it begins to quiver unbearably in
a whole flood of brilliance." This strong contrast of colors is immediately
transferred, the nature referents intact, to Annunciata, a beautiful Italian
girl from the Alban Hills, with her eyes and hair black as "thick pitch," her
face "dazzling snow," and her neck and shoulders "gleaming." We then see
her "hastening of an evening to the fountain with a hammered copper vase
on her head." Perspective further widens as the view acquires a horizon,
then height and depth, in a scene that seems to have been tried out in one
of Gogol's letters: "The wonderful lines of the Alban Hills recede into the

distance more lightly, the depths of the Roman sky are bluer, the cypress soars more erect, and the beauty among southern trees, the Roman pine, is more delicately and purely etched against the sky with its umbrella-shaped top that almost floats in the air."[22] The comparative form of the adjectives suggests movement (from less to more) and thereby creates a kind of visual narrative. The eye then pulls back as the foreground fills with other human figures, positioned picturesquely around the fountain in the manner of genre painting: "the Alban town-girls have already clustered on the marble steps, one higher than the next, conversing with each other in strong, silvery voices, while in a ringing diamond arc the water gushes into each in turn of the copper vats placed beneath it."[23] However, the focus remains on Annunciata, who is said to compose all into a "wonderful harmony": the crowd and the fountain exist only so that she can "*display* more vividly her triumphant beauty, so that it *can be seen* how she surpasses all, just as a queen surpasses her court officials." This entire scene is to be imagined as if it were a painting: "Wherever she goes," we are told, "she takes with her a picture."

With the words "Whether on a holiday [*V prazdnichnyi li den'*]," the eye is drawn to the next scene, in intimation of narrative movement: "when the dark wooden gallery leading from Albano to Castel Gandolfo. . . ." The contrast of height and depth, darkness and brightness runs through this passage too, and the color scheme is fundamentally the same, with blacks, whites, and greens predominant. Picturesque touches prevail: "the festively dressed people"; "donkeys with half-closed eyes" that "amble along or gallop, picturesquely carrying shapely and strong Albano and Frascati women, their white headgear shining in the distance"; "an artist wearing a smock, with a wooden box on a strap and a jaunty Van Dyck beard." By way of contrast (the predominant device here), another donkey is seen to be "dragging, not at all picturesquely, with effort and stumbling, a long, immobile Englishman wearing a pea-green macintosh, his legs twisted at a sharp angle so as not to touch the ground" (218). But this figure is immediately subordinated, like everything else, to the constant play of "shadow and sunlight over the entire crowd," out of which again emerges Annunciata in the same contrastive terms that serve to unify the entire picture: "the depths of the gallery deliver her, all gleaming, all in brilliance, from their gloomy darkness."

The sudden appearance of the painter provides a pair of eyes within the picture. Other onlookers then materialize: "And, on encountering [Annunciata], all stop as if rooted to the spot: the foppish *minente* [nobleman] with the flower in his hat . . . the Englishman in the pea-green macintosh, displaying a question-mark on his immobile face; and the artist with the Van Dyck beard." The young prince himself is described as a particularly avid spectator: "But who is the one who simply could not take his eyes off her footstep? Who keeps watch on what she says, her movements, and the movements of thought on her face?" (218–19). All these characters observe the "pictures" of life that unfold before them, and are in turn observed by us. As the story progresses, the angles of vision multiply. For instance, the crowd at the Carnival is also represented as a spectator, its attention drawn by "a daredevil who was walking on stilts." This crowd in turn is being watched by others, who are being watched by the prince, who himself is observed by women looking out the windows. Annunciata, although the focus of this scene too, is at the same time an observer: "written on the face of the beautiful woman was merely attention to the Carnival: she was looking only at the crowd and at the masks, without noticing the eyes directed at her" (249).

Gogol's letters contain frequent references to the "spectacle [zrelishche]" of Italian life. He was especially fascinated by the Carnival festivities and by religious processions.[24] Such highly formalized public spectacles are also a kind of theater, where the crowd and the leading actors are simultaneously participants and spectators. Gogol's interest in the theater remained unabated in Italy, where he eventually commanded the language well enough to grasp the nuances of the action. He was also an opera lover. While still in St. Petersburg, he had seen Rossini's *Semiramide*, Meyerbeer's *Robert le Diable*, and Auber's *Fenelle*, and he attended performances in some of the great European opera centers, like Vienna and Paris. All these art forms undoubtedly helped shape his perceptions of Italy. But it is especially landscape and genre paintings with Italian settings that proclaim their presence in "Rome": scarcely a motif in these scenes is without its equivalent on canvas. Rome had always attracted painters from northern Europe, but since the late eighteenth century they had been coming in droves, especially from France, England, and Germany. Many of them, like Corot and Turner, were dedicated to landscape painting, which the recently regnant neoclassicists had despised as lacking in moral content.[25] Also popular were genre scenes, especially if they featured peasants. Drawing on a long tradition, these painters had worked out a repertory of motifs. The Albano and Castel Gandolfo mentioned in Gogol's story constituted one such motif, which Corot, among many others, honored in his *Lake Albano and Castel Gandolfo* of 1826–28. Marc-Gabriel-Charles Gleyre's *La Nubienne* (1838) is only one of countless renditions of colorfully dressed and dazzlingly beautiful girls clustered around a fountain. Sharp contrasts of light and dark, relieved by patches of color, had long been remarked as typically "southern" features. In 1800, for example, Pierre-Henri de Valenciennes observed: "The warmth of the climate of Rome endows all the vegetation with a character of vigor that one does not find in Northern countries; the earth has a warmer color, the rocks stand out forcefully, the greens there are darker and more varied, the skies, bluer, and the clouds, more colorful." These comments could have been inserted unobtrusively into the opening scenes of Gogol's "Rome."[26]

Gogol even attempts to convey purely painterly ineffabilities in words. One is bright light: "a flood of *brilliance* [*bleska*] . . . they shone [*blistali*] . . . the dazzling [*siyayushchii*] snow . . . the gleaming [*sverkayushchaya*] neck . . . to display more brightly [*yarche*] . . . with bright [*yarkimi*] belts . . . like a golden [*zolotistym*] blossom . . . shining [*blistayushchikh*] head-dresses . . . all gleaming [*sverkayushchuyu*], all in brilliance [*bleske*]." Here the different words for "shining" are not individually charged, as is usually the case in Gogol, but are near-synonyms that, taken together, create an impression of brightness so overwhelming as to blind us. The technique is reminiscent of the so-called "word-weaving" (*pletenie sloves*) of medieval Russia, as practiced, among others, by Epiphanius the Wise (Epifanii Premudryi):

> [H]ow shall I call [*nareku*] you, my bishop?
> How shall I name [*imenuyu*] you?
> How shall I appeal [*prizovu*] to you?
> How shall I announce [*proveshchayu*] you?
> How shall I regard [*menyu*] you?
> How shall I proclaim [*proglashu*] you?
> How shall I praise [*pokhvalyu*] you?
> How shall I esteem [*pochtu*] you?
> How shall I gratify [*ublazhyu*] you?
> How shall I present [*razlozhu*] you?
> How shall I weave [*s"pletu*] lauds to you?

And so on. The chantlike quality of the parallel syntax comes across in translation; even the repetition of the English pronoun "I" creates much the same effect as the untranslatable repetition in Russian of the vowel (*-u, -yu*) that marks the first-person singular of the verbs.[27] Epiphanius suggests that his subject is so exceptional that no one word or image can adequately account for it. But Gogol is never comfortable with sustained impressionism. In the passage just excerpted, he abruptly descends almost to earth with a concrete image: "The purple fabric of her Alban attire, when touched by the sun, flashes out like a *burning coal* [*ishcher'*]" (218). This last word is all the more effective because it is highly unusual, perhaps even a neologism. With it, the writer steps forth, asserting in effect that however exotic a visual image may be, he can find a corresponding word for it.

The picture of Rome is amplified when the prince leaves the city to visit the "Roman fields," or Campagna, which is dotted with ancient ruins. In effect, he is retracing the steps of the Sentimentalist *promeneur solitaire*;[28] but once again, the more immediate source may well be the painting of Gogol's own time. The palette is by now familiar, being built on a contrast of brightness and darkness, with a few other colors splashed here and there for intensification or contrast. The prince stands amid the fields and sees "four marvellous views in four directions." Each is treated like a picture with its own subject. In the first, the fields "were directly joined to the horizon in a single, sharp, even line, the arches of the aqueducts seemed suspended in air and, as it were, glued onto the gleaming silver sky." The second picture reveals mountains, "not shooting up impetuously and shapelessly, as in the Tyrol or Switzerland [both of which border "Europe," a negative concept in this story], but rising and falling in harmonious flowing lines." They seem "ready to fly off into the sky," but they are well anchored: "at their foot ran a long arcade of aqueducts, like a long foundation, and the top of the mountains seemed like an airy continuation of a marvellous building." The third picture is also delimited by mountains, only "nearer and higher," and through the "light-blue air" the "houses and villas of Frascati" are barely visible. The appearance of man-made structures as part of the natural landscape facilitates the transition to the fourth picture, that of Rome itself. It is described in the same terms as the "natural" scenes preceding: "the angles and lines of the houses gleamed sharply and distinctly," like the contours of a mountain range. This view of Rome also includes works of art: "the statues of St. John Lateran" and especially "the majestic cupola of St. Peter's rising higher and higher the further one moved away from it," eventually "remaining alone" like some great mountain "on that segment of the horizon after the rest of the city had disappeared." At this point there has been a merging of "nature, the arts, and antiquities," as the narrator puts it (238–39); and the use of the word "glued [*naklee-nymi*]" suggests artifice.

The Roman Campagna had also been discovered by painters of the early nineteenth century. Turner's *The Roman Campagna, with the Tiber, from Castel Giubelio* (1819), and Corot's *The Roman Campagna, with the Tiber* (1826–28) were but two of the most illustrious in a spate of paintings on the subject. Preferences ran to panoramic views, usually as seen in the full brightness of the midday sun. Man-made objects, particularly ruins, frequently aqueducts, were often set amidst the vast expanses, and helped establish what Peter Galassi has called "a fugue of nature, a scheme of balance and enclosure, from which excess and accident have been banished" (118). We see a tiny, decrepit aqueduct in the Turner painting, and a somewhat larger one in Carl Rottmann's *Ruined Aqueduct in the Roman Campagna* (1826–27), and in Théodore Géricault's *Evening: Landscape with Aqueduct*.[29] More generally, Gogol's comparison of the skyline of Rome to

distant mountains reminds us that the natural and the man-made complement each other in many paintings of the time; and his emphasis on sharp
lines and angles looks to a favorite device not only of neoclassical painters
but of many contemporary landscapists as well when dealing with natural
or artificial objects. Finally, the idea that Rome is a blend of all periods and
styles was entirely conventional by Gogol's time.

The habit of looking at scenes as if they were paintings was deeply ingrained in other observers of the Italian scene. Among them was Goethe.
In *Italian Journey*, he acknowledges his "tendency to look at the world
through the eyes of the painter whose pictures" he has "last seen." An "animated scene" in the north of Italy "makes one think of some painting by
Heinrich Roos." A view of the lagoons in Venice inspires the feeling that
he is "looking at the latest and best painting of the Venetian school." On
his walks in the Villa Medici, he notes: "a haze hovers over the earth like
that I know from the drawings and paintings of Claude Lorrain." In gazing
out on the Gulf of Palermo, he remarks: "The enchanting look which distant objects like ships and promontories take on in this haze is most instructive for a painter . . . as I discovered when I walked to the top of a
hill. I no longer saw Nature, but pictures; it was as if some very skilful
painter had applied glaze to secure a proper gradation of tone. . . . [A]ll
conjured up images of the island of the blessed Phaeacians." In a further,
quite characteristic literary distancing, he concludes: "I hurried off to buy
myself a Homer [*Odyssey*] so that I could read the canto in which he
speaks of them" (79, 22, 163, 228–29). Here Goethe is following a long
tradition: people had been taught how to look at the landscape by painters
from Claude Lorrain onward, by the makers of *vedute*, and by the guidebooks, which by Goethe's time were chock full of literary and historical
references. He himself used Johann Jakob Volkmann's *Historisch-kritische
Nachrichten von Italien*.[30]

It is impossible to know how many of the omnipresent paintings and
sketches Gogol might have seen, but he was certainly familiar with the
landscape genre and its conventions. He had known many painters in St.
Petersburg, and he began to visit the studios of painters in Rome shortly
after arriving. Apparently he found the Germans and the English most con-
genial; the Russians by and large he did not regard as serious; the French
seem to have stirred no interest. Sigrid Richter has provided a list of these
painters, with brief characterizations of their work.[31] All cultivated the
then fashionable areas of landscape, genre scenes, portraits, and historical
or biblical subjects. Among the classical landscapists, Claude Lorrain
stood high in Gogol's esteem. Otherwise, landscape seems to have ranked
rather low in his priorities, probably because it did not feature human
beings and did not tell a story. (Even Claude Lorrain took care to paint in

people, however tiny, and devise titles that invited "reading" the work as a human drama.) Gogol's favorite painters were Raphael, Perugino, and Pinturicchio, none of them landscapists. Among his Russian contemporaries, those he most admired were Karl Bryullov, whose *Last Day of Pompeii*, as Gogol interpreted it, focuses on the human aspects of a natural disaster; Fyodor Iordan, who worked for ten years making an engraving of Raphael's *Transfiguration of the Lord*; and especially Aleksandr Ivanov, for his *Appearance of Christ to the People*. The most famous Russian landscape painter of Gogol's generation was Ivan Aivazovsky, whom he met in 1840 in Venice but who seems to have made no impression. Gogol's tastes obviously owed much to the precepts of neoclassicism as reflected in *paysage historique*. Undoubtedly he had in mind icons as well, where human or humanlike figures are always present, and where a narrative is at least implicit. Insofar as his views of art were molded by Western painters, it was those Germans known as the Nazarenes, and their Italian counterparts, who were especially influential. We will have more to say about them when we discuss "The Portrait," a work whose revised version appeared the same year as "Rome" (1842).

In "Rome," then, Gogol is following a venerable tradition of using painting to mediate a landscape. One thing that gives the result an unmistakably Gogolian touch is the extreme to which he takes it. Before long, everything the prince sees is aestheticized. Any attempt to establish a reference point outside the "picture" is brushed away. This is especially evident in the treatment of Annunciata.

Her real-life prototype has been found, in the person of Vittoria Cardoni (also attested as Caldoni), the daughter of a vintner in Albano.[32] But that scarcely matters, so stylized is the fictional counterpart. It resembles the idealized portraits of beautiful women in some of Gogol's other works, such as Alkinoe in the essay "Woman" (1831), various villagers in *Evenings on a Farm Near Dikanka*, and Ulinka in *Dead Souls* (Part 2), but it is carried much farther. At the outset, Annunciata is compared to a statue "from ancient times, when marble came to life and sculptors' chisels gleamed," and is turned this way and that for our inspection, like a painter's model (217). Somewhat later we are told that she "certainly would be a wonderful model for a Diana, a proud Juno, the seductive Graces," and this insight is extended to "all women [who] were ever transferred to canvas" (219). In these respects, Gogol looks to the classicizing tendencies of the painters who followed the precepts of *paysage historique*. Annunciata also resembles the central figure of an icon, which imposes its qualities on everything around it, as the narrator states in a strange but striking choice of words: "A marvelous holiday flies from her face to meet all" (218). This impression is reinforced by her name, which of course suggests the Annunciation, and by the comparison to a queen, which is one of the attributes of the Virgin Mary.

The process of aestheticizing human beauty is extended and generalized by the introduction of other arts. One is architecture: "all the women seemed like the buildings in Italy: they were either palaces or wretched hovels, either beautiful or ugly; there was no middle, there were no merely pretty ones." Poetry figures too: "[The prince] enjoyed [beautiful women] as he enjoyed those lines in a long poem which stood out from the others and visited a refreshing tremor on the soul." At one point, sculpture and poetry come together in a composite image: "suddenly there appears a countless multitude of beautiful women whose existence was hitherto unsuspected—beauties whose images are glimpsed only in bas-reliefs and in ancient anthology-poems." Conventional distinctions between animate and inanimate are obliterated as human beings are likened to artifacts and artifacts are represented as living. The world of nature in this story has a purely aesthetic function too: in "looking at [Annunciata], it became clear why the Italian poets compare beautiful women to the sun. This indeed was the sun, complete beauty" (246–48). Finally, the reactions of those who behold Annunciata, men and women both, are identical to the reactions that Gogol thought great art, or any great truth, must call forth:

This was complete beauty, created in order to dazzle all equally! Here there was no need to have any special taste: here all tastes were to come together, all were to prostrate themselves: believer and non-believer would fall before her, as before the sudden appearance of a divinity. [The prince] saw how the people, as many as were present, stared at her, the women's faces wearing an involuntary expression of astonishment mixed with pleasure, and repeating: "O bella"—he saw how everything there, no matter what, seemed to have turned into an artist and was looking intently at her alone. (248–49)

We think of the scene in the revised version of "The Portrait," published the same year as "Rome," where the picture painted by the "true" artist has been put on display at the Academy:

A profound silence, such as is rare in a large assembly of connoisseurs, prevailed everywhere on this occasion. . . . With an involuntary feeling of astonishment the experts were contemplating a new, hitherto unseen brush. . . . It was almost impossible to describe that extraordinary silence in which all who directed their eyes at the picture were involuntarily enveloped—there was not a rustle, not a sound. . . . Involuntary tears were ready to run down the cheeks of the visitors who stood around the picture. It seemed as though all tastes, all daring and mistaken deviations of taste, were blended into a silent hymn to the divine work of art.[33]

The mute scene in The Inspector General is a secularized version of this same idea, as is Gogol's much later observation, "everyone alike is struck

by [female] beauty, even those who are insensitive to everything and without an aptitude for anything," so that "the most dissolute of our young
men" have admitted to him that in the presence of such beauty "nothing
bad comes into their heads, that they do not dare utter not only the kind
of ambiguous word with which they regale other favored ones, but any
word at all."[34]

Such an aestheticized world forms as tightly bounded a space as anything in the early stories. Consequently, violations tend to come in the form
of nonaestheticized reality. Let us again consider the scene where the prince
goes into the Roman Campagna. As the day draws to a close, he stations
himself on the veranda of a villa and looks out over the fields. This is one
of the most beautiful landscapes in all of Gogol, and it inspires ecstasy in
the prince. (Sunset views were also a common motif of paintings with this
setting.) Suddenly a mundane detail intrudes: "an awkward winged insect,
known by the name of the devil, whizzing along in a standing position, like
a human being, kept blindly hitting him in the eyes." This "devil" violates
the boundaries of the prince's aesthetic realm, as do its more humanoid
counterparts in the earlier stories. He can no longer "see" aesthetically, as
his abrupt awareness of physical discomfort and practical necessity indicates: "Only then did he feel penetrated through and through by the on-
setting cold of the southern night, and he hastened into the city streets so
as not to catch the southern fever" (240). One wonders whether Tolstoy, a
great admirer of Gogol, had this episode in mind when, in *Cossacks* (Ka-
zaki, 1863), Olenin, alone in the stag's lair, is bitten by insects and begins
to put aside his romantic, book-mediated notions of the Cossacks. Gogol's
prince does abandon his excursions through the landscape to undertake a
study of the history of Italy, "heretofore known to him in episodes and fragments," through an avid perusal of "archives, manuscripts, and notes."
The result is a reaffirmation not only of the past splendors of his native land
but of his own conviction that she will again rise to greatness, in and
through the uncorrupted "people." Both motifs had long since been ex-
ploited by artists, the second in genre paintings of Italian peasants, the first
in views of the Campagna, where, as Galassi puts it, "the warm tones of
sunset create an elegiac effect, a romantic nostalgia for Roman glory"
(120). The prince's rediscovery of them in written form means that he
learns nothing new, not even how to look in any new way. Ever the aesthete, he contemplates old manuscripts as he does old paintings, statues,
and buildings.

Two further opportunities for a truly different way of seeing present
themselves. We know what a Tolstoyan character would make of them, but
the prince is no Tolstoyan. We find him in the streets of Rome observing
the Carnival festivities. As an inveterate spectator, however, he does not

wish to participate and is therefore not costumed; he merely tries to "make his way through the Corso to the other half of the city." But the crowd is too thick to allow easy passage, and it becomes the equivalent of the insect in the veranda scene:

Scarcely had he squeezed between two people when he was regaled with some flour from above; a motley-colored harlequin struck him on the shoulder with a rattle . . . confetti and bunches of flowers flew into his eyes [cf. "kept blindly hitting him in the eyes" in the veranda passage]; on either side people began buzzing in his ears [*zhuzhzhat'*: the verb is usually associated with insects]. . . . He was physically unable to break through, because the crowd had grown. . . . Finally the whole crowd moved forward . . . the movement of people knocked off his hat, which he now hastened to pick up. (247–48)

He then encounters Annunciata and is entranced by her beauty, but is "awakened" by a shout and sees a "huge cart" standing before him:

The crowd of masks in pink blouses in the cart called him by name and began joggling flour on him, to the accompaniment of a long drawn-out exclamation: "Oo, oo, oo!" [an intensification of the "buzzing" in the previous scene, and an evocation of the earlier insect?]. And in an instant he was covered with white dust from head to foot, to the loud laughter [also an equivalent of buzzing?] of all the neighbors surrounding him. All white as snow, even his eyelashes white, the prince quickly ran home to change clothes. (249)

Similarly, he is noticed and mockingly commented upon, in another version of the annoying-sound motif, by the women who hang out of the windows of the houses "in one of those remote streets of which there are many in Rome," where "everything is open and above board, and the passer-by can get to know every detail of all the domestic secrets" (251). But the prince wishes only to avoid such mundanities, which he cannot reconcile with the life he hopes to spend "in the contemplation of nature, the arts, and antiquities" (240), as well as in the contemplation of Annunciata. There is never a question of approaching her, let alone of possessing her physically. His admiration is voyeuristic. When he sees her at the Carnival, he thinks: "This is a flash of lightning and *not a woman*. . . . I absolutely must *catch a glimpse of her*. I do not want to *see her for the purpose of loving her*, no—I would merely like to *look at her, look at all of her, look at her eyes, look at her hands, at her fingers, at her shining hair. Not to kiss her*. I would merely like to *gaze upon her*." As if suddenly embarrassed at being caught out, he tries to remove her even farther: "Complete beauty is given to the world so that everyone might see it, so that everyone might forever preserve the idea of it in his heart. If she were merely beautiful, and not such a height of perfection, then she would have the right to belong to one man, he could carry her off into the desert and hide her from the world.

But complete beauty ought to be visible to all" (250). Annunciata, now safely desexualized, remains aestheticized. Like Poprishchin, however, the prince keeps on watching while remaining concealed. In the final scene, he has lost sight of her and is about to hire Peppe to locate her, but again the mundane intrudes: he "glanced around and saw that all the Signore Grazias, Susannas, Barbaruchis, Tettis, Tuttis—all, however many—had leaned out the windows in curiosity, and poor Signora Cecilia had practically fallen into the street" (257). Not wishing to reveal himself, he leads Peppe away, through street after street, until they reach a spot where he can speak without being overheard. This is "a small square from which all Rome opened out" in "a wonderful shining panorama" that is "powerfully illuminated by the brilliance of the sunset." We will consider this scene in some detail later on.

We have often compared Gogol's and Goethe's approaches to Italy, but we have not yet remarked one obvious and crucial difference. Goethe represents himself as a direct observer of what he describes. Gogol, in "Rome," resorts to a mediator in the prince. We may wonder why he needs this character, since his views of Rome are already mediated through conventional representations of the city. "Character" is actually a misnomer: we do not know what the prince looks like; he does not even have a name; his mental world is that of the naive observer recording what he sees for the benefit of an impersonal narrator, who passes it on to us. Yet the sights are those that Gogol himself saw, and the prince's thoughts and opinions are for the most part Gogol's own, as we know them mainly from the letters he wrote between 1836 and 1842. Richter, for one, has discovered extensive parallels (126–35). Both the prince and Gogol travel to Paris through Switzerland; both are disturbed by the wild grandeur of the Alps; both are attracted by the vivacity of Paris, but come to see and loathe the superficiality and frivolousness of that city, Gogol almost immediately, the prince gradually; both yearn for Italy and follow the same route there from Paris, breaking the journey in Genoa; both at first are disappointed in Rome, but come to love and cherish it, especially for what remains of the Renaissance; both treasure the "people" as the vital center of the nation and the guarantee of its future greatness; both venerate beauty, especially in art. The parallels extend to details of descriptions as well. I would add that both men are natives of countries that stood on the margin of Europe geographically, economically, politically, and culturally. As the prince sees it, the "real Europe" lies "on the other side" of a well-defined boundary, in this case the Alps. For Gogol, as for most Russians, Europe is not so physically set apart from the homeland, but is psychologically just as difficult of access. In his hands, Italy even looks similar to Russia in topography: "The wild irregularity of the Swiss mountains, towering without perspective, without any weightless distances, somewhat terrified his eye, which was accustomed to the highly peaceful, caressing beauty of Italian nature" (221). We think of the last chapter of *Dead Souls* (a contemporaneous work), where the Russian landscape, though utterly flat and lacking anything to "beguile and ravish the eye," is contrasted with spectacular mountain scenery, presumably Alpine and therefore partly Swiss. In leaving Paris for Rome, Gogol not only enacts the prince's later itinerary but reenacts his departure from St. Petersburg (the Russian Paris) for his "real" native land. The prince soon realizes that he is estranged from his family and society, for in their dedication to isolation, excess, and artificiality, they are but imitations of Europe. He then uses his alienated state to try to discover the true identity of the nation to which he nominally belongs. Gogol's course is virtually identical, although more complex because he has two homelands. He feels comfortable in Rome, yet he is a foreigner there; at the same time, the city provides him with a vantage point from which he can discern the healthy national life of Russia under a veneer of Europeanization.

Despite this evidence, Gogol, when pressed, denied any connection between himself and the prince. In the review of "Rome" to which I alluded earlier, Belinsky disapproved of Gogol's unfavorable picture of Paris and his contrasting picture of Rome as a repository of enduring values. Gogol took exception in a letter to Shevyryov: "I would have been to blame," he wrote, "if I had imposed my view of Paris even on a Roman prince. Because, although I can certainly get off the track as far as artistic intuition is concerned, generally speaking I cannot be of the same opinion as my hero." This is disingenuous, as is his version of the idea of the story: "It consisted in showing the significance of a nation that has lived out its existence, and done so splendidly, with regard to living nations," among which he counts Russia.[35] But in "Rome," the "significance" is located in art and in the "people," both of which are eternally young and therefore exemplary, especially for a "young" nation like Russia. We are left with no real distinction here either.

Although the prince is an intellectual and cultural lightweight, his views and activities are presented with only an occasional touch of irony or sarcasm; we are obviously meant to take them seriously. Why does Gogol find it necessary to deny what must have been obvious to his close friends then and is obvious to his close readers now? There are several possible reasons. One might be disappointment over Belinsky's dislike of the story, and a corresponding desire to distance himself from it. Another might be politics. Gogol, through the prince, makes a distinction between the vital energy of the people and the lifeless state bureaucracy. This is a familiar theme in much of his fiction with Russian settings. But he goes considerably farther in "Rome," intimating that the bureaucracy is utterly irrelevant to the real life of the nation and should simply be ignored. He never explicitly says that about Russia, but it would not have been hard for readers to infer it from what he does say, especially readers of a radical cast of mind. Finally, Gogol may have felt nervous about the image of Rome conveyed by the prince. There is nothing unusual or even particularly interesting in what he sees or thinks: it had all been recorded by others, and would have been familiar to anyone who had spent time in Rome or studied paintings and books about the city.

To be sure, "originality" had no place in Gogol's aesthetic, in the sense of ideas or insights emanating from the mind or the "imagination." The artist's subject was the world outside him, which he was expected to see in ways that escaped ordinary onlookers yet would compel their recognition and assent. For Gogol, as we know, the observation of that world could not be direct, but must be mediated. In "Rome," however, he carries the process of mediation to such extremes that we detect the workings of an acute anxiety, far more so than we might suspect from his rather peculiar uses of Pushkin. Rome is set at three removes, with a faceless narrator observing a nearly faceless prince who observes pictures, verbal and plastic, produced by numerous anonymous others. Given the general familiarity of the material, might Gogol have feared that we would wonder whether he was really just copying and trying to conceal it with artful distancing? Given too his view of how the artist works, the problem of imitation was bound to arise. Did his handling of it in "Rome" betoken insecurity about his own theory of creativity? The fact that imitation was a prominent theme of much of his fiction from all periods, but particularly the one we are now discussing, suggests that these questions were fundamental. And it is to them that we shall devote the next two chapters.

9

Imitation: "The Portrait"

THE question of imitation arises not only from Gogol's psychological makeup, theories of creativity, and literary practices but from his adopted nationality as a writer. To be a Russian in the early nineteenth century, or for that matter, at any time, was to risk anxiety when it came to self-definition. More often than not, the obsession with Russianness, which lay at the heart of cultural discourse in the eighteenth and early nineteenth centuries, moved between two poles: an imitation of European ways and a discovery of indigenous values.

IMITATION AS A RUSSIAN PROBLEM

Imitation had been a central tenet of European neoclassicism, whence it passed into Russia in the eighteenth century. It did not of course mean "copying," any more than *mimesis* had for most Greeks, or *imitatio* for most Romans. The protracted and often arid debates about versification around which public literary life centered in the mid-eighteenth century all agreed in disapproving of the use of foreign models that did not recognize the peculiarities of the Russian language. Boosterism was common too. As early as 1770, Nikolai Novikov had published *Attempt at a Historical Dictionary of Russian Writers* (Opyt istoricheskogo slovarya o rossiiskikh pisatelyakh), which lists the names of 317 figures, including some that predated Peter the Great. The sparse commentary he provides is favorable, in the spirit of what has been called "social criticism," which is aimed at raising the prestige of literature by encouraging readers to read and writers to write. It was the kind most often practiced publicly by Nikolai Karamzin.[1] In 1802 he published an article entitled "The Pantheon of Russian Authors" (Panteon rossiiskikh avtorov), which amounted to a brief survey, hardly more than an annotated listing, of Russian writers from Boyan, the mythical author of the recently discovered *Song of Igor's Campaign*, to the present. Karamzin also chided his predecessors, particularly the neoclassicists, for their lack of interest in the national literature.

It is not difficult, however, to detect in the eighteenth-century men of letters a note of doubt, even apprehension, about the vitality and validity of the up-to-date national literature they were trying to create according to international standards. Even Karamzin, the most polished and cosmopolitan of them all, remained skeptical to the end of his life about the Russianness of his own culture. In a speech delivered in 1818 to the Academy of Sciences, he insisted that Russia had a "national mind and feeling," of which literature was "the mirror," but then repeated the already conventional view that Peter the Great, through his reforms, had forever severed the ties between ancient and modern Russia, thereby making upperclass Russians like other Europeans: "We do not want to imitate foreigners, but we write as they write: for we live as they live; we read what they read; we have the same models of mind and taste." Unsure about whether to place the weight on "Russian" or on "European" qualities, he opts for a balance: "It is good to write for Russians; it is still better to write for all people."[2]

The burgeoning of Russian literary life after the defeat of Napoleon in 1812 might have deracinated doubt. Works by Russian writers appeared in fresh editions. New literary histories strove to identify a Grand Tradition. The study of Russian literature entered the curriculum of higher education, largely through the efforts of Aleksei Merzlyakov, a well-known poet and a professor at Moscow University. Literary circles were formed by many of the important writers of the time. Solid new literary journals were established from the turn of the century on, and became the main forums for poetry, criticism, and especially prose fiction, the predominant form of literature by the 1830's. A new breed of professional critics appeared, as distinct from poets, prose writers, and journalists. Vissarion Belinsky was the first to achieve celebrity; the fact that his career virtually coincided with Gogol's was to be of no small consequence for both.[3]

What Merzlyakov said in 1817 became a truism: literature is the highest achievement of a people, "a sign of political and moral successes." Writers were obliged, as the poet Batyushkov put it, to undertake "a beautiful, great and sacred work: enrich and shape the language of a most renowned people, which populates almost half the world; make the glory of its language equal to its military glory, the successes of its mind equal to its successes in arms." Literature, in fact, became the focus of the culture, and has remained so ever since. William Mills Todd has aptly observed: "The greatest public debate of the 1800's and 1810's—on the origins and future of the Russian language—was an obviously literary one, but it encompassed the cultural and political issues of the day, especially the eternal Russian problem of relations with the West."[4]

By the 1820's, neoclassicism was long dead, and with it, "imitation" as a living mandate to artists. They were now to "create *not from nature*, but *as nature*," seeking an organic form or inner idea that "constructs the material from within."[5] Still, many observers continued to voice dismay at the seemingly ingrained Russian habit of looking abroad for self-validation. Writing in 1825, Aleksandr Bestuzhev-Marlinsky fretted: "There was a time when we sighed inopportunely in a [Laurence] Sternean way, then we paid court in the French manner, and now we have soared off into the nether regions in the German manner." The result, he thought, was a "lack of nationality [*beznarodnost'*]," "an admiration only of what is foreign," and a tendency to "belittle even that which exists" instead of feeling "a zeal to create that which we do not have."[6] So many other famous writers of the time—Venevitinov, Ivan Kireevsky, even Pushkin—insisted that Russian literature did not exist that the idea became almost a commonplace. Pyotr Chaadayev went much further. The first essay of his *Philosophical Letters* dismissed the national culture as being "based wholly on borrowing and imitation," and concluded: "we have given nothing to the world . . . we did not bother to invent anything, while from the inventions of others we borrowed only the deceptive appearances and the useless luxuries." As a final touch, he signed this letter as emanating from "Necropolis." This was to carry public ruminations on the national identity too far. The reaction was swift and decisive. Chaadayev was declared insane, put under house arrest, and two years later freed on condition that he never write again.[7]

Chaadayev's "letter" was published in 1836 in the journal *The Telescope* (Teleskop), which was closed down as a result. Its editor, Nikolai Nadezhdin, was exiled to northern Russia, from which he was allowed to return only in 1838. In many respects he agreed with Chaadayev: in 1831 he too had stated that there was no Russian literature. Yet with time he became more interested in finding ways of making Russian culture a viable reality. His cautious conclusion was: "We have a literature; we also have a literary life, but its development is being inhibited by the one-sided tendency to imitate [Europe], which is fatal to nationality, without which there cannot be a full literary life!"[8] As late as 1834, Belinsky could open his famous article "Literary Reveries" (Literaturnye mechtaniya) by stating: "We have no literature"; and a year or so later he noted "the insignificance . . . and doubtful nature of its existence." If by "literature" he meant Russian novels and drama, this statement might have had some foundation. By the end of the decade, however, there was no doubt in Belinsky's mind that Russia did have a literature. The difference was the appearance of Gogol, whom Belinsky proclaimed a genuinely Russian writer, and the greatest of them all.[9]

Gogol himself contributed to the discussion. In 1836 he wrote an article on the Russian drama, in which he insisted that the time had come to stop imitating the French and instead write plays that reflected "the general elements of our society, its moving springs." A decade later, he took up the topic again in a far broader context. In introducing European ways, he argued, Peter the Great had intended that Russians "examine [them]selves more deeply." Instead, mindless imitation became the norm, as Russia put herself "under the influence of French, German and English tutors, under the influence of immigrants from all countries, from all possible classes, with different ways of thinking, different rules, different turns of mind." In consequence, educated society "grew up in ignorance of its own land amidst its own land." The national essence persists, however, preserved first in folksongs, proverbs, and sermons, and, more recently, in the works of great poets like Lomonosov, Derzhavin, Krylov, Pushkin, Batyushkov, Yazykov, and Zhukovsky. To be sure, Russians have not yet recognized themselves in this literature, but Gogol is confident that they will eventually do so, and that the result will be an amalgamation of native and foreign elements to create a truly national character.[10]

The coexistence of insecurity and confidence about the future greatness of the nation (fed, ironically enough, by a foreigner, Herder)[11] has been typical of the Russian experience from that day to this. In these articles, Gogol's rhetoric is cast in terms of the entirely conventional antithesis of Russia and Europe. Yet he does not really seem to have doubted that his own work was "Russian." Belinsky in that sense knew very well what he had discovered. For that reason, the issue is somewhat artificial when it surfaces in Gogol's nonfiction, and we are likely to suspect him of intellectual laziness. Where we see a truly original and deeply pondered treatment of imitation is in his fiction. It is in fact one of his major themes. But it is viewed less as a cultural than as a spiritual problem. Although the issue is still structured as an antithesis between "imitation" and "authenticity" broadly speaking, "Russia" and "Europe" are no longer present, except perhaps inferentially or subtextually. Instead, Gogol brings in a whole array of images to stand on one side or the other of the opposition.

FICTIONAL IMITATIONS

At its most primitive, imitation is mere copying, and is confined to material objects. Much of the conversation of the two ladies who meet in chapter 9 of *Dead Souls* is devoted to dress patterns, which can of course be reproduced indefinitely. But fashion is less about clothes than about the people who wear them; here the ladies are really talking about the identity of Chichikov. They expect him to cut himself to the pattern of styles for seducers and rogues. But he does not: convention, itself a form of imitation, bears no necessary relation to the underlying realities. In any event, Gogol seemed to think that human beings cannot, or should not, be expected to imitate things.

Some of Gogol's characters attempt to do so. Lieutenant Pirogov, in "Nevsky Prospekt," lays siege to the pretty blond wife of the German Schiller, and is deterred neither by her protests nor by the beating her husband administers to him. Undoubtedly he has a highly developed sense of well-bounded place, but, like all obsessives, he hurtles into the larger community like a projectile. The wife herself is of the same type: though frightened by Pirogov and aware of what he wants, she agrees to dance with him because "all German girls are passionately fond of dancing" (I, 236). These are cases of the kind of self-copying for which machines and instinct-driven creatures are designed.

On a somewhat higher level, the numerous paired characters often look like self-replications. Such are Bobchinsky and Dobchinsky, in *The Inspector General*. According to the stage directions, both are "short, squat little men; extremely alike and very inquisitive; both have little potbellies; both speak very rapidly, and eke out their words with emphatic gestures." Yet "extremely alike" does not mean "exactly alike," as the characterization goes on to indicate: "Dobchinsky is a little taller and more serious than Bobchinsky, but Bobchinsky is livelier and more free and easy."[12] The logical absurdity disguised by the syntactic parallelism reinforces the point: unless Gogol is using chiasmus here, which I doubt, "taller" and "livelier" belong to entirely different semantic categories. Again we are being reminded that each person occupies a unique place. He may try to imitate another's, perhaps from habit or from fear of his own uniqueness, but the result is at best comedy, at worst tragedy.

As a copy-clerk, Akaky Akakievich is an imitator in a very literal way, and, for a time, a highly successful one. Copying confers on him the condition of virtual anonymity he craves, but it is of no use when his basic need for love and recognition is awakened. By contrast, Poprishchin considers copying demeaning, and tries to create a "real" identity outside the office. Even here, as we have seen, he is ever the copyist, for he borrows fragments of literary conventions and patches them together as best he can in service of a philistine and therefore imitative vision. Considerably more interesting and successful as a worker in words is Khlestakov. Though lower intellectually and officially than Akaky and Poprishchin, he is well versed in one powerful and respectable aspect of the Russian literary tradition, and knows how to imitate it to great effect.

In Act III of *The Inspector General*, Khlestakov is presented to the mayor's wife (Anna Andreevna) and daughter, and promptly initiates the conversation with formulas drawn from the lexicon of Sentimentalism, a literary movement already obsolete but recent enough to command instant recognition on the part of any moderately experienced reader or theatergoer of the time.[13] "*How happy* I am, madam, to have, in a sense, the *satisfaction* [*udovol'stvie*] of *seeing* [*videt'*] you." "In a sense [*v svoem rode*]" might be more literally rendered as "in my own way." It attests to Khlestakov's fuzzy-mindedness, and signals that he is going to use the terminology idiosyncratically. It also sets off and marks the terms that follow, "satisfaction" and "see," so that the audience will be more aware that they *are* terms and not merely the small talk that oils social discourse. What follows is built on a pattern of repetition and hyperbole.[14] Anna Andreevna says: "It is *even more pleasant* to us to *see* so distinguished a visitor." "Pleasant [*priyatno*]," another code word of Sentimentalism, is virtually synonymous with "satisfaction," and Khlestakov promptly picks it up: "Upon my soul, madam, it is quite the opposite: it is *even more pleasant* [*eshche priyatnee*] for me," a statement that is not an "opposite" at all, but a repetition and hyperbolization. Anna Andreevna then introduces two topics that are new but also drawn from the Sentimentalist repertory: "I suppose that *after the capital* [*posle stolitsy*] your *journey* [*voyazhirovka*] must have been *very unpleasant* [*ochen' nepriyatnoyu*]." The pattern of hyperbolized imitation is now sufficiently established to make Khlestakov's reply almost predictable: "*Extremely unpleasant* [*chrezvychaino nepriyatna*]. After being used to living, *comprenez-vous*, in the *world* [*svete*, meaning also 'high society'], to find oneself *on the road* [*v doroge*] in dirty inns, in the depths [*mrak*, lit., 'gloom'] of ignorance. . . ." "Road" is a response to Anna's *voyazhirovka*, as well as to "after [*posle*] the capital." *Comprenez-vous* has been triggered by her use of a Russianized French word for "traveling"—*voyazhirovka*—which would have brought smiles to the lips of contemporary audiences as a hyper-genteelism straight out of the eighteenth century. This in turn can be seen as an inflated version of an earlier statement she has made—"You are pleased to say that only for the sake of a *compliment* [*dlya komplimenta*]"—which began its linguistic life in France as well. As real French, *comprenez-vous* represents the final stage of a process that gets under way with *kompliment*—completely Russianized French—and continues with *voyazhirovka*—half-French and half-Russian.

Anna Andreevna's "capital [*stolitsa*]" is neutral and inclusive of all social classes. It evokes Khlestakov's "world" or "high society" (*svet*), which, ironically, is socially exclusive. But the primary meaning of *svet* is "light," as contrasted with *mrak*, "darkness," which also carries literal and figurative meanings. In turn, the pairing of light and darkness prepares us for the contrast of affirmation and denial that structures the following passage:

> *Anna Andreevna:* Indeed, you must find it *unpleasant* [*nepriyatno*].
> *Khlestakov:* At this moment, madam, I find it *very pleasant* [*ochen' priyatno*].
> *A. A.:* How can you! You do me too much honor. I *don't deserve* it [*ne zasluzhivayu*].
> *Khl.:* Not deserve it [*ne zasluzhivaete*]? You *do deserve* it [*zasluzhivaete*], madam.

She explains her lack of merit—"I live in the country"—to which Khlestakov responds with even more grandiosity: "Yes, but the *country* [*derevnya*], too, has its *hillsides and brooks* [*prigorki, rucheiki*] ... though, of course, there is no comparing it with Petersburg! Ah, Petersburg! What a life it is! Perhaps you think I am only a copying-clerk [*chto ya tol'ko perepisyvayu*]." He begins with a gainsaying ("yes, but"), which introduces the two requisite features of Sentimentalist landscape, but promptly undoes it by invoking Petersburg, the "capital," which Anna Andreevna has set up in favorable contrast to the country town in which she is stuck. This marks a reversal of the Sentimentalist formula, where the city represents negative qualities and the country positive ones. If the country "too" has "hillsides and brooks," then such features are potentially present anywhere, the observation is absurd, and the whole exchange is revealed as an exercise in the employment of a fragmented Sentimentalist lexicon to which no effective meaning attaches.

One aspect of the humor here is that Khlestakov is doing what a writer can do: drawing on a set of literary images and conventions from the past. He even quotes from Karamzin's story "The Isle of Bornholm" (Ostrov Borngol'm, 1794)—"Only the laws condemn it" (658)—and identifies the author. He also seems aware of a more obvious subtext, Karamzin's story "Poor Liza" (Bednaya Liza, 1792), as any moderately well-informed reader of the time would have been, given its enormous and enduring popularity on all levels of society. In fact, Khlestakov has much in common with Erast, the city-bred hero of that story. Not, to be sure, a "decent mind," but certainly a "good heart": according to the stage directions, Khlestakov is possessed of "candor and simplicity." Then too, Erast is called "weak and flighty," thinks "only of his own pleasure," seeks this "in worldly amusements," and has "a rather lively imagination," which is fed on "novels and idylls." Khlestakov's "imagination," however, is utterly pedestrian. He protests that he is no mere copy-clerk, but that is precisely what he is here: a copyist of the language, sentiments, and dynamics of a Sentimentalism now vulgarized into small talk. But he cannot even copy accurately: "We shall flee beneath the shade of streams," he says, in a ludicrous conflation of Sentimentalist images.[15] Anna Andreevna is undoubtedly familiar with Karamzin's story too. Unlike his heroine, she is neither young nor a maiden; but her susceptibility makes it easy enough for her to play a willing Poor Liza. This in turn prompts Khlestakov's proposal of marriage first to her and then to her daughter. Anna is already established as a rival of her daughter in the matter of attractive gowns, and she vies for Khlestakov's affections too. There may be an oblique reference to "Poor Liza" here as well: Erast, the young man from the city, flattered and reassured the mother to the point where she "willingly accepted this proposition [that Liza should sell the cloth she weaves only to him] without suspecting any bad intention in it," and at length she says, "Oh, Liza! How kind and good he is! If only your fiancé is like that!"[16]

All this is of course funny. But there is a more serious side to it. Presumably Khlestakov does not really understand what he is doing in mechanically trying to copy an outmoded style. Yet it has a very real and by no means funny effect on Anna and her daughter. Furthermore, he literally becomes a writer at the very end of the play, when he pens a letter to his friend. Like Gogol's own works, it draws on several very different literary traditions, the anecdotal, confessional, and characterological, among others. It is also the "truest" version of the preceding events that is available to the characters who hear it read aloud. And because it has a decisive effect on their lives, it also satisfies one of Gogol's own requirements for "good" literature.

The use of French by Anna Andreevna and Khlestakov can itself be taken as a reference to another vigorous genre of eighteenth-century literature, the satire of the Russian who apes foreign ways. Though the phenomenon was still vital, and commented on by many, including Gogol, it was no longer a particularly productive theme for fiction. Far more important, certainly for Gogol, was the larger question of originality on the part of Russians generally and creative artists in particular. We have described his views of the matter. But the fact is that his fictional representations betray far less confidence than his nonfiction. Akaky Akakievich, Poprishchin, and especially Khlestakov do many of the things that writers do, and even have an "audience" for their "creativity." Because they are on a far lower level than the presumed author of the works in which they appear, Gogol can keep himself safely distanced from them. But they are treated without satire and only to a limited extent with humor, for their "copying" entails serious consequences, sometimes for them, as in "The Overcoat" and "Diary of a Madman," and sometimes for others, as in *The Inspector General*. Furthermore, Gogol returned to the theme of artistic imitation in a far deeper and more significant way in another story, centered around a character who is intellectually and culturally on the same level as the reader and the presumed author. Predictably, however, this character is distanced, although in a predictable way, by being made a painter, not a writer. The character is Chartkov, and the story, "The Portrait."

"THE PORTRAIT"

"The Portrait" can readily be assigned to the then-fashionable genre of stories about failed artists. In its mixture of the fantastic and the ordinary, it is reminiscent of some of the *Dikanka* tales and of E. T. A. Hoffmann. The 1835 version, as published in *Arabesques*, is virtually unknown even to Russian readers and has been neglected by critics. But Gogol obviously regarded it as an important work. He subjected it to a thorough revision, and republished it in 1842. This is the text that is invariably included in selected works in Russian and translated into foreign languages.[17] Critics have not been particularly kind to this recast text either, perhaps because it requires serious attention to Gogol's new-found interest in religion. But it does offer the most sustained and substantial fictional exploration of his view of the mission and responsibilities of the artist, in the context of the problem of imitation.

One part of the story that passed intact into the final version—when virtually nothing else did—is the beginning, which encompasses roughly the first two pages. Here the question of imitation is raised straightaway. The narrator introduces us to a little picture-shop at an open-air market in St. Petersburg. Displayed there are three kinds of pictures: oils, engravings, and *lubki* (cheap woodblock prints). Each features subjects designed to appeal to viewers of different tastes, sensibilities, and educational backgrounds. The *lubki* are being ogled by apprentices, footboys, "dissipated footmen," a "soldier in a greatcoat, a cavalier of the flea market, and a peddler woman from Okhta." The engravings—"a portrait of Khozrev-Mirza in a sheepskin cap, and portraits of generals with crooked noses in three-cornered hats"—aim higher. Finally, the oil paintings "bespoke pretension to a rather high level of art, though its most profound degradation was displayed in them," with subjects like "A winter scene with white trees, an absolutely red sunset that looked like the glow of a conflagration, a Flemish peasant with a pipe and broken arm" (252–54). Regardless of au-

dience, however, all these pictures have one thing in common: they are imitations of familiar motifs in styles so familiar as to be instantly
recognizable.

This sociology of art is amplified by Chartkov, the impoverished young
artist who is the hero of Part 1. He is prepared to tolerate *lubki* and engravings as being "well within the grasp and comprehension of the people"
(253). Such condescension amounts to indifference. Like Gogol himself,
Chartkov has no interest in art for the masses, but only in "high" art, which
potentially includes anything painted in oil. The specimens here displayed
baffle him, for they reveal "a total lack of talent, the feeble, faltering, dull
incompetence of a born failure that impudently pushes himself among the
arts, while his true place is among the lowest crafts, a failure which is true,
nevertheless, to its vocation, and drags its trade into art." Such artists, in
other words, do not know their proper place. We might also rephrase
Chartkov's reactions in terms of imitation. *Lubki* and engravings, being
mass-produced, are imitations in the most literal sense of the word, but can
be tolerated because they are not real art. Paintings, as the creations of individuals, should all be different, but here are not: like their humbler counterparts, they show the "same colors, the same manner, the same practiced,
accustomed hand which seemed to belong to a crudely fashioned autom-
aton rather than to a man" (254). Among other things, Gogol is establishing code words for imitation: "usual," "the same," "practiced," and "accustomed," which will recur in various forms throughout the story.

What Chartkov is not prepared for is the portrait of the moneylender
that hangs inside the shop. It stands in contrast to the predictable specimens outside. Especially striking are the eyes, which "seemed to glare,
glare out of the portrait" (255), disconcerting everyone who sees them.
Even so, he takes it home, only to discover that he cannot escape the "horrible eyes": "[They] actually destroyed the harmony of the portrait. They
were alive, human! It was as if they had been cut from a living man and
inserted in the canvas" (260). He is profoundly disturbed, and asks himself
why this is so: "After all, this is only nature, this is living nature. Where
does this strange and discomforting feeling come from?" He immediately
knows the answer, even though he frames it as a rhetorical question: "Or
is it a crime to make a slavish, literal imitation of nature, which seems like
a shrill, discordant shriek?"[18] Crime or not, such an imitation fails to create art because it is simply a copy, unmediated by "feeling" or "thought":
"if you take a subject dispassionately, unfeelingly, having no sympathy for
it, must it confront you only in all its dreadful reality, being unilluminated
by the light of some intangible idea that is hidden in everything, must it
confront you in that same reality that is revealed when, desirous of understanding what makes a human being beautiful, you arm yourself with a

scalpel and dissect his insides and see only a human being that is disgusting?" As an example of a painstakingly detailed painting that actually is a work of art, Chartkov remembers that his professor had told him about a work by Leonardo da Vinci in which the eyes stood out prominently: "The most minute, almost invisible veins were not overlooked and were committed to the canvas." Since Leonardo, for Gogol, is never less than a supreme master, we may have taken for granted, as does Chartkov himself here, that the eyes have been "illuminated by some idea" (260–61).[19]

At this early point in the story, Chartkov serves as Gogol's mouthpiece in his ruminations on good and bad art. We might recast them somewhat, in the light of his creator's larger preoccupations, and say that imitation is bad because it is a violation of proper place. As we learn in Part 2, the portrait has been painted on commission from the moneylender, who states that the artist has "already sketched his prominent features, and if [the artist] would accurately [or 'truly': verno] reproduce them [the moneylender's] life would be preserved in some supernatural manner in the portrait, and then he would not die completely, for it was necessary for him to remain in the world" (296). The word here rendered as "reproduce," peredast, more literally means "transfer," or "move from one place to another," in this case from "real life" to canvas, so that the result is "no longer a copy of nature" but "a strange kind of life that might have lit up the face of a corpse arisen from the grave" (261). Like all displacements in Gogol, this one opens the way to the demonic. The painter later comes to understand that "his brush had been a tool of the devil and that a part of the moneylender's life had somehow or other really passed into the portrait and was now plaguing people, inspiring diabolical ideas, beguiling artists from the righteous path, inflicting the horrible torments of jealousy, and so forth" (299–300).

Even though the portrait is a prime example of bad art and is recognized as such by Chartkov, he is fated to create art very much like it. After Chartkov takes the portrait home, he finds a hoard of gold coins in the frame. His life is transformed. No longer need he be poor and unknown. He acquires a magnificent apartment, announces his availability in the newspaper, and before long becomes a rich and famous society painter. He expresses utter contempt for all other painters until one day he sees a work executed by one of his contemporaries who had pursued his vision, nurtured his talent, and, despising fame and comfort, gone off to study in Italy. Chartkov is thunderstruck by the unmistakable mark of genius, realizes that he has betrayed himself, tries to recapture the old fire, fails, and in a frenzy of despair uses his enormous wealth to buy up and destroy any masterpiece he can find. At length he goes mad and dies. So ends Part 1 of the story.

Chartkov's encounter with his first customer, the society lady who wants a portrait of her daughter, figures in each version of the story and is crucial in determining what he will become. But it is very differently handled in the two versions. The lady of the 1835 story is a haughty and stupid aristocrat for whom a painter is merely a servant, like a French hairdresser, who must do as he is told. "A certain languor has always been noticeable in her eyes and even in all her facial features; my Annette is very sensitive, and I confess I never allow her to read any new novels! . . . I would like you to depict her simply in a family circle or, even better, alone in the out of doors, in a verdant shade, so that there is nothing to show that she attends balls" (414). Although Chertkov—for so he is named in this version[20]—detects no signs of "languor," he says nothing and adopts the servile role into which he has been cast. In the 1842 version, the lady is presented in a very different way. The result is not only a gain in subtlety but a new thrust. She begins by flattering Chartkov and making him feel almost an equal. Though a philistine, she is well informed about art, having visited Italy and gone through the galleries. Ultimately she is far more dangerous to Chartkov's integrity as an artist than her brainless, autocratic predecessor. One simple but deadly question makes that clear: "Were you in Italy?" Chartkov in embarrassment replies: "No, I have not been there, but I have always had the desire ... I have put it off for a while" (271). The lady already knows that society considers study in Italy an essential stage in the training of a serious artist, and she hereby establishes her moral right to demand that Chartkov depict not his vision of the subject (renamed "Lise" in the 1842 version) but hers.

What she really wants is a replication of the artist who painted Lise's portrait when she was twelve. His name was Monsieur Nohl, which means "zero" in Russian (*nol'*), and obviously betokens an artist with no identity of his own. In comparing Chartkov's studio to "a room in the style of Teniers," she has already revealed that she regards him in much the same light, and has unwittingly forecast his fate. Unlike her 1835 incarnation, she has a clear idea of what she expects, derived no doubt from paintings she has seen in the stylized pastoral mode: "I'd like to see her dressed quite simply and to be sitting in some verdant shade, with a vista of some fields, and with flocks or a grove in the distance ... with nothing to indicate that she attends balls or fashionable parties. Our balls, you know, kill the spirit and murder the last traces of feeling ... Let there be simplicity, as much simplicity as possible!" (273).[21] This is the very opposite of Lise's true appearance: "Alas," the narrator remarks, "it could be clearly seen from the faces of the mother and daughter that they had so exerted themselves dancing at balls that they were now like wax figures" (273). Chartkov sees it too, but says nothing, and sets out to do the lady's bidding: "He seated the model, thought a minute. . . ." Here "thought" renders *soobrazil*, which carries the idea of "pondered," "reasoned," "considered," "weighed," or more literally, "put together." As we have seen, it is a word that describes the creative process for Gogol; thus it invites us to assume that Chartkov's artistic instincts are healthy. His next responses to the situation confirm the diagnosis: "[He] forgot everything else. He even forgot the presence of the aristocratic ladies and began to display some adroit artistic gestures, uttering strange sounds, occasionally humming, as is common with an artist who is totally immersed in what he is doing" (273).[22] The crucial thing here, however, is that the mother's version of the girl is not simply one piece of information that the artist is free to use as he sees fit but represents an entire vision that he is expected to transfer literally to the canvas. This is signaled by her power to interrupt him and bring him forcibly into the world of time and money, which will eventually prove to be his ruination. "Enough, that's enough for the first time!" she commands. He protests: "No, please, just a little more." But she is adamant: "'No, it is time to stop! Lise, it is already three o'clock!' said the lady, taking out a watch that hung from her waist on a gold chain" (273).

At the second sitting, Chartkov again begins to work well. Several days have passed. He has apparently forgotten all about the lady's vision of her daughter—that is, he has achieved some distance—for he begins to paint what he sees before him. His ambition is to express "something which others [have] not yet noticed," and Gogol means us to understand this as a necessary condition for true art. Yet there is danger here too: "He captured every shade, even the slight sallowness, the almost imperceptible blueness under the eyes, and he was making ready even to paint in a little pimple on her forehead" (274). The lady registers a strong objection, explaining that "Lise was just a little indisposed on that particular day only, that she normally showed no signs of any sallowness and that her face was particularly striking for its fresh color" (275). This is a typically philistine argument for ideal resemblance, but the lady is right for the wrong reasons. Chartkov has put no distance between himself and his subject; the result is a literal copy of nature, which cannot be art. He then backs off, only to surrender to another kind of imitation, one that disregards the particularity of the subject in favor of the commonplace: "*Unfeelingly*, he added to the canvas that *common* coloring which comes *automatically* [*naizust'*, lit., 'by heart'] and turns even faces taken from life into *coldly* ideal ones of the kind that can be seen in exhibits in art schools" (275). The emphases identify some of Gogol's code words for bad art. Chartkov himself uses them in his initial appraisal of the portrait of the moneylender; the suggestion that he cannot (or will not) see them now shows how far he has moved toward artistic and spiritual ruin.

In the next scene, however, he manages for a time to achieve a promising distance. Alone in his studio, he effects what amounts to a combination of his first and second approaches. He takes an old sketch of Psyche, itself a conventional subject that he has rendered in an utterly impersonal way, as suggested by the now familiar code words: "It was a pretty, girlish face, cleverly painted, but *entirely idealized, cold*, consisting of nothing but *general* features and belonging to *no living* being" (275). He now recalls the features of his living model and adds them to Psyche: "he began retouching it, putting into it all that he had observed in his aristocratic sitter. Those features, tints and tones which he had captured now appeared on it in the refined [*ochishchennoe*, lit., 'purified'] form in which they appear when the artist, after closely studying nature, moves away from it and produces a creation equal to it."[23] As a result, "Psyche began to come alive, and the faintly dawning idea began gradually to be clothed in a visible form. The type of face of the aristocratic young lady was unconsciously transferred to Psyche, and thereby [Psyche] took on a unique expression, which entitled her to be called a truly original work of art. He seemed to make use of everything, the parts and the whole, that the original offered him, and he devoted himself completely to his work" (275). The idea and the observed subject combine to make an original work, or so we are invited to think. But preexisting ideas can never be the basis for art in Gogol's world. It soon becomes clear that something is amiss. The lady and her daughter reappear just as Chartkov is finishing up the portrait. Both "uttered a cry of joy and clasped their hands in amazement":

"Lise, Lise, ah, how like you. *Superbe! Superbe!* What a wonderful idea to dress her in a Greek costume. Oh, what a surprise!"
    The artist did not know how to disillusion the ladies of their pleasant error. Shamefacedly, with drooping head, he said softly:
    "This is Psyche."
    "In the form of Psyche? *C'est charmant!*" said the mother with a smile, and her daughter smiled as well. "Don't you agree, Lise, that it suits you best to be depicted in the form of Psyche? *Quelle idée délicieuse!* What art! It's a Correggio!" (276)

This verges on one of those so-called "conversations of the deaf" that are so common in Gogol, where one interlocutor keeps repeating a word or phrase that the other hears imperfectly or not at all.[24] Chartkov and the mother seem to be talking about the same thing but are not. Chartkov sees a portrait of Psyche, not of the daughter. The mother sees a portrait of the daughter *in the form of Psyche*, an imitation of a style labeled "Correggio," which her visits to galleries have taught her to regard as respectable, even "great." Neither point of view makes for an original work of art.

    In both versions of the story, Chartkov feels a pang of conscience and wants to impart at least a slight resemblance to the original. His solution in 1835 is desultory and conventional: "He quickly dressed his Psyche in a costume of the nineteenth century, added a slight touch to the eyes and lips, lightened the hair slightly . . ." (418). The mother leaves satisfied. In 1842, he tries to move the portrait closer to what he had achieved in the first sitting, as if suddenly aware of having gone too far in the direction of idealization. As the face of Psyche begins to resemble the girl, her mother, "anxious that the resemblance might be too clearly expressed," reaffirms her vision and imposes it on him: "Enough!" Chartkov instantly does her bidding, and reaps his reward accordingly: "The artist was paid in every possible way: smiles, money, flattery, gentle pressure of the hands, invitations to dinner—in a word, he was overwhelmed with a thousand flattering words" (276). These words spread throughout high society, and he finds himself in tremendous demand.

These first sessions set a pattern from which Chartkov does not deviate until the fateful moment when he visits the picture that has been put on exhibit in the Academy. He paints not what he sees but what his clients want:

The ladies insisted that mind and character should be the chief qualities represented in their portraits, and that nothing else was important. . . . Because of this those who sat for him sometimes assumed expressions which completely amazed the artist: one made an effort to express melancholy; another, meditation. . . . As for the men, they were no better than the ladies: one insisted upon being painted with an energetic, masculine turn to his head; another on being painted with upturned and inspired eyes; a lieutenant of the guard insisted absolutely that Mars be visible in his eyes; an official in the civil service strove to create an impression of as much honesty and nobility in his face as possible, with his hand resting on a book in which the following words, plainly printed, stood out: "He always stood for truth." . . . A word was sufficient to indicate to Chartkov how someone wanted a portrait painted. (277–78)

The sitters are probably imitating portraits they have seen. But literary prototypes also serve: "[T]hose who wanted to look like Lord Byron, he painted in Byronic pose and attitude. If the ladies wanted to be shown as Corinne, Undine, Aspasia, he avidly agreed and imaginatively supplied an adequate measure of good looks, which as everyone knows can do no harm, and for the sake of which an artist may even be forgiven for any lack of resemblance" (278).[25] The result is a complete "lack of resemblance" between prototype and subject. Some five years earlier Pushkin had hinted at the same theme in the beginning of "A Journey to Arzrum" (Puteshestvie v Arzrum, 1835). There the narrator meets General A. P. Ermolov, one of the heroes of the War of 1812, and since 1816 commander-in-chief of the Caucasus: "At first glance I did not see the slightest resemblance to his portraits, which are usually done in profile. A round face, fiery gray eyes, gray hair standing on end, the head of a tiger on the torso of a Hercules. A smile that was unpleasant because it was unnatural. But when he fell pensive and frowned, then he became handsome and bore a striking resemblance to the poetic portrait painted by Dawe." Pushkin may be saying that Dawe saw through to a "real" Ermolov; more likely, the point is that Ermolov too had seen Dawe's portrait of himself, and assumed its expression on public occasions like the one in question.[26]

More than mere vanity is at issue in Gogol's version of the theme. He says in effect that the disparity between the real and the painted kills the living subject by failing to account for its uniqueness, moving it from its own place to one occupied by others. Life imitates art and in turn is imitated by art. And in painting what his subjects demand, Chartkov is denying his own vision and merely imitating the already imitative expectations of others, thereby setting himself at a double remove from his subjects, rendering an illusion of an illusion. In the process the "real" Chartkov is obscured and forgotten. Put another way, he really "becomes" everything he imitates: he is not an artist but merely another version of each of the poses he renders.

THE IMAGERY OF IMITATION

The theme of imitation in "The Portrait" is also conveyed by a tightly organized system of recurrent images. The most striking have to do with rapid and impulsive movement, bright color and light, loud sounds, habit or routine, and money. Often they cluster, as here for example: "[such a person] with nothing but a *practiced* [or 'routine,' *privychnoi*] manner, *boldness* [*boikost'yu*] of brush and *brightness of colors* [*yarkost'yu krasok*] was able to cause a general *commotion* [*shum*] and amass a *fortune* [*denezhnyi kapital*] almost *immediately* [*v mig*]" (259). For our present purposes, the three most important are self-display, money, and habit; but as we shall see, they interconnect with the others, which in turn spawn more.

The urge to self-display first takes the most obvious form of looking into a mirror:

The very first thing he did [upon finding the money in the frame] was to go to a tailor and clothe himself in fresh attire from head to foot and, like a child, he began to *examine himself* incessantly [presumably in a mirror]. . . . Then he rented the first elegant apartment, *one with mirrors and plate-glass windows*, which he came across on Nevsky Prospekt . . . and he went to a French restaurant in town about which he had heard rumors that were as vague as the rumors concerning the Chinese Empire. And there he dined in majestic style, with his arms akimbo, *looking* disdainfully at the other diners, and continually fixing his hair *in the mirror*. (269)

Mirrors of course glitter and sparkle, and in that sense extend the imagery of rapid movement and light. Painting is almost immediately invoked and associated with mirrors: we are told that Chartkov moves into his new apartment, where he "arranged the best of [his pictures] in conspicuous [lit., 'visible,' *vidnye*] places . . . and he promenaded up and down the handsome rooms, constantly *looking into the mirrors*" (270). The association is strengthened in the next sentence: "An inexorable desire to . . . *show himself* to the world awakened in his soul. He could already hear the *shouts* [*kriki*]. 'Chartkov! Chartkov! Have you *seen Chartkov's picture?*'" This is as ambiguous in Russian as in English: it can mean either "the picture representing Chartkov," or "the picture painted by Chartkov." The references to France and China associate the mirror motif with foreignness, much as in "Diary of a Madman." All this precedes the visit of the lady and her daughter, but it foretells the outcome: any picture painted by Chartkov will be a picture of himself as prescribed by others, and alien to his real self. A further broadening of the self-display motif comes when Chartkov takes "ten gold coins" from the small fortune in the picture frame and visits "the publisher of a popular daily [newspaper]." The next day an article appears in the paper under the title "Chartkov's Enormous Talent," praising "the extraordinary brightness [*yarkost'*] and freshness of the brush!" (270). Although he regards the article as an objective piece of reporting, he has paid for it himself and has supplied the contents. As we have seen, this is not the only occasion in Gogol's works when a newspaper, or something like it, functions as a mirror.

The 1835 version has no newspaper at all, and no mirrors at this point in the story, only "solid" and "large" windows in Chertkov's new apartment (262–63). Nor does another, related object figure in that earlier version: the lorgnette. This is one of the first things Chartkov buys with his newfound wealth. It was an essential item of the toilette of a young dandy: we may remember the "double lorgnette" that Eugene Onegin haughtily trains upon the audience at the ballet. But it is more than that here. Chartkov's very first customer comes armed with a lorgnette, through which she has looked at the paintings in Italian galleries and now looks at his work. The fact that Chartkov also has one suggests that their views of art are identical, as proves to be the case: both see only versions of themselves through an instrument that is itself mass-produced, that is, self-imitating. In this sense, the lorgnette functions like the other framed objects in the story—pictures, mirrors, and the newspaper article. When the lady introduces herself, she juxtaposes "article," "portrait," and "lorgnette" as if there were a natural progression: "'So much is being *written* about you. Your *portraits*, they say, are the height of perfection.' Having said this, the lady raised her *lorgnette* to her eyes" (271). The magnifying property of the lorgnette is present here too: "so much is being written" refers to only one article; "height of perfection" is certainly an exaggeration when applied to an unknown and inexperienced artist, although it merely reproduces or imitates the exaggeration already contained in the article.

"They say," in the quotation just above, connects the desire to be seen with the desire to be talked about. Both are covered by the word *slava*. It can be translated not only as "praise" and "fame" but also as "rumor," "reputation," and "glory," what people say about you. In these senses, it is a version of the "noise" or "sound" (*shum*) imagery that we have already noted. *Slava* attaches to Chartkov as soon as he finds the gold and decides to become "a first-rate artist [*slavnym khudozhnikom*]," more literally, an artist much talked about. He obtains a "splendid apartment [*slavnye kvartiry*]," one that will cause people to talk. The piece about him in the newspaper urges him to "glorify" himself and his public (*ProSLAVlyaite sebya i nas*). After his initial session with the lady and her daughter, he "rewarded himself with a first-rate [*slavnym*] dinner." With more and more commissions, "his fame [*slava*] increased"; and even though he paints the same thing over and over, his works continue to "enjoy fame [*slavoyu*]" (269, 270, 274). But the "fame" is as self-referential as the mirrors and the paintings: "Whenever *the papers* [mirror images] printed words of *praise* [*slava*] about him, he was as happy as a child, *even though he himself had bought the praise with his own money*. . . . His fame [*slava*] grew" (279). This is why he cannot "see" the paintings of other artists: "He declared that too much credit had been bestowed upon the old masters and that all that the artists could paint before Raphael was herrings, not figures . . . that not even Raphael himself always painted well . . . that Michelangelo was a braggart because he chose merely to display his knowledge of anatomy, and that there was not any grace about him." What he admires instead are "real *brilliance* [*blesk*] and *power* [*silu*] of drawing and *splendor of colors* [*kolorit*]"; and because these are surface qualities, it is not surprising that Chartkov finds them best represented in the work being done "now, in the present century" (278–79).[27] It is not surprising, either, that he has felt no compelling need to study in Italy, for Italy represents distance, past, and the "height" of painting by most of the old masters he affects to despise. For a man who consigns himself to an endless present, mirrors are an ideal substitute for true art.

Gold coins comprehend most of the important repeating images of the story. They glitter brightly; they jingle; they resemble portraits (and are thereby connected with mirrors, newspapers, and lorgnettes) in being framed and having a head on one side, albeit in profile; if of the same denomination, they are exact replicas or imitations of each other, like Chartkov's portraits. They also evoke a new image, heaviness. At first it is linked with sound. The coins hidden in the picture frame come in "*heavy [tyazhe-lye]* rolls shaped like long little pillars" that "fell on the floor with *a dull thud [s glukhim zvukom]* . . . his hand could still feel that but a minute before there was *something heavy [tyazhest']* in it . . . the molding fell on the floor, and with it, *heavily clanking [tyazhelo zvyaknuv]*, fell a roll wrapped in blue paper . . . he clasped it convulsively in his hand, which sank *from the weight [tyazhesti]*." In the presence of the gold, Chartkov experiences physical symptoms of heaviness, for which the same terminology serves: "Overpowered by an *oppressive feeling [tyagostnogo chuvstva]* . . . the *heaviness [tyagost']* in his chest was unbearable . . . the dream was so *oppressively alive [tyagostno zhiv]* in his imagination . . . he said, with a *heavy* sigh *[tyazhelo vzdokhnuv]*" (262–65). Later, as his fame increases, and with it his wealth, he begins "to *grow heavier [tolstet']*, to broaden out visibly" (280); and he experiences related symptoms of artistic and spiritual obesity, in the form of repetition, habit, coldness, boredom, and self-enclosure: "His brush grew *cold* and *dull*, and he *unfeelingly enclosed himself* [isolation] in *monotonous, pre-determined*, long since *exhausted* forms. The *monotonous, cold, forever immaculate* and, as it were, *buttoned up* [enclosed and isolated] faces of the government officials, soldiers, and statesmen did not offer his brush adequate scope." Heaviness is a common symbol of death. We may think of the scene in the *Iliad* where Zeus weighs the fates of Achilles and Hektor on the golden scales: "and Hektor's death-day was heavier / and dragged downward toward death," that is, toward the grave and the underworld.[28] Like a slowly dying body, Chartkov's world disintegrates and fragments: "Before him were only a uniform, and a bodice, and a dress coat before which the artist is unmoved [*chuvstvuet kholod*, lit., 'feels cold'] and before which all imagination withers and dies" (280).

His reaction to the picture on exhibition in the Academy of Arts looks at first like a miraculous rebirth: his "whole being, his whole life had been *awakened in one instant* . . . as though the *extinguished*[29] *sparks* of talent had *burst into flame* again. . . . He *snatched up* a brush and approached a canvas" (282). But he cannot put off his habit of making "hackneyed forms" in a "stereotyped manner." What he does is but a parody of life, like the spasms that may attend the moment of expiration, as suggested in the violent movements and the drastic foreshortening of time that call us back to the sorcerer's frantic horseback ride in "A Terrible Vengeance." He buys up "all the finest works of art," destroys them, and then falls ill: "*Acute* fever, combined with *galloping consumption* [lit., 'rapid consumption'], took such a *violent* hold on him that in *three days* he was but a shadow of his former self" (284).

As the story ends, Gogol does something he usually reserves for beginnings, clustering the other major images in a densely textured restatement of the main theme:

He began to be haunted by the long-forgotten, living *eyes* of the strange *portrait*, and then his frenzy was terrible [*uzhasno*, a word, like *strashno*, invariably associated with the portrait and with the demonic world in this story]. *All* the people who stood around his bed seemed to him like *dreadful* [*uzhasnymi*] *portraits*. The portrait was *doubled, quadrupled* [repetition and intensification, a reminder of the basic structural pattern of the story] before his eyes, and at last he imagined that *all the walls* [intensification] were hung with these portraits, *all* fastening upon him their *unmoving, living eyes* [a recapitulation of the essential paradox of animated death]. *Terrible* [*strashnye*] portraits *looked at him* from the ceiling, from the floor, the room widened and extended endlessly into space to provide more room for the *unmoving eyes*. (284–85)

These eyes are not only shaped like the other framed objects in the story—portraits, mirrors, lorgnettes, newspaper articles—but perform the same function as the grotesquely multiplied portraits in this scene. They mirror and thereby mock the version of himself that Chartkov has created in imitation of the expectations of others. The unique self has been concealed, isolated, and thereby consigned to the realm of death, which is also the realm of the demonic. No trace can be found of the gold Chartkov has accumulated. The accurate but prosaic explanation is that he has spent it all on his mad scheme. The deeper truth is that he has turned himself completely into money, and in spending the money, he spends himself. When it is gone, so is he.

10

An Anxious Eye

IF Part 1 of "The Portrait" can be read as a series of statements about what art is not, then we have only to perform an easy reversal to arrive at what Gogol thinks it should be. Besides, Chartkov himself outlines them before he succumbs to a combination of temptations and character flaws; and they surface to bedevil him after he sees the picture at the Academy. The most important concerns the boundaries of art. In the 1835 version of the story, Chertkov, contemplating the unsettling presence of the portrait, draws a distinction between "art" and "some supernatural magic that has peered forth in defiance of the laws of nature"—that is, the force contained in the portrait. On this basis he posits the possibility of a "line [*cherta*]" that "has been set as a boundary for the imagination," beyond which we must not step lest we encounter "that horrible reality into which the imagination, once given a push *from outside* [*postoronnim tolchkom*, the same adjective used in 'Old-World Landowners' to introduce Afanasy's 'little jokes,' which invoke the realm of placelessness, or extraneity], leaps from its axis" (III, 405–6). It is a reality that may nonetheless enter the world through works of art, to our incalculable cost. Certain subjects, then, are off-limits to the artist, and there seems to be no mediating vision that would allow ultimate reality to find its way into his creations. All this is in keeping with the first version's rather primitive demonism. In 1842, there is no supernatural realm, only nature—one, indivisible, and informed by "some thought, inscrutable and hidden in everything." The true artist must reveal this thought and let it permeate all his work. This is why "in the work of one artist, simple, lowly nature appears so illumined that there is no sense of degradation," whereas "in the hands of another artist, the same subject seems low and sordid, though he was true to nature, too" (260–61). Thus, there are no subjects alien to art. In this view—which is also Gogol's—there is no question of "self-expression" on the part of the artist, no question of his pursuing a vision or an idea of his own and shaping the subject of his work accordingly. This would amount to self-imitation. The artist must be a discoverer; the "idea" or "thought" inheres in the subject; all the artist can do is penetrate the surface and see it as straightforwardly and honestly as possible.

Gogol, however, may well have been reluctant to entrust reflections on the nature of true art to a character as flawed as Chartkov. At any rate, he added an extensive second part, which tells of the origin of the portrait and amplifies his theories of art.

"THE PORTRAIT": PART 2

The opening scene, virtually identical in the two versions, is set in an auction house, and sounds a familiar note of disapproval at the commercialization of art. The crowd's attention is directed to the portrait of the moneylender, when suddenly a man—old in the first version, 35 in the second—intrudes to state that this is the picture he has been looking for; he is the son of the artist who painted it. He then tells its story. There are substantial differences between the two versions in the treatment of the cityscape and the moneylender, which need not concern us here except to say that in 1835 they are far more detailed and far more indebted to the aesthetics of the physiological school. It is the figure of the artist that is most important for our purposes.

In 1835, he is immediately established as "a modest, pious painter of the kind that lived only during the religious middle ages" (433). He could easily make a good living painting secular subjects, but he prefers to specialize in religious ones, even though they condemn him and his family to poverty. At one point he becomes so destitute that he nearly resorts to the moneylender, but the temptation is lifted, or so he thinks, when he hears that the man is dying. Thereupon the moneylender's servant appears and announces that her master needs the artist urgently, with paints and brushes in hand. The artist goes out of "curiosity," tempted by the "unusual subject," and agrees to execute a portrait of the dying man. The artist of 1842 is not really poor; he earns just enough to support his family and buy art materials. Eventually he undertakes Christian subjects and secures commissions to decorate churches. One painting requires him to represent "the spirit of darkness," and as he ponders the subject, he suddenly thinks of the moneylender as the perfect model. The moneylender himself then appears at his door and requests a portrait; the artist agrees not because he needs the money but because the subject is "unusual" and answers so well to his "idea." In both versions the artist abandons the portrait in fear and revulsion. In 1835, it mysteriously keeps reappearing on the wall of his studio, despite his efforts to get rid of it. In 1842, consistent with the greater realism of the story as a whole, the portrait is brought to the house by the moneylender's servant. In both cases, however, the artist's character changes for the worse, his wife and children die, and he enters a monastery.

The account of his cloistered life is significantly different in the two versions. In 1835, he immediately obeys his superior's order to paint icons for the church, creating, among several lesser works, his masterpiece, the Virgin blessing the people, whereupon he is no longer visited by the "terrible image of the moneylender" (440). In 1842, he balks: "he was unworthy of touching a brush . . . it had been contaminated . . . he must first purify his spirit with hard work and great sacrifice before he would deem himself worthy of undertaking such a task" (300). Purification accomplished, he sets about painting the Birth of Christ. (We will presently comment on the significance of the change of subject.) Finally, there are profound differences in the message the artist imparts to his son (who is an army officer in the first version, an artist in the second). In 1835, a holy man has told him of the imminent coming of the Antichrist, who "will gallop past on a gigantic horse"; the Virgin herself has promised that as a reward for his labors, "this demon will not exist supernaturally in the portrait for all time, that if, at the end of fifty years, anyone solemnly proclaims its history during the first new moon, its power will fade and dissipate like dust" (443–44). All this is in keeping with his passive nature and his susceptibility to the supernatural. At the end, the portrait changes into an innocuous landscape before the eyes of the people who are listening to the son's story. In the final version, the artist is spiritually tough, moved from within by his own experience of the nature of creativity and art. Appropriately enough, the portrait of the moneylender now undergoes no supernatural transformation but simply disappears, perhaps quite plausibly: "Someone had succeeded in taking it away, taking advantage of the fact that the attention of the listeners was distracted by the story" (303).

MEDIATING SUBTEXTS

The very presence of a sizable section devoted largely to explaining what has come before is unusual in Gogol's fiction. Even the final chapter of *Dead Souls*, while offering a kind of summary and commentary, does so only in highly selective fashion. The closest structural parallel to Part 2 of "The Portrait" can be found in "A Terrible Vengeance," where the blind bard enters at the end to give an account of the curse that has underlain and moved the story; but this constitutes only one short chapter, and is more in the nature of a coda.

What might Gogol have had in mind? For one thing, this entire section is built around a "positive" figure, who is supposed to stand as an exemplum for artists, indeed for all of us. Such figures are rare enough in Gogol. Usually he relies on the reader to deduce the desirability of what they represent from the blighted lives that preponderate in the fiction. But in a story where the forces of evil are so compellingly and interestingly at work, and where Chartkov, as a late version of the figure of the doomed Romantic artist, might even awaken a certain sympathy, Gogol perhaps wanted to make sure we do not mistake the proper priorities and emphases. I suspect too that he wants us to measure this ideal artist against a hero figure that appeared in another story published the same year as the first version of "The Portrait": Taras Bulba. At first they seem to have little in common. Bulba is a man of action, a seventeenth-century Cossack warrior who is endowed with a flaw or two to make him seem human, but whose masculine virtues and muscular Christianity dominate the story from beginning to end. The artist-monk belongs to Gogol's own times, is a painter, not a warrior, and leads a reclusive life even outside the monastery; yet his task, Gogol would have us conclude, is just as demanding of moral and physical courage as Taras's, perhaps even more so, in that he must find his way from sin to redemption, whereas his Cossack counterpart needs only to uphold what he has known since childhood.[1] The juxtaposition of these two characters becomes even more plausible when we realize that "Taras Bulba" is also a story about art, only it is the art of the word, as we shall see below in Chapter 14. I suspect these affinities explain why "The Portrait" and "Taras Bulba" were the only stories that Gogol subjected to a painstaking and thoroughgoing revision, the results of which appeared in 1842.

Finally, the presence of Part 2 in a story about artists betrays an uneasiness about the whole process of imitation as it might bear on Gogol personally. We can easily imagine his using Chartkov as a way of examining his own credentials. There are more than a few similarities between his fictional hero and himself, or, more accurately, a version of himself that he feared he might become. The most important is Chartkov's need for mediation in order to create, and his grotesque misuse of it. At the same time, Part 2 could have enabled Gogol to address and dispel any uneasiness by demonstrating how mediating subtexts could be masterfully handled, thereby creating a poetics of imitation. Here he works in much the same manner as his artist-monk, drawing upon certain religious and aesthetic traditions. Two in particular stand out: Christianity and German Romanticism, although, as we shall see, they cannot readily be distinguished.

Christianity

Several Christian subtexts are present in Part 1, sometimes for the purpose of parody, sometimes not. One may well be the parable of the talents, especially as recorded in Matthew 25:14–30. This tells of a man who, before going on a journey, distributes his goods, in the form of talents—gold or silver pieces—among his servants, "to every man according to his several ability," in the words of the King James version. One servant receives five talents; this is a sizable sum of money, which is rendered in modern translations as "five thousand silver pieces" (*The New American Bible*) or "five bags of gold" (*The New English Bible*). He invests them and doubles their value. Another receives two talents, also invests them, and earns two more. But the servant who is given one talent buries it in the ground. When the master returns and demands a reckoning, he is pleased by the initiative of the first two servants, and rewards them. But toward the servant who buried his talent, out of fear of the "hard" master, he acts severely, taking away the one talent and giving it to the servant who now has ten: "For unto every one that hath shall be given, and he shall have abundance; but from him that hath not shall be taken away even that which he hath." Now, "talent," in the more familiar sense of an artistic gift or ability, is derived from the Latin *talentum*, which is used only to designate a unit of weight or a sum of money. The word in Russian is *talant*, which has the same range of meanings as the English "talent." There is no mention of this parable in Gogol's story, and no evidence that he had it in mind while he wrote. But it fits Chartkov's situation so well that most readers who know their Bible (as Gogol's contemporaries surely did) cannot help but find it silently present, as Gogol may well have intended. The proper investment of talent involves much self-deprivation, according to the aesthetics of the story. But Chartkov fears the hard regimen of poverty, and buries his talent in service to the false values of quick fame and wealth. When he tries to recover it, after seeing the picture exhibited at the Academy, he realizes, in despair, that it is gone.[2]

Another Christian subtext is hinted at in the portrait of the moneylender, with his prominent eyes and confrontational manner. This reminds us of figures in Orthodox icons, through which a divine power (or a demonic one, in Gogol's case) enters the world. A biblical text may be at work here too. I am thinking of chapter 17 of that book deemed apocryphal by Protestants but not by Roman Catholics and Eastern Orthodox: *Wisdom*, or, as it is also known, *The Wisdom of Solomon*. It tells of the darkness that afflicts the Egyptians as punishment for their sin of enslaving the Israelites:

For they who supposed that their secret sins were hid under the dark veil of oblivion [w]ere scattered in fearful trembling, terrified by apparitions. For not even their inner chambers kept them fearless, for crashing sounds on all sides terrified them, and mute phantoms with somber looks appeared. . . . So they, during that night . . . [w]ere partly smitten by fearsome apparitions and partly stricken by their soul's surrender; for fear came upon them, sudden and unexpected.

We vividly remember what happens to Chartkov in the "darkness" of his insanity: he is fixed by staring eyes that seem to see his secret sin, and he dies in terror. The text from *Wisdom* came to fascinate Gogol. Five years later, one of the letters in *Selected Passages from Correspondence with Friends* would bear a title, "The Fears and Terrors of Russia," that is taken from this chapter of *Wisdom*, and would paraphrase most of it, although with a significant omission that we will consider in the last section of this book.[3]

Another subtext that is Christian, though not uniquely so, associates evil with physical ugliness and goodness with beauty.[4] Chartkov's mania for buying up and destroying paintings that show signs of talent (and are therefore "beautiful") is called "the most *hellish* [*adskoe*] design which the heart of man has ever cherished." The narrator describes how

with *frenzied* [*beshenoyu*, lit., "demonic"] *violence* he *flew* to carry it out [rapidity of movement, especially when conjoined to violence, is a demonic trait] . . . with the *fury* [*beshenstvom*, lit., "demonicalness," or "rabies"] of a tiger he fell upon it, tore it, rent it, cut it up into *little scraps* [fragmentation is also a demonic trait]. . . . The enormous wealth which he had amassed enabled him to gratify this *fiendish* [*adskomu*, lit., "hellish"] desire. . . . No ignorant *monster* [*chudovishche*] ever destroyed so many wonderful works of art. . . . It was as if a wrathful heaven had sent this *terrible scourge* [*uzhasnyi bich*] into the world specifically to *deprive it of its harmony* [one traditional function of the devil]. . . . It was as if that *terrible demon* which Pushkin had described had been reincarnated in him. (284–85)[5]

In the process, he becomes hideous: "[H]atred *distorted* his features. He ground his teeth and devoured [the paintings] with the eyes of a *basilisk*. . . . A *horrible* color created by this passion suffused his face. On his features were expressed scorn for the world, and blame [*otritsanie*, lit., 'negation']. . . . [I]n three days he was only a *shadow* of his former self. . . . His corpse was *dreadful* to behold" (284–85). We are reminded that several of Pseudo-Dionysius's criteria of evil have an aesthetic dimension as well: "lack," "weakness," "non-symmetrical," "non-intention," "non-beauty," "non-life," "non-complete," "undefined," "limited," "obscure."[6] In fact, virtually all Gogol's characters are unattractive, physically and morally, or, if conventionally attractive at first glance, prove on closer scrutiny to be askew in some way. Ulinka, for instance, in Part 2 of *Dead Souls*, though strikingly beautiful, is as lifeless as a marble statue or a cameo. The same can be said of Annunciata in "Rome," even though Gogol intends us to see her in a positive light too.

By contrast, most of the characters in Gogol's works who are physically attractive are also beautiful in spirit, like Kostanzhoglo in Part 2 of *Dead Souls*. To this small company belongs the artist-monk in "The Portrait." His son goes to visit him for the first time in twelve years and, having "heard some comment about his austerity," expects to "meet a recluse of *rough exterior*, a man who had *become estranged from everything in the world* but his cell and his prayers, a man who was *worn out and shriveled* from eternal fasting and penance." So the standards of the world would dictate. Instead, the son is astonished to find "a *handsome* [*prekrasnyi*: used for both physical and spiritual qualities], almost *inspired* [*bozhest-vennyi*, lit., 'divine'] old man! And on his face there was *no trace of exhaustion. It shone* with the *light* of heavenly *joy*. His beard was *white as snow*, and his thin, almost *transparent* hair, of the same *silvery* hue, fell *picturesquely* over his breast" (301). Such physical beauty is standard in Russian medieval saints' lives, with the virtually unique exception of Efrem's thirteenth-century *Life of Abraham of Smolensk*, where the holy man is emaciated from fasting. In fact, Gogol's monk bears a stronger resemblance to a figure in an icon. This not only is more appropriate in a story about painting but picks up an image much favored by theologians in their accounts of the process of spiritual perfection, of moving closer to the "image and likeness" of God. As Gerhard Ladner observes: "the Greek Fathers ever so often described this process as the cleaning of a painting, spoiled but not completely ruined by the application of wrong colors and especially by accumulation of dirt and dust." Origen even represented Christ as a painter ("Filius Dei est pictor"). Related to painting, as Ladner points out, is the image, found for example in Gregory of Nyssa, of the soul as a "living mirror," which "again begins to express in itself the pure form of the unmixed beauty" after it has "thrown off all material blemish."[7] Similarly, it is only after a lengthy cleansing process that Gogol's artist-monk declares himself ready to paint the kind of icon his superior had originally requested. His regimens as a painter and as a hermit are identical: the painting is also in effect a "mirror" that must not be sullied but be kept clean to reflect the "mirror" of the soul, both mirrors in turn reflecting God in all His glory, and both contrasting with the false mirrors that abound in Part 1.

The story of the monk makes it easier to understand how a writer brought up in a culture saturated by Christian Neoplatonism could so readily move between aesthetic, religious, and moral judgments; how, ultimately, all were synonymous for him; and why he rested such enormous moral weight on art. Some students of Gogol detect a movement from "aesthetic" to "religious." As Mochulsky puts it: "For Gogol the artist, the worship of beauty [in the works of the middle period] made a natural transition to a religious attitude."[8] I would qualify this statement only to say "an *overtly* religious attitude," inasmuch as "religious" and "beautiful" co-existed in Gogol's mind from the beginning and were interchangeable. In "The Portrait," particularly in the 1842 version but even in 1835, all the flaws in Chartkov's life are "aesthetic" since they are expressed in and through his painting, but they are at bottom spiritual—ambition, haste, impatience, intolerance, and moral cowardice.

Vasari and German Romanticism

The combination of religion and art in "The Portrait" suggests that we look in two other directions for more immediate sources. First, let us consider the German Nazarenes, a group of painters who, as students at the Vienna Academy in 1809, conceived a distaste for the neoclassical pitch of the curriculum, especially its pagan thematology. Aspiring to create a Christian art, this group formed an organization called the Brotherhood of St. Luke (*Lukasbund*), after the evangelist who is the patron saint of painters. For inspiration they looked to the so-called "primitives" of the Italian *quattrocento*, to the early Raphael, and to Dürer. One of their guiding spirits and ultimately their most important painter was Friedrich Overbeck, whose *Joseph Being Sold by His Brothers* (1816–17) is typical of their subject matter. The Brotherhood moved to Rome in 1810, and shortly thereafter renamed itself "Followers of Dürer" (*Düreristen*). The corresponding Italian movement, known as Purism, found its most influential representative in Tommaso Minardi. Some of the religious paintings of Ingres, who lived and worked in Rome from 1806 to 1809 and again from 1835 to 1841, reflect the concerns of these groups as well.[9] By the time Gogol set about revising "The Portrait," he was certainly familiar with their work.

A far more important source, however, is to be found in a literary work that had enormous influence on the Nazarenes: Wilhelm Heinrich Wackenroder's *Confessions of the Heart of an Art-Loving Friar*, which was written with Ludwig Tieck and published in 1796. The first Russian translation appeared in 1826.[10] Wackenroder's celebration of Italy as the home of true art and the model for all serious painters was nothing new. Nor were his characterizations of Italy: "[the place] where my soul's thoughts are dwelling constantly, where is the native land of the most beautiful hours of my life" (112), and where one finds "the clear sky, the vast delightful views through which invigorating air blows playfully" (132). Similar phrases and sentiments crop up in many other responses to Italy, including Gogol's. But there are more important parallels.

Like Gogol, Wackenroder is interested less in scenery than in the spiritual dimensions of the Italian experience, particularly as expressed in works of art, Raphael, Leonardo, and Michelangelo being the supreme masters. As he puts it: "They made the art of painting into a faithful servant of religion. . . . [I]n chapels and on altars their pictures inspired the holiest sentiments in the one who knelt down and prayed before them" (145). His ideal, in fact, is the artist who is at the same time a monk or a priest, with characteristics familiar to readers of Part 2 of "The Portrait." In describing Fra Angelico (Giovanni da Fiesole), for instance, he notes: "He did not concern himself with the world at all, even declined the office of archbishop which the Pope offered to him, and always lived quietly, peacefully, humbly and in solitude. He used to pray every time, just before he began to paint; then he set to work and carried it out as heaven had presented it to him, without pondering over it and criticizing it further. For him, painting was a holy penance" (145). For Wackenroder, as for Gogol, such dedication stands in glaring contrast to the practices of the painters of his time, who strive for merely "external beauty" and effects of light and gaudy color, to the detriment of the human figure. Yet for all the magnificence of the Italians, Wackenroder believed that Germany had an equally great national artist in Albrecht Dürer. Gogol might have found a comparable master in Andrei Rublyov (ca. 1360/70–1427/30), and perhaps this painter is silently present in the figure of the artist-monk. Certainly Gogol put none of his contemporaries in that league, although Aleksandr Ivanov would have seemed a plausible candidate, having spent two decades creating his masterpiece *The Appearance of Christ to the People*. (Five years later, in *Selected Passages from Correspondence with Friends*, Gogol devoted an entire admiring article to him.) The Nazarenes even envisaged a kind of cooperative venture between the German art of their day and the Italian Renaissance.[11] Gogol does not go that far. But he does suggest, without explicitly making the comparison, that the artist-monk might well become a Dürer-like figure, insofar as he is strictly a local product who never visits Italy and need not do so, for he is of equal magnitude with the great Italian masters.

Gogol's view of the way great art affects its audience would be familiar to readers of the *Confessions*. When Wackenroder complains of the commercialization of art, wherein galleries are "regarded as annual fairs" whose visitors appraise the "new products," we think of the noisy auction room at the beginning of Part 2 of "The Portrait." Instead, galleries should be "temples where, in peaceful and silent humility and in heart-lifting solitude, one might admire the great artists" (126). To create such works, the artist must himself have achieved serenity, for he is not the subject of art but only "a useful instrument to receive all of Nature within [himself] and give birth to it again, beautifully transformed, animated with the spirit of man" (125). Annibale Carracci, for one, "felt the *silent greatness* of art very deeply" (142). Yet silent contemplation leads to activity, for Wackenroder as well as for Gogol: one "kneels" before the work, and arises "happier and more melancholy, with a fuller and lighter heart, and applies his hand to a large, good enterprise" (126).

Wackenroder's account of Fra Angelico is taken from Giorgio Vasari, with very little embellishment, as are several other accounts of painters in the *Confessions*.[12] Vasari was not translated into Russian until the 1930's. But Gogol read Italian and French with ease, and may have studied him after taking up residence in Rome. He attributes the story of Leonardo da Vinci's portrait with "living eyes" specifically to Vasari, in a passage that was added to the 1842 version: "Suddenly he [Chartkov] remembered he had long ago heard from his professor a story of a portrait by Leonardo da Vinci. The great master regarded it as unfinished though he had labored on it for several years, but despite that, Vasari considered it the most complete and finished example of his art. The most finished thing about it was the eyes, which amazed Leonardo's contemporaries; the most minute, almost invisible veins were not neglected and were committed to the canvas" (260). In Vasari: "Whoever shall desire to see how far art can imitate nature, may do so to perfection in this head, wherein every peculiarity that could be depicted by the utmost subtlety of the pencil has been faithfully reproduced. The eyes have the lustrous brightness and moisture which is seen in life, and around them are those pale, red, and slightly livid circles, also proper to nature, with the lashes, which can only be copied, as these are, with the greatest difficulty."[13] This information is missing from Wackenroder's accounts of Leonardo. However, the larger context in which Gogol embeds it—the behavior of the portrait once it is removed to Chartkov's quarters—comes not from Vasari but very possibly from Wackenroder, where—in a double distancing—it refers not to Leonardo but to Raphael. According to the *Confessions*, Raphael had always been obsessed with the Madonna, but could not imagine how to paint her. Finally, he made a tentative beginning. One night, just after he woke up with a start,

his eye was attracted by a bright light on the wall opposite his bed and, when he had looked closely, he had perceived that his picture of the Madonna, still uncompleted, had been hung upon the wall, illuminated by the gentlest light, and had become a perfect and truly living image. . . . It had looked at him with its eyes in an indescribably touching manner and, at each moment, had seemed as if it wanted to move; and it had seemed to him as if it also really were moving. (84)

Could this be the source of Gogol's account of the moneylender's picture after Chartkov takes it home? "The light of the moon, illuminating the room, fell upon it and invested it with a singular lifelike quality. . . . Almost the whole face seemed to have come alive, and the eyes looked at him in a way that made him shudder, and jumping back, he exclaimed in a loud

voice full of astonishment, 'It looks, it looks at you with human eyes!'"
(260). He goes to bed, and then:

> Through the chink in the screen he could see the illumination of the moon in the
> room, and he saw the portrait immediately in front of him, hanging on the wall.
> The eyes were fixed upon him . . . [the portrait] stared straight at him; stared
> straight into his heart. . . . [S]uddenly he saw that the old man began moving and,
> presently, supporting himself on the frame with both arms, he raised himself on his
> hands and, thrusting out his legs, he leaped out of the frame. (261–62)

If in fact this is a demonized version of Wackenroder's story of Raphael, it
reinforces the intimations that Chartkov is an evil parody of a true artist.

Far more specific is the parallel between the Vasari/Wackenroder account of Francesco Francia's reaction to Raphael's painting of St. Cecilia
and Gogol's account of Chartkov's reaction to the painting (subject unspecified) sent to the Academy of Arts by the Russian artist living in Italy.
Here, paraphrased and somewhat abridged, is Vasari's account. Francia,
living in Bologna, and Raphael, living in Rome, had never met but had
heard high praise of each other. Raphael, having painted a picture of St.
Cecilia on commission from a church in Bologna, wrote Francia asking
him to supervise its installation and, in the process, to repair any scratch
and correct any defect. Francia agreed. On seeing the picture, however,
"such was the astonishment it caused him, and so great was his admiration
for it" that he perceived "his own error and the foolish presumption with
which he had weakly believed in his own superiority." The painting is described as "divine—not painted, but absolutely alive." Francia compares
"the beauties of this most exquisite picture with his own works, which he
saw around him," and "felt as one terrified and half deprived of life." He
goes ahead with the installation, but "having become like a man beside
himself, he took to his bed a few days after [the installation], appearing to
himself to be now almost as nothing in art, when compared with what he
had believed himself, and what he had always been considered. Thus he
died, as many believe, of grief and vexation," although there is also a hint
of a darker reason that brings him closer to Chartkov: "incurring the same
fate from so earnestly contemplating the living picture of Raphael, as that
which befell Fivizzano, from too fixedly regarding his own beautiful painting of Death" (II, 313–14).

Wackenroder repeats this story, with credit to Vasari, but embellishes it
in ways that passed into Gogol's "Portrait": he "wept bitter, smarting tears
that he had consumed his life in conceited, ambitious toil and, in the process, had only made himself increasingly foolish and that he now, close to
death, had to look back with open eyes upon his entire life as upon a
wretched, uncompleted bit of bungling." As he left the room, he saw some

of his own paintings, especially a St. Cecilia (not identified in Vasari), and "almost passed away in pain." Thereafter he became unhinged: "his emotions were in constant turmoil and there was almost always a certain absentmindedness about him" (90). As for Chartkov,

confused tears and sobs broke from him in response, and he ran out of the hall like one possessed . . . he stood senseless and motionless in the middle of his magnificent studio. . . . . Good God! To have ruined so ruthlessly all the best years of his youth, to have destroyed, to have quenched, the spark of fire that glowed perhaps in his breast. . . . 'Did I ever really have any talent?' he finally said. 'Didn't I deceive myself?' And having uttered these words he turned to his old paintings . . . and with great care began to examine them all. (282–83)

The difference is that Chartkov has willfully betrayed his own talent and served himself, whereas Francia has cultivated his gifts for the greater glory of God.

Finally, Wackenroder tells us that Francia's own paintings "now darted through his soul with distorted features and were the tormenters which frightened him in his fevers" (90). Shortly thereafter he is found dead. This does not occur in Vasari, but finds an amplified echo in the "symptoms of hopeless insanity" that Chartkov experiences while in an "acute fever": "Terrible portraits [all of the moneylender] looked at him from the ceiling, from the floor, and to crown it all he saw the room grow larger and extend into space to provide more room for those staring eyes. . . . At last he died in a final paroxysm of speechless agony" (284–85). Although Chartkov has not literally painted the portrait of the moneylender, his paintings have all been "demonic" because they have been copies of one another while pretending to be unique. So the staring eyes function as a symbol of his own art, and in that sense are like Francia's as well.

In the *Confessions*, Wackenroder moves on to consider poetry and music as well, and deals with them more extensively than does Gogol in "Sculpture, Painting and Music." Nonetheless, the emphasis remains solidly fixed on painting, possibly because of the interesting anecdotal material it provided him, through Vasari, and certainly because Wackenroder, like Gogol, tended to think of artistic perception in terms of seeing and to make painting stand for the other arts. In a version of Horace's dictum, he calls painting "a poetry with pictures of human beings," and goes on to make the point that poets and painters work with the same end in view; only the means are different. Words and expressions, he thinks, are analogous to brush strokes. Michelangelo, for example, "wanted to stamp into every nerve of his figures the sublime poetic power with which he was filled," working in this way like "poets in whom an inextinguishable lyrical fire is burning" and who are "not content with great and mighty *ideas*, but also strive particularly to imprint their bold and wild strength in the visible, sensual instrument of their art, in expression and words" (129–30).

However, Wackenroder insists here and there that words are inadequate to describe works of visual art. In the case of the Carracci brothers, for example, Annibale could only draw and paint, but Agostino could also write, and "liked to talk at length about artistic matters." After the brothers saw the Laocoön group, Agostino described it to a group of acquaintances in great detail; Annibale stood silent and "lost in a dream, as if he were not comprehending." When Agostino asked him if he had felt nothing, Annibale "silently took a piece of charcoal, went up to the wall, and quickly sketched the outlines of the entire Laocoon group from memory so accurately and correctly that one believed he was seeing it before his own eyes. Then he smilingly stepped back from the wall,—but all those present were amazed and Agostino acknowledged his defeat and recognized him as the victor in the competition" (142–43). This does not really unmake Wackenroder's point that the visual and the verbal accomplish the same thing through different means; but Annibale clearly prefers the visual, and raises the possibility of the inadequacy of the verbal (or the incommensurability of the two arts), as Gogol would also come to do.

BACKING OFF

In his articles, Gogol insisted that the artist must not invent but avail himself of ready-made materials. In a sense, the artist is a translator, as Gogol suggested in a glowing testimony, written late in his career, to Vasily Zhukovsky, much of whose professional life was devoted to turning the work of other writers into Russian. "You look through the titles of his poems," Gogol says, "and you see: one [poem] is taken from Schiller, another from Uhland, a third from Walter Scott, still another from Byron, and everything is a true copy, word for word, the personality of each poet is preserved, and there is no place for the translator to push himself to the fore." However, "when you have read several of these poems, you suddenly ask yourself: whose poems have I been reading? And it is not Schiller, nor Uhland, nor Walter Scott who appears before your eyes, but a poet who is different from them all, and worthy to take his place not at their feet but beside them, as equal to equal." What may look like an apology for so much translating implicitly rests on the distinction between "imagining" and "assembling" that Gogol elsewhere makes to describe the workings of his own artistic mind: it is not that Zhukovsky lacked creative power, but that he "did not feel like inventing his own," any more than Gogol, as he tells it, was able to "invent" plots for his own works.[14]

Gogol himself made lavish appropriations of themes, ideas, and styles from his predecessors. His works alone would enable us to deduce much of the history of Russian literature, along with its borrowings from the West. Many of his characters have readily identifiable prototypes: the *picaro* for Chichikov, the "little man" of the French physiological school for Akaky Akakievich, Greek mythology for Afanasy Ivanovich and Pulkheria Ivanovna. But it is what he does with these materials that is ultimately important. This elementary point is sometimes lost on scholars who like to run down the sources, most notoriously V. V. Vinogradov, in whose ramblingly detailed articles Gogol often disappears completely.[15] Actually, Gogol may have been afraid not so much of disappearing as of being thought unoriginal. As we have seen, the way he handles the prince in "Rome" indicates anything but an abundance of self-confidence. Late in his career, he made a special point of his distress with readers who charged that the moral and spiritual teachings in *Selected Passages from Correspondence with Friends* were derivative: "I cannot conceal that fact that I was even more pained when equally intelligent people . . . proclaimed in print that there was nothing new in my book, and that what might be new was a lie, not the truth. That seemed cruel to me." In what amounts to a restatement of his artistic credo, he declares his indebtedness—in this case to the spiritual teachers of the past—but insists that he is "not like others in all respects," has "certain qualities that are his alone," and therefore could not help but write a book that had "something new" in it.[16]

As late as 1847, then, we see evidence of a persistent anxiety about what we have called imitation. Perhaps it was inspired in part by a growing awareness of the kind of problem that Plato so famously addresses in Book X of *The Republic*. A real artist, Plato says, "would be interested in realities and not in imitations"; but all poets from Homer on are "only imitators; they copy images of virtue and the like, but the truth they never reach." Consequently, "[t]he imitator or maker of the image knows nothing of true existence; he knows appearances only," inasmuch as imitation is "concerned with that which is thrice removed from the truth" (599–601, Jowett translation). If for "appearances" we read "mediation," as I think we legitimately can in the case of Gogol, then we come closer to an understanding of Gogol's growing reservations and apprehensions about the proper functions of the artist.

These explorations of the dangers of mediation were made almost entirely in the context of painting, in "The Portrait" explicitly, in "Rome" implicitly. (Indeed, Plato, in the passage excerpted above, begins his argument with reference to the painter as "a creator of appearances.") It is as if the visual mode is particularly open to outright copying, perhaps because dazzling surfaces can blind artists to the truer things underneath. We have considered some of the ways in which Gogol tried to ensure that this would not happen to him. At the same time, he was showing signs of greater skepticism about seeing as the right way of apprehending the world. It is evident even in "The Portrait" and "Rome," those two stories that look like celebrations of the joy of seeing, at least, seeing of the proper kind.

Let us look first at the closing pages of "The Portrait." The 1835 version shows a visual concreteness lacking in 1842. The cloister to which the artist repairs is described as "a solitary monastery amidst a pale and bare nature," with "long galleries rotted through in places, green with moss," all of which inspires in the narrator a "poetic oblivion": it gives "a strange, indefinite direction to my thoughts, of the kind we usually feel in late autumn, when the leaves rustle beneath our feet, and there is not a leaf above our heads, when the sky shows through a web of sparse black branches, the ravens croak far aloft, and we involuntarily quicken our step, as if trying to collect our scattered thoughts" (441). None of this is original, being derived, in theme and style, from the literature of Sentimentalism, perhaps from the opening pages of Karamzin's "Poor Liza."[17] Nonetheless, it fixes the scene graphically in our minds. As Sentimentalist convention dictates, the old monk has a "pale, exhausted face"; but more interesting, vivid, and memorable are the Gogolian touches of his dispassionate eyes, which burn with an "unearthly fire" that makes him look like an artist in the throes of inspiration; his motionless body, which reminds his son of a saint in an icon; his religious name, Grigory, whose Russianness contrasts with the Frenchness of the son's name, Leon; and his account of the coming of the Antichrist, to which we have already referred. By contrast, the icon on which he toils for so long, the Virgin blessing the people, is described in the sketchiest possible way, with the Virgin wearing a "profound expression of divinity on her face" (442); yet the subject is unusual enough to single it out from the usual run of icons.

The 1842 version eliminates nearly all these particulars. We find no description of the monastery. Instead we are told only that the old man, who now has no name,

retired into the wilderness so that he could be absolutely alone. And there he built a hut of tree branches, and he ate only uncooked roots, and he dragged a large stone from place to place, and he stood on the same spot with his hands lifted to heaven from the time the sun went up until the time it went down, and, without stop, he recited his prayers. . . . He experienced every possible degree of suffering and pitiless self-abnegation, examples of which can be found only in some lives of the saints. (300)

Indeed, such scenes are virtually topoi in hagiographies. The only striking thing about the man is his healthy and cheerful appearance, which is unusual for an ascetic. The subject of his painting has also undergone a change. It is now the Nativity of Christ, one of the most common motifs in Christian art:

[The monks] were all struck by the wonderful holiness of the figures. The expression of divine humility and gentleness on the face of the Holy Mother as she bent over the Child; the profound intelligence in the eyes of the Holy Child, as though they perceived something from afar; the triumphant silence of the Magi, amazed by the Divine Miracle as they prostrated themselves at His feet, and finally, the ineffable tranquillity which pervaded the entire picture—all this was presented with such harmonious strength and great beauty that the impression it created was magical. All of the brethren fell on their knees before the new icon. (300–301)

On first reading this looks far more detailed than the description of the painting in the 1835 version. But Gogol is actually relying on us to call to mind the countless paintings of the Nativity we have all seen, and to transfer their details in our mind's eye to a literary canvas that is virtually devoid of particulars.

We may also remember, as I think Gogol intends, the religious painting that appears in Part 1 of the story and occasions such a turn in Chartkov's mind. Again we find substantial differences in the way each version accounts for it. In 1835:

Pure, stainless, lovely as a bride, the painter's work stood before him. There was not the faintest sign of desire to dazzle, of pardonable vanity, no thought of showing off to the crowd, none, none at all! It rose modestly. It was simple, innocent, divine as talent, as genius. The amazingly lovely figures were grouped unconstrainedly, freely, not touching the canvas, and they seemed to be bashfully casting down their lovely eyelashes in amazement at so many eyes fixed upon them. The features of those divine faces breathed with the mysteries which the soul has no power, no means to convey to another. The inexpressibly expressible rested on them; and all this had been put on the canvas so lightly, so modestly and freely, that it might have seemed the fruit of a moment's inspiration suddenly dawning in the artist's mind. The whole picture was a moment, but it was a moment for which all human life had been only a preparation. Involuntary tears were ready to run down the cheeks of the visitors who stood around the picture. It seemed as though all tastes, all daring and mistaken deviations of taste were blended into a silent hymn to the divine work of art. (421–22)[18]

Work, artist, and audience are all considered here. But the painting receives by far the most attention. Presumably it "stands" on an easel, or is propped against a wall. We may therefore wonder how it can be said to "rise modestly." The Russian is rather odd too: *voznosilos' skromno*. Garnett/Kent's rendition into smooth English—"It excelled with modesty"—is not wrong, but selects only one of the possible meanings. I think Gogol wants us also to have in mind the religious idea of the Ascension of Christ, which in Russian is *voznesenie*, a gerund formed from the same verb. At the same time, he may be alluding to an important technique of Baroque and Mannerist art, whereby painted and sculpted figures appear to float or rise, in defiance of the laws of gravity, like the figures in this particular painting when they are said not to be touching the canvas. (Garnett/Kent has "as if not touching," but there is no such qualification in the Russian.) Visitors to the interiors of many Roman churches of the seventeenth and eighteenth centuries, with ceilings painted to resemble the sky, will be familiar with this phenomenon. So Gogol is inviting us to think of paintings of a specific style and period, which we may use to fill out the details, otherwise all but nonexistent, of the canvas in his story. Vague as the painting is—we do not even know the subject—it does nonetheless dominate the passage.

The first line of the 1842 version is an almost exact repetition of 1835, and the three or four lines that follow, ending in "fixed upon them," are a close but compressed restatement, which includes the "rising" verb and the detail of the feet and thereby invites us to continue thinking of the Baroque. But substantial change then gets under way: "Everything seemed to have been joined together: intensive study of Raphael, as reflected in the lofty nobility of the postures; intensive study of Correggio, which permeated the ultimate perfection of the brush." Gogol moves us back to an earlier period, where, as he says elsewhere in the story, the true greatness of Italian art resided, and by specifying two towering figures, makes it even easier for us to picture what the Academy painting probably looked like. But the visual details are even sketchier than in 1835. He is now far more interested in the other two aspects of the scene. Picking up the 1835 idea of "inspiration suddenly dawning in the artist's mind," he shifts almost entirely away from the canvas: "But most forceful of all was the creative power that had already been contained [*zaklyuchennaya*] in the soul of the artist himself." It is not clear whether in 1835 the inspiration entered the artist, muse-like, from outside; but in 1842, the "power" is clearly the same as that found in nature itself: "Captured everywhere was that flowing roundness of lines contained [*zaklyuchennaya*, as in the soul] in nature, which can be seen only by the eye of the artist-creator and which comes out all angles in the hands of the mere copyist." Gogol is still concerned with the way energy manifests itself in visually apprehensible forms, which pass, apparently intact, to the canvas. What we actually see is "how everything extracted from the outside world the artist first included [*zaklyuchil*] in his own soul and then, from his spiritual source [*rodnika*], directed it out in a single harmonious, triumphant song." Apparently we are supposed to imagine what a "song" looks like, but Gogol has in fact moved entirely away from the visual. The process of creation described here could apply to any of the arts, as could the general statement that follows: "And it became clear even to the uninitiated how immeasurable was the chasm separating a creation and a mere copy from nature." Gogol then turns to the viewers. In the 1835 version, it is they who direct the "silent hymn" to the painting; in 1842, the "song" emanates from the artist, and is not described as "silent." Now it is the viewers themselves who stand in "extraordinary silence," an attitude that presumably allows them to hear, as it were, the "song." They look at the canvas but do not see it since, in an expansion of the "rising" image of 1835, it seems to move "higher and higher," first becoming transfigured and then altogether decorporealized: "more brightly and miraculously it detached itself from everything and finally turned entirely into a single instant [*mig*], the fruit of a thought that had flown onto the artist from the heavens [not, as before, from the earth], and a moment for which all human life had been only a preparation." Then comes, in the same words as 1835, the detail of tears about to run down the cheeks of the viewers; only now it has been somewhat defamiliarized because it supports the theme of vision obscured. In Chapter 12 below, we will see how this same shift from the concrete or visual to the abstract, rendered in somewhat the same terms, occurs at the end of *Dead Souls*. What is striking is that it is present in a story about painting and that it is present, at least embryonically, as early as 1835.

Because this is the only other religious picture in the story, it inevitably determines the way we see the icon painted by the old monk in the closing pages of Part 2. Lest we miss the lesson, several key images are transferred from that earlier scene and clustered within the icon itself: "solemn silence [*torzhestvennoe molchanie*]," "inexpressible quietness [*nevyrazimaya tishina*]," the "harmonious power and might of beauty [*soglasnoi sile i mogushchestve krasoty*]," and "higher power [*vysshaya sila*]" (III, 134; this passage occurs in Garnett/Kent, II, 300–301, but is not translated literally enough for my purposes). But the result, oddly enough, is a further despecification of the icon. We have been told that as a young man, the artist had seen works by Raphael, Leonardo, Titian, and Correggio; but more important is the information that he was "one of those natural geniuses," a "self-taught artist who without teachers or schools discovered in his own soul the rules and laws of art" (294) and who has never studied in Italy. Even when we try to fill in the unspecified details of his painting from what we know of these Italian masters, we are aware that the more relevant context is that of Russian icon painting, which is virtually anonymous. The one tradition seems to cancel the other, and we are left with no firm visual reference point. But that is how Gogol wants it. The effect of this whole concluding passage is to suggest that holiness is not only essential for good art but ultimately more important and more real. The artist in "The Portrait" achieves authenticity not so much by imitating the divine, admirable though that may be, as by seeking to become as nearly divine as possible himself, a condition in which art is no longer necessary. This further removes the monk from the "ordinary" world, which Gogol elsewhere insisted was the real subject of art, and accounts, I think, for our sense that this figure is ultimately too abstract to speak to us in any meaningful way.

The portrait of the moneylender also undergoes visual despecification in the final paragraph. The son ends his story, and his listeners turn their faces to the wall where the portrait is hanging. In the 1835 version, it gradually changes: the eyes of the moneylender lose their lifelikeness, the outlines of the figure fade, and "something indefinite" remains, which proves, on closer inspection, to be just "an innocent landscape." One picture has been replaced by another. In 1842, the son first looks at the wall, and the listeners then follow suit "in one instant." This is the same word (*mig*) that described the disappearance of the painting in Part 1; if we remember it, we are prepared for what now happens: "it was no longer on the wall." There is no innocent landscape, nor even an empty frame, but simply a blank space, leaving the viewers to speculate whether the portrait was stolen or whether it was "merely a dream which had flashed before their eyes, strained from long examination of old pictures" (303).

At issue here is the failure not so much of imitation as of "seeing." In effect, the story "sees" itself out of existence. So does "Rome," but in a very different way.

In groups and singly, one from behind the other, emerged houses, roofs, statues, airy terraces and galleries; there the entire mass shimmered in a motley play of delicate belfry-tops and domes, with the patterned capriciousness of lanterns; there a dark palace emerged complete; there the flat dome of the Pantheon; there the decorated pinnacle of the Column of Antoninus [Marcus Aurelius], with the capital and the statue of the Apostle Paul; still more to the right the Capitoline buildings, with their steeds and statues, raised their tops; still more to the right, above the gleaming mass of houses and roofs, majestically and austerely soared the dark breadth of the Colosseum's bulk; there another play of walls, terraces, and domes, bathed in the blinding dazzle of the sun. And at a distance, above this entire gleaming mass, darkly rose the blackish green tops of the stone oaks of the Ludovisi and Medici villas, and standing over them, in the air, was a whole herd of Roman pines, raised on slender trunks, with cupola-shaped tops. And then all along the entire length of the picture rose the azure heights of the transparent hills, light as air, embraced in a phosphorescent light. . . . The air was so pure and transparent that the slightest small feature of buildings far distant was clear, and everything seemed close enough to be grasped with the hand. The tiniest architectural ornament, the patterned decoration of a cornice—everything was etched in incomprehensible purity. (III, 258–59)

Surveys of Rome—a theme perhaps initiated by the meeting between Evander and Aeneas in Book VIII of the *Aeneid*—had attracted painters for centuries. Gogol's scene, or "picture," as it is called here, certainly owes much to the tradition, and is also a composite of the earlier ones in the story, with their buildings and statues, old and new, and their landscape of sky and trees. The familiar palette is here too, with its contrasts of light and dark relieved by spots of color. In the transition from full daylight to dusk, Gogol introduces a large-scale narrative movement that could be imitated only by series or groupings of paintings, then much in fashion, of the Romantic landscape at different times of day. The illusion of a dynamic canvas is also created by constant shifts of perspective, as the eye now picks out and scrutinizes individual details, now draws back to survey the whole. Suddenly sound intrudes, as a "cannon shot" signals "the end of the Carnival day." If this represents an equivalent of the insects and the hooting, buzzing people of the earlier scenes, with a corresponding opportunity for fresh perception, it too is lost, as all dissolves into touristy enthusing— "Lord, what a view!"—and then into nothingness: the prince "forgot himself, and the beautiful Annunciata, and the mysterious destiny of his people, and everything that exists in the world" (259). Vision fails and the story ends.

"Lord, what a view!" would be an appropriate reaction for the prince, being obvious and even philistine. It raises the question of just who is responsible for the elegantly crafted text that precedes it. We cannot imagine the prince capable of creating it any more than the scenes of the Roman Campagna earlier in the story. Clearly it is the narrator who now intervenes to create a brilliant tapestry, woven from striking turns of language. This is one of Gogol's more impressive sustained performances in the high style, and would be far beyond the capacities of the plodding prince. The teller now seems privileged over the observer. Are we to conclude that the mere onlooker is an aesthete, fated to contemplate nothing more than dead albeit interesting ruins? If so, then the prince disappears perhaps because he is incapable of using language in a creative way.

Yet the writer, for all his skill, still remains at least doubly distanced from his ostensible subject: writer—prince—paintings of Rome—Rome itself. Of this he seems suddenly aware when, in mid-paragraph, he observes: "Neither with word nor with brush was it possible to convey [*peredat'*, literally, 'transfer,' as in "The Portrait"] the marvellous harmony and blend of all the planes of this picture." If neither observer nor writer can fully account for what lies before them, then art has limits, as Gogol would discover in the 1840's. For a writer who tried to think of his particular kind of art as painting, the limits would prove unacceptably constricting. A verbal text, after all, is apprehended only as linear, left-to-right movement through time and space. A painting, by contrast, is immediately apprehended as a whole, its impact enhanced as the viewer moves closer or farther away. These simple and obvious truths may be the best explanation of Gogol's ultimate decision to dispense with painting as a model for himself.

In 1836, artistic crisis had been followed by a drastic change of geography and the adoption of what Gogol expected would be a new life. This was true of 1842 as well. It was now time to leave Rome, as he had left Russia six years earlier, in search of new distance and fresh perspective.

THE ABANDONMENT OF ROME

Gogol had been extremely happy in Rome for the first three years. He customarily took the waters in Western Europe during the hot Italian summers, but he always looked forward to returning in the fall. The spring of 1839, however, offered a first portent of change. On May 30, he wrote to M. P. Balabina expressing a familiar regret: "You can't believe how sad it is to leave Rome for a month, and my clear, my pure skies, my beautiful lady [Rome], my beloved land," and go to Germany, a land "mean, nasty, soiled and blackened with clouds of tobacco smoke" (XI, 229). He departed for Vienna shortly thereafter, spent July and part of August in Marienbad, returned to Vienna for about a month, set out for Russia in late September, and left for Italy only the following May. En route, however, he stayed for three months in Vienna, where he did much writing and fell seriously ill. This was the great "crisis" of which we have spoken. After recovering, he reached Venice in early September, and was back in Rome three weeks later. "A month" had stretched to fifteen.

He insisted that "the road" was essential to his health and his art. As he told Stepan Shevyryov: "While I am travelling, my material usually develops in my mind; almost all my subjects have been worked out on the road." After 1840, traveling took on a compulsive quality. The trips became more frequent and prolonged, as a rough chronology shows. From September 1840 until the following August, he lived in Rome. Then he journeyed to Frankfurt-am-Main to visit Zhukovsky, and from there, in September, to Russia, where he remained until June 1842, when he went to Germany to spend his usual summer at the spas. He returned to Rome only in October: this absence also ran to nearly fifteen months. Again he was off in May 1843, first to Florence, then to Germany, then on to Nice and other non-Italian spots for the remainder of 1843, all of 1844, and most of 1845, not seeing Rome until November of that year: two and a half years elapsed on this occasion. Always strapped for money, Gogol admitted that he would spend far less if he stayed in one place; but "travel and changes of place are as essential to me as my daily bread," he informed Shevyryov in another letter, because "[m]y head is so strangely constructed that at times I suddenly have to dash off for several hundreds of versts and cover a distance in order to exchange one impression for another, clarify my spiritual vision and have the strength to encompass what I need and turn it into the one thing I need." This is a restatement of the "distance" theme, but it is now a mobile distance, not so much from anything in particular as from everything in general.[19]

An entirely new attitude toward Rome began to surface after the "crisis" in Vienna. He informed Danilevsky in 1841: "I am writing you nothing concerning the events in Rome that you ask about. *I no longer see anything before me*, and I have none of the lively attentiveness of the new arrival. Everything I needed I have taken and enclosed in the depths of my soul." Two years later, in a far stronger statement to Shevyryov, he declared: "everything around me here has long since died, as far as I am concerned, and my eyes most often turn only to Russia." In 1846, he said much the same thing in a letter to Nikolai Yazykov: "I don't know what to write you about the news in Rome; I for one have no interest in it. . . . The most important thing that happened was the arrival of our tsar [Nicholas I]. I admired him only from a distance [the usual Gogolian stance], and prayed for him in my soul."[20]

His cooling toward Rome brought a change of attitude toward Russia. In 1837, he had called it a land of "snows" and "scoundrels" in a letter to Zhukovsky. By 1838, he was telling Balabina that his "anger" toward Russia was "beginning to abate," and he struck a wistful, even homesick note:

I am very glad that you are beginning to find Petersburg bearable. . . . Your description of the railway and of your trip on it is very lively . . . and I confess—secretly and in confidence—that I really envied you. After all, my heart is Russian. Even though at the sight, that is, at the thought of Petersburg a cold shiver runs through me . . . I would still love to take a ride on the railway and hear the jumble of words and speech from our Babylonian populace in the cars.

A year later the older stance is struck as he tells Pogodin: "There's no living in Russia for first-rate people. Only pigs can live there." But another year passes, and he writes to Sergei Aksakov: "Yes, I sense that my love for Russia is strong. Much that once seemed to me unpleasant and intolerable now strikes me as being far less trivial and insignificant, and, now equable and serene, I marvel at how I could have taken those things so close to heart." Toward the end of this same letter he goes even farther: "I don't know why in general young people cannot develop in the fulness of their powers on Russian soil too," although he had felt himself unable to do so. Distance was doing its predictable work, whereas proximity was undoing his old passion for Rome.[21]

Predictably, once he had returned to Russia, he began again to despise it. He wrote to Yazykov on February 10, 1842, "however solitary a life I live here, still, everything oppresses me: the local gossip, and the talk, and the tittle-tattle" (XII, 34). Rome now looked newly alluring. As he put it to Pletnyov: "[A]bout Russia I can write only in Rome. Only there is it present to me in its entirety, in all its immensity. Whereas here [in Moscow] I am lost and mingled in with the others. There is no open horizon before me." He is assailed with a whole catalogue of physical ailments he knew nothing of in Rome:

[I]f it's cold in the room, my cerebral nerves ache and freeze, and you cannot imagine what torment I feel every time I try to master myself, take charge of myself and force my head to work. But if the room is heated, then the artificial heat is utterly suffocating, the slightest exertion produces a strange thickening in my head as if it wanted to crack open. In Rome I used to write in front of an open window, fanned by a salutary breeze that worked miracles for me. . . . My head is stupid, my soul uneasy. Lord, little did I think I would endure such agonies on the occasion of this visit to Russia!"[22]

Eventually, however, Rome was no better. He came to feel quite alone there too. Even his malaise followed him. "My health at first seemed to improve considerably," he wrote Yazykov on January 8, 1846, "but now it is getting worse again. I feel the cold to such an extent that I cannot find any way of getting warm. At first I resorted to running, which helped me; but now my legs are starting to hurt and refuse to work" (XIII, 30). This represents a complete reversal: Rome, once the epitome of warmth, is now "cold."

His accounts of the changes he had undergone since the "crisis" of 1840 apparently found no responsive soul. He wrote to A. O. Smirnova on March 4, 1846: "In Rome I see and spend time with few people. The ones that my soul might have a strong desire to see are not here now. . . . I don't feel like bumping into people for no good reason, and I haven't the time" (XIII, 42). His ideal was solitude spent in the company of loving, understanding friends. These apparently contradictory requirements are not uncommon among creative people. A settled life, whether in Rome or Russia, had proved unsatisfactory. So more and more did the life of "the road." Gogol continued to insist that travel was the best medicine, but it was a medicine he seemed increasingly reluctant to take. He left Rome once more—and for the last time—in May 1846. Soon he settled in at the German spa of Greffenberg, from which he wrote to Yazykov that he ought to move on but was afraid to do so: "I am suffering from an ailment [suggesting that the spas no longer worked], which gets worse and worse. I feel I should move somewhere, but I haven't the strength—or for that matter the spirit or resolve either—because I fear that I will remain alone, which can happen especially in Gastein, and that is dangerous for me."[23] He could not stay; he could not move; this is one of the simplest yet most profound expressions of Gogol's spiritual condition in the mid-1840's. When he did return to Italy in November of that same year, it was to Naples, not to Rome. But he felt no better: "I am tired. I tire very quickly now, because my health has once again taken a turn for the worse. Soon it will be two months since insomnia has gotten the better of me (the reason for which I cannot understand)."[24] Once more he departed for Western Europe in mid-1847, and in September of that year returned to Naples, which seems to have made little impression on him, to judge by a letter he wrote a few months later: "Before me again is Naples, Vesuvius and the sea! The days speed by in activities, time flies so that you don't know where to snatch a spare hour."[25]

In January 1848, he told Aleksandr Ivanov that he was planning to leave the city "in a matter of days" because of an uprising against King Ferdinand II, which brought much political and social unrest.[26] He proceeded to Malta, after a nightmarish voyage of unremitting seasickness, and from there to Jerusalem, by way of Tyre, Sidon, and Nazareth, to visit the tomb of Jesus. He had been looking forward to this pilgrimage, although he felt that he was spiritually unprepared, with his soul still "cold, coarse, unable to detach itself from earthly, self-loving, low pursuits and even from those defects it sees in itself and itself hates."[27] He found the experience "astounding," and pronounced himself "healthy the whole time—healthier than ever before"; yet he complained that he was unable to pray or even to appreciate: "my unfeelingness, coarseness and woodenness have never been so palpably in evidence."[28] In late March and early April, he traveled to Beirut, Smyrna, and Constantinople, and on April 10, returned through Odessa to Russian soil. There he was to spend the five years of life that remained to him.

We have no reason to doubt the sincere anguish of this spiritual quest and disillusionment, to which we shall devote more attention in the next section of this book. Interestingly enough, however, it too parallels a larger movement in European art, a movement first away from Rome to other Italian cities, such as Pisa, Florence, Naples, and Genoa, particularly as interest in the very early Renaissance developed, and next, by 1840, away from Italy generally, as artists from northern Europe—with the notable exception of the Germans—began to discover other landscapes.[29] Once again, Gogol stepped to the rhythm of his times; but once again he reached an artistic dead end, as "Rome" and "The Portrait" so eloquently attest. A mere change of scene was no longer sufficient, for, in a very literal sense, scenery was no longer meaningful. But as in 1836, there was a way out. It required serious, eventually desperate attention to the one obvious aspect of his own work that he had contrived to neglect or play down in his wider ruminations on the nature and purpose of his vocation: the word.

PART THREE

WORD

11

From Eye to Word

THE contrast of verbal and visual adumbrated at the end of "Rome" finds fuller representation in many of Gogol's other works. The first few pages of "The Fair at Sorochintsy," which opens *Evenings on a Farm Near Dikanka*, are a revel for the eye, a portrait of a luxuriant summer landscape and its picturesque inhabitants. The scene is static and timeless. Suddenly spoken words intrude, followed by movement, change, development, the beginning of the action, and a disclaimer of the power of seeing: "Our fair maiden mused, *gazing at the glorious view*, and even *forgot* to crack the sunflower seeds with which she had been busily engaged all the way, when *all at once the words*, 'What a girl!' *caught her ear.*" She looked around to see who could have uttered them, noticed a young man with "fiery *eyes*, which seemed to *look* right through her," and then "*lowered her eyes*"—disconnecting, as it were, from the visual—"at the thought that *he might have uttered those words*" (I, 11). Like the scene before her, the girl had been immobile as long as she had been using her eyes alone.

Five years later, in "The Two Ivans," the contrast is posed far more starkly and with far weightier consequences. Ivan Ivanovich is a "visual" being, who inhabits a well-ordered, scrupulously detailed physical world, in contemplation of which he spends many satisfied hours. He takes for granted that he can possess and therefore control anything that swims into his line of sight. When he enters Ivan Nikiforovich's room to ask for the gun, however, he not only discovers that his eyes fail him but even experiences a visual dislocation:

The room into which Ivan Ivanovich stepped was quite dark, because the shutters were closed and the sunbeam that penetrated through a hole in the shutter was broken into rainbow hues and painted upon the opposite wall a multicolored landscape of thatched roofs, trees, and clothes hanging in the yard, but *all upside down*. This made *an uncanny twilight* in the whole room.

"God's blessing!" said Ivan Ivanovich.

"Ah, good day, Ivan Ivanovich!" *answered a voice* from the corner of the room. *Only then* did Ivan Ivanovich observe Ivan Nikiforovich lying on a rug spread out upon the floor. (II, 177)

The answering "voice" betokens an entirely different mode of apprehending the world. Correspondingly, Ivan Nikiforovich's "place" is never described in any detail; we can form no mental picture of it; he himself is seen in a state of nudity, that is, as unadorned to the eye as one can be. The "gander" scene, which shortly follows, shows just how dynamic this "voice" can be, not only in these shadowed surroundings but throughout the story. When the attempted reconciliation fails as Ivan Nikiforovich repeats the deadly word, Ivan Ivanovich responds by casting on his enemy "a glance—and what a glance! *If that glance had been endowed with the power of action* it would have reduced Ivan Nikiforovich to ashes" (212). But neither here nor anywhere else in the story is his eye so endowed. Nor is the narrator's. On one occasion, the narrator represents himself as a would-be painter, who could successfully portray (*izobrazit'*) a night scene in Mirgorod but "could hardly have depicted" what we would call really important, the many "different emotions *written* [*napisano*]" on the face of Ivan Ivanovich as he goes out to saw down the offending goose-pen (II, 186). A "seeing" narrator brings the story to an end too, in contrast to the "speaking" narrator who opens it. He records not only the interior of the church and the appearance of the two aged Ivans but also, as is appropriate to the visual mode, the permanently static nature of their relationship.

"The Two Ivans" was published in *Mirgorod*. So was "Viy," where the visual/verbal contrast is far more explicit, and far more indicative of the directions that Gogol's art would eventually take.

"VIY"

It is summer vacation. Khoma Brut and two schoolmates from the seminary are taking part in the great "migration" of students out of Kiev. They spend the night in a small, remote homestead that is kept by an old woman. Khoma, who is also known as "the philosopher," that is, an upperclassman, is assigned to a sheep's pen. Presently the old woman comes in and moves toward him with "glittering eyes" and "outstretched arms." Without a word she leaps on his back and rides him through the air like a horse.

Below he sees entirely new things, most spectacularly a sensuous water-nymph. Through prayers and exorcisms he dispels the tempting yet troubling vision, overcomes the witch, beats her with a stick, and stands amazed as she changes into a beautiful girl. But when he "look[s] into her face," and she in turn looks "upward with eyes full of tears," he is once again reduced to a state of powerlessness, "overcome by pity and a strange emotion and timidity, feelings he [can]not himself explain" (II, 139–42).[1]

Khoma then returns to Kiev and gives no more thought to "this extraordinary adventure" (142). Soon he is summoned to the house, some 40 miles distant, of a rich Cossack captain, whose dying daughter has requested that he, and he alone, "should read the prayer for the dying over her and the other prayers for three days after her death." Khoma has a presentiment of evil and does not wish to go, but is compelled to do so by the rector of the seminary. Although the girl turns out to be the witch he has mortally beaten with a stick, he does not at first recognize her, and cannot imagine how she knows him. Presently she dies, and he prepares to pray over her body for three nights running. To each of these sessions Gogol devotes a lengthy scene. All are structured identically, but with rising intensity.

The description of the Cossack captain's house makes for a richly detailed visual tour, which carries no hint of menace. It is only when Khoma is told "this isn't the sort of establishment you can run away from" that we know he has landed in the Gogolian equivalent of a magic locale to which access is difficult and from which escape is virtually impossible. The visual particulars then become a kind of ballast that hinders easy movement. (Korobochka's house in *Dead Souls* is a later equivalent.) A suffocating visual sumptuousness, with more than a touch of the Gothic, introduces the first prayer-scene too: "The whole floor was covered with red cotton material. On a high table in the corner under the holy images lay the body of the dead girl on a coverlet of dark blue velvet adorned with gold fringe and tassels. Tall wax candles, entwined with sprigs of guelder rose, stood at her feet and head, shedding a dim light that was lost in the brightness of daylight" (150–51). Seeing and not seeing are the prevalent gestures here, as they have been since the beginning of the story: "The dead girl's *face was hidden from him* by the inconsolable father, who sat down *facing her*," and who pronounces a curse on her murderer—"that he should *not see* his children again, if he be so old as I, nor his father and mother"—without knowing that it is Khoma. "[I must] live out my days without comfort, wiping with the skirt of my coat the trickling tears that flow from my old *eyes*," the father laments, giving in to "an outburst of sorrow, which found vent in a *flood of tears*" (151). Khoma begins reading aloud, "paying no attention to anything else and *not venturing to glance at the face* of the dead girl." But his attention wanders to the extent that he "*noticed* that the cap-

tain had withdrawn. Slowly he turned his head to *look at* the dead [girl]"
(151). She was extremely beautiful, but then he "*saw* something terrible
and poignant," and "dreadfully familiar in her face," and realized who she
was: "'The witch!' he cried in a voice not his own, as, turning pale, *he
looked away* and *fell to repeating his prayers*" (152).

These opening scenes, like the story as a whole, are built on a counterpoint of the visual and the verbal. But in contrast to "The Two Ivans," it is
now the visual that seems powerful, evilly so, and the verbal that is ineffectual but "good" insofar as it is cast in religious language. However, matters are by no means so clear-cut. As a seminarian, with the rank of "philosopher," Khoma is presumed to be the custodian of sacred language. But
the emotions he experiences as he prepares to read suggest that he is incompetent. "Witch [*ved'ma*]" is a taboo word, which has no place in
prayers for the dead. The fact that he pronounces it "in a voice not his own
[*ne svoim golosom*]" suggests that this word has begun to control him.
Before the service he stammers: "[A]ny man versed in Holy Scripture may,
as far as in him lies ... but a deacon or a sacristan would be better fitted
for it. They are men of understanding, and know how it is all done, while
I ... Besides I *haven't the right voice for it*, and I *myself am the devil knows
what*" (150). The Garnett/Kent translation has merely "I myself am good
for nothing," but this is to blink the crucial "demonic" theme of the story,
which attaches not only to the witch and her cohort but to Khoma himself.
There have been many other references to the devil up to this point, which
in ordinary discourse would simply be manners of speaking. In this story,
however, they quickly become marked.

It is easy enough to see why the witch is demonic. But what about
Khoma and the rector? The seminary to which they are attached claims to
teach the verbal arts and skills in the categories of grammar, rhetoric, philosophy, and theology. However, the effectiveness of the teaching is open
to question, for the students mainly occupy themselves with eating and
fighting. One of the drunken Cossacks at the captain's house asks Khoma:
"I should like to know what they teach you in the seminary. Is it *the same
as what the deacon reads in church, or something different?*" Specifically,
he wants to know "what is written there in those books? Maybe it is quite
different from what the deacon reads" (145). This Cossack unwittingly
calls into question the "sacred" language with which the seminarians have
been entrusted. It seems at best ineffectual, at worst perverted to mundane
and therefore potentially demonic purposes. In this sense, Khoma is not
an adversary of the devil but his ally; and the "sacred" verbal formulas to
which he resorts cannot possibly work in the ways they are supposed to.

The second reading over the girl's corpse takes place inside the church.
Again the scene appeals to the eye and is cast in the Gothic manner. As

Khoma makes ready to read, his eyes fall on "some bundles of candles" and he decides instead to "light up the whole church so that it may be as bright as daylight," thereby empowering the visual to do its work. Once the church is "flooded with light," he goes over to the coffin, looks at the "brilliant beauty" of the corpse, and is transfixed, a posture that almost always attends seeing and being seen in Gogol. "He turned and tried to move away; but . . . he could not, as he withdrew, resist *taking another look*. And then . . . he *looked again*. . . . [I]t seemed to the philosopher that *she was looking at him with closed eyes*. He even fancied that a tear was oozing from under her right eyelid, and, when it rested on her cheek, *he saw distinctly* that it was a drop of blood" (157–58).

Small wonder that his words are even less effective than before. He further diminishes them through profanation: "to give himself more confidence he began reading in a very loud voice." He decides to take some snuff, and his thrice-reiterated declaration seems to parody the structure of liturgical formulas: "I'll have a pinch of snuff: ah, what good snuff! Wonderful snuff! Great snuff!"[2] Finally he raises his voice and begins "singing in various keys," not to serve the prayers but "to drown the fears that still lurked in him" (158). Personal apprehensions are neither here nor there in prayer services for the dead, but it is the snuff-taking that is the greater profanation. As an irritant to the nose that causes a violent discharge of mucous fluids, it suggests masturbation in this context of voyeuristic or self-indulgent sexuality. The long tradition of noses as surrogate penises apart, we have only to look at a story Gogol wrote the following year, "The Nose," where that obviously sexual organ goes into a church and is followed by Kovalyov, who notices an attractive young lady and prepares to pay her court. In "Viy," Khoma keeps looking at the beautiful young girl's coffin, fearful that the corpse may rise at any moment. Finally she does: "He looked at her wildly and *rubbed his eyes* [another hint at masturbation?]. . . . He looked away, and again *turned his eyes* with horror on the coffin. . . . [He] kept *gazing at* the narrow coffin of the witch . . . [he] saw it almost over his head" (158–59), that is, virtually in the same position the witch first occupied when she straddled him. All this looking puts him behind in his reading, thereby profaning it further: when dawn breaks and the corpse returns to the coffin, Khoma is "emboldened by the cock's crowing" and "read[s] on more rapidly the pages he *ought to have* read through before" (160). The only thing that saves him for the time being is the magic circle he draws around himself; but since that is a pagan practice, we can expect that it will not long be protective.

The next night, on returning to the church, Khoma again "drew a circle around him, pronounced some exorcisms, and began reading loudly, resolving not to raise his eyes from the book and not to pay attention to anything" (161).³ Here we see a subtler perversion of sacred language. Khoma is using it not to mediate worldly reality but to avoid that reality altogether. His resolve not to look holds for an hour or so. But once he directs a "timid look" at the coffin, the earlier scene is replayed in a drastic foreshortening: "the corpse was *already* standing before him on the *very edge* of the circle, and her dead, greenish *eyes* were *fixed upon him*." His now practiced response is to avert his eyes and raise his voice as he reads the prayers and exorcisms. Although the witch cannot see him, she now engages him on his own ground, muttering "terrible words" that he understands to be an incantation. It proves effective, if only because his own language is not: "A wind blew through the church at her words, and there was a sound as of multitudes of flying wings. He heard the beating of wings on the panes of the church windows and on the iron window frames, the dull scratching of claws upon the iron, and numberless evil creatures thundering on the doors and trying to break in." Predictably, he counters by "closing his eyes" and "reading prayers and exorcisms." Suddenly the cock crows; dawn breaks; and the evil creatures disappear. When Khoma is found, "his *eyes*" are "almost popping out of his head" and he is "*looking motionlessly* at the Cossacks who [are] nudging him" (161–62), in mimicry of the same staring gestures of the witch and the evil creatures that soon enter the church.⁴

As the third night begins, a terrified, balking Khoma is virtually dragged to the church. He repeats the familiar gestures of drawing the circle, recalling the spells and exorcisms, and flooding the space with light. But now, even before the visual distractions begin, the words go astray: he "turned one page, then turned another, and noticed that he *was not reading what was written in the book*." To restore his courage and set himself back on the track, "he crossed himself and began chanting," after which "the reading made progress." Since the ingredients of this scene are identical to those of the two preceding, what happens next is predictable, albeit intensified: "[T]he iron lid of the coffin burst with a crash and the corpse rose up. . . . [I]ncantations came from [its lips] in wild shrieks. A whirlwind swept through the church. . . . The doors were burst from their hinges and a countless multitude of monstrous beings flew into the church of God. . . . All flew and raced about *looking for the philosopher*" (167). Within the magic circle, Khoma cannot be seen by the corpse or by any of the strange and horrible creatures. And he remains untouched until Viy is brought in, "a squat, thickset, bandy-legged figure [*cheloveka*]," who is "covered all over with black earth," whose "arms and legs grew out like strong sinewy roots," whose "face was of iron," and, most strikingly, whose "long eyelids hung down to the very ground" (167). Much critical ink has been spilled over the etymology of this name. However, as Leon Stilman has pointed out, the important thing is that "the long eyelids . . . and his name . . . are both associated with a glance, with eyes, with vision."[5] The encounter unfolds as follows:

[Viy was] led straight to the spot where Khoma was standing.

"*Lift up my eyelids. I do not see!*" said Viy in a voice that seemed to come from deep in the earth, and all the creatures flew to *raise his eyelids*.

"*Do not look!*" an inner voice whispered to the philosopher. He could not restrain himself, and *he looked*.

"There he is!" shouted Viy, and thrust an iron finger at him. And all pounced upon the philosopher together. He fell expiring to the ground, and his soul fled from his body in terror. (167)

What is it that endows Viy with the special power of breaking the circle? For one thing, there is the utter failure of sacred language as Khoma employs it: he "kept crossing himself and repeating prayers *at random [kak popalo]*," that is, disconnecting them from the organic, living text. His last hold on a saving word may be the "inner voice" that "whispers" to him; but he cannot heed it. In the second place, Viy is designated as *chelovek*. Garnett/Kent translates this word as "figure," and that is not incorrect, but it is likely to obscure the crucial fact that *chelovek* means "human being." In this respect he is different from the witch, who has supernatural powers, and from the creatures in the church, who are out-and-out monsters, with wings, tails, and claws. Only Viy's eyelids are odd, although no more so than the exaggerated traits of physiognomy found elsewhere among many of Gogol's human characters. In other words, Viy is a kind of projection or mirroring of Khoma himself, who presumably has normal eyelids but an exaggerated interest in seeing. There can therefore be no barrier between them, magic circle or not.

As a mirrored Khoma Brut, Viy is gross, coarse, threatening, ultimately lethal, and, as a clincher, unambiguously male. Khoma's sensualist fantasies have until now revolved around women. There are unmistakable suggestions of sexual intercourse—perhaps imagined, but very vivid—in the first encounter with the witch, where Khoma was "aware of an exhausting, unpleasant, and at the same time, voluptuous sensation. . . . The sweat was streaming from him. He was aware of a fiendishly voluptuous feeling; he felt a stabbing, exhaustingly terrible delight" (140–41). Sexual stirrings, though not so overtly physical as these, accompany his ogling of the white-breasted water-nymph and the beautiful young girl into which the witch turns as he beats her. But since these are otherworldly female creatures, he can fail to see them as self, and feed his voyeuristic hankerings as he looks on from what he thinks is a safe distance. The experiences in the church, however, show that he is anything but distanced; and the appearance of a male figure, in Viy, makes it clear that these "others" are only versions of himself. In effect, Khoma ends by imitating himself. Had he remained true to his calling of seminarian, and faithfully copied the for- mulaic words of the prayers, as one must do to profit by their power, they would have worked, and he would have been saved. But his sensuality is more powerful, and eventually even the words he recites become a reflec- tion of him as well.

We see too that the circle he draws is another form of self-enclosure and can therefore offer no real protection. As such, it is the most developed form of the condition in which Khoma enters the story: alone in the world, without father, mother, or siblings, and without hope of "escaping what has to be" (136). He is neither intelligent nor sensitive enough to be num- bered among the Romantic solitaries who peopled the literature of Europe before Gogol. Instead, he is another version of the isolated characters in which Gogol's works abound, such as the sorcerer/father, Poprishchin, and later, Akaky Akakievich and Chichikov, all of whom are sensualists too. Isolated sensualists are usually demonic figures in Gogol, however innoc- uous they may seem to be. They are earlier versions, perhaps even sources, of the most famous of Russian literary demons, who is "wandering / In the desert of the world without a refuge."[6] Christian theology teaches us why demons are as they are. Gogol suggests that even though Khoma has done nothing to deserve his orphaned state, it is nonetheless the place assigned him, a place he transgresses in the ways that create the story's plot.

In a kind of epilogue, Khoma's former schoolmates hear of what has befallen him, and try to contrive explanations. Khaliava says simply: "Such was the lot God sent him. . . . He was a fine man! And he came to grief for nothing." Tibery Gorobets, who in the meantime has himself become a "philosopher," ventures a more complex and eloquent explanation, as be- fits his new academic dignity: "[I]t was because he was afraid; if he had not been afraid, the witch could not have done anything to him. You only have to cross yourself and spit right on her tail, and nothing will happen. I know all about it. Why, the old women who sit in our market in Kiev are all witches." Both explanations may be partly true, but neither begins to account for all that has happened. As exercises in verbalization, they ex- emplify the inadequacy of words in a purely narrative sense, as Khaliava at least intuits: "observing that *his tongue was incapable of uttering a sin- gle word*, he cautiously got up from the table," and "lurching to right and to left [from drink], went to hide in a remote spot in the rough grass [pre- sumably to move his bowels]; from the force of habit, however, he did not forget to carry off the sole of an old boot that was lying on the bench" (168).

With this suggestion of Romantic irony, "Viy" ends. It is a story about proper and improper ways of seeing. It is also about proper and improper ways of employing words. Gogol had not yet worked out a thematics of the word, as he would after 1842; but "Viy" represents his first serious attempt to put forth fictionally what would later develop into a compelling theme of his own life: the right words, rightly used, can prevail in an essentially evil world; words cannot be entrusted to the likes of those who make their living from using them in corrupt ways, whether seminarians, Poprishchins, or, much later, Chichikovs. Only an artist, he would come to believe, was capable of handling "sacred" words responsibly and effectively. Through the 1830's, he was unwilling to see this artist as anything more than a painter in words. But from the time of the religious "conversion" in 1840, he found himself compelled to acknowledge that his work, with two exceptions, was not painting and never had been.

NARRATIVE VOICES

Gogol's works were printed in the format common to prose, fictional or not. With its uniform typefaces and its justified margins, it is supposed to be unobtrusive enough to encourage rapid, silent reading. However, this works against Gogol's purposes. He wants us to read slowly, even word by word. He would probably be pleased if we moved our lips and whispered out the syllables. Otherwise we are likely to miss much. Other prose writers with similar purposes may try to overcome the impersonality of print by indulging in typographical eccentricities. Gogol's method is different. He tries to make us imagine that we are actually hearing the stories narrated by a speaking voice, mainly by using dictions that we have long associated with oral storytelling.

This voice is especially strong, even obtrusive, at the beginnings of the stories. Almost always it is conveyed in one of three types of speech: the oratorical, the reportorial or anecdotal, and the *skaz*.

The Oratorical

Evenings on a Farm Near Dikanka abounds in this type of speech. The very first story in the collection, "The Fair at Sorochintsy," opens as follows: "How intoxicating, how magnificent is a summer day in Little Russia! How luxuriously warm the hours when midday glitters in stillness and sultry heat and the blue fathomless ocean covering the plain like a dome seems to be slumbering, bathed in languor, clasping the fair earth and holding it close in its ethereal embrace! Upon it, not a cloud; in the plain, not a sound" (I, 8). And so on, for many more lines. The sentences are long, hypotactical, and rhythmic, and they almost hypnotize us into languorous assent. Verbal music enhances the effect. It can consist in simple alliteration, as in "*serye stoga sena*" ("gray haystacks"), or in phonic devices of far greater complexity, as in the sentence beginning "*Lenívo i bezdúmno*,

búdto gulyáyushchie bez tséli, stoyát *podóblachnye dubý*" ("The towering oaks stand, idle and apathetic, like aimless wanderers"), which is built
on a repetition of the italicized sounds, with a profusion of internal, mostly
assonantial rhymes: *dúmno/búdto/gulyáyu-*; *-yat/po[a]d*; *-ob/dub-*. The
voice is that of the poet, but in Gogol it is identical to that of the rhetor,
preacher, and prophet, as heard in the articles on history, literature, and
religion, and in many of the letters. It constitutes one of the important links
between the fiction and the nonfiction. In fact, the passage just quoted,
though "fiction," is structured like a sermon. The theme is set out in the
first sentence—*Kak upoítelen, kak roskóshen létnii den' v Malorossíi!*—
then is amplified and explicated, and finally is restated, with the same
sound-system, in the closing clause of the paragraph: *kak pólno sladostrá-
stiya i négi malorossíiskoe léto!* ("how full of voluptuousness and languor
is the Little Russian summer!").[7]

The Reportorial or Anecdotal

An extraordinarily strange incident took place in Petersburg in March, on the
twenty-fifth day. The barber, Ivan Yakovlevich, who lives on Voznesensky Avenue
(his surname is lost, and nothing more appears even on his signboard, where a
gentleman is depicted with his cheeks covered with soapsuds, together with an in-
scription "also lets blood")—the barber Ivan Yakovlevich woke up rather early and
was aware of a smell of hot bread. Raising himself in bed he saw his wife, a rather
portly lady who was very fond of drinking coffee, engaged in taking out of the oven
some freshly baked loaves. ("The Nose," II, 216)

Like many of Gogol's works, "The Nose" is really an extended anecdote.
The styling of the date provides a touch of officialese that seems more appropriate to a police report or a newspaper article.[8] Yet the paragraph lacks
the economy of expression found in competent journalism, and the asides,
not to speak of the rambling manner, betray the presence of an oral
narrator.

Skaz

Ivan Ivanovich has a splendid coat. Superb! And what astrakhan! Phew, damn it
all, what astrakhan! Purplish-gray with a frost on it! I'll bet anything you please
that nobody can be found with one like it! Now just look at it—particularly when
he is standing talking to somebody—look from the side: isn't it delicious? There is
no finding words for it. Velvet! Silver! Fire! Merciful Lord! St. Nikolai the Wonder-
Worker, Holy Saint! Why don't I have a coat like that! He had it made before Agafya Fedoseevna went to Kiev. You know Agafya Fedoseevna, who bit off the tax
assessor's ear? ("The Two Ivans," II, 169)

Skaz has been defined as an oral narration "told by a fictitious narrator
rather than by the author directly." However, it is more usefully restricted,

following the lead of the Russian Formalists, to narrations told, as Victor Erlich puts it, "in such a manner as to emulate the phonetic, grammatical and lexical patterns of actual speech and produce the 'illusion of oral narration.'"[9] In Gogol's practice, this tends to favor narrators like the one in the passage just quoted: his enthusiasms outrun common sense; he obviously has little formal education and little idea of how to develop an argument, let alone talk in an eloquent and persuasive way about his feelings, although he wishes to be considered informed and observant; he tends to ramble and digress, and cannot distinguish the trivial from the important.

By contrast, let us look at one instance of the rarest kind of narration in Gogol: the impersonal. We have a sense here not of a voice speaking but of some penman at work behind the scenes:

Nowhere were so many people standing as before the little picture shop in Shchukin Court. The shop did indeed contain the most varied collection of curiosities: the pictures were for the most part painted in oils, covered with dark green varnish, in dark-yellow gilt frames. A winter scene with white trees, an absolutely red sunset that looked like the glow of a conflagration, a Flemish peasant with a pipe and a broken arm, more like a turkey cock in frills than a human being—such were usually their subjects. ("The Portrait," II, 253)

Despite two instances of heightened verbal texture that are more appropriate to oral narration—the hyperbolic "nowhere" and the faintly grotesque simile ("a turkey cock in frills")—this narrator is self-effacing, and does not prompt us to wonder who he is. (Narrators in Gogol, at least at the beginning of the stories, are invariably males.) In its impersonality, the passage approaches the reportorial, but it is more consciously crafted, more "literary" in intent. It aims at showing us a scene, not telling us about it. Significantly, this kind of narration predominates in the two stories that are mainly concerned with seeing: "The Portrait" and "Rome."

The openings of Gogol's other stories represent one of these three basic types of narration, or combinations of them. But we must resist any impulse to make neat classifications. What would such an impulse make, say, of the opening of "Nevsky Prospekt"? It could be *skaz*. But it is also the work of a narrator who knows the "physiological" tradition of urban literature, with its passion for pigeonholes and generalizations, and who therefore is something of a reporter as well. Insofar as the first sentence states a thesis—"there is nothing finer than Nevsky Prospekt"—and then proceeds, over the next several pages, to elaborate, it draws on the rhetorical arsenal of the orator or preacher. At best, we can speak of tendencies and emphases in these openings. The important thing is that, with almost no exceptions, they are so fashioned that we think we hear a speaking voice.

Unquestionably the speech of these narrators contains a substantial oral residue. Nearly all the verbal devices we have discussed are oral in origin. More pervasively, an oral mind-set can be seen in the preference for the concrete over the abstract, a focus on the external world, a tendency to typologize human beings, a fondness for paired characters, even a conservative attitude toward life and an enormous respect for those who embody it. Such narrators, in Walter J. Ong's terms, are "word-attentive," not "object-attentive."[10] At the same time, there are clear signs of a powerful rhetorical tradition as well, not only in a readily identifiable arsenal of devices and themes but again in certain mind-sets. In contemplating the reasons for the usually lengthy introductions to the stories, for instance, we might remember Aristotle's assertion, "no introduction ought to be employed where the subject is not long and intricate."[11] Gogol's introductions tend to be not only intricate, but long in proportion to the total length of the text, thereby intimating that the story waiting to be told is of high importance. This is very much in keeping with the rhetorical principle of *copia*, which in turn looks back to the tendency of oral cultures to prize a fluent and tireless tongue.

Many scholars have identified particulars of oral residue in Gogol's works. This is certainly an interesting and useful pursuit. But several cautions are in order. "Devices" have too often been treated in isolation, with insufficient regard for their function in particular texts. Then again, as Ong points out in his *Orality and Literacy* (esp. 115), it is not always easy or possible, certainly not as late as the nineteenth century, to distinguish oral tradition from written "rhetorical" styles that may have arisen from it, as in Baroque poetics. Most important, we must always remember that we deduce the presence of a speaker from a printed text, imagining that we are listening when in fact we are reading. In this way we are party to a paradox that has existed since ancient times. As Ong and others have shown, the paradox involves not only the medium of telling but also the way things are told: oral and written modes each have their own vocabulary, syntax, and ideology.

We must of course beware of anachronism as well. The topic of "orality and literacy" is really an achievement of the twentieth century.[12] We cannot assume that Gogol was aware of it in the same way we are. In fact, we can adduce at least one text from the mid-1840's that demonstrates a conscious disregard of the difference: the section entitled "A Definition of the Word and of Literature" in the detailed outline for the never completed *Textbook of Literature for Russian Youth*. Here Gogol uses three different words for "literature": *literatura* (which was borrowed in the eighteenth century, when it was usually spelled with two t's, like the French original), *pis'mennost'* (derived from the word *pisat'*, "to write"), and, most capacious of all, *slovesnost'*, which comes from *slovo*, "word," and which ultimately refers to the spoken language but embraces both oral and written modes of discourse. He makes them all interchangeable, and even goes on to equate the oral and the written: "Literature [*pis'mennost'yu*], *or* the art of the word [*slovesnost'yu*], is the name given to the sum of man's entire spiritual formation, which at one time was transmitted by word [*slovom*] *or* by writing [*pis'mom*]."[13] However, theory was never Gogol's strong point; most important, his practices as a writer of fiction recognized the distinction and made it an important theme.

Each of the two parts of *Evenings on a Farm Near Dikanka* is introduced by a "Foreword," in which the old beekeeper Rudy Panko[14] informs us that his job is merely to write down the stories that are told by the villagers when all assemble of an evening in his hut. He goes on to provide brief descriptions of some of the ways these oral narrators operate. One "fine young gentleman" will sometimes "hold up his finger, and looking at the tip of it, begin telling a story—as choicely and cleverly as though it were printed in a book!" (I, 5). Another "has such a store of frightening tales that it makes the hair stand up on one's head." The result is enough tales "stored away for ten volumes, if only I am not too damned lazy to rack my brains for them" (6). The only tale that he need not write down is "Ivan Fyodorovich Shponka," which, he informs us, was transcribed by one Stepan Kuzmich Kurochka, although the ending was lost when Panko's wife used the paper for baking *pirogi*. This transcript creates a counterpoint to the prevailing oral narrations, and its partial destruction puts into question the vaunted permanence of print. The transcript also reminds us that here, and in later stories too, Gogol not only does not try to conceal the fact that his narratives, though "spoken," are actually printed texts but even flaunts it with devices that belong only to the written mode. For example, he may attach epigraphs, as in "The Fair at Sorochintsy" and "A May Night," footnotes, as in "The Two Ivans," and lists of unusual words, as in the two forewords to *Evenings on a Farm Near Dikanka*. He may create enormously long paragraphs, sometimes extending over several pages, as in "Nevsky Prospekt." Or he may divide stories into chapters, sometimes with headings, as in "A May Night," "Ivan Fyodorovich Shponka," and "The Two Ivans." In "Diary of a Madman," he employs a form that by definition can only be written, but he tells the story through a voice that conveys the "orality" of the story as unmistakably as do the voices in any of his other stories.[15] One of the important differences between the two modes has been succinctly put by Ong: "Oral structures often look to pragmatics (the convenience of the speaker . . .). . . . Chirographic structures look more to syntactics (organization of the discourse itself)" (37–38). Gogol wishes to have it both ways.

This in itself is evidence that we are dealing with a special kind of oral narrator, at least at the beginning of the *Dikanka* stories. Gogol did not invent him in all particulars, but he established him in Russian literature, where he has been widely imitated. This narrator differs in fundamental ways from traditional oral narrators. For one, he can read and write, although he is not always intelligent or cultivated. For another, except in the stylized folk tales, as in *Evenings on a Farm Near Dikanka*, he is not concerned with the preservation and transmission of a body of knowledge, lore, or custom. Nor, as we have seen, does he consistently or even regularly observe the "rules" of oral discourse. He usually projects a far stronger individual personality than is ever apparent in specimens of presumably genuine oral narration. Perhaps most important, his relationship to the listener/reader is far different from that of a traditional oral narrator.

In his first Foreword, Rudy Panko imagines the reader saying: "What oddity is this: *Evenings on a Farm Near Dikanka*? What sort of *Evenings* have we here? And thrust into the world by a beekeeper! God protect us! As though geese enough had not been plucked for pens and rags turned into paper! As though folks enough of all classes had not covered their fingers with inkstains! The whim must take a beekeeper to follow their example!" (I, 3).[16] Presumably a man of the lower classes has nothing worthwhile to tell. But the quotation turns the imaginary reader into a narrator, a presumptuous one at that, and at the same time makes Rudy himself a reader, who is prepared to pass judgment. It is a gentle enough judgment. Although willing to grant the reader's superior sophistication and social position, he makes clear that he possesses knowledge the reader does not, by appending an annotated glossary of unfamiliar words the reader will need to know for a proper understanding of the stories to come. The tone in this first Foreword is one of helpfulness and deference: "In any event, so that no one has a bad word to say about me, I am writing out, in alphabetical order, those words that not everyone understands in this book."[17] In the Foreword to Part 2, he is altogether feistier and touchier: "Only don't scold me! It's not nice to scold at parting, especially when God only knows whether one will soon meet again. . . . I tell you what, dear readers, there is nothing in the world worse than these high-class people." Here too he provides a glossary, but grudgingly, almost matter-of-factly, as if daring us to take it or leave it: "This little book contains many words that not everyone understands. Here almost all are indicated."[18] Now he is no longer content with serving as a scribe for stories told by others; he wants to tell his own, but demurs: "for my story I should need three books of this size." So much for high-toned readers who may think the lives of people like Rudy are impoverished and meager. Besides, the reader "would be laughing at the old man," and he refuses to offer us the occasion to do so (89–91). We discover that on Rudy's territory, we are at a considerable disadvantage: he is the one who decides whether to let the stories be told, not we, and much apparently depends on our good behavior.

The reader is cast as an antagonist here, though hardly of the same order as he is, say, in Fielding, where he is often uncooperative, stupid, and treacherous, and where he is, in his guise as a critic, "a little reptile," "a common slanderer," "odious vermin," and "monster."[19] Only in "An Author's Confession" would Gogol approximate the spirit (though never the language) of such invective. By and large, the narrators of his fictions are far more benevolent than even Rudy Panko. They satisfy at least two of the three criteria that Aristotle specifies as essential to effective "modes of persuasion": they tend to be of "good" character, and they put us into a receptive frame of mind. "We believe good men more fully and readily than others," Aristotle says. "Our judgments when we are pleased and friendly are not the same as when we are pained and hostile." Gogol knows that we feel more relaxed and cooperative with equals and inferiors, more willing to be persuaded by what Aristotle identifies as the third criterion of good rhetoric: "proof, or apparent proof, provided by the words of the speech itself." It is our assent—not, as is so often the case in Dostoevsky, our antagonism—that is essential to the proper workings of the stories.[20] On the face of it, these narrators seem to be facilitating what Ong identifies as yet another mark of an oral culture, "achieving close, empathetic, communal identification with the known," in contrast to writing, which "separates the knower from the known and thus sets up conditions for 'objectivity,' in the sense of personal disengagement or distancing" (45–46). However, the closeness is illusory in Gogol. In their non-antagonistic, often gentle way, the narrators take great care to keep us at a distance. They never assume that they and the reader are engaged in the kind of cozy intercourse we find in Sentimentalist writers like Karamzin and even in a writer as late as Tolstoy, who speaks about a "special type of reader" and defines him as follows: "he should be an *understanding* person, one of those people to whom, when you meet him, you see that you don't have to explain your feelings or your drift, but instead you see that he understands me, that every sound in my soul finds an echo in his."[21]

The job of distancing is easiest for the oratorical narrator. Oratory invites awe, reverence, admiration. It can be intimidating; we are not inclined to question what is being said or how it is presented; we merely listen. In stories like "The Fair at Sorochintsy" and "A Terrible Vengeance," the effect can be disturbing, since the narrators are all villagers and therefore "lower" than the presumed reader; yet their oratory is skillful and effective, far beyond what most of us presumably "superior" readers are capable of. But we soon forget who is doing the telling and even what he has to say, and instead yield to the sound of the voice. As Frank O'Connor has described it in an entirely different context, there is not "what you could call a human voice speaking, nobody resembling yourself who is trying to persuade you to share in an experience of his own, and whom you can imagine yourself questioning about its nature—nothing but an old magician sitting over his crystal ball, or a hypnotist waving his hands gently before your eyes and muttering, 'You are falling asleep; you are falling asleep; slowly, slowly your eyes are beginning to close; your eyelids are growing heavy; you are—falling—asleep."[22]

The *skaz* narrator enables us to feel superior, as in "The Two Ivans" and "The Overcoat." He may be quaint and colorful, even buffoonish and stupid, albeit likable. It is partly our natural tendency to underrate him that gives him power. We do not expect him to present the story material in a complete or coherent fashion, or to distinguish the "important" from the "unimportant." We tend to assume that he is incapable of inventing things or practicing to deceive, and that any attempts to pull such tricks will be so inept as to ensure immediate detection. The less the narrators are like us, the more likely we are to perceive them as veracious. This is why they are effective at unobtrusively planting the basic images and themes of the story in the first few paragraphs (such as the apparently casual remark about the two Ivans' being tied together by the devil): we often do not notice them until, like time bombs, they explode later on. This kind of narrator stands "lower" than the reader, but "higher" than the characters and situations of the story he tells. So positioned, he can manipulate our emotions in ways that are essential to the proper functioning of the story. For instance, "The Overcoat" will not work as it should if the reader considers Akaky Akakievich too low and ridiculous a character to become plausibly tragic. To forestall that possibility, Gogol deflects our psychic energies, as it were, by presenting us at the outset with a narrator who launches into a lengthy, elaborate and rambling discourse that sets the scene for Akaky's appearance. Since the narrator is inferior to us in intellect and sophistication, and is laughable to boot, he draws onto himself much of our condescension and mockery, which would otherwise fall directly on Akaky. In this sense he is like a lightning rod.

Sometimes the opening narrator appears to be our equal in education, intelligence, and social standing, as in "Old-World Landowners," "The Carriage," and perhaps even "The Nose." For this reason, we tend to assume that anything he has to say is likely to be interesting, even if it looks obvious or trivial. Another way in which this kind of narrator establishes at least a momentary illusion of equality with the reader is through clichés, in which Gogol's works abound. Familiar instances are the ending of "The Fair at Sorochintsy" ("Sad is the lot of one left behind!"), the "pathetic" passage in "The Overcoat" ("[H]ow much inhumanity there is in man"), and the lament about lost youth at the beginning of chapter 6 of *Dead Souls*. Like all clichés, these provide us with momentary islands of comfort and reassurance in an otherwise turbulent textual world. But because they are common property, they cannot be the private language of soul mates. The fairly sophisticated narrator of "Old-World Landowners" takes for granted that we immediately recognize the clichés, in this case the ideas and devices of Sentimentalism; and by way of letting us know that he also knows they are out of date, he says: "It is sad! I feel sad in advance!" (II, 2).[23] This creates a presumption of equality: we too know how to ironize. But so debased had Sentimentalism then become—even Khlestakov, who would be incapable of narrating anything, is familiar with its language— that the irony is ultimately for naught; it is merely comical; and we maintain our sense of superiority and therefore distance.

Finally, distancing is achieved in a more literal way. Because most narrators are vividly present at the beginning of their stories, we tend to endue them with flesh, and try to follow them throughout. In fact, they usually step aside in favor of one or more other narrators. For example, the "pathetic" passage just referred to obviously does not emanate from the same narrator who opened the story just a few pages earlier. Narrative functions may also be assumed by various characters who have no connection with the first narrator. Often a strongly marked narrator enters as the story ends, in order to provide a summary and a commentary. Because he speaks in the first person, we may take for granted that he is the same narrator who introduced the story. But the voice, perspective, and personality are usually very different. The ending of "The Two Ivans" is an instructive case in point:

The lean horses, known in Mirgorod by the name of the post-express horses, set off, making an unpleasant sound as their hoofs sank into the gray mass of mud. The rain poured in streams onto the Jew who sat on the box covered with a sack. The damp pierced me through and through. The gloomy gate with the sentry box, in which a veteran was cleaning his gray equipment, slowly passed by. Again the same fields, in places black and furrowed and in places covered with green, the drenched cows and crows, the monotonous rain, the tearful sky without one gleam of light in it.—It is a dreary world, gentlemen! (II, 214)

Just as the story gets under way on an exclamatory note ("superb!"), so it ends.[24] Here too all is subordinated to a single mood, only now it is melancholy, even despairing, with details highly selected to match. And the thrust is no longer horizontal, as at the beginning, but vertical, as is appropriate to musings on the ravages of time when undertaken in a church whose "long [vertical] windows were streaming with tears of rain." This narrator is meditative and reflective; he forms his sentences like a well-educated man and tops his account off with a sententious commentary on what he has observed; he is in fact far more a seeing than a speaking narrator. It is implausible, although some readers insist on it, that the addle-pated bumpkin who opens the story could, even with the passage of twelve years, evolve into the world-weary commentator who closes it. They are two different voices (and we hear others in the course of the story), not two aspects of one "character." In fact, they are not characters at all.

That can be said of Gogol's "narrators" generally. Probably only Rudy Panko and Poprishchin are full-blown characters in their own right, Poprishchin because he tells his own story from beginning to end, Rudy because he establishes himself as a kind of impresario in the two forewords. Otherwise, "narrators" have no real identities beyond their voices. Understandably, then, the overworked idea of the "unreliable narrator" does not apply in Gogol. What we find instead is something far more disorienting to us as readers: a welter of voices, none of which possesses enough authority in itself to account for the whole story. Our natural desire for clarity and closure is frustrated. There are a few exceptions, particularly in the early works. One is the account of the curse that "explains" the story of Katerina, Danilo, and the sorcerer; but Gogol sets it at the end to prevent us from reading the story as the enactment of that curse. Another is the first version of "The Portrait," where we see Chertkov moved against his will by the power embodied in the moneylender. In the revised version, however, Gogol makes sure that we can identify no one causative factor; we find it very hard to decide why matters take the course they do, even though the artist-monk and his son proffer various interpretations. More often than not, there are no explanations at all. At best, we may hear a final baffled voice, as in "The Nose": "I am absolutely unable to understand it! . . . [I]t is quite beyond my grasp. . . . I really do not know what to say of it ..." (II, 239). Indeed, we do not know why Kovalyov loses his nose, why a nose (whether his or another's) turns up in a loaf of bread, or why he eventually recovers it. Since he is a habitual liar and womanizer, psychology-minded readers may consider these facts explanation enough; but the narrative voice offers no enlightenment.

It is this uncertainty, as the stories close, that puts reader and narrator on the same footing. We have no sense that we are potential rivals who must be flattered and kept closely apprised of what the author is up to, as Fielding, for one, insists: "In so doing, we [the narrator] do not only consult our own dignity and ease, but the good and advantage of the reader: for besides, that, by these means, we prevent him from throwing away his time, in reading without either pleasure or emolument, we give him, at all such seasons, an opportunity of employing that wonderful sagacity, of which he is master, by *filling up these vacant spaces of time with his own conjectures*." No Gogolian narrator would indulge in such sarcasm, for he would never grant, even in jest, that his reader could bring "his own conjectures" into play and move beyond the always well-defined boundaries of a given story. In fact, he makes it impossible for us to do so. In the absence of vivid plot lines and solidly fleshed narrators, we are compelled to listen to the voices: they are all we have; they derive their authority, such as it is, entirely from within the text.[25]

VERBAL UNITS

From the very beginning of his career, Gogol tended to mark individual words or word clusters in highly conspicuous ways. "Word," of course, resists easy definition. For the most part, I use it in the sense of "lexeme," as betokening "the minimal *distinctive* unit in the semantic system of languages."[26] Not all of Gogol's usages can be covered by this rather simple definition; but I see no need at this point to venture terminological refinements: what I mean (or what Gogol means) should become apparent from the comments that follow.

I should say, however, that I regard *every* word in any text, Gogolian or not, as meaningful. Some readers of Gogol would take issue. Cathy Popkin, for one, disapproves of the tendency to view "each detail as inherently meaningful" or to insist on "the absolute expressiveness of each and every element and the coherence of the whole." Instead, she prefers to acknowledge the reality of "verbal clutter" in Gogol—his digressiveness, "endless elaboration," and "exhaustiveness," for example—the reality of "a narrative syntax that exhibits about as much connexity as the items on Ivan Nikiforovich's clothesline [there is actually a great deal, as I have shown in Chapter 3]," all of which may have no function beyond "frustrating" and "derailing" the reader. Certainly she identifies important textual strategies with an astuteness and elegance that I admire. Our differences, I think, turn on the word "meaningful." Unquestionably, not every detail is "meaningful" in the sense of yielding to paraphrase or even explanation; but every detail does form a necessary part of an organic whole and affects the way we perceive that whole, even if it is an accident or a misprint. I believe this to be true of any work of art, as of any life; and one does not have to be an "orthodox Freudian" to subscribe to it, as Popkin suggests. (My own inclinations point me more toward Augustine.) There are of course better and worse ways of "reading" the details; but I think, as apparently she does not, that all these details must be considered *actually* "meaningful," in the sense I have just indicated, even if we cannot say how.[27]

Obviously, then, any attempt at a full study of Gogol's language would run to many volumes. Some preliminary work has been done, mostly by way of classification.[28] My own task here is far more modest. I propose to identify a few of Gogol's more salient verbal devices and show how they function in the service of the text as a whole.

Wordplay

The simplest instance of wordplay, though the hardest to bring off in translation, is represented by so-called "speaking names," which abound in Gogol: Poprishchin (from *poprishche*, "career," or possibly *pryshch*, "pimple"), Bashmachkin (from *bashmak*, "shoe"), Piskaryov (from *pisk*, "squeak"), Sobakevich (from *sobaka*, "dog"), and so on. Our immediate impulse is to read such names as tags. Often they do have this function: Bashmachkin ("The Overcoat") is downtrodden, Piskaryov ("Nevsky Prospekt") is effete, Sobakevich (*Dead Souls*) is crude and blustering. Gogol can be more subtle too. In "The Carriage," Chertokutsky's name is manufactured from *chert* ("devil") and *kutsyi* ("bob-tailed"). The latter may connote emasculation, and thereby comment on his infantile relationship with his wife. Why he is also devilish is harder to fathom, unless Gogol means us to think of his passion for self-concealment, a typically demonic trait, or of the tails that sometimes attach to devils. Frequently a name looks like a tag but is not descriptive in any obvious way. Why should "Chichikov" be derived from the verb "to sneeze" (*chikhat'*), unless Gogol is alluding to the popular connection between sneezing and the devil, or "Nozdryov" from the word for "nostril" (*nozdrya*), unless we are supposed to see this character as a version of the sneezer, Chichikov himself? Otherwise, Gogol may be merely teasing our expectations, tempting us to pointless exercises in paraphrase, thereby forcing us to attend to the sound and texture of words themselves. This is certainly true of those names that are merely comic, with no tag function, like "Chipkhaykhilidzev," "Makdonald Karlovich," and "Maklatura Aleksandrovna" (all in *Dead Souls*).

Sometimes tagging and sound combine in interesting ways. "Akaky Akakievich," for instance, arises out of repetitions of *ka-* and *kak* (reinforced by the rhyming *ta-/tra-/tak*) in the sentences immediately preceding the first mention of the full name: "Mózhet byt', chitátelyu onó pokázhetsya néskol'ko stránnym i vyískannym, no mózhno uvérit', chto egó nikák ne iskáli, a chto sámi sobóyu sluchílis' takíe obstoyátel'stva, chto nikák nel'zyá bylo dát' drugógo ímeni, i éto proizoshló ímenno vot *kak*: rodílsya Akákii Akákievich . . ." ("Perhaps it may strike the reader as a rather strange and contrived name, but I can assure him that it was not contrived at all, that the circumstances were such that it was quite out of the question to give him any other name. Akaky Akakievich was born . . . ," II, 305).

As critics have noted, the recurring *Ka[k]* readily forms into the word *kaka*, or "feces," which also helps establish Akaky as an "anal" (or, in Gogol's term, "hemorrhoidal") character, who is obsessed with routines and rituals. Since his patronymic echoes his given name, we are also told that his biology is his fate, and are prepared for the self-isolated world in which he lives. Not least, Akaky was a sixth-century saint famous for his asceticism and his forbearance despite a difficult superior, qualities that also mark his nineteenth-century namesake.[29]

Other kinds of wordplay depend on various techniques of defamiliarization. One works by making the figurative literal. In "Ivan Fyodorovich Shponka," for instance, we are told: "The P—— infantry regiment was not at all of the class to which many infantry regiments belong, and, although it was for the most part stationed in villages, it was in no way inferior to many cavalry regiments" (I, 176). The word for "infantry" in Russian is *pekhota* (adjective form *pekhotnyi*), which is derived from the root that means "walk"; English has a rough equivalent in "foot soldier." With this in mind, let us make a more literal translation of this sentence: "The P—— *foot regiment [pekhotnyi polk]* was not at all of the class to which many *foot regiments [pekhotnye polki]* belong, and, although it for the most part *stood [stoyal]* in villages, it nonetheless was on such a *footing [na takoi noge, omitted in Garnett/Kent]* that it did not *step back [ustupal,* or 'yield']* to many cavalry regiments." Less obvious, and perhaps more characteristically Gogolian, is the realization of metaphor. Again in "Shponka": "One of the boys entrusted to [Shponka's] charge tried to induce his monitor to write *scit* ['he knows'] on his report, *though he had not learned his lesson,* by bringing into class a *pancake* soaked in butter and wrapped in paper" (I, 175). The Russian of the italicized phrase is *togda kak on svoego uroka v zub ne znal,* the expression *v zub znat'* being a colloquialism for "know thoroughly," "know by heart." Literally it translates as "know onto or into the tooth"—perhaps one could translate it as "sink one's teeth into"—but no one now thinks of the individual lexical components, least of all "tooth *[zub].*" However, the sudden appearance of the word "pancake *[blin],*" the referent of which Shponka promptly undertakes to devour, does tend to prise the "tooth" from the idiom and set it to its usual task.

A more complex instance of the realization of metaphor can be seen in the first Foreword to *Evenings on a Farm Near Dikanka.* Rudy Panko says: "Foma Grigorievich's fingers were moving as though to *make a fig* [lit., 'give a fig,' *dat' dulyu,* a graphically rude gesture]. Fortunately my old woman chose that moment to set *hot rolls and butter [knish s maslom]* on the table. We all set to work on them. Foma Grigorievich's hand, instead of *forming the rude gesture [pokazat' shish],* stretched out for a *hot roll* [*knish*]" (I, 6). It is far more common to "show [*pokazat'*]" a fig in Russian than to "give [*dat'*]" one. The substitution of the unusual verb shakes the stability of the expression and makes *dulyu* potentially detachable from it. We may then become more aware of the literal meaning of *dulyu* (nominative case *dulya*), which is "pear." The fact that another food, *knish*, is juxtaposed to it helps further defamiliarize the expression by pulling *dulya* into the same semantic field. The sound of the word *knish* echoes that of *kukish*. It does not occur in this passage, but is likely to spring to the reader's mind, not only because it also means "pear" but also because it is commonly found in the expression *pokazat' kukish*, which means the same thing as *pokazat'* (here *dat'*) *dulyu*. *Kukish* is further made silently present and stretched by Rudy's mention of the word *maslo*, "butter," in the sentence we are discussing. A Russian reader immediately summons up the common expression *poluchit' kukish s maslom*, which translates literally as "receive a *kukish* with butter," and means "come away empty-handed," or "receive a snub." This may hint at Rudy's perception of his lowly position vis-à-vis polite society, which even a well-told story can do little to improve. Or it may be a joke on the readers with active imaginations! Finally, *knish* also rhymes with *shish*, which is used mainly in the expression *pokazat' shish*, as in this text, and is synonymous with *pokazat' dulyu* and *pokazat' kukish*, although it lacks any associations with food. With these four apparently simple sentences, Gogol gives us a lesson in the ways his words work, and, as early as 1831, establishes a connection between food and sex, thereby foreshadowing one of the major themes that will inform much of his fiction to come.

Another kind of play involves words that are so "neutral" on first encounter as to escape notice until they become defamiliarized by what follows. Then they are seen to function as what we might call "pivot words," providing transitions from one semantic field to another, as instances of *e praecedentibus sequentia, e sequentibus praecedentia*, or "the understanding of what follows from what precedes and what precedes from what follows."[30] For example, in the account of Ivan Fyodorovich Shponka's military service we are told: "while the others were driving about with hired horses, visiting the less important landowners, he, sitting at home, spent his time in pursuits peculiar to a mild and gentle soul: he either polished his buttons, or read a fortunetelling book or set mousetraps in the corners of his room, or failing everything he would take off his uniform and lie on his bed" (I, 177). The pivot phrase here is "polished his buttons [*chistil pugovitsy*]." In a military setting, this is a normal occupation for a soldier; and since it is set in contrast to the frivolous pastimes of Shponka's comrades, it suggests that he is a model officer. However, fortunetelling books and mousetraps are certainly not the business of soldiers but the preoccupation of fearful housewives; in this context, button polishing also becomes potentially a housewifely act; and the military associations are further distanced when Shponka removes the button-bearing uniform altogether and takes to his bed. Then too, a soldier-housewife is a hermaphroditic being; the hermaphrodite is sterile, and in this sense is equivalent to the self-gratifier, who is hinted at in the detail of the unclad figure lying alone on his bed.

More subtly, Gogol's titles can also do duty as pivot words. They run to the low-key and the modest, and usually consist of a single word or phrase, like "The Nose," "The Overcoat," "The Carriage," "Nevsky Prospekt," "The Portrait." Immediately elicited by these titles is the whole range of received meanings and usages, as well as our own idiosyncratic definitions: we all "know" what a "carriage" and an "overcoat" are. But then follows the entire story, which in effect is an essay in defining the title. The result is an array of new and unpredictable definitions, against which the received meanings are constantly evaluated. Hence the feeling of insecurity, even bafflement with which we are often left at the end of the story. Gogol's method is the opposite of the mystery writer's. He does not rely on the sort of cryptic or teasing title with which readers of, say, Sir Arthur Conan Doyle are familiar, no "Hound of the Baskervilles," "The Adventure of the Speckled Band," or "The Red-Headed League." We are prepared for strange and unusual happenings, yet find that the stories end in very ordinary ways, when Sherlock Holmes explains, often with great condescension, what he claims any reasonably intelligent and observant man can deduce on the evidence of his own senses. Gogol, on the contrary, moves from a title that seems perfectly plain and obvious, to the conclusion that nothing can be fully understood, that the ordinary yields to the extraordinary, and that puzzlement is the normal condition after events have run their course.

Densification

Densification, or a thickening of texture, is a very common way Gogol has of making us advert to individual verbal units. Among the varieties is enumeration.

An excellent man is Ivan Ivanovich! What a house he has in Mirgorod! There's a porch all round it on oak posts, and there are seats under the porch everywhere. When the weather is too hot, Ivan Ivanovich casts off his coat and his underwear, remaining in nothing but his shirt, and rests under his porch watching what is passing in the yard and in the street. What apple trees and pear trees he has under his very windows! You need only open the window—and the branches thrust themselves into the room. That is all in the front of the house; but you should see what he has in the garden at the back! What hasn't he got there! Plums, white cherries, black cherries, vegetables of all sorts, sunflowers, cucumbers, melons, peas, even a threshing barn and a forge. (II, 169–70)

The objects listed here could not be more ordinary: porch, posts, seats, yard, street, room, trees, produce, and farm structures. However, the profusion of prepositions and adverbs—all around, everywhere, under, in, into, in front of, in back—creates for the viewer a multiplicity of angles and distances suggesting that these objects have a density and palpability that mere labeling cannot convey. The two sentences ending in exclamation points (which always heighten content) function as pivot phrases by forcing us to look back and ahead. We might paraphrase them as follows: if you think that what's *in front* of the house is impressive (just in case you may not have thought so at the time), then you should see what's *behind* the house: that's really something! The suggestion that what is to come is still more important throws everything that has preceded into higher relief. "What" and "what not" call for definition, which ensues in the listing of the ten nouns. In itself, enumeration tends to endow each component with a certain weight; but it is even more marked here because of the way it ends: "even a threshing barn and a forge." "Even [*dazhe*]" signals that what follows is worthy of greater attention than what has gone before, and at the same time intimates that the preceding eight nouns are more significant than we might have thought.[31] This is one of the ways in which Gogol prevents us from reading in our usual fluent, rapid manner, where we are largely unaware of constituent words. One result is a certain blurring of boundaries, for if everything enumerated is potentially extraordinary, then everything is of equal importance. Our natural penchant for ordering and classifying is set at naught.

Retardation is another variety of densification. It frequently appears as negation. In the "earliest morning" scene of "Nevsky Prospekt" (I, 208), for example, we are first told that the street is "empty." But in a kind of preterition, the narrator goes on to specify what is absent: "the stout shopkeepers and their assistants are still asleep in their linen shirts." Then follow some ten lines relating what goes on away from the Nevsky, and concluding with a statement that reinforces the idea of absence: "It may be confidently stated that at this period, that is, up to twelve o'clock, Nevsky Prospekt is *not* the goal for any man [still absence through negation], but simply the means of reaching it: it is filled with people who have their occupations, their anxieties, and their annoyances, and are *not* thinking about the avenue [presence through absence]" (208–9). Then come some ten lines specifying just who these people are. By now our attention is fully engaged: if all these carefully specified features represent absence or purposelessness, then the Nevsky is likely to seem far more solid, real, vivid and full when it is finally shown in all its presence.

Syntactically, retardations may be created by parataxis, which is a variety of enumeration, and Gogol uses it lavishly in many of his stories. Nonenumeratively, it may depend on hypotaxis, which is Gogol's method in "Nevsky Prospekt": "Not only the young man of twenty-five summers with a fine mustache and a splendidly cut coat, but even the veteran with white hairs sprouting on his chin and a head as smooth as a silver dish is enthusiastic over Nevsky Prospekt" (207). This in turn illustrates another technique of Gogolian retardation: backtracking. For this sentence is only a repetition and amplification of the one that precedes, "I know that not one of the poor clerks that live there would trade Nevsky Prospekt for all the blessings of the world," which in turn repeats and amplifies the opening statement, "There is nothing finer than Nevsky Prospekt" (207). This statement is a truism, as are all the generalizations about the Nevsky in this opening paragraph: "it is the making of the city . . . the fairest of our city thoroughfares," and so on. On first occurrence, they inspire skepticism in the reader, as does any cliché. The narrator must play rhetorician, persuading us, and rather quickly, to find them interesting enough to continue reading. Unlike the narrator who opens "The Two Ivans," he does not need to demonstrate the importance of the Nevsky; rather, he must defamiliarize it precisely because everyone knows it is important. Each of these two narrators works in his own distinctive way, as he brings to prominence material we would otherwise disregard; but the result, defamiliarization, is the same. Objects take on fullness and importance; truisms become assertions of facts that had not occurred to us before. Some twenty lines down, for instance, we read: "Nevsky Prospekt is the general channel of communication in Petersburg." To that we all assent. But in the preceding ten or so lines, we have been taught to look with new eyes:

And indeed, to whom is it not agreeable? As soon as you step into [*vzoidesh'*, lit., "ascend into"] Nevsky Prospekt you are in an atmosphere of gaiety [*gulyan'em*]. Though you may have some necessary [*nuzhnoe*] and essential [*neobkhodimoe*] business, yet as soon as you step into it [*vzoshedshi*, lit., "having ascended"], you forget, most likely, about all business. This is the one place where people put in an appearance not out of necessity [*ne po neobkhodimosti*], without being driven there by need [*nadobnost'*] and by the commercial interests that embrace all of Petersburg. A man met on Nevsky Prospekt seems less of an egoist than on Morskaya, Gorokhovaya, Liteinaya, Meshchanskaya and other streets, where greed, *and* selfishness, *and* need [*nadobnost'*] are expressed in all who walk *and* speed along in carriages and droshkies. Nevsky Prospekt is the general channel of communication in Petersburg. (207–8; with considerable modifications)

The first sentence is a trite rhetorical question. But it is promptly defamiliarized by wordplay: *gulyan'em* can mean "walking" and "gaiety" (i.e., diversion), both of which fit here. The subordinate clause that begins the

next sentence creates syntactical and psychological anticipation, and requires resolution. "Necessary and essential business" looks like new information, because it contrasts with "agreeable" and "gaiety"; the "yet"
that follows, however, undoes the contrast and creates a new sense of anticipation with a subordinate clause introduced by a weighty-sounding ad-
verbial participle (*vzoshedshi*), which is simply a different form of the verb
employed in the preceding subordinate clause. The resolution of the sentence is further delayed by "most likely [*verno*]," which is made more conspicuous by the straddling commas. When the resolution does come—"you
forget . . . all about business"—it feels like an anticlimax after the anticipation quickened by "ascending," as if into a holy place; yet it is not ironic
because it repeats the idea of carefreeness conveyed at the beginning in
"agreeable" and "gaiety." The words *neobkhodimost'*, *neobkhodimoe*,
nuzhnoe, and *nadobnost'* are virtual synonyms (though different parts of
speech), and thus here become lexical forms of backtracking. "Commercial interests"—an amplified synonym of "business [*delo*]," twice repeated
in the first sentence—are said to "embrace all of Petersburg." Hereby they
echo yet contradict the first sentence of the story, which tells us that the
Nevsky in itself "comprises everything." But the following sentence con-
tradicts the statement about "commercial interests" by situating these undesirable qualities not in "all of Petersburg" but in particular streets famous for housing tradesmen of various kinds (omitted in Garnett/Kent),
and contrasting them with the Nevsky ("less of an egoist [there]"), which
is thereby restored to its original grandeur and capaciousness. Again, syntax helps make the point: the sudden lapse into parataxis, with the insis-
tently repeated "and," fragments the components of the non-Nevsky parts
of Petersburg, and helps play up the contrast with the "all," which is the
true scope of the great and magnificent main street.

By the time we get to the truism about "the general channel of communication"—so colorless that it might have been lifted from a guide-
book—we react with relief, not with skepticism, at being back on familiar
ground after such a tortuous, obstacle-strewn course. Yet we also understand that truisms do not begin to give an accurate picture of what this
particular world is really like; and we are more inclined to assume that
familiar reality contains more than meets the eye and ear. Gogol is teaching
us how to read him.

Repetition

Repetition is an obvious but effective technique for highlighting detail and
fixing it in a reader's or listener's mind. It abounds in Gogol's works, taking
many different forms. At its simplest, it involves the literal reduplication
of a word or phrase:

[*Ivan Nikiforovich*]: "Who has ever heard of swapping a *gun for two sacks of oats*? . . ."

[*Ivan Ivanovich*]: "But you forget, Ivan Nikiforovich, I am giving you the *sow*, too."

[*I. N.*]: "What, *two sacks of oats and a sow for a gun*!"

[*I. I.*]: "Why, isn't it enough?"

[*I. N.*]: "*For the gun*?"

[*I. I.*]: "Of course *for the gun*!"

[*I. N.*]: "*Two sacks for a gun*?"

[*I. I.*]: "*Two sacks*, not empty, but full of *oats*; and have you forgotten the *sow*?"

("The Two Ivans," II, 180–81)

Rhetorically, this bears some resemblance to what Slonimsky has called "conversations of the deaf."[32] One purpose is to create suspense: we wonder who will break through the verbal impasse, and how. Another is to mark the ordinary in such a way as to enable it to become extraordinary. Still another is to alert the reader-listener to the importance of the components: here it is gun, sow, and sacks of oats that matter, not any other words that might be chosen if mere suspense-building were the only aim. Gogol's task is to invest these particular words with a presence large enough to guide the course of the story. What Frank O'Connor says about Hemingway's use of detail applies here as well:

[T]he repetition of key words and key phrases . . . slows down the whole conversational movement of prose, the casual, sinuous, evocative quality that distinguishes it from poetry and is intended to link author and reader in a common perception of the object, and replaces it by a series of *verbal rituals* which are intended to evoke *the object as it may be supposed to be*. At an extreme point it attempts to *substitute the image for the reality*. It is *a rhetorician's dream*.[33]

This is especially apt for a story like "The Two Ivans," which is about the magic power of words that in turn depends on exact repetition and a highly developed sense of verbal ritual.

But is repetition really possible in anything but the most formal sense? Certainly it seems to be in such oral narrative devices as tropes and, more recently, in what Lidiya Ginzburg calls "the poetics of stable styles [*poetika ustoichivykh stilei*]," which presupposes the "repeatability of poetic means" from writer to writer, work to work, often regardless of content and theme. Repetition was a feature of eighteenth-century poetry, but claimed the allegiance of many writers well into the nineteenth century, long after it had been killed off by Pushkin. It creates the impression that "each . . . [repeated] verbal image is isolated from the others, and the associations aroused by it are shut up within its boundaries and do not carry over into the neighboring semantic series." Whether the reader actually perceives such images in this manner is open to question. I would agree with Yury Lotman that literal repetition in any artistic text is impossible, if only because "all the orderings in it are meaningful," and with each recurrence a word carries "a different syntactic or semantic load."[34] Certainly any text by Gogol could be brought in by way of confirmation. Although his repetitions are always specific to a particular text, they never function as tropes.

One notable practice, found in every period of his work, is the repetition of words and phrases that do not consistently attach to one character or situation. In Section IV of "Ivan Fyodorovich Shponka," for example, the hero goes to dinner at the house of Grigory Grigorievich Storchenko, a neighboring landowner. It is an occasion made memorable by the odd assortment of characters, the enormous meal, and the inane conversation. One of the guests, Ivan Ivanovich (the name itself could not be more inane), comments on the turkey that is being served: "Hm! do you call this a *turkey?* . . . Is that what a *turkey* ought to look like? If you could see my *turkeys*! I assure you there is more *fat [zhiru]* on one of them than on a dozen of these. Would you believe me, sir, they really are a repulsive sight when they walk about my yard, they are so *fat [zhirny]* . . . !" Storchenko calls him a liar and a fool three times (virtually mandatory on ritualistic occasions). Ivan Ivanovich then "said no more, but began downing the *turkey*, even though it was not so *fat [zhirna]* as those that were a repulsive sight" (I, 189–91). This is a comic set piece, invoking two stock Gogolian types: the boaster (Ivan Ivanovich) and the bully (Storchenko). It is also a conversation of the deaf, with Ivan Ivanovich going on "as though [Storchenko's] words could not possibly refer to him," thereby fixing "turkey" and "fat" in our minds.

It is easy enough to associate Storchenko with the turkey. He presides over the dinner where it is the centerpiece, seems unnecessarily bothered by Ivan Ivanovich's blather, and is as stupid and vain as a barnyard Tom. Furthermore, we already know that he is a "fat *[tolstyi]* man," whose "head rest[s] immovably on his short neck, which seem[s] even fatter *[tolshche]* because of a double chin" (180; Garnett/Kent has "thicker," but that misses the repetition). Although in Russian *tolstyi* is used only of persons and *zhirnyi* only of animals, at least in polite discourse, the two merge in Storchenko, not only associatively but almost explicitly in a statement the aunt makes after Ivan Fyodorovich returns from the dinner. She wants to know all the details, primarily what he has found out about the deed (*zapis'*) in which one Stepan Kuzmich (presumably his father) left him the adjoining estate that is now occupied by Storchenko. Her first question is: "Well, did you get the deed out of the old reprobate?" To which Ivan replies: "No, Auntie. . . . Grigory Grigorievich has no deed!" She retorts: "And you believed him? He was lying, the damned scoundrel! Some day

I'll come across him and I will give him a drubbing with my own hands. Oh, *I'd get rid of some of his fat for him* [*ya emu pospushchu zhiru*]!" (191) We would expect her to use the common expression *ya emu spushchu shkuru*, "I will give him a good hiding." Instead, for "hide [*shkuru*]" she substitutes "fat [*zhiru*]," alters the verb slightly, and thereby destabilizes the idiom so that new elements can easily be introduced. Such elements will of course be marked, and since in this case *zhir* is the intruder, we are likely to think back to Ivan Ivanovich's discourse on turkeys and tie Storchenko even more tightly to that bird, particularly since *zhir*, in its noun form, can be used of both animals and humans. We may also remember that in its turkey context, Ivan Ivanovich considers "fat" evocative of plenty, but also "disgusting." These apparently contradictory qualities fit Storchenko rather well too, and further attest to the instability of the image, which is symbolically cut loose by the aunt's threat against her rival.

The aunt abruptly changes the subject (always an attention-getting device in Gogol), asking: "Well, was the dinner good?" Presently she introduces the essential bird as she inquires whether there was "a turkey with pickled plums" (191–92). "Dinner" and "turkey" remain within the same semantic field as "fat," but a new context is established when Shponka, in an amusing non sequitur (another call for the reader's attention), juxtaposes "turkeys" and "young ladies": "Yes, there was a turkey too ... ! Very handsome young ladies, Grigory Grigorievich's sisters, especially the fair one!" Now, it is conventional to compare pretty girls to birds like swans, swallows, pigeons, or chickadees, but certainly not turkeys. The unexpected substitution in a conventional figure of thought creates new associations. "Girl" is now linked, in a complex cluster, not only with "turkey" but also with "fat" and with Storchenko. Food and sex have been put together—but not for the first time. We may remember the scene at the very beginning of the story, where Shponka, acting as class monitor, was bribed by one of the other students, who offered him "a pancake soaked in butter." Hungry and unable to resist, "he took the pancake, held a book up before him, and began eating it, and he was so absorbed in this occupation that he did not observe that a deathly silence had fallen upon the class" in response to the arrival of the "terrifying teacher," who snatched the pancake from Shponka's hands and flung it out the window. He indulges in an illicit pleasure, which he has hoped to conceal, and is punished for it. The method of punishment is specified in some detail, and makes clear that more than eating is involved: "Then he proceeded on the spot to whack Ivan Fyodorovich very painfully on the hands; and quite rightly—the hands were responsible for taking it and no other part of the body" (176). The hands are also of course responsible for the one illicit and hidden sexual practice typical of adolescents, masturbation.

All the ingredients of this scene are present when Shponka, on his way home from the army, stops for the night at a shabby inn, and there for the first time meets Storchenko. When they discover they are neighbors, they kiss: "[Storchenko] folded Ivan Fyodorovich in an embrace and kissed [*oblobyzal*] him first on the right cheek and then on the left and then on the right again." The Russian word for "kiss" here is old-fashioned, roughly equivalent to the English "osculate." One thinks of maids and swains in eighteenth-century poetry. In this context, it is amusing. It also alerts us to something out of the ordinary. What is notable is not the kiss itself, for that was and still is a normal form of greeting between men in Russia, but rather Shponka's reaction: "Ivan Fyodorovich was much gratified by this kiss [*lobyzanie*], for his lips took the stranger's large cheeks for soft pillows" (180). We are meant, I think, to remember the earlier instance in which Shponka's lips encounter something rounded, soft, and pleasurable, namely, the pancake, and the consequences of that encounter. In the exchange with Storchenko, punishment does not follow immediately. But it is anticipated by an expansion of imagery. The other part of the body traditionally subjected to flogging is the buttocks. They do not figure in the pancake scene, but they suggestively appear in the inn scene as "pillows" and as "cheeks," which can denote either end of the body in both English and Russian. In this context, a kiss becomes homoerotic, the more so when we remember that pillows are normally located on a bed.[35] Later, when Shponka visited Storchenko at his estate, "[his] lips found themselves again in contact with the same pillows" (186). One more step and Shponka's lips may begin to "eat" Storchenko's cheeks/buttocks, as they did the pancake, and as they will the "turkey" that Storchenko is soon to become. But homoerotic practices are illicit too, far more so than the equally sterile practice of masturbation. If self-gratification, or pancake eating, is punished by flogging, what might be the penalty for the crime of "eating" another man? However, if the turkey is metamorphosed into the girl, as happens through Shponka's odd juxtaposition, then "eating" might be permissible, certainly within marriage, and might not incur punishment. In Shponka's case, however, "turkey" and "eating" have accumulated an array of "forbidden" associations, and the punishment, though delayed, is far worse for him than mere flogging. Ironically, it consists in the very ritual, marriage, which would legitimize his erotic desires, at least legally. The polysemantic imagery has ensured that he will also be "marrying" Storchenko, who is simultaneously an object of his desire and a threatening authority figure, simultaneously appealing and disgusting.

One function of the dream that ends the story is to make these feelings clear to Shponka and to us by repeating and clustering the major images. However, turkey and fatness are nowhere to be found. They have undergone the kind of transmutations that are common in dreams. Now the wife has "the face of a goose," as does "another wife"; he then sees a third and a fourth wife—and a fifth, sixth, and seventh, and even more. "Fatness" may well be present in the very profusion of wives. But how does a turkey become a goose? As nasty, hissing creatures, geese better fit Shponka's idea of women. These same qualities are found in various predatory birds, but not all are edible, as a goose is, and do not therefore reinforce the all-important link between food and sex. Furthermore, turkeys have already undergone transformation into another bird in one of Ivan Ivanovich's disquisitions at the dinner: "he would pop his head out of his chaise and make faces from which one could almost, it seemed, read . . . how large were the melons of which he had been speaking, and how *fat* [*zhirnye*] were the *geese* that were running about in his yard" (191). Transformation also works here to produce a new image, melons. They may suggest plump buttocks and breasts, therefore Storchenko and the girl. (The aunt is too mannish to count.) But they also point back to Shponka's father: "Your poor father [says Ivan Ivanovich] . . . used to have melons such as you never see anywhere now. Here, for instance . . . they'll set melons before you on the table—such melons! You won't care to look at them! Would you believe it, sir, he used to have watermelons . . . God bless me, they were as big as this!" (188). Structurally, this is identical to Ivan Ivanovich's discourse on turkeys; it therefore ties the question of paternity to the images of fat, turkey, pancake, buttocks, cheeks, girl, and, perhaps most important, Storchenko. He has somehow obtained the deed left by Shponka's progenitor, and thus becomes a surrogate father, with the power to evoke secret longings in the surrogate son, and the power to punish them. But these longings are as illegitimate as Shponka himself; so the question of his legitimacy as a person is once again raised. Insofar as Shponka defines personhood as self-isolation and self-gratification, he is doomed to become a nonperson: "[T]o get married ... ! It seemed to him so strange, so peculiar, he couldn't think of it without horror. Living with a wife ... ! Unthinkable! He would not be alone in his own room, but they would always have to be together ... !" (196).

His apprehensions about the loss of self are amply confirmed by the dream. Even his most secret places—his ear, his pocket, his hat—are inhabited by his wife. No longer can he hide; to the contrary, he now has a public identity as a "married man" and can be seen by all. This may be the meaning of the "bell" that suddenly appears: "He went toward her, but his aunt was no longer an aunt but a belfry, and he felt that someone was dragging him by a rope up the belfry. 'Who is it pulling me?' Ivan Fyodorovich cried plaintively. 'It is me, your wife. I am pulling you because you are a bell.' 'No, I am not a bell, I am Ivan Fyodorovich,' he cried. 'Yes, you are a bell,' said the colonel of the P—— infantry regiment, who happened to be passing" (197). Confinement in a belfry is an effective dream equivalent of feeling trapped in a marriage. But the belfry is the aunt, who has masterminded the union, and probably will continue to do so, since her real interest, as one of Gogol's acquirer-figures, is in the children it may produce. Why a belfry? Perhaps because it is tall, like the aunt, provides a vantage point from which she can keep an eye on her nephew, and also offers him, as the bell enclosed within, a revealing if unwelcome panoramic view of his own true situation. Yet it is a very limited panorama. The Russian reader will probably think of the idiom *smotret' so svoei kolokol'ni*, "look out from one's own belfry," or "take a narrow, parochial view of things," which would suit Shponka's personality and position very well. It is the aunt once more who calls the tune, as it were, with the help of the wife; and the tune they call, like any tune played on a bell, can be heard far and wide, even by the colonel of Shponka's old regiment, which is stationed hundreds of miles away. The bitter experience of the pancake long ago has taught Shponka the perils of being seen, and he has no reason to think that in his newly exposed position, where he is not only seen but heard, an even fiercer punishment will not inevitably follow, presumably in the form of eternal subservience to domineering women.

The story contains several other important repeating images—clothing, lying, the ear, and so on—which constitute part of that large image-world of which different characters and situations may partake. A more modern instance of this technique is found in Andrei Bely's novel *Petersburg*.[36] Of course a dream provides a convenient motivation for the displacement of all kinds of material. But a careful look at the story reveals that virtually all the important imagery has already been displaced, and therefore has the capacity to move anywhere. The fact that the story lacks an "ending" (Rudy informs us at the beginning that is has been lost) leads us to suspect that this basic stock of imagery could undergo still other recombinations, and that the dream therefore represents only one version.

Repetitions in Gogol heighten our awareness of the presence of particular words, but paradoxically, can sometimes make the point that words are arbitrary and even expendable. This is mostly a theme of his later work. One brief example will suffice for now. In chapter 1 of *Dead Souls*, the men of the town are divided into two groups, the stout (*tolstye*) and the thin (*tonkie*), in keeping with the contrastive poetics of the then-popular physiological sketch. In chapter 9, the same contrast is restated, but the terms have shifted in a fundamental way. "[The ladies'] dresses displayed an infinite variety of taste: muslins, satins, chiffons were of the pale fashionable shades for which even a name could not be found (such a degree of *refinement* [*tonkost'*] has modern taste reached) . . . (it must be noted that, in general, the ladies of the town of N. were rather *plump* [*polnye*], but they laced themselves so skilfully and carried themselves so charmingly that it was quite impossible to notice how *plump* they were [*tolshchiny nikak nel'zya bylo primetit'*])" (173). It is not so much that the terms now apply to women instead of men as that they are no longer used to describe two different kinds of people. "Thin," in its secondary meaning of "refined," now coexists with "plump," in the same body; but because "plump" refers only to a physical condition, "thin" retains its physical dimension as well. Two contrasting qualities have been merged into one, and it is up to the reader to wonder how "thinness" and "fatness" can coexist, whether the contrast has any meaning at all, whether the constituent elements of these two passages are meaningful, and if so, in what senses.

12

The Word in *Dead Souls*

GOGOL worked on the first part of *Dead Souls* for some six years, mostly while living abroad. It betrays much of the same uncertainty about the visual that we find in "Rome" and in "The Portrait," but it goes farther than either of these works in establishing the word as a theme and as a viable way of engaging the world.

The very title of the book thrusts the problem of the word to the fore. Ambiguously it suggests either the aliveness of dead souls or the deadness of living souls. Gogol's censor, smelling heresy, made him rename it *The Adventures of Chichikov* (Pokhozhdeniya Chichikova), with "dead souls" relegated to the subtitle. But theological issues pale before linguistic ones.

CHAPTER I

Definitions shape the opening paragraph. The "carriage" that rolls through the gates of the inn is mentioned seven times. First it is introduced by the narrator. Then it is said to be the locus of "bachelors" and of the "gentleman" sitting in it. Then it attracts the attention of "two Russian peasants." Finally it is observed and inspected by a "young man." In the process, it acquires three different names: *brichka* (registered three times), *koleso* (twice), and *ekipazh* (twice).[1] *Brichka* is a word of Polish provenance (*bryczka*), which the *Oxford English Dictionary* registers as "britzka," or "britzska," and defines as follows: "An open carriage with calash top, and space for reclining when used for a journey." *Koleso*, which is pure Russian, translates as "wheel," sums up the practical function of the vehicle, and, as synecdoche, marks a sudden narrowing of focus. *Ekipazh* can be rendered as "turn-out." Of French origin, its nearest English equivalent is "equipage," which the *OED* defines as "a carriage with or without horses and the attendant servants." It stretches *brichka* to make room for both horses and carriage. Implicitly raised in this first paragraph is the question of the adequacy of any one word to account for one object.

The human characters are named in different ways as well. The "bachelors [*kholostyaki*]" are a genus, members of which are identified by species, like taxonomic specimens: "retired lieutenant-colonels, majors, and landowners with about a hundred serfs." With the "gentleman [*gospodin*]" in the carriage, we move from plural to singular, that is, to a specific instance, and to a semblance of individualization: "*not* handsome, but *neither* was he particularly bad-looking; he was *neither* too fat, *nor* too thin; he could *not* be said to be old, but he was *not* too young, either. His arrival in the town did *not* create any [*no*] great stir, *nor* was it marked by anything [*nothing*] out of the ordinary" (17). Negation is a technique characteristic of Gogol's style in all periods; here it indicates that definitions are elusive; yet enumeration, however imprecise, does lend this "gentleman" a certain weight and presence, certainly enough to make us wonder who and what he is—questions the narrator wants us to ask about Chichikov (though we do not yet know his name) at every turn in the book.

Then come the "two Russian peasants [*dva russkie muzhika*]," who seem more palpable not only because they view the carriage in a more concrete way, but because they provide the only instance of direct speech in this paragraph. It marks an abrupt shift in diction, from the relatively "high" style of the narrator to the "low" conversational, and is thrown into even greater prominence by being framed ("made certain remarks. . . . That was the end of the conversation"): "'Lord,' said one of them to the other, 'what a wheel! What do you say? Would a wheel like that, if put to it, ever get to Moscow or wouldn't it?' 'It would all right,' replied the other. 'But it wouldn't get to Kazan, would it?' 'No, it wouldn't get to Kazan,' replied the other. That was the end of the conversation" (17). I think Vladimir Nabokov overloads this passage when he calls it "a kind of to-be-or-not-to-be meditation in a primitive form." More to the point is his characterization of the expression "Russian *muzhiks*" as "a typical Gogolian pleonasm," by which he means that *muzhik* in itself can mean only a *Russian* peasant: no attributive adjective is required.[2] If this is more than sheer oversight on Gogol's part—as we must always be ready to assume, given his careful working habits—then the pleonasm is consistent with his handling of details: he wishes to train us to notice them, however trivial they may seem, so that we will ask: what other kinds of peasants could there possibly be in a Russian provincial town? Or: how are Russian peasants, these two in particular, different from French, German, or Italian ones?

Finally comes the "young man," who does not speak but is described in the kind of detail denied all the other characters in this opening paragraph: "wearing very narrow and very short white canvas trousers, a swallow-tail coat with some pretensions to fashion, disclosing a shirt-front fastened with a pin of Tula manufacture in the shape of a bronze pistol," this last particular fixing the portrait indelibly in our minds. Furthermore, he is not merely driving like the bachelors, sitting like the gentleman, or standing like the peasants, but is endowed with a series of gestures: "The young man *turned round, took a look* at the carriage, *held on* to his cap which a *gust* of wind *nearly blew off* his head, and *went* on his way" (17). Compared to the others, he is virtually a fully developed personage. Yet he promptly disappears from the story. Nabokov, much taken with this fact, observes: "With any other writer of his day the next paragraph would have been bound to begin: 'Ivan, for that was the young man's name' ... But no: a gust of wind interrupts his stare and he passes, never to be mentioned again" (77). Nabokov offers no explanation for this character, beyond seeing him as another instance of the kind of "spontaneous generation" (83) that creates such a wealth of secondary personages in the book. No doubt that is true. But Gogol is also teasing us, as is his wont, and in doing so, again raising questions of definition in our minds. Who is this young man? Why has he no name, if he is so fleshed out? What part will he play in the story? What is the significance of the striking pin he is wearing? We do not yet know whether these are important questions, or even the right questions. At the very least we may suppose that Gogol is warning us to develop the habit of sharpening our eyes.

Like the other characters in this paragraph, the young man is an observer who at the same time is himself being observed by the reader, the narrator, and perhaps the gentleman in the carriage as well.[3] Each of the terms for "carriage" brings into play a different angle of vision, and implicitly a value judgment too, not only of the object being viewed but also of those who view it in that way. Seeing is established from the outset as potentially an important way of getting at the meaning of this world. Yet we already know that we cannot be sure of what we see, or of what is seen for us by the personages. And we will discover that multiple points of view characterize the book to its very end.

One problem is trying to find a language adequate to account for what appears before us. The varieties of speech in the first paragraph lead us to suspect that this will be no easy task. The rest of the first chapter reinforces this impression. For one thing, there is no uniform level of discourse. We find journalese, as in the newspaper report about "some public fete" (21);

a Homeric simile occasioned by the party at the governor's house (24); a
small-scale physiological sketch built on a contrast between two types, fat
and thin men (24–25); the private language of the "names with which they
[the guests at the party] had christened the different [card] suits among
themselves," "Hearts! Heartache! Spades! or Spadefulls! Spade-a-little-
lady! or simply, Speedy!" (26).[4] Many others could be identified. Besides
grounding the theme of language, these passages attune our ear to verbal
texture. Such attunement is essential if we are to catch some of the subtler
instances of verbal play.

For one, when Chichikov enters the public room of the inn, "there was
the same grimy ceiling, the same grimy chandelier with a multitude of pen-
dant glass drops, vibrating and tinkling every time the waiter ran across
the worn oil-cloth, smartly brandishing a tray with as large a number of
teacups as there are birds on the seashore" (19).

The reader has been prepared for the teacup-bird association by the fragmentation and animation of the chandelier in the preceding sentence.
"Glass drops [*steklyshek*: cf. Guerney, 'bits of glass']" are said to be "vibrating [lit., 'jumping,' *prygali*: cf. Guerney, 'leaped and bounded']" in response to the waiter's heavy tread. It is then only a short step to bits of
porcelain on the same waiter's tray looking as if they are about to take off
like seagulls. But the potential for animation has already been embedded
by a subtle point of word usage that is hard to render in translation: "the
same grimy ceiling, the same grimy chandelier." Magarshack really ought
to attach different adjectives to "ceiling" and "chandelier." The Russian
does, with *zakopchennyi* and *kopchenaya*. Both are derived from the verb
koptit', "to cure in smoke," "to blacken with smoke" (*Oxford Russian-
English Dictionary*). *Kopchenaya*, however, applies primarily to foods that
have been smoked: for a native speaker, it is almost invariably followed by
vetchina ("ham") or *kolbasa* ("sausage"). When followed by *lyustra*
("chandelier"), it sounds grotesque, especially when juxtaposed to the
"correct" *zakopchennyi potolok* ("smoke-blackened ceiling"), because it
intimates that the object was once alive.[5] Most interesting is the new visual
reality that emerges from the purely phonic environment created by "teacups." The Russian reads: *bezdna CHAInykh chashEK* ("a large number
of tea cups"), where the syllables I set off in capital letters combine to form
cha[i]ek, the genitive plural (as the grammar requires) of *chaika*, or "seagull." No mention is made of "seagull" as such, but this is the bird most
commonly found on seashores.[6] All this happens in a passage prefaced by
assurances that the public room, and everything within it, is ordinary and
familiar: "*Every* traveller has *a very good idea* of what these public rooms
are like: the walls are *always the same* . . . the merchants repaired there
regularly . . . to drink their *customary* two cups of tea . . . *the same* grimy

ceiling . . . *the same* grimy chandelier . . . *the same* oil paintings" (19). But the wordplay of the teacups-turned-seagulls is anything but customary: it is yet another instance of ordinary words that may become extraordinary, in ways that cannot be predicted and that mock the narrator's penchant for generalization.

The "gentleman" or "traveller" who arrives at the inn acquires no other labels until the waiter asks him to write out "his rank, his Christian name, and his surname on a piece of paper, so that it might be communicated to the proper quarters, namely the police." The gentleman complies, and we learn for the first time that he is "Collegiate Councillor [Grade 6 in the Table of Ranks, considerably higher than Poprishchin or Akaky Akakievich], Pavel Ivanovich Chichikov, landowner, travelling on private business." We note that it is Chichikov himself, not the narrator, who provides this information (20). The statement is brief, to the point, fixed on paper. Of course we do not yet know what any of these terms may mean, but by now we are old enough hands at reading Gogol to distrust appearances of linguistic permanence.

With the publication of this information, Chichikov gains a considerable advantage over the narrator, who is never named, and only occasionally emerges as "I." In fact, the narrator is not a "character" at all, but a succession of personae, each with his own point of view and voice, whereas Chichikov gradually emerges as a personage in his own right. In this first chapter, however, he shares at least two important traits with the narrative persona: a keen interest in looking and a fascination with words. For the narrator, objects as observed and described constantly turn into something else. But Chichikov takes for granted a stable world, and he seems capable of finding the "right" words. This is why he "apparently [is] satisfied" with the town as he sets out to explore it, and why, after examining everything in detail, he gives it a final look "as though wishing to make sure that he would remember where everything was situated" (20–22). To what purpose we do not yet know. That there may be no purpose beyond looking is a possibility raised by his scrupulous interest in the playbill he tears off a display-post to read at leisure back in his room. The reading is preceded by an elaborate, almost pedantic specification of gestures: "Having had his tea, he sat down at the table, ordered a candle, took the playbill out of his pocket, moved it nearer to the lighted candle, and began to read it, screwing up his right eye a little as he did so."

This heightens our expectation that what follows will be worthy of close attention as well:

There was very little of any interest in the bill, however: it announced the performance of a drama by Herr Kotzebue in which the part of Rolla was to be played by Mr. Poplyovin, and that of Cora by Miss Zyablov, the rest of the cast being even less distinguished [as if he or we have ever heard of the two leading actors!]; *however*, he read through *all their names*, getting *even* to the prices of the stalls and discovering that the bill had been printed at the printing works of the provincial administration; he then turned the playbill over to find out if there was anything on the back of it, but *finding nothing*, rubbed his eyes, folded it neatly, and put it in the mahogany box in which he was *accustomed to stow away everything he happened to pick up*. (22)

The words on the playbill establish that the town will welcome a certain amount of culture. Otherwise it does not seem to matter who is playing what role in the Kotzebue play. The reading accomplished, Chichikov takes elaborate care to preserve the document on which these words are printed. Anything so treated is undoubtedly of value; and the very expenditure of so much verbal energy hints at some larger significance as well. Although the words do not seem to "mean" anything to him, he does have a use for them, which becomes evident as he moves through the book. All we know for the moment, however, is that Chichikov collects words as well as views and pieces of paper, all of which come ready-made by others. We cannot conceive of his playing linguistic games like the narrator's.

MANILOV

In chapter 2, Chichikov leaves town and travels to Manilov's estate, thereby setting in motion his scheme of trying to persuade local landowners to sell him their dead souls. Lexically, this entire chapter is built on certain code words of Sentimentalism, to which Manilov swears allegiance:[7] "kindness [*milost'*]," "pleasant [*priyatno*]," the etymologically related "friend [*priyatel'*]," "good [*dobryi*]," "heart [*serdtse*]," "estimable [*pochtennyi*]," and others, repeated over and over again. Chichikov proves adept in this language too. The first dialogue is built on the pattern of cue/exaggerated response that we have learned to appreciate in *The Inspector General*:

"And how did you like our *town*?" Mrs. Manilov said. "Have you *passed your time agreeably [priyatno]* there?"
"It's a *very excellent [good] town [ochen' khoroshii gorod]*, ma'am," Chichikov replied. "A *magnificent town [prekrasnyi gorod]*. And *I've spent a most agreeable time [priyatno]*: the society there is most *affable [obkhoditel'noe]*." (37)

Chichikov is to the Manilovs as Khlestakov is to Anna Andreevna, but he opens his first response not by mimicking the "like" and "agreeable" of his hosts but by introducing the concept "excellent," or "good." This may at first look like an entirely new topic until we remember that the Sentimentalist ethos was often summed up in the formula "pleasant and useful" (*priyatnoe i poleznoe*), or, to use the more familiar Latin tag, *dulce et utile*. By starting with "good," a word that clearly belongs in the *utile* column, then moving to one that signifies either physical or moral qualities (*prekrasnyi*), and only then bringing in the unmistakably *dulce* concepts of "agreeable" and "affable," Chichikov shows that he has a far greater understanding of Sentimentalism than Khlestakov ever did. Manilov, with his very next utterance, which now links the *dulce* and the *utile*, demonstrates at least an equal familiarity with the code: "Don't you think [the governor] is a *most estimable* [*prepochtenneishii*] and *most obliging* [or "amiable": *prelyubezneishii*] person?" Since either the prefix *pre-* or the suffix *-eishii* would in itself be enough to make a superlative in normal Russian, the use of both for each of these two words creates an amusingly ungrammatical double superlative, which might be rendered as "most extremely estimable." In any event, it is entirely in character for Manilov, who wears an expression that is "not merely sweet, but cloyingly sweet" (39, a kind of superlative of "nice"), and who has already told Chichikov: "'You have everything. . . . You've got *everything and even more*" (37). In effect, he now challenges Chichikov, whose role has been that of hyperbolizer, to come up with something that will top "most [extremely] estimable" and "most [extremely] obliging." Usage aside, Russian has other superlativizing prefixes that he might use, such as *nai-* and *arkhi-*. But the result—*naiprepochtenneishii? arkhiprelyubezneishii?*—would be ludicrous monstrosities that might rattle even Manilov, and work against Chichikov's entirely serious purpose in this chapter. His reply safely apes Manilov: "Perfectly true. . . . A *most estimable person* [*prepochtenneishii*]. And how admirably he performs his *duties* [*dolzhnost'*]! How well he *understands* [*ponimaet*] them! I wish we had *more* [*pobol'she*] people like him." We may notice, however, that he does not repeat Manilov's word for "obliging" or "amiable" in any form, or cite any *dulce* quality at all, but instead adds two "useful" concepts, "duties" and "understands," to the one Manilovian term he does repeat ("estimable"), for a total of three, and performs a kind of hyperbolization by wishing there were "more" people with qualities like these. What he does here, and continues to do for the rest of this exchange, is to tilt the equation in favor of the *utile*. When Manilov asks, "And the vice-governor . . . don't you think he is a most charming [or 'nice': *milyi*] person?" Chichikov answers: "A *most, most worthy* [*dostoinyi*] man." Even when, in responding to another of Manilov's questions a few lines later, he returns to the *dulce* by replying that the chief of police is "an *extraordinarily* [*chrezvychaino*: Manilov has only said 'a very,' *ochen'*] *agreeable* [*priyatnyi*] man," he adds three *utile* qualities: "and what an *intelligent, well-read man* [*umnyi, nachitannyi*]. . . . A *most, most worthy man* [*ochen' ochen' dostoinyi chelovek*]" (37–38).

Chichikov is not only displaying a knowledge of the code but making a calculated use of it to persuade Manilov to give him the dead souls. Manilov operates almost entirely in the realm of the "pleasant," although he knows that the useful is essential too, particularly since a business transaction rather obviously falls into that category. He has serious misgivings about the legality of transacting in dead souls. Chichikov assures him that it is all quite legal, that "duty is sacred in my eyes," and that "I'm speechless when confronted with the law." These are all vaguely "useful" concepts, to which Manilov cannot object. But it is not until Chichikov says "I think it would be a *good* thing [*Ya polagayu, chto eto budet khorosho*]" that his misgivings instantly vanish: "Ah, if it's *a good thing* [*esli khorosho*], then it's a different matter, I've nothing against it" (45).[8] When Chichikov first puts his proposition, Manilov, in some bafflement, looks to see whether he is joking or even insane, but concludes that "everything about him was respectable and in perfect order [*prilichno i v poryadke*]," and therefore, by automatic extension, "pleasant" as well. Such a conclusion is possible only because manipulations of the kind we have described have lodged in Manilov's head that what is "useful" is also "good," and therefore, in his world, eminently acceptable.

As a man who is absurd but entirely sincere, and who desperately wishes to find in Chichikov a friend (as Sentimentalism would dictate), only to be deceived by him, Manilov is a sad and perhaps even tragic figure. Sentimentalism was passé by Gogol's time, and easily ridiculed. But Chichikov shows how its language could be empowered under the right circumstances, and used for entirely new ends.

KOROBOCHKA

After leaving Manilov, Chichikov sets out for Sobakevich's estate. But he soon loses his way: Selifan, the driver, is drunk; they run into pelting rain, pitch blackness, and axle-deep mud; and the carriage finally overturns, spilling Chichikov out. Nothing can be seen. Suddenly "fate" intervenes in the form of barking dogs in the distance, whose racket guides them to a house, and who prove, on closer acquaintance, to compose a whole humanlike chorus:

[O]ne of them, his head tossed upwards, was howling in such a drawn-out voice and so painstakingly as though he were getting goodness only knows what wages for it; another was snapping it out rapidly like a sacristan; between them, like a postman's bell, the voice of what sounded like a puppy rang out in a restless treble; all this was capped by a bass voice, probably of an elderly hound endowed with a sturdy canine nature, for he was as hoarse as a *basso profundo* when a concert is in full blast and the tenors, in their anxiety to take a high note, are standing on tiptoe and every man in the choir is straining upwards, tossing back his head, while the bass alone, his unshaven chin tucked into his necktie, squatting on his haunches and almost sinking to the floor, lets out from there a note which sets the window-panes shaking and rattling. From the very barking of the dogs composed of such musicians, it could be concluded that the village was of a decent size. (53)

This passage existed in rudimentary form in the first draft;[9] it was considerably expanded in the second and third. One of its functions is to establish that this new world is organized by sound, and that sight is ineffectual. Even close up, "[a]ll Chichikov could see through the thick curtain of the pouring rain was something that looked like a roof. . . . [T]he carriage stopped before a small house which was difficult to make out in the darkness." Then he stumbles on the steps and nearly falls.

Once inside, Chichikov discovers that his hostess is Korobochka, the only woman among the five landowners he visits. She looks muddled and innocuous, like "one of those dear old ladies." All at first seems cozy and hospitable as she prepares to accommodate her guest for the night. But light, even comic notes of sexual menace are sounded when she offers to rub his back and tickle his heels, as she used to do for her late husband, and when the maid, after taking away his clothes, makes up an enormous feather bed, which sinks to the floor under his weight as he climbs in. Chichikov's helplessness is emphasized by his inability to see any more distinctly inside the house than outside: He was "too tired to notice anything else. He felt that his eyes were sticking together, as though someone had smeared them with honey" (54). Suddenly sound intrudes again, as an old clock hisses like a "roomful of snakes," then wheezes, and "finally, straining with all its might . . . struck two with a sound as though someone were hitting a cracked earthenware pot with a stick, after which it went on again ticking quietly to right and left" (54). This too is comic, but the mention of snakes and beating hints at grimmer possibilities. It is as if Chichikov has wandered into an enchanted realm that is difficult to reach and, as he will soon discover, difficult to escape. Presiding is a woman who, in the gallery of Gogol's female characters, combines the mistresses of two earlier Gogolian fairy-tale realms: Pulkheria Ivanovna, in "Old-World Landowners," with her dedication to acquisitiveness and suffocating hospitality, and the witch-beauty in "Viy," with her sexual blandishments. These are worlds in which transformations can easily occur; even the dead can come to life. Korobochka's house needs only an animating word—and that is soon to come.

When Chichikov awakens the next morning, he can see again: "The sun was shining *straight into his eyes*. . . . Glancing round the room, he *now perceived* that the pictures were not all of birds." He goes over to the window and begins to "contemplate *the scenes before him*," which are carefully arranged and related in considerable detail (56–57). Once more he inhabits what looks like an orderly world, visible in its smallest parts, where animals are animals and clocks are clocks. Gogol obviously attached much importance to this scene, since it is considerably expanded in its second and in its final versions.[10] Chichikov, his powers of sight now fully restored, approaches Korobochka in a confident, even aggressive manner, anticipating no resistance to his proposal to buy dead souls. No doubt his expectations are buttressed by his easy victory over Manilov; a woman ought to be no match at all for him in business matters. (The order in which he encounters the landowners is significant but is not our topic here.) To our surprise—and his—she offers considerable resistance. In fact, she seizes control of the negotiation, and in a complete reversal, makes Chichikov the victim.

On first meeting Korobochka the night before, Chichikov wishes to know "into what parts he had strayed and whether it was far from here to the estate of Sobakevich. The old lady replied that she had never heard that name and that there was no such landowner" (55). Nor has she heard of Manilov—again she denies that such a landowner exists, this time coming back with a list of names that mean nothing to Chichikov. That there will be no dealing with her on his linguistic terms is quite clear. When they meet the next day, she gives him her full name and social position ("a collegiate secretary's widow"), but he withholds both his name and his title. So strong is her need to name, however, that she persists: "You are not a tax assessor, are you?" Chichikov replies: "Why, no, ma'am . . . I'm certainly not a tax assessor. I'm just travelling on a little business of my own." Since she obviously cannot guess his name or rank, she proposes another label: "Oh, so you're a dealer [*pokupshchik*, lit., 'buyer']." Chichikov neither confirms nor denies it, and so it sticks (59). Linguistically speaking, Korobochka creates the buyer. By default, Chichikov establishes her as the namer, and therefore, quite unwittingly, as the one who will control the dialogue that follows.

For Korobochka, words are labels that adequately define the objects to which they are attached. A "buyer" is someone who trades in hemp and hay; therefore, that is what Chichikov, once so labeled, is and does. Put another way, she insists on word-boundaries; Chichikov disregards them or shifts them to suit his purposes. Two different language-systems are in use. He argues from the general category of "agricultural products" (without using the term as such), which he defines only as including any product that can be bought and sold. In this sense, hemp, honey, and dead souls are all the same. Not only is this a rhetorical ploy aimed at conning the old woman; it also answers to his own habits as an indiscriminate collector, for whom all objects that find their way into his box have identical value. Korobochka of course knows that serfs can be bought and sold, but they bear a label that is different from "hemp," if only because they are "dead," just as hemp is different from "honey," and must each be reckoned with individually. She is incapable of recognizing abstractions, let alone dealing with them. Therefore she cannot grasp what Chichikov wants, until, in utter exasperation with her literal-mindedness, he finally admits, "Hemp is all right *in its own way [pen'ka pen'koyu]*," that is, hemp is one thing, dead souls are another.[11] Since "dead souls" is an abstraction too, she still does not understand what he wants, but finally goes along—"I must be nice to him"—only in hopes that he will return and buy some solid, palpable things. This is one of the more comic scenes in the novel, again resembling a conversation of the deaf; but it helps foreground the incompatibility of the two ways of treating language. It finds linguistic resolution only when Korobochka deconstructs the abstraction "dead souls" by identifying individual "souls," at which point they are no longer "souls," and no longer even "dead," because they acquire names that not only label but even characterize them: Pyotr Saveliev Neuvazhai-Koryto ("don't respect the feeding trough"), Korovii Kirpich ("cow brick"), and Koleso Ivan ("Ivan the Wheel"). And she does this orally, her words in their movement through time and space not only mimicking but conferring life. Chichikov, by contrast, writes them down as she speaks and puts them away in his box, which is elaborately described at this point. The fixity of writing mimics and reconfers death, and it is not hard to see the box as a metaphor for the grave.

We must not, however, make too much of Korobochka's capacity to call the dead to life. The Russian reader is well aware that her name means "little box" and therefore suggests that she has more in common with Chichikov than might at first seem to be the case. She too is a collector; she too regards the souls as objects, albeit highly idiosyncratic ones. But her way with objects, or so I think Gogol invites us to speculate, is the right way. For it is also a way with words that, however primitive, respects their capacity to embody and confer life.

NOZDRYOV

The encounter between Chichikov and Nozdryov, to which chapter 4 is devoted, amplifies aspects of the word that have been set forth in the Manilov and Korobochka chapters.

It is built on one of those great reversals that Gogol cherished and that he may well have borrowed from eighteenth-century comedy. Nozdryov usurps several of the functions that until now have been reserved to Chichikov. It is he who invades Chichikov's space; he who is the swindler; he who is the stickler for detail; he who employs violent language. The Gogolian technique of hyperbolized repetition operates here as well. Chichikov's abuse of Korobochka has been merely verbal; Nozdryov's abuse of

Chichikov begins verbally, but then becomes physical, as he throws a punch at Chichikov and summons his servants to administer a sound thrashing, which is averted by the unexpected arrival of the captain of police. Words may indeed have very palpable consequences.

From the very beginning, Nozdryov is established as an indiscriminate acquirer of objects: "If he had the good fortune to come across a simpleton at a fair and fleece him, then he would buy whatever he happened to see in the shops: horse-collars, tapers, kerchiefs for the nurse, a stallion, raisins, a silver wash-basin, holland linen, fine wheaten flour, tobacco, pistols, herrings, pictures, a grindstone, pots, boots, china—for as much money as he had on him" (81). But he differs from other Gogolian acquirers in one essential way. It is the process of acquiring things that intrigues him, not the keeping of them: "it rarely happened that all this was carried home; almost on the same day it was all lost to another and luckier gambler" (81). Here the narrator is talking about a fair, which is not a real "place" but merely a temporary repository of objects, events, and occasions that otherwise are not related. His estate looks considerably more orderly and purposeful, at least on first glance. This impression is largely created by the care the narrator lavishes on the description of objects that belong to a particular space. For example, the numerous dogs (a look back at Korobochka's house, although they are now silent) "had all sorts of names and most of them in the imperative mood: Shoot, Swear, Dash, Fire, Bully, Blast, Plague, Scorcher, Hurry, Darling, Reward, Guardian," and all sorts of coats and colors: "black and tan, black and white, white with brown spots, brown with black spots, red and white, with black ears and with grey ears" (82).[12] Chichikov is taken on a highly particularized tour of the estate, even as far as the boundary, "which consisted of a small wooden post and a narrow ditch" (83). The interior of the house is object-ridden too, with swords, guns, Turkish daggers, a hurdy-gurdy, and pipes. Yet there is no order, and no real bounded space either. Nozdryov announces, everything on "this side of the boundary is mine *and even* on the other side too" (83); in the study "there were no signs of what is usually to be found in studies, that is, books or papers" (84).

Nozdryov's way with words is no different. The first intimation comes even before he drives Chichikov to his estate, in his account of how he drank with the officers of a regiment of dragoons stationed nearby. "Major Potseluyev—such a fine fellow! Such glorious mustachios, my dear chap! Never calls Bordeaux anything but slops [*burdashkoi*]. 'Fetch me some slops, waiter,' he says."[13] Later in the paragraph: "We had champagne— why, compared with it the champagne we had at the governor's was nothing but *kvass*! Just imagine, not Clicquot, but Clicquot-Matradura, which means double Clicquot. And he also got us a nice little bottle of French wine called Bon-bon" (74). The boasting is harmless at this point. What is significant, however, is that this man, who is obsessed with detail, resists calling the wines by their proper names, coming up with "slops" instead of "Bordeaux," and simply inventing "Matradura" and "Bon-bon." Ten pages or so later we are told, "Nozdryov was very particular about wines," and this seems more in character. He offers his guests port, Haut Sauternes, and Madeira. So far so good. But matters take a new turn as he orders a "special bottle to be fetched which, so he said, was a mixture of burgundy and champagne. . . . After a short time a rowanberry liqueur was put on the table which, according to Nozdryov, tasted exactly like cream, but which, to their surprise, tasted strongly of raw brandy. Then they drank some sort of balsam which had a name difficult to remember and, indeed, their host himself called it by a different name afterwards" (84–85). The blends of spirits become less familiar to the palate, and the labels more inaccurate or fanciful. This further confirms our growing suspicion that Nozdryov's world is arbitrary and chaotic. He treats words as he does objects. Just as one thing is as good as another, so one word is as good as another in referring to it. More things and more words are even better; if anything counts, it is the sheer energy that must be expended to acquire or generate them. Word-boundaries are as meaningless as estate-boundaries.

This is the mentality that informs Nozdryov's negotiations with Chichikov about the dead souls. "Listen, I'll give you the hurdy-gurdy *and* as many dead souls as I've got *and* you give me your carriage *and* three hundred roubles thrown in" (90). This looks like a mocking version of Chichikov's dialogue with Korobochka, where he tries to persuade her that honey, hemp, old rags, and dead souls are commensurate in value and therefore interchangeable. Now, however, he finds Nozdryov taking that tack, while he, Korobochka-like, insists that hemp is one thing, souls are another, and horses are not hurdy-gurdys.

Here Nozdryov and Chichikov are operating within different language-systems. No agreement is possible, for an agreement is a contract, and a contract, however crude, depends on a language comprehensible to all the interested parties. Nozdryov breaks the impasse by proposing that they play cards, with the dead souls as the stake. However, games are like languages too, in that they operate by rules that must be understood and honored by all the participants. There is an element of chance, which finds an analogue in the range of individual usages permitted in any language; but even chance has to operate within the general system. Chichikov balks at cards, rightly suspecting that Nozdryov will cheat, that is, willfully violate the rules of the game, and thereby confront his opponent with yet another foreign language. Nozdryov then proposes checkers (or "draughts," in Magarshack's British English), another silent language whose rules need not be verbalized. Aware of Chichikov's misgivings, Nozdryov assures him:

"[T]his is not cards: there's no question of luck or cheating here. It's all a matter of skill, you know." Chichikov assents. But Nozdryov, a man to whom boundaries are meaningless, will certainly not follow the rules here either. He begins to cheat almost immediately, and Chichikov refuses to continue playing. Nozdryov's only recourse is coercion: "No, you can't refuse. . . . The game's begun!" This, in slightly different wordings, becomes an obsessive refrain: "[Y]ou can't refuse to go on. You must finish the game. . . . I'll make you play! . . . So you won't play? . . . [Y]ou tell me straight, are you going to play or not? . . . So you won't finish the game? . . . So you won't finish the game? . . . Oh, so you can't, you dirty dog!" (93–96). This covers nearly three pages in the text, with Chichikov standing his ground and reiterating his refusal to play, and Nozdryov growing angrier and angrier. In its repetitiveness it resembles other conversations of the deaf that we have looked at, particularly the one in "The Two Ivans." However, the purpose here is not to make certain words conspicuous, but to show that words as such do not matter: they have become sheer, intimidating sound; in fact any words would do. This is why verbal violence can so easily turn physical, as it does when Nozdryov summons his servants to beat Chichikov up. Such an action violates still other rules, those governing the code of gentlemanly behavior.

Once again, Chichikov becomes the victim. And again, he is a deserving one. Nozdryov, after all, merely enacts in more extreme fashion what Chichikov himself has done in earlier scenes, mixing up categories of things and words, becoming verbally threatening when he does not get his way, keeping his belongings in a disorderly receptacle (the box he carries everywhere with him, which is the functional equivalent of Nozdryov's chaotic house). Another connection is made by Nozdryov's name. It is derived from *nozdrya*, "nostril"; Chichikov's comes from *chikhnut'*, "to sneeze," or *apchkhi*, "hachoo." Comicality aside, Gogol is once again creating characters that are mere fragments, not the wholes they think they are. Looked at in this way, Nozdryov is part of a part, merely one feature of a nose, which in turn is but one feature of a face, and so on. But in what sense are nostrils and sneezes really part of anything? A nostril is essentially just a hole, a sneeze essentially just a gust of wind. Nozdryov may seem more substantial than Chichikov if only because he already possesses land and an estate; but his name reveals a deeper truth, and hints at the fate of Chichikov's dreams of becoming a landowner in his own right.

SOBAKEVICH

At length Chichikov reaches Sobakevich's estate. All of it—the landscape, the outbuildings, the house, and the inhabitants—is solid, graceless, rough and ready, cut to the pattern of the owner, who in appearance and name resembles a bear.[14] Particularly striking is the interior of the house, with its portrait of "the Greek heroine Bobelina, whose one leg seemed to be larger than the whole body of one of those dandies who fill our drawing-rooms nowadays," its thrush in the cage, "who was also very much like Sobake-vich," and its furniture: "everything was solid and clumsy to the last degree and everything had a strange kind of resemblance to the master of the house . . . every object, every chair, seemed to be saying: 'I'm a Sobakevich too!' or 'I, too, am very much like Sobakevich!'" (104–5).

The resemblances spring first to Chichikov's mind, and are developed through his eyes. This makes his opening remarks, after an awkward silence, all the more surprising: "We were talking about you at Ivan Grigo-ryevich's, I mean, the President of the Court of Justice. . . . We spent *a very pleasant* [*ochen' priyatno*] evening there." This is the language of Manilov, and as such, is ludicrously out of place here. So much so that Sobakevich simply does not pick up his cue, as Manilov and Chichikov himself would have done: "'I'm afraid,' replied Sobakevich, 'I *wasn't at the president's* that day.'" Chichikov tries again, this time with a word drawn from the *utile* column: "A *splendid man* [*prekrasnyi chelovek*]." Again no connection is made: "'Who's that?' said Sobakevich, staring at the corner of the stove." Chichikov elucidates—"The president," he says—but Sobakevich is long in reacting, and when he finally does, his reply completely reverses the expectations generated by the code: "Well, I suppose you must have imagined it: he may be a freemason, but he's the biggest fool on earth." Chichikov is "a little taken aback" at this point, but regains his composure:

"Of course, every man has his weakness, but you must admit that the governor is *a superb person* [*prevoskhodnyi chelovek*; Magarshack has "delightful," but that is a *dulce* word]."
     "The governor a *superb person*?"
     "Yes. Don't you think so?"
     "He's the biggest brigand on earth!"

And so it continues, until Sobakevich finishes off a long tirade by asserting: "There's only one decent [*poryadochnyi*, also a Sentimentalist term] man among them, the public prosecutor," but "even he, to tell the truth, is a dirty swine." If someone can be both "decent" and a "swine" at the same time, some new language is being spoken, one obviously unfamiliar to Chichikov, and he simply gives up in confusion, realizing "that it would be a waste of time to mention any other officials" (105–6).

This dialogue serves several purposes. One is of course to mock the language of Sentimentalism by showing it to be irrelevant in dealing with an interlocutor who can in no way be a soul mate. Another is to advance the characterization of Chichikov. His eyes have enabled him to draw a full picture of the Sobakevich household, even at close range, and to detect the organizing principle behind it: bearishness. For once, they seem adequate to the situation at hand. Yet the style of his opening remarks takes no account of what he has seen. How otherwise could such an observant man make such an egregious error in the way he addresses his host? He is obviously caught unawares by Sobakevich's rudeness, even though it is quite in keeping with the world around him. In his literal-mindedness and stubbornness, Sobakevich reminds us of Korobochka. But he is far more intelligent. She cannot deal in abstractions or understand Chichikov's way of talking; Sobakevich simply refuses to. He quickly understands what Chichikov wants, and, in a reversal of roles—deceiving the deceiver—he even proposes the deal before Chichikov can get it out of his mouth, then asks a price that is far beyond what his guest is prepared to pay. In balking, Chichikov resorts to a version of Manilov's statement "the souls of the dead peasants were, in a way, absolutely useless" (46): "[The dead souls] are no good at all now, you know. They're all dead. You can't even prop up a fence with a dead body, as the proverb has it" (111–12). And it is now Sobakevich who adopts Chichikov's earlier role of affirming the value of the merchandise ("Worthless? Not at all!" 46), declaring, "sound as a bell, all first-class: if not a craftsman, then a fine, sturdy peasant" (111).

Are we meant to conclude that Chichikov's eyes are faulty? Or that he cannot find a language that fits what he sees? Or that language matters to him only as a way of easing social intercourse so that truly important matters can be transacted? Certainly the real surprise, for him and for us, comes in the turn now taken by Sobakevich's use of language. Chichikov, still on the defensive, observes that the souls have been "dead a long time. Nothing is left of them but a mere impalpable sound" (110–11). Sobakevich counters by doing what Korobochka has done, only on a much larger scale, as befits his ursine proportions: creating a whole array of palpable sounds, in the form of names, evocations of occupations and character traits, and even small biographies for the souls he wants to sell, all expressed in an articulate, even eloquent manner. This is what is truly out of character for this bearish man. The narrator has no idea "where he got this unceasing flow of words from" (111), but it seems to arise out of the words themselves, which take on a life and energy that in turn create more and more words, Sobakevich serving merely as the medium. He enters, we are told, "into *the very power of speech*, whence came the jog and gift of the word. . . . Sobakevich was obviously *carried away* by his enthusiasm: such *torrents of speech* flowed from him that one had no choice but to listen. . . . [Chichikov was] amazed at such an abundant flood of words to which there seemed to be no end" (111).[15] But the flow finally ceases, and

Sobakevich reverts to character: "'Why, of course they're dead,' said Sobakevich, as though thinking better of it and remembering that they really were dead" (112). The words themselves, their sounds gone, are no longer subject to change; they have become objects, which can be preserved only on paper. It follows, then, that Sobakevich "began writing out with his own hand not only [the peasants'] names, but also a testimonial of their remarkable qualities" (114).

The word lives and procreates only when it is being uttered. Then it can transform even the most unpromising material: a bear can turn into a nightingale. Chichikov has never experienced for himself "the jog and gift of the word"; it is foreign to him, and a little frightening. But perhaps he understands—certainly we do—that it embodies a force that remains invisible to the eye, and can take us where we least expect to go.

PLYUSHKIN

Chapter 6 begins with a large tribute to the power of seeing, and gradually narrows until we are inside one room of Plyushkin's house. First comes the narrator's paean to his own vanished youth, which is defined in terms of what could be seen by "the inquisitive eyes of a child": "nothing escaped my fresh, alert attention . . . I gazed at the cut of some coat I had never seen before . . . I stared . . . I would gaze with curiosity" (119–20). The "eyes" then become Chichikov's, and are directed at Plyushkin's "spacious village," which is described as if it were a picture, much as the estates in the Manilov and Sobakevich chapters. These eyes soon pass to Plyushkin's "overgrown and neglected" garden, "fully picturesque in its pictorial desolation."[16] This is one of the most intricate and beautiful set pieces in all of Gogol. Susanne Fusso regards it as "the apotheosis of the picturesque and the aesthetic heart of *Dead Souls*." I agree with the first statement, but not with the second. In spite of—indeed, because of—its accomplished beauty, this scene is again like a painting, lifeless and static. As such, it is a compelling demonstration of where this "aesthetic," in Gogol's world, is bound to lead. More immediately, it prepares us for the particulars of Chichikov's encounter with Plyushkin. First his eyes turn to a detailed scrutiny of the exterior of the house, which is said to lack "anything that might animate the picture,"[17] and presently fall upon a figure whose appearance is so bizarre that Chichikov cannot at first decide whether it is a man or a woman. The eyes then move into the interior of the house, to which at least a page of description is devoted, and finally fall again on the strange figure, which proves to be Plyushkin himself. His physiognomy and dress are described in the kind of detail that would have been familiar to readers acquainted with the still-popular physiological sketches and with the burgeoning realistic style.

Seeing soon attests to its own limitations and ultimately proves power-less. The narrator who opens the chapter sees sharply only at the remove of childhood; what lies directly before him is observed "with indifference" and "now slips by [him] without notice" (120). Logically, then, he must relinquish control of the story. And so he does: his seeing function passes to Chichikov, who has been established from the beginning of the book as a "visual" character, and who now proceeds to rehearse the various stances, as defined by distance, that have been adopted by observers in Go-gol's other fictions. The garden, for all its magnificence, is as distanced as all the other nature scenes in Gogol. So too are the village and the exterior of the house. It is only when Chichikov steps out of the secure vantage-point of his carriage (which of course can move if things become too threat-ening) and enters the house that he must confront the scene directly. And then his sight is obscured. The entrance hall was "dark"; the room beyond it was "also dark" and "barely lit by a light coming from a big crack at the bottom of the door." On opening the door, "he at last found himself in the light," and perceived utter "disorder," a jumble of dusty and broken fur-nishings, including a chandelier "in a linen cover, so thick with dust that it looked like the cocoon of a silkworm," and a "heap of coarser articles" on the floor in the corner of the room, so thick with dust that it "was dif-ficult to make out exactly what was in the heap." Up close, Plyushkin, though now recognizably a male only because of his whiskers, presents so indeterminate a figure that he must be described by reference to objects and animals: "[H]is entire chin with the lower parts of his cheeks resembled the currycombs made of wire with which horses are groomed in a stable. . . . [H]is tiny eyes . . . kept darting about under his beetling brows like mice. . . . [T]he sleeves and the upper parts of the skirt [of his dressing gown] were so greasy and shiny that they looked like the soft leather of which Russian boots are made. . . . There was also something tied round his neck. It was impossible to make out whether it was a stocking, a garter, or an abdominal band, but it certainly could not be a neck-tie" (123–25).

The greater the distance, the clearer the vision; the closer, the dimmer: here Gogol, through Chichikov, restates one of the great themes of his work and his life. Evidently the problem is no closer to solution here than in "Rome" or "The Portrait." This is perhaps why it is the obtuse Chichikov, not a more intelligent author-figure, whose eyes are employed. He is com-petent to record the externals up to a point (that being determined by dis-tance), but not competent to determine why Plyushkin, once a "very care-ful manager," has ended up a broken wreck.

If the patterns established in the earlier chapters obtain, we expect that a "seeing" Chichikov will now be confronted by a "speaking" Plyushkin, who will take charge of the negotiations. This in fact happens, but not in a predictable way. When the two men meet inside the house, Plyushkin says nothing, and Chichikov is so taken aback that he is uncharacteristically speechless: "[He] could not bring himself to start the conversation. For a long time he could not think of words in which to explain the reason for his visit" (129–30). When the words do come, they are drawn from the lexicon of Sentimentalism, which he knows by heart. He is "about to express himself something in this vein, that having heard of [Plyushkin's] great *virtues* [*dobrodeteli*] and the *rare qualities of his heart and mind* [*redkikh svoistvakh dushi ego*], he had deemed it his *duty* [*dolgom*] to pay his *homage* [*uvazheniya*] personally"; but given the surroundings, he feels that "it would be going a little too far," and decides instead that "the words 'virtues' and 'rare qualities of heart and mind' could very well be replaced by the words 'economy' [*ekonomiya*] and 'good order' [*poryadok*]; and therefore, changing his speech accordingly, he said that having heard of his *economy* and his *rare ability in managing his estate* [*redkom upravlenii imeniyami*], he had deemed it his *duty* to make his acquaintance and pay his *respects* [*pochtenie*] in person" (130). Chichikov frequently does initiate conversations with Sentimentalist rhetoric (it seems to soothe him when he is uncertain of himself, and reminds us of the way Gogol often uses clichés); but it is unexpected here, and all the more comic because it seems as inappropriate to the situation as it was at Sobakevich's, where it very nearly wrecked the negotiations. At Plyushkin's, Chichikov is well aware of the disparity between word and object. This may account for his attempt to fine-tune his vocabulary, coming up with terms that represent qualities Plyushkin used to possess. If anything, however, it is even more pointless here than in the previous chapter, because nothing he says seems to register on Plyushkin, who merely mutters something inaudible, asks Chichikov to take a seat, remarks that he has few visitors, and launches into a recital of his troubles, during which Chichikov ascertains that some 200 of his souls have died (the final list amounts to more than 120, a substantial number nonetheless).

Thereupon Chichikov heaves a sigh and says that "he sympathize[s] deeply [*soboleznuet*]" with his losses. To which Plyushkin replies: "But sympathy [*soboleznovanie*] is not a thing you can put in your pocket" (131). This suggests that Plyushkin is operating with the same system of language as Korobochka, which presupposes a one-to-one relationship between word and object. But he goes much farther. The word by itself means nothing to him; it is, or should be, not only attached to an object but itself an object. This is why there can be no naming scene during the transferal of the souls to Chichikov, no scene, that is, where the words, and what they signify, come to life by being spoken. Names are meaningful to Plyushkin merely as things, and the only things in this case are located in the grave— or on paper, where they are just as lifeless. This paper, we are told, "had been scribbled all over. Peasants' names covered it as thick as flies. There were all sorts of names there: Paramonov and Pimenov and Panteleymonov" (135), which are more manners of speaking (or writing) than signifiers of individuals. Only "Grigory Never-Get-There" (Doezzhai-ne-doedesh') is striking enough to summon up an individual, and as such, would be more in place on the lists of Sobakevich and Korobochka; but Chichikov forestalls the possibility that it might take on life by putting the list "into his pocket," which is equivalent to his box, which, in turn, is a kind of grave.

Unlike his host, however, Chichikov still understands what spiritual qualities are, and occasionally shows himself responsive to them. His expression of sympathy for Plyushkin's losses may be calculated to counteract the "offense" the old man seems to take at his "almost joyful exclamation" over the death of so many souls, but it also springs from his awareness that "such lack of sympathy with another man's troubles was not quite decent" (131). But what will this spark of decency profit him? After Plyushkin delivers his theory of "sympathy," Chichikov, ever alert to cues, declares himself ready to "prove" the sincerity of his "sympathy" "*not in empty words but in deeds*," whereupon he "comes straight to the point and without beating about the bush" puts his offer to Plyushkin. He seems to be moving rapidly toward the kind of materialism that Plyushkin has embraced in his attitude toward language.

It is jarring to find Chichikov drawing on the arsenal of Sentimentalist rhetoric when Plyushkin balks about the runaway serfs, on whom taxes must also be paid:

"My dear sir [*pochtenneishii*, lit., 'most honored,' 'most respected']," said Chichikov, "I'd gladly give you not forty copecks but five hundred roubles! I'd pay it *with pleasure* [*s udovol'stviem*] because I can see that you're a *most worthy and kind-hearted* [*pochtennyi, dobryi*] old man whose misfortunes are due entirely to his own *good nature* [*dobrodushiya*]."

"Yes, sir, that's true, indeed it is," said Plyushkin, lowering his head and nodding sadly. "It's all because of my *good nature*." (138)

Chichikov certainly knows that these words are lost on Plyushkin. Are they prompted by mere habit? By some lingering conviction or hope that the ethos they represent, however faintly, can still be vital and meaningful? (Chichikov may be a budding entrepreneur, but in his emotional makeup there is much of a man of the late eighteenth century.) It does not matter to the business at hand: words have themselves become merely a medium of exchange. It is entirely appropriate that Plyushkin is the last of the landowners to be visited, for with him, a natural stopping-point is reached in the theme of language. Further exploration is possible only in broader venues.

AFTER THE LANDOWNERS

The rounds of the landowners completed, Chichikov returns to town to register his purchases. He then plans to take his leave, only to discover that matters are not so simple. For isolated provincials, any newcomer is a source of novelty and diversion; and when the newcomer is as engaging and as eager to please as Chichikov, efforts must be made to prolong his stay, if not to keep him permanently. At the same time, he is intruding into a tightly bounded space, and therefore poses a threat. As in the opening scene of "A Terrible Vengeance," the inhabitants of this space meet the threat by resorting to ritual. Much of chapters 7 through 10 is given over to accounts of that ritual.

The first instance occurs when the president of the court asks: "[H]ow is it that you're buying peasants without land? Is it for resettlement?" Chichikov, falling into the cue/response pattern that he has consistently though not always successfully employed in his earlier encounters with the landowners, rejoins: "Yes, for resettlement." The president replies: "Oh, well, that's a different matter. And in what part of the country?" This question simply does not fit into the rhetoric of cue/response. A new code has been introduced. Thematically it can be defined as "rich landowner," and rhetorically, as extended parataxis, where small details gradually accrete. Such a code is characteristic of large social entities, like towns, whereas Sentimentalism's rhetoric best suits the one-to-one discourse of soul mates. The most Chichikov can do is address the general theme, simply invent the essential detail—any place-name will do in the rhetoric of accretion—and hope for the best: "Oh—er—in the Kherson province." One can imagine his relief when the president switches codes and picks up the familiar cue/ response pattern:

"Ah, there's excellent land there!" said the president, and expressed his great appreciation of the fine growth of the grass in that province. "And have you sufficient land there?"
    "Yes, as much as I shall want for the peasants I've bought."
    "Is there a river or a pond?"
    "A river. However, there's a pond there, too." (157)

This dialogue serves two purposes simultaneously. As intimate discourse it reassures Chichikov that he has satisfied the requirements of one important interlocutor and has therefore passed an initial test without which he would have no access to society at large. But that society is already silently present, because this exchange also functions as ritual. The town worthies already "know" that Chichikov has bought a large number of souls, which they assume to be living; therefore, he "must be" a wealthy landowner, just as, in *The Inspector General*, Khlestakov, another intruder into a highly structured society, "must be" an inspector general, whereupon elaborate rituals, like bribery, immediately come into play to address that situation. But rituals do not work by inference. They must be enacted in their totality, and in a prescribed order. No component can be omitted or moved out of place. The logic of the "rich landowner" ritual enacted here begins not with the purchase of serfs, but with the possession of land and all that goes with it, as the president's questions and comments show. The verbal ritual is then confirmed as all repair to the house of the chief of police for a sumptuous dinner, punctuated by numerous toasts, which are of course common on ritual occasions. Chichikov himself quickly learns the rules: "He imagined himself already a real Kherson landowner, talked of the various improvements he was going to introduce, the rotation of crops system, the happiness and bliss of two kindred souls." Even back in the privacy of his room, he talks to himself about "a fair-haired bride with rosy cheeks and a dimple in her right cheek, his Kherson estates, his great fortune. He even gave Selifan [his servant] some orders about the management of his estates, such as collecting all the newly settled peasants and taking a roll-call of them"; and once in bed, "he fell asleep like a genuine Kherson landowner" (161–62). Even when alone, he sticks to the rules of social ritual: private fantasy and public discourse are indistinguishable. Gogol reinforces the point by denying him a language of his own in these middle chapters: he is almost always talked about in the third person, and not often quoted directly, even in his supposedly personal musings.

Ritual works well to integrate Chichikov into the society of the local worthies. The next necessary step is to integrate him into the life of the community as a whole. Accordingly, his purchases "became a topic of general conversation" in the town, and are further ritualized. The following passage shows how particular instances—"Chichikov's serfs"—become general instances, "Russian serfs" who are supposed to behave in certain ritualized ways:

[B]ut what will *Chichikov's peasants* do without water? . . . resettlement is a very risky business. You know perfectly well what *a Russian peasant* [simply *muzhik*, with no attributive adjective in Russian] *is like*: settle him on new land . . . and he will run away. . . . I don't agree with what you say about *Chichikov's peasants* running away. *A Russian* is capable of anything and he can get used to any climate. . . . You haven't asked yourself *what sort of peasants Chichikov has got*. You seem to have forgotten than no landowner ever sells *a good man*. I'm willing to bet you anything you like that *Chichikov's peasants* are thieves, confirmed drunkards, bone idle, and rowdy. . . . [I]t's true that no one will sell *good men* and that *Chichikov's serfs* are drunkards. (164)

Since rituals, to be effective, must be complete, the "peasant" ritual must build up to embrace all of Russia, then the whole world, and all of history:

"[They] are rogues, every one of them, but settled on new land they may well become excellent subjects. *There are hundreds of such instances, both in history and in our world of today*" (164). Within the confines of known possibility, ritual always reenacts the familiar.

The town takes for granted that Chichikov is a rich man. In the literal way of rituals, the assumption must be spelled out. If he is rich enough to buy so many serfs and so much land, then he must be very rich indeed, or a "millionaire." In a town like this one, there are presumably no millionaires: no one "knows" how millionaires "really" act, in contrast to the readily verifiable "landowner" and "peasant." Yet a "millionaire" ritual must be constructed if Chichikov is to be brought further into the life of the town, for, like Chichikov, the word (*millioner*) is foreign, as is the idea itself, and therefore represents a potential danger. One source of information is readily available in the popular fiction of the time. This is the point, I think, of the anonymous letter Chichikov receives from a lady of the town, in which she declares her passion for him entirely in the clichés of pulp romances inspired by Sentimentalism (170–71). Later, at the ball, we are told that the reply he is about to make to the governor's wife is "probably no worse than those uttered in our modern novels by the Zvonskys, the Linskys, the Lidins, the Gremins, and all similarly accomplished army officers" (176).[18] The word has taken on a reality, but it is a purely verbal reality, with no basis in verifiable fact, as the narrator emphasizes when he insists, "*the word 'millionaire' alone was to blame*, not the millionaire himself, but *just the word alone*," and when he goes on to explain, "quite apart from the money bags, there is something in the *mere sound of that word* which alike affects people who are scoundrels, people who are neither the one thing nor the other, and good people; in short, it affects everyone" (169), as of course an effective social ritual must.

The "millionaire" ritual is embedded in, and seems to arise out of, a long discussion (167–70) of the social rules that are scrupulously observed by the ladies of the town: "decorum . . . deportment . . . the maintenance of good tone, the observance of *etiquette*, and a multitude of the most refined *rules of propriety*, and especially the *strict conformance to fashion in its minutest details*," are simply more conventional ways of saying "ritual." As with the registration of the serfs, this new ritual is codified in a public spectacle, a fancy-dress ball, and makes way for another ritual, which has been alluded to earlier but not ritualized until now, that of "bachelor." The more complex "millionaire-bachelor" code enables, indeed compels Chichikov to marry a local girl of high social standing and take her away to his estate, which must of course be correspondingly magnificent. In the meantime, it licenses, indeed obliges the ladies to flirt with him, seriously but safely, since he will soon be leaving. Here we see an expanded version of the situation that prevails in *The Inspector General*, with Khlestakov (paralleling Chichikov), the mayor's daughter (the governor's daughter), and Anna Andreevna (the ladies of the town). Again the literary parallel is telling, reminding us that the Chichikov of the townsfolk (and of course, of the author!) is essentially a verbal construct.

As long as this construct remains intact, its rules are absolute and must be obeyed by all. However, another reality suddenly intrudes when Chichikov is introduced for a second time to the governor's daughter: he is instantly smitten, has eyes only for her, and ignores the rest of the company. His action is a gestural equivalent of the one-to-one kind of discourse that has no place in a collective; and in fact, he is soon tête-à-tête with her. This time, however, he carries his old tried-and-true code to an extreme, and in his utter infatuation, he fails to notice that the girl is bored and does not respond. He has withdrawn into himself, thereby returning to the isolated state in which he first enters the collective, and speaks in what is described as a monologue (but is not reproduced directly). He still does not have a language of his own, but he is no longer speaking the language of the ritualized occasion either. The ladies are offended: this is not how "literary" characters are supposed to behave; they would find Khlestakov far more to their liking, if only because he would be unfailingly attentive.

Wacław Lednicki has studied the phenomenon of the "spoiled duel" in Russian literature, whereby one participant in that highly ritualized event acts in such a way that the entire construct collapses.[19] In Pushkin's story "The Shot" (Vystrel, 1830), Silvio's opponent nonchalantly eats cherries as his opponent prepares to fire; in *The Brothers Karamazov*, Zosima discharges his pistol into the air; and so on. We could extend Lednicki's insights to other social rituals in Russian literature. Masquerade balls, for instance, are often spoiled, as in Bely's *Petersburg*, when Nikolai Apollonovich removes his mask before the appointed time. Does Chichikov qualify as a spoiler of the ritual in the ball scene in *Dead Souls*? Only if the town regards him as already one of them. Outsiders, or so I deduce from Lednicki's article, cannot fundamentally spoil public rituals, though of course their behavior invites hostility. The fact that the town does not instantly expel Chichikov when he deritualizes himself at least indicates that they fervently wish to integrate him—after all, one does not dismiss a "millionaire" lightly—and perhaps indicates that they consider him already integrated to some extent. But to the extent that they deem him integrated, or at least richly fantasize the prospect, his behavior spoils the ritual (according to Lednicki's logic), thus rendering him a threat: by his deritualizing, he has displaced himself in this society, and placeless elements are a danger in any tightly regulated collective.

The ultimate deconstruction of the "millionaire" ritual is performed by

Nozdryov, who barges into the party and loudly announces what Chichi-kov is really up to. To be sure, "everyone recoiled from him and refused to listen to him any more"; but his words strike home, as the familiar Go-golian gesture of petrifaction makes clear: "They all stood gazing with a kind of wooden, stupidly interrogative expression" (182). They know that Nozdryov is an inveterate liar. But he does occupy a permanent place in the community, as Chichikov does not, a place that takes account of all his traits of character: he is "their" liar. Even then, however, Chichikov is not shunned or expelled. Instead, the town undertakes a search, increasingly desperate, for alternative identities that will keep him within the collective. For one part of the elaborate ritualistic construct to fail is to threaten all of it.

Various identities are proposed: forger, government inspector, brigand, even Napoleon returned to Russia from exile. The "Napoleon" tag is the riskiest, yet it has a certain plausibility in terms of the bounded space that defines the various worlds of this "poem." Napoleon had invaded a Russia that was still removed from the mainstream of Europe. Chichikov invades a far-off town and isolated estates. To be sure, Napoleon was foreign, but he could have represented an incarnation of the yearnings and envies long present in the Russian admiration for things French. Chichikov is also for-eign in the same sense as any newcomer to the provinces, and he comes to embody unfulfilled desires, as a Russian "bachelor" and a not-so-Russian "millionaire." However, he is a highly disturbing presence, as aliens in-variably are in Gogol, regardless of nationality. So too was Napoleon. Ul-timately, both are defeated by expulsion from the places they have invaded.

The most inventive of the speculations about Chichikov's identity comes with the "Tale of Captain Kopeikin," a *skaz* narrative inserted into chapter 10. Gogol ran into trouble with the censor here, who thought the picture of the government bureaucracy too harsh and that of the rebellious captain too mild. When the first version was rejected, Gogol wrote despairingly to Pletnyov on April 10, 1842 (o.s.): "The elimination of Kopeikin has dis-turbed me deeply. This is one of the best passages in the poem, *without which there is a hole that I am absolutely unable to patch and sew.* I have made up my mind to recast it rather than be deprived of it altogether" (XII, 54). He revised it twice, and on the third try got it through. Why did he attach so much importance to what might seem merely an amusing anec-dote? And why did he want it placed precisely here, in chapter 10? Un-questionably it shows Gogol at his most brilliantly inventive in neologisms and wordplay. It also enables him to introduce another style, *skaz*, among the many that give the "poem" such a rich verbal texture. But if that had been his only purpose, he could presumably have served it at other points in the text. What he tells us here, I think, is that this "tale" is the most elaborate and most absurd of all the public speculations about Chichikov's identity, yet is completely credible in its own terms.

In preparing to narrate it, the postmaster resorts to at least one gesture that the popular imagination associates with oral storytellers. He "had for some minutes been *absorbed in thought* [*pogruzhennym v kakoe-to razmyshlenie*], whether because of some *sudden inspiration* [*vnezapnogo vdokhnoveniya*] that had *visited* [*osenivshego*] him or because of something else." His tone of voice and artful retardations compel instant and unquestioning attention from his immediate circle of listeners: "Do you know who he is, gentlemen? . . . Why, don't you know who Captain Kopeikin is? . . . Captain Kopeikin . . . Captain Kopeikin . . . why, if I were to tell you . . ." (209). He then proceeds to relate an "epic poem of a sort," that is, an oral narrative about a particular case with broad import. His sudden mention of a practitioner of a different mode—"a most entertaining story for some writer"—enhances the veracity of his own account, which is not written down, which will, by implied contrast, not be invented, and which therefore—according to virtual law in Gogol—will inspire all the more trust in its hearers. So caught up are they in the flow of narrative as to be anesthetized to the obvious fact that Kopeikin's brand of Russian (he is a peasant by origin) is simultaneously too substandard and too inventive to be native to the postmaster (let alone Chichikov). Why it is told in this manner nobody seems to question. But we overhearers know. The story is a reenactment of the "millionaire" ritual. The name "Kopeikin" is derived from *kopeika*, "kopeck," and as such, looks backward and forward to make a connection with Chichikov. Both Kopeikin and Chichikov are obsessed with money. Kopeikin's obsession grows out of need and pride. Chichikov's is harder to account for. Perhaps parental example is the most powerful source. In the extended biography provided in chapter 11, we learn that his father had urged him, from his tenderest years, to save every kopeck, a habit he quickly developed, the accumulation growing in keeping with the expansion principle that shapes so many of Gogol's stories. As the last of the speculations on Chichikov's identity, Kopeikin, in the literal meaning of his name, represents a drastic diminution of "millionaire," from many thousands of kopecks to just one, reminding us of the anomalous pattern that had been earlier set by the plot of "Old-World Landowners." Finally, and perhaps most important, the diminished ritual, now replayed in a "low" language, reduces "millionaire" to manageable and safe proportions.

It is a question not so much of the audience's willingness to suspend disbelief as of its willingness to participate, silently and affirmatively, in the ritual itself, which, like all rituals, does not need to be "logical" except in its own terms. This is why no one thinks to question the obvious disparities between Kopeikin and Chichikov, most notably the fact that Kopeikin is missing two limbs. What breaks the ritualistic spell is the postmaster's inability to sustain his role as an oral narrator. He suddenly indicates that his story material has a "thread [*nit'*]" and a "plot [*zavyazka*]," in other words, that it is mere fiction. The ritual is destroyed; his audience balks: "But, look here, Ivan Andreyevich," objects the chief of police, "you said yourself that Captain Kopeikin had lost an arm and a leg, while Chichikov has ————." The postmaster then "uttered a cry and slapped himself violently on the forehead, calling himself a silly ass in public before them all. *He could not understand how a circumstance like that had not occurred to him at the beginning of the story*" (215). Why he acts so is not clear, unless it has something to do with his "real" profession as a postmaster, who must constantly operate in the world of the written word. Yet so powerfully does the oral narrative continue to work its spell that his listeners do not dismiss it out of hand: they are merely "very doubtful whether Chichikov really was Captain Kopeikin and they thought that the postmaster had gone a little too far." In turn, each advances his own speculations, one of which is just as farfetched as Kopeikin, albeit at the opposite end of the social scale: that Chichikov is Napoleon in disguise. "Of course," we are assured, "the officials did not really believe it, but it did make them wonder" (216). Such is the energy of language structured as ritual.

Gary Saul Morson makes a compelling case for this whole section as a "hermeneutic parable," with "nonsense" as the controlling concern. I think he is right, but we should also be alert to other possibilities. Particularly at stressful times, any words, however little they seem to fit, are preferable to none: after all, most of us take for granted that words "mean" something, and they therefore confer meaning, however absurd, on otherwise incomprehensible or unacceptable situations. If not, anxiety rises to an unbearable level. Paul Fussell has remarked this phenomenon in his study of rumor among soldiers in combat: "[R]umor sustains hopes and suggests magical outcomes. Like any kind of narrative, it compensates for the insignificance of actuality. It is easy to understand why soldiers require constant good news. It is harder to understand why they require false bad news as well. The answer is that even that is better than the absence of narrative. Even a pessimistic, terrifying story is preferable to unmediated actuality."[20] The inhabitants of Gogol's town are like combat soldiers in being isolated from the larger realities of life. We do not know exactly where in the Russian Empire they are located, but like the townspeople in *The Inspector General*, they are remote from any of the cosmopolitan centers, particularly Moscow and St. Petersburg.

Beyond the values of sense-conferring "nonsense," however, there remains the larger need of the townsfolk to preserve the elaborate verbal legend that has been created out of the terms "dead souls," "landowner," and "Chichikov." It serves ritualistic purposes, as we have seen. It also resembles the kind of rhetorical structures that lawyers build in court to persuade the jury that their account of the "facts" is true because it is plausible. The defense and the prosecution come up with very different versions of the "facts," but each must be "true" to itself. If any piece of information cannot be made to fit, the whole structure collapses. Gogol does not draw the legal parallel, but we note that the inability to fit Chichikov into the legend creates an "utter whirlwind" of "discussions, opinions, and rumours which for some unknown reason produced their greatest effect [precisely] on the poor *public prosecutor*. They had such an effect on him that on returning home he began to think and think and suddenly, *without rhyme or reason*, as they say, dropped dead" (220). After this, the construct collapses. The town then shuns Chichikov; he takes that as a sign to move on; the collective finally rids itself of the alien element.

By the end of chapter 10, the dead souls have become far more than merely a means to Chichikov's personal ends. And Chichikov himself is no longer the smooth, faceless character who has conned Manilov. Each encounter has compelled him to reveal more and more of himself. He betrays vulnerability to anger, frustration, and bewilderment, as well as to increasingly complex emotions such as love and compassion. He may even be a man of some substance, breeding, and intellect. More to our immediate point, he increasingly assumes functions that have been reserved to the narrator at the beginning of the "poem." But even though Chichikov is a full-blown character, not merely a "voice," he does not necessarily compel greater credibility, not only because he remains deeply flawed but because Gogol provides no narrative center, at least not in the first ten chapters.

We have seen a simple instance of Chichikov's budding narrative-function in the Plyushkin scene, where he is little more than a pair of eyes that see what the "author" then records. By chapter 7, he has become much more. In addressing himself to the list of peasants he has acquired, "he was seized by a strange feeling, a feeling he found it hard himself to understand. Each list seemed to have a character of its own and through it the peasants themselves seemed to acquire a character of their own" (144). He then proceeds, for some four pages, to invent lives for these peasants, as any narrator might. Now he too possesses the gift of making words come to life. He goes even farther than Sobakevich, who, like Korobochka, does not "invent" anything about the serfs he names but simply recalls their characteristics. As Chichikov reaches the end of his creative musings, another narrator takes over almost imperceptibly:

"Abakum Fyrov! [This is still Chichikov talking.] What about you, my dear fellow? Where, in what places, are you roaming about now? Have you got as far as the

Volga? And have you got attached to a life of freedom and joined the Volga boat-men?" At this point Chichikov paused and fell into thought. What was he thinking about? [Another narrator now enters.] Was he thinking about Abakum Fyrov's lot or was he just thinking about nothing in particular as all Russians of whatever age, rank, or condition do when they start thinking of a riotous life in wide open spaces? And indeed, where is Fyrov now? He leads a gay, rollicking life on some grain dock, bargaining with merchants for a better wage. (148)[21]

By chapter 11, Chichikov has become the Muse, if not quite the author: "It was in this way that this strange *scheme* took shape in our hero's head, and I don't know if my readers will be grateful to him for that, but no words can express the author's gratitude, for, say what you like, if this *idea* had not occurred to Chichikov, this *epic poem* would not have seen the light of day" (252). The Russian word here rendered as "scheme," *syuzhet*, means specifically a literary scheme, or plot;[22] and in a further refinement, Chichikov becomes virtually the creator, and the "author" virtually a scribe: "The reader must therefore not be indignant with the author if the characters who have so far appeared are not to his taste; it is Chichikov's fault, *he is complete master here*, and *we have to follow him* wherever he thinks fit to go" (252). Two pages later, however, Chichikov is abruptly returned to his place as a character: "But what is so hard to bear is not that *my* readers will be dissatisfied with *my hero*" (254).

In some ways the interrelationship of narrator and hero reminds us of *Eugene Onegin*. Yet the similarities cannot be pressed. Pushkin's narrator is a solid presence who remains identifiably the same persona throughout the poem, and unmistakably in control. Onegin undergoes no significant change; Chichikov does, and also takes an increasingly greater part in narrative functions. Paradoxically, however, as he becomes more palpable and rounded, he seems to understand less and less of the world around him, and can no more manage it than anyone else in the first ten chapters of this highly complex work. No one version of "dead souls," or "Chichikov"—whether the townspeople's, the landowners', or the various narrators'—is definitive; all taken together do not add up to an explanation of what has occurred. Everyone uses the same words, and assumes that they compel general assent. Actually, they "mean" very different things, and once set in motion, move beyond the grasp of any one individual.

THE FINAL CHAPTER

After the Kopeikin story, the turmoil in the town, and the death of the public prosecutor, Chichikov is shunned by everyone, and has no idea why un-til Nozdryov appears and informs him that he is suspected of plotting to abduct the governor's daughter. This is among the least improbable of the rumors that have been circulating, most of which he has not heard, but it is enough to convince him that he must leave as soon as possible. As the final chapter opens, he is frustrated by delays, but at last drives out of town.

In this way, the basic plot of Part 1 of *Dead Souls* winds down. But other substantial business is under way, in the form of large excursuses on the "devious paths" chosen by humanity in its attempt to "attain eternal truth" (220–21), the destiny of Russia (231–33, 258–59), the nature of literary heroes and authorship (234–35, 252–57), and an account of Chichikov's earlier life (235–52). Most important for our purposes, there is a final reckoning with the theme of the word as it has developed throughout the book.

As Chichikov's carriage enters the highroad, the objects that swim by diminish in number, and are registered mostly as plurals, which establish categories rather than things in themselves: "a quick succession of milestones, station-masters, wells, strings of village-carts, drab villages with samovars," and so on for another ten lines. This lightens the verbal and visual ballast, and creates a sense that the carriage is rising: "furrows flashing by on *the steppes*, a song struck up *somewhere far away*, the *tops* of pine-trees in the mist, the peal of church bells *fading away in the distance*, cows thick as flies," and finally, "a horizon *without an end*." The narrator, who now seems to be in the carriage with Chichikov, attains the perspective that makes possible the first of the famous pronouncements on Russia in this chapter, or, in the poetic form he uses, "Rus":

Rus! Rus! I see you, from my wondrous beautiful afar: I see you now. Everything in you is poor, straggling, and uncomfortable: no bold wonders of nature crowned with ever bolder wonders of art, no cities with many-windowed tall palaces built upon rocks, no picturesque trees, no ivy-covered houses in the roar and the everlasting spray of waterfalls will rejoice the traveller or startle his eyes; the head will not be thrown back to gaze at the huge rocks piled up endlessly on the heights above it . . . through dark arches he will catch no glimpse in the distance of the eternal lines of gleaming mountains soaring into bright silvery skies. Everything in you is open, empty, flat; your lowly towns are stuck like dots upon your plains, like scarcely visible marks; there is nothing to beguile and ravish the eye. (231)

This scene is surveyed from a distanced height, and therefore reenacts the stance that Gogol thought essential to creativity throughout much of his career. It is also built on a series of negations that ultimately undo it altogether. For it says, in effect, that mere sight is powerless to grasp what Russia really is: from the "beautiful afar" Russia is "scarcely visible" and offers "nothing to beguile and ravish the eye." The little the narrator can see is so unspectacular as to be virtually invisible. The Alpine scenery that he invokes, only to reject, draws on the picturesque landscapes that are a staple of Romantic literature and painting of the 1820's and 1830's, and that can be found in a number of Gogol's own works, particularly

"Rome."[23] In that story, Gogol casts doubt on seeing as a way of grasping reality; now doubt is even stronger. And he makes what looks like a final dismissal of the possibility of the sublime as well, in asserting that "the head will *not* be thrown back to gaze."

Suddenly, however, the narrator is aware of a "force" that draws him, something he cannot see but can hear as "song":

But what is the incomprehensible, mysterious force that draws me to you? Why does your mournful *song* [*pesnya*], carried along your whole length and breadth from sea to sea, echo and re-echo incessantly in my ears? What is there in it? What is there in that *song*? What is there that calls, and sobs, and clutches at my heart? What are those *sounds* [*zvuki*] that caress me so poignantly, that go straight to my soul and twine about my heart? (231–32)

The tone is now contrastingly affirmative. But why it is not "word" (*slovo*) that he hears, we may ask, remembering the long celebration of the "Russian word" that ends chapter 5. That passage is too long to quote here in full: readers may consult pages 117–18 of the Magarshack translation. It is motivated by a peasant's characterization of Plyushkin as "Oh, the —— in tatters! [*A! zaplatannoi, zaplatannoi!*]." The narrator comments: "He had added a noun before the word 'in tatters,' and a very apt one, too, but one that cannot be used in polite conversation, and so we omit it." He then goes on to praise the uncanny ability of the Russian peasant to confer just the right "nickname" or "little word" (*slovtso*) on a person, which then sticks to him forever. This is a curious passage because it is informed by two very different views of how the word works. One regards it as a spoken utterance, bounded only by the territory that Russians inhabit: "there is not a word that is so sweeping, so vivid, none that bursts from the very heart, that bubbles and is tremulous with life, as a neatly [*metko*] uttered Russian word." The other converts the word into the fixed and permanent state conferred by writing: the "indigenous, living and ready Russian wit . . . does not fumble for a word or brood over it like a sitting hen, but comes out with it at once and *sticks it on at once* [like a label] to be carried *like a passport* all one's life." Elsewhere in the passage, the narrator even equates the spoken and written word: "A neatly uttered word is like a word that has been written down [*proiznesennoe metko, vse ravno chto pisannoe*] and that, according to the Russian proverb, cannot be cut out with an axe." What surprises us, I think, is that at this point in Gogol's career we expect the spoken to be privileged over the written. Three possible explanations come to mind. To a large extent, *Dead Souls* restates the major themes of all Gogol's work, and even recapitulates the order in which they develop. The passage we are now discussing occurs fairly early in the book, at a point that might correspond to the mid-1830's in Gogol's own development as a writer. If so, it reflects his earlier preoccupation with place and with seeing, but also his ever more explicit acknowledgment of the spoken language, these modes cohabiting uneasily in the narrator's mind for the time being. As the story moves on, we would expect the oral or verbal to stake out a stronger claim. This begins to happen as early as the Korobochka scene, and there is clear evidence of it on the narratorial plane immediately after the passage we have been considering. As chapter 6 opens, the narrator draws a contrast between the "curious eye of the child," which discerns wonders, and the bored and apathetic eye of the middle-aged man, that is, the narrator himself, which merely glides over surfaces.

Gogol could have continued to use "word" if he had established a historical perspective. For the first few centuries of Russian literature, *slovo* had a much broader range of meanings. For one, it is the generic designation of the twelfth-century *Igor* epos, which Vladimir Nabokov renders as "song," with the following explanation: "The obvious translation of *slovo* is 'word,' in the sense of 'discourse,' 'oration,' 'sermon'; but these terms stress too heavily the didactic character of a work to the exclusion of its poetry. The term *slovo* is looser and more comprehensive than 'discourse,' etc.," and it covers, in the case of *Igor*, "a merging of prose and poetry, with apostrophic intonations of oratory mingling with the lyrical strain of melodious lamentations."[24] In all these senses, "word" would seem adequate where Gogol has "song" and "sounds." It may be, however, that he wished to reserve "word" for the denotative function that he assigned it in chapter 5 and that, as we shall see, he always thought it should have. Yet he knew that mere denotation could make it as static as a passport entry.

The discussion of "song" in the later *Textbook of Russian Literature* offers a clearer idea of what Gogol might have had in mind. Here he talks about "song" primarily as a literary genre, a particular kind of modern lyric poetry, with Pushkin the great exemplar. He prizes it especially for its melodious qualities and its celebration of "feelings and sensations," qualities he also finds in the preliterate folksong, the only difference being that the newer version deals with the inner world of the poet, the older with the collective. But the two are, or should be, ultimately indistinguishable. The poet, we might say, referring again to the passage in *Dead Souls*, reproduces in his "song" the "feelings and sensations" of the nation at large; but these are at the same time his own.[25] This presupposes an intimacy between creator and material that is utterly alien to Gogol's old idea of the artist as a distanced observer. Certainly the narrator, in the passage from *Dead Souls* that we are considering (232), comprehends the need for a new look at himself, a new response, a new kind of involvement in what lies before him. He still stands apart—"length and breadth" suggests a panoramic view—but he is now suddenly and directly involved, as the "sounds" penetrate his soul and heart. In what I believe is the only instance in all of Gogol of a narrator's communicating with his milieu, he understands that this "other," this world before him, is aware of his presence and expects something of him: "Rus! What do you want of me? What is that mysterious, hidden bond between us?" He reverts to visual imagery, as Gogol himself does whenever he feels insecure (a topic we will discuss in Chapter 16). But now he is interested less in seeing than in being seen: "Why do you [Rus] look at me like that? And why does everything in you turn eyes full of expectation on me?" He reacts as do other characters in Gogol's works when confronted with a great truth: "I stand motionless." The "truth" in this case may well be an awareness of his duty to convey this "song." But he feels inadequate to the task: Russia is simply too vast. He therefore stands "deep in perplexity." His problem is similar to the one Tony Tanner has identified as that of the American Romantic writer, who also had to deal with what Whitman called the "measureless oceans of space" of his own country. He might try to expand into them, but that would mean diffusion and loss of identity. Gogol's narrator also seems aware of the risk: "And menacingly your mighty expanse enfolds me, reflected with terrifying force in the depths of me." The other recourse, as Tanner sees it, is just the opposite: spinning a web in which the writer "can live on his own terms, assimilating and transforming what the outside world brings his way."[26] It is a natural enough reaction when one is confronted with infinity, but Gogol's narrator does not entertain it. His own thought is "numb"; only Russia's "thought" is legitimate: "Is it not here, is it not in you that some boundless thought [*mysl'*] will be born?" Yet in the very next sentence, he seems to find the "menace" challenging and stimulating: "my eyes are lighted up with supernatural power—oh, what a glittering, wondrous infinity of space the world knows nothing of!" However, this also hints at a desire to revel in a privileged apartness, which may not be so different from Tanner's web but which in Gogol's world would be inimical to the true function of the artist at any time. The terminology alone suggests as much: "power" renders *vlast'*[*yu*], which means "authority" or "domination," not the "force" or "energy" (*sila*) that is usually a positive concept in Gogol since it betokens life and movement. "Supernatural" renders *neestestvennoi*, which would more literally be "*un*natural," and would appropriately label the work of artists who pursue the wrong kind of power.[27]

If we are reading at all well, then we should not be surprised when this flight of rhetoric, with its tinge of self-promotion, is abruptly cut off by another voice that is rude and down to earth: "Stop, stop, you fool!" At first we take this as being addressed to the narrator, since it stands in immediate juxtaposition to his musings. But we then learn that it is Chichikov

talking to his driver, Selifan, and we enjoy the mild joke. We also understand that it has the purpose of reminding the narrator that the artist's true
subject is ordinary reality, albeit refracted through a larger perspective and
thereby made extraordinary. Another reminder is at hand in the sudden
appearance of a military courier in a "government carriage [*ekipazh*],"
who shouts at Chichikov and Selifan to get out of the way. Suddenly his
vehicle is not so mundane: "like a phantom [*prizrak*] the *troika* vanished
with a thunderous rattle and in a cloud of dust" (232). "Troika" can be
used of any conveyance drawn by a team of three horses. But more is hinted
at here. Certainly there is a tinge of the demonic in the "phantom," the
rapid movement, the courier's wish that "the devil flay your soul," as well
as in the motif of transformation. Invariably, though, "troika" has positive
and poetic resonances for Russians. It embodies the national essence as
ekipazh, *brichka* (the usual designation of Chichikov's vehicle), *kolyaska*,
and any of the other words applied throughout this book to horse-drawn
vehicles do not. The shift from *ekipazh* to *troika* is a shift toward
possibility.

Possibility informs the next paragraph, which begins: "What a strange,
alluring, enthralling, wonderful world it is: the open road!" (232). The narrator now occupies a carriage—perhaps Chichikov's, perhaps not—and
from it, in fitful wakefulness, sees the ordinary physical world in surreal-
istic fashion:

. . . moonlight, a strange town, churches with ancient wooden cupolas and spires
standing out darkly against the sky, dark timber houses and white brick ones.
Shafts of moonlight here and there: they look like white linen handkerchiefs hung
on walls, the roadway, the streets; coal-black shadows cut across them slantingly;
the wooden roofs, with the moonlight falling obliquely across them, shine like
gleaming metal, and not a soul anywhere. (232–33)

The play of light and shadow, and the highly selective detail remind us of
the landscapes of the middle-period stories, especially the final scene of
"Nevsky Prospekt." There, however, fear and apprehension prevail: the
narrator tries "not to look at the objects which meet" him, and those he
cannot help seeing he deems untrustworthy: "Everything is a cheat, everything is a dream, everything is other than it seems." The mood in this scene
from *Dead Souls* is benevolent and gentle, and suffuses the sudden upward
swoop of the narrative gaze to the panorama of the night sky, which is the
celestial counterpart to the earlier view of Russia from the "beautiful
afar": "Heavenly powers, what a night is being enacted on high! And the
air, and the tall sky, far, far away, there in its unfathomable depths, spread
out so boundlessly, harmoniously, luminously!" (233). Again the dangers
of privileged reverie are averted by an intrusive "jolt" and a voice saying

"gently, gently," which awaken the narrator, now in broad daylight, to a view of a Russian village, ordinary yet transformed by distance too: "The sun is high up in the sky. . . . The cart is going down a steep hill.[28] Below is a broad dam and a broad clear pond, sparkling like burnished copper in the sunlight. A village. Peasants' cottages scattered on the hillside. The cross of the village church gleams like a star on one side." A careful reading of these three scenes—the village at night, the celestial panorama, the village by day—shows that they share essentially the same content. The heavens: powers (*sily*), height (*vyshina*), tall (or high: *vysokoe*), far away (*daleko*), depths (*glubina*), boundlessly (*neob"yatno*), harmoniously (*zvuchno*, derived from *zvuk*, sound), spread out (*raskinuvsheesya*). The village by day: height (steep hill, *kruchka*; the lofty sky, *na vershine neba*); broadness (*shirokii*); the pond that sparkles or gleams like "burnished copper [*siyayushchii, kak mednoe dno*: cf. the roofs that shine 'like gleaming metal' in the village seen at night, *podobno sverkayushchemu metallu*]"; the cross of the village church gleaming like a star (*kak zvezda, blestit . . . krest sel'skoi tserkvi*: cf. the "shining of the moon," *siyanie mesyatsa*—loosely translated as "shafts of moonlight"—in the nighttime village scene, and the obvious albeit unspoken presence of stars in any unclouded nocturnal vista). Much of this, in turn, is present, literally or suggestively, in the panoramic view of Russia from the "beautiful afar": distance (*daleko*) as seen from a height, sounds (*zvuki*), boundless expanse (*prostranstvo*), and secret powers (*sily*).

We sense that this group of scenes, in fact the entire last chapter, is related by a single narrative voice, which operates in different registers, depending on subject matter. Largely that is because for the first time in the book the voice is embodied, not quite full-bloodedly, but certainly palpably. This body not only shares the carriage with Chichikov but has a biography of sorts too. He is the "author" who is responsible for the work as a whole and who lectures the reader, at some length and not always indulgently, about what he has been trying to do. In fact, we tend to identify him with Gogol, who also surveyed Russia from a "beautiful afar," and loved to travel. Gogol was already a "famous" and "authoritative" public figure, and our culture has taught us, especially if we are Russians, to treat writers with deference and respect. But this narrator's authority mainly flows from the text itself. When he speaks in the oratorical mode, we know, as experienced readers of Gogol, that he commands authority because the matters he treats, without the slightest irony, are of high seriousness, such as the meaning of life and the nature of Russia. When he switches to the reportorial or anecdotal mode, he now sounds authoritative too, as he has rarely done heretofore. This is crucial if we are to believe, as we must, his story of Chichikov's life. The reason may be sheer fatigue on our part as much as anything else, fatigue with the uncertainties and ambiguities that have riddled the book up to this point, making it seem far longer than it actually is. We see the end coming; we naturally anticipate closure; hence we are inclined, and gratefully so, to take as definitive a version of events that sounds as reasonable and plausible as what we are now offered.

If the story ended here (257), we would tend to read this chapter as a celebration of the narrator's maturation. He has achieved the kind of vision that enables him to discern the coherent, patterned reality underlying a chaotic world. To be sure, we would have to overlook some signs to the contrary along the way, unless we set them down to the kind of stumbling that accompanies any learning experience. The most striking comes in the nighttime village scene, when the narrator says: "Everything is asleep. Except, perhaps, for a light glimmering all by itself in some small window: an artisan mending his boots or a baker busy with his oven—who cares?" (233). Does he mean that artisans and bakers are simply too ordinary to be included in a story of this kind? If so, then he puts himself at serious risk as an artist, for he would be impermissibly preselective of the reality he chooses to treat. Significantly, he follows this statement by swinging his eyes up to record the spectacle of the night sky, as if fleeing the earthbound world. Furthermore, he looks out on the world from a safe and comfortable vantage point within the carriage—perhaps too comfortable, we suspect, as he snuggles in the cozy corner, enjoying the pleasant sensation of warmth and the seductive drowsiness. Though Gogol does not comment, we cannot help but wonder whether his narrator has not in fact refused the challenge posed earlier by Russia's staring eyes, retreating instead to his familiar distance and spurning quotidian realities in favor of private reveries. If so, he is as removed from Russia in his carriage as in his "beautiful afar," and is essentially the same narrator we have seen in the stories of the middle period and even earlier.

But *Dead Souls* does not end here. Two or three pages follow, beginning with " 'I say!' said Chichikov to Selifan, 'what are you doing? You there!' " (257). Thereupon, it seems to me, Russia's challenge is flung out anew, and is finally taken up.

The scene begins, by now almost predictably, in the workaday world, but with an explicit denial of seeing, in favor of sound and rapid movement. Selifan "had for a long time been driving *with closed eyes*"; the horses themselves "were also *half asleep*"; Petrushka, Chichikov's man-servant, is fully asleep, his head in his master's lap. When Selifan, in response to Chichikov's remonstrances, sits up and begins driving rapidly, we are not told that he opens his eyes and looks about, as would be natural. Instead we read: "*flourishing the whip* over all the three horses he *cried out*

in a thin, *sing-song* [or 'singing': *pevuchim*] voice: 'Gee-up!' . . . All Selifan did was to *wave his whip and keep shouting*: 'Gee-up, gee-up, gee-up!,'
bouncing smoothly on the box." These gestures and sounds have their effect on the carriage, which begins to move more and more rapidly, "[flies]
up and down the hillocks," now light "as a feather"; and presently it becomes airborne mysteriously, almost supernaturally (and far more explicitly than in the earlier passage we cited): "It is as if some unknown *force*
[again *sila*, 'power' or 'energy,' not *vlast*][29] has caught you up on its *wing*
and you yourself *fly* and everything with you *flies also*," so much so that
nothing can really be seen: "and there is something *terrible* [*strashnoe*, a
word Gogol frequently uses to signal the imminence of a great and unexpected truth] in this *rapid flashing by* of objects which are *lost to sight
before you are able to discern them properly*." Magarshack's rendition,
here reproduced, of this last clause is really a paraphrase; the Russian has
nothing about seeing or discerning. A more literal translation would be
"objects that disappear before they have time to take shape [*ne uspevaet
oznachit'sya propadayushchii predmet*]." This further reinforces the theme
of the impotence of the visual faculty.

This is the same carriage (*brichka*) in which Chichikov entered and left
the town. So far, its flight has occured within the realm of the metaphori-
cally plausible, even conventional: it is light as a feather and swift as a bird.
But the possibility of a more radical transformation is implanted, as the
narrator for the first time calls it a troika, even a "bird troika [*ptitsa
troika*]." This extends the "feather" and "wing" imagery, and may also hint
at the firebird (*zhar-ptitsa*) of folklore, particularly since the syntactic
structure—two juxtaposed nouns, with one functioning adjectivally—is
often used in fairy tales for objects with magic properties, like *stol-
samobranka* ("table/self-setter," that is, "the table that sets itself"), or
kovyor-samolyot ("carpet/self-flier," or "flying carpet"). This in turn may
motivate the content of the passage that immediately follows, where the
high-flying narrator abruptly (and by now predictably) swoops back to
earth to remind us that this vehicle started life with nothing "ingenious
[*khitryi*]" about it, but is just a "travelling contraption [*dorozhnyi sna-
ryad*]" that is not even "held together by iron screws, but has been fitted
up in haste with only an axe and chisel by some resourceful Yaroslav peasant. The driver wears no German top-boots: he has a beard and mittens,
and sits upon goodness only knows what." So too, the unspoken comparison suggests, did the firebird, for all its wondrous properties, originate
among the common folk. It may look like an ordinary bird, stealing apples
and grain, living in a cage, and eluding capture; but it is a transfigured bird,
with golden feathers and a golden cage, and a penchant for rescuing people
from danger and bringing them back to life.[30] What transfigures it is the

"song" of the folktale, just as the "song" of the coachman creates the conditions essential to the change that the carriage begins to undergo: he "has only to *stand up and crack his whip and start up a song*, and the horses *rush like a whirlwind*, the spokes of the wheel become one smooth *revolving disc*," in what also sounds like a transformation, at least incipiently, of the scene in the opening paragraph of the book, where the "two Russian peasants" speculate on the "wheel" that is Chichikov's carriage. But the result looks like anticlimax: "only the road *quivers* and the pedestrian *cries out* as he stops *in alarm*, and the *troika dashes on and on!*" There is no soaring, no flight, no hint of firebirds here, only an acceleration of the ordinary that verges on anticlimax. The troika even disappears entirely: "very soon *all that can be seen in the distance is the dust whirling through the air*" (258–59). But when it reappears, in the next paragraph, it has undergone what amounts to a transfiguration, which is all the more startling for having occurred unseen:

> Is it not like that that you, too, Rus, are speeding along like a spirited troika that nothing can overtake? The road smokes under you, the bridges thunder, and everything falls back and is left far behind. The spectator stops dead, struck dumb by the divine miracle: is this not lightning cast down from heaven? What is the meaning of this terror-inspiring motion? And what unknown power is contained in these steeds, whose like is unknown by the world? Oh steeds, steeds—what steeds you are! Are whirlwinds hidden in your manes? Is there some sensitive ear that burns in your every fiber? You have caught the sound of the familiar song from above, and all as one, and all at the same instant, you have strained your chests of bronze and barely touching the ground with your hooves are transformed all into straight lines, flying through the air, and she [either the troika or Rus] rushes on, all-inspired by God. Rus, where then are you flying to? Answer! She gives no answer. The bells set up a wonderful ringing; the air is torn to shreds, thunders and turns to wind; all things on earth fly past, and, eying her askance, other peoples and states stand aside and give her the right of way.[31]

Here the narrator catches up all the essential imagery associated with the troika in earlier mentions: horses, bells, song, rapid movement, flying, thundering sounds, unknown power, and so on; and in customary Gogolian fashion, hyperbolizes them. If the pattern holds, hyperbolized repetition will effect a qualitative change as well, and that is certainly the case here, where the Russian principle embodied has moved from the workplace of a Yaroslav peasant to the universe at large. This may well be the most quoted passage in all of Gogol. But it presents a number of problems for the interpreter.

For one thing, Chichikov disappears completely. It is tempting to think that he has undergone a transformation too. As Andrei Bely has shown, the ordinary horses, who throughout the story are characters in their own right, display some of the personality traits of Chichikov.[32] If it is these same horses that appear transformed in the final paragraph, then why not their master? We have seen him steadily become a more complex, rounded character, as well as "elevated," not in moral qualities, to be sure, but in narrative functions. The narrator has even shared his carriage on more than one occasion. However, there is never a suggestion that Chichikov speaks with the same authority as the narrator, nor would we believe him if he did. Furthermore, the narrator, now a character himself, tells the story of Chichikov, "my hero," as his own creation, thus setting himself unmistakably apart. In any event, a drastic transformation of Chichikov would not make artistic sense, if only because it would undo the continuation of *Dead Souls*, which Gogol had already decided to write, and in which Chichikov was to see his sinful ways, repent, and be redeemed. In what remains of Part 2, we see Chichikov in his familiar, untransformed state.

The focus, then, remains on the narrator. He has undergone an unmistakable change, almost to the point of being unrecognizable. Most striking is his identification with the troika. He not only rides in it but, for a moment at least, becomes it, and therefore Russia. Before Gogol, Russian literature had offered numerous instances of poets traveling in carriages and being inspired accordingly. Pushkin provides many memorable examples. In a work written three or four years after *Dead Souls*, Gogol himself thought of the writer, in this case a scholar, as a horse and coachman. He argues that only Russians are capable of true scholarship because of their ability to think globally and intuitively, and urges them, when they make their findings public, to

trot along in even and measured steps, neither too fast nor too slow, swiftly, just as a good coachman, who neither excites the horses nor excites himself, speeds along not at a dull canter nor at a full, breakneck tilt, but in the same heart-rejoicing flight with which he began his journey, and arrives at his destination without having exhausted either the horses or himself. . . . Act boldly, like our fabled winged horse: he lets the tiny bushes and blades of grass pass between his legs.

I know of no other instance in the Russian literature of the period, or for that matter earlier, where the narrator-writer becomes carriage and horses and presumably driver too, except of course in *Dead Souls*. The *locus classicus* is *Phaedrus*, where Plato likens the soul to "a pair of winged horses and a charioteer." The connection with this passage and the other "horse" passages in *Dead Souls* has been observed by scholars. Most recently, Mikhail Weiskopf has seen it as Gogol's way of making the point that the narrator is the vehicle of a larger Platonic idea: "Rising up together with Russia into metaphysical space, the narrator communes with lofty Wisdom; Rus itself becomes Sophia providing him with a prophetic knowledge."[33]

I find this appealing as an interpretation of an obscure ending, although such endings are the norm for Gogol. Certainly Weiskopf convincingly demonstrates Gogol's awareness of the Platonism that permeated the cultural circles of his time. However, I think he makes too explicit what Gogol deliberately leaves vague, and relies too much on extratextual evidence.

Undoubtedly we are left with a prophecy in the closing lines. But what of the prophet himself, who is the central figure of this entire last chapter? We note a constant shifting of narratorial vantage points. At first the narrator sees the troika—still identifiably Chichikov's—receding in a cloud of dust; then he himself is sitting in the transformed troika, soaring above the earth and looking down; then he is standing aside and watching the troika turn into "straight lines"; finally he is aloft again, observing how the "peoples and states" react to Russia's majestic flight through the world. Several purposes are being served here. For one, we have further confirmation that there is no longer any steady, reliable point from which reality can be seen, assessed, and interpreted. For another, the narrator's freedom to enter or leave the carriage borders on the supernatural, and further distances him from Chichikov, who has never displayed anything but the most fleshly traits. Most strikingly, what has been carefully constructed during the course of this chapter, a persona for the narrator, is now undone as he becomes disembodied, or rather, embodies himself in all the other actors in this scene. Once his reembodiment has occurred, a final transformation, from which there is no return, seems to occur. The troika, narrator presumably included, becomes "straight lines," then jingling bells, in a final echo of the "song," and then something that can only be called a phenomenon of nature, perhaps pure energy, invisible in itself, detectable only in the effect it has on others. Seen this way, the artistry is logical: the story ends when there is no more to tell, or no one left to tell it. However, it is the kind of logic for which Gogol would have to pay dearly in the years to come. There is strong evidence that he saw this narrator not only as a version of himself but as a model for other writers. If so, what does a verbal narrator do after he has had what seems to be an ultimate vision that is virtually ineffable? The problem is much the same as in "The Portrait," where the artist-monk paints a picture so definitive that there is no need for him to continue painting. I think it is significant that Gogol's "crisis," both spiritual and artistic, began at about the time he completed Part 1 of *Dead Souls*. Perhaps silence is where the Platonic vision ultimately leads, but Gogol was also a professional writer, who, as we shall see, spent the rest of his life trying, with increasing desperation, to find reasons to gratify his compelling urge to keep on producing words.

It is therefore not surprising that the last paragraph also turns on the theme of the word—more accurately, one word. As readers remember this passage, Russia itself is a troika. But all the narrator offers, in the form of a question, not a statement, is the following: "Is it not *like that* that you, too, Rus, are speeding along *like* a spirited troika that nothing can overtake?" The answer is presumably "yes," but the figure is simile, and the word "troika" is not used again; Gogol has simply "you." To be sure, translators cannot resist the urge to supply it. Magarshack: "The troika rushes on, full of divine inspiration." Guerney: "The troika tears along, all-inspired by God!" (332). Only Reavey, among those I am considering here, follows Gogol: "on you rush under divine inspiration" (270). The point is not, I think, as picky as it may seem. In a sense, Gogol is recapitulating the opening paragraph of the book, which deals with a carriage and the ways in which it can best be denoted. The suggestion there is that no one word is adequate to the task. At the end of the book, the subject is again a carriage; and we are invited to consider the ways in which the word "troika," the loftiest designator of a carriage, can be stretched even further to convey the idea of "Russia." But we are told, in effect, that it cannot stretch that far, that we can talk only in likenesses and approximations. "Troika," therefore, has its limitations. "Russia" presumably has none; but even this word, if we look carefully, is absent from the very last sentence. Instead, the narrator gives us *ei*, "for her" or "for it," as he has somewhat earlier in this same paragraph. This little pronoun has, as plausible antecedents, *Rus'* (Russia), *troika*, and even *pesnya* (song), all of which are feminine in gender too. Is this Gogol's way of telling us, once again, that words are inadequate to the phenomena they purport to betoken?

13

The Retrieval of the Past

MOST of Gogol's characters live in a timeless present where movement is mere appearance, a fitful play over impenetrable surfaces. The ending of *Dead Souls* offers a drastic alternative, with its opening into a future where Russia is transformed and energized. From this perspective, present becomes past. Indeed, past was the dimension most commonly invoked by Russian writers who saw the present as Gogol did. Among them was Pushkin. One of the great tensions in *Eugene Onegin* arises out of the contrast between the eponymous hero, who exists almost entirely on life's superstratum, and the poet-narrator, who can share Eugene's activities and thoughts, even to the point of calling him a friend, but who also has access to a richly textured past through which his own present is refracted and vitalized.

Gogol also recognized the need to acknowledge, celebrate, and incorporate the past. For a time, Rome seemed to provide the ideal locus for precisely that: the prince in the story of the same name is speaking for Gogol when he finds "everything equally beautiful: the ancient world stirring from beneath a dark architrave, the mighty middle ages, which everywhere have left traces of artistic giants and the magnificent generosity of the popes, and, finally, adhering to them, the modern age with its teeming modern population. Pleasing to him was the way in which all merged into one" (III, 234). Yet we come to understand that this past is really an assemblage of artifacts, and therefore just as inert as if it had not been seen at all: this is probably another reason why Gogol ultimately became disillusioned with Rome. Indeed, Rome emblematizes his failure to find in the past the living, inspiriting force he knew it should be. To a large extent, this is because of his insistence, throughout much of his career, that the artist is one who sees and who therefore finds it hard to get below surfaces. Artists who cannot do so, however, risk isolation and death. So do ordinary folk, individually and collectively. Only a society with no memory of the past could possibly mistake Chichikov for Napoleon.

Gogol approaches the past largely through the theme of memory. It is of two kinds: personal memory and collective memory, or what is usually called history.

PAST AS PERSONAL MEMORY

Memory had been a prominent theme of belles lettres during the half century or so before Gogol began to write. Both Karamzin and Pushkin used memory as a means of discovering who they were, thereby achieving a unity of self. More commonly, however, writers had dwelt on the irreconcilability of past and present. In Zhukovsky's poem "A Song" (Pesnya, 1816), the past is associated with "fascination" or "charm" (*ocharovanie*), and constitutes the realm of "dreams [*mechty*]" and "recollection [*vospominanie*]." It is instantly recoverable and recognizable through sound and sight. But is the result valid and vital? "Can I perceive in new splendor / the beauty of the faded dream?" The poet concludes that he cannot: let the past be past. Batyushkov's "Elegy" (Elegiya, 1819) is more complex in its advocacy of forgetting as the solution to the tormenting problem of memories of the past, with nature the great solvent:

> With you, O sovereign one [nature], I am accustomed to forget
> Both what I was, how I was when younger,
> And what I have now become, under the coldness of the years.

The result, however, is obliviousness only to "thoughts" and to their vehicles, "words," and a new awareness of feelings, which are summoned up in and through nature, and are immediate and presumably tormenting because they can be neither expressed nor ignored:

> Through you [nature] I come alive in feelings:
> The soul knows no harmonious words to express them,
> And how to remain silent about them, I do not know.

The opening two lines of Delvig's poem "Disenchantment" (Razocharovanie, 1824) echo the first two lines of Zhukovsky's "Song." Delvig: "Enchantments of days gone by, / I am not to return you to my soul! [*Protekshikh dnei ocharovan'ya, / Mne vas dushe ne vozvratit'*]." Zhukovsky: "Enchantment of days past, / Why have you again been resurrected? [*Minuv-shikh dnei ocharovan'e, / Zachem opyat' voskreslo ty?*]." Delvig's poem as a whole, however, has a far more wintry quality than Zhukovsky's or Batyushkov's. Not only can those past days not be returned, but all that the future holds (a dimension not entertained in the Zhukovsky poem) is a monotonous succession of "days" and "years"—time is now fragmented—which must be lived through "unfeelingly [*beschuvstvenno*]."

A famous passage in *Dead Souls* expresses this same view:

Before, long ago, in the days of my *youth*, in the days of my *childhood*, which have *passed away like a dream never to return*, I *felt happy* whenever I happened to drive up for the first time to an unfamiliar place . . . the *inquisitive eyes* [*lyubopytnyi vzglyad*] of a child found a *great deal of interest* [*lyubopytnogo mnogo*] there . . . nothing escaped my *fresh, alert attention.* . . . Now it is *with indifference* that I drive up to every unknown village and it is *with indifference* that I gaze at its *vulgar exterior*; there is a *cold look in my eyes* and I feel uncomfortable, and I am *amused no more*, and what *in former years would have awakened a lively interest* [*dvizhenie*, lit., "movement"] in my face, *laughter, and an uninterrupted flow of words*, now *slips by me without notice*, and my *motionless lips* preserve an *apathetic silence*. Oh, my youth! Oh, my freshness! (119–20)

This passage is built on long-familiar code words for the theme of past and present. "Past" is youth, happiness, curiosity, freshness, alertness, attentiveness, awakening, laughter, movement, unquietness, speaking. "Present" is indifference, vulgarity, exteriority, coldness, motionlessness, apathy, silence. Possibly the passage is to be taken literally and seriously as a mediated statement by the author to the effect that only the young can be writers, or, if they are middle-aged, that their only possible subject matter lies in the past. But it is so perfect a specimen of its kind that our suspicions are aroused, especially when we are aware that everywhere else in Gogol, childhood is of minor importance. In effect he is restating an approach to the problem of memory so familiar as to be a cliché to the readers of his time, and in so blatant a fashion that it does not ring true. For the logic of it would make any writing about the present impossible, not least *Dead Souls*. Apart from its function as a cliché (a topic we have earlier considered), it does suggest the need for some way of making the past relevant to the present, or, conversely, of inspiriting the present with those life-affirming qualities that are contained in the past. This was a chronic concern for Gogol, and informed much of his fiction.

A look at other works reveals Gogolian twists to the familiar theme. One version can be seen in a still understudied little story of 1836 "The Carriage" (translated as "The Coach" in Garnett/Kent). Chertokutsky, following a long and bibulous party, invited a general and his retinue to visit his home the day after to have dinner and look at the carriage of which he had been boasting. But excessive drink and the late hour took their toll: he overslept, and remembered the invitation only when his wife awakened him upon seeing the guests turn in at their gate. In a panic, he ran to hide in the carriage house, whereupon "he flung down the steps of the carriage standing near, jumped in, closed the door after him, for greater security covering himself with the leather apron, and lay perfectly still, curled up in his dressing gown." The general discovered him, expressed astonishment, then simply "slammed the carriage door at once, covered Chertokutsky with the leather apron again, and drove away with the officers" (II, 249–51). Most readers take Chertokutsky's position to be fetal; as such, it is an apt expression of the kind of visceral, even infantile existence he leads with his "pretty young wife." His most nearly adult form of behavior is the kind of boasting to which young boys (and many soldiers) are prone. Just as infants have nothing to forget, and soldiers choose to forget the very real consequences of the profession they follow, so too Chertokutsky—who catches up the theme of both the infant and the soldier—forgets. There is of course an implied contrast with remembering, which involves responsibility and adulthood. Here, forgetting may seem at best a social embarrassment. However, Chertokutsky's attempt to conceal himself, or "forget," reveals (or "remembers") what he really is. The fact that he has so much invested in remembering what he ultimately forgets, and in trying to forget what he suddenly remembers, suggests that the incident is anything but trivial. But we wonder how different the contrasting "adult" self that proposes the dinner party really is from the infantile self that tries to avoid it. After all, the dinner is necessary if he is to maintain his identity as a man who depends on boasting and playing at soldiers—both childish if not infantile traits in an apparently "adult" world. Remembering seems pointless here: Chertokutsky is as puerile in the present as in the past.

In "Old-World Landowners," a story published a year before "The Carriage," memory is handled in a very different and far more developed way. We have already treated this work at some length in Chapter 2, so there is no need to restate the plot. We recall that both Pulkheria Ivanovna and Afanasy Ivanovich seem to be characters almost without memory. Even as she prepares to die, Pulkheria Ivanovna gives no sign that she has acknowledged, let alone come to terms with, the past that she has tried so hard to repress. She accepts death serenely but joylessly. Once she is abandoned by the cat—the emblem of her nurturing and controlling functions, which constitute her very reason for being—she in turn abandons food, decent clothing, Afanasy, and finally, life itself.

One reason why Gogol has her predecease her husband is to give his death a meaning it would not otherwise have. At first Afanasy simply cannot grasp that his wife is gone. He cannot even utter her name ("remember" it, we might say), and any attempts to do so are accompanied by "childish weeping." The important word here is "childish." Just before her death, Pulkheria has said to him: "You are like a little child [*vy kak ditya malen'koe*]. You need someone who loves you to look after you." Thereupon she appoints the housekeeper Yavdokha in her stead (II, 16). These are virtually the same words Vasilisa Kashporovna uses (although in Ukrainian) when she is contemplating the future of her nephew Ivan Fyodorovich Shponka, even though he has reached the age of 38: "He's still only a young child [*Shche moloda dytyna*, I, 192; original italics]." Both males are under the thumb of over-solicitous mother figures. There is no hope for Shponka. At first there seems to be none for Afanasy either. Yavdokha offers no maternal solace; he grows even more childish as he sinks into decrepitude. And he is a child alone, without even the balm of memories. Yet herein lies opportunity. For he has in effect attained to the childlike state that Christ deemed a precondition for salvation.

The work of salvation begins in the garden. Afanasy is described as "pacing slowly along a path with his usual absentmindedness [*bespechnost'yu*, better rendered as 'unconcern' or 'carefreeness'], *without a thought of any kind in his head*" (20). Suddenly he "heard someone behind him pronounce in a fairly distinctive voice: 'Afanasy Ivanovich!'" He searches, finds no one, reflects for a moment, and then concludes: "It's Pulkheria Ivanovna calling me!" In being able to utter his wife's name, he "remembers" her for the first time since her death. Thereupon he "surrendered completely to his inner conviction that Pulkheria Ivanovna was calling him; he *submitted with the readiness of an obedient child*, wasted away, coughed, melted like a candle, and at last flickered out, as a candle does when there is nothing left to sustain its feeble flame. 'Lay me beside Pulkheria Ivanovna' was all he said before his end" (20–21). The voice is not heard from above, as one might expect, but from "behind," and he searches for it "in all directions," without locating its source. Perhaps it is an inner voice, one that he can hear now that he has wandered, so to speak, in a desert of solitude during the years since Pulkheria's death, his material props crumbling. He is now ready to move in the vertical way that death opens to Christians: first down (burial), then up (resurrection).

In effect, the process set in motion by the spoken words—address and response—is a process of remembering. Now, however, remembering is to be no longer resisted but welcomed, as a joyous, liberating experience that connects past to present and opens the dimension of the future, with Afanasy fully aware that he will soon rejoin his wife. Seen this way, death brings healing and wholeness, and the story is an exemplum showing that the existence most of us lead or aspire to lead is false, but can, if sufficiently impoverished, prepare us for a rich, authentic life. Afanasy does not even form a mental picture of his deceased wife, or say anything about "seeing" her again. His salvation comes through words, not visions. In this sense, his experience is not so far removed from that of the inhabitants of primary oral cultures where, as Walter J. Ong reminds us, words are sounds, not objects: "you might 'call' them back—'recall' them. But there is nowhere to 'look' for them. . . . They are occurrences, events."[1]

Voices in gardens have of course been staples of spiritual literature since the Book of Genesis. The most famous Christian instance is to be found in Augustine's *Confessions*, when he hears the words "take and read [*tolle, lege*]": "in an instant . . . it was as though the *light* of confidence flooded into my heart and all the *darkness* of doubt was dispelled."[2] Afanasy's "conversion" is not so dramatic. But there is another character in the story who hears a voice in a garden and undergoes an experience that contains several of the elements of conversion scenes on the Augustinian model. This character is the narrator. Unlike most of Gogol's narrators, he is established as a character in his own right by remaining present throughout the story in a recognizably consistent persona, by speaking in the same voice, by possessing knowledge denied the other characters, and by surviving the old couple and their estate. The experience in question occurred when he was a child, and he reports it as follows:

It has, no doubt, happened to you, some time or other, to hear a voice calling you by name, which simple people explain as a soul grieving for a human being and calling him; and after that, they say, death follows inevitably. I must admit I was always frightened by that mysterious call. I remember that in childhood I often heard it. Sometimes suddenly someone behind me distinctly uttered my name. Usually on such occasions it was a very bright and sunny day; not one leaf in the garden was stirring; the stillness was deathlike; even the grasshopper left off churring for the moment; there was not a soul in the garden. But I confess that if the wildest and most tempestuous night had lashed me with all the fury of the elements, alone in the middle of an impenetrable forest, I should not have been so terrified as by that awful stillness in the midst of a cloudless day. I usually ran out of the garden in a great panic, hardly able to breathe, and was only reassured when I met some person, the sight of whom dispelled this dreadful desert of the heart. (20–21)[3]

Here we find imagery that is common in spiritual and mystical literature: "sunny day" and "night" (cf. Augustine's "light" and "darkness"), "impenetrable forest" (as in the opening of Dante's *Inferno*), and "desert of the heart [*serdechnaya pustynya*, virtually ubiquitous]."[4] The scene is set for a great event: it is brilliantly illuminated; a dead silence prevails; nothing interposes visually between the hearer and the event ("there was not a soul in the garden"). The voice is then heard. But here it is anticlimactic: no instruction follows. And the narrator cannot even fall back on the consolation of the "simple people" that he is being called by a lonely soul and will soon die; he is merely made more acutely aware that he stands utterly alone. All he knows to do is to run away, which is also a fairly common response in spiritual literature, Francis Thompson's poem "The Hound of Heaven" (1893) being a well-known later instance. Why is this remembered event so frightening? One reason may be that as a "real" child—in contrast to the childlike adult Afanasy—the narrator at that age has little or nothing to remember, no "other," as it were, against which to measure the self. (This may also help explain the almost total absence of children in Gogol's fiction.) But how genuine is the fright after all? The whole experience has a bogus quality to it. It lacks the compelling simplicity of genuine spirituality; it is stagy; it strives too much for effect; it flaunts the clichés of the conversion genre. As an account of a supposedly profound personal experience, it is neither very original nor especially singular.

Earlier the narrator reports another personal experience that also finds a parallel in his fictional characters. While describing the interior of the old couple's house, he says that "the most remarkable thing" is the "singing doors":

As soon as morning came, the singing of the doors could be heard all over the house. I cannot say why it was they sang—whether the rusty hinges were to blame for it or whether the mechanic who made them had concealed some secret in them—but it was remarkable that each door had its own voice. The door leading to the bedroom sang in the thinnest falsetto, and the door into the dining room in a husky bass; but the one on the outer room gave out a strange cracked and at the same time moaning sound, so that as one listened to it one heard distinctly: "Holy Saints! I am freezing!" (5)

This passage, with its emphasis on the "music" of the sounds, forms an analogue to the "music" of Pulkheria's creaking carriage that carries her out of the estate and into the forest. And sound in these two passages, like the voice in the two passages set in the garden, effects an involuntary displacement into the realm of memory:

I know that many people very much dislike this sound; but I am very fond of it, and if here [presumably in the city] I sometimes happen to hear a door creak, it seems at once to bring me a whiff of the country: the [a] low-pitched little room lighted by a candle in an old-fashioned candlestick; supper already on the table; a dark May night peeping in from the garden through the open window at the table laid with knives and forks; the [a] nightingale flooding garden, house, and faraway river with its trilling song; the tremor and rustle of branches, and, my God! what a long string of memories stretches before me then! ... (5)

What the narrator encounters and fully acknowledges here is a pleasant series of memories, not the vaguely glimpsed and promptly repressed world of the past into which Pulkheria Ivanovna is transported. However, the setting, while obviously a country house, probably has nothing specifically to do with the old couple—at least, no mention has been made heretofore of a river or a nightingale.[5] And as a personal reminiscence, it is little more than generalized affect, heavily indebted (as Gogol so often is) to the imagery of Sentimentalism.

The obvious parallels between the narrator's personal experiences and those of the old couple help us see that the narrator is treating himself as a fictional character too. But he is a decidedly limited one in comparison to Afanasy and Pulkheria. In the garden scene, he is unable to rise to opportunities for spiritual growth; in the memories jogged by the singing doors, he cannot transcend emotional cliché to individualize either the scene or himself. By offering us a narrator so constricted, Gogol may have had two goals in mind. One is to call into question the appropriateness of taking one's own feelings, good or bad, as a subject for art. Eventually Gogol would explore this theme on a large scale, particularly in "The Portrait"; here we find an early version of it. The problem is that with self as sole subject, there can be no "other"; what may at first look like "other" proves, on closer examination, to be material appropriated to the service of one's own feelings and fantasies. We have seen how this process operates in the stories set in Petersburg, with "Diary of a Madman" representing the extreme of self-referentiality, that is, madness. The narrator of "Old-World Landowners" is more intelligent and sophisticated than Poprishchin; certainly he is not mad; but he is far less interesting when dealing with his own mind.

Gogol's other goal follows from the first one. It is to use self-as-subject by way of contrast with other-as-subject. The "other" is also cast as reminiscence, but it is indubitably separate from the narrator, as he goes to great pains to make clear: he lives in the city (or so we assume) and "descends" from time to time into the country to visit. And it is reminiscence consciously summoned up, not involuntarily triggered by sounds. The memories are reviewed in order; the story ends when there are no more to be remembered. This is signaled by a shift in the last paragraph to the present tense and to a reportorial diction. Gogol probably did not know the famous discourse on memory in Chapter X of Augustine's *Confessions*, but it bears on what we are now discussing. Augustine is mainly interested in the active, conscious process of calling things to mind: "When I use my memory, I ask it to *produce whatever it is that I wish to remember*. . . . *If I wish, I can summon* [sounds] *too*. . . . *I can recall at will* all the other things which my other senses brought into my memory and deposited in it" (214–15). If applied to the making of art, this would prescribe a narrator very much in control of his material and very much detached from "personal" feelings. An excellent example might be found in a story written more than 60 years after Gogol's, yet so close to it in narrative technique and subject matter that the author, Ivan Bunin, must have known it well. I am thinking of "Antonov Apples" (Antonovskie yabloki, 1900). It too is structured as a series of reminiscences of a gradually diminishing past, and ends in a present time of paucity and desolation. The major difference lies in the tone and attitude of the narrator. At every stage, Bunin's narrator proclaims that what he is remembering is "good"; there is not only a matter-of-fact acceptance of things as they are but an almost cheerful sense of the inevitability, indeed the rightness of the decline of the old estate. By contrast, Gogol's narrator conveys a distinct sense of sadness, loss, and, at the end, a muffled grief. And even when he is dealing with the "other"—the estate and its owners—from a spatial, temporal, and intellectual remove, he seems to do so self-consciously, even self-indulgently, as if the process of remembering is more important than what is being remembered. This is another way of reading his statement, at the beginning of the story, that he feels "sad *in advance* [*zaranee*, omitted in Garnett/Kent]," that is, sad because that is how he knows he is supposed to feel when confronting the story he is about to remember, whereupon he selects those memories that will illustrate and support this feeling. We are tempted to question the authenticity of this feeling too, since it is situated firmly in a past of obsolete Sentimentalist rhetoric.

Once again, the distinction between self and other is not so clear cut. What Gogol is doing in this story, if our reading is valid, is posing the problem, in a tentative albeit highly attractive way, of the proper subject and nature of art. In particular, I think he is asking whether the making of art inescapably involves the process of remembering; and if so, how one can distinguish (as he thinks one must) personal memories from the kind of distanced, impersonal memory that creates art.

To judge by this early story, Gogol already understood that art is not ultimately about the mind of the artist but about the world as revealed by the artist. Augustine hints at this too, when he says: "Some things . . . are forthcoming only after a delay, as though they were being *brought out from some inner hiding place*. . . . [F]inally that which I wish to see stands out clearly and *emerges into sight from its hiding place*" (X, 8, 214; italics mine). This helps remind us that for Gogol, the true subject is present from the beginning, but is veiled or hidden. The artist's job is not so much to call it to memory (*anamnesis* in Greek) as to bring it out of hiding—what the Greeks call *aletheia*, whose general meaning is "truth," but whose more literal sense is not letting lie concealed or forgotten (*lethe*). This aptly and succinctly describes what Gogol came to see as the main purpose of quests both spiritual and artistic. The narrator of "Old-World Landowners"—as close to a writer figure as anyone in Gogol's fiction—is not an artist in this highest sense.

This is about as far as Gogol ever went in his fiction in exploring the theme of memory. However, the nonfictional "Author's Confession" offers an extensive discussion of memory, where the idea of revealing, or *aletheia*, is pervasive. It is essentially an explication of ideas set forth fictionally more than a decade earlier, in "Old-World Landowners"; I will have more to say about it in Chapter 15. Although Gogol came, in the 1840's, to believe that personal renewal had to precede any serious commitment to social, political, and national problems, he felt more comfortable, during the early and middle period of his career, in dealing with the past on a far larger scale, as represented by history.

HISTORY

It was in the seventeenth century that Europeans first attempted to write a general history of their continent, as well as accounts of some of its constituent states, notably England, France, and Germany. The Russians took somewhat longer. They began with translations from foreign works, first on "universal" history, then on more specialized topics, particularly military ones. Peter the Great encouraged the serious study of Russia's own past, and with Vasily Tatishchev (1686–1750), the first important national historian appeared.[6]

History was not only the preserve of professionals. Lomonosov, for one, had been commissioned by the state to write a history of Russia in a readable style. Of his projected four volumes, only the first was completed and published, in 1766, under the title *The Most Ancient Russian History, from the Beginning of the Russian People to the Death of Great Prince Yaroslav the First, or to the Year 1054* (Drevneishaya russkaya istoriya ot nachala rossiiskogo naroda do konchiny velikogo knyazya Yaroslava Pervogo ili do 1054 goda). This kind of history has been called "literary" because it cultivates a smooth and readable narrative and reflects a strongly individualized point of view,[7] in contrast to "scientific" history, which concentrates on presenting source materials as dispassionately as possible. By far the most distinguished representative of the "literary" approach was Nikolai Karamzin. Early in the nineteenth century he had already published some articles on history in his journal *The Herald of Europe* (Vestnik Evropy), and had written some short stories on themes from Russian history, like "Natalya the Boyar's Daughter" (Natal'ya boyarskaya doch', 1792). In 1803, the state bestowed on him the title of "historiographer," retention of which was contingent upon his composing a full history of Russia. He was already famous as a poet, essayist, critic, journalist, memoirist, and short-story writer. Even though he began with no training as a historian, he proceeded with his customary diligence, producing the first eight volumes of *History of the Russian State* (Istoriya gosudarstva rossiiskogo) in

1816, the ninth in 1821, the tenth and eleventh in 1824. The twelfth volume remained incomplete at the time of his death, in 1826. This work enjoyed an enormous popular success, the first installments selling 3,000 copies in one month. "Everyone, even society women," Pushkin reported, "rushed to read the history of their native country, which until now had been unknown to them. For them it was a new discovery. Ancient Russia, it seemed, had been discovered by Karamzin just as America had been by Columbus."[8]

As we might expect of the leading exponent of Sentimentalism, Karamzin insists that history is both useful and pleasurable. Its usefulness consists in providing precepts for rulers and lawgivers, and, for "the plain citizen," a justification of the existing order of things, as well as an assurance that people are everywhere essentially the same. It is pleasurable because it provides a "contemplation of variegated events and characters, which engage the mind or nourish the sensibility." Although the historian never has license to "lie," he can and should strive to be an artist, who weighs and refines his material, introduces "order, clarity, power, painting [*zhivopis*']," and strives for "beauty of narration." An "artful narrative," he states, "is the *duty* of the writer of history, and a good individual idea a *gift*: the Reader demands the first, and is grateful for the second, after his demand has been met."[9] Karamzin's criteria for history are essentially the same as the ones that applied to belles lettres. That is one reason why his *History* has not won the unqualified esteem of professional historians. But herein lay its strength for many of his contemporaries. Nadezhdin mentioned it in the same breath with the historical novels of Walter Scott and Mikhail Zagoskin, and concluded: "A majestic monument to prose belles-lettres—a monument against which time will break its scythe!" For Bestuzhev-Marlinsky, himself a celebrated writer of historical fiction, the appearance of the tenth and eleventh volumes of Karamzin's work marked the high point of Russian literature in 1824, "a treasure from the literary point of view," with "a fresh and powerful style, an intriguing narration, and variety in the structure and sonority of its language."[10] Here too history is made virtually synonymous with belles lettres. Conversely, novels were often judged by the standards normally applied to history. Nadezhdin, for instance, saw the novel as "entering into resolute competition with *history*," to which it "does not yield in amplitude or truth to life." And in a silent borrowing from Aristotle, he insists that both address the same reality, although from a somewhat different perspective.[11]

Soon an interest in history was almost the rule rather than the exception among the best writers of fiction and poetry. The most famous Russian historical novel of the time, Mikhail Zagoskin's *Yury Miloslavsky* (1829), dealt with the Polish occupation of Moscow in 1612 and was based on a study of original sources. Pushkin commended it by noting, among other things, that the "novelistic event fits smoothly into the very broad framework of the historical event." Pushkin himself was acquainted not only with works of Russian history, especially Karamzin's, but also with some distinguished foreign instances as well, notably Guizot, Michelet, Thierry, and Thiers.[12] He had drawn heavily from history for a number of poetical works, such as *Boris Godunov*, *Poltava*, and *The Bronze Horseman*; he himself produced one substantial work of history, *The History of Pugachov* (Istoriya Pugachova, 1833); and from it he derived *The Captain's Daughter* (Kapitanskaya dochka, 1833–36), a short novel that deals with the Pugachov rebellion of the 1770's.

Almost from the beginning of his career, Gogol honored both these branches of the literary art. His first, and disastrous, excursion into print had been *Hanz Kuechelgarten*, a versified "idyll in pictures" (1829). This was followed, between 1830 and 1832, by a start at a "Walter Scott" type of historical novel, *The Hetman*, set in the Ukraine in the middle of the seventeenth century. Fragments under different titles have survived.[13] During this same period he wrote the highly successful series of stories, some with a strongly historical cast, that were collected under the title of *Evenings on a Farm Near Dikanka*. From 1830 on, he also turned himself into an avid student of history as such. Ample evidence of his range is provided by his personal letters and by the copious notes he made from his readings in primary and secondary sources. He was generally acquainted with the works of some of the leading Russian historians, like I. K. Kaidanov and I. I. Shulgin, but showed far greater interest in historians of the Ukraine and Western Europe. And from the outset he had ambitions to write and teach history and geography, the two being interconnected in his mind, as they had been for many historians since ancient times. In the early 1830's, he was planning to write a geography for children. By 1833, his ambitions had expanded to encompass a project for a history and geography of the world, "in three if not in two volumes," to be entitled *The Earth and Its Peoples* (Zemlya i lyudi). At about the same time, he was perusing materials, particularly chronicles and folksongs, for a history of Little Russia (i.e., the Ukraine), "in six small or four large volumes."[14] He had already had some experience teaching history, with a position at the Patriotic Institute in St. Petersburg. In 1833, he set his sights higher, as he sought first an appointment in general history at Kiev University, which was denied him, and then an adjunct professorship in the history of the Middle Ages at St. Petersburg University, which he secured in 1834. He began brilliantly. One of the students who was present at the first lecture, "On the Middle Ages," recalled many years later: "I do not know whether even five minutes had passed when Gogol was already fully in command of his listeners' attention. It was impossible to follow his thought with any serenity, because it darted and flashed like lightning, continually illuminating picture after picture in the gloom of medieval history."[15] But he soon ran out of material, could not fake convincingly, and departed from the university after just a few months. None of the projected books was ever completed. What remains of his historical writings—besides the notes and outlines, which fill an entire sizable volume of the complete works—is some nine articles, written and in some cases published in the early 1830's, and brought together in *Arabesques* (1835), as well as some prose fiction on historical subjects, notably "Taras Bulba."

The names we encounter in these articles tend to be ones that would be familiar to any reasonably well-read Russian secondary-school student of the time. Dates are not very precise, if mentioned at all. There are few specifics about the lives, habits, or dress of peoples and individuals. What interests Gogol instead are general trends and ideas, insofar as they fit some larger pattern he is trying to draw. He is much beholden to the kind of "philosophical, "universal," or "general" history, as it is variously dubbed (he prefers the last term), that had been practiced throughout Europe in the eighteenth century. He consistently talks of the need to find a "leading thread" in the study of history, or "the dominion of a single idea" that "embraces all peoples," such as "liberating the tomb of the divine Savior," which characterizes the Middle Ages ("O srednikh vekakh," 18). Like many historians of the previous century, he considered a vital determinant of the historical "idea" to be geography, by which he means primarily topography, but which also includes economics, demography, trade, manufacture and science ("Mysli o geografii," 102–3). This "idea" should be illustrated selectively, not exhaustively, by "the most original, most intense," and most reverberative traits: "An event that has exerted no influence on the world has no right to enter here" ("O prepodavanii vseobshchei istorii," 26).

As for the nature and purpose of history, Gogol adopts a view that the Romantics had already made familiar. History is an endless, ongoing process, in which everything has "connection, purpose, and direction" ("O srednikh vekakh," 16). Yet there is no "progress," for each age, people, and individual is unique and potentially as important historically as any other. Therefore, any segment of the past is worthy of study in its own right. In fact, Gogol prefers periods where he can comfortably set matters on a large scale, periods that strike him as especially contradictory, colorful, fluid, and volatile. Such is the fifth century A.D., which was characterized by a great "movement of peoples" ("O dvizhenii narodov," 115–40). Such too is the Middle Ages, when "a great transformation of the entire world occurred" ("O srednikh vekakh," 14). In a reflection of the organic model that shaped all his thinking, he insists that the historian must study each people "from beginning to end," considering "how it was founded, when it had reached full strength and brilliance, when and why it declined (if it did) . . . if this people has disappeared from the face of the earth, then how a new people formed to take its place and what this new people took from its predecessor" ("O prepodavanii," 36). Gogol, however, prefers the youthful stage of any phenomenon.

He often focuses on great men. But he sees them as merely embodiments and expressions of the "idea" resident in the people as a whole at a given time; they do not create or change events, but follow and at most intensify them ("Al-Mamun"). In the Middle Ages, such a significant individual was the pope—unspecified, but it matters not which one: "the history of the entire Middle Ages is the history of the pope" ("O srednikh vekakh," 17). The pope's historical purpose was to make Europe a unity. Once that was accomplished, he was no longer necessary; the "idea" he embodied passed from the scene, to be replaced by another. Here again Gogol is beholden to newer ideas of historiography: typically, the eighteenth century had tended to see history as the result of the actions of particular individuals (Karamzin's *History* being a late instance).

What gives these ideas, conventional though they be, a certain persuasive power is the language in which they are cast: high oratory at its most florid. Often it takes a close second look to reveal how intellectually imprecise they are. By way of example, let us cite a comically monstrous mixing of metaphor as Gogol attempts to prescribe the way general history should be taught. He begins in the organic realm: "in what manner the consequences of [the event], like broad branches, spread over the ages to come, more and more ramify into scarcely noticeable offshoots, and finally disappear." Then he moves into the sonic: "[the consequences] dully resound even in present times, like a loud noise in a mountain ravine which suddenly dies away"—with a sudden dip back into the organic—"after its [the noise's] birth, but for a long time is still heard as an echo." Then he calls such events "great beacons of general history"; and finally he resorts to geology and anatomy to explain that these events serve as points of support for history, "just as the earth is supported on primordial granites, like an animal on its skeleton" ("O prepodavanii," 28).

As specimens of historical writing, these pieces are insubstantial, impressionistic, unoriginal, and unsophisticated. Gogol himself made no great claims for them. In fact, he treated them almost as an embarrassment. His foreword to *Arabesques* (1835), the collection in which they were gathered, adopts the same tone that would later be heard in the foreword to the second edition of *Dead Souls*. On reading the book over, he says, he was "startled by the presence in many places of carelessness of style, excesses, and omissions"; these he attributed to "imprudence," "lack of time," the inexperience of youth, and unspecified "conditions that were not always pleasant." Some of the pieces might not have passed his own critical muster a year earlier: at that time "I took a more severe attitude toward my old works." But now he has decided, in effect, that they constitute a noteworthy phase in his intellectual development: "to destroy what has previously been written by us seems as unjustified as forgetting the bygone days of our youth." Besides, he hopes that "two or three valid ideas can make up for the imperfection of the whole."[16] These remarks presumably apply to *Arabesques* generally, and therefore to the other works in it—five essays on other topics, as well as three major works of fiction, "Nevsky Prospekt," "The Portrait," and "Diary of a Madman"—but the weight falls on the nine historical essays, if only because they preponderate numerically. Gogol's misgivings were justified. The critics passed over all the essays in virtual silence, while devoting considerable attention to the fiction; and Gogol himself largely abandoned the writing of history thereafter.

Why did he take it up in the first place? Fashion may have had its say. The public appetite for colorful and coherent accounts of the past seemed insatiable; writers aplenty were needed to feed it. The Ukraine especially was in vogue, as a kind of Slavic Italy, and had already attracted the attention of historians; even Pushkin aspired to write an account of it.[17] Gogol wished to become a celebrity as quickly as possible, though he never put it quite that bluntly. The most coherent explanation he ever gave is to be found in his article on general history, where he says that in his teaching (and by extension his writing) he aims to "form the hearts of young listeners by means of the fundamental experience that is developed by history, understood in its true grandeur; to make them firm and courageous in their principles, so that no frivolous fanatic and no momentary agitation can shake them; to make them gentle, obedient, noble, essential and necessary comrades-in-arms of our great sovereign, so that neither in happiness nor in misfortune will they betray their duty, their faith, their noble honor and their oath to be true to the fatherland and to the sovereign" ("O prepodavanii," 39). This invites some skepticism, not only because this article was written in support of his application to the minister of education, S. S. Uvarov, for a teaching position at Kiev University, but also because, as we shall see, he took virtually no interest in Russian history. Yet the statement is really not inconsistent with his larger convictions, as we can extrapolate them from his writings of the mid-1830's and later. He believed that literature, whatever the genre, was essentially didactic, and undoubtedly thought that reading merely for pleasure was misconceived. He was convinced that a knowledge of the past was essential to the right kind of living in the present, which otherwise was fragmented and chaotic, a casualty of the apotheosis of science, abstract thought, and mercantilism. History would not so much explain the present as teach people to look through the glittering surfaces of the present to the "leading idea" that lay beneath. The lesson could be learned from any period of history, in any locale, because people everywhere were essentially the same.

Besides, history, as Gogol conceived it, was not so different from fiction. He was especially impressed by three very different eighteenth-century practitioners of the art (and it was always that for him, never a "science"), whom he groups in a separate article: Schlözer, Müller, and Herder.[18] He esteems Schlözer for his "fiery, rapid glance," Müller for his ability to call up a larger world through the careful selection of particulars, and especially Herder for being a "poet" who "creates and digests everything within himself, in his solitary chamber, filled with a higher revelation, choosing only the beautiful and the lofty, because that is already an attribute of his elevated and pure soul," and conveying it in a style that "more than anyone else's is replete with a gift for painting and a broad scope." All these qualities combined in Herder made him capable of writing a "general history." Yet even so, Gogol says, Herder lacked something that is necessary in the ideal historian: "a high dramatic art," which Gogol finds to some extent in Schiller's capacity to hold our attention, particularly in *History of the Thirty Years' War* (1791–93), in Sir Walter Scott's interesting story-lines and his gift for "observing the finest shades," and finally, in Shakespeare's "art of developing major traits of character within narrow boundaries." The point here is not so much these particular writers and what they stand for—that was utterly conventional by the 1830's—but rather the readiness with which Gogol turns away from history to look in literature for what he finds absent. In fact, he often holds up belles lettres as a model for his ideal historian to follow. Sometimes the two endeavors look indistinguishable. The historian's job is to construct "a single majestic, full epic poem" out of the materials at his disposal. Like the ideal belletrist, he may never invent, or impose order on the past, but only discern what is already there and present it to us in such a way that we perceive it. He too must be endowed with the gift of seeing, which is clearer the farther he stands from his subject: like a man who wishes to "become thoroughly familiar with a town," he must "climb onto an elevated place from which the town is clearly visible in its entirety" ("O prepodavanii," 26, 30).

Gogol followed these precepts in his practice too. The narrative persona of these articles surveys his subject panoramically, from a present that is obviously conceived spatially as an elevation; he speaks in the oracular manner appropriate to his position; he is concerned with telling an interesting story and persuading his reader of its truth. (Like the ancient historians, Gogol seems to have believed that historiography is a branch of rhetoric; several of his articles, in fact, were delivered as public lectures.)[19] In these respects, he is indistinguishable from the oracular narrator of the prose fiction; in fact, Gogol may well have used the essays to locate the pitch of this particular voice. Readers of his fiction would have no difficulty in detecting his characteristic touch in some other respects as well: in the pervasive use of such contrastive pairings as bounded and unbounded place, order and chaos, movement and stasis; in the assumption that the world is an organic, seamless whole, all of whose parts are necessarily interconnected; and in the insistence that individuals matter only if attuned to the rhythms of society as a whole.

The structure of *Arabesques* may reflect the assumption that history and fiction can comfortably coexist. Looked at another way, however, it may reflect just the opposite, like any number of those troublesome, even incompatible juxtapositions of which Gogol was so fond. In turn, it may be an expression of his own uncertainty about the direction his vocation as a writer should take.

In any event, he abandoned history. Was critical indifference decisive? No doubt it played its part for this sensitive, ambitious young man (we sometimes have trouble remembering how young he was: he seems venerable at every stage of his career), as did the critical praise for the fiction in *Arabesques* and also in *Mirgorod*, which came out more or less simultaneously. Undoubtedly too he respected the sheer magnitude of the task before him as a professional historian. He had done much background reading. He could look to Karamzin, a writer of poetry and fiction who had launched into his *magnum opus* after only two or three years of preparation. But standards had been steadily rising. Over the preceding half century, people had come to believe that good history must rest on a thorough knowledge of the sources, although it was not clear what that meant.[20] Even Karamzin, for all the "literariness" of his history, appended an enormous apparatus of notes and references to his *History of the Russian State*. Volume I, for example, contains 170 pages of text, and some 140 pages of notes ("Primechaniya") in print that is almost twice as small as the main body. It was this scrupulous attention to sources and details that prompted Pushkin to remark that Karamzin was Russia's first historian and last chronicler.[21] Gogol never did that kind of hard digging. He was young and still uncertain of the direction his career should take. Might he not have been reluctant to invest so much energy in a pursuit that was so demanding, particularly after his failure as a teacher of history at St. Petersburg University?

The jumble of images I have already quoted from the article on the teaching of general history may hold a clue too. In a nonfictional essay, such a sentence looks amusingly incompetent. But it would pass unnoticed in virtually any piece of Gogol's fiction, which thrives on inconsistency, contradiction, and an appearance of chaos. Another clue is provided by the oratorical narrator. In the historical essays, he remains in full control of his narrative throughout. His world is self-contained and comfortingly patterned. Conflict and contradiction are explained as functions of some larger "idea" or "principle," whose importance is judged by the retrospective and extratextual criterion of "how things turned out." By contrast, one of the great themes of Gogol's fiction is the vanity of attempting to order the world, even the world of the past, in such a fashion. His narrators, try as they may, are incapable of doing so, and look foolish or inept; the presumed author provides no sure guidance. Even in his one piece of sustained oratorical fiction, "A Terrible Vengeance," the narrator steps aside at the end in favor of the blind bard, who "explains" the story up in a far more "normal" kind of Russian.

Many years later, in "An Author's Confession," Gogol wrote: "I never felt any attraction for the past. My subject was the world of today, and life as it now is, perhaps because my mind was always inclined to things that were more substantive and more palpably useful. The older I got, the stronger was my desire to be a writer of our own times."[22] Whether Gogol is ignoring his very real "attraction" for history or limiting himself to his fiction, which, with one or two exceptions, did deal with "contemporary" life, he gets at a major problem. As a historian, he never came closer to the present than the seventeenth century, except in the article on Schlözer, Müller, and Herder, and never dealt with Russia at all. Of what use, then, was the past once it was reconstructed, particularly if, as he believed, any period of the past is unique and valuable in itself? Without creating what for him would have been a radically new kind of history, he probably could not have achieved creative satisfaction. All the evidence suggests that such a new history would have been indistinguishable from his fiction.

14

Word Wielders

GOGOL may have felt that history, as he was discovering it in the 1830's, had little connection with the kinds of fiction he was beginning to write. However, he did produce one substantial piece of historical fiction, "Taras Bulba." It first appeared in *Mirgorod* in 1835. I doubt that many people today read it in that version, which is one of the weakest things Gogol ever committed to print. But he subjected it to a thoroughgoing revision in 1842, in the process adding it to an extraordinary cluster of works that appeared that same year: the first part of *Dead Souls*; an edition of the collected stories, made by the author himself; a completely recast "Portrait"; and the newly created "Rome." These last two are among Gogol's least popular and least studied works. Both deal mainly with the problem of seeing, and in that sense look back, sum up, and take leave. "Taras Bulba" deals with the problem of the word, and in that sense looks ahead, for the word was to preoccupy, indeed obsess Gogol for the rest of his life. But its vantage point is that of a rather remote past, making it the only instance in all Gogol's work in which these two topics, word and past, combine to form the major theme. In this sense it amplifies *Dead Souls*, where the word is prominent but the past is almost entirely absent.

"TARAS BULBA"

"Taras Bulba" has been a staple of the literary diet fed to generations of Russian schoolchildren. It has enjoyed some popularity abroad, even as a

Hollywood film. Serious critics of Gogol have never found it particularly interesting, perhaps because of its fame as an adventure yarn. I cannot claim for it a place in the first rank of Gogol's works. It does not really succeed in moving beyond the particulars of subject matter onto the plane of universality occupied by the great works. But in its final version it is wrought with a sustained skill, conviction, and passion that make it an almost perfect work of art. What particularly commends it to our attention here, however, are the ways it presents aspects of the word, the past, and the artist that had come to preoccupy Gogol.

Gogol seems to have conceived the idea of the story at the end of 1833, when he was planning to write a history of Little Russia, or the Ukraine. For sources, he availed himself mainly of chronicles, memoirs, and folk-songs. He made several tries of the pen. "A Terrible Vengeance" and the uncompleted *Hetman* both deal with the Cossack-Polish war, and are pro-totypes of "Taras Bulba" in certain respects. Two of his articles, "A Look at the Making of Little Russia" and "On Little-Russian Songs," have much in common with the first version of the story, and also appeared in *Arabesques*. Otherwise the textual history is very complicated, and need not detain us here.[1]

The first version (henceforth called *A*) was published in 1835. Gogol later reworked it radically, and a second version (henceforth *B*) appeared in the collected works of 1842. They are as different in their way as the two versions of "The Portrait." *A* is really little more than the outline for a story, or an extended anecdote, told in a rather workmanlike style. *B* is nearly twice as long, running to some 120 pages in the *Complete Works*, and made more novelistic by a far greater wealth of concrete detail, consider-ably amplified characterizations, and—most important for us—a much expanded account of the historical context. The passages on Ukrainian his-tory are cast in the "high" style of the historical articles, which signals that they are to be read as authoritative utterances. And they are informed by the same view of history that Gogol had been developing elsewhere: the Cossacks are represented as a collective character, functioning as an agency of history yet effective only by virtue of a strong leader (Taras Bulba), who embodies their values in a focused, purposeful, and articulate way.[2]

Although Gogol's accounts of leadership in *A* and *B* make use of much of the same material, they differ substantially. In *A*, Bulba is represented as self-involved: he "was beginning to think of how to undertake some new activity as quickly as possible: he could not long remain inactive" (303). In *B*, however, his immediate reference-point is the Cossack entity: "Such an idle life was not to his taste—he longed for action. He was always pon-dering how he could rouse the camp to some bold enterprise in which a warrior might fittingly enjoy himself" (45). But ultimately he is attuned to history, so that even when he acts "at his own initiative," he can summon the collective to perform historically meaningful tasks. Here his most important attribute is the possession of an effective word.

The ordinary Cossack does not possess this word. His role, through the collective, is to let the leader speak, to indicate assent if the word is "true" (something he knows instinctively), and then to act upon it. One such incident begins when a large ferryboat approaches the settlement, carrying some down-at-heels Cossacks. The leader asks and is granted permission to address the assembly. He informs them—with artful retardations that heighten the suspense and ensure that all are bending an ear—that Orthodox churches are being desecrated by Jews, that Orthodox Christians have been turned into dray horses by Polish priests, and that their hetman and their chiefs have been killed by the Poles in a particularly gory and sacrilegious way. The reaction is first collective silence, then collective indignation, as "all at once voices [lit., 'speeches'] arose and *the whole* riverside was talking." These "speeches" recapitulate, in condensed form, the "speech" of the one leader: "What! Allow such tortures in Russia at the hands of the cursed infidels? Let them treat the chiefs and hetman like that? But that shall not be, that shall never be!" Such words fly "from one end of the crowd to another," gather strength, and precipitate in an even more violent outburst—"Hang all the Jews! . . . Drown them all, the heathens, in the Dnieper!"—which becomes gesture or action: "These words uttered by someone in the crowd flashed like lightning through the heads of *all*, and *the crowd rushed to* the outer village, intending to cut the throats of all the Jews" (53–54).

This is a secular use of the word, providing information that sparks practical activity. Most effective leaders, whether in Gogol or in life, are capable of as much. Far more significant are the consequences when the word is employed sacramentally. The first such use occurs in the description of the oath-taking ceremony in which every incoming member of the Cossack community must participate:

The newcomer merely showed himself to the leader, who usually said: "Good health to you! Do you believe in Christ?"
"I do!" answered the newcomer.
"And do you believe in the Holy Trinity?"
"I do!"
"And do you go to church?"
"I do!"
"Well, then, cross yourself!" The newcomer crossed himself.
"Good!" answered the leader. "Go to the unit which you choose."
With that the whole ceremony ended. And all of the camp prayed in one church

and was ready to defend it to the last drop of their blood, though they would not hear of fasting and abstinence. (43–44)

This dialogue occurs in both versions of the story. And both versions preface it with a reference to the variety of individual backgrounds that the newcomers bring, which must be forgotten, even disowned. There is a slight but telling difference, however, in the way this is stated. Version *A* reads: "He [the newcomer] spat, one may say, *upon the entire past* [*On, mozhno skazat', pleval na vse proshedshee*]" (301). This has each Cossack, and by extension the collective, disavowing not merely a personal past but the past in general, which would amount to a disavowal of Orthodoxy, for an ahistorical Christianity is a contradiction in terms. *B* states that each newcomer "spat, one may say, upon *his past* [*pleval na svoe proshedshee*]" (42). This clears the way for allegiance to a common tradition through history as represented in Orthodoxy. It now becomes plain why the enemies of the Cossacks are represented throughout the story as enemies of Orthodoxy. In turn, this suggests a solution to the problem that Gogol could not resolve in his historical articles: how to make the past present. The swearing of an oath does that in a symbolic sense. The celebration of the Divine Liturgy, for a Christian, does it literally. There is no actual representation of this liturgy in the story. But there is a scene that looks very much beholden to it.

In chapter 8, the Cossacks have pitched camp before the walls of the Polish town of Dubno. They are "sad at heart" and "melancholy" because half their number have left to pursue the Tartars. Taras, who remains behind with them, says nothing for the moment, but "in silence he prepare[s] himself to rouse them, all at once and suddenly,[3] by uttering the Cossack battle cry, so that courage might come back anew to the heart of each with greater force than before." He decides to make his words even more effective by having each of the Cossacks drink some wine. This wine has been kept in a special place, first in Taras's own cellar, now in "one of the wagons that stood apart from the rest" and is "larger and stronger than any of the others." It has been held "in reserve for a solemn occasion," which is defined as "some deed worthy to be handed down to posterity." And all without exception must drink this wine, "so that at a great moment a man might rise to the occasion" (95–96). The sense of ritual is heightened by alliterations and internal rhymes (*palashámi pererézyvali krépkie veryóvki, snimáli tólstye volóv'i kózhi i popóny i stáskivali s vóza baklági i bochónki*), by specialized vocabulary that distances the quotidian (*baklági*, "kegs"), and by syntactic parallelism: "One Cossack used a ladle, one a bowl for giving drink to the horses, another a gauntlet, another a cap, while some simply cupped their hands [*u kogo* byl kovsh, *u kogo* cherpak . . . *u kogo* rukavitsa, *u kogo* shapka, a *kto* . . .]." These devices in turn ritualize gesture: "with their broadswords they cut the strong cords, took off the stout ox-leathers and the horsecloths, and brought out the barrels and the kegs" (96, the English translation of the last Russian sentence). Although Taras bids each Cossack take as much as he wants, it is essential that all drink at the same time, and that something else be present as well: "as strong as the good old wine was in itself and well fitted to fortify the spirit, yet if the *right word* [*prilichnoe slovo*] went with it, *the power of the wine and the spirit would be doubly strengthened*" (96). That "word" is formulaic, and comes in three parts: "to our faith . . . to the camp . . . to glory and to all Christians in the world." It is first pronounced by Taras, then responsively by the Cossacks all together. Obviously, we are meant to think of the sacrament of Communion.

The result, at any rate, is a transformation. All the Cossacks stand "with their hands raised," and all experience a distanced elevation that looks very much like the kind of spatial and temporal removal from the ordinary that Gogol considers a prerequisite to the process of artistic creation: "They were looking into the future, like eagles sitting on the topmost crags of rocky mountains, high precipitous mountains, from which they can see the boundless expanse of the ocean, dotted with galleys, ships, and all manner of vessels like tiny birds in the sky, and bordered by faintly visible strips of coast with towns on the shore like tiny insects, and sloping forests like fine grass" (97). They put off mundane concerns, like "gain and the booty of war" and "gold pieces, costly weapons, embroidered coats, and Circassian horses," and see only the essentials: death and future life. "The whole plain with its fields and rocks will be covered with their bleaching bones," and "the eagles will fly down to peck and tear out their Cossack eyes"; but "there will be great comfort in a deathbed so spacious and free! Not one noble deed will perish, and the Cossack glory will not be lost like the little grain of powder from the musket barrel" (97–98). In the final scene, Taras is captured by the Poles: they "dragged him by iron chains" to the trunk of a leafless tree, then "nailed his hands to it, and raising him on high so that he could be seen from all parts, began to build a fire under the tree." In turn, he is able to see "everything plainly" from his elevated position, and to deliver a final word of reassurance that the Orthodox faith will prevail (130–31).

MORE CHRISTIAN SUBTEXTS

Christian ritual and belief form a strong presence in this story, particularly in the wine-drinking ceremony, with the accompanying "right word," and in Taras's death scene, which is manifestly a crucifixion. These scenes are an achievement of the final version, which was prepared after Gogol's "conversion" of 1840. In *A*, there is no sanctification of the wine; Taras simply proposes that they all raise their glasses and toast the principles for which they will fight in the forthcoming battle, which is compared, as in folklore, to a wedding. Then they mount their horses and ride away as "an orderly bunch," filled not with the religious uplift of *B* but only with "assurance," "a certain inspiration of merriment, a certain quiver of greatness," with "their hearts and passions beat[ing] as one in the unity of a general idea" (327–29). (The Russian here sounds as peculiar as my English.) The final scene is entirely different in *A* too: there is no capture by the Poles, no tree, no bonfire, no elevation from which Taras views the future, not the slightest hint, in other words, of a great sacrifice, let alone a crucifixion. Taras does make a speech, but it is self-directed and self-serving, in keeping with his character in *A*: he urges the Cossacks not to "concern themselves" with his fate, expresses the hope that they will "remember" him now and then, and ends by bidding them "come next summer." With that he is hit on the head by a pursuing Pole, and stops talking (355).

In the religiously charged context of *B*, the transformation experienced by the Cossacks atop their spiritual mountain bears some of the marks of a transfiguration and calls to mind one of the central articles of Orthodox belief. The Feast of the Transfiguration, celebrated on August 6, originated in the Eastern Church, was well established there before the year 1000, and has long been one of the Twelve Great Feasts of Orthodoxy. In the Western Church, however, it dates from only the fifteenth century and enjoys far less prominence, not counting, for example, as a Holy Day of Obligation. It commemorates Christ's Transfiguration as related in the gospels of Matthew (17:1–13), Mark (9:2–13), and Luke (9:28–36). In the Transfiguration "we see Christ's human nature—the human substance which He took from us—filled with splendour, 'made godlike' or 'deified.'" This event "reveals to us the full potentiality of our human nature." Since we are all made in the image and likeness (*obraz i podobie*) of God, we have, as Leonid Ouspensky puts it, "the possibility of acquiring the divine likeness." Such likeness "is assigned to man as a dynamic task to accomplish. . . . The rebirth of man consists in changing the 'present humiliated state' of his nature, making it participate in the divine life." We can, in other words, be transfigured. In our present life, this is accomplished through concrete actions, internal as well as external. The point is not to put off our human nature but to spiritualize it. As Ouspensky goes on to say: "[H]uman nature . . . remains what it is, remains whole: Nothing is lost. On the contrary, it is purified just as the iron is purified when in contact with fire."[4] Hryhory Skovoroda, the great eighteenth-century Ukrainian philosopher and poet, describes it in a striking image as a putting on of "heavenly flesh."⁵ In these respects, transfiguration seems to be a function of place in that we are expected to attain to the fullness of which we are capable by virtue of being what we truly are. It is a fullness conditioned, certainly for a Neoplatonist Christian, by the place we occupy in the divine hierarchy. In a gloss on Pseudo-Dionysius, John D. Jones explains that in Neoplatonic thought, "being always points toward completion (*telos*). This means that something is only to the extent that it attains to the unity which is proper to its logos or nature. In attaining to this unity, a being attains to its completion."⁶

Generally speaking, there is no idea in Gogol of escape from the flesh, which is acknowledged concretely and graphically everywhere in his work. One notable exception is the highly ascetic monk-artist in Part 2 of "The Portrait," but as we have seen, he is too abstract to be plausible. Flesh, as it invests most of Gogol's characters, is misused; but the assumption always is that it can be spiritualized to some extent. The Cossacks in "Taras Bulba" offer an instructive case. When they are not fighting, they are prone to heavy drinking, out of idleness and boredom. When that is carried to the extreme of "dead" drunkenness (*p'yan mertvetski*, the identical idiom in Russian), it stands for utter abandonment to the flesh, uninformed by any larger idea, and is literally lethal, for half the men who are "dead" from drink are killed by the Poles; the other half are taken prisoner. But with the presence of a spiritualizing idea—"comradeship"—drinking itself is spiritualized: "There was a fascinating charm in this carousing [*pirshestvo*]. It was not a gathering of people drinking to drown sorrows, but simply the frenzied revelry [*razgul'e*] of gaiety . . . it was like an intimate club of school comrades" (42). What further legitimizes this form of drinking is that the words *pirshestvo* and *razgul'e* are used elsewhere in the story, as in folklore, to describe battles, which, being defenses of the Orthodox faith, are by definition "spiritual."

Such parallels are not surprising in view of Gogol's zealous efforts to lead a Christian life from the 1840's on and his growing conviction that the artist must achieve spiritual purity if he is to create worthily and effectively. But we should proceed with caution. Is transformation in "Taras Bulba" really the same thing as transfiguration in the Christian sense? Paul Valliere, for one, doubts it, and argues, in a letter to me, that the story is "governed more by an apocalyptic-catastrophic sensibility than by a mystical transfigurationist piety." In any event, many of the parallels or subtexts that we have identified are not exclusively Christian. Wine reserved for special occasions and ceremoniously drunk in an ambience of "right words" is found in pagan epic literature as well, notably the *Iliad*, as is the obligation to discover one's true self as the gods have made one, war as the occasion for the most authentic self-quest, and so on. The theme of the transforming word, in various senses, can be found in virtually all cultures, pagan or Christian; and in Gogol's own time, the German and Russian Romantics had been responsible for some of its most compelling secular expressions. In the figure of the bandore player who sings of the deeds of the Cossacks, thereby perpetuating them for all time among all people, there are some traits we could consider at least vaguely Judeo-Christian. He is Ukrainian, presumably Cossack, and therefore Orthodox. He is a "prophet in spirit," and "a white-headed old man," as prophets should be. His word is likened to the pealing of a bell crafted of "sonorous copper" and "precious silver," whose "lovely chime" rings out "afar through cities, hovels, palaces, and villages," and it is obviously a church bell, for it calls "all alike to join in holy prayer" (98).[7] Yet the idea that great deeds and the people who performed them will survive only if celebrated in art is as old at least as Homer: Demodokos, in Book VIII of the *Odyssey*, is a highly skilled oral poet who is much honored at the court of the Phaeacians; Phemios, in Book XXII, represents perhaps a lesser order of talent, but is one of the few people spared by Odysseus in the wholesale slaughter of the suitors, presumably so that he can record and celebrate the deed. Gogol's bandore player in "Taras Bulba" is such a figure (as in "A Terrible Vengeance"), and that seems to privilege him over a mere speaker of words, however holy. This same passage also contains images found in the concluding pages of *Dead Souls* (Part 1), where Christian references are entirely absent. The bandore-player's tale about the Cossacks, we are told, "will rear up [*poidet dybom*] over the whole world." This expression (rendered by Garnett/Kent merely as "race") is normally used of horses, and seems to parallel the horse/troika imagery that we have discussed in the longer work. The equation of word and bell may also be a highly condensed reference to the complex image, also in the ending of *Dead Souls*, of word/music/bell(s)/troika/poet, and even, as we shall see, Pushkin. In any event, the "mighty word" uttered by this teller of tales is far more powerful than the words uttered by Taras, who, being a kind of priest figure, is hedged about with more explicitly Christian allusions. Even though this word does not come at the end of the story, unlike its counterparts elsewhere, it supposedly ensures the immortality of the Cossacks, Taras among them. It is in this sense a last word, or song, and anything but an explicitly Christian one at that.

ENERGY

At one point in the story, Bulba makes a speech to his men about the virtues of the "Russian soul [*russkaya dusha*]" and "Russian feeling [*russkoe chuvstvo*]," as discerned "in the Russian land [*v russkoi zemle*]" (99–100).

The word "Russian" (*russkii* in the nominative singular masculine) is ambiguous. Any Russian reader of Gogol's time or ours would take it as referring in the first instance to the language and culture of the ethnic group known as Great Russians. It is also the adjective formed from "Rus" (*Rus'*), the name of the first Russian state, as Bulba himself indicates when he says: "You have heard from your fathers and your grandfathers in what honor our land was once held among all men; she let the Greeks see what she could do, and took tribute from Constantinople, and her cities were rich, and her temples, and her princes were *of Russian birth* [*russkogo roda*]." A Russian might then think of the two other senses in which the word is commonly used: to designate the territory north of Kiev that is inhabited mainly by Great Russians, and, more capaciously, the Russian Empire. None of these precisely fits the situation that Bulba is talking about. Cossacks are a mixture of ethnic groups "akin in soul, though not in blood," as Bulba puts it, with Russians merely one component. "Rus" had ceased to exist in the thirteenth century, several hundred years before the time-setting of Gogol's story. "Russia," in the loose sense, lay considerably north of Cossack territory: when Bulba goes on to rail against the "Catholic heretics" (presumably the Poles, Lithuanians, and Uniates) and the "infidels [*busurmany*]" (presumably the Turks), he obviously has in mind what was already being called "Ukraine" in his time. Finally, the term "Russian Empire" was introduced only in the early eighteenth century as the official designator of the state—a good hundred years or more after Bulba's time. In his speech, Bulba never uses the noun forms for any of these geopolitical entities (*Rus'*, *Russkaya Imperiya*, *Rossiya*); Garnett/Kent is wrong in doing so on two occasions ("such comrades as in Russia," instead of "such comrades as in the Russian land," and "what comradeship means in Russia," instead of "what comradeship means in the Russian land"). Bulba, then, employs *russkii* in a very imprecise way. Yet I think that is what Gogol intends. He wishes us to have all these possible meanings in mind, even if they are inaccurate or anachronistic in this context. He thereby suggests, without actually saying so, that the Cossack virtues of which Bulba speaks here and throughout much of the story are also the virtues found in "Russians" of all times and geographies. I will presently speculate on the reasons for Gogol's reluctance to be precise. All we need to know now is that the equation of Cossack and Russian has to be interpreted in the context of his idea of energy. This idea appears at the end of *Dead Souls*. But it was first outlined in a very different context, some half-dozen years earlier, in the articles on history. In fact, it is the only productive idea they yielded, in that it offered a way for Gogol to overcome the main problem inherent in his vision of the historical past: how to make it vitally relevant to the present.

The idea of energy stands out most clearly in two of the articles: "A Look at the Making of Little Russia" and "On the Movement of Peoples at the End of the Fifth Century."[8] Both are concerned with the conflict between established political entities and the raw force of less organized and less civilized peoples, all of whom originate in "Asia," which Gogol extends from the Near East into Siberia and China. He dates this conflict from "the depths of antiquity," marks successive instances of it well into the seventeenth century, and finds that the "Asiatic" always triumphs, at least for a time. Among these people are the ancient Germans, whose Asiatic provenance (in a bow to Schlegel) is confirmed by "the strange similarity between certain root words in German and Persian" and by certain traits of character: the Germans had "nothing but the ferocious expression of war on their faces"; they were "like young tigers, filled with daring," ready "at the first summons to fly with their wild forces" to perform "bold and audacious deeds"; they cherished freedom and "had virtually no government." Their main adversary was the Roman Empire, which by then had become so fossilized as to pose no threat.

Such energy, Gogol asserts, is far more dangerous when it is harnessed and directed, especially under a strong leader. Such were the Huns under Attila, who showed "how dreadful an impetuous Asiatic force could be." Such too were the Mongols, or Tartars, whose appearance in the thirteenth century opened the most traumatic episode in Russian history. Prior to the invasion, Gogol reminds us, Russia had fragmented into hundreds of petty principalities, all engaged in "a chaos of struggle for what was temporary and ephemeral" and devoid of "any unifying power"; they were easily overcome by the awesome sweep of energy from the east. Further developments eventually produced two Russias, north and south, Great and Little. The north, which Gogol calls "the true homeland of the Slavs," consisted of a monotonous, flat, and marshy terrain that "showed not a living life filled with movement, but a vegetative state," and remained sunk in "inertia and torpor" under Mongol domination. But the south responded quite differently, manifesting all the essentially positive Asiatic qualities, even though Mongol power had been broken there. As a "plain" and an "open place" (much like the steppes of Asia), it attracted constantly warring peoples, and "therefore" only "a warlike people could unite in it," a "new Slavic generation," "strong in its unity," made up of individuals who "had nothing to lose," whose "ungovernable will could not tolerate laws and authority." These became the Cossacks.

Even though their principal enemies, the Mongols and the Turks, were "Asiatic," they themselves, as Gogol tells it, displayed unmistakably "Asian" traits: "in half-Tartar, half-Polish dress, in which the borderland nature of the earth was so sharply reflected, galloping along in Asian fashion on [their] horse[s] . . . rushing with the swiftness of a tiger out of [their] imperceptible hiding-places or emerging suddenly from a river or a swamp . . . after a raid, when [they] reveled and caroused." Because they "turned against the Tartars their own methods of warfare—the same Asiatic raids," they prevailed; and because they kidnapped and married Tartar women, "the features of their faces, which at first had been diverse," took on "one common physiognomy, more Asiatic." It was an Asiatic dynamism that enabled them to forge a unity, as the Cossacks, out of a welter of families, bands, and encampments. If anyone had pointed out that the Cossacks were Christians, Gogol could have turned that to profit as well. The article entitled "Life" ends with the birth of Christ in "the east"—a synonym for "Asia," as Gogol uses it—and with Him, the affirmation of eternal life, eternal movement, in contrast with the "immobile," "petrified," and "iron" colossi of ancient Egypt, Greece, and Rome. Christianity, then, seems to embody an "Asiatic" principle as well, although Gogol never describes it as such.[9]

The 1835 version of "Taras Bulba" makes explicit the identity of Cossacks and Asians: "Nothing could resist this Asiatic [Cossack] attack" (II, 312). This is omitted in the 1842 version (chapter 5). In fact, there is no mention of the word "Asiatic" anywhere in the later text. Instead, the parallel is now between "Cossack" and "Russian," but the traits are the same: courage, a love of battle, a passion for individual freedom with a corresponding distrust of established authority, and—repeating a point Gogol had made about the ancient "Asiatic" Germans—a "carefree and inactive" domestic life when not fighting, "insensate and lazy, lying about in their huts without budging."

By now, Gogol has made "Asiatic," "eastern," and "southern" synonymous. All combine in the idea of "Cossack." In the article on Little Russia, Gogol broadens this idea to embrace the Ukraine as a whole: "this crowd, growing and multiplying, became a whole people, which cast its character and, one might say, its coloration on the entire Ukraine, and performing a miracle—turning generations of peaceful Slavs into militant ones, known by the name of Cossacks." The next logical step would be to extend this idea to Great Russia as well. Paradigms were available. Historians had been and still are discussing the question of the origin of the Slavs. There was a dominant "Norman" school, which looked to Scandinavia. There was also a "southern" school, which looked to the Black Sea region. In any event, the idea of migratory national traits was common. For example, Aleksei Khomyakov, somewhat later, argued for an "Asiatic" origin of the Slavs (specifically, in Asia Minor). This enabled him to relate them to the Huns, who in turn became "a special kind of old Russian Cossacks, anticipating by a whole millennium phenomena from the history of Muscovite

Rus." He then extended the "Slavic" principle to much of Western Europe, even making the English "Slavs" by virtue of their "religiosity and the stability of their traditions in everyday life," and introducing the kind of etymological buttress so popular in those times, however shaky: *anglichane*, "Englishmen," was supposedly a form of the word *uglichi* (men from Uglich, a northern Russian town). Finally, he confidently foresaw a universal role for the Slavs, as "the lever which will turn mankind to the realization of [the absolute] idea." Moscow would be the center of this movement, but London the "supporting point of the lever's action."[10]

Khomyakov, a Slavophile, at least used Moscow as his ultimate reference point. Gogol never does (and he certainly would not countenance the inclusion of London in any scheme of his!). Moscow virtually does not exist in his accounts of "Russia." Nor does "Russia" itself from the seventeenth century on. Practically everything he has to say about it can be found in two sentences in his article on the teaching of general history, where he states that Napoleon had "courted his own doom by invading Russia, where the unfamiliar expanses, the ferocity of the climate, and the troops trained in Suvorov's tactics destroyed him. And Russia, having crushed this giant against its impregnable strongholds, paused in dread majesty in its immense northeast" ("O prepodavanii," 35). These statements come toward the end of his outline for a study of the "history of mankind," one component of his ambitious program for the teaching of "general history." He sweeps from the ancient Near East to Greece and Rome, then to the Mongols, and finally to medieval and modern Europe, with an emphasis on England and France; but no mention is made of the Slavs at all, and none of the Russians beyond what we have just cited.

Why should this be so? Although Gogol did not carry his histories beyond the seventeenth century, Moscow, or Muscovy, had been an important power long before then, certainly since the later Middle Ages, when it began to expand and incorporate other Russian lands, from which the empire was eventually built. What we may be seeing here is a response to the idea, rather widespread in the generation or so before Gogol and still vigorous in his time, that Russia had no real history antedating Peter the Great, whose reign, 1682–1725, falls outside Gogol's time frame. Nadezhdin, for one, had argued that even though Russia's recorded history goes back to the ninth century, the first six centuries that followed "do not, properly speaking, belong to the biography of the Russian people." He initiates this "biography" with the reign of Ivan III (1452–1505), but even so, he finds that during the next two centuries, "the face [of the Russian people] changed continually, like the face of a child," on which "not a single trait was able to etch itself deeply, not one characteristic mark could be retained for long. All its movements were instantaneous and fleeting; its entire life was impulse, frenzy!" Although this period shows signs of "much epic grandeur and lyrical animation," it offers "little dramatic fullness of life." Since this last quality is essential to successful works of art as Nadezhdin defines them, historical novels and plays that draw on this period are for him necessarily flawed. Pushkin's *Boris Godunov* (1831), for one, suffers from "a lack of dramatic fullness." Even so, Nadezhdin is essentially optimistic. Like many of his contemporaries, he perceived the Russians as a "young" people, "living in the first chapter of [their] history," a chapter that is "so fresh, so new!" This enables him to foresee the possibility of "a *Russian national novel*, as a picture of Russian national life," provided that it is "a *patriotic novel*."[11]

Gogol puts forth the negative side of this view of the Russian past in "A Few Words About Pushkin": "Russian history has taken on brightness and liveliness only since the time of its most recent [form of] government, under the emperors [that is, since Peter the Great]. Before that, the nature of the people was for the most part colorless, they had little knowledge of the variety of passions."[12] This is an early work, but there is no evidence that Gogol ever revised his opinion. He eventually took a brighter view, in *Dead Souls*; but there he looks to the future, not the past. For reasons we have suggested, Gogol may have assumed that his readers on their own would make a connection between "Taras Bulba" and the idea of a vital, energetic new Russia; but it was also obvious that his vision in the last chapter of *Dead Souls* did not entertain such a connection. As in the theme of the Christian word, so in the theme of energy "Taras Bulba" seemed to mark a dead end.

Yet the idea of energy is essential to this vision. Only it derives from a very different source, one that is not specifically mentioned in the "poem," either, but that forms a palpable structure of thought. Once again, it is to be located in Gogol's Roman experiences.

ROME AND RUSSIA

As we have seen, Gogol frequently registered his reactions to Rome by contrast with Russia in a "south/north" antithesis. "South" stood for movement, warmth, wholeness, and life, whereas "north" betokened immobility, coldness, fragmentation, and death. The contrast itself was conventional, as were its terms. What makes it more interesting and significant in Gogol is that it also corresponds to the "Asia/Europe" antithesis that he developed in the articles on history. We have seen how "Asiatic" traits could become "southern" by virtue of translation onto "southern" territory, notably the Ukraine. Some five years later, the story "Rome" would show that these same traits had moved to yet another "southern" clime,

Italy. But "south" was also "east," and its antithesis, "north," or "Europe," could also be "west," hereby fitting the more familiar dichotomy in whose terms Russians have perpetually tried to define themselves.[13]

The prince, who is obviously speaking for Gogol, muses that the ordinary Roman people, or *narod* (he probably means Italians generally), are "childlike and noble" and "untouched by education." In "the manner of strong people," they have a tendency to go all out and reach for extremes: "either good or bad, either spendthrift or miser." At the same time, they are endowed with an instinctive sense of beauty, which enables them to make art out of the simplest things. Spiritually, they are imbued with self-worth, an innate feeling for justice, a genuine religious faith, and a chronic "gaiety," which traits "other peoples do not now possess." In all these respects, they stand in contrast not only to European enlightenment, which "as if by design did not touch them and did not erect in their breast its cold sense of perfection," but also to the established political structures, like the papacy, the aristocracy, and the state bureaucracy. The prince is willing to make an exception for "the government of the clergy, this strange specter that survived intact from bygone days, survived as if for the purpose of preserving the people from outside influence, so that none of their ambitious neighbors should encroach on their personhood [*lichnost'*], so that for the time being their proud national essence [*narodnost'*] should lurk in silence." The "forces hidden within" this people have not "swept them up in a whirlwind": the prince does not add "yet," but probably thinks it, for he concludes that "some future career has been prepared" for the Roman people, and destiny has decreed that it remain "intact," "elemental," "as yet untouched material" (243–45).

Many of these qualities figure in celebrations of the Italian "folk" virtually everywhere in Europe.[14] But as they are formulated here (and in various letters of Gogol), they offer compelling parallels with the Russian situation. Historians had long been concerned with the idea of a national essence that resided in the Russian "people." Some had credited the clergy with keeping it intact during the hegemony of the Mongols. Others, like Ivan Kireevsky, actually argued that the Mongol invasion was a good thing because it had shielded Russia from Western influences and allowed it to preserve its spiritual purity.[15] More pervasively, the idea of "two Russias" had been formulated around the axes of "the people" and of "European enlightenment" as imported and imposed by the aristocracy. This idea ultimately rested on a distinction between the people and the state. For eighteenth-century Russian historians, the organizing principle had typically been the state, conceived as a succession of rulers and periods: Karamzin's *History* was the outstanding example.[16] However, change was under way. Nikolai Polevoy, a friend of Gogol's, had written the six-volume

History of the Russian People (Istoriya russkogo naroda, 1829–33), whose very title "boldly challenged the authority of Karamzin," as Vasily Gippius puts it, "and met with rebuff from many, Pushkin among them." Polevoy argued that the Russian state began to come into existence only after the defeat of the Mongols, whereas the people had been present from the beginning. By the 1840's, the relationship of "people" and "state" was being widely discussed, and figured in the most important polemic of the time, that between Slavophiles and Westerners. The Slavophile Konstantin Aksakov, the son of Sergei, a good friend and frequent correspondent of Gogol's, framed the distinction as follows: "Outer truth is for the State, inner truth is for the Land; unlimited power is for the tsar, full freedom of life and spirit for the people; freedom of action and law is for the tsar, freedom of opinion and the word for the people."[17] Gogol makes roughly the same distinction when he is talking about Italy or the huge political entities of the ancient world. For Russia, he is largely silent about "the state," concentrating instead on "the people," who come to embody for him the same essential qualities as all the other "southern" and "Asiatic" peoples he treats. As we have seen, "Rome" could in many respects be read as a distanced comment on Russia. No explicit parallel is drawn between the Romans and the Russians, but readers would have been aware of a larger cultural paradigm that made the parallels all but an equivalent. Gogol himself never developed it in any of his writings, but he hinted at it often enough to confirm his awareness of it too.

Since the eighteenth century, translations had made the Greek and Roman classics widely available to the literate population of Russia.[18] A knowledge of the ancient masterpieces not only marked the well-educated man but served more practical cultural purposes as well. The Romans offered an especially compelling paradigm to Russians of the eighteenth and early nineteenth centuries. For much of their history, republican and imperial, they had had to contend with the overwhelming presence of a superior foreign culture, the Greek. In the second and third centuries B.C., Ennius and Cato the Elder had each addressed this problem differently, Ennius wishing, in J. Wright Duff's words, to "introduce a flood of Greek ideas—the wide humanity and critical attitude of Euripides, so appropriate to a people whose destiny now called them from circumscribed views to a tolerant cosmopolitanism," but Cato (ironically enough his student) coming forth as "the champion of anti-Hellenism."[19] Russia's Greece was Western Europe, and its Enniuses writers of the eighteenth century too numerous to mention. But Russian Catos were on the rise, and Russian Horaces as well, who, like the great Latin poet, wondered in effect why they "should be grudged the right of adding" their "little fund, when the tongue of Cato and Ennius has enriched our mother-speech and brought to light new terms for things." One was Lomonosov. He held up Augustan Rome as the model of an enlightened policy toward the arts, which, if followed in Russia (as seemed to him likely), would surely produce Slavic Virgils and Horaces. At the same time, he asserted that the Russian language was the equal of any other, ancient or modern, and probably superior to most, since Russian was basically Greek, and Greek was superior to Latin.[20]

Lomonosov was not advocating a return to the classics but in effect preparing the way for a rejection of the French-centered neoclassicism that predominated in his time. That work would be accomplished largely in the context of the ancient authors. One important contributor to it was Aleksei Merzlyakov, a professor of literature, a poet, and a prolific translator of Greek and Latin writers. He addressed the problem in the familiar terms of "imitation":

In considering models [for our poets], it must be admitted that we do not seek them where we should. French literature was undoubtedly elevated to the highest possible degree of perfection, but the French themselves have been imitators, and thereby, in their imitating, have adapted themselves to their own times, to taste, which is so inconstant, to circumstances, which are so diverse! Why should we not, for the preservation of our own character and honor, draw from the pure, changeless treasures of that same first treasure-house from which they drew? Why should we not also make direct use of the precepts of their teachers, the Greeks and Romans? Why do we pride ourselves on being imitators of often weak imitators, since we have the capacity and strength to take from the originals themselves!

He warns of the consequences: "I am not now speaking of what is worst of all, of the fact that in imitating the creations of a living people that has dealings with us, we insensibly imitate its manners and customs and lose our character and our national pride, which can be called the foundation and bulwark of our glory as a people. In short, it is we who are creating intellectual slavery for ourselves!" The only ways in which he thinks the French can be properly and profitably imitated is "in their labors, their researches, their indefatigability; busy yourselves with the study of the ancient writers as they do, and you will reach the desired goal."[21] Implicit here is an assumption that the classics may be safely imitated because they are timeless, universal, and not delimited by national boundaries or by parochial social and political interests.

Many classicizing poets were active in Russia from about 1800 to 1830, none of the first rank, to be sure, but collectively marking an important moment in the use of the classical tradition. This "return" to the classics was also a way of setting Russian poetry and Russian culture on a new basis. Yury Lotman thinks that it helped promote a move away from what was increasingly seen as the frivolous and self-centered aesthetics of Sentimentalism toward a greater seriousness of subject matter, including "civic" issues that might have created political problems if set forth in purely Russian guise. F. F. Ivanov, for example, wrote "An Epistle of Cato to Julius Caesar" (Poslanie Katona k Yuliyu Tsesaryu, 1812) and "A Conversation of Cato and Brutus" (Razgovor Katona s Brutom, 1812) two poems that, as Lotman sees them, invited reading in very specific ways:

> The image of Cato Uticensis [Cato Minor, great-grandson of Cato the Censor], a strict republican, who committed suicide since he did not wish to accept the unlimited power of Caesar, was very popular in the eighteenth-century literature of the Enlightenment. . . . The image of Brutus was widely used in the literature of the late eighteenth and early nineteenth century as a political symbol. His name was linked with ideas of republicanism and tyrannicide.

In fact, such poets, Lotman argues, were interested "not in the affirmation of classicism but in its destruction." That is, "in ancient poetry they saw not the incarnation of the eternal norms of abstract reason, but a real, historically based form of human culture."[22]

Any educated Russian of the time would have been aware of these ideas in a general way. It is likely that Gogol possessed them in some detail if only because of his friendship with Stepan Petrovich Shevyryov, a poet, critic, and author of many scholarly articles on ancient Roman literature. Russian critics before and since the Bolshevik Revolution have tended to regard him as "a talentless pedant, an intriguer, and an ideologue who hymned the praises of the regime of Nicholas I"[23] and have accordingly neglected him, with their foreign colleagues typically following suit. He certainly was a strange and difficult man. But he is one of the most versatile and interesting literary figures of the nineteenth century, and, for our purposes here, particularly important as an astute critic of Gogol's works and as a major presence in his life.

SHEVYRYOV AND GOGOL

Shevyryov was but three years older than Gogol, having been born in 1806. He outlived him by twelve years, dying in 1864. In Moscow he became associated with the Society for the Lovers of Wisdom, a group organized around Dmitry Venevitinov and Vladimir Odoevsky and dedicated to establishing a new philosophical direction under the aegis of German metaphysics, especially as represented by Friedrich Schelling. His first trip to Italy extended from 1829 to 1832, when he served as tutor to the son of Princess Zinaida Volkonskaya, the *grande dame* of the large Russian colony in Rome and a zealous convert to Catholicism. Over the years, he returned frequently to that city. One of his early works, *A History of Poetry* (Istoriya poezii), received a brief and laudatory mention by Gogol in a review intended for but never published in the journal *The Contemporary*

(Sovremennik) (VIII, 773). In addition, Gogol initiated a correspondence on March 10 (o.s.), 1835, by sending him a copy of the recently published *Mirgorod* and asking him to review it for *The Moscow Observer* (Moskovskii nablyudatel'), for which Shevyryov was the principal critic. Obviously Gogol knew that he was approaching a figure of considerable perspicacity and reputation: "I value your opinion. . . . I have admired you for almost ten years, ever since the time you started publishing *The Moscow Herald* [Moskovskii vestnik], which I began to read while still in school, and your ideas lifted from the depths of my soul much that even now has not been completely developed." He goes on to ask for his friendship, recommending himself as follows: "You are getting a man to whom you can say everything straight out and who is prepared to swallow Lord knows what if only he can hear the truth" (X, 354–55). Shevyryov complied with a thoughtful and generally favorable review—others were to follow over the years, especially two important ones on *Dead Souls* in *The Muscovite* (Moskvityanin, nos. 7 and 8, 1842); and soon a friendship grew beween the two men, which would last, even through stormy periods, until the end of Gogol's life. Some 90 letters from Gogol to Shevyryov survive.

During his first sojourn in Rome, long before Gogol's initial approach, Shevyryov wrote several poems on the city and on Italy. Since some are entirely conventional in thought, their direct influence on Gogol cannot be proved. But much of what seems unique to Shevyryov, particularly in imagery, also appears in Gogol, who very likely read the poems, all of which were published in well-known journals. One of the first, "Stanzas to Rome" (Stansy Rimu, 1829), rehearses the idea that mankind would have no history without art. "To Italy" (Italii, 1830) sets the south/north contrast in terms of fire and ice. This is considerably expanded in "The Tiber" (Tibr, 1829), where the Volga River (standing for Russia) boasts that it is

> Mighty as a young people,
> Broad as Russia,
> Thunderous as its language

and certainly capable of swallowing up "like a drop" the "narrow" and "turbid" Tiber, whose "destiny" has passed it by. The Tiber, however, points out:

> Mighty ice did not forge
> My fearless waters
> In a heavy and cold chain,
>   . . .
> The steed, with despicable shoe
> In proud gallop did not strike
> Against my unrestrained billow [apparently an allusion to the
>   Mongols].

Therefore, the Tiber can "run free into the sea / In a ceaselessly murmuring wave" (77–78). Rome, then, is represented not by ruins but by living water, whose freedom of movement contrasts with Russia's frigid inertness. The poem opens itself to a political reading more than anything Gogol himself wrote except, significantly, "Rome" and some of his letters, with their contrasts between the eternal freshness and warmth of Italy and the coldness and coarseness of Russia.

Far more interesting is "To An Unlovely Mother" (K neprigozhei materi, 1829). Here Italy is the "beautiful woman long well-known," with the "burning, voluptuous glance," "loved by the sun and the earth." Russia is "ugly," her voice "hoarse from the bitter frost," her breast "narrow and cold," her "eyes gray," her figure unshapely, her "language coarse." Yet she has overcome the misfortunes visited on her by fate and has produced accomplished and beautiful children, whereas Italy is sterile, her "tribe" in the graveyard. Therefore Russia inspires "hope": the "restless shining of the eyes" prophesies the "quietly smouldering fire of a soul that has not yet burst into flame / And a desire that has not yet been fulfilled." This is true beauty:

> Granted you are ugly, let me senselessly
> Caress the dream within you;
> But you are a mother to me: I adore
> Your ugly beauty. (68–70)[24]

There are suggestive parallels here with *Dead Souls*, where the Russian "people," or peasants, otherwise have almost nothing in common with the Italian "people" as depicted in "Rome" or in Gogol's letters: they are drab, disheveled, and passive, given to excessive drinking out of a desperate urge for oblivion, lacking aesthetic feeling, love of spectacle, and "gaiety." Likewise, they are utterly different from the Italian-like denizens of the *Dikanka* stories and their devotion to singing, dancing, carousing, colorful dress, and ceremony, not to speak of the Cossacks of "Taras Bulba" and their exotic costumes, love of fighting, cleverness at handicrafts, and capacity to abandon themselves to "reckless gaiety, drinking, and merrymaking." Yet for Gogol, as for Shevyryov, the beauty lies in the ugliness: it is a direct, honest quality, unrouged by "enlightenment," and offering no blandishment to the eye (Gogol's peasants are never "picturesque"). As such, it supposedly reveals solid spiritual qualities to anyone who does not need to "see" in the usual way: common sense, realism (as shown in the peasants' ironic commentaries on the gentry), and the energy of "high-spiritedness" and a "quick and boisterous mind."

Most important for Gogol, the people are the custodians of a pure Russian language, in contrast to "readers of higher society," who are unwilling or unable to say things straightforwardly, and who tend to be "over-generous with French, German or English words" (*Dead Souls*, 174–75). Although complaints about the misuse of Russian by the educated classes had been standard since the eighteenth century, Gogol's version bears the marks of a close reading of another Roman poem by Shevyryov, the long "Missive to A. S. Pushkin" (Poslanie k A. S. Pushkinu, 1830). Here we are told that the Russian language has been fed a "Gallic diet," has become "pale, flabby and boring," "capricious," and "sybaritic," fit only for "pretty little songs and cursing," and incapable of accommodating new ideas. He says nothing about the *narod*, but certainly alludes to it when he calls the language "Ilya Muromets," the most famous of the Russian bogatyrs, who slept for 40 years before awakening. Gogol too, we remember, introduces the image of the bogatyr in chapter 11 of *Dead Souls*, without identifying it with the Russian language; yet the identification is there, for the bogatyr comes from the *narod*. At the end of his poem, Shevyryov calls for an awakening of the bogatyr from his "deep sleep," so that he (or "it," the language: the Russian *on* can mean both in this case)

> Should emit a thick and powerful and broad sound,
> So that he [it] should toll forth in glory of the fatherland
> Like a bell cast from Urals bronze [*medi*],
> So that he [it] should step across his [its] native bounds.

> (88–90)

The narrator, at the end of *Dead Souls*, makes no mention of the language, but instead finds the essence of Russianness in the speeding troika. Yet there are striking similarities of imagery. Gogol's troika has "bells" that "set up a wonderful ringing" (Magarshack's "tinkling" is too effete), and it obviously crosses its "native bounds" if "all things on earth fly past," and "other peoples and states stand aside" and give it "the right of way." Shevyryov is addressing Pushkin; Gogol makes no mention of him; yet the fact that the steeds pulling the Gogolian troika have "chests of bronze [*mednye grudi*]" evokes Shevyryov's bells cast from bronze, and through them, the image of Pushkin as a bell, as well as the most famous bronze steed in Russian literature, the one bearing Pushkin's Bronze Horseman.

Shevyryov sees Pushkin as the one means of "raising the Russian language from its sickbed," for he knows the "secret structure" of the language as well as "its sound and disposition," and can "sound the note of Russian feelings in it" (89). In Gogol, this role devolves onto the narrator of the final paragraph of *Dead Souls*. It is he who has earlier remarked the pure Russian of the *narod*; he who has heard the "song" welling up from the vast expanse before him; he who gathers the otherwise dormant and diffuse energies of these phenomena into a verbal embodiment of movement and power; he also becomes Russia. And it is not difficult to detect an echo of Shevyryov's views of Pushkin as well:

Everything that is Russian resounds in the depths [of the sounds
  uttered by Pushkin],

. . .

You are the organ of Russian thoughts in all keys!
Anointed by your forerunner Derzhavin . . .

(87)

Similarly, Gogol saw himself "anointed" by Pushkin. Russia's destiny becomes his own.

This last connection is made more nearly explicit in the Shevyryov poem
as well. The first three stanzas take up the question of the Rome/Russia
relationship. Rome is the place "To which all the tribes of the earth in turn, /
the chosen ones, brought cups [to be filled]," and to which Russians are
now entitled to come as well, "with equal honor" to "drink [Rome's]
health with our cups as well" (87). This was already a conventional notion,
although it would still have had considerable resonance for Russians even
of the nineteenth century, who were claiming their right to do, on an equal
basis, what generations of Europeans had done. Gogol is hardly so def-
erential. What may have struck him was Shevyryov's statement that from
the vantage point of Rome he would "grasp through premonition / The
great mission of the fatherland" (87). This may hint at the old idea that
Moscow is the "Third Rome," politically, religiously, and culturally. But
more germane is the image of a distance that enables one to see one's native
land more capaciously and authentically, especially if one is "winged," as
is Shevyryov here, and as is the troika (along with the narrator) at the end
of *Dead Souls*. For the most part, *Dead Souls* was written in Rome, and
so it is there too that Gogol had his "premonition" of Russia's future mission. Finally, both Shevyryov and Gogol draw heavily on musical imagery
for their vision of Russia. Shevyryov calls Pushkin a "tuning fork," an "organ," and a "bell"; Gogol speaks of the "song" that wells up from the vast
expanses of Russia, and, almost at the end, centers it in the song of the
troika driver. The final and most effective song, however, is sung by the
poet-narrator. For that is really what the final paragraphs of *Dead Souls*
are—tuneless songs, or chants, as in any piece of high oratory. Pushkin
could rise to it, but not Shevyryov, whose poetry at best was competent.

We do find one striking difference in the view of the poet. Shevyryov put
it succinctly in a diary entry for 1830: "The great poet does not create language unless he has heard it in the people. He brings it to life with his
thought, his soul, and then offers the people its own material, but purified,
renewed and transformed by him. . . . [T]he poet is the apotheosis of the
people. A dead language is put forth by the people, the son of the earth;
thought and a living soul are put into it by the Poet, the son of heaven."[25]
Gogol would agree with the first two sentences, but not the last. Never did

he find the language of the people "dead," nor could he entertain any distinction between earth and spirit, as does Shevyryov, in deference, no doubt, to Romantic poetics. The poet is himself of the earth, a bogatyr, and to earth he always returns. He is no necromancer, bringing inert matter to life, but the focus of the otherwise diffuse and ineffective verbal energy of the people.

By and large, then, Shevyryov provided a paradigm that enabled Gogol, when the time came, to transfer his perceptions of Rome to Russia. But that time was short-lived, as we shall see in the section that follows.

15

The Search for a Language
of Self

THE bandore player, Taras Bulba, the painter-monk, Pushkin: by
1843, Gogol had created a number of versions, mostly fictional, of the ideal
artist. In these figures it is not hard to see characteristics that Gogol himself
wished to embody. In Chartkov, Piskaryov, and Poprishchin, he had also
created images of the kind of artist he feared becoming. As he moved into
the final decade of his life, the aspirations and the failures exemplified by
these figures became the dominant theme of his life as well as his work, all
of which, except for the second part of *Dead Souls*, was now nonfiction.
This theme is documented most substantially in the letters, of which some
840 survive from the period 1842 to his death. Some of them formed the
basis of his only published work during this period, *Selected Passages from
Correspondence with Friends* (1847), which deals with a welter of different
matters, among them the problem of authorship. That same year he wrote
"An Author's Confession" as a retrospective account of his development
as a writer. Finally, *Meditations on the Divine Liturgy* (mid-1840's),
though ostensibly a very different kind of document, has a direct bearing
on the problem of the artist as well. We shall take up all three works in this
chapter.

Gogol's persistent need for models could not be gratified by characters
of his own devising: his readers might be served, but he would be enclosed
in a self-created world, much like Poprishchin. The imperative of distance
still spoke. Pushkin had been his paragon in the 1830's. But he apparently

would not do for the 1840's, except for one brief resurrection in mid-decade, which we shall study in the chapter to come. We have no evidence that Gogol undertook a systematic search for a new mentor. But one was at hand, in the person of Homer.

HOMER

Gogol was exposed to Homer in a Greek class at Nezhin, but apparently came away unscathed.[1] His earliest works contain some conventionally adulatory references to Greece. For instance, the only foreign city the wandering hero of *Hanz Kuechelgarten* (1829) visits is Athens, which displays many of the qualities Gogol would later attribute to Rome, such as picturesque ruins that inspire musings on a glorious past, and a dark-eyed, dark-haired beauty with "white marble shoulders" and "hot lips." Alkinoe, the heroine of the essay "Woman" (1831) and the epitome of feminine beauty, is Greek. But it was only in the early 1840's that Homer began to find a significant place in Gogol's ideas about art. In the final version of "The Portrait," the Russian artist who lives in Rome and sends back the astonishing picture that hangs in the Academy has studied the works of many painters, taking from each "only that which was beautiful," but eventually he settles on "the divine Raphael" as his sole teacher. In this respect, he is likened to a "great artist-poet who has read many works of all kinds, filled with many delights and majestic beauties," but who finally takes the *Iliad* as his only "constant companion, having discovered that it contained everything one could want, and that there was nothing that was not already reflected here in profound and great perfection."[2] No Latin or Italian poet is brought in to stand with Raphael. More important, although there is an apparent equation of painting and poetry here, the weight obviously falls on the side of Homer: if the *Iliad* contains "everything," why bother to look at anything else?

By 1847, Gogol's admiration for Homer had grown enormously. He was apparently reading the poet, for in a letter to Zhukovsky, he mentions "a Latin supralinear translation of the *Odyssey*, recently published in Paris along with the original," pronounces it "very satisfactory," and recommends it as "more useful to you than the others." Gogol had modeled *Dead Souls* on Dante's *Divine Comedy*: the completed first part depicted a contemporary Russian inferno, and in the projected second and third parts, Chichikov would eventually understand the error of his ways, undergo further trials, and achieve redemption. In this same letter, however, Gogol now cites Homer, not Dante, as one of his exemplars, particularly in plotting: "I saw and took in many parts separately, but the plan of the whole would not present itself clearly, definitely, and vividly enough for me to sit down and start writing. At every step I felt that I lacked a great deal, that I did not yet know how to entangle or disentangle events, and that I had to learn from the great masters how to construct larger-scale works. I set about studying them, beginning with our beloved Homer."[3]

The key text is "On the *Odyssey* as Translated by Zhukovsky." Gogol first published this essay separately in the seventh issue of *The Contemporary* for 1846, and the following year incorporated it, without change, into *Selected Passages from Correspondence with Friends*, as the seventh "letter."[4] He begins by explaining, in uninspiringly conventional terms, that the *Odyssey* is "the most perfect work of all times." For one thing, it "embraces the entire ancient world, public and domestic life, all the occupations of the people then living, with their trades, their store of knowledge, their beliefs," whereas the *Iliad*, so celebrated in "The Portrait," is now merely "an episode" (236). He goes on in considerably more interesting fashion to note that the poem represents life in the kind of accurate and lively detail that "neither sculpture nor painting nor, generally speaking, any of the ancient monuments" could match (239). Now he has thoroughly revised the priorities set forth more than ten years earlier in "Sculpture, Painting and Music": the word, which went virtually unmentioned then, is superior to any of the plastic or visual arts. Still more significant is his insistence that the *Odyssey* provides a model for the much-needed reform of Russia. Despite "our recent civic spirit and enlightenment," he says, we have achieved only "a slovenliness and disorder, both internal and external," and have become "loathsome to one another," largely, he suggests, as the result of giving too much room to that "European perfection" that is the motto of "our nineteenth century." We are dissatisfied with our Russian lives; we yearn for the kind of "serenity and almost infantile simplicity" exemplified by the *Odyssey*; and careful study of Homer's great work will take us back to the "childishly beautiful" state that is mankind's "legitimate heritage" but that has been lost (243–44). This is possible, Gogol argues, because Russians have a natural "kinship" with those "patriarchal times" (it is not clear whether he refers to the structures of autocracy), and are "endowed with the purity of virginal taste required to have a feel for Homer." And they are fortunate to possess the language they do. Echoing statements made a century earlier by Antiokh Kantemir, Lomonosov, and Tredyakovsky, Gogol proclaims Russian "the fullest and richest of all European languages," certainly "sufficiently rich and full" to "reflect all the innumerable, elusive beauties of Homer himself and of Hellenic speech in general" (236–37). Even the illiterate can profit, for Gogol foresees the translation's being recited publicly, as epics originally were. In the realm of what we now call high culture, Gogol thought that the *Odyssey* could show Russian writers how to achieve "clarity" and "artless simplicity," as well as renew a "tired" and "confused" literary criticism by stimulating "discussions, analyses and judgments, observations and thoughts" that would "resound in our journals for many years to come" (236–37; 241–42).

The responsibility incumbent on the translator of the *Odyssey* is therefore enormous. By making an otherwise closed world available to his countrymen, he can be the instrument of their spiritual and moral regeneration, Gogol believes, but only if he has devoted himself to a lengthy preparatory work. We know from "The Portrait" what Gogol thought that must be for a painter. It is essentially no different for a writer, whether he produces "original" works or translations. Zhukovsky passes the tests. He has acquired the necessary technical resources by translating "from poets of all nations and languages," which endeavor has attuned his ear "to all lyres." Furthermore, he has fitted himself emotionally, morally, and spiritually by "falling in love with Homer" and by living the kind of life that has "brought his own soul into greater harmony and serenity," a state requisite to transmitting "a work conceived in such harmony and serenity." The result is "not a translation, but rather, a reconstruction, a restoration, a resurrection," which Gogol claims, somewhat startlingly, "leads [us] into ancient life even more than does Homer's original." In effect, the *Odyssey* becomes the equivalent of "nature" or "the world," which must be not copied but studied for the underlying "idea" that is then to be presented in heightened form. The twist is that Zhukovsky had worked from a German translation of the original. Gogol makes no mention of this well-known fact, but it would not have affected his argument. (It does, however, rather make a shambles of his insistence that the Russian language is best suited to the Greek.) The important thing is the underlying "idea," as embodied in the "living word [*slovo zhivo*]" of the text (237).

The grammar of this term, which Gogol italicizes, is biblical (the adjective would be *zhivoe* in modern Russian, and would precede the noun), and suggests that Gogol is talking about Word, or Logos, which can be potentially conveyed in any language.[5] In this way, he introduces what looks like a Judeo-Christian idea. In fact, he goes on to denominate Christian belief as one of the essential attributes of a good translator, finding that again Zhukovsky more than measures up. Zhukovsky had had to become "a more profound Christian, so as to acquire that perspicacious, deep look into life which no one but a Christian, who has already grasped the meaning of life, can have" (237). This last statement was mocked by Baron E. F. Rozen in an unfavorable review of this article published in 1846. It does seem strange. Why indeed should a better Christian make a better translator of Homer? Where does that leave any of the ancients? To some extent Gogol is honoring the long tradition of making the illustrious pagan writers unwitting Christians. In much the same spirit, he sets Homer on a level with the more usual kind of spiritual guides: "having devoted myself to my own inner education, having spent a long time over the Bible, Moses and Homer—the legislators of past ages . . . and finally, observing and dissecting my own soul in the desire to acquire a deeper knowledge of the human soul, and in the process encountering Him [Christ] Who more than all of us knew the human soul, I quite naturally became estranged from everything contemporary for a time."[6] But he is also saying that a spiritual impulse is valid wherever it appears; the important thing is to pursue it deeply and sincerely, regardless of what it is called. Thus, Odysseus did not despair because "at any difficult and grave moment he turned to his own dear heart, not even suspecting that through such an inward turning he was already creating that inner prayer to God which any man utters in moments of calamity, even without having any conception of God" (239). A true Christian, in Gogol's view, does much the same. That is why he is sure that the Russian reader will not be confused by Homeric polytheism but will simply look through it to the spiritual essence beneath, and in the process perhaps become a better Christian: "our people will scratch their heads on sensing that they, knowing God in His true form, having in their hands His written law, even having interpreters of the law in the spiritual fathers, are lazier about praying and fulfill their duties worse than the ancient pagan." They will understand why "this same higher power came to the aid even of the pagan, for his good life and his zealous prayer," even though he invoked it under the names of pagan gods (239).

Gogol's enthusiasm for Homer is understandable. Homer was an oral poet who spoke for the community at large and whose speech had been perpetuated and immortalized in writing. This could be a definition of the ideal Gogol set for himself in his own works—the poet as *vates*.[7] Convention had also made Homer blind, and therefore an appropriate symbol of the shift away from seeing that Gogol was trying to make throughout the 1840's. These very qualities may explain, at least in part, his failure to take any account of the literary achievement of ancient Rome. What may seem particularly surprising is the absence of any significant mention of the *Aeneid*. Previous generations of Russians had sought in their own national experience parallels to ancient Rome. Virgil in particular had shown, with brilliance, flair, and originality, how Homer's achievement could be adapted to his own purposes. Such considerations, however, would probably have struck Gogol as outmoded. The old arguments about Russia's identity had been largely resolved, at least for him, in favor of a native culture that was rich and vital. Furthermore, he had no interest in imperial ideologies, whatever the nationality, and would not have found Virgil's celebration of Augustus appealing or pertinent. Perhaps most important, Virgil was centuries removed from a vital oral tradition, very much a "literary" man, writing for a small and exclusive band of readers, and in all these respects certainly not the kind of writer Gogol wished to be.

Fashion may also have left its imprint. In Western Europe and in Russia, the interest in ancient Roman culture had begun to flag at least a generation earlier. People instead had turned to Greek philosophy and culture. Russian translations of Plato had been undertaken in the late eighteenth century, and helped prepare the ground for the enthusiastic reception of German Romantic Neoplatonism a few decades later. Ancient Rome, which had made virtually no contribution to philosophy, receded in all other respects as well. The *Aeneid* came to be perceived as markedly inferior to the Homeric poems. Belinsky commented in 1835: "The *Iliad* was created by the people, it was a reflection of the life of the Greeks, it was a sacred book for them, a source of religion and morality—and this *Iliad* is immortal. But tell me, for heaven's sake, what are these *Aeneids*, these *Jerusalem Liberateds*, these *Paradise Losts*, these *Messiahs*, etc., etc." By the 1830's, Homer was customarily being set beside Dante and Shakespeare as one of the three great figures of world literature. While a professor at Moscow University, Shevyryov offered a course every other year that focused on these writers as representatives, respectively, of epic, lyric, and dramatic poetry. The classicizing tendencies of the time now embraced the Greeks as they earlier had the Romans. Pushkin, for instance, wrote two charming poems in 1836, "To the Statue of a *Svaika*-Player" (Na statuyu igrayushchego v svaiku), and "To the Statue of a Knucklebones-Player" (Na statuyu igrayushchego v babki). Statues as the subjects of poems are an ancient device, as are the Greek meters that Pushkin imitates; but the games they play here are purely Russian.[8]

Gogol's friend Konstantin Aksakov had proclaimed *Dead Souls* the equal of Homer and Shakespeare; Belinsky had demurred; other critics weighed in on this side or that. Gogol was of course aware of these controversies by the time he wrote his "letter" on the *Odyssey*. True enough, he had studied Homer, had subtitled his work *poema*, by which was conventionally meant "epic poem," had even used many devices of the epic in his work (most strikingly the so-called "Homeric simile"), and obviously intended *Dead Souls*, in its final version, to be about "all" of Russia. But he himself never put it on a level with Homer, who was, in his opinion, the only poet to have produced true epics. At best, *Dead Souls* would fit in among what he called "the lesser kinds of epic," that is, works of more or less recent vintage that stood between the novel and the epic, and whose heroes, "though . . . private and insignificant person[s], [were] nonetheless significant in many respects for the observer of the human soul."[9]

"Lesser" defines modesty's province. But it also tells us a great deal about the way Gogol used models. He looked for approximations, not exact fits. Homer suited him best in the mid-1840's, but he really served as a nucleus around which Gogol could cluster other models, past and present, to construct an ideal poet-mentor, against whom he could then measure himself. The picture that emerges is a composite of pagan and Christian elements. Besides a *vates* of Homeric cast, this figure partook of some of the features of an Old Testament prophet. Closer investigation would probably reveal the presence of various Church Fathers and preachers whom Gogol was beginning to read in the 1840's. Fiction had its say too, in the Romantic figure of the poet-prophet, sometimes with a biblical coloration, as in the poems of Fyodor Glinka and, most famously, in Pushkin's "The Prophet" (Prorok, 1826). Whatever the sources, it was imperative for Gogol that this ideal poet be qualified spiritually, temperamentally, and linguistically for his task. Otherwise, his efforts would be wasted, even harmful. But why was Gogol so obsessed with self-definition at a time of life when most successful writers are well aware of what they are doing? Several possibilities are worth considering.

THE SELF-ANNIHILATING WRITER

One possibility surfaced as early as 1835, in the article "Sculpture, Painting and Music." The youngest of the three sisters, and the last in Gogol's scheme, is music. But it is less an art than a life force, which comes out in both gentle and savage ways. On the one hand, it is "invisible, sweet-voiced, it permeates the entire world, diffuses, and breathes forth in a thousand different images." On the other, it is "all impulse," "rebellious," "shattering"; "all of a sudden, at one go, it tears man from his earth, deafens him with the thunder of mighty sounds, and promptly immerses him in its own world," turning him into "one great trembling," so that he himself becomes music. It is at its most powerful "beneath the endless, dark vaults of a cathedral, where it urges into a single harmonious movement thousands of people who are on their knees in prayer, bares the intentions of their hearts to the very depths, whirls and soars with them on high, leaving behind it a long silence and a sound, long in the fading, that quivers in the depths of the pointed tower" (VIII, 11–12). For "cathedral," Gogol uses the foreign word *katedral'*, instead of the native *sobor*, and endows it with a pointed tower, which is non-Russian as well. This suggests that he was looking westward for his idea of music.

In fact, we find once again a close parallel in Wackenroder's *Confessions*, especially in the section entitled "The Strange Musical Life of the Musical Artist Joseph Berglinger" (146–60). Here Joseph was in church, and when the music sounded, "it seemed to him as if suddenly huge wings were stretched forth from his soul, as if he were being lifted up from a barren heath, the gloomy curtain of clouds disappearing before his mortal eyes, and he floating up to the luminous heaven." His inner self was "cleansed of all the earthly trivialities": he left the church feeling "purer and more ennobled," resolved that his "entire life must be one musical composition." When he later attended a concert, he found that he became music, his soul "entirely a medley of sounds;—it was as if it were detached from his body and were flitting about more freely, or as if his body had become a part of his soul." However, there are important differences between Wackenroder's conception of music and Gogol's. Wackenroder involves thought and perception: "[M]any places in the music were for [Joseph] so clear and penetrating that the sounds seemed to him to be *words* [148–49, Wackenroder's italics]. . . . All these manifold sensations always brought forth corresponding *sensual images* and *new thoughts*" (150, my italics). In this way music intensifies an individual's sense of who he really is. Correspondingly, Wackenroder describes the experience of a particular person who has a name. Gogol speaks in generalities about nameless persons, probably because he recognizes no such correspondences: music is sheer energy, and the individual simply does not count. This is the same mentality that informs the ending of "The Portrait" and *Dead Souls*. But it raises anew the question of what is left for the artist (let alone the narrator) to do. Does he not write himself out of existence? How, if at all, does he seek out and represent what Wackenroder calls new "sensual images and new thoughts"? If Gogol was to go on writing, he had to decide who he was and where he wanted to go.

THE PRIMACY OF THE AUDIENCE

Still another reason for Gogol's obsessive search for self-definition was the continuing failure of his works to create the all-important consensus among his readers. His experience with *The Inspector General* was repeated again and again, not much to his surprise. Even before the first part of *Dead Souls* appeared in print, he foresaw the likelihood of hostile reviews and readied his main defense: this volume was merely an introduction. He wrote to Zhukovsky from Berlin on June 26, 1842: "I have reworked it a great deal since I read you the first chapters, but still, I can't help seeing its insignificance in comparison to the other parts that are to follow. In relation to them it strikes me as being like a porch which a provincial architect has hastily attached to a palace that has been conceived on a colossal scale. No doubt it will be found full of faults such as I cannot yet see" (XII, 70). Many reviewers recognized the book as a major event. Belinsky was one. Even though he refused to rank it with Homer, he devoted five substantial articles to it. But there were some contemptuous, dismissive reviews, which faulted, among other things, bad grammar, peculiar turns of language, the generally negative portrait of Russia, and a lack of good taste. Gogol seemed less bothered by them than by the lack of consensus.

These episodes were trivial by comparison with what was to follow. Belinsky himself, as we saw, came to have serious reservations about the oratorical passages in *Dead Souls*, was appalled by the abjectly apologetic tone of the Foreword, which we have looked at in another context, and concluded by accusing Gogol of being "more and more oblivious to his significance as an artist," and instead preferring to be "the herald of certain great truths, which essentially sound like nothing more than the paradoxes of a man who has strayed from his genuine path by virtue of false theories and systems, which are always fatal to art and talent."[10] To reorient Belinsky only slightly, he obviously had begun to understand how important it was for Gogol to define the persona of the artist, far more important, it would seem, than what this artist actually had to say. If there were any doubts in Belinsky's mind, they were dispelled by the appearance the following year of *Selected Passages from Correspondence with Friends*. This book consists of 33 articles on a variety of topics—literary, religious, social, political—loosely based on letters Gogol had written to friends over the years. It provoked a mix of reactions, which Gogol himself summarized as follows: "first, that the book is the work of the unheard-of pride of a man who has taken it into his head that he is above all his readers . . . second, that the book is the creation of a good man, but one who has fallen into temptation and delusion, and whose head has been turned by praise . . . third, that the book is the product of a Christian who looks at things from a correct point of view and sets everything in its rightful place."[11] True to form, he was not interested in this last category but concentrated on the other two, as in fact do most critics.

Any writer whose audience played such an essential role in the literary process could not simply ignore his critics. His response might take one of two directions. One would be to dismiss the readers as stupid, ignorant, and uncomprehending. Gogol had done so in his first wounded reactions to the reception of *The Inspector General*, and in the picture of the misunderstood poet he had created to link himself with Pushkin. But he could not push this approach, for to alienate readers would be the same as to ignore them. Alternatively, he could publicly take the blame upon himself. And so he did, first in the Foreword to the second edition of *Dead Souls*, then even more pointedly in the Foreword and "Testament" of *Selected Passages*. In the first of these two new pieces, he announces that he hopes "to redeem the worthlessness of everything published by me heretofore," declares himself persuaded that this work contains "more that is necessary to people than do my works of fiction," and urges his audience to "read it through several times" and buy up extra copies for those who cannot afford them. Because his health is precarious, and he is preparing for a pilgrimage to the Holy Places in Jerusalem, he craves forgiveness of anyone he might have offended, from his childhood on; he asks that all pray for him. Picking up points he had made in the earlier Foreword, he insists that he has always meant well, and attributes his faults as a writer to "foolishness, immaturity and hastiness," which produced "imperfect" works that "led almost everyone into error with respect to their true meaning." In the "Testament," after reviewing these same points, he allows that "all the attacks made on me have been fundamentally more or less justified."[12]

These statements did nothing to avert the wrath of the great majority of his readers, most famously Belinsky, who called him "proponent of the knout, apostle of ignorance, champion of obscurantism and Stygian darkness, panegyrist of Tartar morals."[13] By way of reply to his critics, Gogol wrote the apologia that came to be known as "An Author's Confession." It is an attempt not only to justify *Selected Passages* but to give an account of his entire career as a writer. His tone at the beginning is anything but abject, as he conjures up the image of a "cruel" and "unjust" reader scrutinizing every word of the book "with suspicion and mistrust." But he quickly shifts the blame to himself for "the disorientation of more than one reader, and the creation of a countless multitude of irrelevant deductions and conclusions" (VIII, 434). More significantly, he introduces another reason for his inability to function, one that had surfaced at intervals throughout his life but became obsessive in the 1840's: that of illness. Tellingly, "An Author's Confession" begins and ends with the image of himself as a sick man. He compares the experience of hearing the reviews of *Selected Passages* to being cut open alive: "A dreadful dissection was performed on the living body of a still living man, such as to make even someone endowed with a strong constitution break out in a cold sweat" (432). In the concluding sentence of the piece, the illness is spiritual, but the operative verb usually describes physical states: "I know of no loftier deed than to extend one's hand to *a person who has fallen sick in spirit* [*iznemogshemu dukhom*]" (467).

SICKNESS AND HEALTH

Gogol had always complained about his indispositions and malaises. Through the 1830's, these were mostly annoyances that made him unhappy, sometimes interfered with his work, and, once he was in Europe, kept him moving around to various climes and spas. He was one of the great hypochondriacs of world literature. At one point he even insisted that his digestive problems were the result of an upside-down stomach. But from 1840 on, illness took on another dimension altogether. That year he fell so seriously sick in Vienna that he thought he was going to die. And he made the kind of vow that people *in extremis* often do: recovery would mean dedication of his life to the service of Christ. Unlike most, he tried to fulfill that vow. No doubt he hoped for health as a result. But he continued to be almost chronically ill. Only now he scrutinized the state of his health as a barometer of the state of his soul.

For anyone reared in Eastern Orthodoxy, that is a very natural thing to do. One familiar literary instance comes in Dostoevsky's *Crime and Punishment*, when the maid Nastasya, observing that Raskolnikov has taken to his bed, asks: "Are you sick, or what? [*Ty bolen, chto li?*]." Of course he is sick, physically *and* spiritually, as she correctly intuits (Part I, chap. 6). No coreligionist would require further explanation: both sickness and sin are understood as alien invasions into a healthy organism, or "place." As John D. Jones explains: "it is neither the body itself, nor the disease itself, nor even the presence of the disease in a body which 'is' the evil in a diseased body. The evil 'is' *the incompatibility of the disease and the body*." Here he is commenting on Pseudo-Dionysius, who speaks of the sinner's "enjoyment of things foreign to his nature," which makes him incapable of achieving "what is proper to that nature." Those "things" are defined as disharmonies, incompatibilities, contraries.[14] This seems to be what Gogol has in mind in *Dead Souls*, when the narrator, speculating on why his hero behaves as he does, says: "And perhaps, in Chichikov himself, the passion that leads him on *is not part of him*" (254). When the alien passion is expelled, health will presumably return; this was to be the business of Parts 2 and 3. It is not clear how this alien passion entered Chichikov, not so clear, at any rate, as in the case of those characters in Gogol's other works who perceive or invent a "lack" (one of Pseudo-Dionysius's criteria of evil) in their lives and proceed to fill it with things they do not need. A prime example is Ivan Ivanovich, in "The Two Ivans," who, in surveying his domain, asks himself: "What is there that I have *not* got? . . . What is there, then, that I *still* have *not* got? . . . I should like to know what there is I have *not* got?" (II, 174; Garnett/Kent omits "then," *zh*, and "still," *eshche*). The rules of Gogolian rhetoric, as we know, create presence through absence, a phenomenon helped along in this case by the magical three-fold repetition and by the power of words themselves to establish realities far beyond the imaginings of their utterers. Ivan Ivanovich proceeds to discover "it" in his neighbor's gun. Such people are not filling their places harmoniously, but are enabling unnecessary, hence polluting, infectious, and sinful elements to enter from outside.

LAUGHTER AS CATHARSIS

This model of sickness and sin is closely related to, perhaps derived from, ancient Greek ideas of catharsis. In the Hippocratic School of Medicine, catharsis refers "to the discharge of whatever excess of bodily elements has produced a state of sickness, and the consequent return of the body to that state of right proportion which is health." It has been argued that the aesthetic usage represents a transferal "from the somatic to the affective," the most famous instance being of course Aristotle's idea that tragedy, if well constructed, will arouse "pity and fear" in such a way as to effect "the proper purgation of these emotions."[15]

Gogol wrote only comedies, not tragedies. Yet his idea of the nature and purpose of the drama is highly reminiscent of Aristotle, less because of any direct borrowing, for which there is no evidence, more because of the image of sickness and restoration to health that runs through both. Perhaps we are guilty of the kind of thing that one of Gogol's characters charges another with: of wanting to "foist onto satire subjects appropriate to tragedy."[16] But Gogol himself paid scant attention to genre boundaries, and we may permit ourselves a similar flexibility on this occasion.

The amplest treatment of these ideas can be found in Gogol's writings on the drama, particularly in the rather late piece in dialogue form entitled "The Denouement of *The Inspector General*" (1846). He first proposes a simple mechanism of repulsion and attraction. The playwright must "present all the rubbish that's in people . . . in such a way that each member of the audience feels revulsion toward it" and wishes to "push [it] away as quickly as possible"; the good characters, on the other hand, should "captivate not only a good person [in the audience] but even a bad one." This develops into the more sophisticated idea that the town in *The Inspector General* is really the "spiritual town" of each individual, and its inhabitants our sinful "passions." The town then expands into a "state" that is presided over by a "good tsar": "Just as, nobly and sternly, he expels the usurers from his land, let us expel our spiritual usurers!" This is to be accomplished through "laughter." Gogol resorts to a variety of metaphors to describe it. First he calls it a "scourge [*bich*]," which presumably the "good tsar" would wield: this picks up the traditional image of the "lash" of satire. He then goes back to his earlier repulsion theory: "Just as we have laughed at all the nastiness in another person, let us laugh magnanimously at our own nastiness, such as we may discover in ourselves!" More important is the comparison of laughter to a bright light, which illuminates the dark areas of the soul, referred to variously as "nastiness [*merzost'*]" and "low passions [*nizkie strasti*]," which are "bad [*durnoe*]" and "sinful [*porochnoe*]." Once we see what has lain hidden, we understand that "it shames [*pozorit*] the true beauty of man," is an intrusion on our natural state, "our noble Russian nature," and is ugly both physically and spiritually. The result is a restoration of the soul to its natural, harmonious condition.[17]

Aristotle apparently did not expect tragedy to work a moral improvement on people, at least not directly or immediately. As one of his more discerning readers puts it, "tragedy acts on the feelings, not on the will"; at best it purges us of dangerous emotions that might undermine the exercise of virtue and stimulates noble ones that in time may affect our conscious actions. Gogol had no such reservations. He expected the drama (and art generally) to make people better. When the viewer leaves the theater, he should find himself "in a happy frame of mind, either dying of laughter or bathed in sweet tears, and carrying some good intention with him." But Gogol goes even farther, in combining the Christian image of light with the pagan image of laughter. In this same article, he talks of the need for "an electric, animating laughter," laughter that bursts spontaneously and freely from the soul, not the "frivolous" or "vulgar" laughter generated by "word-tricks" or "the convulsions and grimaces of nature."[18] The crucial association is that of laughter and life. Gogol amplified it several years later when he called for the kind of laughter that "wings out of man's bright nature, wings out of it because at [this nature's] depths is found [laughter's] eternally flowing source."[19] Laughter and life are often connected in myths and cults. As Salomon Reinach has observed, "ritual laughter signifies the return to life," and cites various ancient regenerative stories. The dead are therefore excluded, as Vladimir Propp, the great Russian folklorist, points out in what reads like a gloss on Reinach: "The dead do not laugh, only the living do. The dead people who have entered the realm of the dead cannot laugh, while the living people who have entered it must not laugh." The reason is that laughter is "the giver of life. . . . [L]aughter not only accompanies the transition to life [as at birth] but also calls it forth." Bergson's idea that laughter is excited by mechanical (that is, unhuman, or dead) behavior is also pertinent here.[20] Gogol seems to have discovered these ideas by himself. When the mayor in *The Inspector General* turns to the audience and says, "What are you laughing at? You are laughing at yourselves," he may mean that laughter will regenerate the audience, which, as audience, is not "in" the kingdom of darkness but distanced from it, like the author himself.

A heavy responsibility lies on the artist to embed laughter in his work so that it generates a healthy response in his audience, and changes their lives. Can he do that unless he himself is filled with laughter, or virtue? Gogol thought not. The Author of the Play, in *Leaving the Theater After the Performance of a New Comedy*, speaks for Gogol himself when he states, "only a profoundly *good soul* is capable of *laughing* a good, *bright laughter"* (V, 170). In a sense, this is also a major theme of one of the three finished works Gogol produced in the decade after 1842 (although it too was published posthumously): *Meditations on the Divine Liturgy.*

ARTIST AS PRIEST:
THE 'DIVINE LITURGY'

This essay is not included in the so-called "complete" works published by the Academy of Sciences. It has been neglected by literary critics, and by readers who are not interested in the question of Gogol's spirituality. However, it is a work of the first importance for understanding his urgent conviction that spiritual leaders, whether priests or artists, be personally worthy of their profession.

Commentaries on the liturgy are a very old genre of Christian literature, and have engaged many illustrious men, like Ambrose of Milan, John Chrysostom, and Pseudo-Dionysius.[21] For Gogol to set himself among them suggests a high order of confidence in the health of his own spirituality, as did his desire to make the book widely available in an inexpensive edition, and without his name attached. What it represents, however, is a personal ideal, not an actuality.

Of particular importance is the substantial section that deals with the priest. Gogol begins by reminding us that the priest's main business is to celebrate the liturgy. This is so obvious to any Christian that we wonder, as with the truisms of the fiction, whether it does not direct us to look farther. If we do, we discover—the inevitable catechetical qualities of any piece of spiritual writing aside—that virtually everything Gogol says about the priest he says elsewhere about the artist, particularly the verbal artist. The priest is an oral performer, like Gogol himself as a public reader of his own texts, and like the great majority of the narrators within those texts. Of course the priest does not invent his text, but instead reenacts and actualizes events that have already occurred and are thoroughly familiar to the attending congregation. The same can be said of the writer as Gogol saw him, though in a broader sense: his texts consist of materials that are embedded in his culture at large and are therefore known, consciously or not, to his audience. All he really does is provide a reminder; he may not simply invent. In both cases, the text must be verbalized in order to do its work. The great moment in the liturgy comes when bread becomes the Body of Christ, when ordinary reality is transformed and spiritualized, when "a word [with a small 'w'] has called forth the Eternal Word" (46). Transformations of the ordinary, in a less explicitly religious sense, are also the business of art.

The priest's audience, or congregation, must adopt the same attitude as the secular reader, onlooker, or listener, one of reverential and silent assent:

"the deep inner meaning of the Liturgy will unfold itself naturally to everyone who listens attentively, repeating each word in his heart" (xv). The
result is an inner transformation, or transfiguration, which Gogol illustrates with the familiar Orthodox image of iron: "While he abides in Christ
he is holy, in the same way as iron in the furnace takes on the quality of fire
but reverts to its former condition of sombre metal as soon as it is withdrawn" (53–54). And as Gogol insisted must be the case with genuine art,
the Word elicits the desire for a corresponding action, as "each of the faithful strives to be both the hearer and the doer" (25):

On leaving the church where he has been present at the divine feast of love he looks
on all men as brethren. Whether he returns to his daily task in business or in the
family, whatever or wherever it be, his spirit will involuntarily retain the lofty imprint of loving fellowship with all men. . . . He will be more lenient and kind to his
subordinates. If he be under the authority of another he will obey the more readily
and happily, as he would obey the Saviour Himself. If he sees one in need his heart
will be more disposed to help than at any other time. . . . If he himself be needy he
will thankfully accept the least bounty. . . . And all who have diligently followed
the Divine Liturgy emerge gentler, kindlier in their dealings with others, friendlier,
quieter in behaviour. (65)

Most striking, perhaps, is Gogol's insistence that the priest must come
to the Liturgy with "an unsullied purity of heart" (2). To this end "he prays
for his own purifying, that he may stand uncondemned before the holy al-
tar, and be made worthy to offer the sacrifice with the testimony of a pure
conscience" (31). In token of such purification, the priest sets himself apart
from ordinary men by donning special vestments and performing certain
ceremonies that are hidden from the congregation, such as the Rite of Preparation, or Proskomidia.[22] For the writer, the parallel here would not be the
wearing of special garments, even though Gogol himself sometimes did so
while working, but rather the maintaining of a necessary distance from the
reader. Gogol would also want us to extend the parallel to spiritual purification. But here he overstates. As any Christian knows, the personal purity of the cleric is not prerequisite for a valid liturgy; the words themselves
are effective, regardless of the human qualities of the medium. Gogol must
have known this, but by now he had much invested in denying it. The idea
that a bad person could turn word into Word, with all the attendant consequences, was simply intolerable. For a Christian, transubstantiation is a
reality, not a symbol; and if such an awesome event could be brought about
by an impure person saying the right words, then how much easier it would
be for his secular counterpart to work his particular kind of transformation, regardless of the state of his soul.

Plato had insisted that physicians must be healthy in mind, for "they cure
the body with the mind, and the mind which has become and is sick can

cure nothing." But he did not extend this requirement to the body. Quite the contrary: "[T]hey had better not be robust in health, and should have had all manner of diseases in their own persons. For the body, as I conceive, is not the instrument with which they cure the body; in that case we could not allow them ever to be or to have been sickly."[23] Gogol demands far more of the artist, at least of himself: health of both mind and body is not only a sign that the work is valid but also a requisite for its effectiveness. (He says nothing about the priest's physical state.)

In any event, Gogol's attempt at self-revelation had no effect on the illnesses, bodily and mental, that continued to plague him to the end of his life. They are well documented in the letters of the late 1840's and early 1850's. On May 24, 1849, for example, he wrote to S. A. Sollogub that he had resumed work on the second volume of *Dead Souls*. It had been going well, he reports, but then—in a characteristic mix of the somatic and the psychic—"my head grew dull [*otupela*]," and two conditions essential to creativity vanished: a "beneficial mood" and—in a peculiar phrasing—a "lofty softening of the soul [*vysokogo razmyagcheniya dushevnogo*]." The consequences of this "dullness" are described in language that calls on the demonic lexicon of coldness, hardness, disorder, and fragmentation embedded in much of his earlier fictional work: "everything within me suddenly grew hard [*ozhestochilos'*], my heart grew coarse [*ocherstvelo*], I lapsed into anger [*dosadu*], melancholy [*khandru*], almost malice [*zlost'*]," and experienced a "cold unfeelingness [*kholodnoi beschuvstvennosti*] of the heart."[24] As punishment, he goes on to say, God afflicted him with "a powerful derangement of the nerves [*nervicheskim sil'nym rasstroistvom*]," which is "an illness [*bolezn'*] that for me is more dreadful than all other illnesses." As a result "[my soul] began to groan at the dreadful cruelty of my heart." Now, he says, "I see with horror that in [my heart] there lies only egotism, and that despite my ability to evaluate lofty feelings, I myself do not have a trace of them in me, that I am getting worse [*khuzhe*], that my character is going bad [*portitsya*, which, as in English, can betoken either physical or moral decay] and that my every action is an offense to someone. I am afraid for myself as never before." He had every right to be afraid. For *Selected Passages* marked the end of his career as a publishing writer.

SELF-CATHARSIS

Where, then, was the cure? Gogol believed that laughter could illuminate one's defects, or sins, so that they could be seen and dispelled. But laughing at himself was certainly not his style. So he tried to accomplish self-illumination in other ways. The Foreword and "Testament" to *Selected Passages* claim that he is making a sincere and full revelation of his deepest thoughts and concerns, in particular the spiritual "sickness" that had prevented him from working to his fullest. In "An Author's Confession," he is uncharacteristically angry in his insistence that his very openness entitled him to more respect than his readers had given him. After all, he argues, society at large is dissatisfied with the state of its soul and thirsts for "inner formation." As a "writer-creator," he has set the example, thereby "recompensing" people for having "instructed" him. And he does not appreciate the rebuff.

As we contemplate these two unusual documents, one question obtrudes: is Gogol as "writer-creator" and Gogol as "I" one or two persons? At the beginning of the "Confession," he seems to opt for two, for he complains, "the subject of this commentary and criticism has become not the book but its author" (VIII, 432). Toward the end, however, he seems to understand that such a distinction would have run counter to the very direction his life and work were taking in the 1840's: "But having ventured a few explanations with respect to my works, I inevitably had to begin to speak about myself, because the works are intimately linked with the business of my soul" (VIII, 463). This, in fact, is the assumption on which he proceeds in *Selected Passages* and "An Author's Confession."

But had he really revealed everything? What might careful readers of the twenty-sixth letter, "The Fears and Terrors of Russia," have concluded if they had noticed an omission from his paraphrase of the passage from *Wisdom* 8:8 that we discussed earlier (Chapter 10): "they who supposed their secret sins were hid / under the dark veil of oblivion / Were scattered in fearful trembling, / terrified by apparitions. / For not even their inner chambers kept them fearless"?[25] Or what might they have thought had they known that in the unpublished "Confession," Gogol was still insisting on his need to gather "all this prosaic vital rubbish of life . . . all the rags, down to the smallest pin, which swirl around a person every day" (VIII, 453)? How could anyone who worked this way be sure that he had really seen everything, that he had not overlooked some "rag" or "pin" that would drastically alter the final product? Might not some "secret sins" likewise have been overlooked, with similar consequences? If so, what were they? Could deliberate or suspected omissions account for the tone of anxiety that pervades much of *Selected Passages* and all of the "Confession"?

Although the immediate impulse for writing this curious piece was Gogol's desire to respond to public reactions to *Selected Passages*, there was another reason too, and it is obviously the more important: "I resolved to endure everything and take advantage of this occasion as an instruction from on high—to examine myself as severely as possible" (VIII, 432). There is no reason to doubt his assertion that the "Confession" is a profoundly spiritual document, a record of the process of self-analysis and self-purification that were now indispensable to his viability as a "writer-creator." But in what sense is it a "confession"? The title is not Gogol's. It was supplied by his old friend S. P. Shevyryov, in his capacity as editor of *Works by N. V. Gogol Found After His Death* (Sochineniya N. V. Gogolya, naidennye posle ego smerti), which appeared in Moscow in 1855. That is why it is enclosed in brackets in all editions of Gogol's works. The piece has much in common with the "literary" confession in the mode established by Augustine, Rousseau, and others; yet the fact that Gogol did not intend it for immediate publication, and subjected it to little or no revision, makes it a private utterance, though not of course sacramentally confessional. Still, as a man with no false modesty about his own importance, he must have known that it would eventually reach print; and once it did, few readers could have found it surprising. For a work designed to show him in newly revealing ways, it did not look so very different from his other writings, especially those in fiction.

THE FICTIONALITY OF "AN AUTHOR'S CONFESSION"

The "Confession" opens with a lengthy introduction, running to nearly one-fifth of the total (VIII, 432–38). It presents a complex and obtrusive narrator (perhaps more than one), who sustains a generally "high" diction throughout; a series of readers; and a protagonist (or protagonists) usually called "the author." Then comes the tale itself, which is punctuated by narratorial comments and digressions. Finally there is a recapitulation and explanation of everything that has gone before (460–67). This is also the structure of much of Gogol's fiction. In fact, he refers to this work a "tale [*povest'*]," a genre that, in his *Textbook of Literature for Russian Youth*, he defines, in rather shaky syntax, as follows: "The tale takes as its subject-matter events which actually happened or could have happened to any person—an event which for some reason is remarkable in a psychological way, sometimes even without any desire to utter a moral admonition, but merely to arrest the attention of someone who is thinking or observing" (VIII, 482). A closer look reveals even more striking parallels between the "Confession" and the fiction, many of them thematic. For example, the themes of "misunderstanding" and of "true" and "false" identity appear in both places. Here, however, I shall consider only one parallel, which has particular bearing: the emphasis on narrative distance.

From his very first words the narrator sets himself at a remove from the story that is to be told, as well as from the presumed reader:

Everyone is in agreement that *as yet no one book* has created *such a variety* of commentary as *Selected Passages from Correspondence with Friends*. And what is *most remarkable of all*, what has perhaps *never occurred to date in any literature*, the subject of this commentary and criticism has become *not* the book *but* its author. *Every word* has been analyzed with suspicion and mistrust, and *everyone has outdone himself* in his *haste* to announce the source from which it has sprung. (432)

The stance and tone are familiar to readers of the fiction too. Consider the opening of "Nevsky Prospekt":

There is *nothing better* than the Nevsky Prospekt, *at least* in Petersburg; for [that city] it is *everything*. *What* does this street *not glitter with*—it is the beauty of our capital! I know that *not one* of its pale and clerkish inhabitants would exchange Nevsky Prospekt *for all the blessings of the world.*[26]

Both passages are specimens of the oratorical manner, in which hyperbole finds a natural place. Hyperbole inspires skepticism in the reader or listener. But toward "Nevsky Prospekt" we are benevolently tolerant. After all, the narrator says nothing very outrageous or improbable: Petersburg *is* the capital city, and the Nevsky *is* its main thoroughfare. No reasonable person (and the presumed reader of Gogol's fiction is almost always that) could fail to agree; we ourselves might well indulge in such harmless enthusings. Where the "Confession" is concerned, however, there can be no common mind about the importance of so recent a work as *Selected Passages*. We all know of greater and more controversial spiritual writings that have appeared throughout the ages. As presumed readers, we are put on our guard at once and thereby distanced.

But we quickly realize that the passage is establishing the presence of another kind of reader, one we may call the reader-as-character, or the fictionalized reader. It is his reactions to *Selected Passages* that are summarized in the "Confession" (and are quoted earlier in this chapter). The narrator takes pains to distance such a reader from himself and from us. "I have no right," he says, "to blame anyone else for all the attacks on my personal moral qualities, however offensive these attacks may have been to a man in whom a sense of nobility has not yet died" (434). There is an implicit appeal here to the presumed reader as one who will honor that "sense of nobility" and be less "offensive." In other terms, the reader-as-character represents a possible but unworthy version of the presumed reader; and his distance from us, as presumed readers, is reinforced by the use of past tenses. This is the reader who is the target of the narrator's sometimes strident, almost insulting tone. But the presumed reader is treated far more gently, as in the fiction.

The presumed reader, then, is challenged to behave more decently than the reader-as-character. In turn, however, the narrator measures us against still another kind of reader, whom we may call the ideal reader. He is defined as a good Christian, that is, one who knows "in what his duty consists, where his place is," and who therefore knows "who is his neighbor, who are his brothers, who should be loved, who forgiven" (462). But how many of us presumed readers would dare claim to be "good Christians"? We too are distanced religiously and morally. However, as if forestalling the possibility of such a claim, the narrator, in the last paragraph but one, redefines the ideal reader in a less specifically Christian and more aesthetic way: "In order to have some sense of this book [*Selected Passages*], one must either possess a very simple and good soul, or else be a very multifaceted person who, along with a mind capable of embracing every aspect, embodies a superior poetic talent and a soul that is capable of loving with a full and deep love" (467). This reader is not a character in the text, but exists outside it as another kind of presumed or ideal reader, who is superior to virtually all of us.

Just as there are several readers in the "Confession," so too there are several authors. One is the author who wrote *Selected Passages*; he is the narrator's main concern toward the beginning of the "tale." But just as the reader-as-character constitutes only one kind, so too this author is only one of the several responsible for the "tale of my authorship." And the narrator tries to distance himself from all of them. At one point the narrator calls the person who wrote *Selected Passages* not "I," not even "the author," but "a human being [*chelovek*]." Elsewhere he speaks of "the author [*avtor*]," or "the writer [*pisatel'*]." He may carry the process of depersonalization further, referring to "authorship [*avtorstvo*]" or "writership [*pisatel'-stvo*]." Even when "author" and "I" are equated, we understand that "author" may be a version of the narrator but is not coextensive with him. In his various guises, then, "author" becomes a character in this tale, quite as much as the various readers. Toward the end (455), the narrator even puts forth an ideal author (without labeling him as such), the "writer-creator [*pisatel'-tvorets*]," who stands in the same relationship to the narrator as does the ideal reader to the presumed reader: the narrator says that he himself is "a writer not lacking in creative ability," but finds himself "far from that to which I aspire" (457).

Like his fictional counterparts, the narrator has a keen sense of the distance separating him from what he observes and comments upon. Indeed, it is in the "Confession" that we find the most concise statement of his need to leave Russia in order to be able to write about it: "I needed this distancing from Russia so as to remain in Russia more vitally in thought. . . . [I]n the midst of Russia I virtually did not see Russia" (449, 451). Spatial distance translates into nonpresent time, and shapes the idea of "authorship," which the narrator can "see" properly only if it is set into the past. "Authorship" is treated as a series of well-articulated phases that are outgrown and discarded. This means that the narrator, who is eternally "present," need not fully identify himself with any of these "authors," and may interpret them as he pleases. He becomes the kind of poet who, as T. S. Eliot observes, "in the course of time . . . may become merely a reader in respect to his own works, forgetting his original meaning—or without forgetting, merely changing."[27]

As in the fiction, here one function of such distancing is to regulate the attitude of the presumed reader toward the characters. We have seen how this works when the characters are "readers." With the authorial selves, the process is more interesting. Like the characters of the fictions, these authors-as-characters tend to be uncongenial. But so powerfully present is the narrator that, as in the fictions, we tend to visit whatever scorn, wrath, or contempt we may feel upon him rather than them. For instance, although the "facts" of the controversy generated by *Selected Passages* are presented in such a way that we find it almost as hard to sympathize with its author as did the readers-as-characters, particularly since the narrator grants that the author was wrong-headed and the book defective in many ways, still the narrator himself is so abrasive that we conclude that this author, even if "wrong," was probably at least "sincere." And that is exactly what the narrator wishes.

The narrator-author-reader relationship can be seen at its most complex when the subject is "Russia." Gogol's system requires that readers, whether fictionalized, presumed, or ideal, be creative collaborators with "the author." Therefore they share his inability to "see" Russia from within. Either they ignore their country altogether, the narrator says, and talk only about Europe, or, if they do look at Russia, they perceive only "two or three facts," from which they draw hasty and inaccurate conclusions. In consequence, "everybody has formed a picture of his own Russia in his head, and the result is endless arguments" (451). The only way we can "see" Russia is to do what the "author" himself did: go abroad. There we can better fulfill our function of providing the author, who is also living abroad, with information about Russia, which will be doubly (and more effectively) distanced, coming as it does from an observer who, once across the border, can no longer observe what he is reporting. Diagrammatically:

Distance creates a necessary otherness. The self requires the "other" of past selves, and of readers who are represented as partial versions of the self yet are also non-selves insofar as they are non-author. Similarly, "Russia" requires the "other" of "non-Russia," which is most conveniently termed "abroad." In effect, Gogol had become a character in his own fiction. Shevyryov, always an astute critic, seemed well aware of this. He could easily have dubbed this work "My Confession" or simply "A Confession," but the attributive "author's" or "authorial" suggest that he appreciated the distancing mechanisms that were so powerfully at work. However, the most important consideration in the public's failure to understand the "new" Gogol may well have been language.

A LANGUAGE OF SELF

For some time Gogol had been conscious of the need to find a new language to describe a newly emerging inner self. On June 20, 1843, he had written to A. S. Danilevsky complaining, "[I cannot convey] the fulness of these inner impressions of mine. . . . For that it is first necessary to create a language" (XII, 197). Later that same year, in a letter of November 4, he seemed to be telling his close friend N. M. Yazykov that he was reading religious books in order to acquire a language in which to express his religious feelings: "By the way, let me know just what you have read or are reading and what has remained in your soul as a result of such reading. We should help each other and share impressions. I have read so little, especially books of a spiritual nature, that every word of yours about them will be a discovery for me" (XII, 237). Sometimes the terminology in letters about his spiritual state is so strange that it suggests an unsuccessful struggle to find some fresh way of talking about himself within old forms. The "lofty softening of the soul," which we have already quoted from his letter to Sollogub, is one such example. Yet what do we find in the "Confession," one of the most intimate and inner-directed documents he ever wrote? That same high oratorical style that is present throughout his work, fiction and nonfiction, from the beginning of his career. It is admirably suited to authoritative pronouncements on the great issues of life, but not to a detailed, intimate analysis of his own soul.

We do not know how the public at the time would have reacted to the "Confession." But *Selected Passages* is written in this same style, and substantial parts of the book display a confessional mode. It is of course true that the expectations of readers may have been deceived. Except for the recipients of his letters and prescient readers like Belinsky, few were prepared for a work of this kind. As Vasily Gippius tells it:

People had been expecting humorous works. There had been rumors of something called "Diary of a Russian General in Italy," which supposedly had already been written and was very funny—and suddenly there appeared a collection of confessions, exhortations, and prophecies. People had been accustomed to thinking of Gogol as a social satirist, because of such works as "Diary of a Madman," *The Inspector General*, and *Dead Souls*—and suddenly there appeared a defense of autocracy and even serfdom.[28]

In the "Testament," Gogol himself makes reference to a work, presumably fictional, entitled "A Farewell Tale" (Proshchal'naya povest'), describes it as "the best thing that my pen has produced," and otherwise speaks of it as if it had been completed; but of this work nothing remains. It is also true that many people objected to the social and political views set forth in the book. But I suspect that insofar as this work addressed Gogol's own spirituality, readers perceived it as grossly inadequate largely because of the language. Its narrator sounded no different from the one with which they had long been acquainted. Since that narrator was obviously a persona, were they now to assume that "another" Gogol speaking in the same language was more "real," more "genuine"? We can imagine them saying: if this is the "real" Gogol, then he has nothing new to say; if it is not the "real" Gogol, then he offends by pretending to be what he is not.

Gogol could neither discover nor devise a language he deemed adequate to express his innermost feelings and spiritual needs. How deep they ran he himself may not have known. The reason for his failure may be that those feelings were so bound up in his work as a writer of fiction that he could not separate them out, could not find either a "true" self that was distinct enough from his fictional and oratorical personas to qualify as authentic or a language that would be particular to this self.

16

The Failure of the Word

___

It is hard to say how Gogol might have resolved the problem of the word. He seems to have grasped that for the purposes of self-examination, self-revelation, and self-cleansing, the languages he had so brilliantly mastered were inadequate. He came to understand too that he must find a new language of fiction, which would depend on first finding a language of self. The quest began in earnest with *Selected Passages*, or so Gogol's Foreword and "Testament" invite us to assume. In fact, this book offers an oratorical narrator familiar to us from various passages in the fictional works, from many of the letters, and from the articles on history. It is nonetheless remarkable for its tone of self-assurance and its sheer spiritual ruthlessness, qualities that Gogol certainly needed to sustain and develop if he was to find a way out of the impasse he had reached. However, all it took was public disapproval of the book for him to beat a retreat. This he did in "An Author's Confession." The route he followed was a familiar one: back to the visual mode. As we have seen, all the old resources of distancing and mediation that inform the fiction are elaborated and amplified in this piece. The imagery is telling too. He assures us that the "writer-creator" (Gogol himself) has an "eagle-like power of seeing," the ability to "paint the word pictorially," a talent for presenting the fruits of his observations "with portrait-like liveliness," as a result of which "the image depicted pursues us everywhere so that we cannot escape" (VIII, 456). It is as if he had never heard of the transforming power of the word. Instead, he once again looks for a world he can see and find comfortingly stable.

The tendency to flee to safe territory when challenged or when faced with "misunderstanding" is especially evident in his later treatment of Pushkin and in the surviving pages of Part 2 of *Dead Souls*.

AGAIN PUSHKIN

We have already discussed the ways in which Gogol used Pushkin as a mediator at a time when his theory and to a great extent his practice of art presupposed that the writer was an observer. Thereafter, Pushkin receded from view, only to resurface in *Selected Passages*. Particularly important is his role in the long thirty-first "letter," entitled "What, Then, Constitutes the Essence of Russian Poetry, and What Is Its Special Quality" (VIII, 369–409). This is a carefully pondered, vividly argued, highly original evaluation of Russian poetry from the eighteenth century to Gogol's own time. Certainly Pushkin is treated as a great poet. Gogol especially admires his verbal conciseness and his ability to handle any subject, however high or low. But significant qualifications now appear. Gogol makes him just another star in an already bright constellation of major Russian poets. He may emit the purest light (to persist in the imagery that is mine, not Gogol's), but purity is not really a virtue, because it means detachment from life: "Pushkin was given to the world in order to show by his own example what a poet as such is, *and nothing more*" (381). Although responsive to everything, Pushkin displayed nothing of his own personality in his work, and said nothing that was "useful to contemporary society," because everything was turned into beautiful poetry (382–83). This gift, Gogol tells us, was a curse for the young poets who fell under the spell of his "harmonious sounds." Not one of them has yet "been able to break out of the charmed circle he drew and to display his own powers" (401), not one has yet understood that "different times have come," and with them, different expectations for poetry: "to give back to society that which is truly excellent [or 'beautiful'] and which has been driven out by the senseless life of today" (408). What Gogol is alluding to here is a new view of life shaped by Christianity and by "national principles" as preserved in folk literature, sermons, hymns, and much of the great poetry of the past, Pushkin's largely excepted.

This is an extraordinary dismissal of the man whom Gogol at one time had set at the very summit of Russian literature. Obviously he no longer requires Pushkin as a mediator, and to judge by the run of the argument, would find such a role just as dangerous for his own creativity as for that of other poets. He now speaks with the confidence of a self-sufficient artist who is capable of serving society in the ways he specifies here and elsewhere, ways that Pushkin no longer exemplifies for him.

In setting Pushkin aside, Gogol may have been reenacting the process that is implicit in his March 1837 letter to Pogodin, where he absolves Nicholas I of all responsibility for the poet's death, emphasizing that "the monarch himself (may his name be blessed for that) honored his talent" (XI, 91). Considering that the tsar could presumably have intervened to save Pushkin, the remark at first sounds sarcastic. But Gogol is entirely serious, and we wonder where he sees the benefit of royal noninterference. One answer, perhaps the only psychologically plausible one, is that Pushkin's death was necessary if Gogol was to cast himself as the successor. But by 1847, he saw Pushkin in an entirely different way, and no longer wished to be a direct successor of a man he now found to be, despite his admitted greatness, decidedly limited.

Pushkin again comes up in the tenth letter of *Selected Passages*, "On the Lyricism of Our Poets" (VIII, 248–61). But the tone is entirely different, or rather, entirely familiar: here is the mediating Pushkin of old, set in a larger political framework. Gogol argues that the Russian tsar is a benevolent ruler who loves and takes pity on everyone in his realm, and who is for this reason the only one "capable of bringing reconciliation to all classes and turning the kingdom into a harmonious orchestra." This will happen when he understands that he is "the image on earth of Him Who Himself is love" (256). The reigning tsar was Nicholas I, but Gogol means his remarks to apply to autocracy generally. He goes on to insist that all the great Russian poets have understood and supported this idea of the monarch, Pushkin among them. But, says Gogol, it was only after Pushkin's death that "his true relationship to the sovereign and the secrets of two of his best works were revealed" (259). One of them is a poem that Gogol calls "To N**" (K N**); this is actually the poem that later became known as "To Gnedich" (Gnedichu, 1832). He reads it as a paean to Nicholas. Here he joins company with Zhukovsky, among others, who had been busy trying to create a posthumous Pushkin as a loyal subject of this very tsar. But Gogol's evidence is false. Even if he did not know that the "N" in the title refers to the poet Nikolai Gnedich, it would strain anyone's interpretive powers to construe the poem the way he does. But these were his own sentiments about the tsar, and they were certain to make him highly unpopular among a sizable segment of the literary establishment, Belinsky in particular. With Pushkin as mediator, they would become safer, or so we can plausibly imagine Gogol thinking, the more plausibly, in fact, because he himself goes on to suppose that anyone of common sense would say: "If Pushkin himself thought so, then it must be the absolute truth" (259).[1] Ironically, Gogol himself passed under an official cloud after his death. Some of his works, especially *Dead Souls*, had been pressed into the service of radical causes by people like Belinsky and Aleksandr Herzen.

According to Vasily Gippius, the government was "even more disturbed" by the "demonstration of popular affection for Gogol" shown in the huge turnout at his funeral, and resorted to "repressive measures," forbidding the publication of a new edition of his works and forbidding any mention of this fact in the press for three years. Ivan Turgenev was even arrested and exiled to his country house for printing an obituary of Gogol in Moscow, where the censor did not know that it had been proscribed in St. Petersburg.[2]

Gogol reverts to his old ways the minute he thinks he may be put on the spot by disapproving readers. We could therefore expect Pushkin to figure prominently in "An Author's Confession," which is Gogol's attempt to defend himself against the loudest voices of disapproval in his entire career. And so he does. In casting an eye over his own development as a writer, Gogol identifies the mid-1830's as the crucial years and Pushkin as the crucial influence. But now the degree of indebtedness is far greater and far more explicitly acknowledged than in his earlier letters to Pogodin and Pletnyov. He no longer merely imagines Pushkin bestowing approval or disapproval but reconstructs (fancifully, no doubt) an occasion when his mentor was actally present, compelled him to recognize the true direction of his talent, and supplied him with the plot for his greatest work:

But Pushkin made me look at things seriously. He had long been trying to persuade me to undertake a large work, and finally, on one occasion after I had read him a brief description of a small scene, but one which nonetheless struck him more than anything I had read to him previously, he said: "With such an ability to put your finger on a person and to represent him as a fully living human being in just a few strokes, with such an ability and not to undertake a large work! That's just sinful!" Then he began to represent to me my weak constitution and my ailments, which could put an end to my life prematurely. He cited the case of Cervantes, who admittedly wrote several very outstanding and good stories, but if he had not undertaken *Don Quixote* would never have occupied the place among writers he now does. And in conclusion, he gave me a plot of his own, from which he had wanted to make something in the nature of a long poem and which, according to his words, he would not have given anyone else. This was the plot of *Dead Souls*. (The idea of *The Inspector General* is also his.) (VIII, 439–40)

In this same article, furthermore, all the themes formerly associated with Pushkin are reintroduced, heightened, and now moved forward to 1847. The first is that of the distanced observer: "It always seemed to me," he says, in discussing his youthful aspirations, "that some great self-sacrifice lay ahead of me in life, and that in the interest of serving my country, I should school myself somewhere far removed from it" (450). Height is not mentioned, as we would expect it to be; but a few lines earlier it is hinted at when Gogol cites his need to "go up [*podnyat'sya*] into foreign parts."

The verb often means simply "move" or "change position." But given the crucial importance of elevated vantage points for Gogol, I think we are justified in taking this word in its more literal, spatial sense here. Gogol had not actually gone abroad in the period under discussion, yet in recounting it he manages to bring in the theme of exile: "I had such a vivid picture of myself in some alien land pining away for my country." "Picture," by now a familiar shorthand for Gogol's way of meeting and distancing the world visually, here is doubly evocative. From the vantage point of 1847, Gogol nervously pictures himself in the early 1830's picturing himself in Romantic exile. And this "exile" was merely imagined, in response to what he calls a "poetic attraction." For this "poetic" exile he also finds a model in Pushkin, not, to be sure, the Pushkin who was packed off to the Caucasus by Alexander I and to whom Gogol had devoted a "few words" in the article of 1835, but a Pushkin who was himself moved by "poetic attraction" to "go to alien lands, solely, as he puts it, 'To sigh for gloomy Russia / Beneath the sky of my Africa [*Pod nebom Afriki moei / Vzdykhat' o sumrachnoi Rossii*].'"

The verse quotation is significant for several reasons. For one, it gives us an entirely fictitious Pushkin as mediated through a text, *Eugene Onegin* (I, 50), in yet another instance of the kind of triple distancing that occurs so frequently in this article. For another, as Gogol uses it, the quotation is a highly compressed image that functions polyvalently. Africa was not Pushkin's place of exile, but it was part of his ancestry, and, most importantly, "southern," as was the Caucasus, and, for Gogol, the Ukraine and Italy as well. As such, it was not only removed but also beneficial. For Gogol, the counterpart to *Onegin* was *Dead Souls*, which was written in Rome; but the theme extends suggestively to his present situation in 1847, which is one of "exile" from a hostile public in punishment for *Selected Passages*, an exile, furthermore, of the supposedly "real" Gogol, the man who is baring his innermost self, just as the "real" Pushkin had been exiled by a hostile government, as every Russian reader knew. The parallel is strengthened a few pages later by the resuscitation, from the 1835 article, of the theme of the "misunderstood artist," framed, as before, in a contrastive pairing between the writer who merely mirrors what the reader wants to see, and therefore reaps the rewards of fame, and the "writer-creator [*pisatel'-tvorets*]," who expresses the real but unacknowledged needs and aspirations of the reader, and suffers contempt and neglect for it. But in the case of *Selected Passages* too, it is a salubrious suffering: "[W]illy-nilly you look at yourself from angles that never occurred to you before; you begin to seek out in yourself defects of a kind you had never before thought to seek. . . . I needed a mirror into which I could look and see myself a bit more clearly; without this book I would hardly have had such a mirror. And so, my book, which was intended in all sincerity to bring benefit to others, has brought benefit primarily to me" (464). The parallelism—"syllogism" might be the more accurate term—also invokes Pushkin without mentioning his name, and encourages us to conclude that the political, social, and religious opinions at the heart of Gogol's essay are also Pushkin's.

'DEAD SOULS', PART 2

Gogol's nonfictional writings of the 1840's reveal the kind of book he hoped to make with the continuation of *Dead Souls*. It would be, he said, "connected with my own inner formation"; it would concentrate less on presenting negative characters and more on examining the reasons why such people exist; for better balance, it would offer more positive phenomena than had been the case in Part 1; above all, it would show readers "clear as day" how to travel "the paths and roads" to the "lofty and the excellent."[3] There is some evidence that as early as 1836, when Part 1 was just getting under way, he was already thinking of a sequel. He refers to it again in several letters of 1840. Word spread, and people began to look forward to a printed work as an imminent certainty. Among the finishing touches applied to Part 1 late in 1841 were hints that the story would be carried farther. In chapter 7, for example, the narrator says: "And for a long time to come I am destined by the mysterious powers to walk hand in hand with my strange heroes" (143). However, the design for Part 2 took solid form, as far as we know, only between August and October of 1841, while Gogol was on the road from Rome to Moscow, and work commenced only in the autumn of 1843. It moved ahead in fits and starts, with many arid spells. He told A. O. Smirnova in a letter of April 2, 1845 that God had taken away "for a long time my ability to create," in consequence of which "I have tormented myself, forced myself to write, suffered painfully on seeing my impotence, and several times have made myself ill with the strain and have been unable to accomplish anything, and everything has come out forced and bad" (XII, 471). In profound dissatisfaction, he burned the greater part of his manuscript in 1845. Later he insisted that this was a blessing in disguise: "No sooner had the flames consumed the final pages of my book than its contents were suddenly resurrected in a purified and bright form, like a phoenix out of the fire, and I suddenly saw how disorderly was everything that I had regarded as being already orderly and harmonious."[4]

Nonetheless, he did not resume work until nearly three years later, in mid-October of 1848, after returning to Russia for the last time. Now it went well, despite his complaints about health, obtuseness, and spiritual deficiencies. He read seven chapters to friends in July 1849, and a revised version of the first four to other friends over the next four months; and he spent 1850 and 1851 in further revision. But fresh signs of trouble had begun to appear. Yury Samarin, the eminent Slavophile, reported in a letter to Smirnova: "I will never forget the deep and oppressive impression that [Gogol] made on [Aleksei] Khomyakov and me one evening when he read us the first two chapters of the second volume. After the reading he asked us: 'Tell me just one thing, in all honesty: isn't it worse than the first part?' We exchanged glances, and neither he nor I had the courage to tell him what both of us thought and felt."[5] On February 2 (o.s.), 1852, Gogol reported to his friend E. P. Repnina: "I have had no luck with my new [works]. Their subject is so important that my weak capacities prevail over my indispositions with difficulty, and only in the event that someone prays really, really hard for me" (XIV, 270). Ten days later, on the night of February 11–12, he burned the manuscript. This time there was no "resurrection." A day later he began to refuse food and fell into apathy; and little more than a week later, he was dead.

What survives of Part 2 was first published in 1855 by Gogol's nephew, Nikolai Trushkovsky. Since then, generations of scholars have made substantial corrections in the text. What we now have consists of the first four chapters and one chapter that was probably intended as the last. Editors distinguish a "lower" or "original" layer and a "higher" or "later" one. Usually two versions are printed in Russian editions and labeled "the first surviving" and "the last surviving." Both, however, may date from the version that was incompletely burned in 1845. The tangled textual history need not detain us here.[6] To help fill in the gaps, scholars have ransacked the memoirs of people who heard Gogol read the work in progress. One of the more intriguing missing pieces is a portrait of a priest, which would have been the first such portrait in Gogol's corpus. But these accounts give no evidence of strategies and language that are substantially different from what we find in the surviving pages.

Most critics agree with Gogol that this book is a failure, even making allowance for the fact that it is a fragment. One explanation, popular in Soviet times, cites faulty ideas and Gogol's stubbornness in clinging to them. The editors of a widely used edition, for example, describe Gogol as hopelessly caught up in "contradictions" arising from his need to promote an ideology he knew was false: "He committed a grave error when he defended the reactionary ideal he had espoused in *Selected Passages*, but at the same time he was tormented by his awareness of the falseness and inadequacy of this ideal."[7] This line of reading finds its source in Belinsky's apprehensions about Gogol's penchant for preaching in Part 1 of the novel (he never saw Part 2, since it was published long after his death). But its crude presupposition that the right ideology would have solved everything and its crass neglect of the fact that Gogol himself certainly did not regard his "ideal" as false are entirely its own; Belinsky wanted no overt ideology at all, nor did he question the sincerity of Gogol's views. Another kind of interpretation rests on the persuasive evidence of Gogol's conviction that the failure to resolve his spiritual problems automatically meant failure as a writer: the fault lay not so much in his material as in his psyche. Least often addressed are artistic issues. In what amounts to a development of Belinsky's insights, Mikhail Bakhtin posits a fatal disparity between two incompatible tendencies in *Dead Souls*, the "novelistic," which is secular, satirical, polyphonic, unfolding in "the zone of familiar contact," and the epic, which demands "authoritative discourse" and "affirmative pathos." With *The Divine Comedy* as his model, Gogol supposedly tried in Part 2 to be epic, but remained novelistic and therefore unable to "manage the move from Hell to Purgatory and then to Paradise with the same people and in the same work; no continuous transition was possible." Neatly formulated though this may be, it does not honor the reality of the surviving text. There are relatively few instances of "authoritative discourse" such as we find in Part 1, where they so obtrude that critics have dubbed them "lyrical digressions." Instead, we find an authorial persona very much like the one who recounts Chichikov's life in chapter 11 of Part 1, an authoritative but not authoritarian manager of the action, who is consistent in tone and manner but no more obtrusive than the narrator of many a "realistic" nineteenth-century novel. The rhetorical or oratorical functions assumed by various disembodied narrative voices in Part 1 are now transferred to more or less full-blooded characters, such as Kostanzhoglo, whose penchant for making pronouncements becomes merely another aspect of their personalities. This may in fact be Gogol's only real innovation in Part 2. Far more to the point, I think, is Hugh McLean's observation that a picture of the "other" Russia of "nobility, splendor, and perhaps even love," such as Gogol intended to show in Parts 2 and 3, "would have required techniques Gogol had not developed and perhaps a temperament he did not possess."[8]

Otherwise, the content of Part 2 has a very familiar look, so much so that critics of an ideological bent feel reassured. Nikolai Chernyshevsky, who showed a greater understanding of Gogol's later period than did most of his other "left"-leaning brethren of the 1860's, expressed confidence that with further revision, "the predominant character of this book . . . will be *the same one* we find in Volume I and in all the preceding works of the great writer"; as an example, he cites the opening lines, with their paean to the Russian countryside. A century later, the Soviet editors of an edition from which I have already quoted single out for praise the depiction of the provincial officials in the last chapter, where "*once again* we recognize Gogol, the merciless satirist and exposer."[9] The structure of Part 2 also has a familiar look, built as it is on Chichikov's rounds of various landowners. In some scenes, Gogol shows a touch that is just as masterful as anything in the first volume: the landscape that opens the first chapter, the treatment of Tentetnikov, parts of the Kostanzhoglo episode. If there is any sign of a new direction in the book, it is toward the kind of realism that was beginning to appear in Russian fiction; we see it in Gogol's striving, albeit in an almost leisurely fashion, for a fullness and capaciousness of character and setting that often remind us of Goncharov and Turgenev. But in terms of his own development as a writer, all this represents a reversion to earlier ways, an attempt to reappropriate the visual mode that had been found wanting.

One sign of a fresh direction is extratextual. As Gogol worked on this new volume, his need for "statistics" became obsessive. On April 15, 1847, for example, he wrote to A. O. Rosset urging him to start keeping something like a daily journal, in which he would note details (which he would eventually send on) like the following:

"Today I heard the following opinion; it was expressed by such-and-such a person; he leads the following kind of life; his character is as follows (in short, a quick portrait of him). But if he is a stranger, then: I'm not familiar with his life, but I think he is such-and-such, his appearance is pleasant and decent (or not decent); he holds his hand this way; he blows his nose this way; he takes snuff this way." In short, without omitting anything the eye can see, from large traits to small. (XIII, 279–80)

This letter was written from Naples. On August 24 of that same year, however, Gogol expressed his intention to return to Russia to see the details for himself. From Ostend he wrote to Pletnyov: "When I get to Russia I will try to look Russia over as best I can, drop in everywhere, chat with all sorts of people, and not neglect anyone, no matter how antithetical his way of thinking may be to mine, in short, I will try to *touch everything myself*" (XIII, 371; the italics are Gogol's). He did return in the summer of 1848, and took up work on *Dead Souls* once again. In so doing, he eliminated the distance that he still insisted was essential to creativity. To be sure, distance had not helped him with the first version of Part 2, which was written abroad; but he was at least able to continue writing nonfiction there. Could he have unconsciously been trying to make his task impossible by doing the observing himself?

But it is the text itself that betrays the renascent observer. For instance, when General Betrishchev is first introduced, we are told: "In critical moments—[he displayed] magnanimity, bravery, boundless generosity, and intelligence in everything he did, but, mixed up with this, capriciousness, ambition, vanity" (292–93). These contradictory traits of character are supposed to create an impression of psychological complexity. But it is the kind of complexity common to most human beings, generals or not, and is quickly forgotten when Gogol picks up his old technique of drawing character in terms of a dominant physical trait, which embraces the inner man as well: "[In] retirement [he] preserved the same *picturesque*, magnificent deportment. Whether he was wearing a frock-coat, a dress-coat, or a dressing-gown, he was always the same. Everything about him, from his voice to his slightest movement, was commanding, dominating, and inspired in those of inferior rank awe if not respect" (293). If this is not quite a painting, then the description of Platonov that follows a dozen or so pages later could easily be transferred to canvas:

All during this conversation Chichikov was scrutinizing the visitor, who astonished him by his quite unusually handsome appearance, his *picturesque* stature [*kartinnym stanom*, whatever that may be], the freshness of his unwasted youth, the virginal purity of his face unblemished by a single pimple. No passions, no sorrows, nothing remotely resembling excitement and restlessness dared touch his virginal face and leave a wrinkle on it. But at the same time they did not enliven it, either. In spite of the ironic smile which brightened his face occasionally, it wore a sort of somnolent expression. (306)

Betrishchev's daughter Ulinka, like Annunciata in "Rome," evokes a series of comparisons to various arts and artifacts, with no pretense of naturalness:

If a transparent *picture* [or "painting"] had suddenly been *lit up from behind with lamps*, it would not have caused such surprise. . . . Such pure and noble features *could not have been found anywhere*, except perhaps on some *old cameos*: straight and light as an arrow, she seemed to tower over everything. *But that was an illusion* [*obol'shchenie*, also meaning "seduction" or "delusion," and hinting at the kind of aestheticized eroticism so prominent in "Rome"]. She was not at all tall. It was due to the exceptionally harmonious symmetry of all the parts of her body [a sign of good art everywhere in Gogol]. . . . [A] piece of uncut material was caught up in two or three places by a needle and it seemed to hang and drape round her in such folds and pleats [like a classical toga] that, *if she were to be painted* in it, all the young ladies dressed in the latest fashion would have appeared like rag dolls. . . . And *if she were to be chiselled in marble* with all her folds and pleats clinging round her body, she would have been pronounced *a copy of the work of some sculptor of genius.* (295)

The return to seeing the world as if it were a work of art is especially evident in the several detailed and beautiful landscapes of Part 2. The most extensive of them opens the book. It runs to three long paragraphs, each of which is viewed from a different vantage point that recapitulates the nature-painting techniques of the earlier stories. The first begins with "Like the gigantic rampart of some immense fortress [*Kak by ispolinskii val kakoi-to beskonechnoi kreposti*]," and goes on to celebrate sheer size and magnificence. The second—beginning "In one place the steep side of the rising hills [*V odnom meste krutoi bok vozvyshenii*]"—is gentler, attentive to the picturesque qualities of variegation and irregularity, and generous enough with glimpses of human works to produce an integrated "assembly of trees and roofs." Both these views betray Gogol's earlier preoccupation with tightly bounded space, in their "ramparts," "fortress," and "steep side." The third paragraph—beginning with "It was a very fine view [*Vid byl ochen' khorosh*]"—looks out on a vast panorama: "*Miles upon miles* of open country . . . *beyond* the water meadows, covered here and there with copses and water-mills, woods formed *several green belts . . . beyond* the woods . . . yellow sands could be seen, and *beyond* them more woods . . . and *beyond* them more sands." It offers the secure vantage point and sense of wonder that Kant, as we saw in Chapter 6, regards as essential to the sublime: "No guest or visitor *could stand unmoved on the balcony.* He would be *breathless with surprise* and he could only exclaim: 'Lord, what a *magnificent view!*'" (262). All this is so carefully crafted that we have a sense of looking at pictures of nature rather than at nature itself. As in all the earlier work, man is still separated from his world by a seemingly un-bridgeable distance. The narrator then turns to Tentetnikov, the first of the major personages to appear in Part 2, and sets himself the task of showing "what his character was like and to what extent his life corresponded with the beauty of his environment" (263). The answer is that there is no cor-respondence at all: "And so this thirty-three-year-old young man spent his time, *all alone in the whole world*, sitting *indoors in a dressing gown*," that is, within two enclosures. Understandably, then, "the beautiful view of the countryside which no visitor could gaze upon with indifference did not seem to exist for the owner himself" (265). Here, far more explicitly than ever before, a Gogolian narrator regards a situation as undesirable, identifies a cause, and proposes a solution.

The root cause in this case is exposure in school to a variety of courses that did not cohere into any whole, "stuck in his mind in shapeless bits and pieces" (269), and left him incompetent to deal with any aspect of later life. Like many a landowner in Russian literature, Tentetnikov at first wanted to improve his estate and the lot of his peasants, but "he had no idea how [things] are done or even how to begin doing them." Even though "he talked like an educated man," we are told, "he had no real knowledge" of the kind that comes from participation in the work of the estate" (274). He is the man who does *not* see, and for whom words are just a meaning-less jumble. The solution, predictably enough, is the kind of education that enables the student to perceive the vital whole in all its interconnections and to undertake the kind of hard, purposeful labor that both imitates and serves it. Tentetnikov probably understands this, since he looks back nostalgically on one brief exposure to good education. However, it is Kostanzhoglo who most fully embodies the ideal of purposeful, creative activity.[10]

In what is presumably the first surviving version of this chapter, Kostanzhoglo is called Skudronzhoglo. The root is *skud-*, which means "meager" or "scant," and is no doubt meant to connote its bearer's qualities as a waste-not, want-not estate-manager. But it does not quite go with the plenteousness he so effortlessly creates. In the second version, it is changed to the name most translators honor (Guerney notably excepted), whose root word is *kost'*, "bone," a worthy tag for the tough, unyielding figure we see before us. The same suffixes remain, however, giving the new name, as they did the original one, a curiously non-Russian, even Turkish sound. In fact, we are told that Kostanzhoglo is "not a pure Russian," that "he himself did not know where his ancestors had come from." The brief description of his physiognomy, however, makes it clear, even before we are so informed, that he is of "southern" provenance: "Chichikov was struck even more by the swarthiness of his face, the coarseness of his black hair, gone prematurely grey in places, the lively expression of his eyes, and a kind of choleric residue of his passionate southern origin."[11] By now, "southern" has become a code word for vitality, energy, and creativity; and we are evidently supposed to conclude that when these qualities are implanted in the native soil, the result is a new and superior breed of Russian. Gogol has obviously not forgotten his decade-old article on the making of Little Russia, where the Cossacks root their "Asiatic" traits deep in biology by marrying Tartar women, the result being not a dilution but a strengthening of true Cossack attributes.

Kostanzhoglo's face bears a striking resemblance to the picture of the moneylender in "The Portrait":

[He had] a face of a bronze hue. . . . [I]t seemed as if the features of his face had been caught in a moment of convulsive agitation [a hint at a 'choleric residue,' or the 'irritable' and 'embittered' expression of Skudronzhoglo?], and there was a puissance [*sila*, which can also be translated as 'energy,' 'strength,' or 'power,' and evokes an important image from the concluding pages of Part 1] about the face which bespoke the fact that it was not of the north. The torrid south was imprinted upon the features. About his shoulders a voluminous Asiatic costume was draped. . . . The eyes were the most singular of all the features. (II, 255)

We have remarked on the resemblance of that portrait to an icon, due especially to the prominent eyes. In Kostanzhoglo's case, the resemblance is made almost explicit: "[He lifted] his face from which the wrinkles had suddenly disappeared. Like an emperor [*tsar'*] on the day of his solemn coronation, he looked transfigured [*siyal on ves'*, lit., 'all of him shone'] and it seemed as though rays of light were issuing from his face."[12] The difference is that this portrait has the properties of a real icon, whereas that of the moneylender is only a demonic parody. The key to the difference lies in the light that emanates from "all" of Kostanzhoglo, hinting at transfiguration, which affects the entire person. By contrast, it is only the eyes of the moneylender that are illuminated. They are very powerful indeed, and can work transformations, but not in a positive, life-giving way, for they are only a fragment and therefore devoid of true life.

An icon is centered on a human or humanlike figure of great holiness. There are secular saints in the Russian tradition (the sixteenth-century Yuliana Lazarevskaya being the most famous); but it would have been problematical to put Kostanzhoglo in that category, since he is supposed to serve as a role model for Russian landowners. "Emperor" is far more appropriate, and has the advantage of combining both worldly and religious functions. One of the abiding images of Christ is that of King. There are many icons of Him, particularly in the Orthodox tradition of Christ Pantocrator, which resemble the "emperor" to whom Kostanzhoglo is compared. In turn, Gogol does not need to remind us of the divine status of kingship in Byzantine political culture. "King" could also describe the relationship of a Russian landowner to his serfs. Finally, just as a king makes his person felt in every corner of his realm, so the central figure of an icon shapes everything around him. As Leonid Ouspensky reminds us, "we find [in the icon] that everything which surrounds a saint changes its aspect. The world surrounding man—the bearer and announcer of the divine revelation—becomes an image of the world to come, transfigured and renewed. Everything loses its usual aspect of disorder, everything acquires a harmonious order—men, landscape, animals and architecture."[13] Every component of Kostanzhoglo's estate is imbued with his energizing, central presence, and forms a harmonious world, in which there is "not an inch of emptiness. . . . It is completely full" (328). Nothing is superfluous or wasted, be it time, work or materials; all is turned to fruitful use. Even the fish scales that traders have been dumping on the banks of the river find their proper place: "Well, what was I to do with [them]?" asks Kostanzhoglo. "I began making glue and I got thirty thousand for it" (323). Nor is nature exempt. On reaching a prospect that admits a pleasant view, Chichikov reacts like many an earlier character in Gogol: "'If one were to plant woods here,' Chichikov said, 'the view would be more beautiful than ——.'" He is brought up short by his host, who sets forth the priorities: "'Oh, so you're an admirer of fine views, are you?' said Kostanzhoglo with a sudden stern look at him. 'Let me warn you, if you start chasing after views, you'll be left without bread and without views. Always think of what is useful and not of what is beautiful. Beauty will come of its own accord'" (337). Accordingly, "[n]ot a single blade of grass was wasted here. Everything looked like a huge park" (334).

This is perhaps the best single description of Gogol's ideal of place. It could serve for his ideal work of art as well, where every detail is utilitarian, never merely decorative, never hidden but always visible, even foregrounded, as in an icon, and functioning dynamically in service to the idea that informs the work as a whole. In Kostanzhoglo's case, this idea would presumably be "good management." It is the harmonious working together of the constituents that creates beauty and excellence, or *prekrasnoe*, one word serving for both ideas, as in ancient Greek (*to kalon*). Other examples in Gogol's own work are the set pieces in *Dead Souls* that introduce the chapters on Manilov, Sobakevich, and especially Plyushkin. Gogol is also instructing his readers that no detail can be overlooked, and I have been trying to follow this instruction throughout my own examination of his works. But we cannot profitably follow him all the way. To look for the one idea that underlies a given work is to limit ourselves drastically as readers and impoverish Gogol as a writer. In this sense, Gogol himself is a bad reader of his own work. As I hope this book has shown, there is a plethora of "ideas" in any work by Gogol, together with a polyvalence of detail, which make for an always rich, sometimes baffling complexity. Yet every reader senses that it all hangs together, even if we cannot always determine how.

Gogol does not assert that all Russia must follow Kostanzhoglo's example, but we can safely assume that he wishes us to draw that conclusion, provided we understand that "all Russia" means all estate owners. Relatively few would have "southern" or "Asiatic" blood running in their veins. But they would presumably be Christians. And Christ was from the Middle East, a region that in Gogol's geography of energy is synonymous with "Asia" or "South." (In still another parallel, the moneylender in the first version of "The Portrait" bears the name Petromikhali, which sounds Greek and is therefore also Eastern or Asiatic for Gogol.)

Kostanzhoglo, however, is a caricature, and as such, an unlikely role model. To be sure, his "choleric" and "passionate" nature would not be inconsistent with the Christ who inveighed against "lukewarmness" and could treat fools and hypocrites harshly. These are very human qualities of the kind that lend plausibility and appeal to the Christ of the first three Gospels, as well as to Gogol's own Taras Bulba and artist-monk. Kostanzhoglo, however, is ruthless and unforgiving. And it is a ruthlessness of the eye, glaring forth at all it can see, brooking no errant blade of grass or merely feral animal. "Even the pig . . . had the air of a nobleman," we are told. In another setting, this would be a joke; but here it is presently followed by the sinister detail of the "glass watch-tower from which the whole countryside for ten miles around could be seen" (313). Again we wonder how different Kostanzhoglo's eyes really are from those of the money-lender. His anger weakens what at first looks like a solution to the problem of man and nature at odds, for it shows him bending nature to his will and simply eliminating what does not fit. That is bad ecology and very un-Russian.

PHILOSOPHICAL GRAMMAR

Once more, a visually apprehended world brings Gogol to a dead end. We cannot legitimately generalize this statement to account for his sense that Part 2 of *Dead Souls* fails as a whole, simply because we do not have the whole. Perhaps, though, it helps explain why he thought he was repeating himself, and why his letters of the 1840's register a growing conviction that he was losing his gift. It was a conviction made even more poignant by his apparent inability to follow the new direction in which he had been moving since at least 1842. Although he was far more aware than ever before of the word, in the senses we have noted, he found himself bound to certain assumptions about language that he had held from the very beginning of his career. These were ultimately to prove fatal to his art.

Let us go back to the passage on the *metkoe slovo* in chapter 5 of *Dead Souls*, Part 1. Magarshack's "neat word" is not an entirely satisfactory translation. *Metkoe* is related to the verb *metat'*, "throw," and thus carries the sense of something that is well aimed and on target.[14] We have seen how this idea of the word is undone at the end of Part 1 of *Dead Souls*, and how, in turn, this undoing threatens the validity of the very process of writing. Yet Gogol never got away from the idea that words ought to have meanings agreed upon by all, and not subject to the whims of individual users. Ideally, the word should be like the "nickname" that the Russian peasant unerringly finds to bestow on someone:

[I]t will stick to him all through his life and will pass on to posterity, he will carry it with him into the service and into retirement and to Petersburg and to the ends of the earth. And however much he may try to ennoble his nickname, even if he may get the writing fraternity for a consideration to trace it back to an ancient, princely house, nothing will be of any use: like the loud cawing of a crow it will raise its own croaking voice and proclaim clearly where the bird has flown from. (118)

In turn, this view of language is beholden to what has been variously called "universal," "general," or "philosophical" grammar. Though ancient, this idea is a constant presence in linguistic theory, sometimes recessive, sometimes dominant. In more modern times, the end points are conveniently marked by René Descartes and Noam Chomsky.

On November 20, 1629, Descartes wrote to Father Mersenne about a proposal for a universal language that the priest had sent him. Although he finds it wanting, he does not dismiss the idea, saying it would be "possible" provided that one could "discover the Science on which it depends." That would amount to working out a "true Philosophy." Specifically, "if someone had given an adequate definition of the simple ideas in the imagination of men, of which all their thought is composed, and if that had been accepted by everyone, then I would dare to hope for a universal language that would be extremely easy to understand, pronounce and write, and, most important of all, a language that would be an aid to the judgment, representing to it all things so distinctly that it would be almost impossible to err." However, as matters stand, he continues, "the words we possess have almost confused meanings, to which the mind of men has been accustomed for a long time, that being the reason why they understand almost nothing perfectly." With a universal language, even peasants would be better able to "judge the truth of things, which the philosophers do not now do."[15]

These remarks speak to at least two of the main concerns of universal grammar: first, the essential identity and universality of logical and linguistic categories, and second, the assumption that words should and can be signs of ideas. It was, however, a book published in Paris in 1660 by two men of more modest talents that was to prove decisive for the development of this science: *Grammaire générale et raisonnée*, by Antoine Arnauld and Claude Lancelot. It is often referred to simply as the "Port-Royal grammar," owing to its place of origin. It was Cartesian in thrust, having been preceded 23 years earlier by Descartes's *Discours de la méthode*. In 1662, a companion volume to the grammar appeared, *La Logique ou l'Art de penser*, by this same Arnauld, in collaboration with Pierre Nicole. The juxtaposition of the key words of the two titles, *grammaire* and *logique*, neatly defines the approach. In the words written more than a hundred years later by one of its numerous disciples, the Port-Royal grammar was "the rational science of immutable and general principles of Language as pronounced and written in any given tongue."[16] Even though it took French as the norm of "generality," its influence was soon felt throughout Europe, and endured for a century and a half. The French text was reprinted in London as early as 1664, although a translation into English had to wait for nearly a hundred years.[17]

Universalist ideas quickly spread into Russia, along with neoclassical aesthetics. Aleksandr Sumarokov, for one, was reflecting them when, in 1774, he insisted:

> And with the help of the words of a capacious language
> Everything can be expressed, no matter how deep the thought,

> We describe everything: both passions and feelings,
> And thoughts we divide with the voice into small parts.

He went on to say that all thoughts are available to all people; the challenge is to find the right words, which will promote general understanding. Thought can therefore survive translation, for it is provided by the original creator and can be conveyed in any well-developed language. The same ideas informed Lomonosov's theory of rhetoric, which supposed that certain words stimulate predictable responses in listeners or readers. They also underlay the system of so-called "word-signals [*slova-signaly*]," a striking feature of eighteenth-century poetry. Lidiya Ginzburg aptly describes it as follows: "Each genre was a form, established by the rational faculty, of the artistic expression of this or that sphere of life: firmly attached to each genre was a fixed style. . . . For each style there existed a fixed range of words, which gave particularly precise expression to the world-view that lay behind it."[18]

The first philosophical grammar in Russian seems to have been a book of modest size, extant in but a single copy, written in 1730 by Ivan Gorlitsky and entitled *A French and Russian Grammar of the Present-Day Language, Presented with a Small Lexicon in the Interest of Convenient Communication* (Grammatika frantsuzskaya i russkaya nyneshnego yazyka, soobshchena s malym leksikonom radi udobnosti soobshchestva). Of far greater import were the writings that flowed from the restless pen of Lomonosov, the most versatile genius of Russia's eighteenth century. He was a poet, a scientist, a philosopher. He also occupied himself with problems of language, in such works as "A Short Guide to Rhetoric" (Kratkoe rukovodstvo k krasnorechiyu, 1748), *A Russian Grammar* (Rossiiskaya grammatika, 1757), and the brief but consequential "Foreword on the Utility of Ecclesiastical Books in the Russian Language" (Predislovie o pol'ze knig tserkovnykh v rossiiskom yazyke, 1757). Even though he was mainly interested in the particularities of Russian, the marks of philosophical grammar are everywhere present: the noun represents "being" and the verb, "action"; the sentence is an expression of "judgment"; words are "signs" of thoughts or ideas; and so on. Such ideas were soon accepted as commonplace, and eventually found their way into the school curriculum. In 1804, the government prescribed the teaching of "general" or "philosophical" grammar in all high schools (*gimnazii*), along with other "philosophical" disciplines, like logic, psychology, and morals. Russian grammar as such was reserved to the lower schools. Well-known books like Nikolai Grech's *A Practical Russian Grammar* (Prakticheskaya russkaya grammatika) and *An Extensive Russian Grammar* (Prostrannaya russkaya grammatika), both dating from 1827, are prime specimens of philosophical grammar, and helped extend its influence well into the nineteenth century, long after the government had reversed itself in 1818 and banned it from the schools.[19]

Gogol no doubt absorbed the precepts of philosophical grammar from extensive reading in eighteenth-century literature and from his school texts at Nezhin, such as Aleksander Nikolsky's *Foundations of Russian Literature* (Osnovaniya rossiiskoi slovesnosti, 1809), and Yakov Tolmachev's *Rules of Literature* (Pravila slovesnosti, 1815–22). If in his early career he virtually ignored literary and linguistic theory, it was probably because he regarded such matters as self-evident. After all, anyone reared on philosophical grammar could easily talk about one thing in terms of another, "words," say, in terms of "thoughts" or "ideas," just as Gogol was then talking about literature in terms of painting. Certainly his writings on history reflect the "universalism" prevalent among historians since Voltaire's *Essai sur les moeurs* (1756). Another sign of his indebtedness to philosophical grammar was his passion for word collecting. "A Book of Odds and Ends, or A Handy Encyclopedia," which Gogol compiled between 1836 and 1842, contains, among other things, sections entitled "A Little-Russian Lexicon," "Names Given at Baptism," "A Commercial Dictionary," "Little-Russian Dishes and Foods," and "Little-Russian Proverbs, Sayings, Saws and Phrases." Here Gogol draws heavily on printed sources, notably lexicons, glossaries, and dictionaries, with only a few items registered directly from folk speech (IX, 495–538). His passion for list-making never abated. Far more ambitious and substantial were the compilations he made between 1848 and 1851, to which later editors have assigned the title "Materials for a Dictionary of the Russian Language" (IX, 441–85). They run to more than 40 pages in the *Complete Works*, and consist preponderantly of relatively rare terminological substantives about whose "meaning" there can be little doubt. Again they were taken mainly from earlier lexicons, but Gogol expanded some of the definitions, and added other words. One of his ultimate purposes was to "present the Russian word straight out, so to speak, in its direct meaning." The audience would include Russians living abroad, among whom "the direct, true meaning of native Russian words is distorted: some are given a different sense, others are forgotten altogether" (441).

Another famous philosophical grammarian, Samuel Johnson, noted that English had been "suffered to spread, under the direction of chance, into wild exuberance; resigned to the tyranny of time and fashion; and exposed to the corruptions of ignorance, and caprices of innovation."[20] "Constancy" and "stability" were his aim, which he hoped to ensure by drawing from literary sources no farther back than the time of Elizabeth; by relying on his own experience and taste; and by eschewing dialects, "vulgar" (i.e., everyday) usage, and what he calls "fugitive cant," or specialized language. He is not troubled by a multiplicity of meanings, provided he can locate them in the literature of the past. Gogol also requires constancy and stability. But he shows no concern for the history of words, sticks by and large to current usage, and draws his material from both written and spoken sources. What then is his authority? He seems to take for granted the existence of some level where the word has its own fullest and best meaning that subsists despite distortions and corruptions. That level is accessible to what he calls a "linguist [*lingvist*]," one "who has an inner ear that can hear the harmony of the language" (IX, 441). He regards himself as such a person, not because he is endowed with any "great capacities for the business of linguistics," but because he has "a love for the Russian word, which has been alive in me since childhood and has made me think about its inner essence and expression" (IX, 442).[21] By "harmony," he seems to mean not the sound of the language but a sense of the inherent meaning of its constituents; and he believes that such meanings have only to be recorded to become permanent and thereby normative. As models he cites the Polish dictionary of Samuel Bogomił Linde (*Słownik języka polskiego*, 6 vols., 1807–14) and the Czech-German dictionary of Josef Jungmann (*Slovník česko-německý*, 5 vols., 1835–39). Such works he regards as the achievement "primarily of the Slavic lands" (442), but curiously enough, he does not mention any Russian dictionaries, although he draws heavily on them for his own compilation.

As late as 1848, then, Gogol still believed that a word is a "sign" of a "thought," the two ideally forming a perfect match that precludes the possibility of misunderstanding. But even the adherents of philosophical grammar were aware that words are quirky. For one thing, individual languages were demonstrably very different, especially as knowledge of them spread beyond the Indo-European. Leibniz even concluded that they entailed different patterns of thought.[22] For another, word and idea often made an awkward fit. In the Preface to his *Dictionary*, Dr. Johnson states, in good universalist fashion, "Language is only the instrument of science, and words are but the signs of ideas." But he immediately goes on to lament the unreliability of the signs: "I wish, however, that the instrument might be less apt to decay, and that signs might be permanent, like the things which they denote." More specifically: "Words are seldom exactly synonymous . . . names, therefore, have often many ideas, but few ideas have many names." The result is an "uncertainty of terms and commixture of ideas" that defy clear distinctions (280, 286, 287).[23]

Gogol would certainly have understood what Johnson was saying. He never offered a systematic and coherent account of his own philosophy of language, but had he done so, it might have run something like the following. In effect, he recognized a distinction that the Swiss linguist Ferdinand de Saussure (1857–1913) was later to make between *langue* and *parole*. As a recent scholar explains it: "*Langue* represents the abstract system of structural relationships inherent in language, relationships that are held in common by all members of a speech community. *Parole*, on the other hand, represents the individual act of speaking, which is never performed exactly the same way twice. Saussure compared language to a symphony. *Langue* represents the unvarying score, *parole* the actual performance, no two of which are alike."[24] Gogol seemed to think that something like this distinction existed outside artistic texts: language was available to all, and could be employed in an almost infinite variety of purposes. As a product of the Romantic age, he took a great interest in all kinds of speech from all levels of society. The artist could legitimately appropriate as many of them as he wished—the more, in fact, the better. (Gogol's own works are virtually an anthology of the spoken and written Russian of his time.) However, once incorporated into a text as the result of a writer's performance, these languages formed a closed system, and semantically became either monovalent or polyvalent, the latter only insofar as the rules of the system permitted. In effect, the text itself became *langue*, and therefore available for extratextual use, but only on its own terms, to which all users must give assent. It was not to provide the occasion for other performances. Although individual users of a language were of course "performers," their performances were irrelevant, even harmful to the Gogolian text.

However, experience taught him better. He wrote to A. O. Smirnova on December 6 (o.s.), 1849: "A person will idly and often stupidly let drop a meaningless word that he might not even have intended to say. This word starts making the rounds; apropos of it someone else idly lets some other word drop; and little by little a tale weaves itself, without anyone's being aware of it. It's pointless to try to find its real author, because you won't find him" (XIV, 154). He is talking here not about literary texts but about the origins of gossip in society. Yet he could easily be referring to the exasperation and fear he felt at the variety of reactions to his works, the welter of individual performances they engendered. What also worried him was that inadequate, even bad people could produce beautiful and effective verbal utterances. This is the case with the Jew Yankel, in "Taras Bulba," who is depicted as a character with no place of his own, capable of adjusting to any situation he encounters, and in these respects demonic. Taras tells him: "You can cheat the very devil; you know every dodge" (II, 114). These qualities are served by his verbal resourcefulness and eloquence, which successfully echo the language and the expectations of the people he is trying to manipulate. Certainly Gogol would not have been surprised by Horace's famous Second Epode, "Beatus ille," which, when we are through admiring its skill and beauty, turns out to have been written not by "Horace" but by "the usurer Alfius."[25] In fact, he may have feared that he himself would prove to be an Alfius, not a Horace. That is undoubtedly why, unlike Johnson, he was not impressed with authorities when it came to matters of language: they too could be rotten human beings. But if he was to establish himself as the authority, the "linguist," purity of soul was all the more essential. If his language was still faulty, then it was surely better to plead incompetence, ignorance, or unworthiness than to admit to spiritual deficiency, let alone insincerity. So at least his letters and essays of the 1840's and 1850's suggest, particularly with respect to his fiction:

Everything that comes easily to a natural writer has come hard to me. No matter how much I struggle, I have so far been unable to work my style and language, the basic and essential tools of any writer, up to perfection: so far they are in such a slipshod state, the likes of which you don't find even in the worst of writers, that the rawest of schoolboys has a right to make fun of me. Everything I have written is noteworthy only for its psychological significance, but it can in no way be a model of literature, and any teacher who would advise his pupils to study the art of writing from me or to depict nature as I do would be acting irresponsibly: he would be compelling them to produce caricatures.[26]

This could also be read as a nervous apology for the enormous success of his earlier prose works, all of which were published while he was still in what he now regarded as a spiritually unenlightened state. To rephrase in Saussurian terms, those works were examples of *parole*, not of *langue*—otherwise, they would have compelled assent.

TOWARD SILENCE

Of two other possibilities for language raised implicitly by his fiction and by his own interpretations of how people reacted to his work, Gogol showed little or no awareness, and would certainly have dismissed them had they been brought to his attention.

One is an idea of language that is familiar from the writings of certain poststructuralists, although Russians would very likely look back to the Formalists of some 75 years ago. Roland Barthes, for one, has accorded literature a privileged position because it "*stages* language instead of simply using it. . . . Through writing, knowledge ceaselessly reflects on knowledge, in terms of a discourse which is no longer epistemological, but dramatic." Thus, "Writing makes knowledge festive."[27] Among Gogol's stories, "The Nose" might seem to qualify, verging as it does on nonsense, with a baffled narrator unable to account for the capricious ways of a very ordinary bodily appendage. We could well be dealing here with an instance of what French theorists have called *jouissance*, "the very essence of language as surplus of signifier over what is signified."[28] If so, we could adduce a few other instances in Russian literature before Gogol, such as Pushkin's "Little House in Kolomna" (Domik v Kolomne, 1830), and many after him, like Chekhov's "A Horsy Name" (Loshadinaya familiya, 1885), Bely's *Petersburg* (1916), Mikhail Zoshchenko's "The Poker" (Kocherga, 1939), and much of the work of Daniil Kharms (1905–42). However, Gogol himself would have been appalled, at any stage of his career, by the notion that language can be divorced from "thought" or "knowledge." Readers who see "The Nose" as merely a joke miss the sad, even tragic spectacle of a compulsion-driven hero who ultimately learns nothing from his experiences. And with few exceptions (some Futurist poets among them), Russian writers and readers have held too deep a belief, as Andrei Sinyavsky puts it, "in the power of words, in their magic," to spare much time for *jouissance*; literature is "a serious business for us." Harsh experience has taught them that language can be readily appropriated and played around with by unscrupulous people, and even made an instrument of violence and oppression. Linguistic irresponsibility, with political consequences, is one of the great themes of Dostoevsky's *The Possessed* (Besy, 1872), Pasternak's *Doctor Zhivago* (1955), and, more recently, Andrei Bitov's *Pushkin House* (Pushkinskii dom, 1978). Indeed, Solzhenitsyn has made it a primary duty of the Russian writer to defend and preserve the national literary heritage, protecting it, as far as possible, from latter-day depredations. We think of the scene in *The First Circle* where some of the scientists confined to that refined version of the concentration camp known as the *sharashka* begin talking about *The Song of Igor's Campaign* and wonder what would have happened if the hero had not been forgiven by the Great Prince, whose orders he disobeyed, and instead had been charged with treason. They amuse themselves by staging a mock trial. After it is over, however, Rubin, the chief instigator, feels uneasy at having shown disrespect toward a national classic, and goes back to studying his dictionaries, where words are unambiguously registered. One can scarcely imagine American intellectuals indulging in such a pastime, let alone feeling guilty about it if they did; but Solzhenitsyn has illuminated one of the most sacrosanct areas of Russian culture.[29] Gogol would undoubtedly have approved.

The other possibility is one with which we are also richly, obsessively acquainted as our century draws to a close: that there are realms of experience untranslatable into language. Alfred Kazin writes that the Holocaust is "inevitably more real, urgent, terrible, than the writing that came out of it," and goes on to broaden the observation: "To be a Jew is to know that words strive after the reality but can never adequately capture the human situation." What he says has become a truism for our culture as a whole. People either revel in the possibilities for ambiguity and indirection opened by such inadequacy or yearn for a language that would create certitude.[30] This too is a very old theme, reaching back at least to Plato, who insisted that true knowledge is to be found not "in vocal utterance or in bodily forms but in souls."[31] Among Gogol's immediate predecessors, Wackenroder offered an influential version. He thought that language had been given to man by God so that he could "name all the things which the Highest One had placed around him in the world and all the spiritual images which He had implanted in his soul and could exercise his mind in the diverse play with this abundance of names." But words have drastic limitations: "Only *the invisible force which hovers over us* is not drawn down into our hearts by words." That realm is represented by "*two wonderful languages*" that are nonverbal: the language of nature (spoken by God) and the language of art (spoken by only a few elected humans).[32]

Once Gogol had truly committed himself to a career as a writer, a commitment I would date from the creation of *The Inspector General* (1836), he assumed that there was no area of experience that could not be translated into words. There was solid ground for such an assumption not only in philosophical grammar but in Orthodoxy as well. As Lossky has put it: "nothing of what is revealed and makes itself known can remain strange to [the word] . . . icons, just as well as the Scriptures, are expressions of the inexpressible."[33] He is talking about the religious word, but the same holds true for the artistic word as Gogol conceived it from the beginning. Yet perhaps Gogol too came to see that there were realms of experience that resisted verbalization, at least by him. How else can we read the following statement in *Selected Passages*?

One must handle the word honestly. It is God's highest gift to man. Woe unto the writer who utters it . . . before his own soul has achieved harmony. . . . Even with the purest desire to do good he can create evil. . . . It is dangerous for the writer to trifle with the word. . . . All the great educators used to impose a long silence precisely on those who used the word to no purpose, and precisely on those occasions and at those times when they wanted more than anything else to make a great show of the word and even when their souls were bursting to say much that was useful to people. They heard how it is possible to discredit that which one is trying to elevate, and how at every turn our tongue is our betrayer.[34]

Particularly arresting is the emphasis on silence, which here, as in the fiction, acknowledges the presence of a great truth. Silence strikes deep into the Christian tradition as well. Pseudo-Dionysius wrote:

> Into the dark beyond all light
>   we pray to come,
>   through not seeing and not knowing,
>   to see and to know
>   that beyond sight and knowledge,

itself: neither seeing nor knowing.
For by the denial of all that is
one sees, knows, and beyond-beingly hymns
the beyond being.

In this context, discourse, as a recent student has put it, "culminates in the cessation of all discourse. . . . Beyond all discourse: a total silence and unity with the ineffable—the darkness of unknowing."[35] But the parallel, in this case, defines entirely different moods. In the quotation from *Selected Passages*, silence is conceived as a punishment for misusing words. And this seems to be the kind of silence Gogol imposed on himself as part of a fiercely ascetic regimen during the last few days of his life, when he lay scarcely speaking, deep in a despair that is utterly alien to the silence of ecstatic assent that Pseudo-Dionysius attempts to describe. Surely no one can ever fully comprehend the enormous failure of will and nerve that must have imposed a silence of this kind. The silence was to prove permanent. For at eight o'clock on the morning of February 21, 1852, he died.

Reference Matter

Notes

CHAPTER I

1. Nabokov, Foreword to *Song*, 2. This ancient work has been translated into English several times, under different titles, such as *The Lay of the Host of Igor*, *The Igor Tale*, etc., but the best translation is Nabokov's. The passage from the *Primary Chronicle* is from Cross's translation, *Russian Primary Chronicle*, p. 145. A highly abridged version of this work, under the title *Primary Chronicle*, is included in S. A. Zenkovsky, *Medieval Russia's Epics* (the cited passage is on p. 50).

2. Douglas, *Purity and Danger*, 115, 114, 138.

3. A notable exception is the sizable chapter in Driessen, *Gogol*, 87–109.

4. Douglas, *Purity and Danger*, 51. Douglas also observes: "The Hebrew root of k-d-sh, which is usually translated as Holy, is based on the idea of separation" (8).

5. Garnett/Kent's smoother translation eliminates several of the negatives.

6. Turner, *Ritual Process*, 49.

7. For the ordinary Russian *eto on*, Garnett/Kent has the far from ordinary "it is he." For the wedding sorcerer, see Ivanits, *Russian Folk Belief*, 105.

8. The name is derived from the word for "deaf," *glukhoi*, and may therefore suggest that this exemplary tale falls on deaf ears, that fratricide, curse, and revenge are the inescapable lot of humankind.

9. A large literature exists on the phenomenon of pollution and purification. For an interesting approach to Homer from this perspective, with a heavy and acknowledged debt to Douglas, see Redfield, *Nature and Culture*, esp. chap. 5. A special study of the problem in Gogol would undoubtedly be rewarding.

10. The Russian is not explicit, but I think this is the way we tend to picture the

scene. For example, the illustration by A. Laptev in Gogol's *Sobranie sochinenii v semi tomakh*, I, 166, shows the corpses, many times larger than life, atop the steep embankment.

11. As translated by Clark, in Pushkin, *Covetous Knight*, 149.

12. The point is lost in Garnett/Kent, which has simply: "faith and speech are different."

13. Breck, *Power of the Word*, 219. For Mann, see "Gogol's Poetics," 75–76.

14. The two-volume paperback of the Garnett/Kent translation does not include the plays, but the one-volume hardcover edition does, and I am using that here (*The Collected Tales and Plays*). Actually, I prefer the translation by Ehre and Gottschalk, but it is not literal enough for my purposes.

15. See Merezhkovsky, "Gogol and the Devil."

16. "Stupid as a gray gelding" (*glup kak sivyi merin*) is attested by the Ushakov dictionary (*Tolkovyi slovar'*, II, 186), but is said to be "rare," and is supported by precisely this quotation from *The Inspector General*. One therefore suspects that Gogol himself invented it.

17. "Preduvedomlenie," IV, 118–19. See also the speech of Pyotr Petrovich in "Razvyazka *Revizora*," IV, 128. For a brilliant analysis of this scene, see Mann, "Gogol's Poetics," esp. 84–88.

CHAPTER 2

1. For an interesting recent study of the Russian idyll, see Hammarberg, *From the Idyll to the Novel*. For Likhachev, see "Sad i kul'tura Evropy," 478. For a more extensive treatment, see his *Poeziya sadov*.

2. Garnett/Kent soften *uvez* to "eloped with," which of course eliminates any suggestion of violence.

3. See, e.g., Douglas on the Coorgs of India, whom she describes as "a people obsessed by the fear of dangerous impurities entering their system." (She refers specifically to the body, but has already made the point that "the symbolism of the body's boundaries" can be used to "express danger to community boundaries.") The Coorgs "treat the body as if it were a beleaguered town, every ingress and exit guarded for spies and traitors. *Anything issuing from the body is never to be re-admitted, but strictly avoided. The most dangerous pollution is for anything which has once emerged gaining re-entry*" (*Purity and Danger*, 122–23, italics mine).

4. The children are present in the two surviving earlier drafts of *Dead Souls*, under the names of Alcibiades (Alkiviad) and Menelaeus (Menelai). These are of course the names of actual historical characters, not the comical monstrosities that Gogol invents for the final version. The detail of future diplomatic service is also present. See *PSS*, VI, 260–61, 351–52.

5. Schleiermacher, "On the Concepts," 175. For Aesop, see *Fables*, 150; for Livy, *From the Founding of the City* (Ab urbe condita), II, XXXII; for Shakespeare, *Coriolanus*, beginning in Act I, Scene 1, and culminating in Act III, Scene 1; for Maikov, "Golova i Nogi" (The Head and the Legs, 1763–67); for Sumarokov, "Edinovlastie" (Autocracy, 1781); for Plato, *Republic*, V, 462; for Aristotle, *Politics*, II, 3.

6. Again Garnett/Kent prettifies, rendering *dryan'* as "stuff" (7) and *dryazg* as

"trifles" (9). The "heap of all sorts of refuse" mentioned in my next sentence comes out as "heaps of trifles of all sorts."

7. Ovid, *Metamorphoses*, VIII, 455–57.

CHAPTER 3

1. Slonimsky, "The Technique," 355.

2. Dr. Richard C. Borden, in a private conversation.

3. The literature on curses is vast. For a compact but informative treatment of the topic, see Little, "Cursing." I have also found highly suggestive, not only for Gogol but for Russian culture generally, the discussion of the dynamic word in ancient Hebrew thought in Boman, *Hebrew Thought*, esp. chap. 1.

4. Turner, *Ritual Process*, 45, 49.

5. In addition, Gogol palatalizes the *z* of "Golopuz" ("Golopuz'"), but not of "Pupopuz."

6. Another possible explanation is that we may be dealing with a different narrator at the beginning and the end of the story. See Chapter 11 below for a discussion of Gogol's narrators.

7. Peace, *Enigma of Gogol*, 76.

CHAPTER 4

1. See Gippius, *Gogol*, 79.

2. Notably Gustafson, "Suffering Usurper."

3. "Issued on January 24 (February 4), 1722 by Peter I, the Table of Ranks [*Tabel' o rangakh*] provided a system for establishing equivalencies of ranks among the various branches of service in the Russian army, navy, guards, civil service and court bureaucracy. It thereby established as well a ladder of promotion that governmental servitors at higher echelons had to follow. . . . The fourteen ranks were numbered in ascending order from the greatest rank to the least significant" (Wieczynski, *Modern Encyclopedia*, 152–53).

4. Karlinsky, *Sexual Labyrinth*, 122.

5. I am indebted to my student Nicole Monnier for this observation.

6. See Chapters 7 and 8 for a detailed discussion of Gogol's views of how the writer should work.

7. Garnett/Kent misses the important elements of the syllogism: "is suddenly discovered to be a great gentleman or baron, or what do you call it . . ."

8. *The Northern Bee* was founded in 1825 by Faddei Bulgarin, who, according to D. S. Mirsky, had "the reputation of a vile sycophant whom all honest men abhorred. He was a clever, but essentially vulgar, journalist. His paper had a far larger sale than any other. His influence was used to combat all that was young, talented, and independent" (*History*, 125).

9. See Gustafson, "Suffering Usurper," for an ingenious and convincing interpretation of the system of dating.

10. Yury Olesha may have been thinking of this story when, in his novel *Envy* (*Zavist'*, 1927), he had Kavalerov, drunk in a tavern, diminish the threatening presence of a group of other drunks by fragmenting, transforming, and progressively lowering them: "Your face is a harness. . . . Your chin is a nag; your nose, a leprous

cartman. And the rest of you is the load of dung. . . . You, do you have any idea how you laugh? You sound like an enema" (11). There are several other instances in the novel where Kavalerov handles threats in the same way (at the airport, the construction site, the conservatory), and is himself fearful of being fragmented and turned into an object (as in the proofreading scene).

11. See, for example, Odoevsky, "Dva dni" (1828), in which two encounters of the earth with heavenly bodies are envisaged, one dreaded, the other eagerly anticipated. In the first, a giant comet approaches and seems about to hit, but the earth is spared. So sobering is the experience that people drastically change their lives. This was Odoevsky's contribution to an extensive literature on Halley's Comet (which was due to appear in 1832). In the second, the approaching millennium is signaled by dramatic astronomical phenomena: "The earth was slowly approaching the sun, and a gentle heat, like the fire of inspiration, spread over it. A moment more and heaven became earth, and earth heaven, the sun became earth and the earth sun" (222). When the merger is complete, utopia results. See also the brief philosophical dialogue "Anaksagor" (1825), by Dmitry Venevitinov, a member, like Odoevsky, of the Wisdom-Lovers Circle (*Lyubomudry*) in Moscow in the 1820's, which was much beholden to Neoplatonism, particularly as mediated through German Romanticism. It ends with Plato's confident prediction of a return of the golden age in the following terms: "Then let the ancient Egyptian prophecy come to pass! Let the sun swallow up our planet. . . . It will disappear, but having fulfilled its destiny, it will disappear like a clear sound in the harmony of the universe" (137).

12. Carlo Ginzburg has studied one version from sixteenth-century Italy, involving a miller named Menocchio: "all was chaos, that is, earth, air, water, and fire were mixed together; and out of that bulk a mass formed—just as cheese is made out of milk—and worms [putrefaction] appeared in it, and these were the angels." To make the parallel with Gogol even more intriguing, Menocchio's reasoning processes are not dissimilar to Poprishchin's, and he also falls into the hands of the Inquisition (albeit the Italian, not the Spanish). There is no question of a direct influence on Gogol in this particular case since it reposed in archives until uncovered by Ginzburg; but Ginzburg attributes the Menocchio story partly to "a substratum of peasant beliefs, perhaps centuries old, that were never wholly wiped out," and to an unconscious echo of "ancient myths," many of which are of course universal. (Ginzburg, *The Cheese*, 5–6, 20–21, 58.)

13. For the English saying, see Smith, *Dictionary of English Proverbs*, 542. The "cheese" definitions in Dal"s dictionary, *Tolkovyi slovar'*, fall under the general entry *syroi*. Dal' lived from 1801 to 1876. Although he gained some recognition as a writer of fiction, especially "physiological" sketches, his life's work was the dictionary, for which he spent nearly half a century collecting materials. Its first edition appeared in four volumes between 1863 and 1866 (meaning of course there was no possibility that Gogol could have seen it). For a useful account of the dictionary's publication history and of Dal"s activity as a lexicographer, see Babkin, "Tolkovyi slovar' Dalya," iii–x.

14. For a study of the "nosological" theme and its influence on Gogol, see Vinogradov, "Naturalisticheskii grotesk," 5–44. As for the moon-lunacy link, it is not

so linguistically neat in Russian. *Luna* means "moon," but *lunatizm* means "sleep-walking," not "lunacy," and *lunatik* "sleepwalker," not "lunatic." For some other strata recently found, see Weiskopf, "Bird Troika," esp. 132.

15. For the quotations pertaining to Diana, see Wright, *Lemprière's Classical Dictionary*, 204. "Sophie" may also suggest Sophia the Divine Wisdom.

16. See, e.g., the ending of chap. 7 of *Dead Souls*, where a young lieutenant, alone in his room, is described as "a great lover of boots, for he had already ordered four pairs and kept trying on a fifth. He went up to his bed several times to take them off and to lie down, but he could not bring himself to do so. . . . [F]or a long time he kept raising his foot and examining the cleverly and wonderfully shaped heel" (Magarshack, 163). In "The Overcoat," Akaky Akakievich's surname, Bash-machkin, is derived from the word for "shoe" (*bashmak*), as the narrator pointedly reminds us; there is scarcely a more self-involved, self-gratifying character in all of Gogol. For a discussion of other instances, in Gogol's fiction and in his own life, see Yermakov, "The Nose," 171–73.

17. Cf. Hermann, the hero of Pushkin's story "The Queen of Spades" (Pikovaya dama, 1833), who ends by going mad (not by killing himself, as in Tchaikovsky's opera) and constantly muttering the names of the cards on which the story turns: "Three, seven, ace! Three, seven, queen!" In Russian, the term for "circular mad-ness" (which Gogol nowhere uses) is *krugovoe pomeshatel'stvo*. For a useful dis-cussion, see Rozenbakh, "Krugovoe pomeshatel'stvo."

CHAPTER 5

1. Kant, *Critique of Judgement*, 503.

2. See Likhachev, "Sad i kul'tura Evropy. Sad i kul'tura Rossii," 481, 507.

3. Bakhtin, "Forms of Time," 227–28.

4. Virgil, *Georgics*, I, 51–52; IV, 170, 204–5.

5. This is the Ukrainian version of the name as Gogol uses it consistently throughout the story. Garnett/Kent russianizes it to "Andrei."

6. Gogol, "Ob arkhitekture," VIII, 62, 56–57. Further page references will be in the text.

7. It is not clear whether this is the same building, now seen at close range, that strikes Andrii's eyes when he emerges into the marketplace from the church (we are told that he had "already" seen it "from the distance"). That structure is described as "a higher building, quite different from the rest, probably the town hall or some government office. It was a two-story building, and above it there was a belvedere built in two arches, and inside it a sentry standing watch" (69).

8. For an informative survey of the theme of Petersburg in Russian literature, see Antsiferov, *Dusha Peterburga*. The theme ended after the capital was moved to Moscow in 1924. Bely's *Petersburg* (1916) was the last great instance, although the theme survived a change of locale to the One State of Evgeny Zamyatin's distopian novel *We* (My, 1920), which is in general heavily indebted to Bely's book, and to Moscow, as, for example, in Yury Olesha's *Envy*, Leonid Leonov's *The Thief* (Vor, 1927), and, more recently, Aleksander Solzhenitsyn's *The First Circle* (V kruge per-vom, 1968).

9. Pushkin, *Bronze Horseman*, trans. Arndt, 411.

10. *Karamzin's Memoir*, 126–27.

11. Gogol, "Peterburgskie zapiski," VIII, 177–80. The contrast was already well established in Russian literature.

12. Pushkin, *Bronze Horseman*, trans. Arndt, 401, 403.

13. Fonvizin, "[Pis'ma iz Frantsii]," 339, 342: the first quote is from a letter dated March 20/31, 1778; the second from a letter of June 14/25, 1788.(The bracketed title is not Fonvizin's but one supplied later and traditionally used.)

14. Gogol, "Peterburgskie zapiski," VIII, 177–79. See Kirpichenko, *Arkhitekturnye teorii*, esp. 78–81, for a useful summary of nineteenth-century versions of the contrast between the two cities.

15. Gogol, "Peterburgskie zapiski," VIII, 178. The theme is perhaps derived from *Eugene Onegin*, Canto VII, where Tatyana, who embodies a "feminine" and "Russian" principle, is taken to Moscow (not the "masculine" Petersburg, Onegin's territory), which is dominated by women who talk much of dress styles and husband-catching.

16. Fedotov, *Russian Religious Mind*, I, 369.

17. De Man, "Wordsworth," 51, 59. For Karamzin, see *Izbrannye sochineniya*, II, 54. The quote following the Karamzin is from Volkmann-Schluck, "Novalis' magischer Idealismus," 46.

18. "Brozhu li ya vdol' ulits shumnykh" (1829), as translated (under the title "Whether I wander along noisy streets") by Arndt, *Pushkin Threefold*, 235.

19. Tanner, "Notes," 31.

CHAPTER 6

1. The last quote is from a letter to his sister Olga (O. V. Gogol), Jan. 20, 1847, XIII, 181. The letter to Pogodin is dated May 15 (o.s.), 1836, XI, 46.

2. Lossky has argued that the kind of spirituality represented by Kempis's *Imitation of Christ* is alien to Orthodoxy, stressing as it does the "humanity" of Christ. See Lossky, *Mystical Theology*, 243. However, as Florovsky points out (*Puti*), it was studied in Russian seminaries in the early nineteenth century, along with other classics of Western spirituality, especially of a mystical cast.

3. Gogol to S. T. Aksakov, M. P. Pogodin, and S. P. Shevyryov, Jan. 1844, XII, 249. See also Gogol's letter to P. A. Pletnyov, written between Dec. 1 and 14, 1844, in which he quotes from the French translation (XII, 385).

4. Gippius, *Gogol*, 15. For a scrupulous study of Gogol's religious views, and an attempt to link them to his creative work, see V. V. Zen'kovsky, *Gogol'*. See also Kline, "Russian Religious Thought," for a compact and stimulating study of several important ideas in Russian theology. He deals mostly with the middle to late nineteenth century, but in ways that can illuminate Gogol as well.

5. For a good brief account, with a useful bibliography, see Shapiro, "Gogol' and the Baroque Heritage," 95–104.

6. Gogol to M. I. Gogol (his mother), Oct. 2 (o.s.), 1833, X, 281–82. Gippius, who also quotes these lines, comments that the remarks about his sister "are usually ignored by the biographers, either out of embarrassment or out of a desire not to detract from their picture of a religious Gogol" (*Gogol*, 15).

7. Mochul'sky, *Dukhovnyi put'*, 21. For Amberg, see *Kirche*, 24–80.

8. Gogol, ⟨"Avtorskaya ispoved'"⟩, VIII, 461–62. For *Selected Passages*, see "Zhenshchina v svete," VIII, 225.

9. Gumilevsky translated *The Celestial Hierarchy* (as *O nebesnoi ierarkhii*) and *The Ecclesiastical Hierarchy* (as *O tserkovnom svyashchennonachalii*). The 1855 translation of *The Ecclesiastical Hierarchy* is entitled "Svyatogo Ottsa nashego Dionisiya Areopagita kniga o tserkovnoi ierarkhii," and appears in *Khristianskoe chtenie*, I, 1855, Supplement, 1–6. The 1957 translation of *The Divine Names* is by Igumen Gennady, and is entitled *O Bozhestvennykh imenakh*. For a history of the translations of Dionysius and a review of the question of his authenticity, see Gennady's introduction ("Vvedenie"). A new English translation has recently been published by the Paulist Fathers in the series "The Classics of Western Spirituality," under the title *Pseudo-Dionysius. The Complete Works*. It contains useful prefatory material by several specialists. However, I am not using it here, because it has eliminated the quirkiness of the original in the interest of smoothness.

10. Campbell, in Pseudo-Dionysius, *Ecclesiastical Hierarchy*, 13. He provides a good account of bibliographical and textological problems.

11. Gogol, ⟨"Zapisnaya knizhka 1846 goda"⟩, IX, 563.

12. Pseudo-Dionysius, *Divine Names* (*DN*), trans. Jones, IV, 20, p. 150.

13. Lossky, *Mystical Theology*, 120, 123–24. The concept of "image and likeness" is very complex. For a stimulating discussion of the Orthodox version, see Lossky's *In the Image*. For some concise formulations, with indications of important differences between the Orthodox and the Roman Catholic traditions, see Ladner, *Idea of Reform*, esp. 83–107.

14. Borisov, "Personality," 210, 212. This translation inexplicably omits the last sentence quoted in my text. See the Russian version, "Natsional'noe vozrozhdenie i natsiya-lichnost'" (which translates literally as "National Rebirth and the Nation-Person"), 210. The italics are partly Borisov's and partly the translator's (or translators').

15. Ouspensky, *Theology*, 186. Italics mine.

16. Lossky, *Mystical Theology*, 26, 25.

17. Pseudo-Dionysius, *Mystical Theology*, in *"Divine Names" and "Mystical Theology,"* V, 221–22.

18. Gogol, "Razvyazka *Revizora*," IV, 125.

19. Hosking, review of Pipes, 3.

20. Wackenroder, *"Confessions" and "Fantasies,"* 167.

21. See esp. Karlinsky, *Sexual Labyrinth*.

22. Wackenroder, *"Confessions" and "Fantasies,"* 167. I have made a small modification where the English breaks down.

23. Gogol to M. P. Pogodin, May 10 (o.s.), 1836, XI, 41; Gogol to M. S. Shchepkin, Apr. 29 (o.s.), 1836, XI, 38. For Mochul'sky, see *Dukhovnyi put'*, 43.

CHAPTER 7

1. Shenrok, *Materialy*, II, 85. Shenrok's term is *zanyat'sya zhivopis'yu*, "occupy oneself with painting," which does not make clear whether Gogol took classes, copied existing paintings under supervision, or worked entirely on his own.

2. Gogol, "Skul'ptura," VIII, 9–13. Gogol dates the article 1831, even though

it was written three years later. Perhaps it was conceived then, or perhaps he wished to forestall possible criticism, especially in view of its derivativeness, by suggesting youthful inexperience. One possible source is Wilhelm Wackenroder's *Confessions of the Heart of an Art-Loving Friar* (Herzensergiessungen eines kunstliebenden Klosterbruders, 1797), which had been translated into Russian in 1826. A more immediate source might be Dmitry Venevitinov's article of the same title as Gogol's, which was written in the mid-1820's and published posthumously in 1829; it is really the outline of a theory, and is far more optimistic in tone than Gogol's, which is also a criticism of the materialistic nineteenth century.

3. Gogol, "Neskol'ko slov," VIII, 50–55. Further page references will be in the text.

4. Kristeller, "Modern System," 169. For a discussion of the meaning of "music" in ancient Greece, see Grube, "Aristotle," xiii–xiv.

5. Ware, *Orthodox Church*, 209.

6. For an outstanding guide to rhetoric by a Ukrainian of the Kiev Academy, see Prokopovich, *De Arte rhetorica*.

7. Tred'yakovsky, "Mnenie," 181. For Horace, see *Ars Poetica*, l. 361.

8. Vergara, *Rubens*, 15. For studies of the idea in Horace, his predecessors, and followers, see esp. Brink, *Horace*; and Trimpi, "Horace's 'Ut pictura poesis.'"

9. Johnson, "Pope," 238.

10. Hussey, *The Picturesque*, 16, 18. For a more recent though far shorter treatment of the subject, see Ross, "The Picturesque." For a brief discussion of picturesque gardens in Russia, see Likhachev, "Sad i kul'tura Rossii," 509. For an illuminating discussion of Gogol's use of the idea, see Fusso, "Landscape of *Arabesques*."

11. The first quotation is from Karamzin, *Letters of a Russian Traveler*, 315. The term translated as "descriptive" is *zhivopisnoi*, which also renders "picturesque." It is in italics in Karamzin's original. The comparison of Thomson to Shakespeare (and within the article to Milton as well) is from Karamzin, "O Shekspire," 79–80. The words about Thomson's teaching him poetry come from Karamzin, "Poeziya," 11.

12. Gogol, "V chem zhe nakonets," VIII, 378. The Zhukovsky poems are "Letnii vecher" (Summer Evening, 1818), which Gogol calls "Otchet o solntse" (An Account of the Sun), and "Podrobnyi otchet o lune" (A Detailed Account of the Moon, 1820), which he calls "Otchet o lune" (An Account of the Moon).

13. Gogol to A. O. Smirnova, Dec. 23, 1850, XIV, 218. Belinsky's remarks are in "A Survey," 35. The italics are mine except for the word "only."

14. For his appraisal of Bryullov, see Gogol, "Poslednii den' Pompei," VIII, 107–14. For Ivanov, see Gogol, "Istoricheskii zhivopisets," VIII, 328–37.

15. McLean, "Gogol and the Whirling Telescope."

16. Karamzin, "Neskol'ko slov," 155–56. The original is in French, but I translate from the Russian version as provided in this edition. For Novalis, see "Das Allgemeine Brouillon," 536–37. Italics are Novalis's, except for the Latin phrases.

17. Batyushkov, "Nechto o poete," 56.

18. Karamzin, "Rech'," 240–41. The italics are Karamzin's.

19. Hoffman, "Golden Pot," 185, 217. For "true passion [*wahre Passion*]," this translation offers "enjoyed enormously."

20. Zhukovsky, "Pisatel' v obshchestve," 393–402.

21. Gogol, "Neskol'ko slov," VIII, 54.

22. Gogol, "Ob arkhitekture," VIII, 62.

23. Likhachev, "Sad i kul'tura Rossii," 504.

24. Lomonosov, "Oda na vzyatie Khotina," 47.

25. Gogol, "V chem zhe nakonets," VIII, 371

26. The first letter from Gogol to Smirnova is dated Dec. 24, 1844 (XII, 412); the friend is Yury Samarin. The second letter is dated June 6, 1846 (XIII, 69–70).

27. For the Foreword to the second edition of *Dead Souls*, see Gogol, ⟨"Predislovie ko vtoromu izdaniyu"⟩, VI, 587–90. The italics are Gogol's. He never reworked Part 1; the first edition was reissued as a "second" edition, and this Foreword was appended. The letter to Smirnova is dated Jan. 27, 1846 (XIII, 31).

28. Gogol, ⟨"Avtorskaya ispoved'"⟩, VIII, 439, 446–47, 443.

29. Gogol, "Neskol'ko slov," VIII, 50–55; further page references will be in the text. The earlier article by Gogol is "*Boris Godunov*. Poema Pushkina," VIII, 148–52.

30. Mar. 30, 1837, XI, 91–92. The letter to Pletnyov is dated Mar. 28/16, 1837, XI, 88–89.

31. V. I. Dal' to M. P. Pogodin, Apr. 1, 1842, *Literaturnoe nasledstvo*, LVIII (*Pushkin. Lermontov. Gogol'*) (Moscow, 1952), 617. Much has been written about the coexistence of Ukrainian and Russian elements in Gogol. See, e.g., Malaniuk, "Hohol—Gogol," and Luckyj, *Between Gogol' and Ševčenko* (esp. chap. 6, pp. 88–127). Gogol himself was aware of the problem, but denied (disingenuously, I think) that he could distinguish the two elements: see esp. his letter to A. O. Smirnova, Dec. 24, 1844, XII, 418–19.

32. Belinsky to Gogol, July 15, 1847, as cited in Matlaw, *Belinsky*, 92. Belinsky's remarks on Pushkin are in his "Literary Reveries," 67, 84. The italics are Belinsky's.

33. Gogol to V. A. Zhukovsky, June 28, 1836, XI, 49.

34. V. V. Gippius calls it "starvation typhus [*golodnyi tif*]," whatever that may be: see *Gogol*, 174, 213.

35. See also, e.g., Belinsky, "Literary Reveries," 15, where he speaks of the need to choose one of "two roads, two inescapable paths": love of self or love of neighbor. Such pairings are a common device of German Romanticism and the French physiological school, both of which were major influences on Belinsky, Gogol, and their entire generation.

36. Here I modify the Magarshack translation, which creates a potentially misleading impression: "that the glasses through which suns are beheld and through which the movements of microscopic insects are studied . . ." (143). This suggests that the glasses are being used by an observer, and a rather calculating one at that. In the Russian, however, the glasses themselves do the observing, as does the "optical glass" in the article on Pushkin.

CHAPTER 8

1. This was not his first trip to Europe. In 1829, he had spent a couple of months in Lübeck, Germany, for reasons that are still not clear. See Gippius, *Gogol*, 25–27.

2. Gogol to M. I. Gogol, July 24, 1836, XI, 56–57. Some of the primitivism of thought and style may be due to the addressee, whom he consistently patronized.

3. Gogol to Nikolai Prokopovich, Sept. 27, 1836, XI, 61–62.

4. For a reproduction of these two pictures, and details of their acquisition and exhibition history, see *From Poussin to Matisse*, 44–47, 154. It is unlikely that Gogol ever saw them, since they were in the Yusupov private collection in Moscow until 1839, and were subsequently transferred to the Yusupov Palace in St. Petersburg, which did not become a museum until 1918.

5. For a brief but compelling account of the status of Russian art and artists during the reign of Nicholas, see Valkenier, *Ilya Repin*, 5. The author also writes that Bryullov's picture "stunned the Western public . . . [and] was shown in numerous exhibits," and that Ivanov's "created more of a stir by being some twenty years in the making than by affecting the viewers' moral outlook, which had been the artist's intention" (5).

6. See, e.g., Venevitinov, "Italiya" (1826), which, though much shorter than Gogol's poem, manages to parade many of the clichés. For Gogol's "Italiya," see *PSS*, IX, 9–10. According to an editorial note, the poem is to be only "ascribed to Gogol," although his authorship is "almost indubitable" (614–15). For Gogol's readings in ancient history, see *PSS*, IX, 85–87, 106–25, 132–38, 156–57, 162–64.

7. Garnett/Kent simply omits most of the extensive discourse on Italy. See the Russian of the 1842 version in *PSS*, III, 110–11, from which I translate. The quotation from the 1835 version is found in *PSS*, III, 421.

8. Gogol to M. P. Balabina, Apr. 1838, XI, 141.

9. The first quote is from a letter to his sisters, A. V. and E. V. Gogol, Oct. 15, 1838, XI, 176; the second is from a letter to V. A. Zhukovsky, Oct. 30, 1837, XI, 112.

10. Gogol to M. P. Balabina, Apr. 1838, XI, 142, 141.

11. Goethe, *Italian Journey*, 136. Further page references will be in the text. Since this edition makes abridgments, often substantial, I have checked all quotations against the original.

12. The first quote is from Gogol to M. P. Balabina, Mar. 15, 1838. This letter is written in Italian, but I quote from the Russian translation supplied in XI, 129. The second quote is from Gogol to M. P. Balabina, Apr. 1838, XI, 144.

13. For example, in 1843 he drew up a detailed sightseeing plan for A. O. Smirnova: see Gogol, ⟨"Zapiska o plane"⟩, IX, 489–91.

14. Gogol to M. P. Balabina, Apr. 1838, XI, 142.

15. Auden and Mayer, Introduction to Goethe, *Italian Journey*, vii.

16. Richter ("Rom und Gogol'") is a notable exception. Even Debreczeny, in a generally ample accounting of Gogol's reception by his contemporaries, devotes no space to it in his *Nikolay Gogol*. In Garnett/Kent, "Rome" is mentioned in a "Chronological Listing of Gogol's Works" and is characterized only as "a long fragment containing interesting impressions" (II, 336).

17. Belinsky, "Ob"yasnenie na ob"yasnenie," 427.

18. For an interesting discussion of this genre, see LeBlanc, *Russianization of Gil Blas*, 149–55.

19. Gogol, "Rim," *PSS*, III, 234; further page references will be in the text. Since there is no readily available English translation, I have made my own throughout.

20. As printed in Lidiya Ginzburg, "Russkaya lirika," 359. Ginzburg points out in a note (p. 596) that the addressee of the poem is a real person, Princess Aleksandra Ivanovna Laval.

21. Vogel, "Gogol's Rome," 147.

22. See Gogol's letter to M. P. Balabina, Apr. 1838, XI, 144.

23. Richter also points out that the opening scenes are "painted like a picture," and she reckons that "[h]alf of all the adjectives, almost half of all the substantives, and perhaps a third of the verbs have to do with light and shadow." She discusses the ways in which Annunciata is given a central place in the picture, "through the structure of the language (the middle sentences belong to her), through the structure of the picture (through color and light she is the central image), and through her effect on other people" ("Rom und Gogol'," 155, 157). My own reading of the "picture" differs substantially.

24. See, e.g., Gogol's letter to A. S. Danilevsky, Feb. 2, 1838, XI, 122, and to his sisters (A. V. and E. V. Gogol), June 30, 1838, XI, 161. Goethe, among many others, also took a great interest in Italian public spectacles.

25. James Harding has defined the prescribed list of topics for neoclassicism, "in diminishing order of importance," as follows: "episodes from classical history and mythology, events from national history, from military and naval engagements, noble or moving modern-life subjects . . . religious subjects, portraits showing a heroic aspect of the sitter, and last—the least respected—landscape and still life" (*Artistes Pompiers*, 31).

26. Valenciennes, *Élémens de perspective pratique*, as quoted by Galassi, *Corot in Italy*, 90. For the Italian version of these practices, see Broude, *The Macchiaioli*, esp. 38–41. Both these books are lavishly illustrated. For other representative collections, see *Österreichische Künstler* and Naef, *Rome*.

27. Epiphanius the Wise, *The Life of St. Stephen of Perm* (Zhitie sv. Stefana episkopa Permskogo, written probably in 1397), trans. Nicholas Zernov, as quoted in Serge Zenkovsky, 206 (Zenkovsky uses the title "Panegyric to St. Stephen of Perm"). An interesting study of Epiphanius as a writer has been made by Faith C. M. Kitch (*Literary Style of Epifanij Premudryj*).

28. For a discussion of the connection between the rural promenades of the Sentimentalists and the urban ones of Jouy and his imitators, see LeBlanc, *Russianization of Gil Blas*, 154.

29. The Turner and Rottmann as well as the Corot are reproduced in color in Galassi, *Corot in Italy*, 120–22. The Géricault hangs in the Metropolitan Museum, New York City.

30. Volkmann, *Historisch-kritische Nachrichten von Italien*, 3 vols. (Leipzig, 1770–71). For a good characterization of *vedute* and guidebooks, see Galassi, *Corot in Italy*, esp. 83–91. It is hard to know which one place in Homer Goethe might have had in mind, since Odysseus is among the Phaeacians from Cantos VI through XII.

31. Richter, "Rom und Gogol'," 94–110. See also the standard reference sources, such as the Thieme-Becker *Lexikon*.

32. For details, see Richter, "Rom und Gogol'," 138–40.

33. Here I make major modifications in Garnett/Kent (II, 281–82), which omits much of the original (as printed in *PSS*, III, 111–12).

34. "Zhenshchina v svete," VIII, 226. As Yury Mann points out, "petrifaction" is caused by an encounter with either a lower or a higher force ("Gogol's Poetics," 77).

35. Gogol to S. P. Shevyryov, Sept. 1, 1843, XII, 211.

CHAPTER 9

1. For "social criticism," see Lerner, "Criticism. Functions," 158–63. Regarding Karamzin's time, one must distinguish between public criticism, which was often of the "social" variety and almost never *ad hominem*, and private criticism, which was practiced among acquaintances in literary societies and in so-called "familiar letters" (*druzheskie pis'ma*), and was often pointed and personal. See Todd, *Familiar Letter*. For examples of the versification controversy, see Silbajoris, *Russian Versification*.

2. Karamzin, "Rech'," 236.

3. Gogol was born in 1809, Belinsky in 1811. Gogol's first major works appeared in the early to mid-1830's; Belinsky's "Literary Reveries" (his first important article) was published in 1834. Belinsky's large review article on Gogol, "On the Russian Tale and the Tales of Mr. Gogol" (O russkoi povesti i povestyakh g. Gogolya), which appeared in 1835, proclaimed Gogol the heir to Pushkin (who was still alive and only 36 years old). Gogol's *Selected Passages from Correspondence with Friends*, which came out in 1847, prompted an angry reaction from Belinsky and a wounded but forceful reply from Gogol. The following year Belinsky died, and by that time Gogol in effect was already dead as a writer of prose fiction.

4. Todd, *Familiar Letter*, 47. For Merzlyakov, see his "Rassuzhdenie," 46–48; for Batyushkov, see his "Rech'," 47.

5. The first quotation is from A. I. Galich, *Opyt nauki izyashchnogo* (1825), as quoted in Kirpichenko, *Arkhitekturnye teorii*, 51. Kirpichenko aptly characterizes Galich's book as "the first attempt in Russia at a unitary exposition of the aesthetic of Romanticism with all the arts brought in" (49). The second quotation is from N. Ya. Berkovsky, "Esteticheskie teorii nemetskogo romantizma," *Literaturnye teorii nemetskogo romantizma. Dokumenty*, Leningrad, 1934, 65, quoted in Kirpichenko, 289.

6. Bestuzhev-Marlinsky, "Vzglyad," 491, 488–89.

7. Chaadayev's letter is quoted from Edie et al., *Russian Philosophy*, 112, 116. The letter was originally written in French in 1829 (perhaps in another contemptuous gesture to the Russians), but was first published in 1836, and appeared in Russian translation in 1836. His case shows that it was not the Soviets who invented the practice of declaring political dissidents insane.

8. Nadezhdin, "Evropeizm i narodnost'," 89. The title of his 1831 article is "Literaturnye opaseniya" (Literary Apprehensions), which probably suggested the title of Belinsky's article published three years later.

9. For useful studies of the development of Russian prose fiction, including the novel, see Brang, *Studien*, and Striedter, *Der Schelmenroman*. The Russian schol-

arship on this topic is of course vast. The second quotation from Belinsky is from his "O russkoi povesti," 259.

10. Gogol, "V chem zhe nakonets," VIII, 370, 403–05. The earlier article is his "Peterburgskaya stsena," VIII, 555.

11. See Zeldin, "Herder," 11–12.

12. As printed in Garnett/Kent, *The Complete Tales and Plays*, 598.

13. The most important and influential representative of Sentimentalism in Russia was Karamzin, particularly his "Poor Liza" (Bednaya Liza, 1792). Parodies had begun to appear as early as 1807, with Aleksandr Shakhovskoy's comedy *A New Sterne* (Novyi Stern). For a succinct account of this period, see Page, "Sentimentalism," 395–97. In the discussion that follows, I use the Garnett/Kent translation, but make considerable modifications, mostly in the direction of greater literalness.

14. This point is made by Gukovsky, *Realizm Gogolya*, esp. 424–25; I am expanding and developing it.

15. So ludicrous is Khlestakov's conflation, in fact, that translators lose their nerve and "correct" it. Garnett/Kent has: "we shall flee to some happy dale beside a running brook" (658). Ehre/Gottschalk is somewhat closer: "We shall flee to a haven of shady streams" (113). A standard French translation, by André Barsacq, is more courageous and more accurate: "nous nous réfugierons à l'ombre d'un ruisseau" (Gogol, *Oeuvres complètes*, 1020). Gukovsky points out (*Realizm Gogolya*, 428) that even when Khlestakov is boasting of his great station in Petersburg, he remains the copy-clerk, capable only of quantitatively exaggerating the limited world he already knows.

16. Karamzin, "Poor Liza," 53–57.

17. I am making my own translations from the 1835 version, as printed in PSS, III, 401–45. For the 1842 version, I use essentially Garnett/Kent (II, 252–303), but with considerable modifications, sometimes silent, sometimes specified in the notes.

18. Garnett/Kent offers a paraphrase that is somewhat misleading: "After all, this is only an imitation of something from life."

19. See Kent's note: "The reference is very probably to the Mona Lisa. There are also two sketches in which the eyes are singular: his study of the head of St. James (1496), in which the eyes are dominant, and his study of the head of St. Philip (done the same year), a profile, in which both the eyes and the mouth are prominent, but it is unlikely that Gogol knew these" (260). Garnett/Kent, however, omits Gogol's remark about the veins of the eye.

20. "Chertkov" suggests either *chert*, "devil," or *cherta*, "trait" or (more likely here) "boundary." All are important motifs in the story. In its written form, "Chartkov" suggests nothing at all, but when spoken, it sounds identical to "Chertkov," according to the rules of phonetics in standard Russian.

21. I have made considerable revision here in Garnett/Kent, which, for one thing, omits the Sentimentalist code-words "flocks [*stada*]" and "groves [*roshchi*]."

22. "Adroit gestures" is a rather elaborate way of rendering the Russian *ukhvatki*, but it is better than the "mannerisms" of the Garnett/Kent text, which sounds pejorative where the original is not.

23. Here Garnett/Kent makes a serious mistake that will derail the unsuspecting

Anglophone. Instead of "moves away from it" (*otdalyaetsya ot nei*), they have "surrenders to her," which is the opposite of the point Gogol is trying to make. Less seriously, when they have "work of art," the Russian has *sozdanie*, "creation."

24. I borrow the term from Slonimsky, "Technique," esp. 357–58.

25. Kent's editorial note identifying the female characters mentioned here is helpful: Corinne is the heroine "of a novel by Mme. Germaine de Staël (1776–1817)," published as *Corinne* in 1807. Undine is the heroine "of a popular fairy tale, *Undine*, published in 1811, by Friedrich de la Motte-Fouqué (1777–1843)." Aspasia is the "beautiful and learned Greek mistress of Pericles (5th century B.C.)" (278).

26. Pushkin, "Puteshestvie v Arzrum," 641. I am indebted to William Mills Todd for calling this parallel to my attention. George Dawe (1781–1829) was an Englishman who in 1819 "went to Russia, where he painted for the Emperor [Alexander I] about 400 portraits of the chiefs of the Russian army, who had, with the assistance of the snow, vanquished Napoleon" (Williamson, *Bryant's Dictionary*, 16).

27. Garnett/Kent has "the last century," which is a mistranslation of *teper', v nyneshnem veke*, and destroys the typically Gogolian association of brilliant surfaces with an eternal present.

28. Homer, *Iliad*, XXII, lines 209–13.

29. *Potukhnuvshii*: inaccurately, Garnett/Kent has "smouldering" instead of "extinguished." It also omits the next sentence.

CHAPTER 10

1. The artist-monk foreshadows the same path Gogol intended Chichikov to follow in the never completed Parts 2 and 3 of *Dead Souls*.

2. The same parable is found in Luke 19:12–27, but the unit of measure is different (*min* in Russian, *mna* in Latin, "pound" in King James), and the sums involved are smaller. I am indebted to my student Caroline Crutcher for suggesting the possible connection between the parable in Matthew and Gogol's story.

3. Gogol, "Strakhi i uzhasy Rossii," VIII, 343–46. The corresponding passage in *Wisdom* reads: "For they who undertook to banish fears and terrors from the sick soul themselves sickened with ridiculous fear" (*New American Bible*, 745).

4. Cf., e.g., Homer's Thersites "of the endless speech . . . who knew within his head many words, but disorderly, in vain, and without decency. . . . This was the ugliest man who came beneath Ilion" (*Iliad*, II, 212–16). For a brief discussion of the dimensions of the Greek idea of "the beautiful" (*to kalon*), see Jaeger, *Paideia*, 416 n. 9.

5. The reference is to Pushkin's short poem "The Demon" (Demon, 1823), where the following modishly Byronic traits may have gone into Gogol's portrait of Chartkov (as perhaps into Lermontov's later portrait of Pechorin, in *Hero of Our Time*):

> His caustic talk
> Poured a cold poison into my soul.
> With inexhaustible slander

He tempted Providence;
He called the beautiful a dream;
He despised inspiration;
He did not believe in love, in freedom;
He looked mockingly on life—
And there was nothing in all of nature
That he wished to bless [*blagoslovit'*].

Certainly very little of Gogol's world shows evidence that any "blessing" (*blagoslo-venie*) has been conferred.

6. Pseudo-Dionysius, *Divine Names*, IV, 32, p. 160.

7. Ladner, *Idea of Reform*, 91. The quotation from Gregory of Nyssa's *Canticum Canticorum* (homil. XV) is cited in Ladner, 101. Ladner has a more extensive discussion of the image of the mirror (esp. 96–101), specifically of "the soul as a polished mirror in which God himself can be seen even in this life," which he calls "one of the most significant metaphors in Greek patristic assimilation ideology" (96). For a useful summary of the symbol of the mirror generally, see de Vries, *Dictionary*, 323. For an interesting discussion of Efrem and of ascetic holy men in Russia, see Morris, *Saints and Revolutionaries*, esp. 67–70.

8. Mochul'sky, *Dukhovnyi put'*, 48. See also Zen'kovsky's *Gogol'*.

9. I draw this information largely from Broude, *The Macchiaioli*, esp. 24–27. Overbeck's painting is reproduced on 25.

10. Page references to Wackenroder's *Confessions* given in text below will be to the Schubert edition *"Confessions" and "Fantasies."* One of the Russian translators was S. P. Shevyryov, who later became a close friend of Gogol's.

11. See Broude, *The Macchiaioli*, 26, where we find a reproduction of Overbeck's *Italy and Germany* (1811–28), and the explanation that it "shows two female personifications of Italy and Germany seated in the foreground, with landscapes characteristic of their native countries merging behind them. With eyes cast modestly downward, the dark-haired, Raphaelesque Italy, her head crowned with laurel, listens quietly while Germany imparts her new vision—presumably awakening Italy to the modern-day rebirth of her long-neglected and overlooked quattrocento tradition." For Gogol on Ivanov, see his "Istoricheskii zhivopiscts," VIII, 328–37.

12. Vasari, *Lives*, II, 30–48 (in the entry "Fra Giovanni da Fiesole").

13. Ibid., II, 395–96 (in the entry "Leonardo da Vinci"). Kent, in his note to the Gogol passage, says that the reference is "very probably" to the Mona Lisa. In Vasari, it is explicitly so.

14. Gogol, "V chem zhe nakonets," VIII, 377.

15. Vinogradov, "Naturalisticheskii grotesk" and "Yazyk Gogolya." For Vinogradov as a critic of Gogol, see Maguire, "The Formalists."

16. Gogol, ⟨"Avtorskaya ispoved'"⟩, VIII, 436–37.

17. Karamzin: "I go to the same place in the gloomy days of autumn to grieve along with nature. The winds howl frightfully against the walls of the deserted monastery, between the graves overgrown with tall grass and through the dark passageways of the cells. There, leaning on the ruins of the tombstones, I heed the dull

moan of times which have been swallowed up in the abyss of the past—a moan at which my heart shudders and trembles" (54).

18. Garnett/Kent simply substitutes this entire passage for the 1842 text of the story (281–82), perhaps because, as we shall see, without it the painting seems even more abstract (as Gogol intends). Quotations from the 1842 version are my own translations of the Russian in *PSS*, III, 111–12.

19. The first letter to Shevyryov is dated Aug. 10 (o.s.), 1839, XI, 248; the second, Feb. 28, 1843, XII, 145–46.

20. Gogol to Danilevsky, Aug. 7, 1841, XI, 343; to Shevyryov, Feb. 28, 1843, XII, 148; to Yazykov, Jan. 8, 1846, XIII, 30.

21. The quotations in this paragraph are taken, in order, from the following letters: Gogol to Zhukovsky, Oct. 30, 1837, XI, 111; to Balabina, Nov. 7, 1838, XI, 181–82; to Pogodin, May 5, 1839, XI, 224; to Aksakov, Dec. 28, 1840, XI, 323–24.

22. Gogol to P. A. Pletnyov, Mar. 17, 1842, XII, 46–47.

23. He did move on to Karlsbad the following month, and then to Schwalbach, Ems, and Ostend. The letter is dated June 24, 1846. It does not appear in *PSS*, but was first published in the journal *Russkaya literatura*, no. 2, 1962, and is included in Gogol, *Sobranie sochinenii*, VII, 299–300, from which I translate.

24. Gogol to A. O. Rosset, Feb. 11, 1847, XIII, 211.

25. Gogol to V. A. Zhukovsky, Jan. 10, 1848, XIV, 33.

26. Gogol to A. A. Ivanov, Jan. 18, 1848, XIV, 46. See also his letter to A. P. Tolstoy, Jan. 22, 1848, XIV, 46–47, and another to A. M. Vielgorskaya, Jan. 23, 1848, XIV, 48.

27. Gogol to S. P. Shevyryov, Jan. 23, 1848, XIV, 49.

28. Gogol to A. P. Tolstoy, Apr. 25, 1848, XIV, 59. "Astounding [*porazitel'no*]" is the term he uses in a letter to V. A. Zhukovsky, Apr. 6, 1848, XIV, 57.

29. See Galassi, *Corot in Italy*, esp. 213–19.

CHAPTER 11

1. "Viy" can be read in many different ways, most obviously the psychosexual, the mythological, and the folkloric. For instances of the first, see Stilman, "All-Seeing Eye"; McLean, "Gogol's Retreat"; and, at an interesting extreme, Rancour-Laferriere, "Identity of Gogol's *Vij*."

2. Garnett/Kent omits the threefold repetition of the word "snuff [*tabak*]," thereby destroying the suggestion of parody.

3. For "reading loudly," *chitat' gromko*, Garnett/Kent has "reading aloud," which would be *chitat' vslukh*. The mistranslation may seem minor, but it does not convey the image of loudness and its association with profanation.

4. The Russian here reads: *glyadel nepodvizhno na tolkavshikh ego kozakov.* Garnett/Kent has: "he stared at the Cossacks as they came in." Again, this is a paraphrase. The fact that the Cossacks have to "nudge" Khoma suggests that he is practically a corpse himself. The point is reinforced by the word "motionless [*nepodvizhno*]." It may refer just to the eyes, as implied by "stared" in Garnett/Kent, or (the syntax is not clear) it may describe Khoma's entire appearance.

5. Stilman continues: "In a note to the title of the story, Gogol explains that 'Viy

is a colossal creation of the folk imagination. This is the name that the Little Russians [Ukrainians] use to refer to the chief of the gnomes, whose eyelids reach right down to the ground. ...' However, Viy is unknown in Ukrainian folklore; so, in fact, are gnomes, who in all likelihood migrated into Gogol's story from Grimm's fairy tales. Viy therefore is a creation not of the imagination of 'the folk' but rather of Gogol himself. And the word 'Viy' was most likely derived by Gogol from the Ukrainian *viya*, meaning 'eyelash.'" In a note to this last statement, Stilman says: "In the commentary to 'Viy' in *PSS*, II, 742, it is stated that the Ukrainian word *viy* means 'eyelid.' This is incorrect: 'eyelid' in Ukrainian is *povika*, and the word *viy* simply does not exist" ("All-Seeing Eye," 377).

6. Lermontov, *Demon* (1841).

7. Garnett/Kent simplifies the sentence to "how full of delight is the Little Russian summer," thereby obliterating the parallel.

8. In Russian, the date is expressed as "Marta 25 chisla." Garnett/Kent normalizes it to "on the twenty-fifth of March." For an interpretation of the dating, see Yermakov, "The Nose," 176–78.

9. Erlich, *Russian Formalism*, 238. The first definition is by Harkins, *Dictionary*, 360.

10. Ong, *Orality*, 69.

11. Aristotle, *Rhetoric*, Book III, chap. 14 (1415), lines 22–24, p. 202.

12. For a useful summary, see Havelock, *Muse*, esp. 24.

13. Gogol, "Chto takoe slovo," *Uchebnaya kniga*, in *PSS*, VIII, 470.

14. "Rudy" (with the stress on the ending) is Ukrainian for "red," not a nickname for "Rudolph."

15. Richard Peace, without formulating the problem as I have, adduces another interesting instance of the sudden intrusion of the written mode into "The Two Ivans," in the use of letters of the alphabet to characterize the two men: "Ivan Ivanovich is described as having a mouth in the shape of *izhitsa* [like a capital V] and in extreme anger at the insults he has received from his 'friend' this becomes stretched in an 'O.' On the clothes line of Ivan Nikiforovich are a strange pair of trousers in the shape of the Russian letter 'l'" (*Enigma*, 83).

16. Bees have a long and honorable symbolic lineage, stretching back to earliest recorded times. Russians would probably think first of *The Bee* (Pchela), a twelfth-century collection translated from the Greek, which consisted of "short didactic adages and aphorisms culled from 'Holy Writ,' patristic literature, and even from ancient secular writers." It was drawn on and augmented by later Russian writers. (Gudzy, *History*, 56.) As a beekeeper (*pasichnik*), Rudy is the nurturer and protector of the "bees," that is, the various narrators. One might make a case for all of Gogol's narrators as "bees," in that they take material from a variety of sources and create something new and "sweet." In Gogol's own time, the newspaper *Northern Bee* (Severnaya pchela), of which Poprishchin is an avid reader, was a miscellany of popular culture.

17. Translated from the Russian text, *PSS*, I, 107. This sentence is not found in Garnett/Kent, presumably because, understandably, the glossary is omitted.

18. *PSS*, I, 197. Also omitted by Garnett/Kent.

19. Fielding, *Tom Jones*, X, 1, 467; XI, 1, 505–6.

20. Aristotle, *Rhetoric*, Book I, ch. 2 (1356a), line 15, p. 25. Aristotle is of course talking about rhetoric, not poetry; but as he himself says, the line between the two arts is often very thin, as indeed it is in Gogol.

21. Tolstoy, "K chitatelyam," 208. The italics are Tolstoy's.

22. O'Connor, "A Clean Well-Lighted Place," 158. He is talking about Joyce's *Portrait of the Artist as a Young Man* and Hemingway's "In Another Country."

23. Garnett/Kent omits "in advance [*zaranee*]," thereby losing its ironic effect and flattening the whole sentiment: "It is sad! I am sad at the thought!" This may be another case of a translator's failure of nerve when faced with the unusual.

24. Garnett/Kent omits the exclamation point after the last sentence.

25. Leo Braudy makes the point that in *Joseph Andrews* Fielding "emphasizes a totally inductive approach to the phenomena of life" (*Narrative Form*, 115–16). The earlier quotation from Fielding is in *Tom Jones*, III, 1, 121, italics mine. Gogol was probably well acquainted with Fielding. For a brief but useful study, see Elistratova, *Gogol'*, esp. 9–41.

26. Crystal, *A Dictionary*, 178.

27. Popkin, "Distended Discourse," 186, 188–89.

28. See esp. Mandel'shtam, *O kharaktere*, and Vinogradov, "Yazyk." Slonimsky's study "Technique" is one of the few that transcends mere list-making.

29. More has probably been written on "The Overcoat" than on any other work by Gogol. Yermakov is especially interested in the sexual and fecal connotations of the names: see his *Ocherki*, esp. 161–62. See also Kent's note in II, 304: "to a native Russian who has never read or heard of the story, the name is provocative, the resemblance to *kaka* (defecator) being quite impossible to miss." For a discussion of the saint's-life subtext, see Schillinger, "Gogol's 'The Overcoat,'" 36–41.

30. Williams, *Figures*, 23–24.

31. For a discussion of some uses of *dazhe* by Gogol (though not in this story), see Chizhevsky, "Gogol's 'Overcoat,'" 172–95.

32. Slonimsky, "Technique," 357–58.

33. O'Connor, "A Clean Well-Lighted Place," 157. Italics mine.

34. Lotman, *Structure*, 106, 129. Lotman's idea is far more complex that this quotation suggests: see esp. 104–36. For Lidiya Ginzburg, see "Russkaya lirika," 90, 92.

35. Garnett/Kent offers a watered-down paraphrase here: "his lips were pressed against the stranger's fat cheeks as though against soft cushions." "Cushions" (for *podushki*) is not incorrect, but in view of the suggestive sexuality of this scene, I prefer the equally correct "pillows." I do commend "fat," however: even though it is not precisely what the Russian *bol'shie* ("big") means, the cheeks of a fat man are obviously fat, and the word points up the larger pattern we are trying to discern.

36. For further discussion, see Maguire and Malmstad, Translators' Introduction. Generally Bely did not hesitate to acknowledge his enormous indebtedness to Gogol: see his *Masterstvo Gogolya*, esp. the chapter entitled "Gogol' i Belyi," with its revealing parallel passages (297–309).

CHAPTER 12

1. Throughout this chapter I use the Magarshack translation but frequently bring in the versions by George Reavey (1965) and Bernard Guilbert Guerney

(1965) for comparison. In the present instance, Magarshack renders the first and third of these terms as simply "carriage"; Reavey proposes "chaise" for the first and "turn-out" for the third; all three render the second term as "wheel."

2. Nabokov, *Nikolai Gogol*, 76. The expression also occurs at the beginning of "Nevsky Prospekt," and perhaps elsewhere in Gogol too.

3. More literally, the Russian reads: "as the chaise was driving up to the inn, a young man *was encountered [vstretilsya].*" Magarshack has "a young man *happened to walk past*" (17); Reavey, "a young man *strolled past*" (1). Guerney comes closest, with "as the carriage drove up to the inn *it encountered* a young man" (4). The italics are mine.

4. In Russian: "'chervi! chervotochina! pikentsiya!' ili: 'pikendras! pichuru-shchukh! pichura!' i dazhe prosto: 'pichuk!'" Reavey has: "'Hearts!' 'Heartburn!' 'Spadefull!' 'Spadille!' 'Spadefoot!' 'Spadone!' or simply 'Spille!'" (12). For once, Guerney does not rise to the occasion: "or simply exclamations denoting the various diminutives and pet names with which they had rechristened the four suits within their own circle" (15).

5. The Russian language does offer the expression *kopchenoe steklo*, "smoked glass," but this has become fixed and neutral. Reavey has "grimy ceiling . . . sooty chandelier" (3); Guerney has "sooty ceiling . . . chandelier dingy from smoke" (6). "Sooty" is better than "grimy," but "blackened" would be best, since it honors the force of the prefix *za-*, which in this case denotes excess. Why not aim at conveying the oddness of Gogol's usage and call it a "smoked chandelier"?

6. Understandably, there seems to be no way of turning this wordplay into English. Guerney, however, hints at it with "as great a host of teacups as you might find of birds on a shore" (6), for "host" is commonly used of animate objects (the Russian is simply *bezdna*, a very large number of anything).

7. Another devout Sentimentalist was Gogol's own father, whose "esthetic inclinations found expression in a variety of ways: in sentimental serenades to his fiancée; in a no less sentimental passion for horticulture; in the arbors and grottoes he constructed in his garden and the 'valleys of repose' he created in the woods" (Gippius, *Gogol*, 16).

8. Magarshack here renders *khorosho* as "all right" (45). This is not incorrect, but it does obscure the terminological function of the word. Reavey and Guerney do better. Reavey: "I think it would be a *good* proposition" / "Ah, if it is a *good* thing, then I have nothing against it" (34). Guerney: "I think that it will be a *good* thing" / "Ah, if it's going to be a *good* thing then it's an entirely different matter; I have nothing against it" (40). (Italics are mine.)

9. "The dogs were barking in all sorts of voices: one was howling as diligently as though he were getting goodness only knows what wages for it; another was snapping it out rapidly like a sacristan; next could be heard a treble, so irrepressible that one's head rang; all that was covered by a thick basso, evidently an already elderly hound, because he was barking as hoarsely as a general at the front. One could most likely say that there were more than a hundred musicians in this orchestra. That would have allowed Chichikov to observe that the village was of a decent size" (VI, 273).

10. The first version reads: "Glancing out the window, he noticed [very much] that there were quite a few peasant courtyards. 'Why, she has a substantial little

village!' he said to himself: 'really substantial!' he repeated, and began to count on his fingers the courtyards, which proved to number more than thirty. He was very pleased by this discovery" (VI, 277).

11. I borrow this translation from Guerney (63). Magarshack has "There's nothing wrong with hemp" (63), which does not capture the idea that hemp is unique. Reavey does well with "hemp is hemp" (54).

12. Magarshack mistranslates the last attribute, *seroukhikh*, as "with grey eyes." I prefer Guerney's version, as it sounds more terminological, an important point for the characterization of a man who, as we shall see, appears to be obsessed with the proper names for things: "tan, black with markings of white, liver-colored-and-skewbald, tan-and-skewbald, red-and-skewbald, black-eared, gray-eared" (88–89). A much longer list is found in Gogol's notebooks for 1841–44 (⟨"Zapisnaya knizhka 1841–44"⟩, VII, 321–22).

13. Magarshack has "claret" instead of Gogol's "Bordeaux [*bordo*]": I translate literally to preserve the theme of labeling. He also renders *burdashkoi* as "red biddy," which is not likely to mean much to American readers. "Slops" is the translation used by Guerney and by the *Oxford Russian-English Dictionary*, under the entry *burda*, a word of Turkish origin. Reavey's "bawdikins" (66) suggests, misleadingly, that the Russian is a neologism. *Kvass*, in the next sentence, is a mildly alcoholic beverage made of fermented grains.

14. Sobakevich's name is derived from *sobaka*, "dog." His other two names, "Mikhail" and "Semyonovich," are, as Guerney explains in a note, "[t]he first name and patronymic bestowed by the Russian folk on its totem animal, in both affection and respect; when the bear is trained or a pet he is usually called Misha, or even Mishka" (546).

15. A literal translation, even at the expense of smoothness, best makes the point here. The Russian of the first passage cited from p. 111 reads: *Sobakevich voshel, kak govoritsya, v samuyu silu rechi, otkuda vzyalas' rys' i dar slova.* Magarshack paraphrases: "Sobakevich, as they say, had been carried away by his own eloquence, though goodness only knows where he got this unceasing flow of words from." Guerney comes closer with: "Sobakevich had got into the vein, as they say. Whence came this gift of gab and the pace of his speech?" (125–26). Reavey is farthest away with: "Sobakievich had reached the high pitch of oratory and he was borne upon a flow of words" (106). But Magarshack's rendering of the sentences that follow is more or less accurate, and I have let it stand with one slight alteration: *kak vidno* I render as "obviously," in preference to his "it seems."

16. I borrow this phrase from the Guerney translation (139). Magarshack has "truly picturesque in its wild beauty" (121), not a good solution to the difficulty posed by *zhivopisen v svoem kartinnom opustenii*, which contains two different words each translatable as "picturesque." Reavey offers a feeble paraphrase: "the only highly picturesque feature of the place" (117).

17. Again I borrow from Guerney, 140. Magarshack has "there was nothing to relieve the scene" (*nichego ne zametno bylo ozhivlyayushchego kartinu*, 123), which preserves the idea that something (a "scene") is being inspected, but does not repeat the all-important idea of a picture. Reavey falls between the two, with "There was nothing to add animation to the scene" (118). For Fusso, see "Landscape," 123.

18. See Reavey: "The names are meant to sound like those of heroes of Romantic works of the period. 'Gremin:' The idealized hero of a Romantic tale by Alexander Bestuzhev-Marlinsky (1797–1837), *The Test*. The name Gremin was later used by the librettist of Tchaikovsky's opera *Eugene Onegin* (who happened to be Modest Tchaikovsky, the composer's brother) for the husband of the heroine, Tatiana. In Pushkin's work, which served as the source for the opera, the husband is not named" (177).

19. Lednicki, "Dostoevsky," esp. 188–199.

20. Fussell, *Wartime*, 36. For Morson, see "Gogol's Parables," esp. 215–26.

21. I have let Magarshack's Briticisms, including spellings, pretty much stand until now. But here he has "corn wharf," which, although hardly crucial to the sense of the passage, will baffle most Americans. Hence my "grain dock" (thanks to Hugh McLean). Along another line, his "fell into reverie," while not incorrect, renders the verb *zadumat'sya*, which is repeated four times (he registers three) in the following sentence, and perhaps is meant to set up a chantlike rhythm to suggest a verbal artist in the throes of creation.

22. I take the term "scheme" from the Guerney translation (323). Magarshack renders it as "idea," but this obliterates the distinction between *syuzhet* and *mysl'*. Reavey translates *syuzhet* as "theme" (262), which is not so accurate as Guerney, but better than Magarshack.

23. The Alpine scenery is present only in the final version, which Gogol was working on more or less at the same time as the story "Rome." The textual history of *Dead Souls* is highly complicated. For one thing, essentially six different manuscripts are extant. A detailed account can be found in *PSS*, VI, 881–908.

24. Nabokov, Notes to Foreword, in *Song*, 76–77. For pertinent comments on the looseness of the concept of "song" elsewhere, see Hardré, "Song," esp. 779–80.

25. Gogol, "Pesnya," *Uchebnaya kniga*, VII, 474–75.

26. Tanner, "Notes," 28, 26; he cites the line from Whitman.

27. For explicit statements of this position, see Gogol's letters to N. M. Yazykov, Dec. 2 and 26, 1844, XII, 377–79, 421–25, and the article in *Selected Passages* that is based on them, "Predmety," VIII, 278–81.

28. *Telega spuskaetsya s kruchi*. Magarshack has "a cart," which would mean, incorrectly, that it is not the narrator's. Russian word-order requires "the" in English, as does the sense of the passage. Reavey also has "a cart" (240), but Guerney, correctly, "the vehicle" (297).

29. Magarshack mistranslates Gogol's "unknown [*nevedomaya*]" as "unseen" (which would be *nevidimaya*). It would fit my argument well, but obviously one cannot base analyses on translations. Still, there are more than enough of Gogol's own instances of "the unseen" in the sentences that immediately follow.

30. For several stories involving the firebird, see Afanas'ev, *Narodnye russkie skazki*.

31. It is hard to decide where "from above" belongs in the statement about the song. Another possible translation would be: "From above you have heard. . . ." The Russian word-order is ambiguous, perhaps deliberately so: *Zaslyshali s vyshiny znakomuyu pesnyu*. Does the song emanate from above the steeds? Or do the steeds hear it coming from the Russian land below, as did the narrator earlier?

Guerney opts for the former: "Ye have caught the familiar song coming down to you from above" (332). Reavey seems to think that the steeds themselves are actually moving downward (unless he misuses the participle), although the origin of the song is still not clear: "Descending from above you have caught the note of the familiar song" (270). To me it makes more sense for them to hear the sound from below, particularly since it is "familiar"; but I let Magarshack's version stand since it conveys the ambiguity of the original. Reavey, Guerney, and I read this paragraph as an apostrophe to the steeds; hence, "you." Magarshack, who considers them merely "horses," thus disregarding the "poetic" Russian (*koni*), thinks of them as "they." But the verb-ending in Russian could designate either second or third person. I have made other significant modifications in Magarshack's translation here, with a few borrowings from Guerney.

32. Bely, *Masterstvo Gogolya*, 95.

33. Weiskopf, "Bird Troika," esp. 134–35; Plato, *Phaedrus*, 250–51. For similar uses of the horse and carriage among the ancients, see Pindar, Horace, and especially Propertius. The later work by Gogol is "O nauke," *Uchebnaya kniga*, VIII, 470.

CHAPTER 13

1. Ong, *Orality*, 31.

2. Augustine, *Confessions*, VIII, 12, 177–78; italics mine.

3. This scene finds a close parallel in the memoirs of Andrei Bolotov, which were written in 1789 but not published until long after Gogol's death.

> Once in summertime just before evening I took it into my head to go out alone for a walk in the lower garden. This garden was somewhat removed from the yard and was situated on a slope between the river and the top of the hill. Scarcely had I reached it and climbed into the very middle . . . when I suddenly heard a voice calling me by name and patronymic, and the voice was rather loud and seemed to come from close by. I immediately answered: "Here I am!" but to my "I" there came no reply. This surprised me. I immediately shouted: "Who called me?" But I got no reply to this either. I repeated the question, but nothing came back. I proceeded to look here and there, but saw no one. Again I shouted "Who called me? Who needs me?" but again there was no sign of anyone, or the slightest murmur; utter quiet and silence reigned everywhere. . . . Not satisfied with shouting, I began running around the entire garden, searching every nook and cranny, and especially the part from which the voice had seemed to come. I looked on top of the hill, into the grove on the other side, into someone else's garden, and again shouted "Who called me?" several times. But there was no trace of a human being anywhere, and no one answered me. Then I was overcome with fear. I dashed home as fast as I could, and calling all the servants together I asked if anyone had been passing by in the lower garden and called to me, but they all vowed and swore that there had been no one in or near the garden at that time and that no one had called to me. In short, I could not discover then and I still do not know how all that happened and who had called out to me. All I know is that the voice was like a human voice in every respect, and that it was nearby. (Bolo-

tov, *Zhizn'*, I, 253–54. I am indebted to Thomas Newlin for bringing this passage to my attention.)

It is unlikely that Gogol could have seen these memoirs, although this part may have been known anecdotally and disseminated orally. If there is a common source, it may reside in Scripture and in classical pastoral.

4. Garnett/Kent renders *serdechnaya pustynya* as "spiritual loneliness," which conveys the idea but loses the image of the desert or wilderness so common in spiritual literature.

5. Hence my suggested reading of "a" (in brackets) instead of Garnett/Kent's "the." Russian has neither definite nor indefinite articles, so one must rely on sense and context.

6. Tatishchev's work is *Istoriya Rossiiskaya*, 5 vols., 1768–1843. For good accounts of Russian historiography, see Mazour, *Modern Russian Historiography*, and Rubinshtein, *Russkaya istoriografiya*. This last book was published in the Soviet Union in 1941, when historiography had reached a nadir. Despite that, it is useful, stimulating, and often sophisticated, more so, understandably, for the earlier periods than for the twentieth century (the final chapter is devoted, probably of necessity, to Stalin as a historian). In 1948, however, Rubinshtein publicly denounced his own book. See Mazour, 215–16.

7. Rubinshtein (*Russkaya istoriografiya*, 92) credits the nineteenth-century historian Sergei Solovyov with identifying this particular trend in the writing of history, but considers the term "rhetorical" more appropriate than Solovyov's "literary."

8. Pushkin, "Karamzin," 66–67. This is a surviving fragment of "Notes" toward an autobiography, which Pushkin started in 1821 and burned in 1826.

9. Karamzin, "Predislovie," esp. xvii–xviii, xxiv–xxvi.

10. Bestuzhev-Marlinsky, "Vzglyad," 493.

11. Nadezhdin's statements are found in "Sovremennoe napravlenie," 82–83. See also his "Roslavlev," 84–85.

12. As specified by Todd, "Pushkin," 360. Todd gives an interesting account of the interplay of fiction and history in Pushkin's work. The quotation from Pushkin's review can be found in "Yury Miloslavsky," 103.

13. For details, see the notes to these fragments in *PSS*, III, 711–16. The designation "Walter Scott type" belongs to the editors. For a recent study in English, see Karpuk, "Gogol's Unfinished Historical Novel."

14. The first quote is from a letter to M. P. Pogodin, Feb. 1 (o.s.), 1833, X, 256; the second is from a letter to M. A. Maksimovich, Feb. 12 (o.s.), 1834, X, 297.

15. N. I. Ivanitsky, in *Otechestvennye zapiski*, 1853, no. 2, Section VII, p. 120, as quoted in *PSS*, VIII, 752. This lecture was first published in *Journal of the Ministry of Public Enlightenment* (Zhurnal ministerstva narodnogo prosveshcheniya), and later in *Arabesques*. For an excellent brief account of Gogol as a teacher and writer of history, see Gippius, *Gogol*, 54–57.

16. Gogol, ⟨"Predislovie"⟩, VIII, 7. All these articles were published in *Arabesques*, and are found in *PSS*, VIII.

17. Shortly after completing the long poem *Poltava* (1829), which is set in the Ukraine, Pushkin let it be known that he was planning a history of that land. He

read for it during the next two years or so. What remain are the briefest outline of possible topics and a longer précis (in French!). See Pushkin, "Ocherk," 138–42.

18. Gogol, "Shletser, Miller i Gerder," VIII, 85–89. August-Ludwig von Schlözer (1735–1809) lived in Russia from 1760 to 1764, and was particularly well known for his studies of the Russian chronicles. The "Miller" in question is not the famous Gerhard Friedrich Müller, an important collector and compiler of Russian source materials, but Johann Müller (1752–1809), a Swiss who specialized in the history of his native country. Johann Gottfried Herder (1744–1803) is too well known to require identification here, beyond pointing out that his *Thoughts Toward a Philosophy of the History of Mankind* (Ideen zur Philosophie der Geschichte der Menschheit, 1784–91), which has been called "his most systematic and complete historical work" (Garland and Garland, *Oxford Companion*, 373), was published in an abridged Russian version in Moscow in 1829.

19. See Woodman, *Rhetoric*.

20. Mazour describes the problem graphically as it obtained at the beginning of the nineteenth century: "The first and seemingly insurmountable difficulty was that of co-ordinating dispersed efforts in the gathering of materials; another was the evaluation and classification of gathered materials and the order in which these should be published to preclude a haphazard dumping into single volumes. . . . [T]here were also numerous problems concerning methods of publication, introductory remarks, annotations to textual contents, elucidation of stylistic peculiarities, and agreement on the meaning of obscure or obsolete terms; there was the question, too, of whether to reproduce the texts faithfully or change them to more recent spellings and modernized syntax" (*Modern Russian Historiography*, 50–51).

21. "In his critical approach he belongs to history, in his open-heartedness and his apothegms, to the chronicle. His critical approach consists of a scholarly collating of traditional materials, an intelligent prosecution of the truth, a clear and accurate depiction of events. . . . Wherever his narrative is unsatisfactory, he was lacking sources, and he did not deliberately substitute guesses for them" (Pushkin, "Istoriya," 133).

22. Gogol, ⟨"Avtorskaya ispoved'"⟩, VIII, 449.

CHAPTER 14

1. The textual history of "Taras Bulba" is dealt with exhaustively in the notes to the story in *PSS*, II, 701–31. In the discussion that follows, the A version is taken from *PSS*, II, 279–355; the B version is taken from Garnett/Kent, II, 22–132, with some modifications.

2. For a fascinating study of the myth of the Cossacks and Gogol's contribution to it, see Kornblatt, *Cossack Hero*.

3. Garnett/Kent has merely "rouse them all at one moment," whereas the Russian is *razom i vdrug*, a formula that Gogol often uses to indicate the abruptness with which great truths fall on unsuspecting people.

4. Ouspensky, *Theology*, 189–90. See also John Meyendorff, who writes that from the fifth century on, the prayer of ascetics "[would] no longer be a flight from matter but a communion with God *in soul and body*. The divine grace they [sought would] *transfigure both the soul and the flesh*, regarded as bound together in the

New Life and illuminated by the uncreated divine light" (*Orthodox Church*, 203, italics mine). The definition of the Transfiguration is from *Festal Menaion*, 62. The comments on image and likeness are from Ouspensky, *Theology*, 185, 187–88. The Orthodox Liturgy makes frequent references to image and likeness: cf. Great Vespers and Matins, as printed in *Festal Menaion*, 468, 475, 476, 491. The idea is extremely complex. For one stimulating treatment, in an Orthodox tradition, see Lossky, *In the Image*.

5. "A kak ot grekhov voskresnu, kak odenu plot' nebesnu / Ty v mne, ya v tebe vselyusya" (Skovoroda, "Sad Bozhestvennykh pesnei," 60).

6. Jones is commenting on Pseudo-Dionysius, *Divine Names*, IV, 4, p. 136.

7. For "villages [*vesyam*]," Garnett/Kent unaccountably has "plains."

8. Gogol, "Vzglyad na sostavelenie" and "O dvizhenii narodov," VIII, 40–49 and 115–40.

9. Gogol, "Zhizn'," VIII, 82–84.

10. Khomyakov, "Pis'mo," 105–39. One wonders where Khomyakov got the idea that the English were "religious." In the sharp eyes of one of their illustrious countrymen, they were anything but that: the sermons John Henry Newman delivered between 1825 and 1843 are a litany of complaints about rampant materialism to the exclusion of anything but a nominal spiritualism in the vast majority of the population. (See his *Parochial and Plain Sermons*.)

11. The quotes in the last sentence come from Nadezhdin's "Roslavlev," 85; all the others are from his "Letopisi," 86–87.

12. Gogol, "Neskol'ko slov," VIII, 52–53.

13. For a fascinating discussion of this contrast in the *Odyssey*, in terms of *eos* (dawn, light, east, etc.) and *zophos* (dusk, dark, west, etc.), see Austin, *Archery*, esp. 90–100. Many of these attributes appear in the Russian version of the dichotomy as well, usually in political or social contexts, and represent not so much borrowings from Homer as responses to what is probably a universal myth.

14. See, e.g., Goethe, *Italian Journey*: "like children . . . a happy country which . . . breeds a people who are happy by nature, people who can wait without concern for tomorrow to bring them what they had today and for that reason lead a happy-go-lucky existence" (71, 190).

15. See the summary of Kireevsky's idea in Rubinshtein, *Russkaya istoriografiya*, 282. Perhaps arguments similar to Kireevsky's will one day be heard for the benefits of Stalinism during the more xenophobic periods of Soviet history.

16. See Mazour: "[Karamzin's *History* is] a history of the Russian state, not of the Russian people. It is not even that: it is a rhetorical, panegyrical narrative which endeavors to prove that autocracy alone has bestowed all the blessings that the Russian Empire ever enjoyed; it is an album of sovereigns accompanied by descriptions of the most florid style" (*Modern Russian Historiography*, 66).

17. K.S. Aksakov, as quoted in Rubinshtein, *Russkaya istoriografiya*, 276. Rubinshtein gives a useful outline of this problem on 273–79. The quotation from Gippius earlier in the paragraph is in his *Gogol*, 58.

18. For a bibliography of translations and editions of ancient Roman literature in Russian from the eighteenth century to the end of the nineteenth, as well as scholarly writings from this period, see Naguevsky, *Bibliografiya*.

19. Duff, *Literary History*, 104, 100. As far as I know, the classical parallels for

this Russian problem have not been explored in any depth. Such an undertaking would also need to account for the parallels sometimes drawn, after the Bolshevik Revolution, between the fall of the Roman Empire and the fall of the Romanov dynasty, as, for instance, in Pasternak's *Doctor Zhivago* (1958) and Isaak Babel's "Italian Sunshine" (Solntse Italii, 1924), in the collection *Red Cavalry*.

20. Lomonosov, "Predislovie," 270–74. The quotation from Horace is in *Ars Poetica*, l, lines 55–58, p. 455.

21. Merzlyakov, "Rassuzhdenie," 47.

22. Lotman, "Merzlyakov," 43. The earlier quotations from Lotman are from *Poety*, 601, 603. See also Lotman's discussion of V. V. Popugaev's poem "Genius on the Ruins of Nero's Golden Court" (Genii na razvalinakh zolotogo dvortsa Neronova, 1807), with the obvious parallels between Nero and Emperor Paul I ("Russkaya poeziya," 45).

23. Aronson, "Poeziya Shevyryova," vi. Poems will be cited from this edition, with page numbers in the text. Aronson himself is sympathetic toward Shevyryov, but cautiously so, as any scholar under Stalin had to be.

24. Shevyryov does not use the word "Russia" in this poem, but the allegory is obvious, and in any event he spelled it out in a gloss on the title in the margin of the manuscript: "that is, to Russia" (223).

25. *Dnevnik*, vol. 1, Aug. 10, 1830, in *Arkhiv Shevyryova*, Gos. Publ. Biblioteka (Leningrad), as quoted in Aronson, "Poeziya Shevyryova," x–xi.

CHAPTER 15

1. According to V. N. Repnina, the Greek teacher "would read Homer to the students, which none of them understood. After he had read a few lines, he would raise two fingers to his mouth, snap them, and, taking his fingers away, say: 'Magnificent!'" ("Iz vospominanii o Gogole," *Russkii Arkhiv*, No. 3, 1890, 228, as cited in Richter, 136).

2. This entire passage is omitted by Garnett/Kent. It should come on p. 281, second paragraph, following "had hastened without means to a strange land." I translate from *PSS*, III, 111.

3. Gogol to Zhukovsky, Jan. 10, 1848, XIV, 39, 35. For a fuller discussion of Gogol's attitude toward Dante, see Fanger, *Creation*, esp. 167–68; Griffiths and Rabinowitz, "Death," 158–59.

4. Zhukovsky embarked on his translation at the beginning of 1842, and worked on it for some seven years. He was living in Germany, and was often visited by Gogol, who heard him read some of the work in progress and discussed it with him. Gogol wrote his article while the translation was still under way, only the first part having been published. Page references are to Gogol's article as printed in VIII, 236–44.

5. Coincidentally, Goethe uses the same expression in *Italian Journey*, although not in a biblical sense. The idea is not unusual for an adherent of philosophical grammar, as was Gogol (see below, Chapter 16).

6. Gogol to P. V. Annenkov, Aug. 12, 1847, XIII, 362. For a well-known modern instance of the "Christianization" of an ancient classic, see T. S. Eliot, "Virgil": he specifically excludes the ancient Greeks from consideration, deeming them proto-Christians, while finding their literature more admirable than the Roman.

Rozen's article was published in *Severnaya pchela*, no. 181 (1846). In fact, he took issue with all Gogol's main premises: see the summary and discussion in Debreczeny, *Nikolay Gogol*, 51.

7. For an illuminating discussion of the *vates*, though with no reference to Gogol, see Detienne, *Maîtres*.

8. Belinsky, "O russkoi povesti," 265. For a useful summary of the spread of Platonism in Russia, see Weiskopf, "Bird Troika," 126–28; I believe, however, that he exaggerates its influence on Gogol. As for Virgil, even Goethe mentions him only once (and the *Aeneid* not at all), in *Italian Journey*, with a slightly inaccurate quote from the *Georgics* (which is corrected by Auden and Mayer, 25). *Svaika* is an old Russian game in which a large spike is tossed point down into a ring on the ground. See Shevyryov's poem "The Trinity" (Troistvo, 1830), where he speaks of "that sonorous, euphonious world, / Where, harmonizing in triple and full assembly, Homer and Dante and Shakespeare sing" (Shevyryov, *Stikhotvoreniya*, 85).

9. Gogol, "Men'shie rody epopei," *Uchebnaya kniga*, VIII, 478–79. Among the generic categories set forth here, no "poem" (*poema*) is mentioned; hence there is no place, it would seem, for *Dead Souls*, meaning, perhaps, that Gogol saw it as a unique instance. The word Gogol uses for "epic" is *epopeya*. For a summary of the critical reaction to *Dead Souls*, see Debreczeny, 29–50.

10. Belinsky, "Pokhozhdeniya," 51–52.

11. Gogol, ⟨"Avtorskaya ispoved'"⟩, VIII, 433.

12. Gogol, "Predislovie," VIII, 215–16; "Zaveshchanie," VIII, 222. For an interesting study of *Selected Passages* as a whole, see Sobel, *Gogol's Forgotten Book*. Zholkovsky, "Rereading," also makes some good points.

13. Belinsky, "Letter," esp. 85–86.

14. The first Pseudo-Dionysius quotation is from *Ecclesiastical Hierarchy*, 41; the second, from *Divine Names*, IV, 26 [728A], p. 157. Jones's statements come from his introduction to the latter, and are on p. 85. The italics are mine. I owe the Dostoevsky example to Prof. Paul Valliere.

15. The first quotation is from Wheelwright, "Catharsis," 107. As he notes, there is much difference of opinion about the term: "Insofar as there is no agreement yet, and none in sight, all definitions, including this one, must be regarded as interpretations" (108). The second quotation is from Jacob Bernays, as printed in Laín Entralgo, *Therapy*, 187. The quotations from Aristotle come from *The Poetics*, 23.

16. Gogol, "Vtoraya redaktsiya okonchaniya," IV, 135.

17. Gogol, "Razvyazka *Revizora*," IV, 125, 127, 132. For a fascinating modern interpretation of the play in this light, see Ivanov, "Gogol's *Inspector General*."

18. Gogol, "Peterburgskie zapiski," VIII, 562–63, 551. For Aristotle, see Butcher, "Aristotle's Theory of Poetry," 269.

19. Gogol, *Teatral'nyi raz"ezd*, V, 169.

20. Reinach, "Le Rire rituel," 125; Propp, *Folklore*, 145, 131–32; Bergson, *Laughter*, esp. 29–36.

21. For a concise discussion of the genre, see Paul Meyendorff, Introduction, 23–54. As of this writing, a new "complete works" by Gogol is in preparation in Russia. It will apparently include the *Meditations*. I am here using the English translation by Rosemary Edmonds, under the title *The Divine Liturgy of the East-*

ern Orthodox Church; page references will be in the text. Of the history of this work, Edmonds says: "Probably conceived in Paris in 1845, and carefully corrected and revised shortly before his death, it was not published until five years later. He wanted it to be a small octavo book, a 'popular' edition selling cheaply and not bearing his name" (Translator's Preface, xii).

22. Edmonds consistently translates this term as "Office of Oblation," but as Paul Valliere has pointed out to me, this risks confusing it with the different meaning of "oblation" in the Roman Liturgy.

23. Plato, *Republic*, III, 408. See also Plato's specification, in the same work, of the requirements for a good judge ("he will be a good man . . . for he is good who has a good soul"), and for a good dialectician ("temperance, courage, magnificence, and every other virtue"): III, 409; VII, 536.

24. Gogol to S. A. Sollogub, May 24 (o.s.), 1849, XIV, 126–27. For a particularly striking identification of coldness and demonism in Orthodox thought, see St. Seraphim: "And so, if we feel in our hearts coldness, which is from the devil,—for the devil is cold—then let us call upon the Lord, and He will come and warm our hearts" (*Spiritual Instructions*, 25).

25. Gogol, "Strakhi i uzhasy Rossii," VIII, 745. The translation is from *The New American Bible*, 745–46.

26. Garnett/Kent in this case is too free to support my points about style, so I am making my own translation, from the Russian text in III, 9.

27. Eliot, "Modern Mind," 541.

28. Gippius, *Gogol*, 140.

CHAPTER 16

1. This poem did not appear in print during Pushkin's lifetime; part of it was published by Zhukovsky in 1841, under the title "To N**" (K N**), in an edition of Pushkin's works. This was presumably Gogol's source, and explains why he quotes a version that is shorter than, and in some respects different from, the definitive one we now know under the title "Gnedichu." A translation into English of Gogol's article, as of the entire *Selected Passages*, has been made by Jesse Zeldin. It is riddled with mistakes, but does give readers with no Russian a good sense of the original. The use of Pushkin as mediator did not spare Gogol the wrath of Belinsky: see his letter to Gogol dated July 15 (n.s.), 1847, and Gogol's two replies, one not sent (end of July–beginning of August, 1847, XIII, 435–46), and one sent (about June 20, 1847, XIII, 326–28).

2. Gippius, "N. V. Gogol'," 55, 57. My account here comes close to the one in my *Gogol*, 14–15. For the text of Turgenev's obituary notice, see his "Pis'mo iz Peterburga," 72–73. This notice seems politically innocuous, except perhaps for the following statement: "His loss renews our grief for those unforgettable losses, as a fresh wound awakens the pain of ancient sores." This could have been taken (and was undoubtedly meant as) a reference to the deaths of Russian writers that were widely attributed to governmental persecution, interference, or indifference, like Aleksandr Radishchev's suicide and Pushkin's murder.

3. The first quote is from Gogol's letter to Yazykov, July 14, 1844, XII, 332; the second from Gogol, "Chetyre pis'ma," VIII, 298. For a discussion of the need for "balance," see his ⟨"Avtorskaya ispoved' "⟩, VIII, esp. 442–43.

4. Gogol, "Chetyre pis'ma," VIII, 297–98.

5. Samarin to A. O. Smirnova, *Voprosy filosofii i psikhologii*, 1903, kn. 69, 681, as reported in Gogol, *Sobranie sochinenii v semi tomakh* (henceforth abbreviated as *SS*), V, 606.

6. The textual history is exhaustively described in the commentaries to Part 2 in VII. A more compact description can be found in *SS*, V, esp. 612. Although this edition is based on *PSS*, there are considerable discrepancies in the accounts. Translators who include Part 2, like Magarshack, Guerney, and Reavey, tend to make their own composite versions from the existing materials.

7. Commentary, *SS*, V, 602.

8. McLean, "Gogol and the Whirling Telescope," 98–99. For Bakhtin, see "Epic and Novel," 28.

9. Commentary, *SS*, V, 604. For Chernyshevsky, see his "Ocherki," 12. Italics mine.

10. Magarshack transliterates this name as "Kostanjoglo."

11. Magarshack, 316. In the earlier version, the description is less flattering: "Skudronzhoglo's face was very remarkable. It bore the marks of a southern origin. His hair and eyebrows were dark and thick, his eyes expressive [lit., 'speaking'] and very bright. Intelligence shone in every facial expression, and there was nothing at all sleepy about it. Nonetheless, one could observe an admixture of something irritable and embittered" (VII, 189). Gogol's celebration of "southern" admixtures reminds us of the vogue among Russians, particularly in the eighteenth century, of claiming Tartar blood (foreshadowing, though more justifiably, the recent trend among American pop singers of claiming North American Indian ancestry).

12. Magarshack, 329. Unaccountably, Reavey simply omits this last sentence, although he is using the Russian version in which it occurs. It is even found in what scholars take to be Gogol's earlier version, although in somewhat abridged form: "his face was raised, and all his wrinkles had disappeared. Like an emperor on the day of his solemn coronation, he shone" (VII, 204).

13. Ouspensky, *Theology*, 220.

14. Guerney uses "apt" and "aptly" everywhere (it is certainly better than "neat"), except in the one case where he gets at the more literal meaning: "the expression came very close to the mark" (134–35). Reavey uses "telling" on one occasion and "pointed" or "pointedly" on three others (113–14).

15. Descartes, *Correspondance*, 89–93. For Chomsky, see his *Cartesian Linguistics*, where the source of his own "revolution" in modern linguistics is plain to see.

16. N. Beauzée, *Grammaire générale* (1767), as quoted in Donzé, *Grammaire*, 35.

17. The English version—Lancelot and Arnauld, *A General and Rational Grammar* (1753)—is available in a reprint of 1968. An introductory note to the reprint gives a useful summary of the publishing history of the *Grammaire* and the *Logique*. For a concise account of the spread of philosophical grammar, with particular reference to Condillac, see Uitti, *Linguistics*, esp. 77–92.

18. Lidiya Ginzburg, "Russkaya lirika," 11–13. For Sumarokov, see his "Nastavlenie," esp. 134–35.

19. The very title of the French translation of Grech's *Extensive Russian Gram-*

mar indicates its direction: *Grammaire raisonnée de la langue russe I–II*, St. Petersburg, 1828–29. Grech produced several other grammars as well; all enjoyed great popularity, with at least one running to more than ten printings. The government's 1804 decree was entitled "Ustav uchebnykh zavedenii, podvedomykh universitetam"; for a brief discussion, see Berezin, *Istoriya*, esp. 45.

20. Johnson, Preface, 277.

21. "Inner" implies a contrasting "outer," bringing to mind a distinction that had long been made even by philosophical grammarians. In his *Extensive Russian Grammar*, for instance, Grech distinguished two aspects of the word, labeling them respectively "signs of impressions made on outward feelings [*znaki vpechatlenii na chuvstva naruzhnye*]" and "signs of inner mental activities [*znaki vnutrennikh dushevnykh deistvii*]": as quoted in Berezin, *Istoriya*, 55. Here the distinction is purely mechanical. It was Wilhelm Humboldt and his Ukrainian follower Aleksandr Potebnya who developed it in a dynamic way that had enormous consequences for modern linguistics. For a compact discussion, see Fizer, *Potebnya's Psycholinguistic Theory*.

22. See the discussion by Steiner in his "Whorf," esp. 243. He makes a useful distinction between two views of language, "monadist," in which "differences between languages outweigh similarities," and "universalist," where the opposite is true (242–43). He regards Leibniz as the source for all modern versions of the problem.

23. The editors gloss "science" in the first quotation as "knowledge," and "ideas" in the third as "images; conceptions."

24. Newmayer, *Politics*, 32. This is Saussure's most famous dictum, conveniently seen in his *Course*.

25. Horace, "Beatus ille," 364–69. This poem had been widely anthologized throughout Europe since the Renaissance—often with the omission of the last four lines, which identify Alfius as the "author"—and had been translated into Russian in the eighteenth century.

26. Gogol, "O *Sovremennike*," VIII, 427.

27. Barthes, "Inaugural Lecture," 463–64. The classic Formalist instance is represented by Boris Eikhenbaum, who sees "The Overcoat" as a "performance" ("How Gogol's 'Overcoat' Is Made," 269–91).

28. Kearney, *Movements*, 8–9.

29. Most of the participants would be old enough to have been students in the 1920's, when mock trials of literary heroes were a common practice in Soviet universities, as part of the official campaign of "proletarianization." Sinyavsky's statement is quoted in Carlisle, "Voice," 51.

30. To account for the outpouring of literature on the inadequacy of language, particularly in theological discourse, that has appeared in just the last twenty years would be a tremendous task. See, e.g., the problem as discussed by Bruns, in his *Heidegger's Estrangements* and *Modern Poetry*. For Kazin, see his Foreword, x–xi.

31. Plato, Epistle VII, 342C, p. 535. For a useful study of Plato's theories of language, see Rijlaarsdam, *Platon*.

32. Wackenroder, *"Confessions" and "Fantasies,"* 118. The italics are Wackenroder's.

33. Lossky, "Tradition and Traditions," 14. Note Gogol's term "the inexpressibly expressible [*nevyrazimo vyrazimoe*]," used to describe the ideal painting in the 1835 version of "The Portrait" (III, 422).

34. "O tom, chto takoe slovo," VIII, 231–32.

35. Jones, Introduction to Pseudo-Dionysius, *Divine Names*, 22. The quotation from Pseudo-Dionysius is in his *Mystical Theology*, 215.

Works Cited

THE following list of works cited in the Notes and the Preface omits only a few classics that are widely available in various editions.

Aesop. *Fables of Aesop*. Trans. S. A. Handford. London: Penguin, 1964.

Afanas'ev, A. N. *Narodnye russkie skazki*. 3 vols. Moscow: Khudozhestvennaya literatura, 1957.

Amberg, Lorenzo. *Kirche, Liturgie und Frömmigkeit im Schaffen von N. V. Gogol'*. Bern: Peter Lang, 1986.

Antsiferov, N. P. *Dusha Peterburga*. St. Petersburg: Brokgauz-Efron, 1922. Repr., Paris: YMCA-Press, 1978.

Aristotle. *The Poetics*. In Butcher.

———. *Rhetoric*. Trans. W. Rhys Roberts. In *The "Rhetoric" and The "Poetics" of Aristotle*. New York: The Modern Library, 1954.

Arndt, Walter, trans. *Pushkin Threefold*. New York: E. P. Dutton, 1972.

Aronson, M. "Poeziya S. P. Shevyryova." Introduction to Shevyryov, *Stikhotvoreniya*.

Auden, W. H., and Elizabeth Mayer. See Goethe, *Italian Journey*.

Augustine of Hippo. *Confessions*. Trans. R. S. Pine-Coffin. Baltimore: Penguin, 1961.

Austin, Norman. *Archery at the Dark of the Moon. Poetic Problems in Homer's "Odyssey."* Berkeley: University of California Press, 1975.

Babkin, A. M. "Tolkovyi slovar' V. I. Dalya." In Dal', I, iii–ix.

Bakhtin, M. M. "Epic and Novel." In Michael Holquist, ed., *The Dialogic Imagination. Four Essays*. Trans. Caryl Emerson and Michael Holquist. Austin: University of Texas Press, 1981. Pp. 3–40.

———. "Forms of Time and of the Chronotype in the Novel." In Michael Holquist, ed., *The Dialogic Imagination. Four Essays*. Trans. Caryl Emerson and Michael Holquist. Austin: University of Texas Press, 1981. Pp. 84–258.

Barthes, Roland. "Inaugural Lecture, Collège de France." In Susan Sontag, ed., *A Barthes Reader*. New York: Hill and Wang, 1983. Pp. 457–78.

Batyushkov, K. N. "Nechto o poete i poezii" (1816). In his *Sochineniya*. I. *Proza*. St. Petersburg: Smirdin, 1850. Pp. 55–68.

———. "Rech' o vliyanii legkoi poezii na yazyk" (1816). In his *Sochineniya*, I, 36–51.

Belinsky, V. G. "Letter to N. V. Gogol" (Pis'mo k N. V. Gogolyu 15 iyulya n.s. 1847 goda). In Matlaw, pp. 83–92.

———. "Literary Reveries" (Literaturnye mechtaniya, 1834). In his *Selected Philosophical Works*. Moscow: Foreign Languages Publishing House, 1956. Pp. 3–103.

———. "Ob"yasnenie na ob"yasnenie po povodu poemy Gogolya 'Mertvye dushi' " (1842). In his *PSS*, VI, 410–33.

———. "O russkoi povesti i povestyakh g. Gogolya ('Arabeski' i 'Mirgorod')" (1835). In his *PSS*, I, 259–307.

———. "Pokhozhdeniya Chichikova, ili Mertvye dushi. Poema N. Gogolya. Izdanie vtoroe" (1846). In his *PSS*, X, 52–53.

———. *Polnoe sobranie sochinenii* (*PSS*). 13 vols. Moscow: ANSSSR, 1953–59.

———. "A Survey of Russian Literature in 1847: Part Two" (Vzglyad na russkuyu literaturu 1847 goda). In Matlaw, pp. 33–82.

Bely, Andrei. *Masterstvo Gogolya*. Moscow and Leningrad: GIKhL, 1934.

———. *Petersburg* (Peterburg, 1922). Trans., ann., and intro. Robert A. Maguire and John E. Malmstad. Bloomington: Indiana University Press, 1978.

Berezin, F. M. *Istoriya russkogo yazykoznaniya*. Moscow: Vysshaya shkola, 1979.

Bergson, Henri. *Laughter. An Essay on the Comic* (Le Rire, 1900). Trans. Cloudesley Brereton and Fred Rothwell. New York: Macmillan, 1913.

Bestuzhev-Marlinsky, A. A. "Vzglyad na russkuyu slovesnost' v techenie 1824 i nachale 1825 godov." In *Polyarnaya zvezda* (1825). Moscow and Leningrad: ANSSSR, 1960. Pp. 488–99.

Bocharov, S. G. "Around 'The Nose.' " In Fusso and Meyer, pp. 19–39.

———. "O stile Gogolya." In E. El'sberg, ed., *Tipologiya stilevogo razvitiya novogo vremeni (Klassicheskii stil': sootnoshenie garmonii i disgarmonii v stile)*. Moscow: Nauka, 1976. Pp. 409–45.

Bolotov, A. T. *Zhizn' i priklyucheniya Andreya Bolotova, opisannye samim im dlya svoikh potomkov. 1738–1793*. 4 vols. St. Petersburg: V. Golovin, 1870–73.

Boman, Thorleif. *Hebrew Thought Compared with Greek*. Trans. Jules L. Moreau. New York: W. W. Norton, 1970.

Borisov, Vadim. "Natsional'noe vozrozhdenie i natsiya-lichnost' " (1974). In Alexander Solzhenitsyn et al., eds., *Iz-pod glyb. Sbornik statei*. Paris: YMCA-Press, 1974. Pp. 199–215.

———. "Personality and National Awareness." In Alexander Solzhenitsyn et al., eds., *From Under the Rubble* (Iz-pod glyb, 1974). Trans. A. M. Brock et al. Boston: Little, Brown, 1974. Pp. 194–228.

Brang, Peter. *Studien zur Theorie und Praxis der russischen Erzählung. 1770–1811.* Wiesbaden: Otto Harrassowitz, 1960.

Braudy, Leo. *Narrative Form in History and Fiction.* Princeton, N. J.: Princeton University Press, 1970.

Breck, John. *The Power of the Word in the Worshiping Church.* Crestwood, N. Y.: St. Vladimir's Seminary Press, 1986.

Brink, C. O. *Horace on Poetry. The "Ars Poetica."* Cambridge, Eng.: Cambridge University Press, 1971.

Broude, Norma. *The Macchiaioli. Italian Painters of the Nineteenth Century.* New Haven, Conn.: Yale University Press, 1987.

Bruns, Gerald. *Heidegger's Estrangements. Language, Truth and Poetry in the Later Writings.* New Haven, Conn.: Yale University Press, 1989.

———. *Modern Poetry and the Idea of Language.* New Haven, Conn.: Yale University Press, 1974.

Butcher, S. H. "Aristotle's Theory of Poetry and the Fine Arts." In his *Aristotle's Theory of Poetry and the Fine Arts. With a Critical Text and Translation of "The Poetics"* (1894). 4th ed. New York: Dover, 1941. Pp. 113–407.

Campbell, Thomas. See Pseudo-Dionysius, *The Ecclesiastical Hierarchy.*

Carlisle, Olga. "A Voice from the Third Russian Emigration." *New York Times Book Review,* Oct. 30, 1977, p. 51.

Chaadayev, P. Ya. *Philosophical Letters,* Letter I. In Edie et al., pp. 106–25.

Chernyshevsky, N. G. "Ocherki Gogolevskogo perioda russkoi literatury" (1855). In his *Polnoe sobranie sochinenii v pyatnadtsati tomakh,* III. Moscow: OGIZ, 1947. Pp. 5–43.

Chizhevsky, D. S. "About Gogol's 'Overcoat'" (O "Shineli" Gogolya, 1938). In Maguire, *Gogol,* pp. 295–322.

Chomsky, Noam. *Cartesian Linguistics: A Chapter in the History of Rationalist Thought.* New York: Harper and Row, 1966.

Crystal, David. *A Dictionary of Linguistics and Phonetics.* Oxford: Blackwell, 1985.

Dal', V. I. *Tolkovyi slovar' zhivogo velikorusskogo yazyka.* 3d ed. 4 vols. (1880–82). Moscow: Gos. izd. inostrannykh i natsional'nykh slovarei, 1966.

Debreczeny, Paul. *Nikolay Gogol and His Contemporary Critics.* Philadelphia: Transactions of the American Philosophical Society, New Series, vol. 56, part 3, 1966.

de Koven Ezrahi, Sidra. *By Words Alone. The Holocaust in Literature.* Chicago: University of Chicago Press, 1980.

de Man, Paul. "Wordsworth and Hölderlin." In his *The Rhetoric of Romanticism.* New York: Columbia University Press, 1984. Pp. 47–65.

Descartes, René. *Correspondance,* I. Ed. Ch. Adam and G. Milhaud. Paris: Librairie Félix Alcan, 1936.

Detienne, Marcel. *Les Maîtres de vérité dans la Grèce archaïque.* Paris: François Maspero, 1967.

de Vries, Ad. *Dictionary of Symbols and Imagery.* 2nd rev. ed. Amsterdam: North-Holland, 1976.

Donzé, Roland. *La Grammaire générale et raisonnée de Port Royal.* Berne: Editions Francke, 1967.

Douglas, Mary. *Purity and Danger. An Analysis of the Concepts of Pollution and Taboo* (1966). London: Routledge, 1984.

Driessen, F. C. *Gogol as a Short-Story Writer*. Trans. Ian F. Finley. Paris: Mouton, 1965.

Duff, J. Wright. *A Literary History of Rome from the Origins to the Close of the Golden Age* (1909). 3d ed. London: Ernest Benn, 1953.

Edie, James; James P. Scanlan; and Mary-Barbara Zeldin, eds. *Russian Philosophy*, I. Chicago: Triangle Books, 1969.

Eikhenbaum, B. M. "How Gogol's 'Overcoat' Is Made" (Kak sdelana "Shinel'" Gogolya, 1918). In Maguire, *Gogol*, pp. 267–91.

Eliot, T. S. "The Modern Mind" (1933). In Walter Jackson Bate, ed., *Criticism. The Major Texts*. New York: Harcourt, Brace and World, 1952. Pp. 538–45.

———. "Virgil and the Christian World" (1951). In his *Poetry and Poets*. New York: Farrar, Straus and Cudahy, 1957. Pp. 135–48.

Elistratova, A. A. *Gogol' i problemy zapadnoevropeiskogo romana*. Moscow: Nauka, 1972.

Epiphanius the Wise (Epifany Premudryi). *The Life of St. Stephen of Perm* (Zhitie sv. Stefana episkopa Permskogo, 1397). Trans. Nicholas Zernov. In Serge Zenkovsky, pp. 206–8 (abridged), under the title "Panegyric to St. Stephen of Perm."

Erlich, Victor. *Gogol*. New Haven, Conn.: Yale University Press, 1969.

———. *Russian Formalism. History—Doctrine*. 3d ed. New Haven, Conn.: Yale University Press, 1981.

Ermakov, I. D. See Yermakov.

Fanger, Donald. *The Creation of Nikolai Gogol*. Cambridge, Mass.: Harvard University Press, 1979.

Fedotov, G. P. *The Russian Religious Mind*, I. Cambridge, Mass.: Harvard University Press, 1966.

The Festal Menaion. Trans. Mother Mary and Archimandrite Kallistos Ware. London: Faber and Faber, 1969.

Fielding, Henry. *Tom Jones*. Ed. R. P. C. Mutter. Harmondsworth, Eng.: Penguin, 1966.

Fizer, John. *Alexander A. Potebnya's Psycholinguistic Theory of Literature. A Metaphysical Inquiry*. Cambridge, Mass.: Harvard Ukrainian Research Institute, n.d.

Florovsky, G. V. *Puti russkogo bogosloviya*. 2nd ed. Paris: YMCA-Press, 1981.

Fonvizin, D. I. ["Pis'ma iz Frantsii"] (1788). In Makogonenko, pp. 338–48.

Frantz, Philip E., comp. and ed. *Gogol. A Bibliography*. Ann Arbor, Mich.: Ardis, 1989.

From Poussin to Matisse: The Russian Taste for French Painting. New York: The Art Institute of Chicago and The Metropolitan Museum of Art, distibuted by Harry Abrams, 1990.

Fussell, Paul. *Wartime. Understanding and Behavior in the Second World War*. New York: Oxford University Press, 1989.

Fusso, Susanne. "The Landscape of *Arabesques*." In Fusso and Meyer, pp. 112–25.

Fusso, Susanne, and Priscilla Meyer, eds. *Essays on Gogol. Logos and the Russian Word*. Evanston, Ill.: Northwestern University Press, 1992.

Galassi, Peter. *Corot in Italy. Open-Air Painting and the Classical-Landscape Tradition*. New Haven, Conn.: Yale University Press, 1991.

Garland, Henry, and Mary Garland. *The Oxford Companion to German Literature*. Oxford: Oxford University Press, 1976.

Gennady (Eikalovich), Igumen. See Pseudo-Dionysius, *O Bozhestvennykh imenakh*.

Ginzburg, Carlo. *The Cheese and the Worms. The Cosmology of a Sixteenth-Century Miller*. Trans. John Tedeschi and Anne Tedeschi. Baltimore: Johns Hopkins University Press, 1980.

Ginzburg, L. Ya. "Russkaya lirika 1820—1830kh godov." Introduction to L. Ya. Ginzburg, ed., *Poety 1820—1830kh godov*. Biblioteka poeta, Malaya seriya, 3d. ed. Leningrad: Sovetskii pisatel', 1961. Pp. 5–110.

Gippius, V. V. *Gogol* (1924). Trans., ed., and intro. Robert A. Maguire. 2nd ed. Durham, N. C.: Duke University Press, 1989.

———. "N. V. Gogol'." Introduction to Gogol, *PSS*, I, 21–58.

Goethe, Johann Wolfgang von. *Italian Journey* (Italienische Reise, 1786–88). Trans. W. H. Auden and Elizabeth Mayer. San Francisco: North Point, 1982.

Gogol', N. V. *Arabesques*. Trans. Alexander Tulloch. Ann Arbor, Mich.: Ardis, 1981.

———. *The Collected Tales and Plays of Nikolai Gogol*. Trans. Constance Garnett. Ed. Leonard J. Kent. New York: The Modern Library, 1969.

———. *The Complete Tales of Nikolai Gogol*. Trans. Constance Garnett. Ed. Leonard J. Kent. 2 vols. Chicago: University of Chicago Press, 1985.

———. *Dead Souls*. Trans. Bernard Guilbert Guerney. New York: The Modern Library, 1965.

———. *Dead Souls*. Trans. David Magarshack. Harmondsworth, Eng.: Penguin, 1961.

———. *Dead Souls*. Trans. George Reavey. Ed. George Gibian. Norton Critical edition. New York: W. W. Norton, 1985.

———. *The Divine Liturgy of the Eastern Orthodox Church*. Trans. Rosemary Edmonds. London: Darton, Longman and Todd, 1960.

———. *"Hanz Kuechelgarten," "Leaving the Theater" and Other Works*. Ed. Ronald Meyer. Ann Arbor, Mich.: Ardis, 1990.

———. *Letters of Gogol*. Sel. and ed. Carl R. Proffer. Trans. Carl R. Proffer in collab. with Vera Krivoshein. Ann Arbor: University of Michigan Press, 1967.

———. *Oeuvres complètes*. Ed. Gustave Aucouturier. Paris: Gallimard, 1961.

———. *Polnoe sobranie sochinenii* (*PSS*). 14 vols. Moscow and Leningrad: ANSSSR, 1937–52.

———. *Selected Passages from Correspondence with Friends*. Trans. Jesse Zeldin. Nashville: University of Tennessee Press, 1969.

———. *Sobranie sochinenii v semi tomakh*. Moscow: Khudozhestvennaya literatura, 1966–67.

———. *The Theater of Nikolay Gogol. Plays and Selected Writings*. Ed. Milton Ehre. Trans. Milton Ehre and Fruma Gottschalk. Chicago: University of Chicago Press, 1980.

Griffiths, Frederick T., and Stanley J. Rabinowitz. "The Death of Gogolian Polyphony: Selected Comments on *Selected Passages from Correspondence with Friends*." In Fusso and Meyer, pp. 158–71.

Grube, G. M. A. "Aristotle as a Literary Critic." Introduction to Aristotle, *On Poetry and Style*. Trans. G. M. A. Grube (1958). Indianapolis: Hackett, 1989. Pp. ix–xxx.

Gudzy, N. K. *History of Early Russian Literature* (Istoriya drevnerusskoi literatury, 1941). Trans. Susan Wilbur Jones. New York: Macmillan, 1949.

Gukovsky, G. A. *Realizm Gogolya*. Moscow and Leningrad: Khudozhestvennaya literatura, 1959.

Gustafson, Richard F. "The Suffering Usurper: Gogol's *Diary of a Madman*." *Slavic and East European Journal*, IX, no. 3 (1965), 268–81.

Hammarberg, Gitta. *From the Idyll to the Novel: Karamzin's Sentimentalist Prose*. Cambridge, Eng.: Cambridge University Press, 1991.

Harding, James. *Artistes Pompiers*. New York: Rizzoli, 1979.

Hardré, Jacques (J. H.). "Song." In Preminger, pp. 779–81.

Harkins, William E. *Dictionary of Russian Literature*. New York: Philosophical Library, 1956.

Havelock, Eric A. *The Muse Learns to Write. Reflections on Orality and Literacy from Antiquity to the Present*. New Haven, Conn.: Yale University Press, 1986.

Hoffmann, E. T. A. "The Golden Pot" (Der goldne Topf, 1814). In Christopher Lazare, ed., *Tales of Hoffmann*. New York: Grove, 1946. Pp. 139–217.

Homer. *The "Iliad" of Homer*. Trans. Richmond Lattimore (1951). Chicago: University of Chicago Press, 1961.

Horace. *Ars Poetica*. In his *"Satires," "Epistles" and "Ars Poetica."* Trans. H. Rushton Fairclough. The Loeb Classical Library, no. 194. Cambridge, Mass.: Harvard University Press, 1978. Pp. 442–89.

———. "Beatus ille" (Epode II). In *The Odes and Epodes*. Trans. C. E. Bennett. The Loeb Classical Library, no. 33. Cambridge, Mass.: Harvard University Press, 1978. Pp. 364–69.

Hosking, Geoffrey. Review of Richard Pipes, *The Russian Revolutions 1899–1917*. *Times Literary Supplement*, Feb. 1, 1991, pp. 3–4.

Hussey, Christopher. *The Picturesque* (1927). Hamden, Conn.: The Shoe String Press, 1967.

Ivanits, Linda J. *Russian Folk Belief*. Armonk, N. Y.: M. E. Sharpe, 1989.

Ivanov, Vyacheslav. "Gogol's *Inspector General* and the Comedy of Aristophanes" (*Revizor* Gogolya i komediya Aristofana, 1927). In Maguire, *Gogol*, pp. 200–14.

Jaeger, Werner. *Paideia. The Ideals of Greek Culture*, I, 2nd ed. Trans. Gilbert Highet. New York: Oxford University Press, 1945.

Johnson, Samuel. "Pope." In his *Lives of the Poets*, II. The World's Classics, no. 84. London: Oxford University Press, 1975. Pp. 223–344.

———. Preface to *A Dictionary of the English Language*. In Frank Brady and W. K. Wimsatt, eds., *Poetry and Prose*. Berkeley: University of California Press, 1967. Pp. 277–98.

Jones, John D. See Pseudo-Dionysius, *The Divine Names*.

Kant, Immanuel. *The Critique of Judgement*. Trans. James Creed Meredith. In

Robert Maynard Hutchins, ed., *Great Books of the Western World*, vol. 42. Chicago: Encyclopaedia Britannica, 1952, 461–613.

Karamzin, N. M. *Izbrannye sochineniya v dvukh tomakh (IS)*, II. Moscow and Leningrad: Khudozhestvennaya literatura, 1964.

——. *Karamzin's Memoir on Ancient and Modern Russia (Zapiska o drevnei i novoi Rossii, 1810–11)*. Trans. and analysis by Richard Pipes. New York: Atheneum, 1974.

——. *Letters of a Russian Traveler (Pis'ma russkogo puteshestvennika, 1791–95)*. Trans. and abridged by Florence Jonas. New York: Columbia University Press, 1957.

——. "Neskol'ko slov o russkoi literature" (1797). In his *IS*, II, 145–56.

——. "O Shekspire i ego tragedii 'Yulii Tsesare'" (1787). In his *IS*, II, 79–82.

——. "Poeziya" (1787). In his *IS*, II, 7–13.

——. "Poor Liza" (Bednaya Liza, 1792). In Carl R. Proffer, ed., *From Karamzin to Bunin. An Anthology of Russian Short Stories*. Bloomington: Indiana University Press, 1969. Pp. 53–67.

——. "Predislovie." In his *Istoriya gosudarstva rossiiskogo*, I (1818). The Hague: Mouton, 1969.

——. "Rech', proiznesennaya na torzhestvennom sobranii imperatorskoi Rossiiskoi akademii 5 dekabrya 1818 goda." In his *IS*, II, 233–42.

Karlinsky, Simon. *The Sexual Labyrinth of Nikolai Gogol*. Cambridge, Mass.: Harvard University Press, 1976.

Karpuk, Paul A. "N. V. Gogol's Unfinished Historical Novel 'The Hetman.'" Ph.D. dissertation, University of California, Berkeley, 1987.

Kazin, Alfred. Foreword. In de Koven Ezrahi, pp. ix–xii.

Kearney, Richard. *Movements in European Philosophy*. Manchester, Eng.: Manchester University Press, 1986.

Khomyakov, A. S. "Pis'mo ob Anglii" (1848). In his *Polnoe sobranie sochinenii*, 3d. ed., I. Moscow: Universitetskaya tipografiya, 1900. Pp. 105–39.

Kirpichenko, E. I. *Arkhitekturnye teorii XIX veka v Rossii*. Moscow: Iskusstvo, 1986.

Kitch, Faith C. M. *The Literary Style of Epifanij Premudryj*. Munich: Sagner, 1976.

Kline, George L. "Russian Religious Thought." In Ninian Smart, ed., *Nineteenth Century Religious Thought in the West*, II. Cambridge, Eng.: Cambridge University Press, 1985. Pp. 179–229.

Kornblatt, Judith Deutsch. *The Cossack Hero in Russian Literature. A Study in Cultural Mythology*. Madison: University of Wisconsin Press, 1992.

Kristeller, Paul Oskar. "The Modern System of the Arts." In his *Renaissance Thought and the Arts*. Princeton, N. J.: Princeton University Press, 1980. Pp. 163–227.

Ladner, Gerhard D. *The Idea of Reform. Its Impact on Christian Thought and Action in the Age of the Fathers*. Cambridge, Mass.: Harvard University Press, 1959.

Lain Entralgo, Pedro. *The Therapy of the Word in Classical Antiquity*. Ed. and trans. L. J. Rather and John M. Sharp. New Haven, Conn.: Yale University Press, 1970.

Lancelot, Claude, and Antoine Arnauld. *A General and Rational Grammar* (1664, first English trans. 1753). Ed. R. C. Alston. Menston, Eng.: The Scolar Press, 1968.

LeBlanc, Ronald D. *The Russianization of Gil Blas: A Study in Literary Appropriation*. Columbus, Ohio: Slavica, 1986.

Lednicki, Wacław. "Dostoevsky—The Man from Underground." In his *Russia, Poland and the West. Essays in Literary and Cultural History* (1954). Port Washington, N. Y.: Kennikat, 1966. Pp. 180–248.

Legavka, M. I., ed.; M. G. Zel'dovich and L. Ya. Lifshits, comps. *Russkaya literatura XIX v. Khrestomatiya kriticheskikh materialov*. Kharkov: Izd. Khar'kovskogo Universiteta im. A.M. Gor'kogo, 1959 (I), 1961 (II).

Lerner, Laurence D. (L. D. L.). "Criticism. Functions." In Preminger, pp. 158–63.

Likhachev, D. S. "O sadakh. Sad i kul'tura Evropy. Sad i kul'tura Rossii" (1985). In his *Izbrannye raboty v trekh tomakh*, III. Leningrad: Khudozhestvennaya literatura, 1987. Pp. 476–518.

———. *Poeziya sadov*. 2nd ed. St. Petersburg: Nauka, 1991.

Little, Lester K. "Cursing." In Mircea Eliade, ed., *The Encyclopedia of Religion*, IV. New York: Macmillan, 1987. Pp. 182–85.

Lomonosov, M. V. "Oda blazhennyya pamyati Gosudaryne Imperatritse Anne Ioannovne na pobedu nad turkami i tatarami i na vzyatie Khotina 1739 goda." In his *Sochineniya*. Moscow and Leningrad: Khudozhestvennaya literatura, 1961. Pp. 47–54.

———. "Predislovie o pol'ze knig tserkovnykh v rossiiskom yazyke" (1757). In his *Sochineniya*, pp. 270–74.

Lossky, Vladimir. *In the Image and Likeness of God*. Crestwood, N. Y.: St. Vladimir's Seminary Press, 1985.

———. *The Mystical Theology of the Eastern Church*. Cambridge, Eng.: James Clarke, 1968.

———. "Tradition and Traditions." In Leonid Ouspensky and Vladimir Lossky, *The Meaning of Icons*. Trans. G. E. H. Palmer and E. Kadloubovsky. Crestwood, N. Y.: St. Vladimir's Seminary Press, 1983. Pp. 9–22.

Lotman, Yu. M. "Merzlyakov kak poet." Introduction to A. F. Merzlyakov, *Stikhotvoreniya*. Biblioteka poeta, Bol'shaya seriya, 2nd ed. Leningrad: Sovetskii pisatel', 1958. Pp. 5–54.

———. "O Khlestakove." In *Uchenye zapiski Tartuskogo Gosudarsetvennogo Universiteta. Trudy po russkoi i slavyanskoi filologii. XXVI. Literaturovedenie.* Tartu, 1975. Pp. 19–53.

———. "Problema khudozhestvennogo prostranstva v proze Gogolya." In *Uchenye zapiski Tartuskogo Gosudarstvennogo Universiteta. Trudy po russkoi i slavyanskoi filologii. XI. Literaturovedenie*. Tartu, 1968. Pp. 5–50.

———. "Russkaya poeziya nachala XIX veka." Introduction to Lotman, ed., *Poety nachala XIX veka*, pp. 5–112.

———. *The Structure of the Artistic Text* (Struktura khudozhestvennogo teksta, 1970). Trans. Ronald Vroon. Ann Arbor: Michigan Slavic Contributions, no. 7, 1977.

———, ed. *Poety nachala XIX veka*. Biblioteka poeta, Malaya seriya, 3d ed. Leningrad: Sovetskii pisatel', 1961.

Luckyj, George S. N. *Between Gogol' and Ševčenko. Polarity in the Literary Ukraine: 1798–1847.* Munich: Wilhelm Fink, 1971.

Maguire, Robert A. "The Formalists on Gogol." In R. L. Jackson and Peter Rudy, eds., *Russian Formalism: A Retrospective Glance. A Festschrift in Honor of Victor Erlich.* New Haven, Conn.: Yale Center for International and Area Studies, 1985. Pp. 213–30.

———. comp., trans., and ed. *Gogol From the Twentieth Century. Eleven Essays.* Princeton, N. J.: Princeton University Press, 1974, 1976.

Maguire, Robert A., and John E. Malmstad. Translators' Introduction. In Bely, *Petersburg*, pp. vii–xxvii.

Makogonenko, G. P., comp. *Russkaya literatura XVIII veka.* Leningrad: Prosveshchenie, 1970.

Malaniuk, Evhan. "Hohol—Gogol." *Ukrainian Review*, XIV, no. 3, 1967, 55–69.

Mandel'shtam, I. E. *O kharaktere Gogolevskogo stilya. Glava iz istorii russkogo literaturnogo yazyka.* Helsingfors: Huvudstaadsbladet, 1902.

Mann, Yu. V. "Gogol's Poetics of Petrifaction." In Fusso and Meyer, pp. 75–88.

———. *V poiskakh zhivoi dushi. "Mertvye dushi": Pisatel'—kritika—chitatel'.* Moscow: Kniga, 1984.

Matlaw, Ralph E., ed. *Belinsky, Chernyshevsky, and Dobrolyubov. Selected Criticism.* Bloomington: Indiana University Press, 1976.

Mazour, Anatole G. *Modern Russian Historiography.* 2nd ed. Princeton, N. J.: D. Van Nostrand, 1958.

McLean, Hugh. "Gogol and the Whirling Telescope." In L. H. Legters, ed., *Russia. Essays in History and Literature.* Leiden: Brill, 1972. Pp. 79–99.

———. "Gogol's Retreat from Love: Towards an Interpretation of *Mirgorod*." In *American Contributions to the Fourth International Congress of Slavicists, Moscow, September 1958.* The Hague: Mouton, 1958. Pp. 225–45.

Merezhkovsky, D. S. "Gogol and the Devil" (Gogol' i chert, 1906). In Maguire, *Gogol*, pp. 57–102.

Merzlyakov, A. F. "Rassuzhdenie o rossiiskoi slovesnosti v nyneshnem ee sostoyanii." In Legavka, I, 46–48 (abridged).

Meyendorff, John. *The Orthodox Church.* London: Darton, Longman and Todd, 1962.

Meyendorff, Paul. Introduction. In *St. Germanus of Constantinople on the Divine Liturgy.* Crestwood, N. Y.: St. Vladimir's Seminary Press, 1984. Pp. 9–11.

Mirsky, D. S. *A History of Russian Literature. From Its Beginnings to 1900.* Ed. F. J. Whitfield. New York: Vintage, 1958.

Mochul'sky, K. D. *Dukhovnyi put' Gogolya.* Paris: YMCA-Press, 1934.

Morris, Marcia A. *Saints and Revolutionaries. The Ascetic Hero in Russian Literature.* Albany: State University of New York Press, 1993.

Morson, Gary Saul. "Gogol's Parables of Explanation: Nonsense and Prosaics." In Fusso and Meyer, pp. 200–39.

Nabokov, V. V. *Nikolai Gogol.* Norfolk, Conn.: New Directions, 1944.

———, ed. and trans. *The Song of Igor's Campaign.* New York: Vintage, 1960.

Nadezhdin, N. I. "Evropeizm i narodnost' v otnoshenii k russkoi slovesnosti" (1836). In Legavka, II, 87–90 (abridged).

———. "Letopisi otechestvennoi slovesnosti" (1832). In Legavka, II, 86–87 (abridged).

———. "Roslavlev, ili Russkie v 1812 godu (M. N. Zagoskina)" (1831). In Legavka, II, 84–85 (abridged).

———. "Sovremennoe napravlenie prosveshcheniya" (1831). In Legavka, II, 81–84 (abridged).

Naef, Hans. *Rome vue par Ingres.* Lausanne: La Guilde du Livre, 1960.

Naguevsky, D. I. *Bibliografiya po istorii rimskoi literatury v Rossii.* Kazan: Universitet, 1889.

The New American Bible. New York: Thomas Nelson, 1971.

Newman, John Henry. *Parochial and Plain Sermons.* San Francisco: Ignatius Press, 1987.

Newmayer, Frederick J. *The Politics of Linguistics.* Chicago: University of Chicago Press, 1986.

Novalis (Friedrich von Hardenberg). "Das Allgemeine Brouillon" (1798–99). In his *Werke, Tagebücher und Briefe,* II. Ed. Hans-Joachim Mahl and Richard Samuel. Munich: Carl Hanser, 1978. Pp. 473–720.

O'Connor, Frank. "A Clean Well-Lighted Place." In his *The Lonely Voice. A Study of the Short Story.* Cleveland: The World Publishing Company, 1965.

Odoevsky, V. F. "Dva dni v zhizni zemnogo shara" (1828). In V. Guminsky, ed., *Vzglyad skvoz' stoletiya. Russkaya fantastika XVIII i pervoi poloviny XIX veka.* Moscow: Molodaya Gvardiya, 1977. Pp. 215–22.

Olesha, Yu. K. *Envy* (Zavist', 1927). In his *"Envy" and Other Works.* Trans. and intro. Andrew R. MacAndrew. Garden City, N. Y.: Doubleday, 1967.

Ong, Walter J. *Orality and Literacy. The Technologizing of the Word.* London: Routledge, 1989.

Österreichische Künstler in Rom. Vienna: Akademie der Bildenden Künste, May–June 1972.

Ouspensky, Leonid. *Theology of the Icon.* Trans. Elizabeth Meyendorff. Crestwood, N. Y.: St. Vladimir's Seminary Press, 1978.

Ovid. *Metamorphoses.* Trans. Frank Justus Miller. 3d ed. Revised by G. P. Goold. The Loeb Classical Library, no. 42. Cambridge, Mass.: Harvard University Press, 1977.

Page, Tanya (T. P.). "Sentimentalism." In Terras, pp. 395–97.

Peace, Richard. *The Enigma of Gogol.* Cambridge, Eng.: Cambridge University Press, 1981.

Plato. Epistle VII. In *Plato.* Trans. R. G. Bury. The Loeb Classical Library, no. 386. Cambridge, Mass.: Harvard University Press, 1966.

———. "Phaedrus." In his *The Dialogues of Plato,* I. Trans. Benjamin Jowett (1892). New York: Random House, 1937. Pp. 233–82.

———. *The Republic.* In his *The Dialogues of Plato,* I. Trans. Benjamin Jowett (1892). New York: Random House, 1937. Pp. 591–879.

Popkin, Cathy. "Distended Discourse: Gogol, Jean Paul, and the Poetics of Elaboration." In Fusso and Meyer, pp. 185–99.

Preminger, Alex, ed. *Encyclopedia of Poetry and Poetics.* Princeton, N. J.: Princeton University Press, 1965.

Prokopovich, Feofan. *De Arte rhetorica libri X Kijoviae 1706*. Ed. Renate Lachman. Cologne: Bohlau, 1982.

———. *O poeticheskom iskusstve*. Trans. G. A. Stratanovsky. In his *Sochineniya*. Ed. I. P. Eremin. Moscow and Leningrad: ANSSSR, 1961. Pp. 335–455.

Propp. V. Ya. *Theory and History of Folklore*. Trans. Adriana Y. Martin and Richard P. Martin. Ed., with intro. and notes, Anatoly Liberman. Minneapolis: University of Minnesota Press, 1984.

Pseudo-Dionysius the Areopagite. *The "Divine Names" and "Mystical Theology."* Trans. and intro. John D. Jones. Milwaukee: Marquette University Press, 1980.

———. *The Ecclesiastical Hierarchy*. Trans., intro., and ed. Thomas Campbell. Washington, D.C.: University Press of America, 1981.

———. *O Bozhestvennykh imenakh*. Trans. and intro. Igumen Gennady (Eikalovich). Buenos Aires: 1957.

———. *Pseudo-Dionysius. The Complete Works*. Trans. Colm Luibheid. New York: The Paulist Press, 1987.

Pushkin, A. S. *The Bronze Horseman* (Mednyi vsadnik, 1833). In Arndt, pp. 401–27.

———. *The Covetous Knight* (Skupoi rytsar', 1830). Trans. A. F. B. Clark. In *The Poems, Prose and Plays of Alexander Pushkin*. Ed. Avrahm Yarmolinsky. New York: The Modern Library, 1936. Pp. 411–27.

———. "Demon" (1823). In his *PSS*, II, 159.

———. *Eugene Onegin* (Evgenii Onegin, 1823–31). Trans. Charles Johnston. London: Penguin, 1977.

———. "Gnedichu" (S Gomerom dolgo ty besedoval odin, 1832). In his *PSS*, III, 238.

———. "'Istoriya russkogo naroda,' sochinenie Nikolaya Polevogo" (1830). In his *PSS*, VII, 131–40.

———. "Karamzin" (1821–26). In his *PSS*, VIII, 66–69.

———. "Ocherk istorii Ukrainy" (1831). In his *PSS*, VIII, 138–42.

———. *Polnoe sobranie sochinenii v desyati tomakh* (*PSS*), 2nd ed. Moscow: ANSSSR, 1956–58.

———. "Puteshestvie v Arzrum vo vremya pokhoda 1829 goda" (1835). In his *PSS*, VI, 637–712.

———. "Whether I Wander Along Noisy Streets" (Brozhu li ya vdol' ulits shumnykh, 1829). In Arndt, pp. 233–35.

———. "Yury Miloslavsky ili Russkie v 1612 godu." In his *PSS*, VII, 102–4.

Rancour-Laferriere, Daniel. "The Identity of Gogol's *Vij*." *Harvard Ukrainian Studies*, II, no. 2 (June 1978), 211–34.

Redfield, James M. *Nature and Culture in the "Iliad." The Tragedy of Hector*. Chicago: University of Chicago Press, 1975.

Reinach, Salomon. "Le Rire rituel." In his *Cultes, mythes et religions*, IV. Paris: Ernest Leroux, 1912. Pp. 109–29.

Reiss, H. S., ed. *The Political Thought of the German Romantics. 1793–1815*. Oxford: Basil Blackwell, 1955.

Richter, Sigrid. "Rom und Gogol'. Gogol's Romerlebnis und sein Fragment 'Rim.'" Ph.D. dissertation, University of Hamburg, 1964.

Rijlaarsdam, Jetske C. *Platon über die Sprache. Ein Kommentar zum Kratylos.* Utrecht: Bohn, Scheltema and Holkema, 1978.

Ross, Stephanie. "The Picturesque. An Eighteenth-Century Debate." *Journal of Aesthetics and Art Criticism*, XLVI, no. 2 (1987), 271–79.

Rozenbakh, P. "Krugovoe pomeshatel'stvo." In *Entsiklopedicheskii slovar' (Brokgauz-Efron)*, vol. 32 (1890). Reprint, Moscow: Terra, 1991. Pp. 839–40.

Rubinshtein, N. A. *Russkaya istoriografiya.* Moscow: OGIZ, 1941.

The Russian Primary Chronicle. Ed. and trans. Samuel H. Cross. In *Harvard Studies and Notes in Philology and Literature*, vol. 12. Cambridge, Mass., 1930. Pp. 75–320.

Saussure, Ferdinand de. *Course in General Linguistics* (Cours de linguistique générale, 1913). Ed. Charles Bally and Albert Sechehaye, in collaboration with Albert Reidlinger. Trans. and intro. Wade Baskin (1915). New York: McGraw Hill, 1966.

Schillinger, John. "Gogol's 'The Overcoat' as a Travesty of Hagiography." *Slavic and East European Journal*, XVI (Spring 1972), 36–41.

Schleiermacher, Friedrich. "On the Concepts of Different Forms of the State." In Reiss, pp. 173–202.

Seraphim of Sarov, Saint. *Spiritual Instructions.* Vol. 1 of *Little Russian Philokalia.* Ouzinkie, Alaska: St. Herman Press, 1991. Pp. 23–65.

Shapiro, Gavriel. "Nikolai Gogol' and the Baroque Heritage." *Slavic Review*, 45, no. 1 (Spring 1986), 95–104.

Shenrok, V. I. *Materialy dyla biografii Gogolya.* 4 vols. Moscow: A. I. Mamontov, 1892–97.

Shevyryov, S. P. *Stikhotvoreniya.* Ed. M. Aronson. Biblioteka poeta. Leningrad: Sovetskii pisatel', 1939.

Silbajoris, Rimvydas. *Russian Versification. The Theories of Trediakovskij, Lomonosov, and Kantemir.* New York: Columbia University Press, 1968.

Sinyavsky, A. D. See Terts.

Skovoroda, Hryhory. "Sad Bozhestvennykh pesnei, prozyabshii iz zern Svyashchennogo Pisaniya" (Pesn' 1-aya, 1757). In his *Povne zibrannia tvoriv u dvokh tomakh*, I. Kiev: Vidavnytstvo "Naukova Dumka," 1973. Pp. 60–61.

Slonimsky, A. L. "The Technique of the Comic in Gogol" (Tekhnika komicheskogo u Gogolya, 1923). In Maguire, *Gogol*, pp. 323–73.

Smith, William George, comp. *The Oxford Dictionary of English Proverbs.* 3d ed. Ed. E. P. Wilson. Oxford: Clarendon, 1970.

Sobel, Ruth. *Gogol's Forgotten Book. "Selected Passages" and Its Contemporary Readers.* Washington, D.C.: University Press of America, 1981.

Solzhenitsyn, Alexander. *The First Circle* (V kruge pervom, 1955–64). Trans. Thomas P. Whitney. New York: Harper and Row, 1968.

Steiner, George. "Whorf, Chomsky and the Student of Literature." In W. K. Wimsatt, ed. and intro., *Literary Criticism. Idea and Act. The English Institute, 1939–1972. Selected Essays.* Berkeley: University of California Press, 1974. Pp. 242–62.

Stilman, Leon. "The 'All-Seeing Eye' in Gogol" ("Vsevidyashchee oko" u Gogolya, 1965). In Maguire, *Gogol*, pp. 375–89.

Striedter, Jurij. *Der Schelmenroman in Russland. Ein Beitrag zur Geschichte des russischen Romans vor Gogol'*. Berlin: Otto Harrassowitz, 1961.

Sumarokov, A. P. "Nastavlenie khotyashchim byti pisatelyami" (1774). In his *Izbrannye proizvedeniya*. Biblioteka poeta, Bol'shaya seriya, 2nd ed. Leningrad: Sovetskii pisatel', 1957. Pp. 134–39.

Tanner, Tony. "Notes for a Comparison Between American and European Romanticism." In his *Scenes of Nature, Signs of Man*. Cambridge, Eng.: Cambridge University Press, 1987. Pp. 25–45.

Terras, Victor, ed. *Handbook of Russian Literature*. New Haven, Conn.: Yale University Press, 1985.

Terts, A. (Sinyavsky, A. D.). *V teni Gogolya*. London: Overseas Publication Interchange/Collins, 1975.

Thieme, Ulrich, and Felix Becker, eds. *Allgemeine Lexikon der Bildenden Künstler*. 37 vols. Leipzig: Wilhelm Engelmann and E. A. Seemann, 1907–50.

Todd, William Mills, III. *The Familiar Letter in the Age of Pushkin*. Princeton, N. J.: Princeton University Press, 1976.

———. *Fiction and Society in the Age of Pushkin*. Cambridge, Mass.: Harvard University Press, 1986.

———. "Gogol's Epistolary Writing." In Andrew W. Cordier, ed., *Columbia Essays in International Affairs*, V. The Dean's Papers, 1969. New York: Columbia University Press, 1970. Pp. 51–76.

———. "Pushkin." In Terras, pp. 356–60.

Tolstoy, L. N. "K chitatelyam. Glava ⟨34-ya⟩." Second variant to *Detstvo* (1851–52). In his *Polnoe sobranie sochinenii*, I. Moscow: Khudozhestvennaya literatura, 1935. Pp. 207–9.

Tred'yakovsky, V. K. "Mnenie o nachale poezii i stikhov voobshche" (1752). In his *Sochineniya Tred'yakovskogo*, I. St. Petersburg: Smirdin, 1849. Pp. 179–201.

Trimpi, Wesley. "Horace's 'Ut pictura poesis': The Argument for Stylistic Decorum." *Traditio*, XXXIV (1978), 29–73.

Turgenev, I. S. "Pis'mo iz Peterburga" (1852). In his *Polnoe sobranie sochinenii i pisem*, XIV (*Sochineniya*). Moscow and Leningrad: Nauka, 1967. Pp. 72–73.

Turner, Victor W. *The Ritual Process. Structure and Anti-Structure* (1969). Ithaca, N. Y.: Cornell University Press, 1977.

Uitti, Karl D. *Linguistics and Literary Theory*. New York: W. W. Norton, 1969.

Ushakov, D. N., comp. *Tolkovyi slovar' russkogo yazyka*, 4 vols. Moscow: OGIZ, 1938.

Valkenier, Elizabeth K. *Ilya Repin and the World of Russian Art*. New York: Columbia University Press, 1990.

Vasari, Giorgio. *Lives of Seventy of the Most Eminent Painters, Sculptors and Architects*. 4 vols. Ed. and ann. E. H. and E. W. Blashfield and A. A. Hopkins. New York: Charles Scribner's, 1902.

Venevitinov, D. V. "Anaksagor. Beseda Platona" (1825). In his *Sochineniya Venevitinova*. St. Petersburg: Imperatorskaya Akademiya Nauk, 1855. Pp. 130–37.

———. "Italiya" (1826). In his *Sochineniya*, pp. 63–64.

———. "Skul'ptura, zhivopis' i muzyka." In his *Sochineniya*, pp. 149–53.

Vergara, Lisa. *Rubens and the Poetics of Landscape*. New Haven, Conn.: Yale University Press, 1982.

Vinogradov, V. V. "Naturalisticheskii grotesk (Syuzhet i kompozitsiya povesti Gogolya 'Nos')" (1921). In his *Izbrannye trudy. Poetika russkoi literatury*. Moscow: Nauka, 1976. Pp. 5–44.

———. "Yazyk Gogolya." In V. V. Gippius, ed., *N. V. Gogol'. Materialy i issledovaniya*, II. Moscow and Leningrad: ANSSSR, 1936. Pp. 286–376.

Virgil. *The Georgics*. Trans., with intro. and notes, L. P. Wilkinson. Harmondsworth, Eng.: Penguin, 1982.

Vogel, Lucy. "Gogol's Rome." *Slavic and East European Journal*, XI, no. 2 (1967), 145–58.

Volkmann-Schluck, Karl Heinz. "Novalis' magischer Idealismus." In Hans Steffen, ed., *Die Deutsche Romantik*, 3d ed. Göttingen: Vanderbroeck and Rupprecht, 1978. Pp. 45–53.

Wackenroder, Wilhelm Heinrich, and Ludwig Tieck. *"Confessions" and "Fantasies."* Trans. and ann., with critical intro., Mary Hurst Schubert. University Park: Pennsylvania State University Press, 1971.

———. *Ob iskusstve i khudozhnikakh. Razmyshleniya otshel'nika, lyubitelya izyashchnogo*. Moscow: L. Tikom, 1826.

Ware, Timothy. *The Orthodox Church*. Harmondsworth, Eng.: Penguin, 1967.

Weiskopf, Mikhail. "The Bird Troika and the Chariot of the Soul: Plato and Gogol." In Fusso and Meyer, pp. 126–42.

Wheelwright, Philip (P. W.) "Catharsis." In Preminger, pp. 106–8.

Wieczynski, Joseph L., ed. *The Modern Encyclopedia of Russian and Soviet History*, vol. 38. Gulf Breeze, Fla.: Academic International, 1984.

Williams, Gordon. *Figures of Thought in Roman Poetry*. New Haven, Conn.: Yale University Press, 1980.

Williamson, G. C., ed. *Bryant's Dictionary of Painters and Engravers*. 4th ed. (1902–3), II. Port Washington, N. Y.: Kennikat, 1964.

Woodman, A. J. *Rhetoric in Classical Historiography: Four Studies*. London: Croom Helms, 1988.

Wright, F. A., ed. *Lemprière's Classical Dictionary of Proper Names Mentioned in Ancient Authors*. London: Routledge and Kegan Paul, 1949.

Yermakov (Ermakov), I. D. "The Nose" (Nos, 1923). In Maguire, *Gogol*, pp. 155–98.

———. *Ocherki po analizu tvorchestva N. V. Gogolya*. Petrograd: Gosizdat, 1923.

Zeldin, Jesse. "Herder and Some Russians." In Anthony M. Mlikotin, ed., *Western Philosophical Systems in Russian Literature. A Collection of Critical Studies*. Los Angeles: University of Southern California Press, 1979. Pp. 11–24.

Zenkovsky, Serge A., ed., trans., and intro. *Medieval Russia's Epics, Chronicles, and Tales*. New York: E. P. Dutton, 1963.

Zen'kovsky, V. V. *Gogol'*. Paris: YMCA-Press, n.d.

Zholkovsky, Alexander. "Rereading Gogol's Miswritten Book: Notes on *Selected Passages from Correspondence with Friends*." In Fusso and Meyer, pp. 172–83.

Zhukovsky, V. A. "Pisatel' v obshchestve" (1808). In his *Sobranie sochinenii*, I. Moscow and Leningrad: Khudozhestvennaya literatura, 1959. Pp. 393–401.

Index

IN this index an "f" after a number indicates a separate reference on the next page, and an "ff" indicates separate references on the next two pages. A continuous discussion over two or more pages is indicated by a span of page numbers, e.g., "57–59." *Passim* is used for a cluster of references in close but not consecutive sequence.

Library of Congress Cataloging-in-Publication Data

Maguire, Robert A., 1930–
    Exploring Gogol / Robert A. Maguire
        p.   cm. — (Studies of the Harriman Institute)
    Includes bibliographical references and index.
    ISBN 0-8047-2320-6 (cl.) : ISBN 0-8047-2681-7 (pbk.)
    1. Gogol', Nikolaĭ Vasil'evich, 1809–1852—Criticism
    and interpretation. I. Title. II. Series.
    PG3335.Z8M17 1994
    891.78'309—dc20   94-14416
                                                   CIP

⊗ This book is printed on acid-free paper.